God and Nature

GOD AND NATURE

Historical Essays on the Encounter between Christianity and Science

Edited by
David C. Lindberg
and
Ronald L. Numbers

UNIVERSITY OF CALIFORNIA PRESS
Berkeley • Los Angeles • London

University of California Press
Berkeley and Los Angeles, California

University of California Press, Ltd.
London, England

Library of Congress Cataloging in Publication Data

Main entry under title:
God and nature.

   Rev. papers from an international conference held
at the University of Wisconsin—Madison, Apr. 23–25,
1981.

   Bibliography: p.
   Includes index.
   1. Religion and science—History of controversy—
Congresses. I. Lindberg, David C. II. Numbers,
Ronald L.
BL245.G63   1986   261.5'5   85-7548
ISBN 0-520-05538-1 (alk. paper)
ISBN 0-520-05692-2 (paper)

Printed in the United States of America

1 2 3 4 5 6 7 8 9

To
Vern and Barbara Carner,
whose generous support
made this volume possible

Contents

Acknowledgments

This book is the outgrowth of the editors' shared conviction that the interaction of science and Christianity has been of profound importance in the shaping of Western civilization—a conviction nurtured by our respective historical apprenticeships with Edward Grant and Richard S. Westfall (Lindberg) and A. Hunter Dupree and Roger Hahn (Numbers). It is also a reflection of our belief that historians have an obligation to share the fruits of their labors with the reading public. In recent years historians of science and religion have substantially revised many of their opinions but have generally addressed themselves only to fellow professionals. It seemed time to correct this situation. As a first step in that direction we organized an international conference on the historical relations of Christianity and science, held at the University of Wisconsin—Madison on 23–25 April 1981, to which we invited several dozen church historians and historians of science. This book has grown out of that conference.

In organizing the conference and editing this book we have accumulated many debts, which we gratefully acknowledge. The entire project owes its existence to the generosity of the Carner Foundation of Dallas, Texas, and the support provided by the Anonymous Fund, the Humanistic Foundation, and the Knapp Bequest of the University of Wisconsin—Madison. Vern and Barbara Carner adopted our project in its infancy, offering financial and moral sustenance—to say nothing of the coveted "Christianity and Science" coffee mugs given to each conference participant! The Carners are in many respects the true parents of this project.

Early in our efforts we formed an advisory committee to assist us in organizing the conference. For their dedication and wisdom we express gratitude to William Coleman, Edward E. Daub, and Robert M. Kingdon of the University of Wisconsin; John Dillenberger of Hartford Seminary Foundation; Martin E. Marty of the University of Chicago; and Richard S. Westfall of Indiana University.

The conference in Madison was given over entirely to discussion—to defining issues, testing theses, and sharpening arguments. Many papers subsequently underwent substantial rewriting, and none escaped revision. For contributing to these intellectual exchanges we thank, in addition to the contributors to this volume, the following conference participants:

Muriel L. Blaisdell, Miami University
James G. Blight, Harvard University
Paul S. Boyer, University of Wisconsin
T. Dwight Bozeman, University of Iowa
John C. Burnham, Ohio State University
William Coleman, University of Wisconsin
William J. Courtenay, University of Wisconsin
Robert E. Frykenberg, University of Wisconsin
Lawrence T. Geraty, Andrews University
Neal C. Gillespie, Georgia State University
Robert M. Grant, University of Chicago
John C. Greene, University of Connecticut
Thomas L. Hankins, University of Washington
Robert M. Kingdon, University of Wisconsin
Michael MacDonald, University of Wisconsin
W. Newton Maloney, Fuller Theological Seminary
Ernan McMullin, University of Notre Dame
Margaret J. Osler, University of Calgary
Leroy E. Page, Kansas State University
Harry W. Paul, University of Florida
Karl E. Peters, Rollins College
Ernest R. Sandeen, Macalester College
Robert Scharlemann, University of Iowa
A. Truman Schwartz, Macalester College
Robert Siegfried, University of Wisconsin
Phillip R. Sloan, University of Notre Dame
Sabetai Unguru, University of Tel Aviv
William A. Wallace, Catholic University of America

Owen Chadwick of the University of Cambridge, though unable to be present in person, shared his ideas in a paper distributed to participants. Dov Ospovat, a promising young historian of science at the University of Nebraska, had hoped to be with us, but his tragic death made that impossible.

In preparing the papers for publication we have benefited from the splendid secretarial services of Carolyn Hackler and Lori Grant and from the support of our colleagues and students in the departments of the History of Science and the History of Medicine at the University of Wisconsin—Madison, especially those who participated in our memorable seminar on science and Christianity in the spring of 1981. From beginning to end Greta Lindberg and Janet Numbers have shared the joys and frustrations of this venture. To all who lent support we offer our sincerest thanks.

Introduction

For over a century scholars have debated the historical relationship between science and Christianity, some maintaining that the two have been mortal enemies, others that they have been allies, and still others that neither conflict nor harmony adequately describes their relationship. The "terms of the debate," to use Donald Fleming's phrase, were set in the mid-nineteenth century by two Americans, John William Draper (1811–1882) and Andrew Dickson White (1832–1918), whose writings stressed the "conflict" or "warfare" between science and Christianity.

The English-born son of a Methodist minister, Draper immigrated to America in 1832, graduated from medical school four years later, and subsequently joined the faculty of New York University, where he taught chemistry and physiology. Along the way he abandoned the faith of his father for rational theism. Shortly after mid-century he turned his attention to historical matters, authoring in turn a two-volume *History of the Intellectual Development of Europe* (1862) and a three-volume *History of the American Civil War* (1867–1870).[1]

In the early 1870s Edward L. Youmans, America's premier popularizer of science, asked Draper to contribute a *History of the Conflict between Religion and Science* (1874) to his International Scientific Series of books by prominent scientists. Aroused by recent proclamations from Rome declaring papal infallibility and elevating "revealed doctrine" above the "human sciences," Draper welcomed the opportunity to excoriate the Catholic church for its alleged long-standing opposition to science. Although the title of his book suggested an exploration of the relations between *religion* and science, Draper's quarrel was almost exclusively with Roman Catholicism, which, ever since seizing political power in the fourth century, had displayed "a bitter, a mortal animosity" toward science. The Vatican's persecution of scientists and other dissidents, he charged in language calculated to arouse emotion, had left its hands "steeped in blood."[2]

1

Other religious bodies received little but praise. Islamic scholars, he claimed, had laid the foundations of several sciences; the Greek Orthodox church had generally welcomed science; Protestants had cultivated a "cordial union," marred only by occasional "misunderstandings." In fact, Draper regarded the Protestant Reformation, with its insistence on the private interpretation of Scripture, as the "twin-sister" of modern science. If John Calvin caused Michael Servetus to be burned, "he was animated, not by the principles of the Reformation, but by those of Catholicism, from which he had not been able to emancipate himself completely." And if some nineteenth-century Protestant clerics rashly accused scientists of infidelity, they did so for the same reason.[3] To Draper, the historical lesson could not be clearer:

> Religion must relinquish that imperious, that domineering position which she has so long maintained against Science. There must be absolute freedom for thought. The ecclesiastic must learn to keep himself within the domain he has chosen, and cease to tyrannize over the philosopher, who, conscious of his own strength and the purity of his motives, will bear such interference no longer.[4]

Not surprisingly, Draper's narrative of "ferocious theologians" hounding the pioneers of science "with a Bible in one hand and a fiery fagot in the other," as one critic characterized his account, attracted a wide readership. His *Conflict* outsold every other title in the International Scientific Series, going through at least fifty printings and ten translations, including a Spanish version that ended up on the Catholic Index of Prohibited Books. Draper modestly predicted that his book would be only "the preface, or forerunner, of a body of literature, which the events and wants of our times will call forth." In this instance his sense of the future proved more accurate than his knowledge of the past: scarcely a year passed during the late nineteenth century that did not witness the appearance of a new work echoing—or attacking—Draper's views.[5]

By far the most influential historical study of science and religion to follow Draper's was White's *A History of the Warfare of Science with Theology in Christendom* (1896). White, an Episcopal-bred historian, taught at the University of Michigan and served in the New York State Senate before becoming the first president of Cornell University. He began writing on science and religion as part of an effort to discredit religious critics envious of the funds given to his new university in Ithaca and distressed by its thoroughgoing secularism, typified by White's stated desire to create "an asylum for *Science*—where truth shall be sought for truth's sake, not stretched or cut exactly to fit

Revealed Religion."[6] For nearly three decades—from 1869, when he delivered his first lecture on "The Battle-Fields of Science," to 1896, when he brought out his two-volume history—he waged unrelenting war on the detractors of science. Imbibing fully the military rhetoric so pervasive in Victorian culture, he dramatically described not a mere conflict but an all-out war: "a war waged longer, with battles fiercer, with sieges more persistent, with strategy more shrewd than in any of the comparatively transient warfare of Caesar or Napoleon or Moltke."[7]

On the basis of his historical research White concluded that

in all modern history, interference with science in the supposed interest of religion, no matter how conscientious such interference may have been, has resulted in the direst evils both to religion and to science—and invariably. And, on the other hand, all untrammeled scientific investigation, no matter how dangerous to religion some of its stages may have seemed, for the time, to be, has invariably resulted in the highest good of religion and of science.[8]

Although White aimed his earliest broadsides at "Religion" and "Ecclesiasticism," he eventually drew a sharp distinction between theology, which made dogmatic statements about the world and regarded the Bible as a scientific text, and religion, which consisted of recognizing "a Power in the universe" and living by the Golden Rule. Religion, so defined, often fostered science; theology smothered it.[9] White's *Warfare* apparently did not sell as briskly as Draper's *Conflict*, but in the end it proved more influential, partly, it seems, because Draper's strident anti-Catholicism soon dated his work and because White's impressive documentation gave the appearance of sound scholarship.[10]

Well into the twentieth century, militaristic language dominated discussions of science and religion, especially during the 1920s, when Bible-quoting fundamentalists attempted to outlaw the teaching of evolution in public schools.[11] As late as 1955 Harvard's distinguished historian of science George Sarton was still praising White—and suggesting that his thesis be broadened to include non-Christian cultures.[12] Even later, in 1965, the historian Bruce Mazlish, in the introduction to an abridged paperback edition of the *Warfare*, noted that the book still commanded "immense respect and continued reading." In his opinion White had established his thesis "beyond any reasonable doubt."[13]

Such judgments, however, overlooked mounting evidence that White read the past through battle-scarred glasses. A number of scholars, including Alfred North Whitehead and Michael B. Foster, had begun to downplay the conflict between science and Christianity as early as the 1920s and 1930s. Indeed, Whitehead and Foster became convinced that Christianity, rather than impeding science, had actually encouraged it by establishing that nature behaves in a regular and orderly fashion—a basic premise of modern science.[14]

For many scholars the most compelling example of religion in the service of science came from seventeenth-century England, where a large number of Puritans, it seemed, had avidly cultivated science. The classic statement of this thesis appeared in a 1938 monograph by the sociologist Robert K. Merton, who maintained that Puritanism had contributed to the origins of modern science by providing a system of values that sanctioned scientific effort. Since the case of Puritanism and science has often been seen as a microcosm of the larger encounter between science and Christianity, the arguments pro and con deserve more than passing comment.

According to Merton, medieval scholars held the study of nature in contempt, owing to "monastic asceticism and the feeling of the impermanence and relative worthlessness of matter." At best they considered natural science to be useless; at worst they associated it with black magic and judged it altogether illegitimate. In contrast the Protestant Reformation, through the Puritan "ethos," endowed the scientific enterprise with positive value. By viewing natural science as "socially acceptable" and as "a laudable rather than an unsavory occupation," Puritanism directed "talents into scientific pursuits which at other times would have found expression in other fields."[15]

Several elements in the Puritan ethos, Merton thought, promoted such results. Puritans judged the study of nature to be an act of worship, revealing the glory of the Creator. They believed that one might also glorify God by engaging in utilitarian activities that would contribute to the material betterment of the human race. Indeed, the doctrine of predestination encouraged good works as a demonstration of one's membership among the "elect." Diligence in utilitarian pursuits thus became one of the hallmarks of Puritanism.[16] In addition, Puritanism placed high value on reason, while carefully subordinating it to observation. Merton perceived a "point-to-point correlation" between such attitudes and those associated with modern science, writing, for example, that "the combination of *rationalism and empiricism* which is so pronounced in the Puritan ethic forms the essence of the spirit of modern science."[17] Finally, Merton buttressed his conclusions with an impressive numerical study of the membership of the Royal Society of London, the foremost scientific organization in seventeenth-century England, which revealed (by his count) a disproportionate representation of Puritans.

Merton's arguments did not go unchallenged. Some critics objected to his overly broad definition of Puritanism as the "common attitude and mode of life" of Anglicans, Calvinists, Independents, Anabaptists, Quakers, and millenarians—a definition that included virtually everybody except Catholics and "enthusiasts."[18] Merton's definition of science proved equally contentious. In a telling passage he noted that the Protestant ethic "embraced an undisguised emphasis upon utility as well as control of self and the external world, which in turn involved a preference for the visual, manual and concretely manageable rather than the purely logical and verbal."[19] Thus Merton had in mind a highly empirical, utilitarian enterprise—a far cry from the theoretical contributions of Galileo, Kepler, and Newton, which, in the minds of many, epitomized the Scientific Revolution. Further objections were lodged against Merton's analysis of the membership of the Royal Society. Lotte Mulligan, for example, concluded that the "typical Fellow was a royalist, Anglican, university-educated gentleman"—hardly Merton's antiestablishment artisan.[20] In addition, a number of historians criticized Merton's thesis for its inability to account adequately for the major scientific achievements of contemporary Catholic cultures: the anatomical and physiological innovations of sixteenth-century Italians, the astronomical achievements of Copernicus, the physics of Galileo, and the mechanical philosophy of the French clerics Mersenne and Gassendi.[21]

One could, however, reject much of Merton's evidence and many of his conclusions, yet share his conviction that science is a social phenomenon, which in the seventeenth century was stimulated in some way by Puritanism or, more generally, by Protestantism. In a monumental recent study of the relationship between Puritan ideology and the development of various utilitarian pursuits, clustered together under the rubric of science, Charles Webster has argued that, despite the diversity of religious affiliations found within the "active nucleus" of the Royal Society, Puritanism influenced the transformation of the society into an institution dedicated to the cultivation of experimental science.[22]

Although Merton showed the value of searching outside of science, in the social and religious milieus, for factors that may have affected the vigor, shape, and direction of the scientific enterprise, the exact relationship between Puritanism and science remains elusive—as does the larger question regarding Christianity and science. All too often those who have argued that Christianity gave birth to modern science—most notably the Protestant historian Reijer Hooykaas and the Catholic priest-scientist Stanley L. Jaki—have sacrificed careful history for scarcely concealed apologetics.[23] From the fact that modern science developed in Christian Europe they have tended to conclude, without further demonstration, that there was a causal connection between Christianity and science.

The 1950s, a decade that coincided with the maturation of the history of science as an academic specialty, witnessed the appearance of a number of fresh interpretations of the relationship of Christianity and science by such scholars as A. Hunter Dupree, Charles C. Gillispie, Paul H. Kocher, Giorgio de Santillana, and Richard S. Westfall. Writing on topics ranging from Copernicanism to Darwinism, they demonstrated that neither "conflict" nor "harmony" adequately captured the complex interaction between Christianity and science.[24] Typical of this new breed of scholars was John Dillenberger, a professor of historical theology, who in *Protestant Thought and Natural Science* (1960) consciously avoided reciting accounts of conflicts and instances of harmony in order "to penetrate behind the concrete issues . . . to the underlying problems which exercised the major parties in the debates."[25]

Despite a developing consensus among scholars that Christianity and science had not been at war, the notion of conflict refused to die. Many historians, apparently more from habit than from conviction, found it difficult to abandon the warfare metaphor. John C. Greene, for example, in a book otherwise sensitive to the complex relationship between science and religion, insisted that Darwin's influence on Christian thought be viewed "against the background of the historical development of the conflict betweeen science and religion in modern times." Similarly, Paul F. Boller, Jr. entitled a discussion of American responses to Darwin "The Warfare of Science and Religion"—and then proceeded to describe as much compromise as conflict.[26]

Some historians, seemingly enchanted by the notion of warfare, have heard the sounds of battle just over the horizon—shortly beyond the period of their own studies, when peace generally prevailed. Roy Porter, for example, in an excellent study of the origins of geology, asserted that the *"detente"* between theology and the science of the earth in the eighteenth century gave way in the nineteenth (where, significantly, his account ends) to "that sporadic but prolonged atmosphere of 'warfare' between divinity and geology which so troubled the nineteenth century." Herbert Hovenkamp, who surveyed science and religion in America from 1800 to 1860, a time of warfare for Porter, found harmony—until the late 1850s, when Hovenkamp's period drew to a close and Darwin's *Origin of Species* allegedly changed "the honeymoon with science into a pitched battle for the minds of Protestants."[27] And so it went.

In recent years several historians, aware of the distortions involved in pitting science against Christianity but convinced that conflict was more than a rhetorical device invented by polemicists such as Draper and White, have sought to redefine the conflict in less simplistic terms:

as a popular hypostatization of a number of small conflicts (Owen Chadwick), as a battle of ideas within individual minds (James Moore), as a conflict between competing systems of science (Neal Gillespie), or as a struggle between groups of professionals (Frank Turner). Although these particular examples have been drawn from nineteenth-century English studies, their methods and insights are applicable to other times and places.

In two influential works Owen Chadwick addressed the problem of the relationship between science and religion in Victorian England, emphasizing the importance—obvious in retrospect but previously ignored by most scholars—of distinguishing "between science when it was against religion and the scientists when they were against religion." It was one thing to have disagreement between scientific opinion and religious doctrine, quite another for an individual scientist to attack Christianity, because scientists might oppose religion for a variety of reasons having nothing to do with science. In the nineteenth century there was more conflict between "historical study and accepted views of the Bible" than between science and theology, but the public, failing to make such distinctions, labeled any challenge to the Bible as "science." Thus a war between science and religion was "hypostatized . . . out of a number of conflicts," some of which had no connection with science. The war, in this sense, was not "mere legend," argued Chadwick, but a potent intellectual force that greatly influenced thinking about both science and religion.[28]

In a masterly historiographical introduction to his analysis of the post-Darwinian controversies James R. Moore urged historians to forsake the military language of Draper and White for a "non-violent and humane" interpretation of the relations between science and religion. The military metaphor, he argued, implied "sharp polarisation, distinct organisation, and violent antagonism"—none of which characterized the Darwinian debates. On the contrary, Moore found each of these implications to be "entirely misleading if not utterly false":

There was not a polarisation of "science" and "religion" as the idea of opposed armies implies but a large number of learned men, some scientists, some theologians, some indistinguishable, and almost all of them very religious, who experienced various differences among themselves. There was no organisation apparent on either "side" as the idea of rank and command implies but deep divisions among men of science, the majority of whom were at first hostile to Darwin's theory, and a corresponding and derivative division among Christians who were scientifically untrained, with a large proportion of leading theologians quite prepared to come to terms peacefully with Darwin. Nor, finally, was there the kind of antagonism pictured in the discharge of weaponry but rather a much more subdued overall reaction to the *Origin of Species* than is generally supposed and a genuine amiability in the relations of those who are customarily believed to have been at battle.

Conflict arose, not between science and religion as such, but within individual minds experiencing a "crisis of faith" as they struggled to come to terms with new historical and scientific discoveries. It was, wrote Moore, a "conflict of minds steeped in Christian tradition with the ideas and implications of Darwinism."[29]

In *Charles Darwin and the Problem of Creation* (1979) Neal C. Gillespie argued that the conflict between science and religion in the nineteenth century involved competing systems of science or "epistemes," the older of which rested on theological assumptions while the newer one, associated with Darwin, rejected religion as a means of knowing the world and insisted on an interpretation of nature that involved only natural, secondary causes. "Because the new episteme for science differed from the old in having within it no place for theology . . . serious questions were thereby raised that made the conflict, some- times dismissed as an illusion or a mistake, very real indeed," ex- plained Gillespie. "The important thing was to get theology out of science. The conflict, therefore, was both necessary and unavoidable if a positive science were to develop."[30] Conflict, according to this view, arose from transformations within science that had nothing to do with warring scientists and clerics.

A fourth way of viewing the nineteenth-century "conflict" between science and religion has been suggested in a pathbreaking article by Frank M. Turner. The "Victorian conflict between religious and sci- entific spokesmen," he claimed, resulted not from hostility between progressive science and retrogressive theology, but from a "shift of authority and prestige . . . from one part of the intellectual nation to another," as professionalizing scientists sought to banish clergymen from science and end their control of education. According to Turner, the positivist science described by Gillespie

constituted both a cause and a weapon. The "young guard" agreed among themselves that science should be pursued without regard for religious dogma, natural theology, or the opinions of religious authorities. . . . The drive to organize a more professionally oriented scientific community and to define science in a more critical fashion brought the crusading scientists into conflict with two groups of people. The first were supporters of or- ganized religion who wished to maintain a large measure of control over education and to retain religion as the source of moral and social values. The second group was the religiously minded sector of the preprofessional scientific community, which included both clergymen and laymen.[31]

For Turner the conflict had a social as well as an intellectual dimension.[32]

Interpretations like Turner's reflect a growing inclination among historians to take science down from its traditional pedestal and treat it as mere ideological property, intrinsically no different from any other kind of knowledge—religious, political, or social. Margaret C. Jacob, for example, has maintained that liberal Protestantism allied itself with Newtonian philosophy in the late seventeenth century not because the new mechanical philosophy "offered the most plausible explanation of nature" but because it best served the social-political purposes of the ruling classes, providing "an underpinning for their vision of what they liked to call the 'world politick'":

> The ordered, providentially guided, mathematically regulated universe of Newton gave a model for a stable and prosperous polity, ruled by the self-interest of men. That was what Newton's universe meant to his friends and popularizers: it allowed them to imagine that nature was on their side; they could have laws of motion and keep God; spiritual forces could work in the universe; matter could be controlled and dominated by God and by men. Stability was possible without constant divine intervention; the spiritual order could be maintained; the church was necessary and essential; yet at the same time men could pursue their worldly interests. That, briefly stated, was what the world natural, explicated in the *Principia,* meant to churchmen who were primarily interested in promoting their vision of the "world politick."[33]

Historians such as Turner and Jacob not only reject scientific triumphalism but systematically look "for the effects of social circumstances, experiences and interests on the constructed content of scientific knowledge," as Martin Rudwick has pointed out in an essay on recent interpretations of the relations between science and religion. Scholars of this persuasion tend to focus on the *use* of science rather than on its influence. They seek, for example, not only to describe the relationship between science and religion that prevailed at a given time but to ask, "Who put it forward, who used it, and what (and whose) interests did it serve?" This approach to history, says Rudwick, places scientific and religious knowledge on an equal footing— in theory if not always in practice—and thus demythologizes "the old positivist views of the victorious struggle of science against religion just as much as the older view of science as the natural ally of religion." It now seems clear, as Rudwick maintains, that the historical relationship between science and religion has involved a process of "gradual differentiation and divergence, rather than the replacement of one by the other, as the older positivist tradition maintained."[34]

What view of the encounter between Christianity and science emerges from the essays in this volume? Almost every chapter portrays a complex and diverse interaction that defies reduction to simple "conflict" or "harmony." Although instances of controversy are not hard to find, it cannot be said that scientists and theologians—much less science and Christianity—engaged in protracted warfare. Likewise, although cases of mutual support are numerous, it would be a travesty to maintain that Christianity and science have been perennial allies. Some Christian beliefs and practices seem to have encouraged scientific investigation, others to have discouraged it; the interaction varied with time, place, and person. Such an interpretation may lack the drama of militaristic accounts and the inspiration of apologetic history, but, by eschewing a unitary explanation of the past, it shows "the respect for the particularity, individuality and value of each people and age" that the canons of historical scholarship demand.[35]

Old stereotypes about theological suppression of scientific effort during the period of the early church and the Middle Ages are clearly refuted by the first two essays in this volume. Although the early church fathers did not place high priority on the investigation of the visible world, neither did they judge such efforts valueless. They considered knowledge of visible things useful for biblical interpretation and defense of the faith; this undoubtedly reduced science to the status of handmaiden, but that was far from suppression. The church thus contributed to the preservation and transmission of a modest level of Greek scientific knowledge through the social upheavals of the first millennium of the Christian era. Crucial to this dissemination were the writings of the church fathers and the establishment of monastic and cathedral schools and libraries. Of course, the church transmitted Greek scientific knowledge selectively, preferring Plato to Aristotle and steering clear of the obviously heretical.

Greek scientific knowledge also became an important ingredient in Christian worldviews, from Basil of Caesarea (d. 379) and Augustine (d. 430) through the end of the Middle Ages and beyond. The often-repeated notion that Christian thinkers attempted to obtain their worldview from the Bible alone is a ludicrous distortion of the facts. From the beginning of the thirteenth century onward we see a persistent effort to integrate Aristotelian natural philosophy with Christian theology, a goal that was not achieved without soul-searching and struggle. In the end, Christianity took its basic categories of thought and much of its metaphysics and cosmology from Aristotle; in return, science received institutional support and access to new perspectives that enriched and redirected it. But certain aspects of Aristotelian natural philosophy, such as its determinism and its denial of creation, caused a major stir in theological circles and led ultimately to a theological condemnation of these and other philosophical propositions in 1270 and 1277—condemnations that placed a theological lid on certain lines of scientific speculation, while opening the door to others. There was thus a continual give-and-take between medieval theology and medieval science—not always willing but nonetheless mutual.

In 1543 Nicolaus Copernicus, a Catholic church official from northern Poland, proposed a heliocentric cosmology that removed the earth from the center of the universe and awarded it planetary status. According to Draper and White, conservative religious forces quickly suppressed the idea owing to its inconsistency with certain biblical passages that were taken to teach the immobility of the earth. However, a close examination of the historical record reveals quite a different picture. Copernicus's book was written for mathematical astronomers and initially enjoyed little comprehension outside that community. The first sustained response came from a group of astronomers at the Lutheran University of Wittenberg who assimilated certain aspects of Copernican astronomy while ignoring others—who, in the spirit of moderate reform, recognized the mathematical advantages of Copernicus's heliocentric hypothesis and put it to mathematical use, while overlooking or rejecting the radical thesis that the earth really moves. Their reasons for opposing the motion of the earth were both scientific and theological. Heliocentrism unmistakably violated the principles of Aristotelian physics as well as common physical intuition. Biblical interpretation was also an issue, though there were hermeneutic schemes available for those who wished to accommodate apparently geocentric or geostatic passages to a heliocentric cosmology.

Responding to the Protestant challenge in the second half of the sixteenth century, Catholicism grew more conservative and authoritarian; power became centralized, and ideological vigilance increased. One of the most sensitive issues was biblical interpretation, for here Protestant rejection of the Catholic position that only the church interprets the Bible set the two sides in direct opposition. The Roman church assumed a firmer, more literalistic stance, and hermeneutic freedom was accordingly restricted. When Galileo burst on the scene in 1610, he came equipped not only with telescopic observations that could be used to support the heliocentric theory but also with liberal arguments about how to interpret biblical passages that seemed to teach the fixity of the earth. Thus the trouble in which Galileo found himself and which led ultimately to his condemnation was not a matter of clear scientific evidence running afoul of biblical claims to the contrary but of ambiguous scientific evidence (for Galileo was never able to produce a convincing proof of the earth's motion) provoking an intramural dispute within Catholicism over the proper principles of biblical interpretation—a dispute won by the conservatives at Galileo's expense.

Relations between Christianity and science became more intricate as the seventeenth century progressed. The condemnation of Galileo clearly had an inhibiting effect on certain lines of investigation in Catholic countries, particularly Italy. Nevertheless, by the middle of the century the French Catholics René Descartes, Marin Mersenne, and Pierre Gassendi (the second of whom was a friar and the last-named a priest) were among the principal formulators of the mechanical philosophy, an alternative to the natural philosophy of Aristotle and the foundation of much of the scientific work that followed. The mechanical philosophy experienced further development in Protestant England, where scientists such as Robert Boyle and Isaac Newton found support for it in Reformation ideas of the sovereignty of God and the total dependency of matter. Newton himself was convinced that nature demonstrated the existence and activity of God, but not the Trinitarian God of orthodox Christianity. It would be indefensible to maintain, with Hooykaas and Jaki, that Christianity was fundamentally responsible for the successes of seventeenth-century science. It would be a mistake of equal magnitude, however, to overlook the intricate interlocking of scientific and religious concerns throughout the century.

The eighteenth century witnessed the gradual unraveling of the close interaction between Christianity and science. As astronomers increasingly turned to physical explanations to account not only for the stability of the solar system but for its very origin, the concept of God became so superfluous that Laplace declared that the God hypothesis was of no further use to astronomers. Students of the life sciences displayed a similar disdain for miraculous explanations in science and grew noticeably uncomfortable in the presence of such metaphysical notions as that of the soul. The separation occurred, by and large, without rancor. True, some *philosophes* used scientific developments to discredit orthodox beliefs, and some conservative clerics feared that science was drifting too far from its religious moorings. But many persons found the idea of a Divine Architect, who created a smoothly running world machine and left it to itself, more appealing theologically than the image of a Divine Repairman, forced from time to time to fix his imperfect creation. The savior God of medieval and Reformation theology thus gave way to the clockmaker God of eighteenth-century deism. Among Christians in the English-speaking world the Baconian compromise described in chapter 13 helped to preserve congenial relations throughout the century by granting scientists the freedom to interpret the Scriptures in the light of science.

According to the warfare school of historians—and in the minds of many people today—the nineteenth century was the scene of some of the bloodiest battles in the conflict between science and religion. During the first half of the century, we have been taught, clerical defenders of the faith constantly harassed geologists who derived their history of the earth from the rocks rather than from the Bible; and enlightened advocates of uniformitarianism struggled against reactionary, theologically motivated catastrophists, who construed earth history to fit Mosaic history. After 1859 Christian churchmen marshaled their forces against the greatest threat of all—Darwinism, which made man an animal and left God unemployed. The legendary encounter in 1860 between Bishop Samuel ("Soapy Sam") Wilberforce and Thomas Huxley, "Darwin's bulldog," came to symbolize the acrimonious relationship that developed between orthodox clerics and Darwinian biologists. The bishop, as the apocryphal story went, pretentiously dismissed evolution and evolutionists with the insolent query: Was it through their grandfathers or their grandmothers that Darwinists claimed descent from monkeys? Huxley rose to the challenge. He was "not ashamed to have a monkey for his ancestor," he quipped, "but he would be ashamed to be connected with a man who used great gifts to obscure the truth."[36]

Little of this view of the nineteenth century survives in the chapters of the present book. The findings of geologists regarding the history of the earth did indeed depart far from traditional readings of Genesis, but reconcilers experienced little difficulty accommodating the testimony of the rocks. When conflict occurred, it was not along a simple line separating scientists and clerics. Rather, professional geologists, who embraced Charles Lyell's admonition to study geology "as if the Scriptures were not in existence," joined professional biblical scholars, who adopted Benjamin Jowett's advice to "interpret the Scriptures like any other book," in an alliance against amateur geologists and exegetes who refused to accept these maxims. In this version of the encounter between Genesis and geology, critical biblical scholarship played as important a role in fostering scientific geology as did empirical investigation.

The issues raised by Darwin also provoked widespread controversy, but such episodes as the Wilberforce-Huxley exchange represented a mere "tempest in a teapot." Some scientists, like Huxley, flaunted their desire to drive all vestiges of religion out of science, and some clerics, like Wilberforce, scarcely disguised their contempt for Darwin's theory. But the conflicts surrounding Darwin were far more complex than the science-versus-religion formula suggests. They arose between persons who wished to retain an older, theologically grounded view of science, and those who advocated a thoroughly positivistic science; scientists as well as clerics could be found on each side, neither of which was motivated solely by scientific considerations. In contrast with the stereotypical view of Darwin's clerical critics as ignorant obscurantists, the Reverend Charles Hodge, who equated Darwinism with atheism, appears in chapter 15 as a man who saw the issues as clearly as Darwin. For such orthodox Christians the fundamental question was not the incompatibility of Darwinism with the Mosaic account of creation nor the prospect of kinship with apes but the negative consequences of Darwinism for theism.

Even the twentieth-century controversy between creationists and evolutionists involved far more than conservative Christians fighting science. Religious fundamentalists did, to be sure, declare war on the teaching of evolution—not, however, because of hostility toward science in general (some of them were scientists themselves) but because of the social, moral, and theological implications of human evolution. Like the scriptural geologists of an earlier age, creationists regarded Genesis as a scientifically valid text and thus, in the view of their critics, smuggled religion back into science.

Although such mingling of science and Scripture found favor with large numbers of conservative Christians, it enjoyed little popularity among twentieth-century theologians. Liberal and neoorthodox alike rejected the authority of the Bible in matters of science and thus ruled out the possibility of conflict. Even most evangelical theologians, who did continue to look for ways of integrating theological and scientific concerns, went to great lengths to accommodate the findings of science. Only fundamentalists insisted on judging science by the Bible.

NOTES

1. See Donald Fleming, *John William Draper and the Religion of Science* (Philadelphia: Univ. of Pennsylvania Press, 1950).

2. John William Draper, *History of the Conflict between Religion and Science* (New York: D. Appleton & Co., 1874), pp. x–xi, 335, 364; James R. Moore, *The Post-Darwinian Controversies: A Study of the Protestant Struggle to Come to Terms with Darwin in Great Britain and America, 1870–1900* (Cambridge: Cambridge Univ. Press, 1979), pp. 20–29.

3. Draper, *Conflict*, pp. x–xi, 102, 363–364.

4. Ibid., p. 367.

5. Ibid., p. ix; Fleming, *John William Draper,* pp. 129–134; Moore, *Post-Darwinian Controversies,* pp. 28, 46.

6. Bruce Mazlish, preface to Andrew Dickson White, *A History of the Warfare of Science with Theology in Christendom,* abridged ed. (New York: The Free Press, 1965), p. 13. On White see Glenn C. Altschuler, *Andrew D. White—Educator, Historian, Diplomat* (Ithaca, N.Y.: Cornell Univ. Press, 1979).

7. Andrew Dickson White, *The Warfare of Science* (New York: D. Appleton and Co., 1876), p. 7; Moore, *Post-Darwinian Controversies,* pp. 29–40.

8. White, *Warfare* (1876), p. 8. The italics are White's.

9. Andrew Dickson White, *A History of the Warfare of Science with Theology in Christendom,* 2 vols. (New York: D. Appleton and Co., 1896), 1:xii. In the earliest published account of his thesis ("First of the Course of Scientific Lectures—Prof. White on 'The Battle-Fields of Science,'" *New-York Daily Tribune,* 18 Dec. 1869, p. 4), White repeatedly referred to relations between "Religion and Science"; in 1876 (White, *Warfare,* p. 145) he recounted "the long war between Ecclesiasticism and Science"; in 1896 he titled his book the *Warfare of Science with Theology.*

10. Moore, *Post-Darwinian Controversies,* p. 36; Altschuler, *Andrew D. White,* p. 208. For critical evaluations of White's scholarship see, e.g., O[tto] Zöckler, *Geschichte der Beziehungen zwischen Theologie und Naturwissenschaft, mit besonderer Rücksicht auf Schopfungsgeschichte,* 2 vols. (Gütersloh: C. Bertelsmann, 1877, 1879); Thomas Dwight, "Dr. Andrew D. White's *Warfare of Science,*" *Boston Medical and Surgical Journal* 125 (1891): 122–123; James J. Walsh, *The Popes and Science: The History of the Papal Relations to Science during the Middle Ages and Down to Our Own Time* (New York: Fordham Univ. Press, 1908). We are indebted to Rennie Schoepflin for bringing Dwight's comments to our attention.

11. See, e.g., Maynard Shipley, *The War on Modern Science: A Short History of the Fundamentalist Attacks on Evolution and Modernism* (New York: Alfred A. Knopf, 1927).

12. George Sarton, "Introductory Essay," in *Science, Religion and Reality,* ed. Joseph Needham (New York: George Braziller, 1955), pp. 3–22. For a less negative view see Charles Singer's essay in the same volume, "Historical Relations of Religion and Science," pp. 89–152, which was also published as a separate book, *Religion and Science Considered in Their Historical Relations* (New York: Robert M. McBride, n.d.). The Needham volume first appeared in 1925.

13. Mazlish, preface, pp. 9, 18.

14. Alfred North Whitehead, *Science and the Modern World* (New York: Macmillan, 1925); M. B. Foster, "The Christian Doctrine of Creation and the Rise of Modern Natural Science," *Mind* 43 (1934): 446–468; M. B. Foster, "Christian Theology and Modern Science of Nature," *Mind* 44 (1935): 439–466, and 45 (1936): 1–27. For a recent restatement of this position see Eugene M. Klaaren, *Religious Origins of Modern Science: Belief in Creation in Seventeenth-Century Thought* (Grand Rapids, Mich.: Wm. B. Eerdmans, 1977).

15. Robert K. Merton, "Science, Technology and Society in Seventeenth Century England," *Osiris* 4 (1938): 432–434.

16. Ibid., pp. 419–424.

17. Robert K. Merton, "Puritanism, Pietism, and Science," *The Sociological Review* 28 (1936): 6, 8.

18. Merton, "Science, Technology and Society," pp. 416–417.

19. Ibid., p. 474.

20. Lotte Mulligan, "Civil War Politics, Religion and the Royal Society," *Past and Present* 59 (1973): 108; reprinted in *The Intellectual Revolution of the Seventeenth Century,* ed. Charles Webster (London: Routledge & Kegan Paul, 1974), p. 336. Mulligan herself has, in turn, been challenged; see chap. 7 of this volume.

21. A. Rupert Hall, "Merton Revisited, or Science and Society in the Seventeenth Century," *History of Science* 2 (1963): 4; Theodore K. Rabb, "Religion and the Rise of Modern Science," *Past and Present* 31 (1965): 112; François Russo, S. J., "Catholicism, Protestantism, and the Development of Science in the Sixteenth and Seventeenth Centuries," in *The Evolution of Science,* ed. Guy S. Métraux and François Crouzet (New York: New American Library, 1963), pp. 291–320.

22. Charles Webster, *The Great Instauration: Science, Medicine and Reform, 1626–1660* (London: Duckworth, 1975).

23. See, e.g., R[eijer] Hooykaas, *Religion and the Rise of Modern Science* (Grand Rapids, Mich: Wm. B. Eerdmans, 1972), and Stanley L. Jaki, *The Road of Science and the Ways to God* (Chicago: Univ. of Chicago Press, 1978). For a historical and theological critique of the thesis that Christianity officiated at the birth of modern science see Rolf Gruner, "Science, Nature, and Christianity," *Journal of Theological Studies* 26 (1975): 55–81.

24. A. Hunter Dupree, *Asa Gray, 1810–1888* (Cambridge, Mass.: Harvard Univ. Press, 1959); Charles Coulston Gillispie, *Genesis and Geology: A Study in the Relations of Scientific Thought, Natural Theology, and Social Opinion in Great Britain, 1790–1850* (Cambridge, Mass.: Harvard Univ. Press, 1951); Paul H. Kocher, *Science and Religion in Elizabethan England* (San Marino, Calif.: Huntington Library, 1953); Giorgio de Santillana, *The Crime of Galileo* (Chicago: Univ. of Chicago Press, 1955); Richard S. Westfall, *Science and Religion in Seventeenth-Century England* (New Haven: Yale Univ. Press, 1958).

25. John Dillenberger, *Protestant Thought and Natural Science: A Historical Interpretation* (Nashville: Abingdon Press, 1960). Since the 1940s Charles E. Raven has been arguing that the supposed conflict between science and Christianity has been exaggerated; see his *Science, Religion, and the Future: A Course of Eight Lectures* (Cambridge: Cambridge Univ. Press, 1943), and *Natural Religion and Christian Theology, First Series: Science and Religion* (Cambridge: Cambridge Univ. Press, 1953).

26. John C. Greene, *Darwin and the Modern World View* (Baton Rouge: Louisiana State Univ. Press, 1961), p. 4; Paul F. Boller, Jr., *American Thought in Transition: The Impact of Evolutionary Naturalism, 1865–1900* (Chicago: Rand McNally, 1969), pp. 22–48. For additional examples of this tendency see Francis C. Haber, *The Age of the World: Moses to Darwin* (Baltimore: Johns Hopkins Press, 1959), pp. 1–2; William Coleman, *Biology in the Nineteenth Century: Problems of Form, Function, and Transformation* (New York: John Wiley

& Sons, 1971), pp. 86–87; Michael Ruse, *The Darwinian Revolution: Science Red in Tooth and Claw* (Chicago: Univ. of Chicago Press, 1979); and Ernst Mayr, *The Growth of Biological Thought: Diversity, Evolution, and Inheritance* (Cambridge, Mass.: Harvard Univ. Press, Belknap Press, 1982), pp. 307–309. For an idiosyncratic view of conflict see Lewis S. Feuer, *The Scientific Intellectual: The Psychological and Sociological Origins of Modern Science* (New York: Basic Books, 1963), which focuses on the psychological opposition of scientists, motivated by a "hedonist-libertarian ethic," to theological constraints.

27. Roy Porter, *The Making of Geology: Earth Science in Britain, 1660–1815* (Cambridge: Cambridge Univ. Press, 1977), pp. 197–198; Herbert Hovenkamp, *Science and Religion in America, 1800–1860* (Philadelphia: Univ. of Pennsylvania Press, 1978), pp. 48–49. See also Theodore Dwight Bozeman, *Protestants in an Age of Science: The Baconian Ideal and Antebellum American Religious Thought* (Chapel Hill: Univ. of North Carolina Press, 1977), which sees harmony disappearing in the 1850s (p. 104); and Ronald L. Numbers, *Creation by Natural Law: Laplace's Nebular Hypothesis in American Thought* (Seattle: Univ. of Washington Press, 1977), which tends to postpone conflict until the fundamentalist controversy in the twentieth century (pp. 117–118).

28. Owen Chadwick, *The Victorian Church*, Part 2, 2d ed. (London: Adam & Charles Black, 1972), pp. 1–39, and Chadwick, *The Secularization of the European Mind in the Nineteenth Century* (Cambridge: Cambridge Univ. Press, 1975), pp. 161–188.

29. Moore, *Post-Darwinian Controversies*, pp. 80, 89, 94, 99, 103.

30. Neal C. Gillespie, *Charles Darwin and the Problem of Creation* (Chicago: Univ. of Chicago Press, 1979). pp. 12–13, 18, 53. See also Alvar Ellegård, *Darwin and the General Reader: The Reception of Darwin's Theory of Evolution in the British Periodical Press, 1859–1872* (Gothenburg, Sweden: Elanders Boktryckeri Aktiebolag, 1958), p. 337; and Charles C. Gillispie, *Genesis and Geology,* p. ix.

31. Frank M. Turner, "The Victorian Conflict between Science and Religion: A Professional Dimension," *Isis* 69 (1978): 356–376.

32. This point has also been argued by Robert M. Young, "The Historiographic and Ideological Contexts of the Nineteenth-Century Debate on Man's Place in Nature," in *Changing Perspectives in the History of Science: Essays in Honour of Joseph Needham,* ed. Mikuláš Teich and Robert M. Young (London: William Heinemann, 1973), pp. 344–438.

33. Margaret C. Jacob, *The Newtonians and the English Revolution, 1689–1720* (Ithaca, N.Y.: Cornell Univ. Press, 1976), pp. 17–18. See also James R. Jacob, *Robert Boyle and the English Revolution: A Study in Social and Intellectual Change* (New York: Burt Franklin, 1977); and Barry Barnes and Steven Shapin, eds., *Natural Order: Historical Studies of Scientific Culture* (Beverly Hills, Calif.: Sage Publications, 1979).

34. Martin Rudwick, "Senses of the Natural World and Senses of God: Another Look at the Historical Relation of Science and Religion," in *The Sciences and Theology in the Twentieth Century,* ed. A. R. Peacocke (Notre Dame, Ind.: Univ. of Notre Dame Press, 1981), pp. 241–261.

35. For a parallel opinion regarding world histories see Donald Kagan, "The Changing World of World Histories," *New York Times Book Review,* 11 Nov. 1984, pp. 1, 41–42, from which the quotation is taken.

36. J. R. Lucas, "Wilberforce and Huxley: A Legendary Encounter," *The Historical Journal* 22 (1979): 313–330.

1

Science and the Early Church

David C. Lindberg

> The pagan party . . . asserted that knowledge is to be obtained only by the laborious exercise of human observation and human reason. The Christian party asserted that all knowledge is to be found in the Scriptures and in the traditions of the Church; that, in the written revelation, God had not only given a criterion of truth, but had furnished us with all that he intended us to know. The Scriptures, therefore, contain the sum, the end of all knowledge. The clergy, with the emperor at their back, would endure no intellectual competition. . . .
>
> The Church thus set herself forth as the depository and arbiter of knowledge; she was ever ready to resort to the civil power to compel obedience to her decisions. She thus took a course which determined her whole future career; she became a stumbling block in the intellectual advancement of Europe for more than a thousand years.[1]

Thus wrote John William Draper (1811–1882) in a polemic against the excesses of organized Christianity, especially Catholicism. In so doing, he gave shape to what has become a very widespread (probably the dominant) interpretation of the relationship between science and the early church: that the church, if it did not entirely stamp out science, surely retarded its progress.

This theme was echoed near the end of the nineteenth century by Andrew Dickson White (1832–1918). After quoting Augustine on the necessity of yielding to scriptural authority, White commented:

> No treatise was safe thereafter which did not breathe the spirit and conform to the letter of this maxim. Unfortunately, what was generally understood by the "authority of Scripture" was the tyranny of sacred books imperfectly transcribed, viewed through distorting superstitions, and frequently interpreted by party spirit. Following this precept of St. Augustine there

were developed, in every field, theological views of science which have
never led to a single truth—which, without exception, have forced mankind away from the truth, and have caused Christendom to stumble for
centuries into abysses of error and sorrow.[2]

Draper and White believed that Christianity waged war on science
in two ways. First, the early church fathers denigrated the investigation of nature for its own sake: with the kingdom of heaven just
around the corner, there was no time or energy to waste on irrele-
vancies. Second, any truth that might be discovered through patient
observation and reasoning was forced to yield to the puerile opinions
extracted by dogmatic churchmen from sacred writings. White
claimed: "The most careful inductions from ascertained facts were
regarded as wretchedly fallible when compared with any view of
nature whatever given or even hinted at in any poem, chronicle, code,
apologue, myth, legend, allegory, letter, or discourse of any sort
which had happened to be preserved in the literature which had come
to be held as sacred."[3] The result was a tyranny of ignorance and
superstition that perverted and crushed true science.[4]

The thesis of Draper and White has given way to a spectrum of
scholarly opinion in the twentieth century. Some scholars continue
to affirm, although (in most cases) somewhat less militantly, the
Draper-White view.[5] Others have gone to the opposite extreme, arguing that Christianity was good for science—indeed, that modern
science would not have come into existence without it.[6] And some
have sought middle ground.[7] But this is scholarship; in popular opinion the Draper-White view still prevails. It frequently appears in books
aimed at the general reader; moreover, Draper's and White's own
works continue to be reprinted, purchased, and presumably read and
believed.[8]

This chapter will reassess the evidence, while shunning, as far as
possible, the polemical and ideological goals that motivated Draper
and White and continue to motivate many discussions of early Christianity and science. Instead of using the historical problem as an
occasion for attacking or defending Christianity for its detrimental or
beneficial effects on science, we must endeavor to understand the
complexity and subtlety of their interaction. Only thus can we achieve
a fair appraisal and learn something useful.

Discussions of our subject have frequently suffered from the assumption that in antiquity there was an intellectual discipline having
more or less the same methods and the same lines of demarcation as
modern science, to which the term *science* can be properly and unambiguously applied. Thus it was modern science, or its immediate
antecedent, that Draper and White and their followers held Chris-

tianity to have retarded. But the truth is far more complicated. Several of the subdivisions of modern science did exist as recognizable disciplines in antiquity—for example, medicine (with some associated biological knowledge) and mathematics (including astronomy and other branches of mathematical science). But there was nothing in antiquity corresponding to modern science as a whole or to such branches of modern science as physics, chemistry, geology, zoology, and psychology. The subject matters of these modern disciplines all belonged to natural philosophy and thus to the larger philosophical enterprise.[9] Even such distinctions as existed (for example, that between natural philosophy and mathematics) could be easily overlooked, since the disciplines thus distinguished did not represent clearly defined social roles or professions.[10] The natural philosopher and the mathematician were often the same person, and professionally he would probably have identified himself neither as natural philosopher nor as mathematician but simply as a teacher; and his teaching would likely have extended beyond mathematics and natural philosophy to all manner of other philosophical issues. The world of the intellect thus had a unity in antiquity that it does not have today. It was not sharply divisible into separate disciplines, such as metaphysics, theology, epistemology, ethics, natural science, and mathematics, but presented itself as a relatively unified and coherent whole.

The methodology of this scholarly enterprise has often been misrepresented. Members of the Draper-White School have portrayed ancient philosophy as an early version of modern scholarship—the embodiment of the ideals of rationality, objectivity, and whatever other traits they find praiseworthy in themselves.[11] Undoubtedly, there were ancient philosophers and philosophical schools for which such a characterization is more or less apt, and I do not wish to understate or downplay the rationalistic tendencies of Greek philosophy. Certainly the rationalism of Greek thought was one of the greatest achievements of antiquity.[12] But in late antiquity philosophy was changing. The philosophical classics of the past continued to be available and influential, but within the living, contemporary tradition the focus of attention was shifting toward ethics, metaphysics, and theology; and, in some of its manifestations, philosophy was becoming progressively more like a religion, based on inspired authorities, with mystical illumination and personal salvation among its principal goals. Thus Neoplatonic authors such as Porphyry, Iamblichus, Proclus, and Damascius (third through sixth centuries) accepted the *Chaldean Oracles* (esoteric religious writings devoted to theurgy, demonology, and other forms of magic) as an authoritative source of revealed truth, beyond the reach of rational discussion and debate.[13]

Those who would characterize the early Christian tradition as "superstitious" must apply the same term to aspects of contemporary pagan philosophy.

There is also a tendency within the Draper-White tradition to see pagan philosophy as tolerant, committed to a free market of ideas—in contrast with the intolerance of Christians. Indeed, those who regret the triumph of Christianity frequently have this in mind, viewing the struggle between Christianity and pagan philosophy as a battle for freedom of thought. But this too is a misconception. To have it corrected, one need only recall that Plato demanded solitary confinement (and, in extreme cases, execution) for those who denied the existence of the gods and their involvement in human affairs.[14] Intolerance was (and is) a widely cultivated trait, shared about equally by pagans and Christians. Moreover, each party was capable of employing coercive measures when it possessed the political power to do so; Christians, in fact, appear to have yielded to the temptation less often than did pagans.[15]

This is the pagan philosophical culture that the early church confronted. It comprised both a contemporary philosophical tradition and a collection of philosophical classics; it dealt with an enormous range of philosophical issues, covering the spectrum from epistemology to politics; and it furnished the technical tools for reasoned discourse. It did not look very much like modern science. Although we will eventually focus our attention on that portion of its content which pertained to nature, we must (if we wish to understand the church's response) begin by considering it as a whole. We must ask: How did the early church regard pagan intellectual culture? How and to what extent did Christians make use of it? Was Christian theology ever a rational enterprise, employing the tools of Greek philosophy, or did it always involve a retreat from philosophy into the claims of revelation? How were Christian thought and the pagan philosophical tradition affected by their encounter? We must, in short, begin by examining the problem of reason and revelation—the question raised by Tertullian when he inquired: "What has Athens to do with Jerusalem?

ATHENS AND JERUSALEM

Christianity spread rapidly outward from Jerusalem and surrounding Judaea during the first century of the Christian era, particularly to the north and west, into Syria, Asia Minor, and as far as Rome. Beginning as a Jewish sect, appealing largely to Hellenized Jews, it

first broadened its reach into the Gentile world through the efforts
of the Apostle Paul. It was too insignificant a sect to attract serious
attention from the Roman authorities until Christians were blamed
by the emperor Nero for the great fire that destroyed Rome in
A.D. 64. Considered antisocial because of their unwillingness to participate in the traditional religious practices, Christians thereafter attracted sporadic persecution through the third century—persecution
that seems to have contributed more to the growth than to the decline
of Christianity. The conversion of the emperor Constantine early in
the fourth century marked the beginning of a radical change in the
political fortunes of Christianity; by the end of the fourth century it
had become the state religion.[16]

From the beginning Christianity attracted converts from a wide
social and intellectual spectrum. The Apostle Paul is representative
of highly educated Hellenized Judaism; one finds within his writings
ample evidence of familiarity with Greek philosophical systems. As
people committed to sacred writings, Christians were in need of literacy and therefore at least elementary education, but it was not until
the second century that Christianity, under the influence of doctrinal
dissent within and attack from without, developed a significant intellectual tradition. The first major Christian apologist was Justin Martyr, of Greek descent, born in Samaria near the beginning of the
second century and martyred in Rome between 162 and 168. Justin
studied Stoic, Aristotelian, Pythagorean, and Platonic philosophy,
finding satisfaction only in the last-named. Later he converted to
Christianity and became convinced of the fundamental compatibility
between Christian doctrine, Platonic metaphysics, and Stoic ethics.
He firmly rejected pagan polytheistic religion but welcomed such
pagan philosophy as was consistent with biblical teaching. Justin explained the impressive parallels between Christianity and pagan philosophy (particularly Platonism, which not only could be construed
as monotheistic but also taught the immortality of the soul and the
formation of the world at a point in time) by proposing that the Greek
philosophers had studied the Old Testament, and also that all of
humankind, insofar as it thinks rightly, does so through participation
in the universal rational power, the divine *logos*, Christ. Justin thus
expressed deep confidence in the power of reason—a divine gift.[17]

The apologetic work begun by Justin was continued by Athenag-
oras, Theophilus of Antioch, Clement of Alexandria, Origen, and
others. There were varieties of opinion among these apologists, of
course, but all were familiar with Greek philosophy, esteemed portions of it, particularly Platonic philosophy (for its many affinities
with Christian theology), and put it to apologetic use whenever pos-

sible. Clement (d. between 211 and 215), a teacher in a catechetical
school in Alexandria, regarded Greek philosophy as absolutely essential for the defense of the faith against heresy and skepticism and
for the development of Christian doctrine. Central to Clement's
thought was the doctrine that truth is one—that ultimately all truth,
wherever it may be encountered, is God's truth.[18] In his *Stromateis* he
claimed that "barbarian and Greek philosophy have torn off a piece
of the eternal truth . . . from the theology of the Logos who eternally
is. And he who brings together again the divided parts and makes
them one, mark well, shall without danger of error look upon the
perfect Logos, the truth."[19] Like Justin, he argued that Greek philosophy partook of the truth because it was plagiarized from the Old
Testament, and also because pagan philosophers employed their God-
given rational capacities to obtain a portion of divine truth. Thus did
Clement endeavor to rescue Christianity from the charge of intellectual obscurantism by affirming the value of Greek philosophy.

The attitude of Origen (ca. 185–ca. 254) toward Greek philosophy,
particularly Platonic, was even more liberal than Clement's. Origen,
also an Alexandrian teacher, possessed a thorough knowledge of
Greek philosophy—Aristotelian, Platonic, Stoic, and Epicurean. He
adopted the basic elements of Plato's theology, cosmology, and psychology, while borrowing his terminology and definitions from Aristotle.[20] His student Gregory Thaumaturgus, commenting on
Origen's teaching methodology, reveals Origen's remarkable open-
ness to pagan philosophical sources:

> He required us to study philosophy by reading all the existing writings
> of the ancients, both philosophers and religious poets, taking every care
> not to put aside or reject any . . . , apart from the writings of atheists. . . .
> He selected everything that was useful and true in each philosopher and
> set it before us, but condemned what was false. . . . For us there was
> nothing forbidden, nothing hidden, nothing inaccessible. We were allowed
> to learn every doctrine, non-Greek and Greek, both spiritual and secular,
> both divine and human; with the utmost freedom we went into everything
> and examined it thoroughly, taking our fill of and enjoying the pleasures
> of the soul.[21]

Not all Christians shared the opinion of Justin, Clement, and Origen. Tatian, a Syrian Christian who apparently studied under Justin,
was skeptical of the value of Greek philosophy and launched an attack
on the teaching of the pagan schools.[22] In the third century the author
of the *Didascalia apostolorum* warned Christians against the dangers of
pagan literature: "Shun all heathen books. Of what concern to you

are strange ideas or laws or pseudo-prophets, which often lead inexperienced men into error? What is lacking to you in God's word, that you should turn to that heathen nonsense?"[23] And in the fourth century, John Chrysostom, who was willing to concede that pagan schools were not without value, nevertheless pointed out that "the study of eloquence requires good morals, but good morals do not require eloquence."[24] Whether or not such views were typical of Christians, they were portrayed as such by pagan opponents. Celsus (fl. ca. 177–180) accused Christians of enjoining, "Let no one educated, no one wise, no one sensible draw near. For these abilities are thought by us to be evils. But as for anyone ignorant, anyone stupid, anyone uneducated, . . . let him come boldly."[25] Eusebius, probably reporting Porphyry's view, refers to those who "have supposed that Christianity has no reason to support itself but that those who desire the name confirm their opinion by an unreasoning faith and an assent without examination."[26] And the emperor Julian, who promoted a restoration of paganism in the fourth century, argued as follows against the Christians (at the same time giving paganism somewhat more than its due): "Ours are the reasoned arguments and the pagan tradition which comprehend at the same time due worship of the gods; yours are want of reason and rusticity, and all your wisdom can be summed up in the imperative 'Believe.'"[27]

The church father who is generally taken to epitomize the antiintellectualism of the early church is Tertullian (ca. 155–ca. 230), whose views we must therefore consider with some care. Tertullian was a native of Carthage in Roman Africa, of pagan parentage, well educated in philosophy, medicine, and law, and able to write in either Greek or Latin. Etienne Gilson has portrayed him as an implacable foe of pagan philosophy, the archetype of those Christian theologians who wished to substitute faith for reason.[28] In a celebrated denunciation of philosophy, Tertullian exclaims:

> What indeed has Athens to do with Jerusalem? What concord is there between the Academy and the Church? What between heretics and Christians? Our instruction comes from "the porch of Solomon," who had himself taught that "the Lord should be sought in simplicity of heart." Away with all attempts to produce a mottled Christianity of Stoic, Platonic, and dialectic composition! We want no curious disputation after possessing Christ Jesus, no inquisition after enjoying the gospel! With our faith, we desire no further belief. For once we believe this, there is nothing else that we ought to believe.[29]

Elsewhere Tertullian attacks vain curiosity about nature:

Now, pray tell me, what wisdom is there in this hankering after conjectural speculations? What proof is afforded to us, notwithstanding the strong confidence of its assertions, by the useless affectation of a scrupulous curiosity, which is tricked out with an artful show of language? It therefore served Thales of Miletus quite right, when, star-gazing as he walked with all the eyes he had, he had the mortification of falling into a well. . . . His fall, therefore, is a figurative picture of the philosophers; of those, I mean, who persist in applying their studies to a vain purpose, since they indulge a stupid curiosity on natural objects, which they ought rather [to direct intelligently] to their Creator and Governor.[30]

There can be no doubt that Tertullian was not an enthusiast for secular learning; but neither was he the uncompromising opponent of reasoned discourse that these passages, if allowed to stand alone, might seem to imply. It was apparent to him that philosophy led easily to heresy, especially the Gnostic heresy (a dualistic system, which radically separated the transcendent deity from a dark and evil material world). What he therefore opposed was not philosophy generally but heresy or the philosophy that gave rise to it.[31] When not engaged in polemic against heresy, he could express a quite favorable view of mankind's rational capacities. On one occasion he argued that "reason . . . is a thing of God, inasmuch as there is nothing which God the Maker of all has not provided, disposed, ordained by reason—nothing which He has not willed should be handled and understood by reason."[32] He even defended the possibility of rational knowledge of divine things: "One may no doubt be wise in the things of God, even from one's natural powers. . . . For some things are known even by nature: the immortality of the soul, for instance, is held by many; the knowledge of our God is possessed by all."[33] Tertullian is frequently quoted as having said of the resurrection of Christ, "I believe it because it is absurd." However, scholars have adequately established, first, that this is a misquotation, but more importantly that Tertullian was simply making use of a standard Aristotelian argumentative form, maintaining that the more improbable an event, the less likely is anybody to believe, without compelling evidence, that it has occurred; therefore, the very improbability of an alleged event, such as Christ's resurrection, is evidence in its favor.[34] Thus, far from seeking the abolition of reason, Tertullian must be seen as appropriating Aristotelian rational techniques and putting them to apologetic use. Philosophy, despite its dangers, had a place in the armory of the Christian. But Tertullian never forgot to put first things first.

In the long run the most influential statement of the Christian attitude toward philosophy and reason was that of Augustine (354–

430). Augustine obtained a rich classical education, heavily literary in its orientation, in the North African schools of Thagaste, Madaura, and finally Carthage.[35] In his early manhood Augustine yielded to the appeal of Manichaean religion, with its dualism between good and evil and its unwavering rationalism; later he discovered the works of Plotinus and became deeply imbued with Neoplatonic philosophy. Meanwhile he converted to Christianity and began the effort, which occupied him through much of his life, of accommodating Neoplatonism and Christianity.[36]

Augustine's position has frequently been misunderstood as an attempt to substitute faith for reason. But this was surely never his purpose: philosophy and the philosophical life were not to be replaced or repudiated, but to be Christianized.[37] Esteem for human rational capacities pervades Augustine's writings. Reason is a divine gift, which distinguishes humankind from brutes, and its exercise is to be assiduously cultivated. In a letter to Consentius, Augustine spoke of his wish "to arouse your faith to a love of understanding, to which true reason conducts the mind and for which faith prepares it."[38] He went on to point out that heretical reasoning about the Trinity "is to be shunned and detested, not because it is reasoning, but because it is false reasoning; for if it were true reasoning, it would surely not err. Therefore, just as you would be ill advised to avoid all speaking because some speaking is false, so you must not avoid all reasoning because some reasoning is false."[39] Reasoning is indispensable if the faith is to be defended and its content understood; it is also required if one is to grasp that portion of truth which has not been revealed. Augustine's letter to Consentius is a remarkable expression of these themes:

> You say that truth is to be grasped more by faith than by reason. . . . Therefore, according to your rule you ought in this matter . . . to follow only the authority of the saints and not seek understanding by asking me for reasons. For when I begin . . . to lead you to an understanding of so great a mystery, . . . I will simply be giving you reasons, insofar as I am able. But if it is not unreasonable for you to beg me or some other teacher to help you to understand what you believe, then you ought to correct your rule—not to the point of overturning faith, but of permitting you to discern in the light of reason what you already firmly hold by faith.
>
> Heaven forbid that God should hate in us that by which he made us superior to the other animals! Heaven forbid that we should believe in such a way as not to accept or seek reasons, since we could not even believe if we did not possess rational souls. Therefore, in certain matters pertaining to the doctrine of salvation that we cannot yet grasp by reason— though one day we shall be able to do so—faith must precede reason and

purify the heart and make it fit to receive and endure the great light of
reason; and this is surely something reasonable. Thus it is reasonable for
the Prophet [Isa. 7:9] to have said: "Unless you believe, you will not
understand." Here he was doubtless distinguishing between these two
things and advising us first to believe, so that afterwards we might understand what we believe. It is thus reasonable to require that faith precede
reason. . . . If, therefore, it is reasonable for faith to precede reason in
certain matters of great moment that cannot yet be grasped, surely the
very small portion of reason that persuades us of this must precede faith.[40]

Despite his reference in the final lines of this passage to reason that
precedes faith, Augustine usually stresses the movement from faith
to reason or understanding. Without faith there will be no understanding; once faith is achieved, the quest for understanding is
obligatory.

Can we then say that Augustine subordinates reason to faith? Yes,
in the sense that ultimate authority rests with revelation. Augustine
had no hesitation in proclaiming his resolve "in nothing whatever to
depart from the authority of Christ."[41] But to concentrate exclusively
on the question of authority is to adopt a modern perspective and to
overlook Augustine's. Augustine viewed faith not as a taskmaster to
which reason must submit but as the condition that makes genuine
rational activity possible. Christian faith provides the foundation, the
blueprint, and the materials, without which no sound philosophical
structures can be built. Philosophy thus finds its fulfillment within
the framework of faith. For Augustine the highest goal is understanding: "Our Lord . . . says to believers, 'Seek and ye shall find [Matt.
7:7].' But one cannot speak of that being found which is believed
without knowledge."[42] The relationship between faith and reason is
therefore that between the precondition and the ultimate objective,
the means and the end; in that sense we find in Augustine the subordination not of reason to faith but of faith to reason.[43]

What, then, has Athens to do with Jerusalem? No uniform answer
will suffice for all of the fathers of the Christian church. There was a
spectrum of attitudes toward pagan culture, from deep mistrust to
high enthusiasm. But few would have rejected pagan philosophical
culture totally. For the great majority, whether or not to philosophize
was no issue; the question was rather how and about what to philosophize. The classic answer given by Augustine and destined for
enormous influence set philosophy to work on revelation and the
content of Christian belief. But this required philosophical education.
Christians were thus committed to education—and in practical terms
this meant secular education, since no Christian educational system
was developed until much later. Gregory of Nazianzus (329–389) revealed how liberal the Christian position could be, when he wrote:

I take it as admitted by men of sense, that the first of our advantages is education; and not only this our more noble form of it, which disregards rhetorical ornaments and glory, and holds to salvation, and beauty in the objects of our contemplation: but even that external [i.e., pagan] culture which many Christians ill-judgingly abhor, as treacherous and dangerous, and keeping us afar from God. For as we ought not to neglect the heavens, and earth, and air, and all such things, because some have wrongly seized upon them, and honour God's works instead of God: but to reap what advantage we can from them for our life and enjoyment, while we avoid their dangers; not raising creation, as foolish men do, in revolt against the Creator, but from the works of nature apprehending the Worker, and, as the divine apostle says, bringing into captivity every thought to Christ; and again, as we know that neither fire, nor food, nor iron, nor any other of the elements, is of itself most useful, or most harmful, except according to the will of those who use it; and as we have compounded healthful drugs from certain of the reptiles; so from secular literature we have received principles of enquiry and speculation, while we have rejected their idolatry, terror, and pit of destruction. . . . We must not then dishonour education, because some men are pleased to do so, but rather suppose such men to be boorish and uneducated, desiring all men to be as they themselves are, in order to hide themselves in the general, and escape the detection of their want of culture.[44]

There are no data to permit a judgment regarding the average educational levels of pagans and Christians, but it is clear that the Christian intelligentsia were at least as well educated as, and the intellectual equals of, their pagan counterparts.[45]

THE CHURCH AND NATURAL SCIENCE

Although science was neither an autonomous discipline nor a profession during the patristic period, we can nonetheless investigate the relationship between Christianity and those aspects of the philosophical enterprise which were concerned with nature. Did science in this sense benefit or suffer from the appeerence and triumph of Christianity? Did Christianity, with its otherworldliness and its emphasis on biblical authority, stifle interest in nature, as the old stereotype proclaims? Or was there a more ambiguous and subtle relationship?

We must begin our inquiry by briefly surveying the state of science in late antiquity. Was there, in fact, a decline of science for which Christianity might be held responsible? The answer is not simple. Surely there are instances of important scientific work in the early centuries of the Christian era. Ptolemy's work in astronomy and Galen's in medicine (both in the second century A.D.) and Diophantus's mathematical efforts (in the third century) are outstanding examples.[46] And, as we shall see, John Philoponus presented a major and important reassessment of Aristotelian physics and cosmology as late as the sixth century. Nevertheless, it is agreed by most historians of ancient science that creative Greek science was on the wane, perhaps as early as 200 B.C., certainly by A.D. 200.[47] Science had never been pursued by very many people; it now attracted even fewer. And its character shifted away from original thought toward commentary and abridgment. Creative natural science was particularly scarce in the Roman world, where scholarly interests leaned in the direction of ethics and metaphysics; such natural science as Rome possessed was largely confined to fragments preserved in handbooks and encyclopedias.[48]

Can Christianity be held responsible in any way for this decline? Let us first consider Christian otherworldliness. In antiquity there was a broad spectrum of attitudes toward the material world. At one end of the spectrum was pagan cosmic religion, constructed from a mixture of Pythagorean, Platonic, Aristotelian, and Stoic doctrines. This cosmic religion saw the material cosmos, or at least its upper, heavenly part, as a perfect expression of divine creativity and providence, "the supreme manifestation of divinity," and indeed itself a divine being. Moreover, study and contemplation of the cosmos were judged the only ways to God; natural philosophy and theology had been merged.[49] At the other end of the spectrum was the Gnostic attempt to equate the material world with evil. The cosmos was viewed by "pessimistic" Gnostics as a disastrous mistake, the scene of disorder and sin, the product of evil forces, the antithesis of the divine, and a prison from which the soul must escape in order to make its way to its true home in the spiritual realm.[50] Finally, between these extremes there was Platonic philosophy (or, in the hands of certain Neoplatonists, Platonic religion), which distinguished clearly between the transcendent world of eternal forms and their imperfect replication in the material cosmos. Neoplatonists by no means considered the world to be evil; it was the product of divine intelligence and, as A. H. Armstrong puts it, the "best possible universe that could be produced under difficult circumstances."[51] Contemplation of it was even held to play a positive, albeit small, role in leading the soul upward to the eternal forms. Nevertheless, Neoplatonism was fundamentally otherworldly; the material world, for all its beauty, remained the scene of imperfection and disorder; and it had to be escaped before humanity could achieve its highest good, the contemplation of eternal truths.

There was, of course, no unitary Christian view of the material world. But orthodox Christianity, as it developed, emphatically rejected the extremes; nature was neither to be worshiped nor to be repudiated. Christianity was deeply influenced by Neoplatonic philosophy, and most Christian thinkers adopted some form of the Neoplatonic attitude. Gregory of Nyssa (ca. 331–ca. 396) believed deeply in the unreality and deceitfulness of the material world and yet recognized that it could provide signs and symbols that would lead mankind upward to God.[52] Augustine insisted that sin is situated not in the body but in the will. This was a point of extraordinary importance, because it helped to liberate western Christendom from the notion that the soul is contaminated by its contact with the body— and therefore that matter and flesh must be inherently evil.[53] Nevertheless, in a well-known passage from the *Enchiridion*, Augustine expressed serious doubt about the value of natural science:

> When it is asked what we ought to believe in matters of religion, the answer is not to be sought in the exploration of the nature of things, after the manner of those whom the Greeks called "physicists." Nor should we be dismayed if Christians are ignorant about the properties and the number of the basic elements of nature, or about the motion, order, and deviations of the stars, the map of the heavens, the kinds and nature of animals, plants, stones, springs, rivers, and mountains; about the divisions of space and time, about the signs of impending storms, and the myriad other things which these "physicists" have come to understand, or think they have. . . . For the Christian, it is enough to believe that the cause of all created things, whether in heaven or on earth, whether visible or invisible, is nothing other than the goodness of the Creator, who is the one and the true God.[54]

Yet, insofar as scientific knowledge is required, it must be taken from the pagan authors who possess it:

> Usually, even a non-Christian knows something about the earth, the heavens, and the other elements of this world, about the motion and orbit of the stars and even their size and relative positions, about the predictable eclipses of the sun and moon, the cycles of the years and the seasons, about the kinds of animals, shrubs, stones, and so forth, and this knowledge he holds as certain from reason and experience. Now it is a disgraceful and dangerous thing for an infidel to hear a Christian, presumably giving the meaning of Holy Scripture, talking nonsense on these topics; and we should take all means to prevent such an embarrassing situation, in which people show up vast ignorance in a Christian and laugh it to scorn.[55]

A view broadly the same as Augustine's was presented by Pope Leo the Great (440–461). Leo argued that the material world is not to be denigrated:

Man, awake, and recognize the dignity of your own nature. Remember that you were made in the image of God; and though it was spoilt in Adam, it has been remade again in Christ. Use these visible creatures as they ought to be used, as you use earth, sea, sky, air, springs and rivers; and praise and glorify the Creator for everything fair and wonderful in them.

But neither should the material creation be allowed to occupy the center of attention:

Do not devote yourself to the light in which birds and snakes, beasts and cattle, flies and worms delight. Feel bodily light with your bodily senses and clasp with all the strength of your mind that true light which "lightens every man coming into this world." . . . For if we are the temple of God, and the Spirit of God dwells in us, what everyone of the faithful has in his own soul is more than what he admires in the sky. We are not, of course, . . . telling you this to persuade you to despise the works of God, or to think that there is anything against your faith in the things which the good God has made good; but so that you may use every kind of creature, and all the furniture of this world, reasonably and temperately. . . . So, since we are born to things of this present life but reborn to those of the future life, let us not devote ourselves to temporal goods but be set on eternal ones. . . .[56]

The material world is not to be loved but to be used; it is not an end in itself but a means to the contemplation of higher things.

What were the implications of this attitude for the scientific enterprise? If we employ as a standard of comparison some sort of ideal world, a scientist's paradise, in which social values and resources are all marshaled in support of scientific research, Christianity may be judged harshly: the church was certainly not calling for the establishment of scientific research institutions nor urging able young men to undertake scientific careers. Most of the pejorative pronouncements regarding the early church in relation to science seem to spring from the anachronistic application of precisely such a standard. But what we must realize is that the early church was expressing values obtained from the pagan environment. On a spectrum of *pagan* values, from cosmic religion to Gnostic repudiation of the cosmos, the church fathers chose a middle position. There can be no doubt that biblical teaching about the creation as God's handiwork was influential in determining where on the spectrum Christians would land, and therefore it is clear that their Christianity was highly relevant to the issue; but it must be recognized that the alternatives from which they chose were of pagan origin.

It seems unlikely, therefore, that the advent of Christianity did anything to diminish the support given to scientific activity or the number of people involved in it. The study of nature held a very precarious position in ancient societies; with the exception of medicine and a little astronomy, it served no practical function and was rarely seen as a socially useful activity. As a result it received little political patronage or social support but depended on independent means and individual initiative.[57] With the declining economic and political fortunes of the Roman Empire in late antiquity, people of independent means decreased in number, and initiative was directed elsewhere. Moreover, changing educational and philosophical values were diverting attention from the world of nature. Inevitably the pursuit of science suffered. Christianity did little to alter this situation. If anything, it was a little less otherworldly than the major competing ideologies (Gnosticism, Neoplatonism, and the mystery religions) and offered slightly greater incentive for the study of nature.[58] Christians regarded science as important only insofar as it served the faith; but at least it did, on occasion, serve the faith.

PRACTITIONERS OF SCIENCE

We have been proceeding at the theoretical level. What did Christian involvement in science or natural philosophy amount to in practical terms? How much science was known? What did Christians contribute to its preservation and further development? And how did it interact with their theology? These are extraordinarily difficult questions, because the basic research that would make it possible to answer them has, in general, not yet been undertaken. Nevertheless, let us take some preliminary steps toward answers by considering briefly the work of three Christians representing different degrees of involvement in natural philosophy—Basil of Caesarea, Augustine, and John Philoponus.

Basil (ca. 330–379) was from Cappadocia in eastern Asia Minor, where, in the last decade of his life, he became Bishop of Caesarea. In his *Homilies on the Hexaemeron* (the six days of creation) he brought to bear what natural philosophy he could in defense and elucidation of the biblical account of creation. Basil began by attacking the materialists (undoubtedly the Ionians and atomists), who have failed to see that the cosmos is a beautiful and purposeful creation, the work of an intelligent Creator. Basil's own philosophical preferences become clear when he identifies the Creator with Plato's Demiurge and accepts a Platonic hierarchy of celestial intelligences. Also, against the materialists and in concert with Christian and Platonic teaching, he defends a temporal cosmos—that is, one that had a beginning and will have an end.[59]

A good bit of Aristotelian cosmology and physics appears in the *Homilies*—much of it reported (without endorsement) as the useless imaginings and empty noises of the philosophers. Basil accepts the doctrine of the four elements and reports the arguments for a fifth celestial element.[60] He refers to the opinion (of Anaximander and Democritus) that there is an infinity of worlds, but counters with Aristotle's denial, on geometrical grounds, of the possibility of more than a single world.[61] He inquires regarding the position of the earth in the cosmos and recounts the Aristotelian doctrine of a fixed, central earth, situated in the place to which all heavy bodies naturally descend; it is implicit in this account, moreover, that the earth is spherical. According to his custom, however, Basil refuses to commit himself to the truth of this scheme—although he apparently does not think it improbable. He declares simply that we should direct our admiration toward the source, rather than the details, of cosmic order:

> If there is anything in this system which might appear probable to you, keep your admiration for the source of such perfect order, for the wisdom of God. Grand phenomena do not strike us the less when we have discovered something of their wonderful mechanism. Is it otherwise here? At all events let us prefer the simplicity of faith to the demonstrations of reason.[62]

One cannot help being impressed by Basil's considerable command of basic Greek cosmology and natural philosophy—most of it obtained, no doubt, from handbooks and compendia rather than from the original sources. But he is not overcome with admiration for pagan authors. He sometimes labels their arguments "ridiculous" and refers repeatedly to their inability to agree among themselves: "Why torment ourselves to refute the errors of philosophers, when it is sufficient to produce their mutually contradictory books and, as quiet spectators, to watch the war?"[63] Above all, he is adamant in denying these matters any importance for their own sake.

We can learn more about the way in which biblical doctrine and pagan philosophy interacted in Basil's thought by considering his discussion of the various heavens. The problem is the apparent discrepancy between Aristotle, who had argued that beyond the planetary spheres there is a single heaven (bearing the fixed stars), and the opening verses of Genesis 1, where reference is apparently made to two heavens, one created on the first day and another on the second. The relevant passage reads:

In the beginning God created the heavens and the earth. . . . And there was evening and there was morning, one day. And God said, "Let there be a firmament in the midst of the waters, and let it separate the waters from the waters." And God made the firmament and separated the waters which were under the firmament from the waters which were above the firmament. And God called the firmament Heaven. And there was evening and there was morning, a second day.[64]

Basil, who refuses to accept an allegorical interpretation of the passage (and, indeed, attacks his Christian predecessors for so doing),[65] feels compelled to acknowledge the existence of two heavens and, moreover, of a body of supercelestial water between the two. In the long run Basil's distinction between three separate heavenly entities was to give rise to the medieval scheme of three heavens: the outermost or empyrean, which served as the abode of angels, then the aqueous or crystalline heaven, composed of crystallized water, and finally the firmament, to which the stars are affixed.[66] We see clearly how biblical claims could intrude into natural philosophy and shape cosmological theory.

Augustine, who flourished fifty years after Basil, had a much fuller command of pagan natural philosophy than did his predecessor. His works reveal a man broadly educated in the full range of the liberal arts. In his *Confessions* he recalls his discovery of Aristotle's *Categories* and reports reading, in his youth, all the books on the liberal arts that he could obtain, including works on rhetoric, logic, geometry, arithmetic, and music.[67] In *De ordine*, written early in his career, he develops an educational program that includes mathematics and mathematical sciences as studies preparatory to philosophy. And in his *Retractions* he reports that he once intended to write manuals on all of the liberal arts, including arithmetic, geometry, music, and the elements of philosophy.[68] References to many pagan sources are scattered throughout his writings.

Despite his studies Augustine came in the long run to view natural knowledge (for its own sake) with no greater enthusiasm than had Basil. We are, he advised, to set our hearts on things celestial and eternal, rather than earthly and temporal. Nevertheless, the temporal could serve the eternal, and Augustine frequently acknowledged the utility of natural knowledge for the elucidation of Christian doctrine and the exegesis of Scripture. Fragments of Greek natural philosophy are thus sprinkled throughout his works. A good example (but only one among many) is his frequent use of Greek ideas on light and vision for the development of his own theology and epistemology. Augustine employs the Neoplatonic doctrine of emanation, explained by analogy with the radiation of light, to reveal the nature of the

Trinity.[69] He puts the phenomena of illumination to epistemological use, arguing that just as the sun must illuminate corporeal things in order that they may be seen by the corporeal eye, so intelligible things must be illuminated with a divine light if they are to be grasped by the intellect:

> But distinct from these objects [of intellectual vision] is the Light by which the soul is illumined, in order that it may see and truly understand everything, either in itself or in the Light. For the Light is God Himself, whereas the soul is a creature. . . . And when it tries to behold the Light, it trembles in its weakness and finds itself unable to do so. Yet from this source comes all the understanding it is able to attain.[70]

This epistemological use of light is a Platonic motif, taken over and Christianized by Augustine.[71] In the course of his many discussions of the psychology and epistemology of perception, Augustine clearly commits himself to the extramission theory of vision, according to which light emerges from the observer's eye to perceive its object. In his *Literal Commentary on Genesis*, for example, he remarks that

> The emission of rays from our eyes is surely the emission of a certain light. It can be drawn in when we observe that which is near our eyes, thrust out when we observe things along the same line, but far away. . . . Nevertheless, this light which is in the eye is shown to be so scanty that we would see nothing without the assistance of exterior light.[72]

Once again Augustine's sources are Platonic.

A second example of Augustine's use of natural knowledge and efforts to deal with natural questions is his doctrine of *rationes seminales*, or "seedlike principles." The problem is to reconcile the biblical notion that God created everything in the beginning of time with the observational fact that there is a progressive development of natural (particularly biological) forms. To resolve the difficulty, Augustine calls on a Stoic notion, which Plotinus also appropriated, according to which nature contains germs or seedlike principles that direct and determine its subsequent unfolding. According to Augustine, God created all things in the beginning, some actually and some potentially—the latter as seedlike principles, which later developed into mature creatures, much as a seed develops into a mature plant. Augustine thus uses Greek natural philosophy to resolve an exegetical problem—maintaining that God's creative activity is truly completed in the beginning, and yet taking full account of observational and commonsense notions regarding the development of natural things.[73]

It is noteworthy that Augustine applies the doctrine of seedlike principles even to the origin of Adam and Eve.[74]

R. A. Markus has pointed out that from Augustine's doctrine of seedlike principles there follows a conception of natural law. This implication of the theory was acknowledged by Augustine himself in his *Literal Commentary on Genesis:*

> The ordinary course of nature in the whole of creation has certain natural laws in accordance with which even the spirit of life . . . has its own appetites. . . . The elements of the physical world also have a fixed power and quality determining for each thing what it can do or not do and what can be done or not done with it. From these elements all things which come to be in due time have their origin and development as well as their end and dissolution according to their kind.[75]

Each thing behaves according to its God-given inclination—the law of its own nature. From this it is but a short step to the distinction between God as first cause and a created order of secondary causes:

> It is one thing to build and to govern creatures from within and from the summit of the whole causal nexus—and only God, the Creator, does this; it is another thing to apply externally forces and capacities bestowed by him in order to bring forth at such and such a time, or in such and such a shape, what has been created. For all these things were created at the beginning, being primordially woven into the texture of the world; but they await the proper opportunity for their appearance.[76]

There is a kind of double causation: on the one hand, things change and develop according to the natures that God has given them; on the other, God governs his creation "from the summit of the whole causal nexus."

This brings us to the question of miracles. Augustine is not perfectly consistent on the subject. On one occasion he argues that an event is miraculous if caused by direct divine intervention, in violation of the natural pattern embodied in the created secondary causes. More frequently Augustine points out that God's decision to violate the usual order is no less natural (and no more miraculous) than his decision to abide by it: "Just . . . as it was possible for God to create any natures He chose to create, so it is no less possible for Him to change any qualities He chooses to change in any natures He chose to create."[77] Ultimately everything is of divine origin, and the concept of miracle, if it has any meaning at all, represents merely the violation of our expectations:

A portent means, in ordinary parlance, "something contrary to nature," although, in fact, such happenings are not really contrary to nature, for the simple reason that nothing that happens by the will of God can be "contrary to nature." The "nature" of any particular created thing is precisely what the supreme Creator of the thing willed it to be. Hence, a portent is merely contrary to nature as known, not to nature as it is.[78]

A final example of Augustine's relationship to pagan natural philosophy is his opinion of astrology. In the *City of God* Augustine mounts a vigorous attack on the science of astrology, particularly its fatalistic teachings. He argues over and over that if twins, conceived at the same instant and born at almost the same time, differ dramatically in personality, character, and course of life, it surely cannot be sensibly maintained that the stars determine a person's fate.

> [The astrologers] have never been able to explain why twins are so different in what they do and achieve, in their professions and skills, in the honors they receive, and in other aspects of their lives and deaths. In all such matters, twins are often less like each other than like complete strangers; yet, twins are born with practically no interval of time between their births and are conceived in precisely the same moment of a single sexual semination.[79]

Augustine can admit stellar influence on physical things, but the human will must be left untouched; only thus can its freedom be preserved. There was, we can see, a theological motivation underlying the discussion. A final question: if the stars do not determine human fate, if astrologers are the perpetrators of fraud, how can the occasional astrological success be explained? Successful astrological predictions, Augustine maintains, have nothing to do with the casting of horoscopes, but depend on the promptings of evil spirits, "whose business it is to persuade men, and keep them persuaded, of the false and dangerous opinion that men's destinies are settled by the stars."[80]

The last figure in our study is John Philoponus, an Alexandrian Christian of the first half of the sixth century, who illustrates the compatibility between Christianity and very intense involvement in natural philosophy. Philoponus was a professional teacher, holder of a chair in philosophy in the school of Alexandria, and one of the last great ancient commentators on Aristotle. He wrote commentaries on several of Aristotle's logical works, as well as the *Physics, Meteorology, On the Soul,* and *On Generation and Corruption*—works in which he undertook a major attack on Aristotelian natural philosophy. The central point of Philoponus's anti-Aristotelianism was the denial of Aristotle's dichotomy between the celestial and terrestrial regions. To that end he argued that different stars are of different colors, that difference of color implies variations in composition, that composition implies the possibility of decomposition and decay, from which it follows that the heavens are no more exempt from decay than are things in the terrestrial region. He argued that the sun is composed of fire (a terrestrial substance) rather than a fifth celestial substance, the quintessence, and that astronomy (he clearly has Ptolemaic astronomy in mind) destroys the Aristotelian notion that heavenly bodies possess simple motion about the center of the universe. It follows that the heavens are not divine, and this enabled Philoponus to draw a radical distinction between the Creator and all of his creation (heaven as well as earth). A central Aristotelian doctrine thus fell before Christian doctrine. But this does not mean that the attack was philosophically frivolous; on the contrary, Philoponus proceeded intelligently, with considerable rigor, and (historians of science have been quick to point out) with notable benefit for the future course of cosmology.[81]

There was much more to Philoponus's campaign against Aristotelian philosophy. He attacked Aristotle's doctrine of the eternity of the world. He attempted a reassessment of Aristotle's theory of light.[82] And he undertook a major assault on Aristotelian dynamics, denying that in a medium a body falls with a speed proportional to its weight, that the speed of descent would be infinite in a void, and that a projectile is maintained in motion through the action of the medium after it loses contact with the projector. It is noteworthy that Philoponus's attack on Aristotelian dynamics rested not on any kind of theological foundation but to a very considerable extent on arguments from experience.[83] Philoponus's efforts, some of them motivated by Christian belief and some of them not, clearly confute the claim that Christianity and serious natural philosophy were fundamentally and necessarily antagonistic.

CONCLUSIONS

A sober view of the relationship between Christianity and science in the patristic period has proved remarkably difficult to obtain. One reason for this is that studies of the problem have so often been undertaken with polemical or apologetic purposes in view, as expressions of religious preference. Critics of Christianity have seized upon instances of Christian displeasure with pagan learning and inflated them into a systematic rejection by the religious establishment of the scientific enterprise. Defenders of Christianity, playing the same game, have exaggerated Christian contributions to science into representative episodes and symbols of a positive relationship between Christianity and science. But the true relationship was far more complex than either of the extreme positions reveals.

Our attempt to characterize that relationship must begin with a qualification. If we speak of "the Christian position," we can only mean the "center of gravity" of a distribution of Christian opinion, for great variety existed. The church was not monolithic, and there was no universal Christian view of pagan philosophy or natural science. Christian attitudes toward classical culture were perhaps as diverse as the comparable attitudes of pagans. In each community there were people who valued philosophy and others who denigrated it, people who thought natural science useful and those who considered it a waste of time or even a detriment. Such attitudes were determined not merely by the claims of theology but by other forces as well. In late antiquity there were social and intellectual forces tending to discourage and alter the character of philosophical discourse, particularly to divert attention from the impracticalities of natural philosophy toward the quest for true happiness and other matters of ultimate concern.[84] Christians, of course, responded differently to these forces, just as they responded differently to the claims of Christian theology.

How, then, should Christian involvement in science or natural philosophy be characterized? Few Christians regarded study of the natural world as of more than secondary, perhaps even tertiary, importance. Next to salvation and the development of basic Christian doctrine it was decidedly insignificant. There is no cause for alarm, Augustine pointed out, if the Christian "should be ignorant of the force and number of the elements. . . . It is enough for the Christian to believe that the only cause of all created things . . . is the goodness of the Creator."[85] It would be crude distortion to maintain that Christianity offered major stimulus to scientific activity.

But it would also be distortion to create the impression that there was no Christian involvement in natural philosophy or that the church retarded or crushed science. Many fathers of the church not only possessed a significant body of natural knowledge but also considered it useful for scriptural exegesis and defense of the faith. Augustine, in his efforts to formulate a Christian worldview, put considerable portions of Greek natural philosophy (particularly Platonic) to work. Thus the church fathers used Greek natural science, and in using it they transmitted it. We must count this transmission as one of the major Christian contributions to science. Until the twelfth century, when a wave of translation brought an abundance of new sources to

the Latin-speaking West, patristic writings constituted a major repository of scientific learning.

What the church transmitted, it also altered—and had its own
doctrines altered in return. Christian doctrine and Greek natural philosophy must be viewed not as independent, unchangeable bodies
of thought, situated side by side in the patristic period, with an
occasional exchange of fisticuffs, but as interacting and mutually
transforming views of the world. Christianity transformed the philosophical tradition, first, by performing a selective function. Because
the church fathers had a strong preference for Platonic philosophy,
they helped to determine that Plato's view of the world would prevail
for a thousand years, until direct access to Aristotelian philosophy
was gained in the twelfth century. But transformation could also occur
when revelation impinged directly on natural questions. For example,
the eternity of the world was directly addressed in Scripture, and we
have seen how Basil's understanding of the opening verses of Genesis
led to the multiplication of celestial spheres. The heavens were also
de-divinized as a result of the encounter between natural philosophy
and Christian theology. In return, Christians learned to read the Bible
with Greek, particularly Platonic, eyes; and Christian theology became thoroughly imbued with Greek metaphysics and cosmology.[86]
The extent of this mutual transformation was probably unrecognized
by the participants, and unwanted; but unless we take cognizance of
it, we cannot begin to understand the subsequent course of Western
theology, philosophy, and science.

NOTES

This is a revised version of a paper that appeared originally in *Isis* 74 (1983):
509–530. For critical commentary I would like especially to thank Darrel W.
Amundsen, William B. Ashworth, William J. Courtenay, Gary B. Deason,
Edward Grant, Herbert M. Howe, Robert Siegfried, Nicholas H. Steneck,
Robert S. Westman, and Keith E. Yandell.

1. John William Draper, *History of the Conflict between Religion and Science*,
7th ed. (London: Henry S. King, 1876), pp. 51–52. On Draper and his career
see Donald Fleming, *John William Draper and the Religion of Science* (Philadelphia: Univ. of Pennsylvania Press, 1950).

2. Andrew Dickson White, *A History of the Warfare of Science with Theology
in Christendom*, 2 vols. (New York: Appleton, 1896), 1:325. On White see the
biography by Glenn C. Altschuler, *Andrew D. White—Educator, Historian,
Diplomat* (Ithaca, N.Y.: Cornell Univ. Press, 1979); also the excellent historio-

graphical essay by James R. Moore, *The Post-Darwinian Controversies* (Cambridge: Cambridge Univ. Press, 1979), chap. 1.

3. White, *Warfare* 1:376.

4. For the two verbs employed here see ibid., 1:97, 376.

5. For example, George Sarton, *Introduction to the History of Science*, 3 vols. (Baltimore: William & Wilkins, 1927–1948), 1:17, 21; Sir William Dampier, *A History of Science and Its Relations with Philosophy and Religion* (Cambridge: Cambridge Univ. Press, 1929), pp. 66–73; Charles Singer, *Religion and Science Considered in their Historical Relations* (New York: Robert McBride, [1932]), pp. 52–56; J. D. Bernal, *Science in History*, 4 vols. (London: C. A. Watts, 1954), 1:258–262; Ernst Mayr, *The Growth of Biological Thought: Diversity, Evolution, and Inheritance* (Cambridge, Mass.: Harvard Univ. Press, Belknap Press, 1982), pp. 307–309.

6. R. Hooykaas, *Religion and the Rise of Modern Science* (Grand Rapids, Mich.: Wm. B. Eerdmans, 1972); Eugene M. Klaaren, *Religious Origins of Modern Science: Belief in Creation in Seventeenth-Century Thought* (Grand Rapids, Mich.: Wm. B. Eerdmans, 1977); Stanley L. Jaki, *The Road of Science and the Ways to God* (Chicago: Univ. of Chicago Press, 1978). None of these authors addresses himself in any serious way to the patristic period. It is their larger view, however, that Christianity was a necessary condition for the development of science; it would seem to follow that the advent of Christianity was a necessary first step.

7. Marshall Clagett, *Greek Science in Antiquity* (London: Abelard-Schuman, 1957), pp. 130–145; E. J. Dijksterhuis, *The Mechanization of the World Picture*, trans. C. Dikshoorn (Oxford: Clarendon Press, 1961), pp. 89–95; G. E. R. Lloyd, *Greek Science after Aristotle* (London: Chatto & Windus, 1973), pp. 167–171. Lloyd, however, does regard Christianity as having had a generally detrimental effect on science.

8. See Will Durant, *The Age of Faith*, vol. 4 of *The Story of Civilization* (New York: Simon & Schuster, 1950), pp. 78–79; Thomas Goldstein, *Dawn of Modern Science: From the Arabs to Leonardo da Vinci* (Boston: Houghton Mifflin, 1980), p. 43. Between them, Draper's and White's books have gone through more than eighty editions. Draper's book has been translated into Spanish, French, German, Polish, and Russian; White's into French, Italian, Swedish, and Japanese. Draper's book was last published in 1970; White's is still in print.

9. On the classification of theoretical knowledge see James A. Weisheipl, O.P., "The Nature, Scope, and Classification of the Sciences," in *Science in the Middle Ages*, ed. David C. Lindberg (Chicago: Univ. of Chicago Press, 1978), chap. 14.

10. It is true that there were always professional physicians, but even here the lines of demarcation were fuzzy, since many a physician was also a philosopher. On the organization of science in antiquity see Ludwig Edelstein, *Ancient Medicine: Selected Papers* (Baltimore: Johns Hopkins Univ. Press, 1967), pp. 429–439 (the final section of an article: "Recent Trends in the Interpretation of Ancient Science," reprinted from *Journal of the History of Ideas* 13 [1952]: 573–604); G. E. R. Lloyd, *Early Greek Science: Thales to Aristotle* (London: Chatto & Windus, 1970), pp. 125–130; and Thomas W. Africa, *Science and the State in Greece and Rome* (New York: Wiley, 1968).

11. See the quotation from Draper with which this chapter began.

12. On Greek rationalism see Bruno Snell, *The Discovery of the Mind: The Greek Origins of European Thought* (Cambridge, Mass.: Harvard Univ. Press, 1953); E. R. Dodds, *The Greeks and the Irrational* (Berkeley: Univ. of California Press, 1951); G. E. R. Lloyd, *Magic, Reason and Experience: Studies in the Origins and Development of Greek Science* (Cambridge: Cambridge Univ. Press, 1979).

13. Hans Lewy, *Chaldean Oracles and Theurgy: Mysticism, Magic, and Platonism in the Later Roman Empire* (Cairo: Institut français d'archéologie orientale, 1956), pp. 67–76; John J. O'Meara, *Porphyry's Philosophy from Oracles in Augustine* (Paris: Etudes Augustiniennes, 1959); Richard Walzer, *Galen on Jews and Christians* (London: Oxford Univ. Press, 1949), pp. 55–56; Henry Chadwick, *The Early Church* (Harmondsworth: Penguin, 1967), p. 112; Ramsay MacMullen, *Paganism in the Roman Empire* (New Haven: Yale Univ. Press, 1981), pp. 70–72. E. R. Dodds, *Pagan and Christian in an Age of Anxiety* (Cambridge: Cambridge Univ. Press, 1965), p. 122, points out that while Christians were substituting reason for authority, pagans were substituting authority for reason.

14. Plato, *Laws*, book 10. See also MacMullen, *Paganism*, p. 62.

15. This, at least, might be judged from Chadwick's remarks, *Early Church*, pp. 171–173. On Christian use of coercion see MacMullen, *Paganism*, pp. 135–136.

16. For an excellent short history of the early church see Chadwick, *Early Church*. Longer histories are innumerable; I have made greatest use of Louis Duchesne, *The Early History of the Church*, 3 vols. (New York: Longmans, Green & Co., 1914–1924).

17. On Justin see Henry Chadwick, *Early Christian Thought and the Classical Tradition: Studies in Justin, Clement, and Origen* (New York: Oxford Univ. Press, 1966), chap. 1; Chadwick, "The Beginning of Christian Philosophy: Justin: The Gnostics," in *The Cambridge History of Later Greek and Early Medieval Philosophy* (henceforth cited as *Cambridge History*), ed. A. H. Armstrong (Cambridge: Cambridge Univ. Press, 1970), chap. 9; Frederick Copleston, S.J., *A History of Philosophy*, 9 vols. (Westminster, Md.: Newman Press, 1946–1975), 2:16–18.

18. E. F. Osborn, *The Philosophy of Clement of Alexandria* (Cambridge: Cambridge Univ. Press, 1957), pp. 117–126. On Clement see also Chadwick, *Early Christian Thought and the Classical Tradition*, chap. 2; Charles Bigg, *The Christian Platonists of Alexandria* (Oxford: Clarendon Press, 1886), lect. 2; H. B. Timothy, *The Early Greek Apologists and Greek Philosophy, Exemplified by Irenaeus, Tertullian, and Clement of Alexandria* (Assen: Van Gorcum, 1973), pp. 59–80, 88–98.

19. Quoted by Osborn, *Philosophy of Clement*, p. 124.

20. Dodds, *Pagan and Christian*, pp. 127–129; Charles N. Cochrane, *Christianity and Classical Culture: A Study of Thought and Action from Augustus to Augustine* (Oxford: Clarendon Press, 1940), p. 226. On Origen see also Chadwick, *Early Christian Thought and the Classical Tradition*, chap. 3; Bigg, *Christian Platonists*, lects. 4–6.

21. *In Origenem oratio*, quoted by M. L. Clarke, *Higher Education in the Ancient World* (London: Routledge & Kegan Paul, 1971), pp. 126–127 (with minor changes in punctuation).

22. Copleston, *History of Philosophy* 2:18; Etienne Gilson, *Reason and Revelation in the Middle Ages* (New York: Charles Scribner's Sons, 1938), pp. 11–12.

23. *Didascalia et constitutiones apostolorum*, VI, ed. Franciscus X. Funk, vol. 1 (Paderborn: Ferdinand Schoeningh, 1905), pp. 12–14. For another translation from a different edition see M. L. W. Laistner, *Christianity and Pagan Culture in the Later Roman Empire* (Ithaca, N. Y.: Cornell Univ. Press, 1951), p. 50.

24. Quoted in ibid., p. 53.

25. Origen, *Contra Celsum*, trans. Henry Chadwick (Cambridge: Cambridge Univ. Press, 1953), p. 158.

26. Quoted by Walzer, *Galen on Jews and Christians*, p. 54.

27. Ibid.

28. Gilson, *Reason and Revelation*, pp. 5–11; cf. Cochrane, *Christianity and Classical Culture*, pp. 227–230.

29. *On Prescription against Heretics*, chap. 7, trans. Peter Holmes, in *The Ante-Nicene Fathers*, ed. Alexander Roberts and James Donaldson, 10 vols. (New York: Charles Scribner's Sons, 1896–1903), 3:246. I have substituted my own translation of the final sentence.

30. *Ad nationes* 2.4, trans. Peter Holmes, in ibid., 3:133.

31. This theme is nicely developed by Robert H. Ayers, *Language, Logic, and Reason in the Church Fathers* (Hildesheim: Georg Olms, 1979), pp. 25–34. For another useful discussion of Tertullian see Timothy, *Early Greek Apologists*, pp. 40–58.

32. *On Repentance*, chap. 1, trans. S. Thelwall, in *The Ante-Nicene Fathers* 3:657. I was led to this and a number of the other quotations from Tertullian by Ayers.

33. *On the Resurrection of the Flesh*, chap. 3, trans. Peter Holmes, in ibid., 3:547.

34. That is, resurrection of the dead is so improbable an event that the apostles would not have believed in the resurrection of Christ if they had not been faced with incontrovertible evidence that indeed, on this occasion, the improbable had occurred. This truth makes the resurrection of Christ more probable than some other event, the occurrence of which might have been accepted merely on the basis of general plausibility. See Ayers, *Language, Logic, and Reason*, pp. 21–24; Robert Grant, *Miracle and Natural Law in Graeco-Roman and Early Christian Thought* (Amsterdam: North-Holland, 1952), pp. 194, 209; Aristotle's *Rhetoric* 2.23.22. What Tertullian did say is "Certum est quia impossibile est."

35. Peter Brown, *Augustine of Hippo: A Biography* (Berkeley and Los Angeles: Univ. of California Press, 1969); on Augustine's education see chap. 3.

36. On Augustine's Neoplatonism see especially A. H. Armstrong, *St. Augustine and Christian Platonism* (Villanova, Pa.: Villanova Univ. Press, 1967); reprinted in Armstrong, *Plotinian and Christian Studies* (London: Variorum Reprints, 1979), chap. 11. Late in his career Augustine moved away from Neoplatonic assumptions.

37. This is one of the themes of Cochrane's *Christianity and Classical Culture*, which has deeply influenced me.

38. Letter 120, ed. A. Goldbacher, in *Corpus Scriptorum Ecclesiasticorum Latinorum*, vol. 34 (Vienna: F. Tempsky, 1895), p. 708.

39. Ibid., p. 709.

40. Ibid., pp. 705–707.

41. *Against the Academics* 3.20.43, trans. John J. O'Meara, *Ancient Christian Writers: The Works of the Fathers in Translation*, ed. Johannes Quasten and Joseph C. Plumpe, vol. 12 (New York: Newman Press, 1951), p. 150.

42. *On Free Choice* 2.2.6, trans. Carroll Mason Sparrow; quoted by Vernon J. Bourke, *The Essential Augustine* (New York: New American Library, 1964), p. 25.

43. On faith as a condition for understanding see Cochrane, *Christianity and Classical Culture*, chaps. 10–11; Brown, *Augustine of Hippo*, chap. 10.

44. *The Panegyric on St. Basil*, trans. Charles G. Browne and James E. Swallow, in *A Select Library of Nicene and Post-Nicene Fathers of the Christian Church*, ser. 2, 14 vols., ed. Philip Schaff and Henry Wace (New York: Christian Literature Co., 1890–1900), 7:398–399.

45. A. H. Armstrong, "Reason and Faith in the First Millennium A.D.," in *Scholasticism in the Modern World*, Proceedings of the American Catholic Philosophical Association, vol. 40 (Washington, D.C.: American Catholic Philosophical Association, 1966), p. 107; reprinted in Armstrong, *Plotinian and Christian Studies*, chap. 12.

46. The best histories of ancient science are by G. E. R. Lloyd: *Early Greek Science: Thales to Aristotle* and *Greek Science after Aristotle*.

47. On science in late antiquity see Lloyd, *Greek Science after Aristotle*, chap. 10; Clagett, *Greek Science in Antiquity*, chaps. 8–11. Benjamin Farrington, *Greek Science* (Harmondsworth: Penguin, 1961), would push the decline of Greek science even earlier, to the fourth century B.C.

48. On Roman science see William Stahl, *Roman Science: Origins, Development, and Influence to the Later Middle Ages* (Madison: Univ. of Wisconsin Press, 1962).

49. I have closely followed A. H. Armstrong, "The Material Universe," chap. 4 of Armstrong and R. A. Markus, *Christian Faith and Greek Philosophy* (London: Darton, Longman & Todd, 1960). See esp. pp. 31–33, 39–40. The quoted line is from p. 31.

50. On Gnosticism see Hans Jonas, *The Gnostic Religion*, 2d ed. (Boston: Beacon Press, 1963); Robert M. Grant, *Gnosticism and Early Christianity*, 2d ed. (New York: Columbia Univ. Press, 1966).

51. Armstrong, "Material Universe," p. 34.

52. I. P. Sheldon-Williams, "St. Gregory of Nyssa," in *Cambridge History*, ed. Armstrong, pp. 447–456.

53. Armstrong, *Augustine and Christian Platonism*, p. 11. Despite Augustine's influence the tendency to denigrate the flesh persisted in medieval (especially early medieval) Christendom.

54. 3.9, trans. Albert C. Outler, *The Library of Christian Classics*, vol. 7 (Philadelphia: Westminster Press, 1955), pp. 341–342. The qualification contained in the opening line of this passage ("what we ought to believe *in matters of religion*") is often overlooked by those who quote it.

55. *The Literal Meaning of Genesis* 1.19.39, trans. John Hammond Taylor, *Ancient Christian Writers: The Works of the Fathers in Translation,* ed. Johannes Quasten et al., vols. 41–42 (New York: Newman Press, 1982), 41:42–43, slightly altered.

56. *In nativitate Domini sermo VII;* quoted by Armstrong, "Material Universe," pp. 36–37.

57. Edelstein, *Ancient Medicine,* pp. 434–435; Lloyd, *Early Greek Science,* pp. 125–130.

58. It is true that cosmic religion attached great importance to the visible world as a manifestation of the divine being, but its preoccupation with the heavenly bodies and its tendency to venerate them precluded its becoming a major patron of scientific activity; indeed, as Armstrong has pointed out, cosmic religion had its own "curious kind of materialized other-worldliness" ("Material Universe," p. 33). Armstrong has also pointed out that the tendency of cosmic religion to merge science and theology was probably not beneficial for either enterprise (ibid., pp. 39–40). Cf. Armstrong, *St. Augustine and Christian Platonism,* pp. 9–24; and Armstrong, "Man in the Cosmos: A Study of Some Differences between Pagan Neoplatonism and Christianity," in *Romanitas et Christianitas,* ed. Willem den Boer et al. (Amsterdam: North Holland, 1973), pp. 5–14; reprinted in Armstrong's *Plotinian and Christian Studies,* chap. 22. My conclusions about Christian attitudes toward nature are remarkably similar to those recently expressed by Darrel W. Amundsen in regard to Christian attitudes toward secular medicine; see his "Medicine and Faith in Early Christianity," *Bulletin of the History of Medicine* 56 (1982): 326–350.

59. Homily 1, in *Select Library of Nicene and Post-Nicene Fathers,* ser. 2, ed. Schaff and Wace, 8:53–55. On Basil see also I. P. Sheldon-Williams, "St. Basil of Caesarea," in *Cambridge History,* ed. Armstrong, pp. 432–438; Lynn Thorndike, *A History of Magic and Experimental Science,* 8 vols. (New York: Columbia Univ. Press, 1923–1948), 1:481–494. On early hexaemeral literature including Basil's, see Frank E. Robbins, *The Hexaemeral Literature: A Study of the Greek and Latin Commentaries on Genesis* (Chicago: Univ. of Chicago Press, 1912).

60. Homily 4, in *Select Library* 8:74–75; Homily 1, ibid., p. 58.

61. Homily 3, ibid., p. 66.

62. Homily 1, ibid., p. 57.

63. Homily 3, ibid., p. 70; also p. 67.

64. 1:1, 5–8, Revised Standard Version.

65. Homily 3, in *Select Library* 8:71.

66. See *Campanus of Novara and Medieval Planetary Theory: Theorica planetarum,* ed. Francis S. Benjamin, Jr., and G. J. Toomer (Madison: Univ. of Wisconsin Press, 1971), pp. 393–394; Edward Grant, "Cosmology," in *Science in the Middle Ages,* ed. Lindberg, pp. 275–278.

67. *Confessions* 4.16. It is important to realize that Augustine's education, like that of almost every other educated man of the period, was heavily literary in orientation. There might be some attention to quadrivial studies (arithmetic, geometry, astronomy, and music), but among Christians and non-Christians alike these would be heavily overshadowed by concern with grammar, rhetoric, and the literary classics.

68. See Henri-Irénée Marrou, *Saint Augustin et la fin de la culture antique*, 4th ed. (Paris, E. De Boccard, 1958), pp. 187–197; Brown, *Augustine of Hippo*, pp. 121–126. Only the manual on music survives; the others, Augustine notes in *Retractions* 1.5, were only begun and then lost.

69. See *De Trinitate* 4.20.

70. *The Literal Meaning of Genesis* 12.31.59, trans. Taylor, 42:222.

71. On Augustine's theory of divine illumination see R. A. Markus, "Augustine: Reason and Illumination," in *Cambridge History*, ed. Armstrong, pp. 362–373; Etienne Gilson, *The Christian Philosophy of Saint Augustine*, trans. L. M. Lynch (New York: Random House, 1960), pp. 77–96.

72. *De Genesi ad litteram*, 1.16.31, ed. Joseph Zycha, *Corpus Scriptorum Ecclesiasticorum Latinorum*, 28.1 (Vienna: F. Tempsky, 1894): 23. On Augustine's optical knowledge and use of light metaphors see also François-Joseph Thonnard, "La notion de lumière en philosophie augustinienne," *Recherches augustiniennes* 2 (1962): 125–175; and David C. Lindberg, *Roger Bacon's Philosophy of Nature* (Oxford: Clarendon Press, 1983), pp. xxxix–xli.

73. On the seedlike principles see R. A. Markus, "Augustine: God and Nature," in *Cambridge History*, ed. Armstrong, pp. 398–399; Gilson, *Christian Philosophy of Augustine*, pp. 206–208; Jules M. Brady, S.J., "St. Augustine's Theory of Seminal Reasons," *New Scholasticism* 38 (1964): 141–158; Christopher J. O'Toole, *The Philosophy of Creation in the Writings of St. Augustine* (Washington, D.C.: Catholic Univ. of America Press, 1944).

74. *The Literal Meaning of Genesis* 9.17.32, trans. Taylor, 42:92–93.

75. Ibid., 92. The basic point of this paragraph, and also the quotations, I owe to Markus, "Augustine: God and Nature," pp. 398–402.

76. *De Trinitate* 3.9.16, quoted by Markus, p. 400.

77. *City of God* 21.8, trans. Gerald G. Walsh, S.J., and Daniel J. Honan, in *Fathers of the Church*, ed. R. Deferrari et al., 68 vols. to date (New York: Fathers of the Church; Washington, D.C.: Catholic Univ. of America Press, 1947–), 8:362.

78. Ibid., p. 359. On Augustine's view of miracles see Markus, "Augustine: God and Nature," pp. 400–402; Brown, *Augustine of Hippo*, pp. 415–418.

79. *City of God* 5.1, trans. Demetrius B. Zema, S.J., and Gerald G. Walsh, S.J., in *Fathers of the Church* 6:243. The "twins" argument against astrology was not original with Augustine.

80. Ibid., 5.7, p. 254. On Augustine's view of astrology see also Theodore O. Wedel, *The Mediaeval Attitude toward Astrology, Particularly in England* (New Haven: Yale Univ. Press, 1920), pp. 20–24; Thorndike, *History of Magic* 1:504–522.

81. On Philoponus see S. Sambursky, "John Philoponus," *Dictionary of Scientific Biography* 7:134–139; Sambursky, *The Physical World of Late Antiquity* (London: Routledge & Kegan Paul, 1962), pp. 154–175 and passim; I. P. Sheldon-Williams, "The Reaction against Proclus," in *Cambridge History*, ed. Armstrong, pp. 477–483.

82. Jean Ann Christensen, "Aristotle and Philoponus on Light" (Ph.D. thesis, Harvard University, 1979).

83. For translations of some of the relevant documents see Morris R. Cohen and I. E. Drabkin, *A Source Book in Greek Science* (Cambridge, Mass.: Harvard

Univ. Press, 1948), pp. 217–223. For analysis see Clagett, *Greek Science in Antiquity*, pp. 169–176.

84. Many scholars have pointed out that in antiquity the term *philosophy* came increasingly to denote the quest for happiness or salvation.

85. Above, n. 54.

86. For discussion of the influence of Greek thought on Christian doctrine see Edwin Hatch, *The Influence of Greek Ideas on Christianity*, ed. Frederick C. Grant (New York: Harper & Brothers, 1957); Timothy, *Early Christian Apologists*, pp. 81–98.

2

Science and Theology in the Middle Ages

Edward Grant

Science and theology were never more closely interrelated than during the Latin Middle Ages in Western Europe. In this occasionally stormy relationship, theology was clearly the dominant partner. Limited challenges to that dominance occurred only when a sufficiently powerful natural philosophy was available to offer alternative interpretations of cosmic structure and operation. Conflict between science and theology rarely arose in the technical sciences, but developed in that part of natural philosophy concerned with the larger principles of cosmic operation, especially where theology and science sought to explain the same phenomena.[1] Prior to the twelfth century, when the scientific fare of Latin Christendom was meager, science lacked powerful metaphysical foundations and consisted of little more than a few of Aristotle's logical treatises, some medical works, two-thirds of Plato's *Timaeus*, a few astrological books, and, especially, a series of Latin encyclopedic handbooks written by Pliny, Solinus, Calcidius, Macrobius, Martianus Capella, Boethius, Cassiodorus, Isidore of Seville, and the Venerable Bede. An important feature of this body of secular learning was the famous seven liberal arts with their twofold division into language and mathematics or mathematical science, the former consisting of grammar, rhetoric, and dialectic (or logic) and designated by the term *trivium*, the latter embracing arithmetic, geometry, astronomy, and music, collectively known as the *quadrivium*.

The narrow conception of science embodied in the *quadrivium* of the seven liberal arts was expanded into the broader sense of natural philosophy during the twelfth and thirteenth centuries when, in the course of an unparalleled period of translating activity from Arabic and Greek into Latin, the bulk of Greek science and natural philosophy was finally introduced into Latin Christendom, some eleven hundred years after the birth of Christianity.

SCIENCE AS HANDMAIDEN TO THEOLOGY

Through much of the Middle Ages, science was assigned the status of a "handmaiden to theology" (*philosophia ancilla theologiae*), a role first envisaged for it by Philo Judaeus in the first century A.D., subsequently adopted by Clement of Alexandria (ca. 150–ca. 215) and Saint Augustine (354–430) in late antiquity, and fully reinforced centuries later by Hugh of Saint-Victor (d. 1141) and Saint Bonaventure (1221–1274). According to the handmaiden concept, science was not pursued for its own sake but only for the aid it could provide in the interpretation of Holy Scripture. Saint Bonaventure even devoted a special treatise to the ancillary and subsidiary role of the arts to theology. In this work, which he titled *On Retracing the Arts to Theology (De reductione artium ad theologiam)*, Bonaventure interpreted the "arts" (*artes*) as almost synonymous with philosophy and science and believed that he had demonstrated "how all divisions of knowledge are handmaids of theology," for which reason "theology makes use of illustrations and terms pertaining to every branch of knowledge." It was the purpose or "fruit of all sciences, that in all, faith may be strengthened, [and] *God may be honored.*"[2] The glorification of God was the ultimate goal of the scientific study of nature. Some two centuries earlier, Peter Damian (1007–1072) also reflected patristic and early medieval attitudes toward the relationship of God and nature. Because God created the world from chaos, Damian considered Him the direct and immediate cause of nature's laws and its ordered beauty.[3] God encourages the study of the external, visible world with a twofold purpose: to provide in us the contemplation of its invisible, spiritual nature, so that we should better love and adore Him, and to enable us to gain dominion over it as described in Psalms 8:6–9.[4] Achievement of these goals is made possible by the sciences of number and measure in the *quadrivium.*[5] For Peter Damian, as for Bonaventure later, the study of nature and its laws was not an end in itself, pursued merely for the sake of knowledge. It had to serve the higher needs of religion and theology. Under these circumstances the secular sciences could hardly avoid the status of handmaidens.

REVOLT OF THE HANDMAIDENS:
NATURAL PHILOSOPHY CHALLENGES THEOLOGY

The subservience of science to theology, however, was always relative. It was more complete during the early Middle Ages than later, a condition attributable, in no small measure, to the enfeebled state of natural philosophy in the five or six formative centuries of the early medieval period. The bulk of Greek science and philosophy was simply absent from the corpus of secular learning that passed for science. So low was the level of science in this period that it posed no threat whatever to Christian tradition and doctrine. With the exception of Plato's *Timaeus*, most of it was encyclopedic, unintegrated, and frequently confused or contradictory. Devoid of cohesion or guiding principles, it could inspire little by way of new interpretations or insights about the nature of the world that might prove subversive of Christianity.

By the twelfth century, significant changes were under way that would eventually challenge theology's interpretation of the cosmos and the God who created it. The threat to theology and the church did not derive from astrology or magic, which, though potentially dangerous, were successfully contained in the Middle Ages. It came from Greek natural philosophy and science, initially in its benign Platonic and Neoplatonic forms in the twelfth century and then in its powerful and truly menacing Aristotelian form in the thirteenth century. The beginnings of this momentous process are already apparent in the enthusiastic study of Plato's *Timaeus* in the twelfth century. Evidence of significant change is readily available. Inspired perhaps by Honorius of Autun's (fl. 1122) joyous sentiment that "all of God's creation gives great delight to anyone looking upon it,"[6] a sentiment shared by his contemporary, Thierry of Chartres (d. ca. 1155),[7] and by earlier authors such as Peter Damian, scholars came to investigate nature for its own sake. William of Conches (ca. 1080–ca. 1154), for whom physical laws took precedence over ecclesiastical authority, reflected the new attitude when he denounced those who, "ignorant themselves of the forces of nature and wanting to have company in their ignorance . . . don't want people to look into anything; they want us to believe like peasants and not to ask the reason behind things."[8] To explain causes and phenomena by mere appeal to God's omnipotence or a biblical passage was now tantamount to a confession of ignorance.[9] It was the obligation of philosophy, not Holy Scripture, to teach about nature and its regular causes and events. A newfound confidence in human reason and sensory experience had emerged.

Even the Bible, especially the creation account of Genesis, had to conform to the demands of physical science. The bold new emphasis on rational inquiry, with which the names of Adelard of Bath, Peter Abelard, William of Conches, Bernard Silvester, Clarenbaldus of Arras, and others in the twelfth century were associated, marked the beginning of an unsuccessful, though vigorous, attempt to separate science from theology. Separation, however, did not signify that science was to be pursued solely for its own sake. On the contrary, its application to the exegesis of Holy Scripture and to the elucidation of theological problems would produce a role reversal: science began to encroach upon theology. Thus were the seeds of a science-theology confrontation planted, the bitter fruits of which would grow to maturity in the thirteenth century following upon the introduction of Aristotle's scientific works, which formed the crucial core of the new Greco-Arabic science that entered Western Europe. By the early thirteenth century, Latin translations (from Arabic) of Aristotle's scientific, logical, and metaphysical works had taken Europe by storm. No match for the depth and diversity of the Aristotelian treatises with their elaborate scientific methodology and foundational principles, Plato's *Timaeus*, which had formed the basis and inspiration of the twelfth-century worldview, soon fell into abeyance.

Aristotle's treatises on physics, metaphysics, logic, cosmology, the elements, epistemology, and the nature of change furnished the Middle Ages with its conception of the structure and operation of the physical world. They assumed this fundamental role because their introduction into Western Europe coincided with, and probably contributed toward, the establishment of that uniquely medieval institution, the university. For approximately 450 years, from 1200 to 1650, the universities of Western Europe emphasized a philosophical and scientific curriculum based on the works of Aristotle, whose logic and natural philosophy were studied by all who received the master of arts degree. Since the latter was usually a prerequisite for entry into the higher faculty of theology, most theologians were well acquainted with contemporary science.

The impact of Aristotle's thought on the late Middle Ages cannot be overestimated. For the first time in the history of Latin Christendom, a comprehensive body of secular learning, rich in metaphysics, methodology, and reasoned argumentation, posed a threat to theology and its traditional interpretations. Where Plato's creation account in the *Timaeus*, which featured a creator God who sought to share his goodness by fabricating a world from preexistent and coeternal matter and form, was reasonably compatible with Christianity, Aristotle's cosmic system, which assumed a world without beginning or end and a deity who had no knowledge of that world, was not. When to these difficulties were added those concerning the soul (it apparently perished with the body) and a strong tendency to employ naturalistic and even deterministic modes of explanation, it becomes obvious that the Aristotelian world system was not readily reducible to the status of a theological handmaiden. While numerous theologians and almost all arts masters eagerly embraced the new Aristotelian learning at the University of Paris, which possessed the most prestigious and powerful faculty of theology in all Christendom, there was a growing uneasiness amongst more traditionally minded theologians, as evidenced by a ban on Aristotle's natural books issued in 1210 and 1215 and an abortive attempt to expurgate them in 1231.[10] All such attempts were in vain, and by 1255 Aristotle's works were not only officially sanctioned but constituted the core of the arts curriculum.[11]

Those who had hoped for a harmonious relationship between theology and philosophy were to be bitterly disappointed. During the 1260s and early 1270s a fundamental split developed. On the one side were radical arts masters and liberal theologians who found Aristotle's philosophy essential to a proper understanding of God and his creation. Opposed to them were traditional theologians for whom significant aspects of Greek philosophy were dangerously subversive to the Christian faith.[12] Typified by the likes of Siger of Brabant and Boethius of Dacia, the more radical arts masters perceived Aristotle's natural philosophy as the indispensable key to a proper interpretation of the cosmos and concluded that philosophy was not only independent of theology but at least its equal and perhaps its superior. Although they would surely have denied it equality, many theologians regarded philosophy as worthy of independent study and assigned it a central role. The most illustrious member of this group was undoubtedly Thomas Aquinas (ca. 1225–1274), who considered theology the highest science because of its reliance on revelation. Without revelation the truth of the metaphysics that philosophers might devise would be incomplete and imperfect.[13] Yet Aquinas not only embraced philosophy with enthusiasm but regarded Aristotle as the greatest of philosophers, one who had achieved the highest level of human thought without the aid of revelation.[14] Rightly understood, philosophy, which included secular science, could not contradict theology or faith.[15]

Suspicious of the emphasis on philosophy and secular learning that had occurred during the 1260s and fearful of the application of Aristotelian philosophy to theology, traditional and conservative theologians, inspired by Saint Bonaventure, sought to stem the tide by outright condemnation of ideas they considered subversive. Since repeated warnings of the inherent dangers of secular philosophy and the perils of its application to theology had been of little avail,[16] the traditional theologians, many of whom were neo-Augustinian Franciscans, appealed to the bishop of Paris, Etienne Tempier, who responded in 1270 with a condemnation of 13 propositions, which was followed in 1277 by a massive condemnation of 219 propositions, any one of which was held at the price of excommunication.

THE IMPACT OF THEOLOGY ON SCIENCE

Controversial and difficult to assess, the Condemnation of 1277 looms large in the relations between theology and science. Except for articles directed specifically against Thomas Aquinas, which were nullified in 1325, the condemnation remained in effect during the fourteenth century and made an impact even beyond the region of Paris, where its legal force was confined. Hastily compiled from a wide variety of written and oral sources, the 219 condemned errors were without apparent order, repetitious, and even contradictory.[17] Orthodox and heterodox opinions were mingled indiscriminately.[18] A number of the errors were relevant to science. Of these, many were condemned in order to preserve God's absolute power (*potentia Dei absoluta*), a power that natural philosophers were thought to have unduly restricted as they eagerly sought to interpret the world in accordance with Aristotelian principles.[19] If the condemned errors accurately reflect contemporary opinion, some natural philosophers were prepared to deny the divine creation of the world, that God could create more than one world, that he could move the world in a straight line, leaving behind a void space, that he could create an accident without a subject, and so on. In denying to God the capacity to perform these and other actions that were impossible in the physical world as conceived by Aristotle and his followers, philosophers were severely constraining God's power. The theologians who compiled the list of condemned errors sought to curb the pretensions of Aristotelian natural philosophy by emphasizing the absolute power of God to do whatever He pleased short of a logical contradiction. Indeed, article 147 made this quite explicit by rejecting the claim "that the absolutely impossible cannot be done by God or another agent," which is judged "an error, if impossible is understood according to nature."[20] With respect to nature, then, all had to concede that God could do things that were contrary to prevailing scientific opinion about the structure and operations of the cosmos. In short, God could produce actions that were naturally impossible in the Aristotelian worldview. It was thus Aristotelian natural philosophy on which the Condemnation of 1277 pressed most heavily. If we can judge from those condemned errors which asserted that "theological discussions are based on fables," that "nothing is known better because of knowing theology," that "the only wise men of the world are philosophers,"[21] and that "there is no more excellent state than the study of philosophy,"[22] the Condemnation of 1277 may have served as a vehicle of sweet revenge for the theologians who compiled it. It offered an opportunity to humble the professional Aristotelian natural philosophers from whom those hostile sentiments derived.

The Paris condemnation of 219 diverse errors in theology and natural philosophy was a major event in the history of medieval natural philosophy. Whatever the doctrinal and philosophical disputes, or personal and group animosities that produced it, emphasis on God's absolute power was its most potent feature. Although the doctrine of God's absolute power was hardly new in the thirteenth century,[23] the challenge from Aristotelian natural philosophy and physics, and Greco-Arabic thought generally, conferred on it a new significance. The growing tendency prior to 1277 was to interpret cosmic phenomena in accordance with natural causes and explanatory principles derived from Aristotelian physics and cosmology. After 1277, appeals to God's absolute power were frequently introduced into physical and cosmological discussions. Whether by implication or explicit statement, many of the articles of the condemnation proclaimed God's infinite and absolute creative and causative power against those who would circumscribe it by the principles of Aristotelian natural philosophy. As a consequence, natural impossibilities, usually cast in the form of "thought experiments," were hereafter entertained with increasing frequency and occasionally with startling consequences. The supernatural alternatives considered in the aftermath of the condemnation of 1277 conditioned Scholastics to contemplate physical possibilities outside the ken of Aristotelian natural philosophy, and frequently in direct conflict with it. As the means of achieving these hypothetical possibilities, God's absolute power was usually invoked. Indeed, hypothetical possibilities based upon supernatural actions became a characteristic feature of late medieval Scholastic thought. To illustrate these tendencies we need only consider two articles concerned with the possibility of other worlds and the movement of our own.

Both Aristotle and the Bible agreed that only one world existed. With a variety of arguments Aristotle had demonstrated the impossibility of other worlds. For some of his enthusiastic medieval followers it was an easy inference that God could not create other worlds even had He wished to do so. Thus a limitation was placed upon divine power, a limitation that was condemned in article 34, which threatened excommunication to any who held that God could not possibly create more than one world. Although it was in no way required to believe that God had created a plurality of worlds—indeed, no one in the Middle Ages did so believe—but only that He could do so, the effect of article 34 was to encourage examination of the conditions and circumstances that would obtain if God had indeed created other worlds. In this spirit a number of Scholastic authors formulated arguments that sought to make the possible existence of other worlds intelligible. Sometime around 1295 Richard of Middleton (d. ca. 1300) argued in his commentary on Peter Lombard's *Sentences* that if God created other worlds identical with ours, the very kind Aristotle had discussed, each of them would behave just as ours does, since no good reasons could be adduced for supposing otherwise. Hence each world would be a self-contained, closed system with its own center and circumference.[24] It surely followed that if God did indeed create more than one world, no unique and privileged center would exist, an inference that subverted the foundation of Aristotle's cosmology, namely that the center and circumference of our world are unique. This extraordinary result, which would be repeated in the fourteenth century by the likes of William of Ockham, John Buridan, and Nicole Oresme, was achieved merely by considering possible, hypothetical worlds, not real ones.

Consideration of other worlds immediately posed the problem of what might lie between them. Prior to 1277 the possibility that a vacuum might intervene was rejected because Aristotle had demonstrated the impossibility of void space within and beyond our unique world. In light of article 34 of the condemnation of 1277, however, Nicole Oresme and others now boldly proclaimed the existence of intercosmic void space. Indeed, the necessity of conceding the existence of void space beyond our world—and therefore the possibility that void space could intervene between our world and other possible worlds—could be directly inferred from another article (no. 49), which made it mandatory to concede that God could, if He wished, move the last heaven, or the world itself, with a rectilinear motion even if a vacuum were left behind.[25]

A few fourteenth-century Scholastics moved beyond the merely hypothetical and boldly proclaimed the real existence of an infinite, extracosmic void space, which they identified with God's immensity. Late medieval Scholastics introduced God into space in a more explicit manner than that suggested by the vague metaphors found in earlier patristic, cabalistic, and hermetic traditions.[26] In the fourteenth century Thomas Bradwardine, Jean de Ripa, and Nicole Oresme proclaimed the existence of a real, extracosmic, infinite void space filled by an omnipresent deity. Oresme explicitly identified infinite, indivisible space with God's immensity. These ideas were developed further by Scholastic authors of the sixteenth and seventeenth centuries. The medieval Scholastic idea that God must bear an intimate relationship to space remained a viable concept well into the eighteenth century and played a role in the scientific and theological thought of Isaac Newton himself. From the assumption that infinite space is God's immensity, Scholastics derived most of the same properties for space that non-Scholastics did subsequently. As God's immensity, space was necessarily assigned divine properties, such as homogeneity, immutability, infinity, lack of extension, and the capacity to coexist with bodies to which it offered no resistance. Except for extension, the divinization of space in Scholastic thought produced virtually all the properties that would be attributed to space during the course of the Scientific Revolution.[27]

Although no articles of the Condemnation concerned vacua within the cosmos, it followed inexorably that if God could create a vacuum beyond our world and between possible worlds, He could surely create one or more within our world. Throughout the fourteenth century and later, God was frequently imagined to annihilate all or part of the matter within the material plenum of our world.[28] After 1277 all sorts of situations were hypothesized within such wholly or partially empty spaces. The questions raised became an integral part of a large literature on the nature of vacuum and the imagined behavior of bodies therein. Would the surrounding celestial spheres collapse inward instantaneously as nature sought to prevent formation of the abhorred vacuum? Indeed, could an utterly empty interval, or nothingness, be a vacuum or space? Would a stone placed in such a void be capable of rectilinear motion? Would people placed in such vacua see and hear each other? Analyses of these and similar "thought experiments" in the late Middle Ages were often made in terms of Aristotelian principles even though the conditions imagined were "contrary to fact" and impossible within Aristotelian natural philosophy. From such analyses intelligible and plausible alternatives to Aristotelian physics and cosmology emerged and demonstrated that things could be otherwise than was dreamt of in Aristotle's philosophy.

But if the Condemnation of 1277 beneficially stimulated speculation outside the bounds of Aristotelian natural philosophy, it may also have adversely affected scientific development. In emphasizing God's inscrutable will and his absolute power to do as He pleased, the conservative theologians encouraged a philosophical trend in which confidence in demonstrative certainty, and ultimately confidence in the ability of science to acquire certain truth about the physical world, was weakened. The imaginary physical conditions that were frequently conjured up in the Middle Ages were usually contrary to the "common course of nature" (*communis cursus nature*), which represented the operation of nature interpreted in accordance with Aristotelian natural philosophy. But, it was asked, if God could intervene at will in the causal order, how could scientific principles and laws be absolute, so as to guarantee a "common course of nature"? John Buridan (ca. 1295–ca. 1358), perhaps speaking for many arts masters who wished to defend Aristotelian science as the best means of understanding the physical world, conceded, as he had to, that God could interfere in natural events and alter their course at any time. To alleviate the effect of such uncertainty, however, Buridan urged natural philosophers to proceed as if nature *always* acted with regularity and followed its "common course."[29] On this assumption he believed that "for us the comprehension of truth with certitude is possible."[30] The scientific principles from which these certain truths are derivable are themselves indemonstrable, "but they are accepted because they have been observed to be true in many instances and false in none."[31] Since the ultimate principles depend on experience rather than strict logical demonstration or *a priori* grounds, any of Buridan's certain truths could be overturned by a single empirical counterexample. A degree of uncertainty thus lurked within Buridan's concept of certitude. On methodological grounds Buridan also found a place for the principle of Ockham's razor: that if more than one explanation could "save the phenomena," the simplest should be chosen.

But even if one accepted the simplest explanation as true, how could the best and simplest explanation be determined with certainty? Nicole Oresme (ca. 1320–1382), one of the most brilliant natural philosophers and theologians of the fourteenth century, found experience and human reason inadequate for the proper determination of physical truth. Only faith could furnish us with genuine truth. The fourteenth-century emphasis on God's free and unpredictable will, encapsulated in the concept of God's absolute power, had eroded confidence in human ability to arrive at demonstrated truth in both theology and natural philosophy. In the process of defending God's absolute power to act as He pleased, theologians not only showed the inconclusiveness of certain philosophical proofs traditionally employed to demonstrate what God could or could not do, or to prove his existence or attributes, but they also revealed the limitations of natural philosophy by demonstrating the radically contingent nature of the world. Led by William of Ockham (ca. 1285–1349), many theologians concluded that neither reason nor experience could provide certain knowledge of any necessary connection between causes and their alleged effects. Both reason and experience were consequently deemed inadequate to demonstrate fundamental truths about God and his physical creation, both of which were generally perceived as less knowable during the fourteenth century than in the thirteenth. Where demonstrative certainty about nature was the goal of most natural philosophers in the thirteenth century, probable knowledge was the most that was thought attainable by many in the fourteenth century. While the latter were hardly skeptics, their attitude toward nature, when compared with that of thirteenth-century Scholastics, appears to mark a loss of confidence in human ability to acquire certain knowledge—apart from faith and revelation—about the true nature of God and the world. It was within this intellectual environment that a new trend developed in which physical problems were couched in hypothetical form without existential implication. The phrase *secundum imaginationem*, "according to the imagination," was regularly employed to characterize the innumerable hypothetical possibilities that were formulated in both natural philosophy and theology without any regard for physical reality or application to the world. In marked contrast, the key figures in the later Scientific Revolution—Copernicus, Galileo, Kepler, Descartes, and Newton, to name only the greatest—were confident, perhaps naively, that nature's essential structure and operation were knowable. They were thus encouraged to search after nature's true laws of the physical world. With them, hypothetical conditions were but heuristic devices to arrive at physical truth. Things were quite different in the fourteenth century.

THE IMPACT OF SCIENCE ON THEOLOGY

With a diminished confidence in the certainty of theological and scientific claims, theologians of the fourteenth century turned their attention to hypothetical problems posed *secundum imaginationem*. The *Sentences* (*Sententiae*, or opinions) of Peter Lombard (d. ca. 1160), written around 1150, provided a major point of departure for consideration of these problems. Divided into four books devoted, respectively, to God, the Creation, the Incarnation, and the sacraments, the *Sentences* served for some four centuries as the standard text on which all theological students were required to lecture and comment. Although the second book, devoted to the six days of creation, afforded ample opportunity to consider specific scientific topics such as the nature of light, the four elements, the problem of the supracelestial waters, and the order and motion of the celestial spheres and planets, there was an even more direct impact of natural philosophy on theology involving the attempt to define the relationship of God to the world and his creatures. The injection of science, mathematics, and logic into commentaries on Peter Lombard's *Sentences* grew to such proportions that in 1366 the University of Paris decreed that except where necessary those who read the *Sentences* should avoid the introduction of logical or philosophical material into the treatment of the questions.[32] Despite such appeals, however, Scholastic commentators apparently found it "necessary" to introduce such matters frequently and extensively.

That science and mathematics were applied to the exegesis of the creation account in medieval commentaries on the second book of Peter Lombard's *Sentences* comes as no surprise. Since later antiquity, science and mathematics had been used extensively in hexaemeral commentaries on Genesis—for example, by Saints Basil, Ambrose, and Augustine—a practice that continued throughout the Middle Ages (and well into the seventeenth century) and reached enormous proportions in the lengthy (over a million words) popular, encyclopedic commentary of Henry of Langenstein (composed between 1385 and 1393), which employed almost every scientific subject in its biblical exegesis and made apparent the ease with which science could be introduced into the analysis of creation.[33] During the late Middle Ages, however, science and mathematics were also applied extensively to theological problems that were largely or wholly unrelated to the creation account in Genesis. Themes, techniques, and ideas from natural philosophy and mathematics were frequently used in problems that concerned God's omnipresence, omnipotence, and infinity, as well as his relations to the beings of his own creation and to comparisons between created species. Mathematical concepts were regularly drawn from proportionality theory, the nature of the mathematical continuum, convergent and divergent infinite series, the infinitely large and small, potential and actual infinites, and limits, which included boundary conditions involving first and last instants or points.[34]

Not only were these concepts applied to theological problems, but the latter were frequently formulated in the language of mathematics and measurement. Such concepts were employed to describe the manner in which spiritual entities could vary in intensity and how such variations could best be represented mathematically by application of the peculiarly medieval doctrine known as "the intension and remission of forms or qualities" (or occasionally as "the configuration of qualities"); they were also to determine the manner in which upper and lower limits, or first and last instants, could be assigned to various processes and events, as in problems concerning free will, merit, and sin. In the fourteenth century Robert Holkot conceived a dilemma requiring *either* that limits be placed on free will *or* that we concede that God might not always be able to reward a meritorious person and punish one who was sinful.[35] Thus he imagined a situation in which a man is alternately meritorious and sinful during the final hour of his life: he is meritorious in the first proportional part of that last hour and sinful in the second proportional part; he is again meritorious in the third proportional part and again sinful in the fourth proportional part, and so on through the infinite series of decreasing proportional parts up to the instant of his death. Since the instant of death cannot form part of the infinite series of decreasing proportional parts of the man's last hour of life, it follows that there is no last instant of his life and, therefore, no last instant in which he could be either meritorious or sinful. As a result, God does not know whether to reward or punish him in the afterlife, which was an unacceptable consequence of the doctrine of free will.[36] One could only conclude that free will cannot be assumed to extend to every imaginable sequence and pattern of choices, a point that Holkot buttressed with eight more continuum arguments.

The mathematical concepts already mentioned, and others as well, were applied to many other problems, especially those concerned with infinites. In this category were included speculations about God's infinite attributes (namely his power, presence, and essence); the kinds of infinites He could possibly create; the infinite distances that separated Him from his creatures, a problem related to the widely discussed concept of the perfection of species;[37] the possible eternity of the world; whether God could improve upon something He had already made, especially whether He could make endlessly better and better successive worlds or whether He could create an ultimate, best possible world.[38] A host of problems was concerned with the behavior of angels, namely how, if at all, an angel could occupy a place; whether it could be in two places simultaneously; whether two or more angels could occupy one and the same place simultaneously; whether angels moved between two separate places with finite or instantaneous speed. In all these problems about angels, basic concepts that had been developed in discussions of the motion of material bodies were applied directly or used as the standard of comparison. The motion of angels was one of the most popular contexts for the intense medieval debate about the nature of the continuum: whether it consisted of parts that are infinitely divisible or was composed of indivisible, mathematical atoms that could be either finite or infinite in number.[39] In contemplating the range of theological topics to which mathematics and mathematical concepts were applied, one may reasonably conclude that in the fourteenth century theology had been quantified.

Further examples of the quantification of theology could easily be supplied, since the process was ubiquitous in *Sentence Commentaries*. But just as the influence of theology, with its emphasis on God's absolute power, had encouraged, and even facilitated, the formulation in natural philosophy of hypothetical speculations about natural impossibilities, so also did the importation into theology of concepts, ideas, and techniques from mathematics and natural philosophy influence and encourage theology to express many of its problems in a scientific and logicomathematical format that was essentially hypothetical and speculative, or, as would be said in the Middle Ages, *secundum imaginationem*. Why theological arguments should have been expressed hypothetically in a logicomathematical format is by no means obvious. The hypothetical character of the arguments is probably attributable to the Condemnation of 1277 and its long aftermath. Either because it was the safer course to pursue or perhaps because of the widespread conviction among theologians that God's nature and the motives for his actions were not directly knowable by human reason and experience, it became rather standard procedure to couch theological problems in hypothetical form. That the format of the problems was frequently quantitative and logicomathematical and involved measurements and comparisons between all sorts of spiritual and incorporeal entities is perhaps also explicable by the educational background of theological students and masters. With their overwhelming emphasis on natural philosophy and logic, and sufficient training in geometry, they may have found it quite natural to formulate, and even recast, their hypothetical theological problems in the quantitative languages that had formed their common educational background and that had been fashioned by natural philosophers in the first thirty or forty years of the fourteenth century.

Whatever the reasons for the hypothetical and quantitative format, it is no exaggeration to detect in all of this a major change in the techniques of theology, the like of which had never been seen before. Under the seductive influence of science, mathematics, and logic, theology found major expression in a quantified format within which solutions to a host of hypothetical theological problems were sought by various kinds of measurements, especially in problems that involved relationships between God and his creatures.[40] Traditional theological questions were often recast in a quantitative mold that allowed the easy application of mathematical and logical analysis. Yet this massive influx of quantitative apparatus appears to have had little if any impact on the content of theology. But if content was unaffected, the traditional methodology of theology had been transformed by the emphasis on natural philosophy and mathematics. It is this transformation that marks the fourteenth century and the late Middle Ages as an extraordinary period in the history of the relations between science and theology in the Western world.

The impact of science on theology was not all of this kind, however. The application of science to the interpretation of the creation account in Genesis was quite traditional and generally lacked the quantitative and hypothetical, imaginary character that dominated other aspects of theology. Basic procedures for the application of science to the creation account had been laid down by Saint Augustine in his *Commentary on Genesis*[41] and were faithfully summarized by Saint Thomas Aquinas (ca. 1225–1274) in the latter's own commentary on the six days of creation in the *Summa theologiae*. In considering whether the firmament was made on the second day, Aquinas observes that Augustine had insisted upon two hermeneutical points in the explication of scriptural texts:

> First, the truth of Scripture must be held inviolable. Secondly, when there are different ways of explaining a Scriptural text, no particular explanation should be held so rigidly that, if convincing arguments show it to be false, anyone dare to insist that it still is the definitive sense of the text. Otherwise unbelievers will scorn Sacred Scripture, and the way to faith will be closed to them.[42]

These two vital points constituted the basic medieval guidelines for the application of a continually changing body of scientific theory and observational data to the interpretation of physical phenomena described in the Bible, especially the creation account. The scriptural text must be assumed true. When God "made a firmament, and divided the waters that were under the firmament, from those that were above the firmament,"[43] one could not doubt that waters of some kind must be above the firmament.[44] The nature of that firmament and of the waters above it were, however, inevitably dependent on interpretations that were usually derived from contemporary science. It is here that Augustine and Aquinas cautioned against a rigid adherence to any one interpretation lest it be shown subsequently untenable and thus prove detrimental to the faith.

In conformity with his own admonitions Aquinas adopted no single interpretation of either "firmament" or the "waters" above the firmament. Instead he enumerated different historical interpretations that were compatible with Scripture and patiently explained how the

application of different scientific theories implied different and sometimes conflicting consequences. The firmament created on the second
day was susceptible of two interpretations: it could be the sphere of
the fixed stars or part of the atmosphere where clouds condense.[45]
The first of these opinions could be interpreted in a variety of ways,
each dependent on the material nature assigned to the firmament,
that is, whether it was compounded of the four elements (Empedo-
cles), or of a single element such as fire (Plato), or indeed consisted
of a fifth element wholly different from the other four (Aristotle).
For each of these possibilities Aquinas explained in what sense it
was or was not compatible with the creation of a firmament on the
second day.

Aquinas approached the meaning of the "waters" above the firmament in a similar manner. Each of a variety of possible significations
was made to depend on the material nature attributed to the firmament.[46] Thus if the sphere of the fixed stars is the firmament and is
composed of the four elements, the waters above the firmament could
then plausibly be interpreted as the ordinary element water, but if
the firmament is not compounded of the four regular elements, the
waters above the firmament must be something other than the regular
element water. In the latter event, "water" may be interpreted in the
Augustinian manner as the unformed matter of which bodies are
made. Its designation as aqueous may even derive from its transparent
nature rather than its fluidity. After all, those waters may be solid
like ice, that is crystalline, as in the "crystalline heaven of some authors."[47] Should the firmament be construed as that part of the atmosphere where clouds are formed, the waters above the firmament
would be identical with those that are evaporated below and rise up
to fall as rain. Because of the solidity of the celestial spheres these
evaporated waters could not rise beyond the moon and *a fortiori* would
never rise above the celestial region itself. Indeed, they could not
even survive the heat of the fiery region immediately below the moon
and would never reach the celestial spheres. With the presentation
of these differing opinions Aquinas felt he had accomplished his objective. Because they were all compatible with the scriptural text, he
saw no need—and indeed no way—to choose among them.

Occasionally the literal meaning of scriptural statements conflicted
directly with universally accepted scientific theories and observations.
In such instances the scriptural text had to be reinterpreted, as in the
case of Psalms 103:2, where God is said to have stretched out the
firmament like a tent. Because of the near unanimous opinion that
the earth is spherical, it was necessary that the firmament also be
spherical, a condition that a tent could not fulfill. Under these cir-

cumstances Augustine and medieval Scholastics generally agreed that it was the biblical exegete's duty to demonstrate that the description of the firmament as a tent was not contrary to the scientific truth of a spherical firmament.[48] Augustine admonished against the development of a special Christian science that would attempt to explain the literal meaning of difficult texts that conflicted with well-founded scientific truths. Such attempts would undermine the credibility of Christianity. Augustine's attitude was thus compatible with both literal and allegorical interpretations of Scripture. The literal meaning of a text was always preferable, even where multiple interpretations were unavoidable, as with the supracelestial waters. But wherever a scriptural passage conflicted with a scientifically demonstrated proposition—as happened in Psalms 103:2—the scientific interpretation must prevail to prevent any erosion of confidence in scriptural truth. Under such circumstances, an allegorical interpretation was required so that truth and Scripture would be in harmony.

During the late Middle Ages broad and liberal, rather than narrow and literal, interpretations were the rule in biblical exegesis involving physical phenomena. An important illustration of this tendency is the famous passage that describes God's miraculous intervention on behalf of the army of Joshua (Joshua 10:12–14). By commanding the sun to stand still over Gibeon, God lengthened the day and allowed Israel to triumph over the Amorites. Since it was the sun—not the earth—that was ordered to come to rest, it followed that night and day were the consequence of the sun's daily revolution around an immobile earth rather than a result of the earth's daily rotation around its own axis. Here the Bible was in conformity with the best of Greek and medieval astronomy. Yet Nicole Oresme challenged this seemingly routine interpretation. "When God performs a miracle," he explained,

> we must assume and maintain that He does so without altering the common course of nature, in so far as possible. Therefore, if we can save appearances by taking for granted that God lengthened the day in Joshua's time by stopping the movement of the earth or merely that of the region here below—which is so very small and like a mere dot compared to the heavens—and by maintaining that nothing in the whole universe—and especially the huge heavenly bodies—except this little point was put off its ordinary course and regular schedule, then this would be a much more reasonable assumption.[49]

Despite the plain statement of Scripture that the sun stopped in its course, Oresme argued that the same effect could be produced more economically and with less interruption of the common and regular course of nature by the assumption of a *real* daily axial motion for the much smaller earth. The sun's cessation of motion could thus be construed as only apparent and not real, an appearance produced when God caused the real axial rotation of the earth to cease. On the assumption that God always acted in the simplest and least disruptive manner, He surely would have stopped the smaller earth and not the sun, from which it followed that the apparent daily motion of the sun results from a real rotation of the earth. But Scripture plainly states that the sun, not the earth, stood still. Oresme's assumption would conflict not only with this clear biblical statement but with many others that also speak of the sun's motion or the earth's immobility.[50] Such passages, Oresme countered, may not reflect literal truth but merely conform "to the customary usage of popular speech just as it [that is, Holy Scripture] does in many other places, for instance, in those where it is written that God repented, and He became angry and became pacified, and other such expressions which are not to be taken literally."[51]

However, despite persuasive arguments in favor of the earth's axial rotation, Oresme knew that it was beyond his powers to demonstrate it scientifically. In the end, faithful to the admonitions of Augustine and Aquinas, he retained the literal meaning of the Bible and rejected the earth's rotation. Although he adopted the traditional opinion, Oresme's interpretation of the Joshua passage was more daring than Galileo's in 1615. As a confirmed Copernican, Galileo interpreted the Joshua text literally. With the sun at the center of the planetary system, Galileo assumed that it controlled the motions of all the planets. Hence

> when God willed that at Joshua's command the whole system of the world should rest and should remain for many hours in the same state, it sufficed to make the sun stand still. Upon its stopping, all the other revolutions ceased. . . . And in this manner, by the stopping of the sun, without altering or in the least disturbing the other aspects and mutual positions of the stars, the day could be lengthened on earth—which agrees exquisitely with the literal sense of the sacred text.[52]

Oresme's interpretation was radically different and far more striking because it was contrary to the literal meaning of the text, which, in this instance, agreed fully with Aristotelian cosmology and Ptolemaic astronomy. Since Oresme's consideration of the earth's diurnal rotation was in the end merely hypothetical, it caused no apparent theological consternation. Whether the same indifference would have prevailed if Oresme had concluded in favor of the reality of the earth's daily axial rotation is simply unanswerable, as is the question whether he might have suffered a fate similar to that which befell Galileo some 250 years later.

We may reasonably conclude that the application of science to medieval scriptural exegesis was effected without noticeable constraints or interference. Indeed, the text of Holy Scripture was more often compelled to conform to the established truths of science than vice versa. The application of science to Scripture is perhaps best characterized by flexibility. Though the literal meaning was preferred, provision was made for allegorical interpretations. Potential conflict lurked, however, in passages where the literal meaning contradicted what were thought to be scientifically demonstrated truths. While theologians found it easy to place an allegorical interpretation on the passage in Psalms 103:2—no one believed that the firmament was shaped like a tent—they would eventually prove unyielding, as Galileo would learn to his sorrow, on the many passages that mentioned the sun's motion and the earth's immobility. Galileo's insistence on an allegorical interpretation of those passages, on the grounds that he could scientifically demonstrate the earth's motion, clashed with the interpretation of the theologians who rejected his demonstrations and insisted on the traditional, literal sense. Ironically, to legitimate their positions both sides quite properly appealed to Augustine's conception of scriptural interpretation. During the Middle Ages no similar conflict erupted, not even on the always vexing problem of the eternity of the world. The medieval theologian–natural philosopher was generally free to propose and adopt a single interpretation—though encouraged not to embrace it unreservedly if it were not scientifically demonstrated—or to enunciate multiple interpretations without firm commitment to any one of them.

DID THEOLOGY INHIBIT SCIENTIFIC INQUIRY?

We must finally confront an unavoidable question on the relations of medieval science and theology: how, if at all, did the latter affect the freedom of inquiry of the former? The attempts to ban and expurgate the physical works of Aristotle during the first half of the thirteenth century bear witness to theological fears about the potential power of uncontrolled philosophical learning. The Condemnation of 1277 marked the culmination of theological efforts to contain and control natural philosophy. The bishop of Paris and his theological colleagues sought to restrict, under penalty of excommunication, categorical claims for a number of ideas in natural philosophy. It was now forbidden, for example, to deny creation and assert the eternity of the world, to deny the possibility of other worlds, and to deny that God could create an accident without a subject in which to inhere. Although these restrictions fell equally on masters of arts and theologians at the University of Paris, the arts masters were more seriously affected than their theological colleagues. Not only were they obliged to comply with the Condemnation of 1277, but, in the absence of professional credentials in theology, they had been required, since 1272, to swear an oath that they would avoid disputation of purely theological questions and were generally discouraged from introducing theological matters into natural philosophy.[53]

Despite such restrictions, however, arts masters were free to uphold almost all of Aristotle's scientific conclusions and principles, provided that they conceded to God the power to create events and phenomena that were contrary to those conclusions and principles and which were therefore naturally impossible in the Aristotelian system. They were thus free to support Aristotle and deny the existence of other worlds if only they would allow that God could create them if He wished. Even the eternity of the world, which was to the relations between science and religion in the Middle Ages what the Copernican theory was to the sixteenth and seventeenth centuries and what the Darwinian theory of evolution was to the nineteenth and twentieth centuries, could be proclaimed hypothetically when "speaking naturally" (*loquendo naturaliter*), that is, when considering a question in natural philosophy. Indeed, on the assumption that there was a fixed quantity of matter in the world and that the world was eternal, Albert of Saxony concluded in the fourteenth century that over an infinite time this limited quantity of matter would, of necessity, furnish the bodies for an infinite number of human forms. It followed that on the day of resurrection, when every soul receives its material body, the same finite quantity of matter would be received by an infinite number of human souls, a clearly heretical consequence, since one and the same body would have to receive a plurality of souls. To this dilemma Albert's response was typical for natural philosophers who regularly contended with theological restrictions: "The natural philosopher is not much concerned with this argument because when he assumes the eternity of the world, he denies the resurrection of the dead."[54] By such appeals to the hypothetical, medieval natural philosophers could consider almost any condemned and controversial proposition. Nevertheless, they were not permitted to proclaim such beliefs categorically, and to the extent that their discussions touched theology or had theological implications, they were inhibited and frustrated, as when John Buridan complained that in his analysis of the vacuum, which touched upon faith and theology, he was reproached by the theological masters for intermingling theological matters.[55]

With the arts masters forbidden to apply their knowledge to theology, we are left with the theologians as the class of scholars who applied science to theology and theology to science during the Middle Ages. Not only were they thoroughly trained in natural philosophy and theology, but some were also significant contributors to science and mathematics, as the names of Albertus Magnus, John Pecham, Theodoric of Freiberg, Thomas Bradwardine, Nicole Oresme, and Henry of Langenstein testify. Because they were trained in both natural philosophy and theology, medieval theologians were able to interrelate science and theology with relative ease and confidence, whether this involved the application of science to scriptural exegesis, the application of God's absolute power to alternative possibilities in the natural world, or even the frequent invocation of scriptural texts in scientific treatises in support of scientific theories and ideas. Theologians had a remarkable degree of intellectual freedom[56] and, for the most part, did not allow their theology to hinder or obstruct inquiry into the structure and operation of the physical world. If there was any real temptation to produce a "Christian science," they successfully resisted it. Biblical texts were not employed to "demonstrate" scientific truths by blind appeal to divine authority. When Nicole Oresme inserted some fifty citations to twenty-three different books of the Bible in his scientific treatise *On the Configurations of Qualities and Motions,* he did so only by way of example or for additional support, but in no sense to demonstrate an argument.[57]

Ironically, rather than inhibiting scientific discussion, theologians may have inadvertently produced the opposite effect, as suggested by the impact of the doctrine of God's absolute power described above. Theological restrictions embodied in the Condemnation of 1277 may have actually prompted consideration of plausible and implausible alternatives and possibilities far beyond what Aristotelian natural philosophers might otherwise have considered, if left to their own devices. While these speculations did not lead to the abandonment of the Aristotelian worldview, they generated some of the most daring and exciting scientific discussions of the Middle Ages.

That medieval theologians combined extensive and intensive training in both natural philosophy and theology, and possessed exclusive rights to interrelate the two, may provide a key to explain the absence of a science-theology conflict in the extensive medieval commentary literature on the *Sentences* and Scripture. For the host of issues they regularly confronted, the medieval theologian–natural philosophers knew how to subordinate the one discipline to the other and to avoid conflict and confrontation. Indeed, they were in an excellent position to harmonize the two disciplines while simultaneously pursuing all manner of hypothetical and contrary-to-fact conditions and possibilities. Compared to the situation in late antiquity, when Christianity was struggling for survival, and the difficult times that lay ahead, the late Middle Ages—except for the 1260s and 1270s—was a relatively tranquil period in the long interrelationship between science and theology.

NOTES

1. Although there are significant differences between the modern term *science* and the medieval term *natural philosophy*, the two will be used here interchangeably. In practical terms, natural philosophy (or "natural science," as it was occasionally called) was generally identified with Aristotle's "natural books" (*libri naturales*), which treated themes in cosmology, physics, and matter theory. As one of the three major subdivisions of speculative philosophy, natural philosophy was concerned exclusively with mobile bodies and their changes. Although natural philosophy was distinct from mathematics, sciences that used mathematics, such as optics and astronomy, but were also concerned with mobile bodies could also fall under the consideration of natural philosophy. For the place of natural philosophy in the medieval division of the sciences see Robert Kilwardby, O.P., *De Ortu Scientiarum*, ed. Albert G. Judy, O.P. (Toronto: British Academy and the Pontifical Institute of Mediaeval Studies, 1976), pp. 15–29, and Domingo Gundisalvo, *On the Division of Philosophy*, partially translated by M. Clagett and E. Grant in *A Source Book in Medieval Science*, ed. Edward Grant (Cambridge, Mass.: Harvard Univ. Press, 1974), pp. 62–65.

2. See Sister Emma Therese Healy, ed and trans., *Saint Bonaventure's "De reductione artium ad theologiam": A Commentary with an Introduction and Translation* (Saint Bonaventure, N.Y.: The Franciscan Institute, 1955), p. 41. I have added the bracketed word. For the manner in which Roger Bacon subordinated mathematics to theology see David C. Lindberg, "On the Applicability of Mathematics to Nature: Roger Bacon and His Predecessors," *British Journal for the History of Science* 15 (1982): 3–26. The most frequently cited biblical passages in support of the handmaiden idea were Exodus 3:22 and 12:36, which spoke of despoiling the Egyptians of their treasures. In 1231, when he sought to justify the expurgation of Aristotle's physical treatises, Pope Gregory IX referred to the despoiling of the Egyptians by the Hebrews (for the passage see *Source Book*, ed. Grant, p. 43).

3. André Cantin, *Les sciences séculières et la foi: Les deux voies de la science au jugement de S. Pierre Damien (1007–1072)* (Spoleto: Centro Italiano di Studi sull'Alto Medioevo, 1975), pp. 557, 578.

4. Ibid., p. 580.

5. Ibid., pp. 536 ff.

6. From Honorius's *Elucidarium* 1.12 as translated by M. D. Chenu, O.P., *Nature, Man, and Society in the Twelfth Century: Essays on New Theological Perspectives in the Latin West,* preface by Etienne Gilson, ed. and trans. Jerome Taylor and Lester K. Little (Chicago: Univ. of Chicago Press, 1968; original French version published in 1957), p. 8 n. 15.

7. See Tina Stiefel, "The Heresy of Science: A Twelfth-Century Conceptual Revolution," *Isis* 68 (1977): 350.

8. From William's *Philosophia mundi* 1.23 as translated in Chenu, *Nature, Man, and Society,* p. 11. For William's attitude toward the relationship between physical law and the exegetical tradition on Genesis see Helen R. Lemay, "Science and Theology at Chartres: The Case of the Supracelestial Waters," *British Journal for the History of Science* 10 (1977): 229–233.

9. Chenu, *Nature, Man and Society,* p. 12.

10. The bans of 1210 and 1215 were issued by the provincial synod of Sens, which included the bishop of Paris. The order to expurgate the books of Aristotle in 1231 came from Pope Gregory IX, who appointed a three-member committee for the purpose. Whatever the reasons, the committee never carried out its assignment. For a translation of the documents of 1210 and 1231 see *Source Book,* ed. Grant, pp. 42–43.

11. For the document of 1255 see *Source Book,* ed. Grant, pp. 43–44.

12. The different reactions to pagan philosophy are described by John Wippel, "The Condemnations of 1270 and 1277 at Paris," *Journal of Medieval and Renaissance Studies* 7 (1977): 195.

13. See Frederick Copleston, S.J., *A History of Philosophy,* 9 vols. (Westminster, Md.: Newman Press, 1946–1975), 2:318–319.

14. Ibid., p. 319. Edith Sylla observes ("Autonomous and Handmaiden Science: St. Thomas Aquinas and William of Ockham on the Physics of the Eucharist," in *The Cultural Context of Medieval Learning,* ed. John E. Murdoch and Edith D. Sylla [Dordrecht and Boston: D. Reidel, 1979], pp. 354, 363) that despite Aquinas's acknowledgment of the autonomy of philosophy (which includes natural philosophy) from theology, he often subordinated the former to the latter, as exemplified in his discussion of the Eucharist. By contrast, William of Ockham (ca. 1285–1349) refused to bend physics and natural philosophy to the needs of theology, choosing rather to explain physically inexplicable religious phenomena by God's direct intervention.

15. Wippel, "Condemnations of 1270 and 1277," p. 175.

16. For some of these warnings see Leo Elders, S.V.D., *Faith and Science: An Introduction to St. Thomas' "Expositio in Boethii De Trinitate"* (Rome: Herder, 1974), p. 51 and nn. 42, 43.

17. The Latin text of the 219 articles, in their original order, appears in Heinrich Denifle and Emile Chatelain, *Chartularium Universitatis Parisiensis,* 4 vols. (Paris: Ex typis Fratrum Delalain, 1889–1897), 1:543–555; for a methodical regrouping of the articles aimed at facilitating their use see Pierre F. Mandonnet, O.P., *Siger de Brabant et l'Averroïsme latin au XIIIme siècle, IIme partie: Textes inédits,* 2d ed. (Louvain: Institut supérieur de philosophie de l'Uni-

versité, 1908), pp. 175–191. Using Mandonnet's reorganized version, Ernest L. Fortin and Peter D. O'Neill translated the articles into English in *Medieval Political Philosophy: A Sourcebook,* ed. Ralph Lerner and Muhsin Mahdi (New York: Free Press of Glencoe, 1963), pp. 337–354. Their translation was reprinted in *Philosophy in the Middle Ages: The Christian, Islamic, and Jewish Traditions,* ed. Arthur Hyman and James J. Walsh (Indianapolis: Hackett Publishing Co., 1973), pp. 540–549. Selected articles relevant to science have been translated in *Source Book,* ed. Grant, pp. 45–50. For a discussion of each article, including its sources, see Roland Hisette, *Enquête sur les 219 articles condamnés à Paris le 7 mars 1277,* Philosophes médiévaux, vol. 22 (Louvain: Publications Universitaires; Paris: Vander-Oyez, 1977).

18. Wippel, "Condemnations of 1270 and 1277," p. 186.

19. Here and in what follows on the Condemnation of 1277 I follow my article "The Condemnation of 1277, God's Absolute Power, and Physical Thought in the Late Middle Ages," *Viator,* 10 (1979): 211–244. For the distinction between God's absolute power and his ordained power (*potentia ordinata*) see p. 215.

20. *Source Book,* ed. Grant. p. 49.

21. Articles 152, 153, and 154 as translated in *Source Book,* ed. Grant, p. 50.

22. Article 40 as translated in Wippel, "Condemnations of 1270 and 1277," p. 187.

23. It had already been proclaimed by Saint Peter Damian in the eleventh century (for a translation of the relevant sections from Damian's *On Divine Ominipotence [De divina omnipotentia]* see *Medieval Philosophy from St. Augustine to Nicholas of Cusa,* ed. John F. Wippel and Allan Wolter, O.F.M. [New York: The Free Press, 1969], pp. 143–152, esp. 148–149) and by Peter Lombard in the twelfth century (the passage from Peter's *Sentences* is translated in Grant, "Condemnation of 1277," p. 214 n. 10).

24. For the references and further discussion see Grant, "Condemnation of 1277," pp. 220–223.

25. A detailed discussion appears in ibid., pp. 226–232.

26. By "hermetic" tradition is meant the approximately fifteen anonymous Greek treatises written sometime between A.D. 100 and 300 and ascribed to the Egyptian god Hermes Trismegistus ("Thrice-Great Hermes"). A diverse collection of mystical and spiritual works that incorporated popular Greek philosophy along with Jewish and Persian elements, the hermetic treatises exercised some influence during the Middle Ages but had their greatest impact during the Renaissance. For an account of their significant role in Western thought see Frances A. Yates, *Giordano Bruno and the Hermetic Tradition* (Chicago: Univ. of Chicago Press, 1964).

27. The summary presented here of the relations between God and space is drawn from my book, *Much Ado about Nothing: Theories of Space and Vacuum from the Middle Ages to the Scientific Revolution* (Cambridge: Cambridge Univ. Press, 1981), esp. pp. 260–264.

28. See Grant, "Condemnation of 1277," pp. 240–241.

29. Ockham had also adopted this attitude (see Sylla, "Autonomous and Handmaiden Science," p. 359), as did others who sought to assign meaning and significance to the "common course of nature."

30. Buridan, *Questions on the Metaphysics,* bk. 2, question 1. The interpretations of Buridan and Oresme (below) are based on my article "Scientific Thought in Fourteenth-Century Paris: Jean Buridan and Nicole Oresme," in *Machaut's World: Science and Art in the Fourteenth Century,* ed. Madeleine Pelner Cosman and Bruce Chandler, Annals of the New York Academy of Sciences, vol. 314 (New York: New York Academy of Sciences, 1978), pp. 105–124, esp. p. 109. On the quotation from Buridan see also William A. Wallace, *Prelude to Galileo: Essays on Medieval and Sixteenth-Century Sources of Galileo's Thought* (Dordrecht and Boston: D. Reidel, 1981), p. 345.

31. From Buridan's *Questions on the Metaphysics,* bk. 2, question 2, as translated by Ernest A. Moody, "Buridan, Jean," *Dictionary of Scientific Biography* 2:605.

32. Denifle and Chatelain, *Chartularium Universitatis Parisiensis,* 3:144. The statute is cited and discussed by John E. Murdoch, "From Social into Intellectual Factors: An Aspect of the Unitary Character of Late Medieval Learning," in *Cultural Context,* ed. Murdoch and Sylla, p. 276. Some 160 years later, John Major (1469–1550), in the introduction to the second book of his *Sentence Commentary* (1528), declared that "for some two centuries now, theologians have not feared to work into their writings questions which are purely physical, metaphysical, and sometimes purely mathematical" (translated by Walter Ong, *Ramus, Method, and the Decay of Dialogue: From the Art of Discourse to the Art of Reason* [Cambridge, Mass.: Harvard Univ. Press, 1958], p. 144).

33. Henry's *Lecturae super Genesim,* to use its Latin title, has been analyzed by Nicholas Steneck, *Science and Creation in the Middle Ages: Henry of Langenstein (d. 1397) on Genesis* (Notre Dame, Ind.: Univ. of Notre Dame Press, 1976); see esp. p. 21.

34. The basic research on the application of concepts of mathematics and measurement to theology has been done by John E. Murdoch in at least two articles on which I have relied: "*Mathesis in Philosophiam Scholasticam Introducta:* The Rise and Development of the Application of Mathematics in Fourteenth Century Philosophy and Theology," in *Arts libéraux et philosophie au Moyen Âge: Actes du quatrième Congrès international de philosophie médiévale, Université de Montréal, 27 août–2 septembre 1967* (Montreal: Institut d'études médiévales; Paris: J. Vrin, 1969), pp. 215–254; and "From Social into Intellectual Factors," pp. 271–339.

35. The following illustration appears in Holkot's (or Holcot's) *Sentence Commentary,* bk. 1, question 3, the Latin text of which is quoted by Murdoch ("From Social into Intellectual Factors," p. 327 n. 102) from the edition of Lyon, 1518. For the interpretation of this difficult argument I am indebted to my student Mr. Peter Lang.

36. Ockham argued that if God wished, He could save a man who died without grace (see Sylla, "Autonomous and Handmaiden Science," p. 358).

With respect to Holkot's argument, Ockham might have replied that God could save the man regardless of his state of grace at the final moment of life and despite God's ignorance of that state. The startling aspect of Holkot's argument, however, is that God could be in ignorance about a person's state of grace or sin at the last moment of life.

37. On the application of scales and measurements to the perfection of species see Murdoch, "*Mathesis in Philosophiam Scholasticam Introducta*," pp. 238–239.

38. See Steven J. Dick, *Plurality of Worlds: The Origins of the Extraterrestrial Life Debate from Democritus to Kant* (Cambridge: Cambridge Univ. Press, 1982), pp. 31–35; and Armand Maurer, "Ockham on the Possibility of a Better World," *Mediaeval Studies* 38 (1976): 291–312.

39. Murdoch, "*Mathesis in Philosophiam Scholasticam Introducta*," p. 217 n. 4.

40. Murdoch, "From Social into Intellectual Factors," p. 292.

41. *De Gensi ad litteram* 1.18, 19, and 21. These passages are partly translated and partly summarized by Stanley L. Jaki, *Science and Creation: From Eternal Cycles to an Oscillating Universe* (New York: Science History Publications, 1974), pp. 182–183.

42. Saint Thomas Aquinas, *Summa theologiae: Latin Text and English Translation, Introductions, Notes, Appendices and Glossaries*, vol. 10, *Cosmogony* (1a65–74), trans. William A. Wallace, O.P. (New York and London: Black-friars in conjunction with McGraw-Hill Book Co. and Eyre & Spottiswoode, 1967), part 1, question 68, 1 (the second day), pp. 71–73.

43. Genesis 1:7 (Douay-Rheims translation).

44. An opinion expressed by Saint Augustine, *De Genesi ad litteram*, 2.5, and quoted approvingly by Aquinas, *Summa theologiae* (trans. Wallace), part 1, question 68, 2, p. 79.

45. *Summa theologiae* (trans. Wallace), part 1, question 68, 1, pp. 73–75.

46. Aquinas, *Summa*, part 1, question 68, 2, pp. 79–83.

47. Ibid., p. 81.

48. Jaki, *Science and Creation*, pp. 182–183, provides the references to Augustine's *Commentary on Genesis*. Presumably, William of Conches thought he was following Augustine's advice when he insisted upon an allegorical interpretation of "firmament" as air, rather than taking it literally as anything celestial, beyond or above which it was impossible for water of any kind to exist (see Lemay, "Science and Theology at Chartres," pp. 229–231).

49. Nicole Oresme, *Le livre du ciel et du monde*, ed. Albert D. Menut and Alexander J. Denomy, C.S.B., trans. Albert D. Menut (Madison: Univ. of Wisconsin Press, 1968), p. 537. The passage is reprinted in *Source Book*, ed. Grant, p. 509.

50. For example, Genesis 15:12; Ecclesiastes 1:5; 2 Samuel 2:24; Psalms 92:1; Ephesians 4:26; and James 1:11.

51. *Le livre du ciel et du monde*, p. 531; *Source Book*, ed. Grant, p. 507.

52. "Letter to Madame Christina of Lorraine, Grand Duchess of Tuscany, Concerning the Use of Biblical Quotations in Matters of Science," in *Discoveries*

and Opinions of Galileo, trans. Stillman Drake (Garden City, N.Y.: Doubleday, 1957), pp. 213–214.

53. For the statute see *Source Book,* ed. Grant, pp. 44–45. On John Buridan's complaint against theological restrictions in his discussion of the vacuum see pp. 50–51.

54. For the text and discussion based on Albert's *Questions on Generation and Corruption* see Anneliese Maier, *Metaphysische Hintergründe der spätscholastischen Naturphilosophie* (Rome: Edizioni di Storia e Letteratura, 1955), pp. 39–40. Maier also notes (p. 41) that, in coping with the same question, Marsilius of Inghen declared that, in truth, the world had a beginning and will come to an end. Whether, on the assumption of the eternity of the world, an infinity of souls would receive the same matter is a theological question and of no concern in a work on natural philosophy. Although he sought to avoid the question, Marsilius did allow that God could, if He wished, assign one matter to many men.

55. For the text of Buridan's complaint see *Source Book,* ed. Grant, pp. 50–51.

56. For an elaborate defense of this claim see Mary Martin McLaughlin, *Intellectual Freedom and Its Limitations in the University of Paris in the Thirteenth and Fourteenth Centuries* (New York: Arno Press, 1977; Ph.D. diss., Columbia University, 1952), chap. 4 ("The Freedom of the Theologian as Scholar and Teacher"), pp. 170–237, and chap. 5 ("Intellectual Freedom and the Role of the Theologian in the Church and in Society"), p. 238.

57. See Marshall Clagett, ed. and trans., *Nicole Oresme and the Medieval Geometry of Qualities and Motions: A Treatise on the Uniformity and Difformity of Intensities Known as "Tractatus de configurationibus qualitatum et motuum"* (Madison: Univ. of Wisconsin Press, 1968), pp. 134–135.

3

The Copernicans
and the Churches

Robert S. Westman

In 1543, on his deathbed, Nicolaus Copernicus received the published results of his life's main work, a book magisterially entitled *De Revolutionibus Orbium Coelestium Libri Sex (Six Books on the Revolutions of the Celestial Orbs)*, which urged the principal thesis that the earth is a planet revolving about a motionless central sun.[1] In 1616, seventy-three years after its author's death, the book was placed on the Catholic Index of Prohibited Books with instructions that it not be read "until corrected." Sixteen years later—and, by then, ninety years after Copernicus first set forth his views—Galileo Galilei (1564–1642) was condemned by a tribunal of the Inquisition for "teaching, holding, and defending" the Copernican theory. These facts are well known, but the dramatic events that befell Galileo in the period 1616–1632 have tended to overshadow the relations between pre-Galilean Copernicans and the Christian churches and to suggest, sometimes by implication, that the Galileo affair was the consummation of a long-standing conflict between science and Christianity.[2]

In this chapter we shall focus our attention on the long period between the appearance of *De Revolutionibus* and the decree of 1616. It will be helpful if we can suspend polar categories customarily used to describe the events of this period, such as Copernican versus anti-Copernican, Protestant versus Catholic, the individual versus the church. The central issue is better expressed as a conflict over the standards to be applied to the interpretation of texts, for this was a problem common to astronomers, natural philosophers, and theologians of whatever confessional stripe. In the case of the Bible, should its words and sentences in all instances be taken to *mean* literally what they say and, for that reason, to describe actual events and physical truths? Is the subject matter of the biblical text *always* conveyed by the literal or historical meaning of its words? Where does the ultimate authority reside to decide on the mode of interpretation appropriate to a given passage? In the case of an astronomical text, should its diagrams be taken to refer literally to actual paths of bodies in space? Given two different interpretations of the same celestial event, where does the authority reside to decide on the particular mode of interpretation that would render one hypothesis preferable to another? When the subject matters of two different *kinds of text* (e.g., astronomical and biblical or astronomical and physical) coincide, which standards of meaning and truth should govern their assessment? And finally, how did different accounts of the God-Nature relationship affect appraisal of the Copernican theory? Questions of this sort define the issue faced by sixteenth- and early seventeenth-century Copernicans.

COPERNICUS'S ACHIEVEMENT

Before proceeding further, we must ask who Copernicus was and what he proposed. Nicolaus Copernicus (1473–1543) was a church administrator in the bishopric of Lukas Watzenrode, located in the region of Warmia, now northern Poland but then part of the Prussian Estates.[3] Watzenrode was Copernicus's uncle and guardian, and it was through his patronage that the young man was able to study medicine and canon law in Italy before returning to take up practical duties, including supervision of financial transactions, allocation of grain and livestock in peasant villages, and overseeing the castle and town defenses in Olsztyn. Though a member of the bishop's palace, Copernicus was not a priest but a clerical administrator or canon.

In his spare time Copernicus worried about a problem that had long concerned the church—accurate prediction of the occurrence of holy days such as Easter and Christmas.[4] Now calendar reform was an astronomical problem that demanded not primarily new observations but the assimilation of old ones into a model capable of accurately predicting the equinoxes and solstices, the moments when the sun's shadows produce days of longest, shortest, and equal extent. But predictive accuracy had never been the astronomer's only goal. The mathematical part of astronomy was complemented by a physical part.[5] The object of the latter was to explain why the planets moved, what they were made of, and why they are spaced as they are.[6] According to Aristotle's heavenly physics, the sun, moon, and other planets are embedded in great spheres made of a perfect and invisible substance called aether. The spheres revolve uniformly on axes that all pass through the center of the universe. This model yielded an appealing picture of the universe as a kind of celestial onion with earth at the core; but it failed to explain why the planets vary in brightness. As an alternative, the astronomer Ptolemy (fl. A.D. 150) used a mathematical device according to which the planet moves uniformly about a small circle (the epicycle) while the center of the epicycle moves uniformly about a larger circle (the deferent). Such a model could account for variations in both speed and brightness. Ptolemy also invented another device, however, called the "equant" (see fig. 3.1). Here the center of an epicycle revolves *nonuniformly* as viewed both from the sphere's center and from the earth but *uniformly* as computed from a noncentral point (situated as far from the center on one side as the earth is on the other). As a predictive mechanism the equant is successful. But now ask how it can be that the planet, like a bird or fish, "knows" how to navigate uniformly in a circle about an off-center point while, simultaneously, flying variably with respect to the center of the same sphere? In response to objections like this it was quite customary for astronomers in the universities to consider the planetary circles *separately* from the spheres in which they were embedded.[7] This meant that conflict between the mathematical and physical parts of astronomy could be avoided by not mixing the principles of the two disciplines. If, however, an astronomer were determined to reconcile physical and mathematical issues, it would be customary within the Aristotelian tradition (which prevailed within the universities) to defer to the physicist, for in the generally accepted medieval hierarchy of the sciences, physics or natural philosophy was superior to mathematics.[8]

Copernicus, like all great innovators, straddled the old world into which he was born and the new one that he created. On the one hand he was a conservative reformer who sought to reconcile natural philosophy and mathematical astronomy by proclaiming the absolute principle that all motions are uniform and circular, with all spheres turning uniformly about their own centers.[9] But, far more radically, Copernicus argued for the earth's status as a planet by appealing to arguments from the *mathematical part* of astronomy.[10] In so doing he shifted the weight of evidence for the earth's planetary status to the lower discipline of geometry, thereby violating the traditional hierarchy of the disciplines. If anything can be called revolutionary in Copernicus's work, it was this mode of argument—this manner of challenging the central proposition of Aristotelian physics.[11]

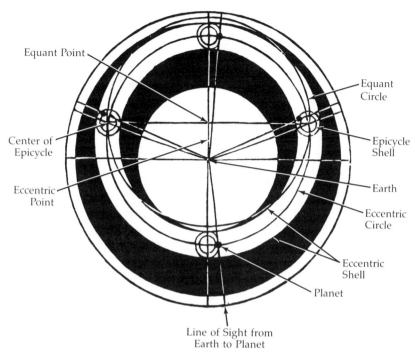

Fig. 3.1. Fifteenth-century representation of planetary mechanism for Venus and the superior planets, from Georg Peurbach, *Novae Theoricae Planetarum* (Augsburg, 1482; first published ca. 1474). The earth is the center of the universe and of the dark shell that contains the eccentric shell. The planet revolves uniformly about the center of the epicycle. The epicycle's center, in turn, defines a circle with respect to the eccentric point. Note, however, that the motion of the epicycle's center is uniform only when viewed from the equant point and not from the earth or from the eccentric's center. In this woodcut the artist shows the equant circle penetrating the eccentric shell, but the author of the text does not explain how this is possible if the shells are made of impermeable aether.

We are now prepared to consider the general logical structure of Copernicus's argument. Briefly, it looks like this: *If* we posit that the earth has a rotational motion on its axis and an orbital motion around the sun, then (1) all known celestial phenomena can be accounted for as accurately as on the best Ptolemaic theories; (2) the annual component in the Ptolemaic models, an unexplained mirroring of the sun's motion, is eliminated; (3) the planets can be ordered by their increasing sidereal periods from the sun; and (4) the distances of the planets from the center of the universe can be calculated with respect to a "common measure," the earth-sun radius (a kind of celestial yardstick), which remains fixed as the absolute unit of reference (see fig. 3.3, p. 97). Although they were certainly among the most important consequences, these four were not the only ones to follow from the assumption of terrestrial motion. However, from the viewpoint of the prevailing logic of demonstrative proof, found in Aristotle's *Posterior Analytics,* there was no *necessity* in the connection between the posited cause and the conclusions congruent with that cause. Thus, while Copernicus's premises certainly authorized the conclusions he drew, there was no guarantee that other premises might not be found, equally in accord with the conclusions. In short, Copernicus had provided a systematic, logical explanation of the known celestial phenomena, but in making the conclusions the grounds of his premises, he failed to win for his case the status of a demonstrative proof.[12]

problems. First, their central premise had the status of an assumed, unproven, and (to most people) absurd proposition. Second, whatever probability it possessed was drawn primarily from consequences in a lower discipline (geometry). Third, even granting the legitimacy of arguing for equivalent predictive accuracy with Ptolemy, the practical derivation of Copernicus's numerical parameters was highly problematic. Fourth, the Copernican system flagrantly contradicted a fundamental dictum of a higher discipline, physics—namely, that a simple body can have only one motion proper to it—for the earth both orbited the sun and rotated on its axis. And finally, it appeared to conflict with the interpretations of another higher discipline, biblical theology—in particular, the literal exegesis of certain passages in the Old Testament.

Under the circumstances Copernicus resorted to a rhetorical strategy of upgrading the certitude available to "mathematicians"—by which he meant those who practiced the mathematical part of astronomy—while underplaying the authority of natural philosophy and theology to make judgments on the claims of mathematicians.[13] Final authority for interpreting his text, he said, rested with those who best understand its claims. Church fathers such as Lactantius had shown a capacity for error in astronomy and natural philosophy, as when Lactantius declared the earth to be flat. Theologians of this sort should stay away from a subject of which they are ignorant.

Copernicus's strategy of appealing to the autonomy and superiority of mathematical astronomy was undercut by a prefatory "Letter to the Reader" that appeared immediately after the title page of *De Re-*

volutionibus. That brief epistle bespeaks the extraordinary circumstances surrounding the publication of the book.[14] It was only at the very end of Copernicus's life that he was finally persuaded to publish his book—not by one of his fellow canons, some of whom were eager to see the manuscript in press, but by a young Protestant mathematics lecturer who had come to visit the old canon from the academic heart of the Lutheran Reformation, the University of Wittenberg. Georg Joachim Rheticus (1514–1574) was permitted by Copernicus to publish a preliminary version of the heliocentric theory (*Narratio Prima,* 1540) and also to attend to the eventual publication of *De Revolutionibus.* But Rheticus lacked the time to oversee the work and so entrusted it to a fellow Lutheran, Andreas Osiander (1498–1552). Osiander, without permission from either Copernicus or Rheticus, took it upon himself to add an unsigned prefatory "Letter" written in the third person singular. Upon reading the manuscript, Osiander had become convinced that Copernicus would be attacked by the "peripatetics and theologians" on the grounds that "the liberal arts, established long ago on a correct basis, should not be thrown into confusion." Osiander hoped to save Copernicus from a hostile reception by appealing to the old formula according to which astronomy is distinguished from higher disciplines, like philosophy, by its renunciation of physical truth or even probability. Rather, if it provides "a calculus consistent with the observations, that alone is enough." *De Revolutionibus* was thus to be regarded as a strictly mathematical-astronomical text unable to attain even "the semblance of the truth" available to philosophers; and both mathematicians and philosophers were incapable of stating "anything certain unless it has been divinely revealed to them."[15]

EARLY PROTESTANT REACTION: THE MELANCHTHON CIRCLE AND THE "WITTENBERG INTERPRETATION"

When Rheticus returned to his teaching duties at Wittenberg after his long visit to Copernicus, he brought back strongly favorable personal impressions of the Polish canon and his new theory.[16] Rheticus himself was Copernicus's first major disciple, and many of the Wittenberger's students read and studied *De Revolutionibus.* Furthermore, Rheticus composed a treatise, recently rediscovered, in which he sought to establish the compatibility of the Bible and the heliocentric theory.[17] All of this tempts us to ask whether Protestants were particularly well disposed toward the Copernican theory.

To answer this question, we must distinguish between the Protestant Reformers and men who happened to be Protestants and were also well versed in the reading of astronomical texts. The Reformers Luther and Calvin were learned men who knew enough astronomy to understand its basic principles; but neither had ever practiced the subject. It used to be thought that Luther played an important role in condemning Copernicus's theory when, in the course of one of his *Tischreden* or *Table Talks*, he said: "That fool wants to turn the whole art of astronomy upside down."[18] But the statement itself is vague on details and, in any event, was uttered in 1539, sometime before the publication of either Rheticus's *Narratio Prima* or Copernicus's *De Revolutionibus*. As for Calvin, there is no positive evidence that he had ever heard of Copernicus or his theory; if he knew of the new doctrine, he did not deem it of sufficient importance for public comment. In short, there are no known opinions by these two leading Protestant Reformers that significantly influenced the reception of the Copernican system.[19]

There was, however, a third Reformer, a close associate of Luther's and the educational arm of the Reformation in Germany, Philipp Melanchthon (1497–1560), known as *Praeceptor Germaniae*. A charismatic man, beloved teacher, and talented humanist, Melanchthon was also a brilliant administrator with a gift for finding compromise positions.[20] In the face of serious disturbances from the Peasants' Revolt of 1524–1525 and plunging enrollments all over Germany, Melanchthon instituted far-reaching reforms that led to the rewriting of the constitutions of the leading German Protestant universities (Wittenberg, Tübingen, Leipzig, Frankfurt, Greifswald, Rostock, and Heidelberg), profoundly influencing the spirit of education at several newly founded institutions (Marburg, Königsberg, Jena, and Helmstedt). Most important of all, Melanchthon believed that mathematics (and thus astronomy) deserved a special place in the curriculum because through study of the heavens we come to appreciate the order and beauty of the divine creation. Furthermore, mathematics was an excellent subject for instilling mental discipline in students. Such views alone would not predispose one toward a particular cosmology, but they did help to give greater respectability to the astronomical enterprise. Thus, a powerful tradition of mathematical astronomy developed at Wittenberg from the late 1530s and spread throughout the German and Scandinavian universities. At Wittenberg itself, three astronomers in the humanistic circle gathered around Melanchthon were preeminent: Erasmus Reinhold (1511–1553), his pupil Rheticus, and their joint pupil and the future son-in-law of Melanchthon, Caspar Peucer (1525–1603). Melanchthon was the *pater* of this small *familia scholarium*. Many of the major elements in the subsequent interpretation of Copernicus's theory in the sixteenth century would be prefigured in this group at Wittenberg.

The "Wittenberg Interpretation," as we will call it, was a reflection of the views of the Melanchthon circle. Melanchthon himself was initially hostile to the Copernican theory but subsequently shifted his position, perhaps under the influence of Reinhold. Melanchthon rejected the earth's motion because it conflicted with a literal reading of certain biblical passages and with the Aristotelian doctrine of simple motion. But Copernicus's conservative reform—his effort to bring the calculating mechanisms of mathematical astronomy into agreement with the physical assumption of spheres uniformly revolving about their diametral axes—was warmly accepted. Reinhold's personal copy of *De Revolutionibus*, which still survives today, is testimony; it has written carefully across the title page the following formulation: "The Astronomical Axiom: Celestial motion is both uniform and circular or composed of uniform and circular motions." As it stands, this proposition simply ignores physical claims for the earth's motion, but commits itself to an equantless astronomy. It is, we might say today, a "research program," one which Copernicus tried to make compatible with the assumption that the earth is a planet. But the Wittenbergers, with the noticeable exception of Rheticus, refused to follow Copernicus in upsetting the traditional hierarchy of the disciplines. Instead, Reinhold and his extensive group of disciples accepted Melanchthon's physical and scriptural objections to the Copernican theory. In the prevalent mood of reform, Copernicus was perceived not as a revolutionary but as a moderate reformer (like Melanchthon), returning to an ancient, pristine wisdom before Ptolemy.

If Melanchthon and Reinhold saw Copernicus as a temperate reformer, Rheticus saw the radical character of his reform. Rheticus returned to Wittenberg in 1542 as an inflamed convert, writing of Copernicus as of one who has had a Platonic vision of The Good and The Beautiful—though in the harmony of the planetary motions. "My teacher," wrote Rheticus, referring to Copernicus,

> was especially influenced by the realization that the chief cause of all the uncertainty in astronomy was that the masters of this science (no offense is intended to divine Ptolemy, the father of astronomy) fashioned their theories and devices for correcting the motion of the heavenly bodies with too little regard for the rule which reminds us that the order and motions of the heavenly spheres agree in an absolute system. We fully grant these distinguished men their due honor, as we should. Nevertheless, we should have wished them, in establishing the harmony of the motions, to imitate

the musicians who, when one string has either tightened or loosened, with great care and skill regulate and adjust the tones of all the other strings, until all together produced the desired harmony, and no dissonance is heard in any.[21]

Even more enthusiastically than Copernicus, Rheticus extolled the "remarkable symmetry and interconnection of the motions and spheres, as maintained by the assumption of the foregoing hypotheses," appealing to analogical concordance with musical harmonies, to the number six as a sacred number in Pythagorean prophecies, to the harmony of the political order in which the emperor, like the sun in the heavens, "need not hurry from city to city in order to perform the duty imposed on him by God," and to clockmakers who avoid inserting superfluous wheels into their mechanisms. Copernicus's unification of previously separate hypotheses had a liberating, almost intoxicating, effect on Rheticus, which Rheticus expressed almost as a personal revelation fully comprehensible only by visualizing the ideas themselves.

A wide spectrum of early Protestant opinion is defined between Melanchthon's cautious promotion of Copernicus's reform and Rheticus's radical espousal of the core propositions of Copernican cosmology. In general, the Wittenberg Interpretation dominated until the 1580s, while Rheticus's vision was typically ignored in public discussions. By the late 1570s, however, there were signs of the emergence of a cosmological pluralism among Protestant astronomers.[22] A Danish aristocrat named Tycho Brahe (1546–1601) established an extraordinary astronomical castle on the misty island of Hveen, near Copenhagen, where he commenced a major reform of astronomical observations and, by the early 1580s, proposed a new cosmology in which all the planets encircle the sun, while the sun moves around the stationary, central earth. This system—the Tychonic or geoheliocentric—adopted Copernican-heliocentric paths for the planets, causing the orbits of Mars and the sun to intersect, while preserving Aristotelian terrestrial physics (see fig. 3.2); but in another quite important respect, Tycho departed from Aristotle by abolishing the solid celestial spheres.[23] In 1600 the Englishman William Gilbert (1540–1603) suggested that the earth possesses a magnetic soul that causes it to turn daily on its axis; but he was cryptic about the ordering of Mercury and Venus.[24]

Throughout the second half of the sixteenth century, Copernicus's book was widely read and sometimes studied in both Catholic and Protestant countries.[25] Compared to the fairly large number of people

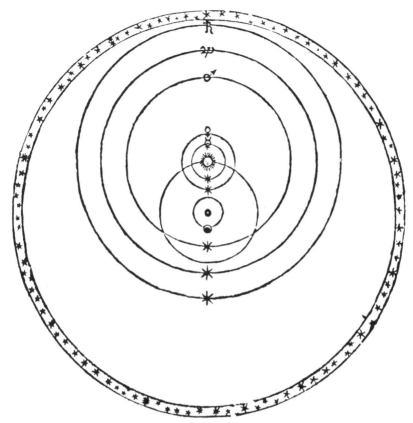

Fig. 3.2. The geoheliocentric system of Tycho Brahe, from his *De Mundi Aetherei Recentioribus Phaenomenis* (Uraniborg, 1588).

aware of the central claims of *De Revolutionibus*, however, there were relatively few who actively adopted its radical proposals and whom we can justifiably call "Copernicans" in that sense. To be precise: we can identify only ten Copernicans between 1543 and 1600; of these, seven were Protestants, the others Catholic. Four were German (Rheticus, Michael Maestlin, Christopher Rothmann, and Johannes Kepler); the Italians and English contributed two each (Galileo and Giordano Bruno; Thomas Digges and Thomas Harriot); and the Spaniards and Dutch but one each (Diego de Zuñiga; Simon Stevin). It is time now to examine the Catholic reaction more closely.

EARLY CATHOLIC REACTION AND THE COUNCIL OF TRENT

De Revolutionibus was published at a time when two powerful so-cioreligious movements converged. The first of these was the Prot-estant Reformation and, of special importance to us, its incursion into the German universities. The second was a movement of reform from within the Catholic church, the Counter-Reformation, driven partly by the need to respond to the Protestant challenge, partly by the need of the papacy to assert its authority in an area where for too long it had avoided reform. In 1545 Pope Paul III (1534–1549), to whom Co-pernicus had dedicated *De Revolutionibus*, called into session a council in the Italian Imperial city of Trent, which was to last until 1563, the year before Galileo's birth. A list of laxities within the church can only hint at the depths of the need for reform: cardinals, bishops, and priests chronically absent from their domains of responsibility; irreg-ularities in clerical training and abysmal literacy levels among par-ish priests; rampant granting of privileges and dispensations; priestly ownership of private land; and unchecked drunkenness, con-cubinage, and hunting among the clergy.[26] No wonder that the overriding issue confronting the Council was the need to give the faithful some feeling of security by restoring clerical discipline and providing a highly structured theology. Whatever real reforms were eventually made, however, the new initiatives created an atmosphere of obsessional control over detail, endless doctrinal clarifications by councils, synods, and theologians, suspicion of deviancy, and a pro-clivity for inflexible, legalistic remedies in areas of social conflict—a climate to which Protestants also contributed.[27]

At Trent the problem of authority surfaced in many ways, not least in the question of the authenticity of the Catholic Bible or Vulgate, the Latin translation prepared by Saint Jerome in the fourth century. After considerable debate it was agreed that the Vulgate, together with the writings of the church fathers, was to be the final authority in all matters of faith and discipline. The Vulgate was the infallible text; matters of hermeneutics were to be referred to the tradition of patristic interpretation. Whatever appeared to be an error in its lan-guage was to be attributed to copyists and in no way admitted to affect the basic sense of the text. Trent did not prohibit *private* ver-nacular translations and readings of the Bible, but the Index of 1559 and 1564 did.[28] Although the Tridentine position on biblical herme-neutics was imposing, it concealed a prolonged battle between two groups, which raged throughout the Council.[29] One group was com-posed of liberal Spanish humanists, mostly from the University of Salamanca, the other of more conservative scholastics. After the

Council the debate continued at Salamanca, led by the Augustinian friar and poet Luis de León (1527–1591). Fray Luis, whose ancestors were Jews,[30] was part of a distinguished lineage of Spanish philosophers and theologians at Salamanca.[31] His group favored the use of Hebrew and Greek in interpreting problematic passages in the Vulgate. The other group, much in the majority, opposed the use of Hebrew. The anti-Hebraists argued that the Jews had corrupted the original texts, that Hebrew was a nuisance to study, that Hebrew should be abolished in biblical studies, and that linguistic exegesis would only lead to controversy and the undermining of church authority.[32] The Hebraists claimed that the Vulgate was not always well translated and that it often came off poorly when compared with texts in the original language. Furthermore, there were good grounds for trusting the ancient Jewish texts: neither Christ nor Jerome nor Augustine had ever accused the Jews of corrupting the Old Testament.

Fray Luis's arguments were sound, but the political atmosphere after Trent was not with him. The problem was not biblical literalism but the Scholastic monopoly over theological discourse. Use of languages other than Latin was seen as a threat to the *unique* meaning of Scripture rather than as a means of defending it. When Luis himself prepared a Spanish translation and commentary on Solomon's *Song of Songs*, he was incarcerated for five years by the Inquisition of Valladolid.[33] Although his sentence was eventually reversed by the Supreme Office of the Inquisition in Madrid, the atmosphere of linguistic conformity in which he was charged was well captured by a remark made in 1576 by one of his primary accusers, Fray León de Castro: "The general congregation holds that nothing may be changed that disagrees with the Latin edition of the Vulgate, be it a single period, a single little conclusion or a single clause, a single word or expression, a single syllable or one iota. . . ."[34]

Copernicus's theory was not discussed at the Council of Trent. In fact, matters of natural philosphy and even calendrical reform were not in any sense primary issues of discussion.[35] But now, thanks to recently discovered evidence, we know that about the time the Council was beginning, there was some considered reaction within certain circles at the papal court. A year after the appearance of *De Revolutionibus*, a Florentine Dominican theologian-astronomer, Giovanni Maria Tolosani (1470/1–1549), authored a large apologetic work entitled *On the Truth of Sacred Scripture*.[36] This treatise, completed in 1544 but never published, concerned itself precisely with certain issues that were about to be debated at the Council of Trent. Between 1544 and 1547 Tolosani added a cluster of "little works" dealing with such topics as the power of the pope and the authority of councils, conflict between Catholics and heretics, justification by faith and works, the dignity and office of cardinals, and the structure of the church. But Tolosani was also an astronomer of no mean ability. He had written a treatise on the reform of the calendar and had attended the Fifth Lateran Council (1515), where calendrical reform was a primary topic.[37] Somehow he obtained a copy of *De Revolutionibus* and wrote in his fourth *opusculum* an extensive critique of book 1.[38] This little work is remarkable. First, in contrast with the Wittenberg Interpretation, it avoided purely technical astronomical issues and made no mention of the equant. Second, Copernicus's theory conflicted with the most basic principles of Aristotelian natural philosophy. And third, the Dominican Tolosani chose to locate *De Revolutionibus* within the Thomist hierarchy of the disciplines and to present the theory as a violation of its principles of classification.

> He [Copernicus] is expert indeed in the sciences of mathematics and astronomy, but he is very deficient in the sciences of physics and dialectic. Moreover, it appears that he is unskilled with regard to Holy Scripture, since he contradicts several of its principles, not without the danger of infidelity to himself and to the readers of his book. . . . The lower science receives principles proved by the superior. Indeed, all the sciences are connected mutually with one another in such a way that the inferior needs the superior and they help one another. An astronomer cannot be perfect, in fact, unless first he has studied the physical sciences, since astrology [i.e., astronomy] presupposes celestial corporeal natures and the motions of these natures. A man cannot be a complete astronomer and philosopher unless through logic he knows how to distinguish between the true and the false in disputes and knows the modes of argumentation, [skills] that are required in the medicinal art, philosophy, theology, and the other sciences. Hence, since Copernicus does not understand physics and logic, it is not surprising that he should be mistaken in this opinion and accepts the false as true, through ignorance of these sciences. Call together men well read in the sciences, and let them read Copernicus's first book on the motion of the earth and the immobility of the sidereal heaven. Certainly they will find that his arguments have no force and can very easily be resolved. For it is stupid to contradict an opinion accepted by everyone over a very long time for the strongest reasons, unless the impugner uses more powerful and incontrovertible demonstrations and completely dissolves the opposed reasons. But he [Copernicus] does not do this in the least.[39]

What we see here is the possibility of exploiting the somewhat ambiguous status of astronomy as a mixed or middle science. Unlike Osiander, who tried to protect Copernicus by stressing the *separation* between the mathematical and the physical parts of astronomy, Tolosani brings out the *dependency* of astronomy upon the higher disciplines of physics and theology for the truth of its conclusions. Physics and theology are disciplines superior to mathematics by virtue of their sublime subject matters, tradition, and demonstrative capacity to reach necessary conclusions. The rejection of *De Revolutionibus* as inconsistent with a very conservative rendering of Aristotle's physics (failing even to mention Thomas Aquinas's notion of impressed force) was entirely consonant with the mood that was to prevail at Trent regarding the exegesis of biblical passages.

Tolosani ends his little treatise with the following interesting revelation: "The Master of the Sacred and Apostolic Palace had planned to condemn this book, but, prevented first by illness and then by death, he could not fulfill this intention. However, I have taken care to accomplish it in this little work for the purpose of preserving the truth to the common advantage of the Holy Church."[40] The Master of the Sacred Palace was Tolosani's powerful friend, Bartolomeo Spina, who attended the opening sessions of the Council of Trent but died in early 1547.[41] As trenchant as Tolosani's critique of Copernicus had been, there is simply no evidence that it received any serious consideration either from the new master or from the pope himself. Meanwhile, Tolosani's unpublished manuscript, written in the spirit of Trent, was probably shelved in the library of his order at San Marco in Florence awaiting its use by some new prosecutor. The result was that sixteenth-century Catholic astronomers and philosophers worked under no formal prohibitions from the Index or the Inquisition.

THE COPERNICAN THEORY AND BIBLICAL HERMENEUTICS

The Protestant Reformers were agreed in emphasizing the plain, grammatical sense as the center of biblical interpretation, thereby making it accessible to anyone who could read. Additional help was sometimes sought from spiritual or allegorical readings, but the literal, realistic meaning always remained central. Now, the literalism of the Reformers was twofold: they believed that the Bible was literal both at the level of direct linguistic reference (nouns referred to actual people and events) and in the sense that the *whole story* was realistic. The Bible's individual stories needed to be woven together into one cumulative "narrative web." This required the earlier stories of the Old Testament to be joined interpretatively to those in the New Testament by showing the former to be "types" or "figures" of the latter. Luther and Calvin were agreed that there was a single theme, a primary subject matter, which united all the biblical stories: the life and ministry of Christ.[42]

Although Protestants rejected the Catholic appeal to allegorical and anagogical interpretations of Scripture as an illegitimate stretching of the plain meaning, both groups of exegetes had available to them a method of interpretation to which they could appeal: the principle of accommodation. One purpose of this hermeneutic device was to resolve tensions between popular speech, wedded to the experience of immediate perception, and the specialized discourse of elites. The necessity of sacrifices or anthropomorphic references to God as a man with limbs were types of references that could easily evoke appeal to the principle of accommodation.[43] In the seventeenth and eighteenth centuries, Jesuit missionaries in China sparked a controversy over accommodation when they allowed Chinese converts to pray to Confucius, worship ancestors, and address God as *Tien* (sky).[44] Like the Jesuit missionaries, the sixteenth-century followers of Copernicus made use of the option of accommodation. For them, however, the problem was not the alien belief-systems of a foreign society but the disciplinary hierarchy of the universities in which theology occupied the highest rank.

Before pursuing this matter further, let us look briefly at four specific classes of biblical passages that were relevant to the Copernican issue—references to the stability of the earth, the sun's motion with respect to the terrestrial horizon, the sun at rest, and the motion of the earth. Both Protestant and Catholic geocentrists customarily cited verses from the first two categories and interpreted them to refer literally to the physical world. Consider, for example, Psalms 93:1: "The world also is stablished, that it cannot be moved"; or Ecclesiastes 1:4: "One generation passeth away, and another generation cometh: but the earth abideth for ever"; Eccelesiastes 1:5: "The sun also ariseth, and the sun goeth down and hasteth to his place where he arose"; Psalm 104:19: "He appointed the moon for seasons: the sun knoweth his going down."[45] The literal interpretation of these passages springs from different sources for Protestants and Catholics. For Protestants, such as Melanchthon, it came from a steadfast faith in the inerrancy of the grammatically literal text; for Catholics, such as Tolosani, the literal meaning was legitimated by appeal to the (allegedly unanimous) authority of previous interpreters. In both cases the geocentrists ignored verses from categories three and four.

The Copernicans had available to them two hermeneutical strategies. The first, which we may call "absolute accommodationism," declares that the verses in all four categories are accommodated to human speech. The virtue of this position is that it draws a radical line of demarcation between biblical hermeneutics and natural philosophy, so that the principles and methods of the one cannot be mixed with those of the other. It is also in keeping with the moderate Christocentric reading of Scripture advocated by the Reformers. Far more dangerous was the second strategy, which we may call "partial accommodationism," according to which the interpreter provides a literal, *heliostatic* or *geomotive*, construal of either Joshua 10:12–13 or Job 9:6 and then accommodates it to verses conventionally read as geostatic. In the Joshua text we read: "Then spake Joshua to the Lord in the day when the Lord delivered up the Amorites before the children of Israel, and he said in the sight of Israel, Sun, stand thou still upon Gibeon; and thou, Moon, in the valley of Ajalon. And the sun stood still, and the moon stayed, until the people had avenged themselves upon their enemies." The construction "stand still" is certainly plain talk to the senses; thus, the heliocentrist, if he wished to pursue a partial-accommodationist line, must point out that we need not intend the horizon as our reference frame and that the sun could be rotating on its own axis, while remaining at rest at the center of the universe. A similar kind of ambiguity of reference frame is present in the Job text: "Which shaketh the earth out of her place, and the pillars thereof tremble." The phrases "out of her place" and "tremble" could be taken to denote either diurnal or annual motion or simply the earth quaking. The sixteenth-century Copernicans, perhaps taking the lead from Copernicus's brief remarks about Lactantius, tended to adopt the position of absolute accommodation. The two most eloquent expressions of this position were by Giordano Bruno (1548–1600) and Johannes Kepler (1571–1630).

Bruno, a Dominican from Naples, was well trained in Scholastic philosophy and Thomist theology, but he had also been receptive to newer, radical intellectual currents, including the cosmology of Copernicus.[46] In 1576 he suddenly left his order in Naples and began a fifteen-year pilgrimage throughout Europe, preaching on a variety of subjects including the deficiencies of Aristotle. Describing himself as an "academician of no academy," Bruno arrived at Oxford in 1583, and there defended Copernicus's theory before a hostile audience of philosophers and theologians. The following year he published a witty and sarcastic humanistic dialogue called *The Ash Wednesday Supper,* where he dealt with the problem of Copernicus and the Bible. Referring to Ecclesiastes 1:5, he wrote ironically:

> So if the Sage, instead of saying, "The sun riseth and goeth down, turneth toward the south and boweth to the north wind," had said: "The earth turns round to the east, leaving behind the sun which sets, bows to the two tropics, that of Cancer to the south and Capricorn to the north wind," his listeners would have stopped to think: "What, does he say that the

earth moves? What kinds of fables are these?" In the end, they would have accounted him a madman, and he really would have been a madman.[47]

Moral and redemptive meaning rather than physical truth was the Bible's message, according to Bruno.

By a different route Kepler reached much the same conclusion in his *New Astronomy* (1609). His argument, appealing in the first place to optics, was that the biblical writers have accommodated their stories to the human sense of sight.[48] Yet, as we can easily demonstrate, the phenomena of sight are often misleading and must be corrected by a theory of visual distortion. Men believe that the sun moves because it appears to be small while the earth appears large. In the Joshua story the phrase "the sun stood still" is an accommodation to Joshua's ocular sense, whereas the biblical writer knew the truth that "the earth stood still." Furthermore, Joshua himself was not an astronomer interested in the cause but rather a warrior concerned about the effect, namely, that the day be lengthened. Elsewhere, we find phrases which, if taken literally and in isolation, appear to be physical propositions, as in the oft-quoted verse from Ecclesiastes. But the Bible's purpose here, as elsewhere, says Kepler, is to teach human truths: "The fable of life is ever the same; there is nothing new under the sun. You receive no instruction in physical matters [from the Bible]. The message is a moral one. . . ."[49]

There was one notable exception to this Copernican consensus on accommodation: Diego de Zuñiga (1536–1597). A student of Luis de León at Salamanca and, like him, a member of the Hermits of St. Augustine, Zuñiga taught theology and philosophy at the universities of Osuna and Salamanca.[50] Zuñiga's writings were Augustinian in theme: in 1577 a treatise on free will, and in 1584 a commentary on the Book of Job.[51] Zuñiga's sentiments were clearly with the liberal Hebraist faction at Salamanca, although he had not been present at Trent and would not go as far as Fray Luis in approving vernacular translations. In his massive commentary on Job, Zuñiga had to face the difficult problem of chapter 9, verse 6. The general theme of this part of Job is the omnipotence and wisdom of God, who "shaketh the earth out of her place, and the pillars thereof tremble." Perhaps wishing to emphasize God's physical and moral power, Zuñiga did not see the language as accommodated to common speech but read it literally as a statement about the physical world; in particular, he explicated the passage according to the Copernican theory![52]

Zuñiga's acquaintance with *De Revolutionibus* is probably to be explained by the fact that the University of Salamanca, like the German

Protestant universities, encouraged the mathematics professors to lecture on *De Revolutionibus.*[53] Although we have every reason to believe that it was taught as a "hypothesis," following the recommendation of the anonymous preface, Zuñiga claimed boldly that Copernicus's theory is "demonstrated" on grounds that it contains a better account of the precessional motions and that it predicts planetary positions "more exactly" than does Ptolemy's. Between 1584 and 1597 Zuñiga revised his position. In a text on natural philosophy he rejected the earth's daily rotational motion as "absurd."[54] When he died in 1597, it was already too late to revise his commentary on Job. His literal reading of Job 9:6, however, would not be forgotten.

THE JESUITS

The Society of Jesus, founded at about the time the Council of Trent began and *De Revolutionibus* was published, was the real sword of the Counter-Reformation. Worldly and militant, the Jesuits eagerly engaged the Protestants in polemics and ingratiated themselves with the royal courts as privileged advisers. Even more impressively, they challenged the Melanchthonian hegemony by founding their own colleges all over Europe.[55] Systematically dividing the Continent into regions, they rapidly established dozens of colleges in the 1550s and 1560s within each area from the Iberian Peninsula to the Provinces of the Netherlands, from the German principalities east to the Hapsburg lands. The flagship of these colleges was the Collegio Romano in Rome. Its professors were among the best in the Society and were the leaders in establishing curricular policy for the college system. Perhaps because of this position of leadership, the Collegio Romano was also a site of controversy among its most important lecturers. Not only was wrangling prevalent within disciplines, but serious debates also occurred between the philosophers and mathematicians. In the 1580s, debates over educational policy came to a head with the promulgation of the *Ratio Studiorum.*[56] A primary author of this document, Christopher Clavius (1537–1612), succeeded in elevating the status of mathematics to an unprecedented level of academic responsibility, arguing for its pedagogical indispensability to philosophy and the other disciplines.[57]

Clavius, an outstanding astronomer and mathematician, disagreed particularly with those philosophers who had no practical experience as astronomers, yet insisted on questioning the physical reality of the mechanisms posited by Ptolemaists like Clavius.[58] The debate then turned on the degree of certitude to which astronomy could aspire in constructing true explanations. In his authoritative textbook, which became the standard of the Jesuits, Clavius argued that astronomy, like physics, was concerned with true causes. The Averroists at the Collegio Romano, who believed in solid, concentric spheres, countered by arguing that, by the rules of the syllogism, a true conclusion could be deduced from false premises; one could, in short, posit any set of eccentrics and epicycles—even if they were not true causes—so long as they saved the phenomena. Clavius answered that this objection *ex falsa verum* could just as well be applied to physics and to all the other disciplines, including theology. An unacceptable skepticism would result. In the midst of this controversy, Clavius introduced the case of the Copernican theory, which successfully uses epicycles and eccentrics to save the phenomena. Are we thereby left with another skeptical dilemma, unable now to choose between Copernicus and Ptolemy? In such a case of (what we would perhaps call) inter-theoretic conflict, Clavius argues, one respects the traditional disciplinary hierarchy and turns to natural philosophy and theology for assistance in discovering true causes. The point is an interesting one because it reveals the limits to Clavius's assertion of the primacy of mathematics over the other disciplines. His deeper aim was to bring *concordance* between Ptolemaic astronomy and natural philosophy. Copernicus's mathematical harmonies were not alone sufficient to induce Clavius to seek out a fundamentally new kind of physics.

Clavius's authority was enormous. The astronomical text in which he stated his views was used throughout the Jesuit colleges. It is thus no surprise that when Jesuit theologians considered Diego de Zuñiga's Copernican reading of Job 9:6, they turned to Clavius for guidance. For example, when the Spanish Jesuit Juan de Pineda (1558–1637), philosopher and theologian, consultor to the Inquisition, and compiler of the Spanish Index arrived at the moot passage 9:6 in his *Commentary on Job*, he declared Zuñiga's interpretation to be "plainly false," as shown "elegantly with firm reasons from philosophy and astrology by Our Christopher Clavius." Scripturally, he followed Zuñiga's literalism but offered an alternative, literal reading, rendering *terrae commotio* not as change of place but as *terrae tremor*—a quivering or shaking of the earth, sign of God's power and displeasure with man.[59] In 1620, four years after the decree against Copernicus and Zuñiga, he published a commentary on Ecclesiastes in which the language was stronger: "Diego de Zuñiga, a man knowledgeable and distinguished in religion, was babbling idly when he wrote on Job 9:6. . . . [His views are] false and dangerous. . . ."[60] Pineda's *Commentary on Job* was immediately influential. At the Collège de France the theologian Jean Lorin (1559–1634) wrote; "Our Clavius . . . and Pineda in Job chap. 9, demonstrate his [Zuñiga's] opinion to be false and rash. . . . This aforesaid opinion can be seen to be dangerous and repugnant to the Faith. . . ."[61] It is also noteworthy that Cardinal Robert Bellarmine, who knew Lorin personally,[62] possessed a copy of Pineda's commentary in his library.[63]

Although the Jesuit theologians took a dim view of what we might call Zuñiga's "commentatorial Copernicanism"—encoded as it was in a biblical commentary—it is important to stress again the moderately progressive spirit of Clavius's astronomy. Clavius's textbooks underwent constant emendation in order to include references to new issues. Copernicus appeared in the 1581 edition; Francesco Maurolyco's discussion of the New Star of 1572 was reported in the fourth edition of 1585;[64] the new stars of 1600 and 1604 received consideration in the 1607 edition; and in the last edition of his *Sphere* (1611), Clavius included a brief reference to Galileo's telescopic discoveries, which, he said, would need to be accommodated to a new system of the world.[65] That this was not intended as support for the Copernican system is certain; yet Clavius was also too cautious to give public support to the new cosmology of Tycho Brahe, although he had been aware of it at least since 1600.[66] Only after Clavius's death in 1612 would his students at the Collegio Romano make Tycho's geoheliocentric cosmology their own.

COPERNICAN THEOLOGIES

In the atmosphere of literalism prevalent in the sixteenth century, the Copernicans had to address the question of the Bible's true sense when it uses the words *sun, earth,* or *moon;* they had to argue that the moral and symbolic meanings of these words were *detachable* from any literal reference to the physical world. But there are other passages in the Scriptures that do not mention the celestial bodies and yet were singled out as containing special meaning about God's relation to nature. Romans 1:20, appealed to by Christians in a tradition reaching back to Saint Augustine, provided a text capable of wide connotation, not least as a basis for legitimating alternatives to Aristotle's philosophy of nature: "For the invisible things of Him from the creation of the world are clearly seen, being understood by the things that are made. . . ." From this evolved an important metaphor, invoked by both Protestants and Catholics: nature is a book through which the invisible God reveals Himself sensibly to man. Now if the intention of the author of the Scriptures was also that of the author of nature, then there could be only one truth revealed—though in different forms of discourse. In what language, then, did God write the book of nature? And which disciplines would yield privileged access to its meaning? The sixteenth-century Copernicans were as diverse in their hermeneutic and disciplinary preferences as they were in their theological assumptions. A few abbreviated examples must suffice here.

The Puritan Thomas Digges (1546–1595?) was the earliest English-man to offer a defense of the Copernican theory. This occurs in the form of a very brief treatise appended to an almanac written by his father, Leonard Digges.[67] Accompanying Digges's account is a diagram of the universe portraying the heliocentric system surrounded by the orb of fixed stars, described by Digges as infinitely extended in all dimensions (see fig. 3.3). If we examine the picture carefully, however, we see that it is not merely a cosmological representation but a hieroglyph with a soteriological message. The orb carrying the earth is labeled the "Globe of Mortality," that is, man in a state of sin after the Fall. The fixed sun lights up the darkness of man's understanding, as Digges writes, "sphaerically dispearsing his glorious beames of light through al this sacred Coelestiall Temple." And the stars are the realm of the saved: "the very court of coelestiall angelles devoid of greefe and replenished with perfite endlesse love the habitacle for the elect." Digges's account thus portrays the world both as a harmonious order displayed in the Copernican arrangement and as the symbolic stage of a great Puritan drama.

The theme of infinitude was handled differently in the other Copernican theologies. While Digges's infinitely spherical, stellar "habitacle of the elect" contains a unique world with a single sun in the midst of it, Bruno waxes rhapsodic in a vision of the necessity (and freedom) of the Deity to manifest his infinite power in an infinite number of worlds, each with a sun at its center.[68] Going even further, he breaks explicitly with the Aristotelian concept of place, maintaining that no place is ontologically different from any other and that space has an existence prior to bodies. In this infinite womb an infinite number of indivisible corpuscles, each animated by the infinite soul of the world, move about with uniform velocities in circles and spirals, unconstrained by celestial orbs. For Bruno, Copernicus was a mere mathematician who had stumbled upon a fragment of a deeper philosophy—not a mathematical one but a grand celebration of God's omnipotence worked out in the infinite expanse of the Creation.

In contrast with Bruno's grandiloquent celebration of God's unlimited power, Kepler's conception is a vast working out of the mystery of the Trinity, where mathematics is primary to the Creation: "There were three things in particular about which I persistently sought the

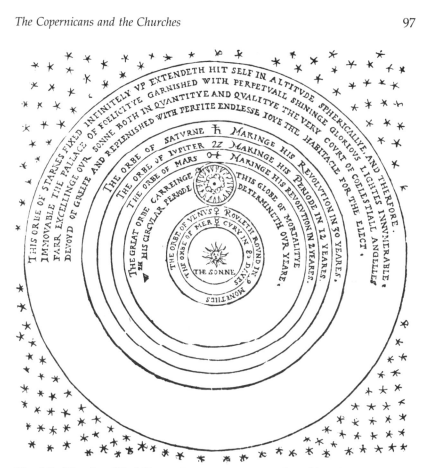

Fig. 3.3. The simplified Copernican system, as produced by Thomas Digges, *A Perfit Description of the Celestiall Orbes* (London, 1576).

reasons why they were such and not otherwise: the number, the size and the motion of the orbs. That I dared so much was due to the splendid harmony of those things which are at rest, the Sun, the fixed stars and the intermediate space, with God the Father, and the Son, and the Holy Spirit."[69] For Kepler, divinity is to be found not in (what he considered) Bruno's unrestrained expression of God's omnipotence, but in God's ordained power—finite, geometrical structures mirroring God's Ideas, just as physical objects are represented like a painting on the retina of the eye.[70] To "see" God's plan and purpose properly, we must form hypotheses, reasoning both *a posteriori* from the visible world (as Copernicus did) and *a priori* from the Idea of the Creation itself. In this way Kepler interpreted his famous discovery— that the planets were spaced according to the inscribed regular sol-

ids—as an insight both into the actual arrangement of the universe
and into the orderly purposefulness underlying it. With Kepler the
search for mathematical and physical causes itself became a kind of
religious calling. Everything for Kepler was a vast hermeneutic endeavor, for he believed that God has given Himself to mankind
through the Word (Bible), through his Son (Christ), and through
natural things and their order (nature).[71] So Kepler wrote of his
polyhedral hypothesis: "I am satisfied to use my discovery to guard
the gates of the temple in which Copernicus makes sacrifices at the
high altar."[72] In their different accounts of the relationship between
nature and the Divinity, the Copernicans strove to justify a belief in
the new planetary arrangement; but, in the end, their heterogeneous
theologies drove them apart rather than together. This as much as
any other cause explains the lack of a Copernican movement in the
period before Galileo.

GALILEO: PROGRESSIVE CATHOLIC REFORMER

It is illuminating to regard Galileo, if only briefly, against this somewhat complex career of the Copernican theory in the sixteenth century. To begin with: he was, at first, an *academic* Copernican.[73] This
in itself was fairly unusual; apart from Zuñiga and Rheticus the only
really comparable example was Kepler's teacher, Michael Maestlin
(1550–1631), at Tübingen; and Maestlin, like the early Galileo, was
fairly cautious about polemicizing on behalf of Copernicus.[74] Second,
we now know that Galileo's astronomical lectures at Pisa were largely
paraphrases of Clavius's *Commentary on the Sphere*.[75] Thus, Galileo's
early exposure to the Copernican problem would have been conditioned by Clavius and his arguments against philosophers at the Jesuit
Collegio Romano who insisted that astronomy could never achieve
certitude.[76] Third, and most significantly, in his defense of the Copernican system Galileo committed himself to a strict notion of proof
in science, according to which true conclusions must be deduced
necessarily from true premises, which are themselves self-evident.[77]
No other Copernican had locked himself into such a tight position.
Fourth, Galileo's advocacy of demonstrative proof in the Copernican
matter was deeply affected by both scientific and political developments. The sudden availability of the telescope in 1609[78] radically
changed what it was now possible to do in the domain of celestial
natural philosophy. Among other things, it provided a conclusive
argument against the Ptolemaic theory by proving the existence of
phases of Venus. This success, which even some Jesuits at the Col-

legio Romano were willing to acknowledge, boosted Galileo's confidence that a grand demonstration could eventually be found that would establish the Copernican system conclusively against other alternatives.

Galileo used his success with the telescope to negotiate a return to Florence—to leave his academic position in Venice, where he was now very secure, well paid, and relatively free from church interference—and to take up a position at the court of the grand duke of Tuscany.[79] He made his move in 1610, against the better judgment of his Venetian friends,[80] and was awarded the title "Chief Mathematician and Philosopher" at his own request.[81] He also received an appointment from the grand duke as chief professor of mathematics at the University of Pisa *without obligation to teach or reside there.*[82] He was now free to break with fixed forms of academic disputation and to express himself in the vernacular Italian of his native Tuscany.[83] No other Copernican except Kepler had hitherto engineered a position with such powerful disciplinary freedom and leverage.

The move to the Florentine court did not, however, provide Galileo with all the immunity from attack that he had hoped to achieve. Although he had received a warm reception from the Jesuits for his telescopic discoveries, he encountered hostility in Florence from two quarters: certain philosophers at Pisa, most notably Lodovico delle Colombe (1565–ca. 1615) and a Dominican preacher, Tommaso Caccini (1574–1648), who was in possession of Tolosani's long-buried, anti-Copernican treatise.[84] Delle Colombe, arguing from the traditional view of the disciplinary superiority of philosophy and theology, claimed that mathematics offered no certitude about what moves and what does not, because it abstracts from matter, whereas philosophy is concerned with essences. In short, one should not assume, as Copernicus did, that the earth moves in order to find out what consequences follow; rather, one asks first whether it is self-evident that the earth is physically suitable for motion. And with regard to Scripture, delle Colombe declared: "All theologians without a single exception say that when Scripture can be understood according to the literal sense, it must never be interpreted in any other way."[85] Caccini's attack was even less temperate. In December 1614 he delivered a sermon denouncing mathematics as a diabolical art, mathematicians as violators of the Christian religion and enemies of the state, and Galileo as the propagator of cosmological absurdities. He cleverly cited a passage from Acts 1:11: "Ye Men of Galilee, why stand ye gazing up into heaven?" thus punning on Galileo's name.[86] It was a popular sermon, not a learned disputation like Tolosani's critique of 1546 or Clavius's commentary of 1581. Galileo's disciple, the Benedictine

Benedetto Castelli, who held the lower mathematics position at Pisa, well described the quality of the opposition when he wrote of "those pickpockets and highwaymen who waylay mathematicians."[87]

The Copernican situation in Italy during this period, as we now see, does not lend itself to facile dichotomies. The most powerful order, the Society of Jesus, was opposed to Copernicanism but not unalterably closed to the novelties revealed by the telescope. Indeed, there were further important divisions within the order itself: some Jesuits were far more willing to criticize Aristotle than is usually recognized.[88] Two nonacademic, reform-minded Dominicans from the socially tumultuous region of Naples, Bruno and Tommaso Campanella, had given vigorous support, respectively, to Copernicus and to Galileo—although both had come to bad ends for their political views.[89] Castelli the Benedictine and, later, Bonaventura Cavalieri, a Jesuate, were faithful Galilean disciples. Zuñiga at Salamanca had been an Augustinian. Now, in January 1615, came unexpected support for the Copernican position from a member of the reformed Carmelite order in Naples, Paolo Foscarini (1580–1616). Foscarini was well read; and, indeed, by 1615 there was more to read than there had been when Zuñiga wrote his commentary on Job in the early 1580s: Galileo's *Sidereal Messenger*, Kepler's *New Astronomy*, Clavius's last edition of the *Sphere*, suggesting the need for a new cosmology, and Copernicus's *De Revolutionibus*. Foscarini knew and cited them all. His *Letter Concerning the Opinion of Copernicus and the Pythagoreans about the Mobility of the Earth* is an ambitious garnering of all biblical texts bearing on the Copernican theory with the object of showing that they can be reconciled with heliocentrism. Building primarily on the evidence of Galileo's telescopic observations of Venus, he rejects Ptolemy's theory, maintains that all physical propositions in the Bible are absolutely accommodated to popular discourse, and concludes that the Copernican "opinion" is "not improbable."[90] Foscarini treats the problem of cosmological choice as though it were a moral problem, falling therefore into the domain of the contingent or that which can be other than it is. Under such conditions, what we can have is *opinionative* knowledge, the best expression of truth at that time—rather than *demonstrative knowledge*, that which must follow all the time from true premises.[91]

Thus, Galileo was not alone. Though not a cleric, he belongs by family affinity within a small movement of church progressives, not all Copernicans, who sought reform of traditional positions on natural knowledge and more liberal rules of scriptural translation and interpretation. They included a considerable range: from the Salamancan humanists Luis de León and Diego de Zuñiga to the Neapolitan probabiliorist Foscarini; from the moderate academic mathematicism of

Clavius at the Collegio Romano[92] to the heterodox Neapolitan metaphysics of friars Bruno and Campanella; and finally, Galileo's numerous, mathematically talented academic disciples in the minor orders. Against this group was the conservative heritage of Trent— represented most formidably by the greatest Jesuit controversialist of the period, Cardinal Robert Bellarmine (1542–1621)—although the young Bellarmine had entertained quite remarkably un-Aristotelian and even un-Ptolemaic notions in his Louvain lectures of 1570–1572.[93] Bellarmine was an old friend and colleague of Clavius, author of the preface to the Clementine Vulgate of 1592 (the very symbol of Tridentine authority), a member of the commission that tried and convicted Bruno in 1599,[94] and head of the Collegio Romano in 1611, when it honored Galileo for his telescopic discoveries. It was the same Bellarmine to whom Foscarini sent his little book in 1615. Yet, in his well-known reply to Foscarini, Bellarmine thundered with the weight of tradition: "The Council [of Trent] would prohibit expounding the Bible contrary to the common agreement of the Fathers." The Fathers *do* agree, according to Bellarmine, on a literal reading of the standard passages concerning cosmology. It is, therefore, a matter of faith because of the unanimity of those who have spoken. Mathematicians should therefore restrict themselves to speaking "hypothetically and not absolutely," for to speak absolutely would injure the faith and irritate all the theologians and Scholastic philosophers. Only if there were a strict demonstration would one be permitted to accommodate Scripture absolutely to popular discourse—and Bellarmine was convinced that no such demonstration existed.[95]

Galileo obtained a copy of Bellarmine's letter and immediately recognized the rejection of Foscarini's probabiliorism.[96] Equally significant, he accepted the conditions of strict demonstration that Bellarmine laid down and which, in any case, he had accepted long before under the influence of his associations with the Collegio Romano. "Our opinion," he wrote in notes to the Bellarmine letter, "is that the Scriptures accord perfectly with demonstrated physical truth. But let those theologians who are not astronomers guard against rendering the Scriptures false by trying to interpret against it propositions which may be true and might be proved so."[97] This brief remark contains much of the gist of Galileo's position developed in his *Letter to the Grand Duchess Christina* (composed in June 1615, not published until 1635). Although Galileo readily appealed to the book of nature as warrant for his mathematical mode of philosophizing about nature, it is interesting to observe that, unlike Bruno and Kepler, he would not try to create a systematic theological justification for the Copernican arrangement. Instead, he chose to fight the battle at the boundaries of natural philosophy, mathematics, and biblical theology.

But the *Letter*, though filled with the *rhetoric* of necessary demonstration and sense experience, failed to specify the true and necessary cause of the earth's motion—even though Galileo had at that time an argument about the tides that he believed to be conclusive.[98] Rather, the principal strategy of the *Letter* was to argue against the disciplinary hegemony of the conservative theologians and philosophers.[99] By this tactic Galileo hoped to convict the conservatives of two charges: first, theology is not "queen of the sciences" by virtue of providing the principles on which the less sublime disciplines are founded. It gains its authority through the dignity of its subject matter, which is eternal and sublime, and the special means by which it communicates to men (revelation). Second, the decree of the fourth session of Trent had been improperly interpreted in the matter of the unanimous consent of the Fathers and thus failed the test of demonstrative truth *in theology*. The Fathers, says Galileo, never debated the question of the motion of the earth. It was not even controversial. Their statements about the stability of the earth were all accommodated to the language of the people. "Hence it is not sufficient to say that because all the Fathers admitted the stability of the earth, this is a matter of faith; one would have to prove also that they had condemned the contrary opinion."[100]

At this point in his discussion Galileo introduced the testimony of Diego de Zuñiga. "Some theologians," Galileo wrote, "have now begun to consider it [the earth's motion] and they are seen not to deem it erroneous."[101] In so doing, he thereby gave implicit approval to the partial-accommodationist line taken by Zuñiga and identified himself with the temper of liberal Salamancan humanism. He could have no way of knowing that a copy of Pineda's critique of Zuñiga's book was in the library of Cardinal Bellarmine. It is significant that his citation of Zuñiga is then followed immediately by a veiled reference to delle Colombe's very conservative interpretation of the Council's position that physical conclusions, when there is a consensus of the Fathers, are a matter of faith. "I think this may be an arbitrary simplification of various council decrees by certain people to favor their own opinion,"[102] wrote Galileo. The motion of the earth, he was trying to say, is not a matter of faith and morals.

The *Letter* ends with a subtle exegesis of Joshua 10:12–13. The logic of Galileo's position here cleverly seeks to shift the exegetical ground to the *astronomical* meaning of the passage, thereby exposing the theologian's astronomical incompetence even in the area of their own subject matter and presaging the structure of his arguments in the *Dialogue Concerning the Two Chief World Systems* (1632). *Even if* physical propositions were a matter of faith, which they are not, astronomically informed theologians could still ask whether Joshua's request for more daylight might be better accomplished on the Copernican system than on the Ptolemaic. More cautious than Zuñiga, Galileo was nevertheless close to the Spaniard in flirting with the construction of the dangerous geomotive interpretation of Joshua.

CONCLUSION

The official Catholic response to Copernicus's theory on 5 March 1616 masks the very complex history that we have constructed—the diversity of Copernican discourses, the variety of disciplinary and exegetical strategies employed by Protestants and Catholics, and finally the struggle *within the church itself* between reformers and traditionalists.[103] The decree published by the Congregation of the Index ordering that Copernicus's *De Revolutionibus* and Zuñiga's *Commentary on Job* be "suspended until corrected" represented a local victory for the conservative Tridentine faction of the church, for the maintenance of traditional hierarchical authority in the universities and within the Jesuit Order. What was the immediate effect of this decree? Catholics could buy and read the books, but they were to know that the doctrines contained therein were false, and they were instructed on which lines to expurgate.[104] The decree was hard to enforce. Of more than five hundred copies of *De Revolutionibus* still extant in the world today, only about 8 percent have been censored by their seventeenth-century owners.[105] The offensive passages in the copy of Zuñiga's extremely rare book in the library of the University of Salamanca have been heavily crossed out. The British Library copy has thick paper pasted over the dangerous sections—so nicely done, in fact, that the book automatically falls open to that section of the commentary! We are uninformed as to other extant copies. Paolo Foscarini's little treatise was "altogether prohibited and condemned." His work was perceived as more threatening because its extensive accommodations of Scripture to the Copernican theory were not as easily handled with scissors, paste, and ink. The name Galileo Galilei appears nowhere in the decree.

NOTES

The author wishes to express his gratitude for numerous critical suggestions made on the first draft by David C. Lindberg and the conference commentator, Ernan McMullin; special thanks also for their comments and reactions to Geoffrey N. Cantor, Gary Deason, Rivka Feldhay, Maurice Finocchiaro, Keith Hutchison, and Winifred Wisan.

1. Nuremberg, 1543; 2d ed., Basel, 1566. For English translations see A. M. Duncan, *Copernicus: On the Revolutions of the Heavenly Spheres* (Newton Abbot: David & Charles; New York: Barnes & Noble, 1976); and Edward Rosen, *Nicholas Copernicus: On the Revolutions*, vol. 2 of *Complete Works* (Warsaw and Cracow: Polish Scientific Publishers, 1978). All citations are to the Rosen translation, although the reader is referred to the caveats of Noel Swerdlow, "On Establishing the Text of 'De Revolutionibus,'" *Journal for the History of Astronomy* 12 (1981): 35–46.

2. The *locus classicus* of this view is Andrew Dickson White, *History of the Warfare of Science with Theology in Christendom*, 2 vols. (New York: D. Appleton Century Co., 1936), 1:126, although elements of it are reflected in Thomas Kuhn's otherwise far more sophisticated *The Copernican Revolution* (Cambridge, Mass.: Harvard Univ. Press, 1957), pp. 191–197.

3. On the life of Copernicus see Leopold Prowe, *Nicolaus Coppernicus*, 3 vols. (Berlin: Weidemann, 1883–1884); Ludwik Antoni Birkenmajer, *Mikolaj Kopernik* (Cracow: Uniwersytet Jagiellonskiego, 1900); and Edward Rosen, "Nicholas Copernicus: A Biography," in *Three Copernican Treatises*, 3d rev. ed. (New York: Octagon Books, 1971), pp. 313–408.

4. See Noel Swerdlow, "On Copernicus' Theory of Precession," in *The Copernican Achievement*, ed. Robert S. Westman (Berkeley, Los Angeles, London: Univ. of California Press, 1975), pp. 49–98.

5. Considerable controversy exists among historians about how the domains of mathematics and physics were defined by contemporaries. See Pierre Duhem, *To Save the Appearances*, trans. E. Doland and C. Maschler (Chicago: Univ. of Chicago Press, 1969; first published in 1908); William H. Donahue, "The Solid Planetary Spheres in Post-Copernican Natural Philosophy," in *Copernican Achievement*, ed. Westman, pp. 244–275; Fritz Krafft, "Physikalische Realität oder mathematische Hypothese? Andreas Osiander und die physikalische Erneuerung der antiken Astronomie durch Nicholas Copernicus," *Philosophia Naturalis* 14 (1973): 243–275; G. E. R. Lloyd, "Saving the Appearances," *Classical Quarterly* 24 (1978): 202–222; Robert S. Westman, "The Astronomer's Role in the Sixteenth Century: A Preliminary Study," *History of Science* 18 (1980): 105–147; E. J. Aiton, "Celestial Spheres and Circles," *History of Science* 19 (1981): 75–113; Nicholas Jardine, "The Significance of the Copernican Orbs," *Journal for the History of Astronomy* 13 (1982): 168–194, esp. 183–189.

6. For an excellent survey of the central elements of medieval cosmology see Edward Grant, "Cosmology," in *Science in the Middle Ages*, ed. David C. Lindberg (Chicago: Univ. of Chicago Press, 1978), pp. 265–302.

7. The nature of medieval and Renaissance objections to the equant are still much disputed by historians. See Willy Hartner, "Copernicus: The Man, the Work, and Its Theory," *Proceedings of the American Philosophical Society* 117 (1973): 413–422, esp. 416–417; Noel M. Swerdlow, "The Derivation and First Draft of Copernicus's Planetary Theory: A Translation of the Commentariolus with Commentary," ibid., pp. 423–512, esp. 424, 435–438; Westman, "Astronomer's Role," pp. 112–116; Aiton, "Celestial Spheres and Circles," pp. 96–97; Jardine, "Significance of the Copernican Orbs," pp. 174–183.

8. In the division of the sciences going back to the thirteenth-century Parisian Aristotelian, Albertus Magnus, the mathematical sciences are conceived as inferior to physics. This tradition of the *divisio scientiarum* was opposed by a Platonic tradition at Oxford that claimed preeminence for mathematics in the whole of natural philosophy; see James A. Weisheipl, "Classification of the Sciences in Medieval Thought," *Medieval Studies* 27 (1965): 54–90, esp. 82–84.

9. *De Revolutionibus* 1.4, pp. 10–11; 5.2, p. 240.

10. Ibid., preface, p. 5; 1.10, p. 22: cf. Westman, "Astronomer's Role," pp. 109–111.

11. For an alternative interpretation, arguing that the sole burden of justification still rests in the domain of natural philosophy, see Jardine, "Copernican Orbs," pp. 183–189.

12. On the concept of demonstrative proof see Aristotle, *Posterior Analytics* 1.6.74b15 ff. Cf. Owen Bennett, *The Nature of Demonstrative Proof According to the Principles of Aristotle and St. Thomas Aquinas,* The Catholic University of America Philosophical Studies, vol. 75 (Washington, D.C.: Catholic Univ. of America Press, 1943), pp. 58–85. It should be observed that Aristotle's own system of the planets does not satisfy the conditions of demonstrative proof.

13. See Westman, "Astronomer's Role," pp. 107–116.

14. See A. Bruce Wrightsman, "Andreas Osiander's Contribution to the Copernican Achievement," in *Copernican Achievement*, ed. Westman, pp. 213–243.

15. *De Revolutionibus*, p. xvi. The modern editor and translator Edward Rosen has labeled the Letter "Foreword by Andreas Osiander," but no such designation appears in the original work.

16. Karl Heinz Burmeister has published all of Rheticus's correspondence, a detailed bibliography of his works, and an excellent biography: *Georg Joachim Rhetikus, 1514–1574: Eine Bio-Bibliographie*, 3 vols. (Wiesbaden: Guido Pressler Verlag, 1967). For a different interpretation of Rheticus's relationship to Copernicus see Robert S. Westman, "The Melanchthon Circle, Rheticus and the Wittenberg Interpretation of the Copernican Theory," *Isis* 66 (1975): 165–193, esp. 181–190.

17. As this article goes to press, R. Hooykaas announces the discovery of an anonymous treatise entitled *Letter on the Motion of the Earth* (1651) that he believes to be Rheticus's ("Rheticus's Lost Treatise on Holy Scripture and the Motion of the Earth," *Journal for the History of Astronomy* 15 [1984]: 77–80).

18. Luther's words are reported here by Aurifaber: "Der Narr will die ganze Kunst Astronomiae umkehren" (*Weimar Ausgabe, Tischreden*, vol. 1, no. 855); cf. the later report of Lauterbach: "Wer do will klug sein, der soll ihme nichts lassen gefallen, was andere achten. Er muss ihme etwas eigen machen, sicut ille facit, qui totam astrologiam invertere vult. Etiam illa confusa tamen ego credo sacrae scripturae, nam Josua jussit solem stare, non terram" (ibid., vol. 4, no. 4638). Andrew Dickson White (*Warfare*, pp. 126–127) and Bertrand Russell (*Religion and Science* [London: Oxford Univ. Press, 1935], pp. 22–23) use the Aurifaber report to argue that Luther's reaction to Copernicanism was severe and influential.

19. On the Reformers' reaction to the Copernican theory see Richard Stauffer, "L'attitude des Reformateurs à l'égard de Copernic," in *Avant, avec, après Copernic: La représentation de l'univers et ses conséquences épistémologiques* (Paris: Albert Blanchard, 1975), pp. 159–163.

20. On Melanchthon and the Wittenberg school see Westman, "Melanchthon Circle," pp. 165–181.

21. Georg Joachim Rheticus, *Narratio Prima*, in Rosen, *Three Copernican Treatises*, p. 138.

22. See Robert S. Westman, "Three Responses to the Copernican Theory: Johannes Praetorius, Tycho Brahe and Michael Maestlin," in *Copernican Achievement*, ed. Westman, pp. 285–345; and Owen Gingerich, "Copernicus and Tycho," *Scientific American* 229, no. 6 (Dec. 1973), 86–101. Gingerich and I have since revised some of our claims about the evidence for Tycho Brahe's views on Copernicus: Owen Gingerich and Robert S. Westman, "A Reattribution of the Tychonic Annotations in Copies of Copernicus's 'De Revolutionibus,'" *Journal for the History of Astronomy* 12 (1981): 53–54, and a longer forthcoming study in *Centaurus*.

23. In 1588, the same year in which Tycho's system was published, Nicholas Reymers Baer proposed a system without intersecting spheres that makes the planets revolve around both the sun and the earth while the latter rotates on its axis at the center of the universe (*Fundamentum Astronomicum*, Strassburg). A furious priority dispute ensued. For brief details see J. L. E. Dreyer, *Tycho Brahe* (Edinburgh, 1890; reprint, New York: Dover, 1963), pp. 183–185.

24. *De Magnete*, trans. P. Fleury Mottelay (London: Quaritch, 1893), 6.3.

25. Owen Gingerich, "The Great Copernicus Chase," *American Scholar* 49 (1979): 81–88.

26. See "The Beginnings of the Catholic Reform in Rome under Paul III," in *History of the Church*, ed. Hubert Jedin and John Dolan, trans. Anselm Biggs and Peter Becker, 10 vols. (London: Burns & Oates, 1965–1980), 5:456–462.

27. See Jean Delumeau, *Catholicism between Luther and Voltaire: A New View of the Counter-Reformation*, trans. Jeremy Moiser (London: Burns & Oates Ltd., 1977; original French version published in 1971), p. 126.

28. Ibid., p. 9.

29. See the excellent study by Salvador Muñoz Iglesias, "El decreto tridentino sobre la Vulgata y su interpretación por los teólogos del siglo XVI," *Estudios bíblicos* 5 (1946): 145–169.

30. See Miguel del Pinta Llorente, *Estudios y polemicas sobre Fray Luis de León* (Madrid: Viuda de Galo Saez, 1956), p. 69.

31. His teachers included the important theologian Melchior Cano (1509?–1560) and the philosopher/theologian Domingo de Soto (1494–1560); see Luis G. Alonso Getino, *Vida y procesos del Maestro Fr. Luis de León* (Salamanca: Calatrava, 1907), pp. 34–35.

32. "I believe that much more would be achieved," wrote one Tridentine conservative, "if we would rid ourselves of old doubts and impose a perpetual silence so that we do not go around saying 'here it says this in Hebrew, there it says that in Greek' (*aliter habetur in hebraeo, aliter in graeco*), which only

weakens and disarms the authority of the Vulgate edition . . . " (Iglesias, "El decreto tridentino," p. 165).

33. Getino, *Vida y procesos*, pp. 528–563.

34. Iglesias, "El decreto tridentino," p. 165.

35. This statement is based upon a careful study of the indices of *Concilium Tridentinum: Diariorum, Actorum, Epistularum, Tractatuum*, ed. Stephanus Ehses et al., 13 vols. (Freiburg im Breisgau: Herder, 1961–1976).

36. Firenze, Biblioteca Nazionale, MS Conv. Soppr. J.I.25, with the provenance of the monastery of San Marco.

37. See Demetrio Marzi, *La questione della riforma del calendario nel Quinto Concilio Lateranense (1512–1517)* (Florence: G. Carnesecchi e Figli, 1896).

38. "De coelo supremo immobile et terra infima stabili ceterisque coelis et elementis intermediis mobilibus." The entire text of this little work is transcribed by Eugenio Garin, "Alle origini della polemica anticopernicana," in *Colloquia Copernicana*, vol. 2, Studia Copernicana, vol. 6 (Wrocław: Ossolineum, 1975), pp. 31–42. All citations are to the Garin transcription. See also Edward Rosen on Garin's discovery: "Was Copernicus's *Revolutions* Approved by the Pope?" *Journal of the History of Ideas* 36 (1975): 531–542.

39. Garin, "Alle origini," pp. 35–36.

40. Ibid., p. 42.

41. Spina presented articles concerning baptism and justification (*Concilium Tridentinum* 12:676, 725); he was succeeded on his death by the Bolognese Dominican Egidius Fuschararus (ibid., 5:728n).

42. See Hans Frei, *The Eclipse of Biblical Narrative: A Study in Eighteenth and Nineteenth Century Hermeneutics* (New Haven: Yale Univ. Press, 1974), pp. 1–37.

43. On the problem of accommodation see Klaus Scholder, *Ursprunge und Probleme der Biblelkritik im 17. Jahrhundert* (Munich: Kaiser, 1966), pp. 56–78; Amos Funkenstein, "The Dialectical Preparation for Scientific Revolutions: On the Role of Hypothetical Reasoning in the Emergence of Copernican Astronomy and Galilean Mechanics," in *Copernican Achievement*, ed. Westman, pp. 195–197.

44. See Johannes Bettray, *Die Akkommodationsmethode des P. Matteo Ricci S.I. in China* (Rome: Universitas Gregoriana, 1955), p. 278.

45. Another verse cited was Isaiah 66:1: "Thus saith the Lord, the heaven is my throne, and the earth is my footstool."

46. There is a considerable literature on Bruno, of which the following works are especially recommended: Frances Yates, *Giordano Bruno and the Hermetic Tradition* (Chicago: Univ. of Chicago Press, 1964); Paul-Henri Michel, *The Cosmology of Giordano Bruno*, trans. R. E. W. Maddison (London: Methuen, 1973; original French version published in 1962); Hélène Vedrine, *La conception de la nature chez Giordano Bruno* (Paris: J. Vrin, 1967). See also Robert S. Westman, "Magical Reform and Astronomical Reform: The Yates Thesis Reconsidered," in Robert S. Westman and J. E. McGuire, *Hermeticism and the Scientific Revolution* (Los Angeles: William Andrews Clark Memorial Library, 1977), pp. 1–91.

47. Giordano Bruno, *The Ash Wednesday Supper*, ed. and trans. Edward A.

Gosselin and Lawrence S. Lerner (Hamden, Conn.: The Shoe String Press, 1977), Dialogue 4, p. 178.

48. Johannes Kepler, *Gesammelte Werke*, ed. Walther von Dyck and Max Caspar, 18 vols. to date (Munich: C. H. Beck'sche Verlag, 1937–), 3:28–34. A recent English translation of the introduction to the *New Astronomy* has been prepared by Owen Gingerich in *The Great Ideas Today: 1983* (Chicago: Encyclopedia Britannica, 1983), pp. 309–323.

49. Kepler, *Gesammelte Werke* 3:31.

50. On Zuñiga's life and work see Marcial Solana, *Historia de la filosofía española*, 3 vols. (Madrid: Aldus, 1940), 3:221–260. On Zuñiga and the Copernican problem see Zofia Wardęska, *Teoria heliocentryczna w interpretacji teologów XVI wieku*, Studia Copernicana, vol. 12 (Wrocław: Ossolineum, 1975), pp. 62–69. I am grateful to Annette Aronowicz for providing me with translations of this and a few other sections of Wardęska's work.

51. *De Vera Religione in Omnes Sui Temporis Haereticos Libri Tres* (Salamanca, 1577); *In Zacharias Prophetam Commentaria* (Salamanca, 1577); *In Job Commentaria* (Toledo, 1584). Zuñiga's aim was nothing less than a full commentary on all books of the Bible.

52. A facsimile of this section of Zuñiga's treatise is conveniently supplied by Wardęska, *Teoria heliocentryczna*, pp. 47a–c (hereafter, this and other facsimiles are cited as "Wardęska Texts"). An English translation of the Zuñiga passage was made by Thomas Salusbury in the seventeenth century: *Mathematical Discourses and Demonstrations* (London, 1665), pp. 468–470.

53. See Juan Vernet, "Copernicus in Spain," in *Colloquia Copernicana*, vol. 1, Studia Copernicana, vol. 5 (Wrocław: Ossolineum, 1972), p. 275.

54. "Certain motions that Nicolaus Copernicus and others ascribe to the earth," Zuñiga wrote, "are not very difficult to comprehend. But the motion of the earth, whereby in the space of twenty-four hours it turns entirely on its axis, is most difficult and appears to me to make absurd this opinion of the earth's motion" (*Philosophia, Prima Pars* [Toledo, 1597]); see J. M. Lopez-Piñero, V. Navarro Brotons, and E. Portela Marco, *Materiales para la historia de las ciencias en España: S. XVI–XVII* (Valencia: Artes Gráficas Soler, 1976), pp. 89–91.

55. See, for example, François de Dainville, S.J., "L'enseignement des mathématiques dans les collèges jesuites de France du XVIe au XVIIIe siècle," *Revue d'histoire des sciences et de leurs applications* 7 (1954): 6–21, 102–123.

56. The full text and translation of the relevant passages is given in A. C. Crombie, "Mathematics and Platonism in the Sixteenth Century Italian Universities and in Jesuit Educational Policy," in *Prismata: Naturwissenschaftsgeschichtliche Studien: Festschrift für Willy Hartner*, ed. Y. Maeyama and W. G. Saltzer (Wiesbaden: Franz Steiner Verlag, 1977), pp. 63–94, esp. 65–66; cf. also Giuseppe Cosentino, "L'insegnamento delle matematiche nei collegi gesuitici nell'Italia settentrionale: Nota introduttiva," *Physis* 13 (1971): 205–217.

57. On Clavius, the Collegio Romano, and their importance for Galileo, the definitive work is now William A. Wallace, *Galileo and His Sources: The Heritage of the Collegio Romano in Galileo's Science* (Princeton: Princeton Univ.

Press, 1984). I am most grateful to Professor Wallace for allowing me to inspect the manuscript of his book prior to publication.

58. Christopher Clavius, *In Sphaeram Ioannis de Sacro Bosco Commentarius, Nunc Iterum ab Ipso Auctore Recognitus* (Venice, 1591), pp. 452–458. See also Nicholas Jardine, "The Forging of Modern Realism: Kepler and Clavius against the Sceptics," *Studies in History and Philosophy of Science* 10 (1979): 141–173.

59. *Commentariorum in Iob Libri Tredecim* (Cologne, 1600), p. 340; Wardęska Texts, p. 31.

60. *In Ecclesiasten Commentariorum Liber Unus* (Antwerp, 1620), pp. 111–118; Wardęska Texts, pp. 32a–h.

61. *In Acta Apostolorum Commentarii* (Lyon, 1606), p. 215; Wardęska Texts, p. 22.

62. See James Brodrick, S.J., *The Life and Work of Blessed Robert Francis Cardinal Bellarmine, S.J., 1542–1621*, 2 vols. (London: Burns & Oates Ltd., 1928), 1:212.

63. This may be inferred from the "Index of Explicators of Holy Scripture" appended to the *Opera Omnia* of Bellarmine, ed. Justinus Fevre, 12 vols. (Paris: Vivès, 1870–1874; reprint, Frankfurt a.M.: Minerva, 1965), 12:478.

64. See C. Doris Hellmann, "Maurolyco's 'Lost' Essay on the New Star of 1572," *Isis* 51 (1960): 322–336.

65. Christopher Clavius, *Opera Omnia*, 5 vols. (Mainz, 1611), 3:75.

66. Tycho Brahe to Christopher Clavius, 5 Jan. 1600, transcription published by Wilhelm Norlind, *Tycho Brahe: En levnadsteckning med nya bidrag helysande hans liv och verk* (Lund: C. W. K. Gleerup, 1970), pp. 376–381, no. 9.

67. Leonard Digges, Gentleman, *A Prognostication euerlastinge of righte good effecte . . . Lately corrected and augmented by Thomas Digges his sonne* (London: Thomas Marsh, 1576). The supplement is entitled: *A Perfit Description of the Caelestiall Orbes according to the most aunciente doctrine of the Pythagoreans, latelye reuiued by Copernicus and by Geometricall Demonstrations approued*, ed. with commentary by Francis R. Johnson and Sanford V. Larkey, "Thomas Digges, the Copernican System, and the Idea of the Infinity of the Universe in 1576," *The Huntington Library Bulletin* 5 (1934): 69–117.

68. See note 46 and Bruno's *De l'infinito universo et mondi* ("Venice" [i.e., London], 1584), in Dorothea Waley Singer, *Giordano Bruno: His Life and Thought, with Annotated Translation of His Work "On the Infinite Universe and Worlds"* (New York: Henry Schuman, 1950).

69. Johannes Kepler, *Mysterium Cosmographicum: The Secret of the Universe*, trans. A. M. Duncan (New York: Abaris Books, 1981), p. 63.

70. As we have seen already with his criterion of scriptural exegesis, there is an intimate connection in Kepler's work between seeing and knowing: just as vision is the making of pictures, so correct knowledge consists in the eye of the intellect forming mathematical pictures that are like an indifferent mirror of the physical world. For Kepler in the context of visual theory see David C. Lindberg, *Theories of Vision from Al-Kindi to Kepler* (Chicago: Univ. of Chicago Press, 1976), pp. 202–203; as the articulator of a pictorial mode

see Svetlana Alpers, *The Art of Describing: Dutch Art in the Seventeenth Century* (Chicago: Univ. of Chicago Press, 1983), pp. 26–71; and for further development of the thesis enunciated here see Robert S. Westman, "Nature, Art and Psyche: Jung, Pauli and the Kepler-Fludd Polemic," in *Occult and Scientific Mentalities in the Renaissance*, ed. Brian Vickers (Cambridge: Cambridge Univ. Press, 1984), pp. 177–229.

71. See Jürgen Hübner, *Die Theologie Johannes Keplers zwischen Orthodoxie und Naturwissenschaft* (Tübingen: J. C. B. Mohr [Paul Siebeck], 1975), esp. pp. 158–228.

72. Kepler to Herwart von Hohenberg, 26 March 1598, *Gesammelte Werke* 13:193.

73. The extent of our *direct* knowledge of Galileo's Copernican views is contained in a well-known letter to Kepler, 4 Aug. 1597: "I have for many years past considered the view of Copernicus, and from it I have been able to discover the causes of many natural phenomena which without doubt cannot be explained by the traditional hypotheses. I have drawn up a list of many reasons and refutations of contrary arguments which, however, I thus far do not dare to make public, being frightened by the fate of our teacher Copernicus, who, having gained immortal fame in the eyes of a few, has been ridiculed and hissed off the stage by innumerable others (for so great is the number of fools). I should indeed venture to disclose my thoughts if there were more men like you; since there are none, I shall desist from such a venture" (*Le opere di Galileo Galilei*, ed. Antonio Favaro, 20 vols. [Florence: G. Barbèra, 1899–1909], 10:68). Cf. the somewhat stronger conviction rendered in Willy Hartner's translation of this passage: "Galileo's Contributions to Astronomy," in *Galileo, Man of Science*, ed. Ernan McMullin (New York and London: Basic Books, 1967), p. 181.

74. See Robert S. Westman, "Michael Mästlin's Adoption of the Copernican Theory," in *Colloquia Copernicana*, vol. 4, Studia Copernicana, vol. 13 (Wrocław: Ossolineum, 1975), pp. 51–61, and "Three Responses," pp. 329–337.

75. See A. C. Crombie, "Sources of Galileo's Early Natural Philosophy," in *Reason, Experiment and Mysticism in the Scientific Revolution*, ed. M. L. Righini Bonelli and William R. Shea (New York: Science History Publications, 1975), pp. 157–175; William A. Wallace, *Prelude to Galileo: Essays on Medieval and Sixteenth-Century Sources of Galileo's Thought* (Dordrecht: Reidel, 1981), pp. 192–252 (containing an impressive content-analysis of Galileo's *Tractatio de Caelo* and Clavius's *In Sphaeram*); and Wallace's *Galileo and His Sources*.

76. The case for Clavius's importance in providing the context for Galileo's earliest methodological convictions has been made eloquently by William A. Wallace (*Prelude*, pp. 137–138, 231–233; *Galileo and His Sources*, pp. 126–148).

77. Historians continue to debate the ways in which Galileo's various proof structures are to be characterized and the contrast between his ideal of science and the way in which he practiced science. See Ernan McMullin, "The Conception of Science in Galileo's Work," in *New Perspectives on Galileo*, ed. R. E. Butts and J. C. Pitt (Dordrecht: Reidel, 1978), pp. 209–257, esp. 227 ff.; Winifred Lovell Wisan, "Galileo's Scientific Method: A Reexamination," ibid., pp. 1–57; William A. Wallace, *Galileo and His Sources*.

78. See Albert Van Helden, *The Invention of the Telescope*, Transactions of the American Philosophical Society, vol. 67, no. 4 (Philadelphia: American Philosophical Society, 1977).

79. The telescope provided Galileo with the institutional leverage that he would need to leave the university and to embark on a series of topics that would have met with resistance from the entrenched disciplinary hierarchy of the university. See Galileo to Belisario Vinta, quoted and translated in Wallace, *Prelude*, p. 139.

80. Galileo's Venetian friend Francesco Sagredo, immortalized in the *Dialogue*, viewed Galileo's move as an error; see his argument, translated in Stillman Drake, *Discoveries and Opinions of Galileo* (Garden City, N.Y.: Doubleday Anchor, 1957), pp. 67 ff.

81. "As to the title of my position," Galileo wrote to the grand duke, "I desire that in addition to the title of 'mathematician' His Highness will annex that of 'philosopher'; for I may claim to have studied more years in philosophy than months in pure mathematics" (translated in Drake, *Discoveries and Opinions*, p. 64).

82. Ibid., pp. 61–62.

83. "The Tuscan language," wrote Galileo, "is entirely adequate to treat and to explain the concepts of all branches of knowledge" (Galileo, *Opere* 5:189–190). See further, Eric Cochrane, *Florence in the Forgotten Centuries, 1527–1800: A History of Florence and the Florentines in the Age of the Grand Dukes* (Chicago: Univ. of Chicago Press, 1973), pp. 168–171; Lauro Martines's excellent discussion of *la questione della lingua*, in *Power and Imagination: City-States in Renaissance Italy* (New York: Alfred A. Knopf, 1979), pp. 317–322.

84. See notes 36 and 37; an annotation by Caccini appears on fol. 3r of the Tolosani MS.

85. Galileo, *Opere* 3:255, 290.

86. See Antonio Ricci-Riccardi, *Galileo Galilei e Fra Tommaso Caccini* (Florence: Successori Le Monnier, 1902), pp. 66–67; Jerome J. Langford, *Galileo, Science and the Church* (Ann Arbor, Mich.: Univ. of Michigan Press, 1966), p. 55; Drake, *Discoveries and Opinions*, pp. 153–154.

87. Galileo *Opere* 12:123. Castelli's comment suggests again that the opposition was not confined to academics and that there was an element of Florentine popular street sentiment. Galileo's followers called themselves *Galileisti*, and their opponents were called *Colombi* (pigeons), a play on the name of Lodovico delle Colombe. That Caccini was aligned with the League of Pigeons seems assured by a letter from his brother, Matteo, who worked at the papal court in Rome: "What idiocy is this of yours to be set bellowing at the behest of pigeons or blockheads or certain *colombi*!" (Ricci-Riccardi, *Galileo e Caccini*, p. 70).

88. See Ugo Baldini, *"Additamenta Galileiana*, I: Galileo, La nuova astronomia e la critica all'aristotelismo nel dialogo epistolare tra Giuseppe Biancini e i Revisori Romani della Compagnia di Gesu," *Annali dell'Istituto e Museo di Storia della Scienza di Firenze* 9 (1984): 13–43.

89. On the political situation in Naples at the end of the sixteenth century see Rosario Villari, "Naples: The Insurrection in Naples in 1585," in *The Late Italian Renaissance, 1525–1630*, ed. Eric Cochrane (New York: Macmillan, 1970),

pp. 305–330; cf. Carolyn Merchant, *The Death of Nature: Women, Ecology and the Scientific Revolution* (San Francisco: Harper & Row, 1980), pp. 115–117.

90. Paolo Foscarini, in Wardęska Texts, pp. 10a–z, esp. 10e and 10z.

91. For an excellent discussion of the concept of probability and moral deliberation in Thomas Aquinas, whose influence on this issue was considerable, see Edmund F. Byrne, *Probability and Opinion: A Study in the Medieval Presuppositions of Post-Medieval Theories of Probability* (The Hague: Martinus Nijhoff, 1968), pp. 213–227.

92. As William Wallace has emphasized, expanding on the work of R. G. Villoslada, there were close connections between the Spanish Jesuits and Dominicans, especially at Salamanca and the Collegio Romano. Clavius himself had studied under Pedro Nuñez at the Portuguese university in Coimbra, and there existed a general tendency for the Roman Jesuits to imitate Parisian and Salamancan academic styles (Wallace, *Prelude*, pp. 229, 241).

93. Ugo Baldini and George V. Coyne, S.J., "The Louvain Lectures (Lectiones Lovanienses) of Bellarmine and the Autograph Copy of His 1616 Declaration to Galileo: Texts in the Original Latin (Italian) with English Translation, Introduction, Commentary and Notes," *Vatican Observatory Publications*, Special Series: *Studi Galileiani*, 1 (1984): 3–48.

94. Xavier Le Bachelet has established that Bellarmine actually played a lesser role in the trial of Bruno ("Bellarmin et Giordano Bruno," *Gregorianum* 4 [1923]: 193–210).

95. Galileo, *Opere* 12:171–172; Drake, *Discoveries and Opinions*, pp. 162–164.

96. We know that Galileo had received a copy of Foscarini's book from his friend Federico Cesi by mid-March 1615 and that the book had been read approvingly by his friends in Rome (pp. 162–163) and in Pisa (p. 165). Much of what we know about Galileo's immediate response to Bellarmine is based upon a critical undated document, apparently composed sometime between March and June 1615 ("Considerazione circa l'opinione Copernicana"), translated in Drake, *Discoveries and Opinions*, pp. 167–170.

97. Ibid., p. 168.

98. In the *Letter to Christina* Galileo employs various locutions: "necessarie dimostrazioni," "certezza di alcune conclusioni naturali," "le causi de quali forse inaltro modo non possono assegnare," etc. (*Opere* 5:311, 316–317). But nowhere does he refer to arguments contained in his *Dialogue on the Tides*, a work completed by January 1616 and later to become Day Four of his *Dialogue Concerning the Two Chief World Systems* (1632). On the tidal arguments see esp. William Shea, *Galileo's Intellectual Revolution: Middle Period, 1610–1632* (New York: Science History Publications, 1972), pp. 172–189.

99. As Galileo puts the point: "Why, this would be as if an absolute despot [i.e., the superior science], being neither a physician nor an architect but knowing himself free to command, should undertake to administer medicine and erect buildings according to his whim—at grave peril of his poor patients' lives, and the speedy collapse of his edifices" (Drake, *Discoveries and Opinions*, p. 193).

100. Ibid., p. 202. See also the very fine analysis of Olaf Pedersen that appeared as this article underwent revisions: "Galileo and the Council of

Trent: The Galileo Affair Revisited," *Journal for the History of Astronomy* 14 (1983): 1–29, esp. 16–24.

101. Galileo continues: "Thus in the *Commentaries on Job* of Didacus a Stuñica, where the author comments upon the words *Who moveth the earth from its place . . .* , he discourses at length upon the Copernican opinion and concludes that the mobility of the earth is not contrary to Scripture" (Drake, *Discoveries and Opinions,* p. 203).

102. Ibid.

103. Galileo, *Opere* 19:322–323.

104. The actual instructions for correcting copies of *De Revolutionibus* were not published until 15 May 1620 (ibid., 19:400–401).

105. See Owen Gingerich, "The Censorship of Copernicus' *De Revolutionibus*," *Annali dell'Istituto e Museo di Storia della Scienza di Firenza* 7 (1981): 45–61.

4

Galileo and the Church

William R. Shea

The condemnation of Galileo (1564–1642) is perhaps the most dramatic incident in the long and varied history of the relations between science and religious faith. Honest seekers after truth have been shocked by the attempt to suppress the claim that the earth moves and have seen in the trial of Galileo decisive evidence that religion is dangerous, not only when willfully perverted to secular ends but also, and perhaps more especially, when pursued by sincere men who consider themselves the stewards of God's revealed truth.[1] But Galileo's condemnation must be seen in historical perspective. We must remember that he was born in 1564, the year after the close of the Council of Trent, which may be considered as setting the tone of Roman Catholicism until a new spirit came to prevail with John XXIII in our own century. The opposition he encountered can only be understood if it is related to a period in which modern liberal values were far from commanding the assent that we have come to take for granted.

AN AGE OF RESTRICTIVE ORTHODOXIES

For the cultural historian and the student of the development of dogma, sixteenth-century Italy is notorious for its return to the rigor of an earlier age. This has conventionally been blamed on the Counter-Reformation, but to see it in this light is to take the symptom for the cause. The Counter-Reformation must not be viewed as an external and reactionary movement or wave of obscurantism that suddenly banished all intellectual creativity. It was rather a crisis of confidence that took place within the Italian mind.[2] The sack of Rome in 1527 and the collapse of the Florentine Republic in 1530, followed by Span-

114

ish domination over most of the peninsula, left Italians sorely disillusioned. Many lost faith in reforms aimed solely at the improvement of political institutions and became not only willing but anxious to exchange the burden of freedom for the security of regulated order. One notices this in the greater emphasis on the authority of princes and the new accent on the importance of titles, even if those who bore them had to be fixed up with spurious genealogies and endowed with the nobility somehow inherent in the cities of their birth.

The writings of Aristotle that had earlier stimulated lively discussion were increasingly turned into rigid dogma and a mechanical criterion of truth. Other philosophical systems were viewed with suspicion. When the Platonic chair of Francesco Patrizi (1529–1597) at the University of the Sapienza in Rome fell vacant at his death, Pope Clement VIII consulted Cardinal Robert Bellarmine (1542–1621), who had recently been called from Naples as papal theologian and counselor to the Holy Office. Bellarmine judged that Platonism contained more insidious subtleties than Aristotelianism—not because it was more erroneous but on account of its deceptive affinity with Christianity. Platonism was therefore more dangerous than paganism, and Bellarmine recommended suppression of the chair.[3] The widely accepted authority of Aristotle helped to make his disciple Thomas Aquinas (1224–1274) the most popular guide to the meaning of the faith in the late sixteenth century. Named a doctor of the church in 1567, Aquinas was considered the supreme authority in theology by Cardinal Bellarmine. The Jesuit *Ratio Studiorum,* although permitting deviation from Aquinas's theology on particulars, prescribed dismissal for any professor who showed himself hostile to the system as a whole. The task of theology under these circumstances was chiefly to systematize and to clarify the faith, conceived as a body of coherent intellectual propositions, in such a way as to maximize its certainty and finality. The articulation of Catholic belief almost became an administrative problem, and Bellarmine an administrator of doctrines. He organized them into systems so that they might be directed, in their most unequivocal and effective form, against doubt and heresy. Indeed, to make confrontation easier he even systematized the views of his opponents.[4]

The cultural authoritarianism of the papacy was greatly assisted by the Italianization of the papal court and the growth of a centralized bureaucracy within the church. At the beginning of the sixteenth century the Sacred College of Cardinals numbered thirty-five, of whom twenty-one (60 percent) were Italians. By 1598, when the number had risen to fifty-seven, forty-six (more than 80 percent) were from Italy.[5] A similar reduction in the proportion of foreigners was occurring at the lower levels of the papal bureaucracy. The Italian influence had already been decisive at the Council of Trent (1545–1563), called to formulate a response to the Protestant challenge; there, of 270 bishops attending at one time or another, 187 were Italian, 31 Spanish, 26 French, and 2 German. Moreover, by the procedural rules adopted in 1545, only bishops and the generals of a few religious orders could vote in the full sessions. This decision strengthened the Italian contingent, many of whom were financially dependent on the papacy and therefore under its influence. The sharp increase in the number of cardinals reduced the importance of individual figures, as, in an aristocratic age, did the elevation of clergy of low social origins. The sudden appointment, in 1583, of nineteen new cardinals by Gregory XIII, without consultation or advance notice, ruffled the feathers of those already belonging to the Sacred College but led to little open resistance. Sixtus V (1585–1590) took the further step of dividing the papal bureaucracy into fifteen smaller bodies that functioned separately and henceforth rarely assembled as a whole. This effectively converted the Curia from a quasi-constitutional agency into an appointive and specialized bureaucracy. In his justification of papal claims, the *Controversia Generalis de Summo Pontifice*, Cardinal Bellarmine argued that a monarchical form of government was preferable to a democratic one because it was more natural.[6] And Bellarmine did not hesitate to tell Catholic princes that they had a moral obligation to enforce true belief among their subjects.[7]

This reassertion of pontifical authority is likely to appear anachronistic. European life had been too thoroughly secularized to give any hope of success to the effort to impose an ecclesiastical tutelage. But none of this was obvious in Italy during the latter half of the sixteenth century: the sufferings, the fragmentation, and the weakness of Italy made the new secular accomplishments appear singularly vulnerable. Ecclesiastical authority appeared to triumph and thus to fulfill the values of the Counter-Reformation.[8] But the aspirations of Rome were also based on faith in the ultimate course of history arising not from a scrutiny of actual conditions but from divine promise. For Rome, what ought to be must eventually be. Meanwhile she would do everything in her power to hasten the event.

At the end of the sixteenth century her efforts intensified. Heartened by signs that the Turks could be beaten, and supported by powerful new religious orders, such as the Jesuits, and a reorganized and efficient bureaucracy, the papacy mounted a systematic campaign against the dangerous political and philosophical ideas of the Renaissance and the Reformation. The chronology of the papal counteroffensive is significant. In 1559 Paul IV issued the first official

Roman Index of Prohibited Books, an undiscriminating list, which included all the works of Erasmus, all the production of sixty-one printers, and all translations of the Bible into vernacular languages.[9] Its harshness was mitigated by the Council of Trent in 1562, but shortly thereafter, under the pontificate of Pius V (1566–1572), it became implacably severe. Pius changed the nature of the Index, intending it no longer as a fixed list of condemned writings but as a continuous action of vigilance and censorship; in 1571 he set up a special Congregation of the Index to oversee this enterprise.

Thus by the end of the sixteenth century, the Catholic church appeared to have emerged from the struggle against Protestantism with renewed strength. It continued to keep an eye on theologians, such as Michel Baius and Bartolomé de Carranza, but it now extended its vigilance to all manifestations of social and spiritual life; that is, it reached beyond the religious realm to ethics, politics, philosophy, art, and even manners and customs.

The last decade of the sixteenth century and the early years of the seventeenth produced a wave of ideological assaults and condemnations. Although Niccolò Machiavelli had been on the Index since 1559, he was systematically refuted only after 1589; in that year Giovanni Botero's *Della ragion di stato* appeared, closely followed by the conservative works of Antonio Possevino and Tommaso Bozio and by Pedro de Ribadeneira's *Princeps Christianus*. The works of Jean Bodin were condemned in 1592; two years later his political doctrines were refuted by Fabio Albergati. It was also at this time that the Platonism of Patrizi was denounced and the old philosopher forced to profess his total submission. The work of Bernardino Telesio was proscribed as subversive in 1596, and nine years later his views were sweepingly condemned. During the same period Pietro Pomponazzi's condemnation was renewed, and Tommaso Campanella, Francesco Pucci, and Giordano Bruno were imprisoned for their ideas. Pucci perished at the stake in 1597, Bruno in 1600.[10]

During the pontificates of Gregory XIII (1572–1585) and Sixtus V (1585–1590) the radical papism of Augustinus Triumphus (fourteenth century) was revived in the form of his *Summa de Potestate Ecclesiastica*. This work, printed four times between 1582 and 1585, encouraged the view that all particular kingdoms and republics are subordinate to a world state under papal leadership. Gregory and Sixtus were convinced that Christendom must become an effective political reality. Any fragmentation of the social order was judged intrinsically evil, the expression and consequence of sin. Individuals and governments were considered subject to a single eternal system of justice based ultimately on eternal and divine law, of which the Catholic church

was sole guardian and interpreter. In this climate of opinion a revolution in science or any other field of human endeavor could easily
be perceived as a threat unless shown to agree with the teachings of
the church.

GALILEO'S EXEGETICAL CHALLENGE

The heliocentric theory had been given scientific status by Nicolaus
Copernicus in his *De Revolutionibus Orbium Caelestium* of 1543, but it
was not until the invention of the telescope in the first decade of the
seventeenth century that it received sufficient confirmation to pose a
problem to the traditional imagery embedded in the Christian worldview. When Galileo turned his looking glass to the heavens in 1609,
he discovered fresh arguments for the centrality of the sun in the
phases of Venus and the satellites of Jupiter. Although the new observations were suggestive, they were by no means conclusive, and
the debate over Copernicanism, which had flagged, received new
impetus. Galileo's *Sidereal Messenger,* published in 1610, was an instant
success, as was his trip to Rome the next year, when the Jesuits
publicly confirmed his telescopic discoveries and Prince Federico Cesi
(1585–1630) made him a member of the Accademia dei Lincei. So great
was the applause that Cardinal Francesco Maria del Monte wrote to
the grand duke Cosimo II: "Were we living in the ancient Roman
Republic, I have no doubt that a statue would be erected in the Cam-
pidoglio in honor of his [Galileo's] outstanding merit."[11]

Galileo was elated by his warm reception in Rome, but an editorial
incident that occurred when Prince Cesi offered to publish his *Letters
on Sunspots* in 1612 should have made him wary of theologians. The
cavils of the censors forced successive revisions upon him, and it is
perhaps in an editorial incident of this kind that we can appreciate
the day-to-day workings of the Counter-Reformation.

The book was to have opened with a letter from Marc Welser in
which he quoted from Matthew 11:12: "The kingdom of heaven suffers
violence, and men of violence take it by force." The censors objected
to the quotation as likely to give the impression that astronomers
hoped to conquer a domain that was the prerogative of theologians.
To allay these fears, the passage was paraphrased to read: "Already
the minds of men assail the heavens, and the more valiant conquer
it."[12] Although there was no significant change in content, the biblical
passage had disappeared! In a second passage Galileo had written
that "divine goodness" had directed him to display the Copernican
system publicly. The censors had him substitute "favorable winds."[13]

A third amendment reveals the censors' desire to save the incorruptibility of the heavens, a doctrine to which they still subscribed.[14] In his original version Galileo had described the immutability of the heavens as "not only false, but erroneous and repugnant to the indubitable truths of the Scriptures," and had attributed the new astronomy to divine inspiration. When the censors demurred, he produced a new draft in which he called his own theory "most agreeable to the indubitable truths of Holy Writ" and praised his predecessors for their subtlety in finding ways of reconciling biblical passages on the mutability of the heavens with the conflicting evidence in favor of their immutability.[15] The tacit implication was that, since theologians had long interpreted the texts to show their agreement with Aristotelian doctrine, there already existed in the church a nonliteral way of reading biblical passages on astronomy. The censors deemed the revision inadequate and demanded a third version, in which Galileo reluctantly excised all mention of Scripture.

The attitudes of both the censors and Galileo are instructive. On the one hand, the censors adamantly refused a layman the right to meddle with Scripture. On the other, Galileo was inclined to describe his own point of view as "divinely inspired" and to brand that of his opponents "contrary to Scripture." The popular conception of Galileo as a martyr for freedom of thought is an oversimplification. That his views were different from those of the majority of the academic establishment did not make him a liberal. In philosophy he replaced the dogmatism of Aristotle with an equally dogmatic faith in the validity of a mathematical interpretation of nature. In politics he was weary of the time-consuming demands of democracy and longed for the haven of a princely court. In 1610 he pointed out in no uncertain terms that he had left the Venetian Republic for the grand duchy of Tuscany because freedom from teaching duties could only be granted by an absolute ruler.[16]

Galileo no doubt cherished the hope that the church would endorse his opinions. Along with many of his contemporaries he looked to an enlightened papacy as an effective instrument of scientific progress. But what Galileo does not seem to have understood is that the Catholic church, attacked by Protestants for neglecting the Bible, found itself compelled, in self-defense, to harden its ground. Whatever appeared to contradict Holy Writ had to be treated with the utmost caution.

Galileo's favorite pupil, the Benedictine priest Benedetto Castelli (1578–1643), was appointed to the chair of mathematics at the University of Pisa in November 1613. In December of that year he was invited to dine with the grand duke Cosimo II, his mother the grand duchess Christina of Lorraine, and several dignitaries. The conversation turned to Galileo's celestial discoveries. Everyone praised them except the grand duchess, who, prompted by a professor of philosophy, began to raise objections from Scripture against the motion of the earth. Castelli replied as best he could and later reported the conversation to Galileo, who sent him a letter in which he outlined his views on Scripture. This was to form the basis of his *Letter to the Grand Duchess Christina* of 1615, the fullest statement of his views on the relations between science and religion.[17]

A Florentine layman, Lodovico delle Colombe, had criticized Galileo as early as 1610 for contradicting Scripture, but it was not until the fourth Sunday of Advent, 1614, that the matter became serious when Tommaso Caccini, a Dominican friar, preached against the motion of the earth and blasted mathematicians for promoting it. Galileo, incensed, complained to a distinguished preacher-general of the order, Fr. Luigi Maraffi, who apologized most courteously for the misdemeanor of a member of his order known for his intemperate and ill-advised rhetoric.[18] Galileo also wrote to Federico Cesi, asking how he could obtain redress. The advice of the religious, yet worldly-wise, prince could have taught him much about the Roman milieu he was so sorely to misjudge:

> Concerning the opinion of Copernicus, Bellarmine himself, who is one of the heads of the Congregation that deals with these matters, told me that he considers it heretical, and that the motion of the earth is undoubtedly against Scripture; so you can see for yourself. I have always feared that if Copernicus were discussed in the Congregation of the Index, they would proscribe him.[19]

Matters were brought to a head by the arrival in Rome, at the beginning of 1615, of a Carmelite priest, Paolo Antonio Foscarini (ca. 1580–1616), who had just published a letter on the *Opinion of the Pythagoreans and Copernicus Regarding the Motion of the Earth*. Foscarini made a forceful but serene plea for the compatibility of the Copernican hypothesis with Scripture. He did not assert that the new theory was true, but argued that the Bible was written to be understood by all men and hence employed popular rather than scientific language. God chose to reveal only what could not be discovered by the light of reason; the rest he left to human disputation.[20] Foscarini was anxious to make his views known and therefore wrote to Bellarmine himself, enclosing a copy of his book. The cardinal tactfully replied that, to the best of his knowledge, the motion of the earth had not yet been proved and that it was best treated as a convenient device rather than a physical truth since it ran counter to clear biblical assertions about the rising and setting of the sun. Bellarmine then added:

> It cannot be answered that this is not a matter of faith, for if it is not a matter of faith *ex parte objecti* [with respect to the subject matter], it is a matter of faith *ex parte dicentis* [with respect to the one who asserts it]. Hence a man who denied that Abraham had two sons and Jacob twelve would be as much a heretic as one who denied the Virgin Birth of Christ, since both are declared by the Holy Ghost through the mouths of the prophets and the apostles.

The cardinal, however, was far from taking an intolerant and inflexible stance:

> If there were a true demonstration that the sun is at the center of the world and the earth in the third sphere, and that the sun does not revolve around the earth but the earth around the sun, then we would have to use great care in explaining those passage of Scripture that seem contrary. . . . But I cannot believe that there is such a demonstration until someone shows it to me.

Bellarmine proceeded to point out that using a theory to compute the position of the planets is not tantamount to affirming its physical reality. He was unmoved by the analogy, already invoked by Copernicus, of the beach that appears to recede when we leave the harbor aboard ship. No one, he pointed out, ever argued that the shore and not the ship was in motion.[21]

The cardinal's letter was sent to Galileo, who wrestled with the theological arguments. Replying to the objection that the motion of the sun is a matter of faith *ex parte dicentis* if not *ex parte objecti*, Galileo claimed that the Council of Trent upheld the authority of Scripture only in matters of faith and morals:

> Having said therefore *in rebus fidei* [in matters of the faith], we see that the Council meant *in rebus fidei ratione objecti* [in matters of the faith by reason of the object]. It is much more a matter of faith that Abraham had sons and that Tobit had a dog, because it is stated in Scripture, than that the earth moves . . . , for since there have always been men who have had two, four, six, or no sons . . . there does not appear any reason or cause why the Holy Spirit should state in such matters anything but the truth, since the affirmative and the negative are equally credible for all men. But this is not so with the motion of the earth and the immobility of the sun. These propositions are far removed from the comprehension of the common people.[22]

GALILEO'S CONCEPTION OF SCIENCE

Galileo seems to have been oblivious to the danger of trying to enlighten the foremost Catholic theologian of the day on the interpretation of the decrees of the Council of Trent. He also jeopardized his case by overstating the degree of proof that he could provide:

> It is prudent to believe that there is no proof that the earth moves until it has been produced, and we do not ask that anyone believe such a thing without proof. On the contrary, for the good of the church, we have no other wish than that what is adduced by the followers of this doctrine be strictly examined and that nothing be granted unless it greatly outweighs the rival arguments. If they are only 90 percent right, we shall consider them refuted. . . . We can afford to be so generous because it is clear that those who are of the wrong position cannot have any valid reason or experiment, whereas for those on the right side everything necessarily fits.

Commenting on the relative motion of the boat and the shore, he wrote:

> The error of regarding the apparent motion of the shore and the immobility of the boat is clear to us once we have observed several times the motion of the boat from the shore, and the shore from the boat. Thus if we could stand on the earth and then go to the sun or some other planet, perhaps we would gain certain and sensory knowledge as to which moves.[23]

But would such sensory evidence in fact yield certainty? A lunar inhabitant would see the earth and the sun revolve around *his* planet, and he would *feel himself* to be at rest.

Why did Galileo thus overstate his case? To make sense of his claims, we must understand his conception of science. We can hardly overestimate the importance of the ideas that a scientist brings to his scientific work, especially those that concern what he looks for and how he goes about finding it. Before a scientist can even begin to work, he must have some idea about what it means to know—that is, to know scientifically—and at least a general plan for advancing toward his knowledge. These ideas we may call the scientist's heuristic structure.

Galileo never vouchsafed a definition of science or a systematic account of scientific procedure. Yet his practice is eloquent. There is no doubt that he considered himself a disciple of Archimedes and that he believed mathematics to be the key to the interpretation of nature:

Philosophy is written in this great book—I mean the universe—which stands continually open to our gaze, but it cannot be understood unless one first studies the language and the characters in which it is written. It is written in the language of mathematics, and its characters are triangles, circles, and other geometrical figures, without which is it humanly impossible to understand a single word of it.[24]

This view of nature is the hidden root of natural science in the Renaissance. Galileo loathed people who reiterated "trumpetlike" everything that was old, but he adhered dogmatically to the notion that the world was written in mathematical symbols. His instinct for theoretical elegance told him that Copernicus was right, and although the actual observations were only partially in his favor, he was certain that he would be vindicated in the end. He displayed a scornful impatience with the complexity of data, a kind of self-righteousness characteristic of minds whose goals, when they address themselves to nature, are order and simplicity.

How did this outlook agree with early-seventeenth-century attitudes? Despite considerable opposition, Aristotle's view that true theories are discoverable still held sway in physics, while astronomy was dominated by the Ptolemaic reliance on geometrical arguments to "save the phenomena" without necessarily claiming that these arguments were true in nature. Hence, the orthodoxy of the day called for naive realism in physics and instrumentalism in astronomy.

Aristotle's position is particularly important because, however much his latter-day opponents attacked him, they usually retained more of his philosophy than they would have been fond of admitting. Galileo attacked several of Aristotle's ideas, but he never queried Aristotle's scientific realism—namely, the view that there is a uniquely true physical theory, discoverable by human powers of reason and observation, and that alternative theories are consequently false. Where Galileo differed from Aristotle was in his conception of the nature of this physical reality. To speak very broadly, Aristotle looked at nature as a process by which things fulfill their potential, and this turned speculation away from questions of structure and mechanism toward questions of function and development. This concern with teleology was allied with the belief that natural philosophy could be built directly on perception and that mathematics could not explain the colorful and qualitatively determined facts of common experience. Galileo considered such an approach naive and misleading, and he sought to transcend the limitations of Aristotelian empiricism by claiming that reality is mathematical in form and that mathematical theory should determine the very structure of experimental research.

In this he was following the ancient mathematician Archimedes, who was commonly regarded by Galileo's contemporaries as a Platonist. Galileo's mathematical essentialism (the view that nature is basically mathematical) must, in fact, be seen against the background of the Platonic revival of the period, especially in Florence, despite the fact that Galileo differed from Plato in the character of his essentialism. Plato had held that the physical world was a copy or likeness of a transcendent, ideal world of mathematical forms; it was an inexact copy, and therefore physics could never yield absolute truth but only likely stories. Galileo, by contrast, held that the world actually consisted of the mathematical primary and secondary qualities and their laws and that these laws were discoverable in detail and with absolute certainty.

CONFLICT AND CONDEMNATION

It was in this frame of mind that Galileo, encouraged by his admirers, expanded the letter to Castelli into a brilliant treatise on hermeneutics, which he dedicated to Cosimo's mother, the grand duchess Christina. His friends, however, warned him "to keep out of the sacristy" and urged him to reiterate frequently his willingness to submit to the proper authorities.[25] The specific shoals Galileo had to avoid were issues that are little dwelt on now but that were of paramount importance to men of his time. The four main ones were the possible existence of rational creatures on other planets, the location of hell, Christ's ascension, and the anthropocentric purpose of creation.

Giovanni Ciampoli (ca. 1590–1643), who was later to be involved in the publication of Galileo's *Dialogue,* wrote from Rome on 28 February 1615, warning Galileo of the dangerous speculations to which his astronomical discoveries gave rise:

> Your opinion of the phenomena of light and shade on the clear and spotted surfaces of the moon assumes some analogy between the earth and the moon. Someone adds to this and says that you assume that the moon is inhabited by men. Then another starts discussing how they could be descended from Adam or how they could have gotten out of Noah's ark, and many other extravagant ideas that you never even dreamed of. It is indispensable, therefore, to remove the possibility of malignant rumors by repeatedly protesting of one's willingness to defer to the authority of those who have jurisdiction over the human intellect in matters of the interpretation of the Scriptures.[26]

That people should have been exercised over the location of hell will come as a surprise to the modern reader, be he Christian or agnostic. Yet the belief that hell was a real place situated in the center of the earth was widely held among Christians well into the seventeenth century. Francesco Ingoli, the first secretary of the *Sacra Congregatio de Propaganda Fide*, one of the most successful ventures of the new bureaucracy of the Counter-Reformation, objected to Galileo on precisely this point.[27] Characteristically, he appealed for support to the Roman authority of the day, Cardinal Bellarmine. The cardinal's influential views are worth rehearsing. In a chapter of his *Controversia Generalis de Christo* entitled "Hell is a subterranean place distinct from the tombs," he gives several arguments, and concludes:

> The last is natural reason. There is no doubt that it is indeed reasonable that the place of devils and wicked damned men should be as far as possible from the place where angels and blessed men will be forever. The abode of the blessed (as our adversaries agree) is heaven, and no place is further removed from heaven than the center of the earth.[28]

Phrases such as "natural reason" and "it is indeed reasonable" illustrate how "reason," like its yokefellow "nature," could be made equivalent, in less guarded moments, to the usual assumptions of contemporary good sense, where "good sense" was implicitly defined by the Council of Trent.

Centuries of theological insight had purged the Christian supernatural order of cruder elements, and by the seventeenth century the spatial location of hell was no longer held by all Christians to be an article of faith. But side by side with this rational religion, or concealed beneath it, there still persisted mental habits more deep-rooted and more ancient, which expressed themselves in the pictorial beliefs Bellarmine was defending. It is, of course, easier to think pictorially than abstractly; hence the vitality, for instance, of popular demonology. The factual basis of Christ's ascension seemed also to be imperiled by the motion of the earth. Here again the diagrammatic representation of theory that placed the sun at the center of the universe and the earth above or below it added to the difficulty of visualizing Christ ascending into the uppermost region of the heavens.[29] Finally, the notion that the world had been created for mankind set up psychological barriers to accepting the earth as merely another planet revolving about the sun. After his interview with the archbishop of Pisa in 1615, Benedetto Castelli wrote to Galileo: "He took but a single reason from his stock, omitting all others, and the gist of it was that

since all things are created for man, it is clearly a necessary consequence that the earth cannot move like the stars."[30]

It was with these difficulties in mind that Galileo set out to reconcile
the Scriptures with the Copernican theory by reinterpreting contentious passages in the Bible and confuting current "misinterpreta-
tions." Galileo's solution was to affirm that the "Word of God" can
be read not only in Scripture, where it is often to be understood
metaphorically (as when God is said to have hands and feet, or that
he is angry and repents) or according to the common parlance (as
when it is stated that the sun rises and sets), but also in nature, where
it is to be interpreted with all the rigor of mathematical language.
Nature, which is the undoubted word of God, we are never to re-
nounce. What, then, are we to do when Scripture, which we acknowledge to be supernaturally inspired, appears to conflict with
nature? In his *Letter to the Grand Duchess Christina*, Galileo offered two
quite different views of the relation between the Bible and natural
science. One series of arguments was to become the characteristic
reply of the latter part of the seventeenth century. According to this
line of argument, there can be nothing in Scripture contrary to reason,
but there are many things that are above reason. Moreover, where
Scripture appears to contradict reason it requires reinterpretation,
since God, the author of the two inspired books, cannot contradict
himself. No one prior to Galileo spoke with such clarity of the relationship between science and Scripture:

> I think that in discusssing natural problems we should not begin from the
> authority of scriptural passages, but from sensory experiences and nec-
> essary demonstrations; for Holy Scripture and nature proceed alike from
> the divine Word, the former as the dictate of the Holy Spirit and the latter
> as the faithful executrix of God's commands. Furthermore, Scripture,
> adapting itself to the understanding of the common man, is wont to say
> many things that appear to differ from absolute truth as far as the bare
> meaning of the words is concerned. Nature, on the contrary, is inexorable
> and immutable; she never transcends the limits of the laws imposed upon
> her, and she is indifferent whether her secret reasons and ways of oper-
> ating are understood by men. It would seem, therefore, that nothing
> physical that sense experience sets before our eyes, or that necessary
> demonstrations prove to us, should be called in question, not to say con-
> demned, because of biblical passages that have an apparently different
> meaning. Scriptural statements are not bound by rules as strict as natural
> events, and God is not less excellently revealed in these events than in
> the sacred propositions of the Bible.[31]

Quoting the *bon mot* of Cardinal Baronius—"The intention of the Holy
Ghost is to teach us how one goes to heaven, not how heaven goes"—

Galileo added that the aim of Scripture is not to disclose what we can know by our senses and intellect (for then why would God have endowed us with these faculties?) but what surpasses human understanding.[32] In his view, therefore, incidental references to physical phenomena in the Scriptures are simply irrelevant to problems of natural science: the conveyance of scientific truth is not the Bible's purpose.

But Galileo also made use of another line of argument that leads to a different conclusion. It was inspired by the traditional hermeneutics of Saint Augustine, who made clear that the literal interpretation of any given biblical passage that is not clearly allegorical or metaphorical is to be preferred at all times. Only when a *demonstrated* scientific truth conflicts with a passage as literally interpreted can that passage be reinterpreted. Galileo quotes Saint Augustine with approval on this point and then proceeds to observe:

> In the books of the sages of this world, some natural things are truly demonstrated while others are merely stated. As to the former, it is the office of wise theologians to show that they are not contrary to the Holy Scriptures; as to the latter, which are asserted but not rigorously demonstrated, if they contain anything contrary to Holy Writ, they are to be considered undoubtedly false and proved so by every possible means.[33]

The question, of course is: into which category does the heliocentric theory fall? Galileo was convinced that he had found a compelling physical proof of the motion of the earth. This is his celebrated, but unfortunately mistaken, argument from the tides. Galileo believed that the ebb and flow of the sea was caused by a combination of the earth's daily rotation on its axis and its annual revolution around the sun.[34] Confident that his new proof would take Rome by storm, Galileo journeyed to the Eternal City at the end of 1615. When the Tuscan ambassador, Pietro Guicciardini, heard that Galileo was coming, he quickly dispatched a letter to the secretary of state in Florence reminding him that Rome was hardly "a place to discuss things on the moon." Pope Paul V (1605–1621), apprised of Galileo's theory by the young Cardinal Alessandro Orsini, immediately replied: "You would do well to dissuade him from holding such a view."[35] The matter was referred to the Holy Office. The result was that Copernicus's *De Revolutionibus* and Foscarini's *Letter* were placed on the Index of Prohibited Books. Galileo, however, was spared any unpleasantness and even given a certificate by Cardinal Bellarmine to the effect that he had not been asked to recant any of his theories.

Galileo had practically resigned himself to silence when Cardinal Maffeo Barberini, a native Florentine, was elected pope in 1623 under

the name Urban VIII (1623–1644). In the following spring Galileo journeyed to Rome where Urban VIII granted him no less than six audiences; gave him a painting, two medals, several *Agni Dei*, and the
promise of a pension for his son; and, last but not least, agreed that
he could write about the motion of the earth provided he represented
it not as reality but as a scientific hypothesis. During his stay in Rome,
Galileo made the acquaintaince of Cardinal Frederic Eutel Zollern,
who offered to discuss the Copernican question with the pope before
his return to Germany. Zollern represented to the pope that the German Protestants were all in favor of the new system and hence that
it was necessary to proceed with the utmost caution before the church
attempted to settle the Copernican question. The pope replied that
the church had never declared the view of Copernicus to be heretical
and would not do so, but that there was no reason to suppose that
a proof of the Copernican system would ever be forthcoming.[36] Galileo
returned to Florence with this encouraging news and set to work on
his *Dialogue on the Two Chief World Systems*. Unfortunately, Cardinal
Zollern died in 1625, and Galileo lost a friend who could have been
a key witness at his trial eight years later. Misfortune also struck in
the form of ill health; between 1626 and 1629 Galileo was unable to
work with any regularity, and it was only in Janaury 1630 that he
managed to finish his long-awaited masterpiece. He hoped that it
would be steered through the shoals of Roman censorship by his
friends Cesare Ciampoli and the Dominican Niccolò Riccardi, who
had become Master of the Apostolic Palace and whose duty it was to
authorize the publication of books.

When Riccardi received the manuscript of the *Dialogue* from Galileo's hands in the spring of 1630, he passed it on to a fellow Dominican, Raffaello Visconti. Visconti was sympathetic to astronomy, but
his interests extended to astrology and the occult sciences as well.
He was a personal friend of Orazio Morandi, the abbot of S. Prassede
in Rome, who was known to have spent a considerable time in the
company of Antonio and Giovanni de' Medici, mastering the secrets
of the Hermetic tradition. In the spring of 1630, probably in the first
fortnight of May, Morandi published certain prophecies based on
astrological computations, among them one that predicted the early
death of the pope. Galileo, who had arrived in Rome on 3 May, was
almost certainly unaware of this incident when he received, on the
24th of May, an invitation to dine with Morandi in the company of
Visconti; but Roman gossip had already linked his name with theirs.
Galileo left Rome on 26 June, and shortly thereafter Morandi was
imprisoned in the Tor di Nona. Galileo requested information from
a mutual friend, who replied on 17 August that the trial was so secret

that there was no way of knowing what was happening. At the trial an "Astrological Discourse on the Life of Urban VIII" bearing Visconti's name was brought forward. Visconti must have been at least partly successful in his plea of innocence, since he was only banished from Rome, while several others received heavy sentences. Morandi himself died in prison on 9 October 1630, before the completion of his trial.

In the spring of 1631 Urban VIII issued a bull (renewing the prescriptions of Sixtus V's bull *Coeli et Terrae Creator* of 5 January 1586) against astrologers who claimed the power of knowing the future and of setting in motion secret forces for the good or harm of the living. Urban commanded that an eye should be kept on such magical arts as were directed against the life of the pope and that of his relatives down to the third degree. Guilty parties were to be punished not only with excommunication but also with death and confiscation of property. That Galileo's name should have been associated with those of Morandi and Visconti was unfortunate, to say the least. Little did he suspect that his intimacy with Ciampoli would prove even more damaging.

Urban VIII was a poet in his leisure hours and enjoyed the company of literary men, one of whom was Giovanni Ciampoli, his secretary of briefs. Ciampoli's relations with the pope were quite intimate, and he became confident that he could read his master's mind. He was also impatient to secure the cardinal's hat that Urban VIII distributed to men whom Ciampoli considered his inferiors. In his frustration he became reckless and allowed himself to be befriended by acquaintances of the Spanish cardinal Gaspare Borgia, the spokesman of Philip IV and a thorn in Urban's flesh. When Cardinal Borgia publicly protested against the pope's position in the struggle between France and the House of Hapsburg in a stormy consistory on 8 March 1632, Urban decided to purge his entourage of pro-Spanish elements. He was particularly incensed upon hearing of Ciampoli's relations with the Spaniards. He stripped Ciampoli of his considerable powers and in August 1632 exiled him to the governorship of the small town of Montalto; Ciampoli was never allowed to return to Rome.

Ciampoli's downfall was to have important consequences for Galileo. In 1630 and 1631 Ciampoli had played a vital role in securing permission for the printing of Galileo's *Dialogue*. Visconti had informed Riccardi that he approved of the book and that it needed only a few minor corrections. Riccardi, after considerable anguish and delay, granted the *imprimatur*, first for Rome, later for Florence where it was to be censored by the local consultor of the Inquisition. He insisted, however, that the preface and the conclusion be forwarded to him. When the Florentine censor gave permission to go to press in September 1630, Riccardi began to raise difficulties and to claim that Galileo had agreed to return to Rome to discuss the final draft. Meanwhile, an outbreak of plague had rendered travel between Florence and Rome difficult, and Riccardi proposed that a copy of the work be sent to Rome "to be revised by Monsignor Ciampoli and myself."[37] Even this requirement was eventually waived, and thereafter Riccardi heard no more of the book until a printed copy reached him in Rome; above the Florentine *imprimatur* he discovered, to his horror, his own approbation. As Urban VIII remarked to the Tuscan ambassador, "the name of the Master of the Holy Palace has nothing to do with books printed elsewhere."[38] Summoned to account for his behavior, Riccardi excused himself by saying that he had received orders to license the book from Ciampoli himself.[39]

The *Dialogue* had gone to press in June 1631. The publisher had decided to print a thousand copies, a large edition for the time, and the work was not completed until 21 February 1632. Copies did not reach Rome until the end of March or early April, thus bursting onto the Roman scene only a few weeks after the consistory in which Cardinal Borgia attacked Urban VIII. Any "Ciampolata," as Urban put it,[40] was bound to be looked at closely. Moreover, the Roman *imprimatur* on a Florentine publication was bound to arouse suspicion. Riccardi was instructed to write to the Florentine inquisitor and have a ban placed on the sale of Galileo's book pending further notice. In the climate of deep suspicion that followed the Borgia incident, even the emblem of three dolphins (which could be associated with Hermetism) on the frontispiece caused concern. It was with relief that Riccardi learned that the device was not Galileo's but the printer's and appeared on all of his publications.

In the summer of 1632 Urban VIII ordered a Preliminary Commission to investigate the licensing of the *Dialogue*. In the file on Galileo in the Holy Office the Commission found an unsigned memorandum of an injunction, allegedly received by Galileo in 1616, "not to hold, teach or defend *in any way whatsoever*" that the earth moves.[41] The authenticity of the document is now contested, but the commissioners considered it genuine and concluded that Galileo had contravened a formal order of the Holy Office.[42] In the light of this discovery Galileo was summoned to Rome, arriving, after much delay, on 13 February 1633; he remained in Rome as guest of the Tuscan ambassador while three theologians read his *Dialogue* to ascertain whether he had presented the Copernican doctrine as a proved fact rather than a hypothesis. The closing paragraph of the *Dialogue* contained a statement, proposed by Urban himself, to the effect that the Copernican view was "neither true nor conclusive" and that "it would be excessive boldness for anyone to limit and restrict the divine power and wisdom to one particular fancy of his own."[43] Unfortunately, Galileo had put these words into the mouth of Simplicio, the Aristotelian pedant, who cuts such a poor intellectual figure throughout the *Dialogue*. The theologians were quick to spot this; and the pope, when it was called to his attention, was personally affronted.

On 12 April Galileo was summoned to the Holy Office; there he was kept in custody and twice interrogated, before being allowed to return to the residence of the Tuscan ambassador. He appeared again before the tribunal on 10 May and 21 June, but at no time was he physically tortured or molested. In the end, despite a vigorous denial that he had intended to argue in favor of the truth of the heliocentric system, Galileo was judged to have contravened the orders of the church. On the morning of 22 June 1633 he was taken to a hall in the convent of Santa Maria sopra Minerva in Rome, where he was made to kneel while the sentence condemning him to imprisonment was read. Still kneeling, Galileo was ordered to abjure his error. He recanted in the following words:

> I, Galileo Galilei, son of the late Vincenzio Galilei of Florence, aged seventy years, tried personally by this court, and kneeling before you, most Eminent and Reverend Lord Cardinals, Inquisitors-General throughout the Christian Republic against heretical depravity, having before my eyes the most Holy Gospels, and laying my own hands on them, do swear that I have always believed, do now believe, and with God's help will in the future believe all that the Holy Catholic and Apostolic Church does hold, preach, and teach. But since I, after having been admonished by this Holy Office entirely to abandon the false opinion that the sun is the center of the universe and immovable, and that the earth is not the center of the same and that I was neither to hold, defend, nor teach in any manner whatsoever, either orally or in writing, the said false doctrine, . . . did write and cause to be printed a book in which I treat of the said already condemned doctrine, and bring forward arguments of much efficacy in its favor, without arriving at any solution; I have been judged vehemently suspected of heresy, that is, of having held and believed that the sun is the center of the universe and immovable and that the earth is not the center of the same nor immovable.
>
> Nevertheless, wishing to remove from the minds of your Eminences and all faithful Christians this vehement suspicion reasonably conceived against me, I abjure with a sincere heart and unfeigned faith, I curse and detest the aforesaid errors and heresies. . . . And I swear that for the future I will neither say nor assert in speaking or writing such things as may bring upon me similar suspicion. . . .[44]

Galileo was not formally incarcerated but was allowed to leave for Siena and later Florence, where he was confined to his country estate.

Galileo sought comfort in work, and within two years he completed the *Two New Sciences*, the book to which his lasting fame as a scientist is attached. When he cast about for a publisher, he came up against a new problem: the church had issued a general prohibition against printing or reprinting any of his books. Through a friend in Venice, Galileo's manuscript reached the famous publisher Louis Elzevir in Holland, a Protestant country over which the Roman church had no power. At once Elzevir undertook the printing; Galileo feigned surprise and pretended not to know how the manuscript had left Italy. Although it is unlikely that anyone believed his story, the church let the publication of the *Two New Sciences* in 1638 go unchallenged. Galileo, however, was never successful in obtaining the pardon he longed for and was still under house arrest when he received the visit of the young English poet John Milton. Of this visit little is known, but the context in which Milton mentions it is highly significant. It occurs in the *Areopagita*, a speech addressed to Parliament against an ordinance requiring the licensing of all books:

> I could recount what I have seen and heard in other countries where this kind of Inquisition tyrannizes . . . that this was it which had damped the glory of Italian wits; that nothing had been there written now these many years but flattery and fustian. There it was that I found and visited the famous Galileo, grown old, a prisoner of the Inquisition, for thinking in astronomy otherwise than the Franciscan and Dominican licensers thought.[45]

In fact, Galileo's condemnation was the result of the complex interplay of untoward political circumstances, personal ambitions, and wounded prides. Nevertheless, Milton was right in believing that the whole episode had the effect of inhibiting scientific speculation in Catholic countries. He was also right in sensing the underlying conflict between the authoritarian ideal of the Counter-Reformation and the nascent desire and need for freedom in the pursuit of scientific knowledge. Had Galileo been less devout, he could have refused to go to Rome; Venice offered him asylum. Had he been less convinced of the truth of his theory, he could have treated it as mere conjecture and remained at peace with the church. But Galileo could not resign himself to either course. He pressed for a prompt acceptance of his theories, and Urban VIII responded with a stern reaffirmation of the authority of the pope. Science and religion were both to suffer from the clash, and what could have been a fruitful dialogue proved to be a bitter feud. It was not until 1832 that Galileo's *Dialogue* was dropped from the Index of Prohibited Books and Catholics allowed to teach Copernicanism with complete freedom.

NOTES

The author wishes to thank the Social Sciences and Humanities Research Council of Canada and the McGill Faculty of Graduate Studies for supporting research related to this paper. He is also grateful to Paolo Galluzzi and Albino Babolin for their helpful advice, and to David C. Lindberg for his editorial assistance.

1. For an introductory account of Galileo's difficulties with the church see Jerome L. Langford, *Galileo, Science, and the Church*, rev. ed. (Ann Arbor: Univ. of Michigan Press, 1971); also Giorgio de Santillana, *The Crime of Galileo* (Chicago: Univ. of Chicago Press, 1955). Pietro Redondi has recently argued, in *Galileo eretico* (Turin: Einaudi, 1983), that the trial for teaching that the earth moves was a cover-up for the more serious charge that Galileo's atomism imperiled the Catholic dogma of transubstantiation. Redondi's case rests on the highly conjectural attribution of an anonymous letter to the Jesuit Orazio Grassi.

2. For a general account of the Counter-Reformation see Arthur G. Dickens, *The Counter Reformation* (London: Thomas & Hudson, 1968); Marvin R. O'Connell, *The Counter Reformation* (New York: Harper & Row, 1974).

3. Luigi Firpo, "Filosofia italiana e contriforma," *Rivista di filosofia* 41 (1950): 166, relying on I. Fuligatti, *Vita Roberti Bellarmini Politiani S.J.* (Antwerp, 1631), pp. 189–190.

4. Another great systematizer was the Dominican Melchior Cano, whose *De Locis Theologicis Libri Duodecim* was published in 1563 and reprinted six times before 1605; see P. Mandonnet, "Melchior Cano," *Dictionnaire de théologie catholique* 2:1538.

5. Jean Delumeau, *Vie économique et sociale de Rome dans la seconde moitié du XVIe siècle*, 2 vols. (Paris: E. de Boccard, 1957–1959), 1:219.

6. Robert Bellarmine, *Controversia Generalis de Summo Pontifice* 1.2, in *Opera Omnia*, 12 vols. (Paris: L. Vivès, 1870–1874), 1:464–465.

7. Bellarmine, *De Officio Principis Christiani Libri Tres* 1.11, in *Opera Omnia* 8:109–110.

8. See H. Outram Evennett, *The Spirit of the Counter-Reformation* (Cambridge: Cambridge Univ. Press, 1968), pp. 109–110.

9. Heinrich Reusch, *Die "Indices Librorum Prohibitorum" des sechzehnten Jahrhunderts* (Nieuwkoop: B. de Graaf, 1961), pp. 176–208.

10. Luigi Firpo, "Il processo di Giordano Bruno," *Rivista storica italiana* 60 (1948): 542–597; 61 (1949): 5–59; Luigi Firpo, "Processo e morte di Francesco Pucci," *Rivista di filosofia* 40 (1949): 371–405.

11. *Le opere di Galileo Galilei*, ed. Antonio Favaro, 20 vols. (Florence: G. Barbèra, 1899–1909), 11:119 (letter of 31 May 1611). On Galileo and Copernicanism see William R. Shea, *Galileo's Intellectual Revolution*, 2d ed. (New York: Science History Publications, 1977); Maurice Clavelin, *The Natural Philosophy of Galileo*, trans. A. J. Pomerans (Cambridge, Mass.: Harvard Univ. Press, 1978); Ernan McMullin, ed., *Galileo: Man of Science* (New York: Basic Books, 1967); *Discoveries and Opinions of Galileo*, trans. Stillman Drake (Garden City, N.Y.: Anchor, 1957); and Alexandre Koyré, *Galileo Studies*, trans. John Mepham (Atlantic Highlands, N.J.: Humanities Press, 1978).

12. Galileo Galilei, *Istoria e dimostrazioni intorno alle macchie solari*, in *Opere* 5:93.

13. Ibid., p. 238, and critical apparatus for lines 29–30.

14. As late as 1618 Federico Cesi found it necessary to argue that the heavens are not crystalline spheres. See his letter of 14 Aug. 1618 to Cardinal Bellarmine, "De caeli unitate, tenuitate fusaque et pervia stellarum motibus natura ex sacris litteris," and Bellarmine's reply, in Christoph Scheiner, *Rosa Ursina* (Bracciano, 1630), pp. 777–783.

15. Galileo, *Istoria e dimostrazioni*, in *Opere* 5:138–139, and critical apparatus for line 24.

16. Galileo's letter to a Florentine correspondent, Feb. 1610, *Opere* 10:233.

17. An incomplete translation of this work is given in Drake's *Discoveries and Opinions of Galileo*, pp. 175–216.

18. Letter from Luigi Maraffi to Galileo, 10 Jan. 1615, *Opere* 12:127.

19. Letter from Cesi to Galileo, 12 Jan. 1615, *Opere* 12:129.

20. Paolo Antonio Foscarini, *Lettera sopra l'opinione de Pittagorici e del Copernico della mobilità della terra* (Naples, 1615).

21. Letter from Bellarmine to Foscarini, 12 Apr. 1615, in Galileo, *Opere* 12:171–172.

22. "Considerazioni sopra l'opinione Copernicana," *Opere* 5:367–368.

23. Ibid., pp. 368–370.

24. Galileo, *The Assayer*, in *Discoveries and Opinions*, trans. Drake, pp. 237–238. Here and in what follows I have made substantial alterations to Drake's translations. See *Opere* 6:232.

25. Letter from Piero Dini to Galileo, 2 May 1615, *Opere* 12:175.

26. Letter from Ciampoli to Galileo, 28 Feb. 1615, *Opere* 12:146. As early as 1611 Campanella had used Galileo's discovery of similarities between the earth and the moon as a peg on which to hang some of his most daring speculations: "There is much to be discussed about the shape of the stars and the planets and the kind of government to be found among the inhabitants of celestial bodies. . . . If the moon is more contemptible than the earth . . . its inhabitants are less happy than we are" (letter to Galileo, 12 Jan. 1610, in Galileo, *Opere* 11:22). As such ideas became widespread, Galileo felt it necessary to write to Cardinal Giacomo Muti in 1616 to deny that he assumed the existence of rational creatures on the moon (letter to Muti, 28 Feb. 1616, *Opere* 12:240–241).

27. Ingoli, *De Situ et Quiete Terrae contra Copernicum Disputatio*, in Galileo, *Opere* 5:408.

28. Robert Bellarmine, *Controversia Generalis de Christo* 5.10, in *Opera Omnia*

1:418. Bellarmine also located purgatory and limbo at the center of the earth, near hell (*Controversia Generalis de Purgatorio*, 2.6, in *Opere Omnia* 3:109–112).

29. This was felt to be a serious difficulty by J. G. Locher, *Disquisitiones Mathematicae de Controversiis et Novitatibus Astronomicis* (Ingolstadt, 1614), p. 23; Paolo Foscarini, *Lettera sopra l'opinione de Pittagorici*, pp. 15–16; Marin Mersenne, *Quaestiones Celeberrimae in Genesim* (Paris, 1624), col. 897. Galileo sought to allay such fears in his *Dialogue Concerning the Two Chief World Systems*, trans. Stillman Drake, 2d ed. (Berkeley and Los Angeles: Univ. of California Press, 1967), p. 357.

30. Castelli to Galileo, 12 Mar. 1615, in Galileo, *Opere* 12:154.

31. *Discoveries and Opinions*, trans. Drake, pp. 182–183; *Opere* 5:316–317. This letter was first published by Matthias Bernegger in Strassburg in 1636, but it had already enjoyed a wide manuscript circulation; for example, in the "Fondo Corsiano" of the Roman Accademia dei Lincei alone, Ada Alessandrini found four manuscript copies (*Galileo Galilei: Celebrazioni del IV centenario della nascita* [Rome: Accademia dei Lincei, 1965], p. 174).

32. *Discoveries and Opinions*, trans. Drake, p. 186; *Opere* 5:319.

33. *Discoveries and Opinions*, trans. Drake, p. 194; *Opere* 5:327.

34. For Galileo's argument see Shea, *Galileo's Intellectual Revolution*, pp. 172–189.

35. Guicciardini to Curzio Picchena, 5 Dec. 1615, in Galileo, *Opere* 12:242.

36. Letter from Galileo to Federico Cesi, 8 June 1624, *Opere* 13:182.

37. Letter from Castelli to Galileo, 21 Sept. 1630, *Opere* 14:150.

38. Letter from Niccolini to Andrea Cioli, 5 Sept. 1632, *Opere* 14:384.

39. From an account of Galileo's trial written by Giovanfrancesco Buonamici, in Galileo, *Opere* 19:410.

40. Letter from Niccolini to Cioli, 26 Feb. 1633, *Opere* 15:56. Ciampoli was not the only dignitary to incur the wrath of the pope. In July 1633 Cardinal Roberto Ubaldini, suspected of sympathizing with the Spaniards, was deprived of "the share of the poor cardinals," namely the emolument paid by the Holy See to prelates who had no independent means of subsistence. Ubaldini was one of the cardinals to have received a telescope from Galileo, and in his letter of acknowledgment had professed himself eager to help Galileo (letter of 29 July 1618, *Opere* 12:401).

41. *Opere* 19:322.

42. On this document see de Santillana, *Crime of Galileo*, pp. 261–274. Langford, *Galileo, Science, and the Church*, pp. 93–97; Stillman Drake and Giorgio de Santillana, in appendices to Ludovico Geymonat, *Galileo Galilei: A Biography and Inquiry into His Philosophy of Science*, trans. Stillman Drake (New York: McGraw-Hill, 1965), pp. 205–225.

43. *Opere* 7:489. The pope's argument had already appeared in print in Agostino Oregio, *De Deo Uno* (Rome, 1629), pp. 193–195; quoted in Antonio Favaro, *Gli oppositori di Galileo VI: Maffeo Barberini* (Venice: Antonelli, 1921), pp. 26–27.

44. *Opere* 19:406–407; see also Langford, *Galileo, Science, and the Church*, pp. 153–154.

45. *The Essential Milton*, ed. Douglas Bush (London: Chatto & Windus, 1949), p. 183.

5
Catholicism and Early Modern Science

William B. Ashworth, Jr.

Whenever the issue of Catholicism and early modern science is raised, it is usually quickly narrowed to the subject of Galileo and the church, which is still such a lively and unsettled question that we have rarely had the time or the stamina to look at the rest of the story. For this one occasion, the great Florentine has been removed from the scene. The background pattern that remains is the subject of this essay.

First a comment about scope: It is clear that my task, if conceived as a comprehensive analysis of the interaction of science and Catholicism in the seventeenth century, is hopeless; such a project, done properly, would take volumes. However, it does seem possible within a limited space to suggest the kinds of questions we ought to be asking and, in a tentative way, the probable nature of the answers. I am encouraged in this enterprise, somewhat perversely, by two rather bleak historiographical observations. First of all, the few essays so far attempted on this subject have aimed far too low, seemingly content with compiling lists of Catholic scientists; such attempts have been further compromised by an obviously apologetic posture.[1] Second, scholarship on the question of Protestantism and science has become hopelessly mired because it started off in the wrong direction, counting heads, collecting Calvinist-sounding quotations, and seeking parallels instead of connections.[2] No one, in other words, has been asking the right questions about either Protestantism or Catholicism and its relation to science. While others may yet rescue the Protestant question, my hope is to divert the inquiry regarding Catholicism and science to more fruitful ground. It seems to me that the essential questions are these: (1) In the case of the individual Catholic

136

scientist, is there evidence that his religious views affected his scientific work, in either his preconceptions, his motivation, his discoveries, or his conclusions? (2) In the case of Catholic scientists viewed collectively, do any tendencies or interpretations emerge that are distinctive enough to be called a Catholic pattern? (3) Were Catholic scientists helped or hindered by the church in its institutional capacity? (4) For the many scientists belonging to religious orders, how, if at all, did the rules and programs of their various orders influence their science?

VARIETIES OF CATHOLIC SCIENTIFIC EXPERIENCE

The seventeenth century witnessed remarkable changes in the philosophy, methodology, and content of science. In a short list of the important developments one might include the establishment of the mechanical philosophy, the discovery that the laws of nature are mathematical, the acceptance of a new cosmology and its ramifications, an increasing reliance on experiment, measurement, and observation, and a growing tenor of anti-Aristotelian sentiment. Many Catholics played roles, large and small, in all facets of this revolution. What we would like to know is whether there was anything in Catholic theology that made such changes harder, or easier, to perceive or to accept. Did Catholic scientists have a view of God, nature, reason, process, Scripture, or authority that one can characterize as peculiarly Catholic, and did these views facilitate, or hinder, any aspect of the metamorphosis of science? In short, what difference did the Catholic faith make for the seventeenth-century scientist?

In order even to begin to answer such a question, we must look first at individual cases. Ideally one would like to consider a large number of Catholic scientists, perhaps compiling tables of absence and presence in good Baconian style, but since an exhaustive analysis is obviously impossible, I present instead a filtered spectrum—a brief discussion of five scientists in sequence. I did not choose these five at random, as a sociologist might wish, but rather selected those I consider to be the most important of the period, a choice that reflects my own conviction that the scientific revolution was perpetrated by great scientists and not by some kind of population pressure or genetic drift. For each of these five, we wish to know the extent to which scientific stances were influenced by religious views and vice versa. With all this in mind, we can then ask whether any common features have emerged that may be said to characterize the Catholic scientist in the seventeenth century.

Marin Mersenne (1588–1648) provides an interesting point of departure for this excursus, since not only was he instrumental in the rise of the mechanical philosophy, but his motivation was, at least initially, exclusively religious.[3] Mersenne was alarmed in the 1620s by the growing threat of atheism (in its seventeenth-century sense of misbelief rather than disbelief). And for Mersenne the greatest danger lay in the philosophies of Italian naturalists such as Pietro Pomponazzi, Girolamo Cardano, and Giulio Cesare Vanini. Italian naturalism was considered dangerous to religion because it confused the natural with the supernatural and physics with metaphysics; essentially, it eliminated the boundaries between science and faith. Miracles, for example, were endangered by the naturalists, because in a world filled with sympathies and occult forces—with what Lenoble calls a "spontanéité indéfinie"—anything could happen naturally.[4] So Mersenne declared war not only on heterodoxy but on all occult philosophies, such as Hermetism, alchemy, and natural magic. His attack on Robert Fludd was not, as was the Kepler-Fludd altercation, a disagreement over the role of mathematics but a disagreement over the operations of nature. And in order to preserve the realm of the miraculous and supernatural, Mersenne was driven to mechanize the natural. He reduced nature to an ensemble of phenomena that proceed according to natural law, recognizing that some kind of natural order is a prerequisite for a miracle that is contrary to nature.[5] The mechanical philosophy, then, was Mersenne's instrument for preserving the realm of faith.

Having advocated a general philosophical position, Mersenne went further. He also maintained, and demonstrated by example, that the world of phenomena was worthy of study—that the laws of nature could be, and should be, determined by human observation and experiment. This attitude does not seem so surprising in the courtly Galileo, but Mersenne was a member of one of the most ascetic orders in all of France; as a Minim, he lived in perpetual Lent, practicing an extremely involved daily ritual. Yet Mersenne found it important and permissible to roll balls down planes, measure the rate of free fall, and determine the speed of sound. His example alone is sufficient to call in question the claim that personal observation of nature was uniquely associated with the rejection of religious authority advocated by Calvinism.[6]

Many consider Mersenne's greatest contribution to science to have been the correspondence network he established and presided over, and it is interesting that here too his motivation seems to have been at least partly religious. Mersenne had no illusions about the ability of humans to penetrate very far beyond the observation of phenomena; he judged absolute knowledge of the essence of things to be beyond our powers. But the Christian does not need absolute knowledge to live a life of faith, nor does a scientiest need to know causes in order to comprehend nature. So Mersenne concluded that the problems of science and faith could be worked out by gathering the opinions of intelligent men; by talking things over, a consensus of some kind could be reached that was good enough for all practical purposes.[7] The idea that group activity could lay to rest the skeptical demon was most unusual; only Francis Bacon at this time was having similar thoughts (for quite different reasons), and Bacon never put such ideas into practice. Mersenne did, and in the process sowed the seeds for the social transformation of the scientific enterprise in the last half of the century.

Before leaving Mersenne, it is important to note that while he was beyond question a man of sincere Catholic faith, many of his theological views were quite untypical of the age. He supported Galileo when it was most unfashionable; he saw no theological problems in Gassendi's proposed revival of Epicurean atomism; he encouraged Samuel Sorbière to publish a translation of Thomas Hobbes; he supported the trend in biblical criticism that culminated in the work of Richard Simon.[8] He was, in other words, tolerant beyond the norm of the times, whether Catholic or Protestant.

The religious beliefs of René Descartes (1596–1650) may have aroused the suspicions of Blaise Pascal, but Queen Christina had no qualms about the genuineness of his faith, for she converted to Catholicism in 1655 and gave the credit to Descartes. She was shrewder than many later critics, for Cartesian philosophy is quite inexplicable without God. The existence of God can be demonstrated by both causal and ontological arguments, and the proof of his existence is perhaps the most important link in the entire chain of deductions that gave rise to the Cartesian system. God's perfection alone can lay to rest the threat of the evil genius of the *Meditations*. He is the guarantor of right reason and of the reliability of clear and distinct ideas. It is God's immutability that ensures the existence of laws and nature and necessitates the conservation of motion in the world. It is God's continuous presence that conserves those laws. So God is considerably more than first cause for Descartes.[9]

Although Descartes believed that certain questions of theology could be answered by reason—the existence of God, the distinction of soul and body—he was very much opposed in general to rational theology. Matters of faith could be determined only by revelation; but matters of fact were the domain of reason and observation. Men abuse Scripture, he said, who use it to answer questions of reason, as do those who attempt to reason about faith. In truth, Descartes would have prefered to eliminate theology altogether, at least as represented by Scholasticism; it was an unnecessary middle ground between religion and philosophy, and the two realms of knowledge were better kept entirely separate.[10]

Descartes had a similar disdain for theological arguments drawn from nature. The world was not for Descartes a collection of signs that demonstrated divine attributes or pointed the path to God. He rejected outright any doctrine of final causes, stating that whatever the purposes of God, they were too impenetrable to be discerned by mere observation of nature. His stance was quite similar to that of Bacon and rather different from that of most contemporary Christians, Catholic as well as Protestant.[11]

Descartes's decision to ignore all theological questions except the ultimate one gave his work a flavor that could easily be disagreeable to more conventional philosophers and theologians. For all the attention he gave to God, his world of vortices was not noticeably Christocentric, a defect that Malebranche would later try to remedy. Descartes's assertion that doubt was a suitable vehicle for the acquisition of knowledge certainly came as a surprise to those weaned on Aquinas and seemed to many critics to undermine the very basis of religion (although Descartes himself did not apply his method to matters of faith). There are also passages in his work—particularly the posthumous treatises—that suggest dissimulation, as when Descartes asks us "in our imagination" to move out of sight of the world God actually created five or six thousand years ago and to consider a new world where the laws of nature, acting on chaotic matter, produced a world very much like our own.[12] Had Pascal been alive to read that, he would have had even more doubt about Descartes's sincerity.

But the most severe theological objection to Cartesianism would come from the implications of his theory of matter. Descartes's assurance that the worlds of faith and nature do not intersect ignored the reality of contemporary theology; and he failed to anticipate that, by equating matter with extension and denying the reality of secondary qualities, he had completely undermined the doctrine of the Eucharist. If accidents have no real existence, how could the accidents of bread remain while the substance was miraculously transformed into the body of Christ? Descartes was taken to task for this by Antoine Arnauld in the "Fourth Set of Objections" to the *Meditations*; and, while Descartes attempted to defend the compatibility of his matter theory with transubstantiation, he was not noticeably convincing, and most of the ensuing problems faced by Cartesians would grow out of this one deviation from Scholasticism, as we shall see in due course.[13]

At first glance Pierre Gassendi (1592–1655) seems to have traveled the same intellectual path as Descartes and Mersenne. Like his two contemporaries, he was adamantly opposed to Scholastic philosophy and Aristotelian science, and he bore a similar antipathy toward nature philosophies and alchemy. He too was profoundly affected by the skeptical revival of the period and was led ultimately to embrace a thoroughly mechanical philosophy of nature. But a closer look reveals that, while Gassendi may have started from the same point and reached some of the same conclusions, he really took an entirely divergent route, defended his conclusions quite differently, and held a view of the relation between science and religion that distinguished him markedly from both Descartes and Mersenne.[14]

Gassendi was by inclination a Christian humanist in the tradition of Erasmus. When he began in the 1620s, along with Mersenne, to rebel against Scholasticism, his dissatisfaction did not lead him to a rejection of all authority, as it had Descartes; instead he instituted a search for a better ancient authority, which he ultimately found in Epicurean atomism. As a Catholic priest he readily saw the atheistic implications of this mechanical philosophy of antiquity, but he believed that, properly refurbished, atomism could be completely compatible with Christian theology—certainly more compatible than Aristotelianism. And so he tailored an atomic philosophy according to Christian guidelines. Since an infinite number of atoms was incompatible with the idea of a provident God (in such a universe, everything possible will happen), Gassendi determined that the universe of atoms is finite. He added to the human corporeal soul a separate, incorporeal mind that God creates *ex nihilo*. By such careful custom-fitting, Gassendi fashioned a Christian atomism that, to his mind at least, suffered none of the inconsistencies inherent in Scholasticism (although in his later days he began to have some doubts).[15]

Gassendi thus ultimately arrived at a view of nature that was as mechanical as that of Descartes (although the two differed on important points, such as the possibility of a void and the divisibility of matter). But having gained a similar position, Gassendi defended it in quite a different way. It was evident to Descartes that matter was only extension; this conclusion could be rationally demonstrated. For Gassendi, by contrast, no fact of nature could be rationally demonstrated, and very few things, certainly not the nature of matter, were evident. Gassendi defended atomism because it was compatible with phenomena, whereas Aristotelianism was not. But it was one thing to say that atomism was plausible, quite another to say that we can learn precisely how the interaction of atoms causes sensible effects. Gassendi denied the possibility of gaining knowledge of such causes; only phenomena may be known, only effects may be observed, and the scientist need concern himself with nothing else.[16]

Gassendi's strict scientific empiricism seems to have been the product of his fideistic theology. In Gassendi's view, reason was useless for religious purposes, since all religious truth comes by faith. Consequently he opposed all forms of rational theology, objecting strongly, for example, to Descartes's attempts at a rational proof of the existence of God. But if certainty comes only through revelation, then the study of the sensible world, beyond the pale of faith, is doomed to uncertainty. And so the scientist must be satisfied with the observation of phenomena, and he must resist the temptation to reason about causes that he can never know.[17]

Gassendi's fideism led him to disagree with Descartes in one further respect. Descartes tried to insulate science from religion; Gassendi sought to remove the barriers. If our only certain truths are theological ones, it would be foolish indeed to ignore these when observing nature. And thus many of the premises of his atomic philosophy have an explicitly Christian origin. Consistent with this proposition is Gassendi's favorable opinion of arguments from design. Descartes rejected final causes out of hand, but Gassendi saw purpose in all of nature, and he suggested to Descartes that if he wanted to prove the existence of God, he should abandon reason and look about him; the order and harmony of the universe demonstrate God's existence and his attributes of goodness and providence.[18] For Gassendi, the Two Books (nature and Scripture) were not to be kept on separate shelves.

One last feature of Gassendi's thought is noteworthy: his adamant stand against occult causes and effects. His vehemence on this subject is a little strange, since if the knowledge of true causes is beyond our ability, then all causes are in a sense occult.[19] His antipathy does not seem to derive from a wish to preserve the supernatural, as it did for Mersenne; we can only conclude that Gassendi's atomistic philosophy, assumed as a hypothesis of convenience, took on the trappings of certitude as time went on, and thus any effect that could not be explained mechanically, by the interaction of atoms, was thrown out of court. Gassendi was neither the first nor the last scientist to proclaim the impossibility of certain knowledge while simultaneously proposing a host of rather certain explanations.[20]

If Gassendi still resists categorization, Blaise Pascal (1623–1662) positively defies it. At once Christian pessimist, Cartesian rationalist, scourge of the Jesuits, mystic, skeptic, and experimental physicist, he remains an enigma impossible to resolve. He was clearly a man of different faces at different times (and occasionally at the same time), and his observation about nature—"a sphere whose center is everywhere and circumference nowhere"—might be better applied to Pascal himself. Yet if we ignore temporarily the unsettled question whether the barometer experiments and the *Pensées* were the product of the same Pascal, I think we can make several general observations about the interplay of science and religion in this singular mind.[21]

Perhaps Pascal's most novel insight was his realization that authority plays different roles in religion and science. In his remarkable scientific manifesto, the preface to the unpublished "Treatise on the Vacuum," he asserted that in theology the authority of Scripture and the Fathers is the sole source of truth, so that we must "confound the insolence of those foolhardy souls who produce novelties in theology." In those matters subject to reason and the senses, however, authority is totally useless, and we should "pity the blindness of those who rely on authority alone in the proof of physical matters."[22] This striking bifurcation of authority allows us to make sense of many of the supposed inconsistencies in Pascal's thought—to understand how he could claim, on the one hand, that "to give complete certainty to matters incomprehensible to reason it suffices to show them in the sacred books" and, on the other, that "all the powers in the world can by their authority no more persuade people of a point of fact than they can change it!"[23] Even the pope drew Pascal's fire when he trespassed on the world of sense and reason. Pascal must join Mersenne as another counterexample to the notion that Protestants were better able to disregard authority in scientific matters.

Given this clear demarcation of the provinces of reason and faith, it is not surprising that Pascal spurned the very premise of rational theology. His distaste for reasoners in religion was evident early in his career, when he pursued Sieur de Saint-Ange all the way to the archbishop, disputing his claim that even the Trinity could be demonstrated by reason.[24] When the Jesuit Etienne Noël casually mentioned God in connection with the void in the barometer, Pascal replied—somewhat nastily—that the mysteries of the Divinity should not be profaned by scientific disputes.[25] In the "Preface" we are urged to be filled with horror at the wickedness of those who use reason alone in theology.[26] And this position is held, of course, all through the *Pensées*. Pascal's *coeur*, whatever it means, is certainly not reason discovering God.[27]

Pascal's feelings about religious arguments drawn from nature were more complex.[28] Unlike Descartes, Pascal *did* believe that nature expressed the handiwork of the Creator—that "God has represented the invisible in the visible."[29] And he did occasionally offer a religious truth gleaned from nature, as when he wrote: "Nature possesses forms of perfection to show that it is the image of God, and faults to show that it is only his image."[30] But this latent theology of nature is nipped in the bud by Pascal's deeper conviction that God is not manifest, but irretrievably *hidden* in nature. "God has hidden [truth] behind a veil," Pascal claims, and the study of nature will never lift that veil.[31] If truth lay in nature, then anyone might discover it and know God. But for Pascal, such knowledge comes only through Scripture and grace.

Nature became even more isolated from Pascal's theology because, as he so famously confessed, the contemplation of nature's immense complexity scared him to death. Because nature is graven with God's image, she too is infinite, and no matter how much we learn about nature, we still know nothing.[32] So Pascal pulled back from the brink, and his final position was that the road to God is not a walk through His garden. If you wish to convert the irreligious, abandon arguments from nature, for "to tell them that they have only to look at the smallest things that surround them, and they will see God openly . . . is to give them grounds for believing that the proofs of our religion are very weak."[33]

There is, I think, a coherent structure that unites Pascal's views of nature, reason, and authority; it is admittedly a unique structure, but nonetheless still definable. There remains, however, one aspect of Pascal's career that refuses to bond with the rest: his foray into experimental physics. From the perspective of the historian of science his investigations of the barometer constitute a most brilliant achievement. But the Pascal we have portrayed had, quite simply, no business pursuing experimental science. His feelings about nature, even in his early years, should not have justified such concern as to whether air has weight or a void exists. The inconsistency does not lie in the belief that such studies are possible; the "Preface" and the *Provincial Letters* both emphatically declare that the world of the senses must be studied by the senses. No, the fact that jars is that Pascal *himself* became so engaged in this physical world, at the very time he was telling Mme Perier that tending to nature is idolatry, the worship of the creation rather than the Creator.[34] There is of course no requirement, then or now, that a man live a life consistent with his beliefs, but I think it quite probable that Pascal felt the dissonance within and that he ultimately abandoned scientific inquiries because he could not justify them to himself. I make this point because it seems to set Pascal apart from the other Catholic scientists we have discussed. I think Descartes, Mersenne, and Gassendi were, to varying degrees, motivated in their science by religious factors. With Pascal such is not the case.

Pascal was certainly a great Catholic and a great scientist. But if there is a causal thread that runs from the former to the latter, I fail to detect it.

Nicolaus Steno (1638–1686) is seldom mentioned in the same breath with Pascal or Descartes, yet he was arguably a more original thinker than either. His proposal that the surface of the earth contains the evidence of its own history—indeed, that an individual rock or fossil exhibits clues to the place and manner of its production—is as brilliant an insight as one can find in this marvelous century, and Steno's consequent unraveling of the geological history of Tuscany and his proposal of the organic origin of fossils shows that insight was coupled in his case with an extremely capable scientific methodology. Steno, in short, belongs on any list of great seventeenth-century scientists.[35]

He belongs here, however, because he was a Catholic scientist, and he was so in a different sense from the others discussed. With Pascal or Descartes one never escapes the feeling that science and theology were in unstable equilibrium, that tensions existed between their worlds of faith and reason. With Steno one finds no hint of conflict. Raised a Protestant, Steno came to the Catholic faith quite deliberately, converting shortly after completing his treatise on the shark's head; and, wrapped in his newly acquired religion, he proceeded to write his great geological work, the *Prodromus*. It is true that his religious fervor would shortly carry him right out of the scientific arena, as he became priest, then archbishop (and soon it appears, a saint). But in those fruitful years between 1667 and 1670 he was equally at home in the spiritual and material realms, and his thoughts on certainty, nature, and Scripture are illuminating.

Steno had little use for the deductions of Cartesian rationalists, but he was also impatient with skeptics who argued that we can know nothing with certainty.[36] There is indeed a great deal that is uncertain, admits Steno; with matter, to use his example, we do not know whether it is divisible or indivisible, whether it has other attributes than extension, or whether interstitial vacuums exist. Nevertheless, amid all this uncertainty we can still be sure that larger objects are aggregates of smaller ones; that in the case of rock strata, aggregates on top must have been formed after those beneath; that in the case of solids within solids, the object that takes the form of the other must have solidified later.[37] Steno took skepticism further than Gassendi did by dismissing the questions that are unknowable and concentrating on others—many heretofore unasked—that can be answered.

In many cases Steno was able to solve problems only by stringing together a complex series of deductions based on observation; witness his remarkable performance in the treatise on the shark's head; where he begins with eleven observations, from which follow six conjectures and the conclusions, with both observations and conjectures cited by number in the margin, in good Euclidean fashion, as the argument proceeds.[38] Such a method reveals what Steno elsewhere makes explicit: he had complete faith that nature operates according to law, not whimsy. If a body is a solid and if it was produced according to the laws of nature, then it was produced from a fluid.[39] Since according to nature solids dissolve in fluids, then the fluids flowing through the earth must dissolve the solids there.[40] Again and again Steno argues in this fashion, so that Nature becomes almost his coauthor. This is not to say that things cannot happen contrary to nature. Steno is most emphatic about this; not only can God produce supernatural effects, but even man can effect the unnatural.[41] But when things do happen naturally, they happen regularly. This belief in the regularity of nature leads Steno to speak critically of those who abuse the phrase "according to nature"—who would have nature produce "ex quolibet quodlibet" (anything from anything whatsoever). "Nature" used in this way, like "form" and "quality," is a thing known only by name, says Steno, and therefore not known at all.[42]

But by far the most arresting feature of Steno's geological thought is his failure to find any incompatibility between nature and Scripture. He was, after all, attempting to reconstruct the early history of the earth, a story which in his time was known *only* through the account in Genesis; but none of his findings, in his eyes, suggested disagreement with Scripture. Discussing the earliest phases of Tuscany's geological history, he points out that "Scripture and Nature agree" that everything was once covered with water; as to how long it lasted, "Nature says nothing, while Scripture speaks." In other cases nature supplements Scripture, or neither provides an answer, but in *no* instance does nature suggest one thing and Scripture another.[43]

Some scholars have interpreted this sanguinity as blindness and a tragic failing, and have lamented that the continued development of geology was held back for a century by Steno's reluctance to break away from a scriptural history of the earth.[44] Such criticism misses the point. Steno would indeed have achieved towering greatness had he been able to anticipate every eighteenth-century development. But it is even more marvelous, and more instructive, that he was able to set down most of the principles of modern geology *without* departing from the traditional religious framework.

If there is anything to regret in Steno's career, it is that he was unable to hold on to his vision of the natural world as his theological interests expanded in the early 1670s. Already in 1673 he was extolling the unknowable over the world of observation,[45] and in his last geological essay, the "Treatise on Ornaments" of 1675, we see him reverting to a hermeneutic view of nature as a collection of signs and symbols, where each gem or stone evokes a religious truth or draws our minds to God.[46] What this change tells us about Steno, or about science and religion in general, is difficult to ascertain. Some will think that Steno slid from the summit, but others will contend that he went on to better things. Not many geologists, after all, achieve sainthood.

What can we conclude from these portraits of five Catholic scientists—Mersenne, Gassendi, Descartes, Pascal, and Steno? Are they part of a larger picture? Do they, collectively, project something we can call a Catholic pattern? The answer, I think, is obvious; the term "Catholic science," judging from these five individuals, has no meaning whatsoever. Once you have listed Catholicism as a common feature, you have exhausted the list of similarities. All were motivated by religious considerations, but each was led in a different direction, to positions that were mutually irreconcilable. Five is of course a tiny sample, but were you to enlarge it by including Ismael Boulliau, Marcello Malpighi, Giovanni Alfonso Borelli, Francesco Redi, and Evangelista Torricelli (and, of course, the implicitly present Galileo), the resulting overall picture would be even more confusing and a pattern even less evident.

The failure of a pattern to emerge is very significant. It means that nothing was inherently denied to the Catholic scientist by his personal faith. He could be, and was, rationalist, empiricist, skeptic, mechanical philosopher, mystic, natural theologian, atomist, or mathematizer. And the lack of a Catholic pattern considerably weakens the case for a Protestant one. To demonstrate this point, I suggest a thought experiment. Place our original Catholic five in a room with the Protestants Francis Bacon, Johannes Kepler, Christiaan Huygens, Robert Boyle, and Isaac Newton; add Galileo and Gottfried Wilhelm Leibniz for good measure; and divide the resulting dozen into two halves on any criterion *other* than religion. I doubt that anyone could produce in this manner a contingent exclusively of Catholics facing a side entirely of Protestants.

If Catholicism were just a personal creed, this discussion could end here, and we could conclude that the Catholic faith was rarely a hindrance, and often a considerable source of inspiration, for the architects of the scientific revolution. However, to be a Catholic in the seventeenth century was not just to subscribe to a creed; it was to be part of an institution, one of the most bureaucratically complex institutions of the era. The Catholic church could and did set policy on many matters of faith and conduct, and the true Catholic not only accepted these decisions but believed, as an essential ingredient of his faith, that the decisions of the church were necessarily correct. Because of the important role played by the church in determining questions of faith for the individual believer, it is vital that we now ask how the church, in its institutional capacity, reacted to the new developments of seventeenth-century science and what effect these reactions had on the Catholic scientific community.

SCIENCE AND THE INSTITUTIONAL CHURCH

Religions are not, as a rule, novelty-seeking institutions, and it should come as no surprise that the Catholic church of the seventeenth century was decidedly reluctant to embrace many of the novel discoveries and reinterpretations of contemporary science. One could, after all, make the same statement about every other religious institution of the period, to say nothing of political and even educational institutions. Any religion more than a few hours old is going to take a dim view of radical theories that undermine its own dogma, and the Catholic church, as one of the most venerable and traditional of faiths, can hardly be faulted for resisting assured claims that the earth moves, that color is an illusion, that space is empty, and that in general modern scientists know more about nature than all the philosophers of antiquity.

The Catholic church, however, stands out from all other seventeenth-century institutions in that it not only criticized unwelcome ideas but was uniquely equipped to censor and repress such ideas and even to punish their advocates. This capacity for policing the faith was a legacy of the Counter-Reformation and two innovations of the Council of Trent—the Congregations of the Index and the Holy Office (Inquisition)—that were regularly used to identify heretical or dangerous ideas and ensure their containment and elimination. Moreover, since the church was both centralized and hierarchical, considerable pressure could be brought to bear on offenders by archbishops and bishops, generals of religious orders, and theological faculties at various universities. The resulting machinery of ideological suppression was formidable.[47]

This apparatus, of course, was not established to deal with earth-movers or mechanical philosophers, but with those who would insinuate such Protestant heresies as consubstantiation or the priesthood of all believers into the mother church. Nevertheless, by the beginning of the seventeenth century several Renaissance philosophers of nature had become entangled in the machinery.[48] Girolamo Cardano and Giambattista della Porta had been the subject of inquisitorial proceedings, and several of their books were prohibited. Francesco Patrizi's major philosophical treatise had been first censored and then, posthumously, banned completely, along with an important work of Bernardino Telesio.[49] Tommaso Campanella and Giordano Bruno suffered extensive imprisonment, and each saw his entire corpus of writings prohibited—in the case of Bruno, not the only corpus he would lose to the Inquisition. Since this short list includes some of the most original minds of the Renaissance, and since their significance lies in their contributions to science and cosmology rather than theology, it seems appropriate to ask how the church found itself in what was, in hindsight, the regrettable position of adjudicating questions of natural philosophy.

The ground was laid by the desire at Trent to protect the faith from magic. Magic was anathema to mainstream Catholicism for many reasons. Natural magic could easily become supernatural magic, which involved trafficking with demons. Just as offensive, the supernatural often became natural in magical treatises, leading to explanations of the miraculous. Magic usually involved forms of divination, and the implication that the future is ordained by the lines on one's palm smacked of Calvinist predestination. Magic also gave an inflated role to the individual magus, which again suggested the taint of Protestantism. So from the very first edition of the Roman Index all magic was prohibited, and all astrological works were subsequently forbidden, since astrology also risks denying the essential Catholic dogma of free will.[50]

The church had in mind by this campaign the suppression of various disreputable followers of the sixteenth-century magicians Agrippa von Nettesheim and Johannes Trithemius. Unfortunately the inquisitorial powers did not adequately distinguish between practical magicians and philosophers who admitted magical forces into their universe. This is strange, since no Catholic theologian would have dreamed of denying that cosmic forces exist, that stars influence human behavior, or that sympathies and correspondences are effective. Indeed, if such forces did not exist, there would be no danger in trifling with them. But somehow the distinctions were not made, the net grew too large, and the likes of Cardano and Patrizi were hauled in with the rest. Unfortunately, they were not thrown back.

To exacerbate matters, when the works of these magical philosophers of nature were examined, other distasteful features also emerged, and these were included in the process of inquisition. Bruno (1548–1600), for example, was charged not only with defending magic and teaching that Moses and Christ were magi but with maintaining that stars have souls and that the number of worlds is infinite.[51] Similarly Patrizi (1529–1597) was forbidden to advocate that there is only one heaven and that stellar space is infinite.[52] These are doctrines that are not so much dangerous to the faith as they are anti-Aristotelian. By choosing to become the watchdog of Aristotelian philosophy as well as of Catholic theology, the church in 1600 was setting course for most of its confrontations with seventeenth-century science.

One of the roads down which the church was drawn led to the prohibition of heliocentrism and the condemnation of Galileo, events discussed elsewhere in this volume (see chaps. 3 and 4). Another led to an attack on Cartesian philosophy that will be discussed momentarily. But since I have argued that the origins of the church's position lay in its war on magic, I would first like to pursue this subject down a third path, which led to a rejection of alchemy, chemistry, and chemical medicine.

Alchemy was not included in the original church proscriptions against astrology and magic, perhaps because alchemy was in temporary eclipse at the time of the Council of Trent, perhaps because its foremost Renaissance champion, Paracelsus, was a Catholic (although certainly of a heterodox variety). A Paracelsian revival began around 1580, however, and most of the first wave of Paracelsians such as Joseph Duchesne and Oswald Croll were Protestants. Even Andreas Libavius, the principal early critic of Hermetic excess in chemistry, was a Lutheran, and as a result chemistry and chemical medicine in the first decades of the seventeenth century became an exclusively Protestant affair.[53] Probably because of this, and certainly because Paracelsianism shared with magic the danger of tampering with the supernatural, the church tried to stamp it out.[54] An early victim of this attempt at repression was the great physician Jan van Helmont (1579–1644). Helmont was one of the first Catholics to pick up the banner of Paracelsus, and as a result he suffered life-long persecution from ecclesiastical authorities. His treatise on the weapon salve and sympathetic cures was denounced by the Spanish Inquisition in 1625 as smacking of heresy.[55] In 1630 Helmont was convicted by the Louvain theological faculty of perverting nature with magic and diabolical art. He later spent some time in prison, and proceedings against him were abandoned only in 1642. Consequently, he was able to publish nothing for most of his remaining years, and his significance became apparent only with the posthumous appearance of his works.[56]

At about the same time, the physician Marco Severino (1580–1656) ran afoul of the Inquisition in Naples, and while the charges are not known, he was thought to have suffered for his anti-Galenic medical views (and possibly for his anti-Aristotelian philosophy in general). Somewhat later Sebastian Bartoli (1630–1676), a disciple of Severino and also an ardent chemical physician, had his book condemned and destroyed by the Neopolitan ecclesiastical authorities. When it was republished several years later in Venice, it was placed on the Index, burned, and never reprinted.[57] Meanwhile, every Jesuit scientific treatise that found the opportunity continued to denounce alchemy and chemical medicine as magic and diabolical.[58]

The impact of this chemical persecution is not difficult to characterize: very few Catholics entered the field of chemistry, and except for the beleagured Helmont, there was no Catholic contribution to the discipline in the seventeenth century. Not that the science was mightily advanced by Protestants. But still, Libavius, Jean Beguin, Daniel Sennert, Niçaise Le Febvre, Nicolas Lemery, and Boyle—Protestants all—were at least able to make a start on the chemical revolution. No Catholic lent a hand. And it was not that chemistry in Protestant countries was free of criticism; many English opponents of Paracelsianism were even more vitriolic than the Jesuits.[59] But in England neither side was suppressed, and out of the controversies emerged Boyle and the Newtonian school. In Italy nothing emerged at all. The Catholic failure to contribute to chemistry should give pause to those who would argue that bureaucratic interference, while regrettable, was only token interference, and that under the surface the search for truth went on.

The Catholic church's campaign against Cartesian philosophy is less notorious than its opposition to heliocentrism, but in many ways it is more illuminating, since it involved censorship at practically every level of the church hierarchy. Descartes, as is well known, was worried about the acceptability of his work in the 1630s; concerned about the Galileo affair, he abandoned plans to publish *Le monde*. Ironically, it was not Copernicanism at all, but his theory of matter, that eventually brought him into conflict with the authorities. As pointed out earlier, Descartes's denial of real accidents challenged the Thomistic explanation of the miracle of the Eucharist, which stipulated that the accidents of the bread remain while the substance is transformed into the body of Christ.[60] Descartes attempted to reconcile his matter theory with transubstantiation in his reply to Arnauld, and all seemed well for a while. But after Descartes's death, when his philosophy was becoming increasingly popular in France, his views on the Eucharist were brought to the attention of Honoré Fabri (1607–1688), papal penitentiary in Rome, and an accomplished Jesuit scientist. As a result, Descartes's *Meditations* were placed on the Index in 1663. The previous year, Descartes had been condemned by the theological faculty at the University of Louvain, and the ecclesiastical pressure against Descartes began to build. In 1671, at the king's request, the archbishop of Paris requested his faculty to cease teaching Cartesian philosophy. The university of Angers took an even stronger stand in 1675, resulting in the condemnation and expulsion of the Cartesian Bernard Lamy. In 1677 the theological faculty at Caen also became officially anti-Cartesian and exiled several offenders. Even religious orders became involved. Nicholas Poisson, like Lamy an Oratorian, was forbidden by his superiors to write a biography of Descartes, and distribution of his Cartesian commentary was suspended. In 1675 the Benedictine Maurists forbade teaching of the Cartesian claim that matter equals extension. And in 1678 the Oratorians, purportedly coerced by the Jesuits, officially subscribed to substantial forms, real accidents, and the Thomistic soul, thereby repudiating Cartesian positions.[61]

Did such persecution make any difference? Cartesian philosophy, unlike alchemy, continued to find support among Catholics. Probably the most serious result was personal distress, since most followers of Descartes seem to have been sincere Catholics and did not consider themselves heretics in the same class with Bruno.[62] But occasionally the consequences of personal religious crisis manifested themselves in ways that are sad to witness. Jacques Rohault (1620–1675), one of the leading Cartesians in Paris in the 1660s, authored the most widely used Cartesian textbook of the last quarter of the century. But in his subsequent *Entretiens sur la philosophie*, which appeared after the archbishop's warning in 1671, he stated: "I have no other principles than those of Aristotle. I recognize, as he does, privation, matter, and form. I agree with his general notions and his understanding of the words: substance, accident, essence, and quality."[63] It is, in its quiet way, an abjuration fully as tragic as that of Galileo.

Apart from these examples, and a few other skirmishes against atomism and the plurality of worlds, the church took little interest in the content of contemporary science, and most work passed unscathed through the censorship machinery. The threat of censorship and inquisitorial proceedings was always in the air, however, and it may be that the most devastating effect of church intervention in science was the dampening of the spirit of inquiry that had bubbled through Italian thought in the late Renaissance. This argument has been made before, although usually so overstated as to maintain that the church killed science in 1633 with one blow, which is of course nonsense.[64] Nevertheless, it would be an overreaction to such hyperbole to assume that the flavor of Italian science was unaffected by the activities of the Curia. Cosmological discussion ceased except among the Jesuits (see below), and astronomy, with the single exception of Giovanni Borelli, was reduced to the making and using of telescopes. Medicine remained so traditional that Marcello Malpighi (1628–1694) lamented the repressive atmosphere at Bologna and was forced to turn to the Royal Society of London for encouragement and a forum for his discoveries.[65] Even in physics, where the Italians excelled through the middle of the century, there was a noticeable reluctance to speculate about such things as the nature of matter or the significance of the vacuum. This philosophical apathy is most apparent in the activities and publications of the Accademia del Cimento, for which science became anonymous and philosophy invisible.[66] The same lack of interest is evident in the work of Francesco Redi (1626–ca. 1698), who refused to comment on the significance of his microscopical discoveries or place them in any grander scheme.[67] Some modern scholars of positivist persuasion have praised the non-speculative nature of Italian science in this period, perhaps believing that Newton did not frame hypotheses either and that science is better off without philosophy.[68] But the simple fact is that Newton, Boyle, Leibniz, and Descartes spun off hypotheses in profusion, and science flourished in their wake. In Italy after 1650, a hypothesis could hardly be found, and by 1700 science was struggling to survive.[69]

But it is time we allowed an objection. Defenders of the institutional church who have read this far will be wondering if I have not overlooked an important point: if the church was so resistant to the content of contemporary science, why was it that so many Catholics in Holy Orders were engaged in various scientific investigations? Does this not suggest that the church positively encouraged many types of scientific inquiry, even if it did outlaw Copernicanism and certain points of philosophy? The objection is well taken, and it requires us to take a closer look at the role of religious orders in the seventeenth-century scientific enterprise.

SCIENCE IN THE RELIGIOUS ORDERS

The number of scientists within Catholic religious orders is impressive, as is the quality. We have noted already that Mersenne was a Minim, and he was joined in his scientific pursuits by his brethren Emmanuel Maignan and Jean-François Niceron. Jean-Baptiste Du Hamel and Nicholas Malebranche were both Oratorians, and the Jesuati could boast of the mathematicians Bonaventura Cavalieri and Stefano degli Angeli. Vincenzo Coronelli was a Minorite, Valeriano Magni a

Capuchin, and Benedetto Castelli a Benedictine. Priests who were not in orders include Gassendi, Steno, and Ismael Boulliau. The list could be extended considerably by including lesser-known scientists. There is much we do not know about the policies of the various orders toward science, or the effect of the different rules in encouraging or discouraging scientific activity. One would like to know, for example, why the Minims, with their very strict vows, produced three eminent scientists, while the Benedictines of St. Maur, another monastic order that practiced a similar ritual, spawned no scientists but a number of excellent historians. Despite the deficiency of our knowledge, we can say with some assurance that taking vows was no barrier to becoming a scientist—in many cases a very good scientist indeed.

There is one order, however, that stands out from all others as the scientific order without rival in seventeenth-century Catholicism, and that of course is the Society of Jesus. I wish to focus the rest of my discussion on this remarkable group, for not only do we know a great deal about them, but the nature of Jesuit science raises many important questions concerning the influence of religious beliefs on scientific thought.

A complete bibliography of Jesuit scientific treatises of the seventeenth century would fill the space of this chapter.[70] If we listed only the most important Jesuit scientists, we would have to mention Christoph Scheiner, Giambattista Riccioli, Francesco Grimaldi, Francesco Lana Terzi, Honoré Fabri, Athanasius Kircher, Niccolo Cabeo, and Gaspar Schott, and the roll could be extended considerably without great drop-off in quality. The Jesuits had a particular zest for experimental science; they were interested in every newly discovered phenomenon, from electrostatic attraction to the barometer to the magic lantern, and Jesuits played a major role in discovering many new effects on their own, such as diffraction and electrical repulsion. A recent history of early electrical science awarded the Jesuit order the honor of being the single most important contributor to experimental physics in the seventeenth century.[71] Such an accolade would only be strengthened by detailed studies of other sciences, such as optics, where virtually all the important treatises of the period were written by Jesuits.

More significant than their numbers or their inventiveness is the fact that many of the Jesuits had a keen sense of the value of *precision* in experimental science—a sense that was not widely echoed by many of their more illustrious contemporaries. Riccioli's attempt to develop an accurate one-second pendulum by persuading nine Jesuit colleagues to count eighty-seven thousand oscillations over the course of a day, enabling him to identify an error of three parts in a thousand, is as amazing in its own way as Kepler's more famous dissatisfaction with an error of eight minutes of arc.[72] It is instructive to remember that it was Riccioli—not Galileo, and not Mersenne, and certainly not Descartes—who first accurately determined the rate of acceleration for a freely falling body.

Another admirable feature of the Jesuit scientific enterprise was their appreciation of the value of collaboration. One might well argue that the Society of Jesus, rather than the Accademia del Cimento or the Royal Society, was the first true scientific society. Kircher (1602–1680), the impresario in Rome, was more than a match for Mersenne and Boulliau in Paris or Henry Oldenburg in London, in his ability to collect observations and objects from a worldwide network of informants.[73] More important, Kircher published all this data in massive encyclopedias, which, together with similar efforts of Schott and Riccioli, were as vital as the early scientific journals in disseminating scientific information. If scientific collaboration was one of the outgrowths of the scientific revolution, the Jesuits deserve a large share of the credit.

Thus the Jesuits practiced science on a wide scale, were able (and often inspired) investigators, made many important discoveries and inventions, and encouraged the involvement of others. They do indeed seem to merit the praise they have frequently received. And yet when all this is said and acknowledged, there still remains the unavoidable feeling that Jesuit science was somehow seriously deficient. One does not appreciate this deficiency when reading *about* the Jesuit scientific achievements, but one certainly will by spending a few hours with a volume of Kircher, Scheiner, or Lana Terzi. It is hard to pinpoint what is wrong—indeed, as far as I know, no one has tried—but I wish to suggest what I see as the principal shortcomings.

One problem is that the Jesuit writers were, almost to a man, overly eclectic. Now eclecticism might be thought a virtue in an age when intolerance was the principal vice, and in fact Jesuit eclecticism has been singled out for praise.[74] But an extended encounter with a typical Jesuit treatise leaves the impression not of eclecticism but of a total lack of discrimination. Kircher, for example, in his *Mundus Subterraneus*, sandwiches descriptions of fossil fish between accounts of gems bearing the images of cities and stones in the shape of John the Baptist, and he can sustain such a mélange for hundreds of pages.[75] There is no suggestion that some authorities might be more reliable than others; every fact or observation seems to be given equal weight. Even contemporaries who were equally fascinated by curiosities thought that Kircher was overly credulous, and Leibniz would later deride Kircher for believing tales of rocks sporting the features of Luther and for placing such fancies on the same ontological level as true figured stones.[76]

A second deficiency of Jesuit scientific treatises, less obvious but more serious, is the lack of any philosophical superstructure holding together the facts being presented. There was surprisingly little interest in drawing conclusions about how nature operates. No doubt this dearth of Jesuit natural philosophy is partly a product of Jesuit eclecticism, for if one accepts at one and the same time the existence of corpuscles, effluvia, sympathies, and occult and manifest qualities, as Lana Terzi (1631–1687) does, then it is difficult to frame a consistent thesis concerning the mechanisms of nature.[77] There are many instances in Jesuit works where a collection of mutually irreconcilable facts or hypotheses seems to call for a choice, or at least an order of preference, and yet a stance is rarely taken. Riccioli (1598–1671), in a remarkably erudite discussion of new stars, lists fourteen possible explanations for their appearance, along with the strengths and shortcomings of each. This is eclecticism at its best.[78] But he never chooses one, not even his own offering; he does not seem to care which one is correct, or even to realize that there can be only one true explanation, and that this one, when separated from the rest, will tell us something important about the cosmos. Riccioli and his fellow Jesuits present science as a game to be played or to be watched and admired, but the outcome of which is irrelevant. As a result, no Jesuit comes even remotely close to the stature of Descartes, Galileo, Pascal, or even Gassendi as a natural philosopher.

How is one to explain this Janus-faced character of Jesuit science? How could so many intelligent scientists invest all that time and energy, become masters of the experimental method, discover all sorts of genuine natural effects, write all those magnificent treatises, and yet play such a small role in the essential developments of the scientific revolution? I am going to offer several possible explanations, and I wish to caution that these are conjectural and unproven, since the necessary supporting scholarship does not yet exist. I hope that in the near future we will see the rise of at least a cottage industry in the history of Jesuit science to test such conjectures, because until we finally solve the Jesuit enigma, we cannot be said truly to understand the role of religion in seventeenth-century science.[79]

My first suggestion is that the Jesuits were handicapped by an emblematic view of nature, which they retained long after it had been discarded by other scientists. An emblematic worldview, which sees nature as a vast collection of signs and metaphors, was a staple feature of Renaissance thought, but in the seventeenth century Bacon, Descartes, Galileo, and their followers rejected the notion that everything in nature carries a hidden meaning.[80] Nature instead was to be taken at face value and investigated on its own terms. The Jesuits, however, had become deeply committed to an emblematic view of the world, because in the late sixteenth century they had begun using emblems and images in their missionary program to attract the faithful. The Jesuits believed that a skillfully constructed emblem could teach a religious truth more effectively than a sermon, and the order became the single most important and prolific producer of emblem literature in the seventeenth century.[81] When the Jesuits in 1640 issued a volume to celebrate the centennial of their order, it is significant that they chose to publish not a history or a panegyric but a lavish emblem book, which opens with the Society's own emblem: a sun shining on the world, carrying the epigram, "There is no one who can hide from its glow."[82]

Not surprisingly, this emblematic approach to the world of the spirit carried over into Jesuit investigations of nature. A precedent of sorts was established by the immensely influential Robert Bellarmine (1542–1621), who in one of his most popular treatises, *The Ascent of the Mind to God,* interpreted the hidden meanings of every aspect of the natural order; to Bellarmine, for example, the observation that the moon sometimes shines on the earth while keeping a dark side to heaven, became a reminder that man too will often turn his back on God.[83] Bellarmine was writing a devotional treatise, not a natural history, but exactly the same outlook is apparent in most of the Jesuit scientific encyclopedias. Kircher included stories about Christo-morphic stones because they are signs of God, and they are signs whether the objects really exist or not. This of course is the crucial point. As long as one holds the view that nature is an elaborate hieroglyph, important only as a source of mystery and wonder, then the separation of true phenomena from false becomes secondary, if not irrelevant. Such a worldview produced enchantingly elaborate works of art and literature, but its dissolution was an essential feature of the revolution in science. The Jesuits were never able to abandon their emblematic world.

My second suggestion is that the Jesuits' reluctance to commit themselves to any one viewpoint or authority may be related to their probabilist stance in matters of moral theology. I do not pretend to understand the nuances of seventeenth-century casuistry, but the Jesuits were well known, indeed notorious, for their willingness to condone actions that other orders rejected as sinful.[84] The Jesuit position, called probabilism, was that an action could be deemed moral if at least one respectable authority had judged it so, even if his opinion was less probable than that of authorities who denied its morality.[85] The Jesuits found such a "morally eclectic" position necessary if their missionary work was to be successful, but it meant that they became accustomed in theological questions to giving less probable opinions the same weight as more probable ones. And how interesting that they followed precisely the same course in their scientific writings! They recorded the opinion of every authority, provided he was a reasonable man, and they refused to reject a viewpoint merely because it was less probable than others. This is a striking parallel. We are a long way from making it more than a parallel, but it is my suspicion that the Jesuits embraced, consciously or not, a form of scientific probabilism that prevented them from taking any firm position, not only on matters of opinion but on questions of fact, and that this provided an insurmountable barrier to the development of any consistent natural philosophy.[86]

A third factor that seems to have had an impact on Jesuit science was the legacy of fictionalism that the Jesuits inherited from Bellarmine, in the aftermath of the Inquisition's edict of 1616. Bellarmine, like Clavius before him, had subscribed to the opinion that astronomical systems were all fictional devices designed only to save the appearances of things, and that appearances have nothing to do with reality, which is the business of philosophers rather than astronomers.[87] Fictionalism was common enough in the sixteenth century, but after Kepler the practice of using hypotheses that could not possibly be true fell rapidly out of favor. The Jesuits, however, were in an awkward position following the condemnation of Galileo, for they were the order charged with defending a geocentric cosmology. Initially they tried invective; as they grew more expert in science, they tried to disprove Copernicanism on scientific grounds; but by the time of Riccioli it had become evident to them that no system could be strictly proved or disproved by scientific means. How then to deal with the increasing superiority of heliocentric celestial mechanics? If the Jesuits had been realists, they would simply have proclaimed the system false, citing Scripture and church decrees, and refused to sanction the utility of an erroneous hypothesis. Such a position, while theologically quite sound, would have been very weak strategically; therefore Riccioli and other Jesuits instead revived the fictionalist stance, discussing heliocentric astronomy with great erudition and even considerable enthusiasm, but always with the caveat that it was merely a hypothesis, like dozens of other hypotheses that scientists adopted for convenience.[88] The problem with fictionalism is that, like probabilism, it leads to excessive eclecticism and discourages the asking of larger questions. The Jesuits did take a position on Copernicanism—as mandated by Scripture and the Holy Office—but on matters where Scripture was silent, their fictionalist posture kept them from asking which hypothesis describes the way things really are. Thus Lana Terzi collected "models" that fit the phenomena—effluvia for electricity, sympathies for magnetism—but he did not require them to be true or even to be consistent with other models.[89] The goal was simply to save the phenomena. In the late Renaissance that was a laudable program. In 1670 it was not enough.

One final point should be made concerning the Jesuits' role as defenders of the church's stance on Copernicanism. Non-Jesuit Catholic scientists reacted in differing ways to the pronouncements on Galileo and heliocentrism. Descartes chose silence, at least temporarily, although he did not change his mind. Mersenne waffled, while Boulliau, to Descartes's amazement, went right ahead with the publication of a Copernican work. Gilles Roberval pretended to find a lost treatise of Aristarchus; Pascal ridiculed the pope for trying to change the facts; and Borelli disguised his Copernican treatise as an exercise on the satellites of Jupiter.[90] These varying reactions make one point: that while most Catholics did genuinely believe that the church was one of the twin pillars of the faith, they were willing to admit that the church was occasionally wrong, or at least misguided. Such a tolerant attitude was denied the Jesuits; for them the church was never wrong, and its every pronouncement was to be accepted without question and defended without misgiving. The thirteenth Rule of Loyola is explicit: "If we wish to be sure that we are right in all things, we should always be ready to accept this principle: I will believe that the white I see is black, if the hierarchical Church so defines it."[91] I think modern historians have failed to appreciate the significance of this point of faith and have misinterpreted many of the Jesuits' actions. Riccioli, Fabri, and others were not acting out of duty in defending geocentrism but out of *belief*. There is no reason to question the sincerity of such belief; indeed, Riccioli's *New Almagest* would make little sense if it were not sincere. Fabri, in the controversy over Saturn's rings, was not being stupid, or obtuse, or malicious; he was trying quite hard to reconcile new facts with a conflicting belief that he knew, in his heart, to be true.[92] This was not an easy task for the Jesuits; it is hard to see white as black, especially when others keep shouting "White! White!" and the effort no doubt colored their views of other matters. I strongly suspect that the Jesuit proclivity for eclecticism, fictionalism, and probabilism, and their mistrust of the larger questions, were at least partially an outgrowth of a sincere attempt to accommodate a point of faith to a recalcitrant world of phenomena.

The Society of Jesus demonstrates, better than any other seventeenth-century case study, the difficulties that could ensue when religious concerns intruded into scientific affairs. The Jesuits were, after all, a missionary order; they were active in proselytizing for the church and keeping heretics at bay. It is not surprising that they would not, or could not, put aside such interests when contemplating the natural order. But when they allowed missionary concerns to shape their epistemology and view of nature, their scientific work was inevitably affected. It seems that the very factors that made the Society such a successful religious order, and set it apart from all others, also figured strongly in Jesuit scientific work, isolating it irretrievably from the main currents of the scientific revolution.

NOTES

1. The only essay to address explicitly this topic is François Russo, "Catholicism, Protestantism, and the Development of Science in the 16th and 17th Centuries," in *The Evolution of Science*, ed. G. Métraux and F. Crouzet (New York: New American Library, 1963), pp. 291–320. The various works of Stanley L. Jaki, such as *Science and Creation* (Edinburgh: Scottish Academic Press, 1974), are learned, informed, and so biased as to be useless. See also Eric Cochrane, "What Is Catholic Historiography?" in *God, History, and Historians: Modern Christian Views of History*, ed. C. T. McIntire (New York: Oxford Univ. Press, 1977), pp. 444–465.

2. The worst offender to my mind is R. Hooykaas, *Religion and the Rise of Modern Science* (Grand Rapids, Mich.: Wm. B. Eerdmans, 1972). But see the other works cited in the essays by Deason and Webster in this volume.

3. For this discussion I have relied primarily on Robert Lenoble, *Mersenne ou la naissance du mécanisme* (Paris: J. Vrin, 1971); John S. Spink, *French Free-Thought from Gassendi to Voltaire* (London: Athlone Press, 1960), pp. 3–47; P. J. S. Whitmore, *The Order of Minims in 17th-Century France* (The Hague: Nijhoff, 1967). See also Richard H. Popkin, *The History of Scepticism from Erasmus to Spinoza* (Berkeley, Los Angeles, London: Univ. of California Press, 1979), pp. 129–140; A. C. Crombie, "Marin Mersenne (1588–1648) and the Seventeenth-Century Problem of Scientific Acceptability," *Physis* 17 (1975): 186–204; William L. Hine, "Mersenne and Vanini," *Renaissance Quarterly* 29 (1976): 52–65.

4. Lenoble, *Mersenne*, p. 314.

5. Ibid., pp. 380–382; William Hine, "Marin Mersenne and Italian Naturalism," in *Actes du XIIᵉ Congrès international d'histoire des sciences*, 12 vols. (Paris: Albert Blanchard, 1971), IIIB, 50–53; Whitmore, *Minims*, pp. 144–147.

6. Lenoble, *Mersenne*, pp. 461–477, 482–486; Whitmore, *Minims*, pp. 149–150.

7. Ira O. Wade, *The Intellectual Origins of the French Enlightenment* (Princeton: Princeton Univ. Press, 1971), pp. 144–145.

8. Wade, *Origins*, p. 165; Whitmore, *Minims*, pp. 71–72.

9. Descartes discusses the divine attributes in the third *Meditation* and the *Principles of Philosophy*; see *The Philosophical Works of Descartes*, trans. Elizabeth

S. Haldane and G. R. T. Ross, 2 vols. (Cambridge: Cambridge Univ. Press, 1931), 1:165, 228. An additional observation on God's immutability comes later in the *Principles*, pt. 2, no. 37 (not in the Haldane-Ross translation). For good discussions see Gary C. Hatfield, "Force (God) in Descartes' Physics," *Studies in the History and Philosophy of Science* 10 (1979): 113–140; and Margaret J. Osler, "Descartes and Charleton on Nature and God," *Journal of the History of Ideas* 40 (1979): 445–456.

10. Descartes's distaste for rational theology is best manifested in his "Notes against a programme" of 1647, *Works*, trans. Haldane and Ross, 1:431–450, esp. 438–439.

11. *Works*, trans. Haldane and Ross, 1:230–231 (*Principles*, pt. 1, no. 28). See also Edward J. Kearns, *Ideas in 17th-Century France* (Manchester: Manchester Univ. Press, 1979), p. 32.

12. René Descartes, *Le monde* (1664), trans. Michael S. Mahoney (New York: Abaris Books, 1979), pp. 50–51.

13. Arnauld's objection is in *Works*, trans. Haldane and Ross, 2:95; Descartes's reply follows, pp. 116–122.

14. Gassendi's views of God and the natural order are discussed in Spink, *Free-Thought*, pp. 85–102; Popkin, *Scepticism*, pp. 141–146; Kearns, *Ideas*, pp. 68–72; Wade, *Origins*, pp. 206–230; see also the more definitive studies of Bernard Rochot, *Les travaux de Gassendi: Sur Epicure et sur l'atomisme, 1619–1658* (Paris: J. Vrin, 1944); Olivier R. Bloch, *La philosophie de Gassendi: Nominalisme, matérialisme, et métaphysique* (The Hague: Nijhoff, 1971).

15. Some scholars, such as Bloch, find a tension between Gassendi's atomism and his Christianity. Others, such as Rochot, find Gassendi quite consistent. See Bloch, *Gassendi*, pp. 288–302, and the discussion in Lillian U. Pancheri, "The Magnet, the Oyster, and the Ape, or Pierre Gassendi and the Principle of Plenitude," *Modern Schoolman* 53 (1976): 141–150, esp. p. 148. This debate is related to the older one as to whether Gassendi was a humanist or a *libertin*; see Popkin, *Scepticism*, pp. 104–106.

16. Popkin, *Scepticism*, pp. 141–142.

17. See Gassendi's "Objections" to Descartes's *Meditations*, where he attacks, among other things, Descartes's ontological argument and impishly asks what Descartes would know about God if he had been born with no senses and had spent his life just thinking about the divine attributes (*Works*, trans. Haldane and Ross, 2:175–176).

18. Gassendi argues in the "Objections" that Descartes, in refusing to use final causes, has rejected the principal argument for establishing God's wisdom and existence (ibid.). See also Bloch, *Gassendi*, pp. 350–378; Spink, *Free-Thought*, pp. 92–93; Wade, *Origins*, pp. 219–220.

19. Pierre Gassendi, *Opera Omnia*, 6 vols. (Lyons, 1658), 1:449–457. See also Keith Hutchison, "What Happened to Occult Qualities in the Scientific Revolution?" *Isis* 73 (1982): 233–253; Hutchison does not discuss Gassendi, but he does include Gassendi's English spokesman, Walter Charleton.

20. Alexandre Koyré, "Gassendi and Science in His Time," in his *Metaphysics and Measurement* (Cambridge: Harvard Univ. Press, 1968), pp. 118–130.

21. Several good general treatments of Pascal are Jean Mesnard, *Pascal: His Life and Works* (New York: Philosophical Library, 1952); Ernest Mortimer, *Blaise*

Pascal: The Life and Work of a Realist (London: Methuen, 1959). For a briefer but more provocative discussion see Alexandre Koyré, "Pascal Savant," in *Metaphysics and Measurement,* pp. 131–159.

22. The fragmentary "Preface" may be found in Blaise Pascal, *Oeuvres complètes,* ed. Jean Mesnard, 2 vols. (Paris: Desclée de Brouwer, 1964–1970), 2:777–785. Quotations are from p. 779.

23. The first sentiment is from the "Preface," ibid., 2:778; the second is from the eighteenth Provincial letter, in Pascal, *Oeuvres complètes,* ed. Louis Lafuma (Paris: Editions du Seuil, 1963), p. 467.

24. Mesnard, *Pascal,* pp. 28–31.

25. Koyré, "Pascal," pp. 153–155.

26. Pascal, *Oeuvres,* ed. Mesnard, 2:779.

27. Pascal's most famous *pensée:* "The heart has reasons that the reason never knows," does not really mean what the English translation says. What *coeur* does mean has been widely discussed; see Kearns, *Ideas,* pp. 99–116.

28. See A. W. S. Baird, "Pascal's Idea of Nature," *Isis* 61 (1970): 297–320; Robert Lenoble, *Esquisse d'une histoire de l'idée de nature* (Paris: Albin Michel, 1969), pp. 334–337.

29. Pascal's letter to Mme Perier of 1 April 1648; in *Oeuvres,* ed. Lafuma, p. 273.

30. This is *pensée* 580 in the Brunschvicg ordering, or 262 in that of Lafuma; see *Oeuvres,* ed. Lafuma, p. 624, no. 934.

31. *Pensée* 843 (Brunschvicg), 878 (Lafuma); ibid., p. 609, no. 840. Historians often use the expressions "natural theology" and "rational theology" interchangeably and assume that an individual who employs a variety of the design argument is thereby trying to provide rational foundations for Christianity. The examples of Descartes, Gassendi, and Pascal suggest that rational arguments and arguments from nature were not only carefully distinguished but often contraposed.

32. Arthur O. Lovejoy, *The Great Chain of Being: A Study of the History of an Idea* (New York: Harper Torchbooks, 1960), pp. 129–130.

33. *Pensée* 242 (Brunschvicg); *Oeuvres,* ed. Lafuma, p. 599, no. 781.

34. *Oeuvres,* ed. Lafuma, p. 273.

35. See the collection of papers edited by Gustav Scherz, *Dissertations on Steno as Geologist* (Odense: Odense Univ. Press, 1971), as well as Scherz's introduction to his edition of *Steno: Geological Papers* (Odense: Odense Univ. Press, 1969), pp. 11–47.

36. *Papers,* ed. Scherz, p. 145.

37. Ibid.

38. Ibid., pp. 95–107.

39. Ibid., p. 153.

40. Ibid., pp. 103, 145.

41. Ibid., p. 147.

42. Ibid., pp. 143, 149.

43. Ibid., pp. 204–207.

44. Tore Frängsmyr, "Steno and Geological Time," in *Dissertations,* ed. Scherz, pp. 204–212, esp. 210.

45. In a lecture in Copenhagen which also provided the epigram "Pulchra sunt quae videntur; pulchriora quae sciuntur, longe pulcherrima, quae ignorantur." This essay is not in *Papers,* ed. Scherz; see Nicholaus Steno, *Opera Philosophica,* ed. Vilhelm Maar, 2 vols. (Copenhagen: Vilhelm Tryde, 1910), 2:249–256.

46. The "Treatise on Ornaments" is reprinted and translated in *Papers,* ed. Scherz, pp. 249–267; see esp. pp. 250–253.

47. Owen Chadwick, *The Reformation* (Baltimore: Penguin, 1964), pp. 269–273, 299–305.

48. Lynn Thorndike has a chapter on "The Catholic Reaction: Index, Inquisition, and Papal Bulls," in his *History of Magic and Experimental Science,* 8 vols. (New York: Columbia Univ. Press, 1923–1958), 6:145–178.

49. Paolo Rossi, "Francesco Patrizi: Heavenly Spheres and Flocks of Cranes," in *Italian Studies in the Philosophy of Science,* ed. Maria Luisa dalla Chiara (Dordrecht: Reidel, 1980), pp. 363–388, esp. 383.

50. Thorndike, *History* 6:147, 156

51. Frances Yates, *Giordano Bruno and the Hermetic Tradition* (London: Routledge & Kegan Paul, 1964), pp. 348–356.

52. Rossi, "Patrizi," p. 384, containing some of Patrizi's censored passages.

53. See the outstanding work by Owen Hannaway, *The Chemists and the Word: The Didactic Origins of Chemistry* (Baltimore: Johns Hopkins Univ. Press, 1975). Hannaway is unusual among historians of science for his attention to and knowledge of theological issues.

54. Gassendi got right to the heart of the matter in 1630, when he attacked Robert Fludd for making alchemy the only religion, and the alchemist the only religious person. See Allen G. Debus, *Robert Fludd and his Philosophical Key* (New York: Science History Publications, 1979), p. 18.

55. Walter Pagel, *Joan Baptista van Helmont: Reformer of Science and Medicine* (Cambridge: Cambridge Univ. Press, 1982), pp. 12–13. It probably did not help for Helmont to suggest that in place of the moss from a dead thief's skull for the weapon salve, one could just as well use that from a Jesuit's skull.

56. I find it interesting that Eugene M. Klaaren spends thirty pages extolling the "Spiritualist" theology of Helmont without mentioning, as far as I could tell, either his Catholicism or his troubles with the ecclesiastical authorities; see *Religious Origins of Modern Science* (Grand Rapids, Mich.: Wm. B. Eerdmans, 1977), pp. 53–83.

57. Max H. Fisch, "The Academy of the Investigators," in *Science, Medicine and History: Essays in Honour of Charles Singer,* ed. E. A. Underwood, 2 vols. (London: Oxford Univ. Press. 1953), 1:521–563.

58. One example is Athanasius Kircher's diatribe in *Mundus Subterraneus,* 2 vols. (Amsterdam, 1665), 2:231–325.

59. P. M. Rattansi, "The Helmontian-Galenist Controversy in Restoration England," *Ambix* 12 (1964): 1–23.

60. The impact of Descartes's matter theory on the doctrine of the Eucharist has been studied by Henri Gouhier, *Cartésianisme et augustinisme au XVIIe siècle* (Paris: Vrin, 1978), pp. 71–79; Richard A. Watson, "Transubstantiation among

the Cartesians," in *Problems of Cartesianism*, ed. Thomas M. Lennon et al. (Kingston and Montreal: McGill-Queen's Univ. Press, 1982), pp. 127–148, with a response in the same volume by Ronald Laymon, pp. 149–170. For the following discussion I have relied heavily on Trevor McClaughlin, "Censorship and Defenders of the Cartesian Faith in Mid-seventeenth Century France," *Journal of the History of Ideas* 40 (1979): 563–581.

61. It is important to realize that Catholic authorities were not alone in trying to suppress Descartes; the curators at Leiden, goaded by Reformed clerics, tried for thirty years, until 1676, to eliminate Cartesianism. It is also important to realize that they failed to do so, perhaps because they lacked the institutional machinery of enforcement. See Edward G. Ruestow, *Physics at 17th- and 18th-Century Leiden* (The Hague: M. Nijhoff, 1973), pp. 44–78.

62. McClaughlin, "Censorship," p. 574.

63. Ibid., pp. 578–580.

64. For an example see Leonardo Olschki, *The Genius of Italy* (New York: Oxford Univ. Press, 1949), p. 389.

65. Howard B. Adelmann, *Marcello Malpighi and the Evolution of Embryology*, 5 vols. (Ithaca, N.Y.: Cornell Univ. Press, 1966), 1:67, 86.

66. W. E. Knowles Middleton, *The Experimenters: A Study of the Accademia del Cimento* (Baltimore: Johns Hopkins Press, 1971).

67. Anto Leikola, "Francesco Redi as a Pioneer of Experimental Biology," *Lychnos*, 1977–1978:115–122.

68. For example, Leikola, "Redi," p. 122.

69. W. E. K. Middleton, in "Science in Rome, 1675–1700, and the Accademia Fisicomatematica of Giovanni Giustino Ciampini," *British Journal for the History of Science* 8 (1975): 138–154, argues that there was complete freedom to discuss the most sensitive scientific questions in Rome in the last quarter of the century. He is unconvincing, in that nothing of importance comes out of the Ciampini group.

70. There is no such bibliography, to my knowledge, although one could be gathered, rather arduously, from the monumental *Bibliothèque de la Compagnie de Jesus*, ed. Augustin de Backer and Carlos Sommervogel, 10 vols. (Brussels: O. Schepens, 1890–1909).

71. John L. Heilbron, *Electricity in the 17th and 18th Centuries: A Study of Early Modern Physics* (Berkeley, Los Angeles, London: Univ. of California Press, 1979), p. 2.

72. Alexandre Koyré, "An Experiment in Measurement," in *Metaphysics and Measurement*, pp. 89–117.

73. Only a fraction of Kircher's correspondence network has been examined; see, for example, John E. Fletcher, "Astronomy in the Life and Correspondence of Athanasius Kircher," *Isis* 61 (1970): 52–67; "Johann Marcus Marci Writes to Athanasius Kircher," *Janus* 55 (1972): 95–118.

74. Heilbron, *Electricity*, pp. 108–112.

75. Kircher, *Mundus* 2:32–36.

76. Southwell wrote to Boyle in 1661 that Kircher was apt to put into print any strange story: "he has often made me smile" (quoted in Thorndike, *History*

8:177). Gottfried Wilhelm Leibniz, *Protogaea* (Göttingen, 1749), pp. 44–45. The *Protogaea* was composed around 1693.

77. Thorndike, *History* 7:610–613; Heilbron, *Electricity*, pp. 110–111.

78. Giovanni Battista Riccioli, *Almagestum Novum*, 2 pts. (Bologna, 1651), 2:174–177.

79. It would be gratifying, for example, if the history of science could produce the equivalent of Rudolph Wittkower and Irma B. Jaffe, eds., *Baroque Art: The Jesuit Contribution* (New York: Fordham Univ. Press, 1972).

80. Michel Foucault, *The Order of Things, An Archaeology of the Human Sciences* (New York: Random House, 1970), pp. 15–45, 128–130; Paolo Rossi, "Hermeticism, Rationality, and the Scientific Revolution," in *Reason, Experiment, and Mysticism in the Scientific Revolution,* ed. Maria Luisa Righini Bonelli and William R. Shea (New York: Science History Publications, 1975), pp. 247–273. See also my forthcoming article, "Natural History, Antiquarianism, and the Demise of the Emblematic Cosmos," in *Reappraisals of the Scientific Revolution,* ed. David C. Lindberg and Robert S. Westman.

81. Mario Praz, *Studies in 17th-Century Imagery*, 2 vols. (London: Warburg Institute, 1939–1947), 1:155–185. Praz states that emblems were "the honey of humanism which the Jesuits used in order to make palatable the wormwood of Faith" (p. 158).

82. Ibid., 1:170.

83. Robert Bellarmine, *De Ascensione Mentis in Deum* (1615), trans. as *A Most Learned and Pious Treatise . . .* (Douai, 1616), p. 244. This work is discussed in detail and extensively quoted in James Brodrick, *The Life and Work of Blessed Robert Francis Bellarmine*, 2 vols. (London: Burns, Oates & Washbourne, 1928), 2:381–391.

84. The notoriety derived in great part from Pascal's inspired assault on Jesuit casuistry in his *Provincial Letters* of 1657. See Dale Van Kley, *The Jansenists and the Expulsion of the Jesuits from France, 1757–1765* (New Haven: Yale Univ. Press, 1975), pp. 13–17.

85. Ibid., p. 16. See also the article on "Probabilism" in the *Catholic Encyclopedia.*

86. Benjamin Nelson mentioned probabilism as a possible factor in Catholic science in "The Early Modern Revolution in Science and Philosophy: Fictionalism, Probabilism, Fideism, and Catholic 'Prophetism,'" in *Boston Studies in the Philosophy of Science*, vol. 3 (Dordrecht: Reidel, 1968), pp. 1–39. Thorndike also mentions probabilism (*History* 7:578) but seems to equate probabilism with "smokescreen," which is unfair to the Jesuits.

87. Ernan McMullin, "Empiricism and the Scientific Revolution," in *Art, Science, and History in the Renaissance,* ed. Charles S. Singleton (Baltimore: Johns Hopkins Press, 1967), pp. 331–369; Edward Grant, "Late Medieval Thought, Copernicus, and the Scientific Revolution," *Journal of the History of Ideas* 23 (1962): 197–220; Nelson, "Revolution."

88. Although for the most part Riccioli did not try to confront heliocentrism on physical grounds, he did temporarily reverse his tactics when he stumbled on what is called the "Galilean argument" against a moving earth. But sub-

sequent Jesuits, such as Andre Tacquet, rejected all physical arguments, including Riccioli's. See Alexandre Koyré, *A Documentary History of the Problem of Fall from Kepler to Newton,* Transactions of the American Philosophical Society, n.s., vol. 45, pt. 4 (Philadelphia: The Society, 1955), pp. 329–395, esp. 393.

89. Heilbron, *Electricity,* pp. 110–111.

90. William L. Hine, "Mersenne and Copernicanism," *Isis* 64 (1973): 18–32; Robert A. Hatch *The Collection Boulliau: An Inventory* (Philadelphia: American Philosophical Society, 1982), p. xxx; Leon Auger, "Les idées de Roberval sur le système du monde," *Revue d'histoire des sciences* 10 (1957): 226–234; Alexandre Koyré, *The Astronomical Revolution: Copernicus-Kepler-Borelli,* trans. R. E. W. Maddison (London: Methuen, 1973), pp. 471, 517.

91. Ignatius Loyola, *The Spiritual Excercises,* trans. Anthony Mottola (Garden City, N.Y.: Doubleday, 1964), pp. 140–141.

92. John L. Heilbron, "Honoré Fabri, S.J., and the Accademia del Cimento," *Actes du XIIᵉ Contrès international d'histoire des sciences,* 12 vols. (Paris: Albert Blanchard, 1971), IIIB, 45–49.

6

Reformation Theology and the Mechanistic Conception of Nature

Gary B. Deason

FROM ARISTOTELIANISM TO THE MECHANICAL PHILOSOPHY

Historians of the Scientific Revolution have identified the development of mathematical physics as the watershed separating ancient and modern science. Without demeaning the other achievements of the Scientific Revolution, we are compelled to acknowledge the widespread application of mathematical methods to the physical world as the single most significant change made by the seventeenth century in the scientific tradition that it inherited. From Galileo's formulation of the law of falling bodies to Descartes's programmatic reduction of nature to geometry, to Wren's laws of impact and Huygens's law of centrifugal force, to Newton's *Mathematical Principles of Natural Philosophy*, the seventeenth century progressively and successfully described the world using the tools of mathematics.

The mathematization of nature in the Scientific Revolution represented the reassertion of a Platonic view of mathematics over the view of Aristotle, which had dominated natural philosophy since the thirteenth century. For Plato the highest reality was Intellectual Form, or pure Ideas, embodied imperfectly in physical things and more perfectly in mathematics. Because mathematics reflected truth more perfectly than physics, Platonic science exploited it in the analysis of nature, with the ultimate goal of reducing physical reality to numbers and geometrical shapes. Aristotle rejected Plato's mathematicism, believing that mathematics and physics study separate kinds of objects.

167

For Aristotle the quantities and shapes of mathematics were abstractions from physical entities. They captured certain qualities of material things but left unexplained the true natures, which could not be reduced to mathematics.

Among these irreducible qualities was the natural tendency (*nisus*) of objects to change. For Aristotle the world had within it principles and powers of development. Natural things changed as a result of their inherent tendency to embody more perfectly the rational form or essence that defined them. Since rational essences did not change, the end of nature was the perfect embodiment of changelessness, a goal that is never achieved because of the changeability and obstinacy of matter. Aristotle's world of inherent tendencies, continual transformations, and teleological development eluded mathematical description. Consequently, Aristotelian physics employed philosophical tools rather than mathematical ones.

The successful application of mathematics to the physical world in the seventeenth century called in question the Aristotelian conception of the world and necessitated the development of a new conception that allowed the applicability of mathematics to nature. In developing this new conception, seventeenth-century thinkers did not return directly to Plato, whose description of the world in *Timaeus* had fallen into some disrepute as a result of its association with magic and Paracelsian medicine in the sixteenth century. Instead, they constructed a new view of the world by revising and expanding ancient philosophy into a mechanistic conception of nature.

The mechanical world view rested on a single, fundamental assumption: *matter is passive*. It possesses no active, internal forces. Nothing in matter compels it to develop or to move toward an ultimate goal. The matter of the seventeenth century possessed only the passive qualities of size, shape, and impenetrability. Change did not result from the operation of internal principles and powers, as in the Aristotelian view; instead, motion was explained by the laws of impact and the new principle of inertia. The seventeenth century replaced Aristotle's conception of nature as an organic being achieving maturity through self-development with the view of nature as a machine whose parts undertook various movements in response to other parts doing the same thing.

In the absence of internal principles governing change, material bodies in the mechanical worldview were controlled by external laws. The laws of nature, as understood by the mechanical philosophers, prescribed the movement and interaction of material bodies without themselves being part of the inherent nature of matter. With the exception of the German philosopher Gottfried Wilhelm von Leibniz

(1646–1716), who reiterated Aristotle's belief that the laws of nature must be internal to nature itself, virtually every thinker who accepted mechanistic physics claimed that material bodies followed laws imposed on the world much as good citizens followed laws imposed on society. One major difference between the laws of nature and the laws of society, however, was the emerging recognition of the laws of nature as mathematical. The driving force behind the development of mechanism was the belief that recent discoveries by Kepler, Galileo, Descartes, Stevin, and others of mathematical formulae describing physical phenomena could be given conceptual foundation if nature were seen as a collection of inert material particles governed by external mathematical laws. In half a century, nature came to be seen as a machine, and the natural philosophy of Aristotle gave way to the new promise of mathematics.

Until recently, historians have seen the overthrow of the Aristotelian concept of nature as a change of worldviews antagonistic to Christianity. Centuries before the rise of mechanism, Thomas Aquinas (1224–1274) produced a majestic synthesis of Aristotelian natural philosophy and Christian theology that became a prominent form of Christian thought throughout the medieval period. Thomas interpreted Aristotle's principles inherent in nature as powers instilled there by God, which God used in his providential work. God *cooperated* with natural powers in a way that respected their integrity while accomplishing his purposes. When the mechanists rejected Aristotle's understanding of nature, they simultaneously rejected the theory of God's cooperation with nature. Older histories of the rise of science and some modern textbook accounts interpret the latter rejection as the expurgation of theological dogma from scientific knowledge. Usually influenced by a positivistic conception of science, these studies disallow any contribution from theology to the Scientific Revolution. For example, Andrew Dickson White's *A History of the Warfare of Science with Theology* (1896) claimed that the growth of mechanism "cleared away one more series of dogmas." "As in so many other results of scientific thinking," White added, "we have a proof of the inspiration of those great words 'THE TRUTH SHALL MAKE YOU FREE.'"[1]

The antagonism between theology and science portrayed in White's work has disappeared from certain recent studies. These have argued that mechanism did not entail the rejection of theology but represented a furtherance of theological convictions first expressed by late medieval nominalists. Francis Oakley and Eugene Klaaren have placed the seventeenth-century conception of laws of nature in the history of debates about the freedom of God following the Condemnation of 1277.[2] At issue in the debates was the extent to which an

Aristotelian conception of nature limited the freedom of God. The Condemnation asserted that certain Aristotelian claims (such as "God cannot create a vacuum" or "God cannot move the universe rectilinearly") implied God's inability to choose freely what kind of world to create. Nominalist theologians imbibed the spirit of the Condemnation and scrutinized the cogency of Aristotle's arguments. From their questioning developed the belief that the Creator did not follow Aristotelian principles out of necessity and that he might have chosen to create the world differently. Oakley and Klaaren see the mechanists' insistence that the laws of nature might have been different as a continuation of the nominalist emphasis on divine freedom. Seen in this light, the mechanists' belief that God imposed laws of nature on the world was not simply a timely answer to the need for conceptual grounding of mathematical methods but also a culmination of theological changes begun four centuries earlier.

This essay further qualifies older accounts by tracing ties between the passivity of matter in the mechanical philosophy and the doctrine of the radical sovereignty of God in Reformation thought, especially in the theologies of Martin Luther (1483–1546) and John Calvin (1509–1564). By *radical* sovereignty of God I mean an understanding of sovereignty peculiar to the Reformers and to some of their followers, such as the English Puritans, which held that God's sovereignty excluded the active contribution of lesser beings to his work. Unlike the medieval theory of cooperation, which held that God's cooperation with lesser beings did not compromise his sovereignty, the Reformation believed that an adequate understanding of sovereignty necessitated the exclusion of any contribution to divine providence from human beings or nature. To protect the glory of God and to avoid making God's actions contingent on the actions of created beings, the Reformers affirmed the concept of radical sovereignty against the medieval view of accommodating sovereignty, or cooperation.

In this chapter I will argue that the mechanical philosophers turned to the Protestant doctrine of the radical sovereignty of God in arguing for the passivity of matter. The conviction that matter could not possess active powers if God were sovereign in the Reformation sense provided mechanical philosophers with an important argument against Aristotelianism. Moreover, as many of the mechanists were Protestants, the compatibility between their theological views and their view of nature reinforced their commitment to the mechanical philosophy and made their arguments for it more acceptable to other Protestants. This essay concludes that the mechanists' belief in the passivity of matter gained prominence in the seventeenth century in part because of the recognized affinity between it and the Protestant doctrine of the radical sovereignty of God.

Before turning to these matters, I must say a word about other themes in the literature of Protestantism and science and their relation to this essay. Two themes have been prominent in recent discussions. The first considers the relationship of Protestant biblical interpretation to new scientific hypothes 's, especially the Copernican hypothesis. Studies published in the past few years have revised the views of earlier historians who believed that biblical literalism encouraged Protestants to reject Copernicanism more vehemently than did Catholics. John Dillenberger and Brian Gerrish have argued convincingly that Protestant exegetical theory included many elements allowing for rapprochment between biblical claims and astronomical hypotheses.[3] For example, Luther recognized the significance of contexts of discourse in which the same object can be described in either a religious or a scientific way. The light of the moon, he observed, can be seen by the believer as a sign of divine providence, even though the astronomer may understand it as a reflection of the sun.[4] Similarly, Calvin's influential principle of accommodation attributed a degree of poetic licence to the biblical text, by which divine truths were presented in a nontechnical language for the lay reader. In his commentary on Genesis, Calvin stated:

> Moses wrote in a popular style things which, without instruction, all ordinary persons endued with common sense, are able to understand; but astronomers investigate with great labour whatever the sagacity of the human mind can comprehend. Nevertheless, this study is not to be reprobated, nor this science to be condemned, because some frantic persons are wont boldly to reject whatever is unknown to them. For astronomy is not only pleasant, but also very useful to be known: it cannot be denied that this art unfolds the admirable wisdom of God. . . . Nor did Moses truly wish to withdraw us from this pursuit in omitting such things as are peculiar to the art; but because he was ordained a teacher as well of the unlearned and rude as of the learned, he could not otherwise fulfil his office than by descending to this grosser method of instruction. . . . Moses, therefore, rather adapts his discourse to common usage.[5]

Recognizing the accommodation of the text to the general reader, the interpreter could avoid conflict with contemporary astronomy by claiming that the biblical author described the heavens as they appear to the unlearned eye, not as they might be understood by the astronomer.

In addition to the subject of Protestantism and Copernicanism, recent discussion has concerned the "Merton thesis." In *Science, Technology, and Society in 17th Century England* (1938), Robert K. Merton focused on the ethos of the Puritan branch of English Calvinism and argued that it provided a context of social values promoting the attractiveness of science as a vocation. The Puritan ethos, Merton believed, was epitomized in the often repeated phrase, "To the glory of God and the good of mankind." Science seemed predestined to fulfill these goals. It promised to reveal the intricacies of creation and to improve the standard of living. As a result, between 1640 and 1660, when Puritans were the dominant power in English government, natural science became for the first time an attractive vocation. Merton cited figures showing a sharp rise in numbers of students entering scientific fields during and shortly after this period and concluded that Puritan values had contributed significantly to the growth of science in mid-seventeenth-century England.

Since its initial statement in 1938, the Merton thesis has fueled a large controversy among historians of religion and science.[6] Some critics have seen Merton's sociological analysis as unimportant for the history of science, which, they believe, has more to do with scientific ideas than with values that may have influenced the place of science in society. Others have accepted Merton's general approach but have criticized him for restricting his data to the period 1640–1660 and for taking Richard Baxter as a representative Puritan. Both lines of criticism have resulted in heated debates about the definition of *Puritanism* and *science* in the seventeenth century, about the proper focus for writing the history of either, and about the real significance for science of any putative relation between them. Not even Charles Webster's recent, exhaustive study has silenced the controversy. Webster's expanded focus and well-substantiated claims leave little doubt about a relation between Puritanism and science, but questions of method, definition, and significance remain and will continue to be debated for years to come.[7]

Although the last word has not been said, the above-mentioned discussions have resulted in the generally accepted view of a *rapport* between certain aspects of Protestantism and the new science. This rapport, however, cannot be taken as grounds for claiming that the Reformation caused the Scientific Revolution, or even that it was a necessary precondition for the rise of science. Numerous factors having no apparent connection with Protestantism influenced the emergence of science, and modern science probably would have developed had there been no Reformation. Recent studies of Protestantism and science, including this essay, have not located the origins of science in Luther's revolt, but they have disputed earlier views that the Reformation and the Scientific Revolution had nothing in common. Whether we focus on Copernican astronomy, on Puritan values implicit in the new science, or on the passivity of matter in the mechanical worldview, Protestantism possessed qualities of thought and practice that had significant affinities with early modern science.

JUSTIFICATION AND RADICAL SOVEREIGNTY IN REFORMATION THOUGHT

In a discussion of threads common to the thought of the Reformation and that of mechanical philosophers, it is tempting to turn immediately to the Reformer's view of the natural world. To do so, however, would suggest that the leaders of the Reformation had interests in nature resembling those of seventeenth-century natural philosophers or that their writings gave comparable emphasis to natural philosophy. In fact, the concerns of Luther and Calvin differed widely from those of the mechanists, and these differences must be taken into account.[8] The theology of the Reformation cannot be said to have contained a systematic or detailed view of nature. Very little of the Reformers' work would count as natural philosophy per se, although some of the insights of natural philosophers were employed in their theological reflections, and some of those reflections held implications for natural philosophy.

The Reformers' own emphasis can be maintained if we turn first to the doctrine of justification, for it was the focus of the Reformation and offers the key to its theology. "The article of justification," Luther wrote, "is master and head, lord, governor, and judge over all the various branches of doctrines."[9] According to Luther, human beings are not justified by endeavoring to becoming righteous but by accepting on faith that God through Christ has made them righteous. Luther drew a sharp distinction between "active righteousness" (trying to become righteous by acting virtuously) and "passive righteousness" (accepting on faith the righteousness offered by God). Active righteousness, he maintained, had a role in everyday affairs, but no place in the gospel. The gospel of Christ concerned only passive righteousness:

> This most excellent righteousness, the righteousness of faith, which God imputes to us through Christ without works, is neither political nor ceremonial nor legal nor work-righteousness but is quite the opposite; it is a merely passive righteousness, while all the others, listed above, are active. For here we work nothing, render nothing to God; we only receive and permit someone else to work in us, namely, God. Therefore it is appropriate to call the righteousness of faith or Christian righteousness "passive."[10]

Luther's insistence that passive righteousness formed the heart of the gospel departed sharply from medieval teachings on justification, which acknowledged the active participation of human beings in salvation. For Thomas Aquinas, believers initially received a free gift of grace that enabled them to cooperate with God in their salvation. Once in a state of grace, they performed works of charity that engendered righteousness and enabled union with God. For William of Ockham (1285–1349), God provided the initial infusion of grace only when the believer had done everything possible to perform good works without it. Upon receipt of grace, as in the Thomistic scheme, believers actively participated in their salvation by performing charitable deeds, becoming righteous, and accepting eternal life.[11]

To Luther and the Reformation such teaching compromised God's sovereignty. Even though medieval theology recognized that grace was required for salvation, works were required as well. Salvation would not be awarded unless the pilgrim made an active effort. The Reformers argued that this made salvation contingent on human actions and detracted from God's sufficiency. "For God is He who dispenses His gifts freely to all," Luther wrote, "and this is the praise of His deity. But He cannot defend this deity of His against the self-righteous people who are unwilling to accept grace and eternal life from Him freely but want to earn it by their own works. They simply want to rob Him of the glory of His deity."[12] To maintain God's glory the Reformers emphasized his radical sovereignty. Salvation did not depend on human actions but on God alone. Against common sense and church tradition Luther boldly proclaimed this conclusion about salvation: God does everything, human beings do nothing.

Rejecting the active role of human beings in salvation, the Reformers also rejected the medieval use of Aristotle's *Ethics* in theories of salvation. In the *Ethics* Aristotle claimed that moral virtue did not develop without effort and practice. A person had the potential for being virtuous but became virtuous only by performing virtuous acts. Medieval theology adopted this premise, claiming that active moral cooperation in a state of grace engendered righteousness and enabled the pilgrim to draw closer to God. On this view the grace of God helped to perfect human nature by cultivating the potential for virtue inherent within it. Aristotle provided the analysis of human nature; medieval theology explained how grace cooperated with nature, perfected it, and made salvation possible.

Quite the opposite view of virtue prevailed in Protestant thought. For the Reformers, human nature could not be improved by virtuous actions, at least not in any way important for salvation. For this reason they resolutely denounced the use of Aristotle's *Ethics* in theology. In his *Disputation against Scholastic Theology* Luther asserted: "Virtually the entire *Ethics* of Aristotle is the worst enemy of grace. This in opposition to the scholastics."[13] "According to him [Aristotle], righteousness follows upon actions and originates in them. But according to God, righteousness precedes works. . . ."[14] This difference was the crux of the Reformation. For the Reformers any effort aiming to perfect human nature for salvation was built on an overassessment of human ability and an atrophied view of divine grace.

The discerning reader may have anticipated that the mechanical philosophers made the same argument against Aristotle's view of the world. Insofar as Aristotle attributed change in the world to the striving of the world for perfection, the mechanists believed that he attributed too much to nature and not enough to God. Against Aristotle they argued that nature contributed nothing to its formation or development. It was not a being capable of any power or purpose apart from the hand of God. To attribute intrinsic powers and purposes to the world, as Aristotle had done, falsely anthropomorphized nature and detracted from the exclusive role of God in forming and sustaining the world. However, before discussing the arguments of the mechanists, let us turn to the Reformers' view of the natural world. Even though natural philosophy was not central to their theology and their view of nature cannot be called "mechanistic," their understanding of natural things as passive recipients of divine power was entirely consistent with the mechanical philosophy.

GOD AND THE NATURAL WORLD

Luther and Calvin based their understanding of God's relation to nature on the belief that God created the world *ex nihilo*. In their view, God did not shape preexistent matter; he merely spoke, and the world was. In creating the firmament and giving motion to the celestial bodies, He did not depend on nature, which, Luther says, "is incapable of this achievement."[15] By his Word He called the heavens into existence, and by the same Word He created the things of the earth. Calvin saw the Word as the instrument by which God "preserves all that He created out of nothing." Were it not for the continuous presence of the Word, the world would slip back into nothing.

While preserving the world, God continues to perform a creative role. However much appearances may suggest a natural cause, Luther and Calvin believed that procreation does not occur unless God commands it. In discussing Aristotle's claim that mice originate from decaying matter, Luther said,

> If you should ask by what power such a generation takes place, Aristotle has the answer that the decayed moisture is kept warm by the heat of the

sun and that in this way a living being is produced, just as we see dung
beetles being brought into existence from horse manure. I doubt that this
is a satisfactory explanation. The sun warms; but it would bring nothing
into being unless God said by His divine power: "Let a mouse come out
of the decay."[16]

Luther chided physicians and philosophers for ascribing procreation
to "a matching mixture of qualities which are active in predisposed
matter." "Aristotle," he claimed, "prates in vain that man and the
sun bring man into existence. Although the heat of the sun warms
our bodies, nevertheless the cause of their coming into existence is
something far different, namely the Word of God."[17] Similarly, Calvin
believed that "fruitfulness proceeds from nothing else but the agency
of God."[18] Commenting on Genesis 1:1, he wrote, "Hitherto the earth
was naked and barren, now the Lord fructifies it by his Word. . . .
For neither was it naturally fit to produce anything, nor had it a
germinating principle from any other source, till the mouth of the
Lord was opened."[19]

In his discussion of Providence in the *Institutes*, Calvin formulated
a systematic view of God's relation to the natural world. He made
clear that God's activity in nature is ever-present and that nothing in
nature can be attributed to natural causes alone. God sustains the
existence of creatures, He invigorates created beings with power and
movement, and He determines the ends of natural things and of
nature as a whole. Under no circumstances can nature be seen as an
independent entity running under its own power toward inherent
ends. In the *Institutes*, Calvin repudiated all views of nature that made
it a complete or even partial cause of events. Natural things are only
instruments through which God acts; He could choose to use different
instruments, or none at all. For example, in discussing the sun as a
cause of propagation of plants, Calvin pointed out that Genesis describes the creation of herbs and fruits *before* the creation of the sun.
He concluded, "Therefore a godly man will not make the sun either
the principal or the necessary cause of these things which existed
before the creation of the sun, but merely the instrument that God
uses because he so wills; for with no more difficulty he might abandon
it, and act through himself."[20]

As instruments of God's work, natural things do not have an inherent activity or end. Although they may have received a certain
nature or property at creation, this constitutes only a "tendency" that
is ineffective apart from the Word of God. For Calvin, as for Luther,
the behavior of a thing depends entirely on God.

And concerning inanimate objects, we ought to hold that, although each one has by nature been endowed with its own property, yet it does not exercise its own power except in so far as it is directed by God's ever-present hand. These are, thus, nothing but instruments to which God continually imparts as much effectiveness as he wills, and according to his own purpose bends and turns them to either one action or another.[21]

Depending on his purpose, God may command natural things such as water, wind, or trees to behave according to their natures or against them. In both cases their action and end depend on Him. For example, Calvin agreed with Aristotle that earth is heavy and has a natural tendency toward the center of the universe. Water, which is lighter, has less tendency toward the center. "Why then," Calvin asks, "does not water . . . cover the surface of the earth?" Because God holds back the waters to make the earth inhabitable: "In short, although the natural tendency of the waters is to cover the earth, yet this will not happen because God has established, by his Word, a counter-acting law, and as his truth is eternal, this law must remain stead-fast."[22] In contrast, at the time of the flood, God removed the counteracting law and allowed water to follow its natural course. Here again Calvin saw the complete subjugation of the elements to the Word of God.

It must always be remembered that the world does not properly stand by any other power than that of the Word of God, that secondary causes derive their power from Him, and that they have different effects as they are directed. Thus the world was established on the waters, but they had no power themselves, but were rather subject to the Word of God as an inferior element. As soon as it pleased God to destroy the earth, that same water showed its obedience in a death-carrying flood. We can now see how wrong people are who stop at the bare elements as though perpetuity was to be found in them, and not rather that their nature is amenable to the will of God.[23]

On the basis of these texts several conclusions can be drawn about God's relation to nature in Reformation thought. As a result of their belief in the radical sovereignty of God, the Reformers rejected Aristotle's view of nature as having intrinsic powers. In place of the Aristotelian definition of nature as "the principle of motion and change," the Reformers conceived of nature as entirely passive.[24] For them the Word or command of God is the only active principle in the world. The Reformers, moreover, rejected Aristotle's belief that the inherent tendencies of things determine their ends. Whereas Aristotle understood teleological change as "the fulfillment of what exists potentially," Luther and Calvin denied that the potential of a thing determines its end because only God controls its behavior and purpose.[25] In effect, the Reformers' view of God rendered Aristotelian essentialism pointless by denying that essences contribute causality or purpose to nature. Unlike Thomas Aquinas, who asserted that God's respect for created things imparts "the dignity of causing" to them, the Reformers took away nature's dignity in order to enhance God's.[26]

Before turning to arguments by which mechanical philosophers rejected Aristotle, let us reiterate a caution expressed earlier. The work of the Reformers differed too much from that of the mechanists for us to see in Reformation thought a nascent philosophy of nature that blossomed, as though inevitably, into a mechanical worldview. In fact, many Protestant thinkers after Luther and Calvin departed from their mentors' extreme formulation of divine sovereignty by returning to an Aristotelian view of nature and restoring the balance between primary and secondary causes.[27] Despite this departure, the doctrine of radical sovereignty lived on among some Protestant groups in France, Holland, and England and, under the complex vicissitudes of the next century, became incorporated into the mechanical philosophy.

THE SOVEREIGNTY OF GOD AND THE PASSIVITY OF NATURE

The basic source of the ideas of mechanical philosophers was the Renaissance revival of ancient atomism. Although the tenets of atomism had been known to the medieval Schoolmen, their source was Aristotle, whose comments about the atomists in *De caelo* and *De generatione et corruptione* were uniformly critical. The rediscovery of Lucretius's *De rerum natura* in 1417 provided a new source for the atomic philosophy, and by the middle of the sixteenth century there was "fairly widespread interest in the atomic view of matter."[28]

Yet the revival of atomism was only the first step in the emergence of the mechanical philosophy. Atomism in its ancient form faced serious problems as a philosophy of nature, problems that Plato and Aristotle had been quick to point out. Foremost among these was the difficulty of accepting the claim that the order and regularity evident in nature originated in the chance encounters of atoms moving in the void. A closely related problem of the atomic doctrine was the association of atomism with atheism. For Leucippus, Democritus, Epicurus, and Lucretius, atoms were not created, but eternal. The gods themselves had been created by the concourse of atoms, they were subject to chance, and they were unable to legislate principles that might give nature a rational order or goal. Unlike other ancient philosophies of nature, atomism, because of its emphasis on randomness and materialism, offered no basis for rationality or purpose in this world. For this reason the revival of atomism in Christian Europe was not a serious possibility until significant changes in the ancient doctrine had been made. The move that circumvented these problems and established atomism as a viable worldview was the introduction of God as a cosmic lawgiver, who imposed laws on atoms for the purpose of creating an orderly universe. By giving God this function the mechanists provided cosmic principles and purposes that had been lacking in the ancient doctrine, removed its atheistic associations, and cleared the way for the establishment of a mechanical worldview.

The French priest Pierre Gassendi (1592–1655) was among the most influential revivers of ancient atomism. His *Philosophiae Epicuri Syntagma* (1649) followed Epicurean teachings and was thoroughly anti-Aristotelian.[29] It recognized the existence of a vacuum and accepted the primary qualities of matter as solidity, hardness, resistance, impenetrability, and extension. Unlike Epicurus, however, Gassendi did not claim that motion was inherent in matter. As a first step in removing the atheistic taint of the ancient doctrine, Gassendi held that God imposed motion on atoms at the creation of the world. His introduction of God as the source of motion helped to overcome the independence of nature in the ancient doctrine and to establish its contingency on God.

In Gassendi's attribution of atomic motions to God, Walter Charleton (1620–1707), sometime physician to King Charles of England, saw new possibilities for ancient atomism as a religiously acceptable philosophy of nature. In *The Darkness of Atheism Refuted by the Light of Nature* (1652), Charleton went beyond Gassendi, turning the motion of matter into a proof of the existence of God. The brute, passive matter of the atomic doctrine could never account for activity and order in the world. Therefore, Charleton reasoned, the world as we know it could not have come about without God. Charleton became such a devoted adherent of Gassendist views that he published a lengthy English paraphrase of the arcane *Syntagma*, entitled *Physiologia Epicuro-Gassendo-Charltoniana; or, A Fabrick of Science Natural upon the Hypothesis of Atoms* (1654). The *Physiologia* soon became the major source of Epicurean views in England. It enunciated the same relation of God and atomic matter as Charleton's earlier work:

To a sober judgment it appears the highest *Impossibility* imaginable, that either the Chaos of Atoms could be eternal, self-principate, or increate, or dispose and fix itself into so vast, so splendid, so symmetrical, so universally harmonical, or Analogical a structure as this of the World. For, as the Disposition of the Chaos of Atoms into so excellent a form, can be ascribed to no other Cause, but an *Infinite Wisdom*, so neither can the *Production* or Creation of the same Chaos be ascribed to any other Cause, but an *Infinite Power*, as we have formerly demonstrated in our *Darkness of Atheism*, cap. 2.[30]

Robert Boyle (1627–1691) was a prolific critic of the Aristotelian concept of nature and one of the strongest advocates of the mechanical philosophy. In *A True Inquiry into the Vulgarly Received Notion of Nature* (1686) he described the medieval Aristotelian view of a personified nature and argued that it detracts "from the honor of the great author and governor of the world, that men should ascribe most of the admirable things, that are to be met with in it, not to him, but to a certain nature. . . ."[31] Seeing nature as a living, active being, he added, "seems not to me very suitable to the profound reverence we owe the divine majesty, since it seems to make the Creator differ too little by far from a created (not to say imaginary) Being."[32] A sharp distinction between the Creator and the creature, Boyle believed, was fundamental to Christian faith. He claimed that the failure to make this distinction sharply enough by ascribing to nature what belonged to God was "the grand cause of the polytheism and idolatry of the gentiles." The Bible, he said, makes no reference to nature as a cause (not even as a secondary or cooperating cause) but sees all of creation as the direct work of God.

Moses in the whole history of the creation, where it had been so proper to bring in this first of second causes [i.e., nature], has not a word of nature: and whereas philosophers presume, that she, by her plastic power and skill, forms plants and animals out of the universal matter, the divine historian ascribes the formation of them to God's immediate *fiat*.[33]

Boyle's insistence on the radical distinction between the Creator and creation, and his belief that any attribution of activity or purpose to nature denied the distinction, followed closely the Reformer's understanding of sovereignty. Insofar as active qualities were attributed to nature, they detracted from the sufficiency of grace and denied God his full glory. Interpreting Scripture as had Calvin before him, Boyle argued against views of nature incorporating any force, principle, or agent that might be construed as an active or purposeful being. The world soul of Plato, the plastic power of the Cambridge

Platonists, and the substantial forms of Aristotle became unnecessary metaphysical constructs whose existence denied "the ability of the sovereign Lord and Governor of the world to administer his dominion over all things." "For my part," Boyle said, "I see no need to acknowledge any architectonic being besides God. . . ."[34] "Those things which the school philosophers ascribe to the agency of nature interposing according to emergencies, I ascribe to the wisdom of God. . . ."[35]

In an early notebook entitled *Quaestiones Quaedam Philosophicae* Isaac Newton (1642–1727) reveals that during his years at Cambridge he read Gassendi, Charleton, and Boyle. The first entry is taken almost verbatim from Charleton, and the entire notebook exhibits a commitment to the tenets of mechanical philosophy.[36] An essay written several years later, however, shows more clearly the extent of the mechanists' influence on Newton and especially on his belief in the dependency of nature on God. In *De Gravitatione et Aequipondio Fluidorum* he attempted to work out the relations among space, matter, and God. The discussion of space may have been influenced by Boyle's previous criticism of Gassendi and Charleton, both of whom accepted the Epicurean doctrine of the independence of space from God. Newton made clear, however, that space cannot be conceived as a *substance* because it is neither absolute in itself nor does it act on other things. Nor is it an *accident*, because it can exist without bodies. Having eliminated these alternatives, Newton proposed that space is the necessary effect of the existence of God. Because God exists as a ubiquitous being, space exists.

Material bodies, in contrast, do not follow from divine existence necessarily, but were created by "an act of the will alone." Newton suggested an account of creation by which God endowed parts of space with certain sensible qualities (shape, mobility, impenetrability, and perceptibility) simply by his will. Distinguishing his view from accounts that held that God had created through an intermediary, Newton said:

> some may perhaps prefer to suppose that God imposes on the soul of the world, created by him, the task of endowing definite spaces with the properties of bodies, rather than to believe that this function is directly discharged by God. . . . But I do not see why God himself does not directly inform space with bodies; so long as we distinguish between the formal reason of bodies and the act of divine will.[37]

Making matter directly contingent on the will of God, Newton maintained, is more acceptable theologically than the views of Descartes and Aristotle because "we cannot postulate bodies of this kind without at the same time supposing that God exists and has created bodies in empty space out of nothing."[38] Like Charleton and Boyle before him, Newton sought to ensure the sovereignty of God by adopting a concept of a material body as an entity having no independent reality, but totally dependent on the Creator. Material bodies, he said, "cannot be truly understood independently of the Idea of God." Matter is a created substance and hence "the idea of it no less involves the concept of God than the idea of accident involves the concept of created substance."[39]

Although these were the thoughts of the young Newton, speculating freely about metaphysical concepts, the ideas formed in these early years reappeared in his later work. Again and again he returned to the sovereignty of God and the dependency of matter in seeking to comprehend the phenomena of nature. Especially after the publication of the *Principia* (1687), when the question of the cause of gravity emerged as an issue, Newton pondered the attractive force of matter in a way that recalled his early commitment to the contingency of matter on divine volition. While he explored many explanations of gravitational forces, characteristically avoiding definitive claims where he felt the evidence was weak, the picture of the immediate presence of the divine will moving material bodies according to freely established laws was never far from his mind. It was a picture consistent with the early Protestant and mechanist view that nature is completely passive and that God is the exclusive source of activity in the world.

By design, Newton had presented the *Principia* as a descriptive work. His purpose, he said, was to describe mathematically the relationships among celestial and terrestrial bodies. His great achievement was to unify the description of these relations by the inverse-square law of gravitational attraction. In doing so, however, he introduced into the mechanical philosophy the concept of gravitational force, which quickly became a controversial issue among mechanists who previously had limited the notion of force to impact alone. In particular, Leibniz criticized Newton for reintroducing into physics "occult causes," which the mechanical philosophy had banished. The concept of gravity as a force acting between bodies, Leibniz said, reverted to Aristotelian essentialism by making attraction a mysterious, unseen property of bodies. Newton, however, denied that he had offered any explanation of gravity, repeatedly stating that he described only its effects while leaving the explanation of its cause for posterity. In a famous statement in the General Scholium of the *Principia*, he wrote,

But hitherto I have not been able to discover the cause of those properties of gravity from phenomena, and I frame no hypotheses; for whatever is not deduced from the phenomena is to be called an hypothesis; and hypotheses, whether metaphysical or physical, whether of occult qualities or mechanical, have no place in experimental philosophy. In this philosophy particular propositions are inferred from the phenomena, and afterwards rendered general by induction. Thus it was that the impenetrability, the mobility, and the impulsive force of bodies, and the laws of motion and of gravitation, were discovered. And to us it is enough that gravity does really exist, and act according to the laws which we have explained, and abundantly serves to account for all the motions of the celestial bodies, and of our sea.[40]

Yet it hardly appeared satisfactory to leave hanging the question of the cause of gravity, especially since Newton all but denied the possibility of a mechanical cause (that is, one resulting from impact alone). If gravity were caused by the impact of small particles against bodies (as Descartes, Huygens, and Leibniz held), then its action should be proportional to the surface areas of bodies. In the General Scholium, however, and indeed throughout the *Principia*, Newton made clear that gravity "operates not according to the quantity of the surfaces of the particles upon which it acts (as mechanical causes used to do), but according to the quantity of solid matter which they contain."[41] Having thus apparently denied mechanical causation, Newton naturally appeared to his critics to hold privately that gravity was an essential property of matter.

In attributing this view to Newton, however, the critics were wrong. Although he never found an explanation of gravity that satisfied him, Newton vehemently rejected the possibility that matter possessed inherent powers such as attraction. "I desired that you would not ascribe innate gravity to me," he told Bentley in 1693. "That Gravity should be innate, inherent and essential to Matter . . . is to me so great an Absurdity, that I believe no Man who has in philosophical Matters a competent Faculty of thinking, can ever fall into it."[42] Newton appears to have had two reasons for this denial. First, like other mechanists, he accepted the doctrine of the passivity of matter. Second, the radical sovereignty of God required the animation of nature to come from God alone and not from matter.[43]

Consistently maintaining these two commitments, Newton struggled between the publication of the *Principia* in 1687 and that of the *Opticks* in 1704 to arrive at a satisfactory solution to the problem of gravity. Although he never accomplished this aim, in the course of these struggles he developed a view that separated the phenomena of nature into two fundamental principles: a "passive" principle, which he associated with matter, and an "active" principle, which he associated with God. Given only the passive principle, the world as we know it could never have formed, nor could it continue. From the passivity of matter alone neither motion nor the conservation of motion would be possible. Active principles, in contrast, initiated and conserved motion. Newton identified them with such forces as gravity, fermentation, and cohesion. He came to believe that the life and structure of the world resulted from active principles. Without them the world would collapse into lifeless matter.

> For we meet with very little Motion in the World, besides what is owing to these active Principles. And if it were not for these Principles, the Bodies of the Earth, Planets, Comets, Sun, and all things in them would grow cold and freeze, and become inactive Masses; and all Putrefaction, Generation, Vegetation and Life would cease, and the Planets and Comets would not remain in their Orbs.[44]

Bifurcating the world into passive and active principles, Newton (even more than his mechanist predecessors) came to see nature per se as a lifeless world, but permeated by the life of God. Active principles become a manifestation of God's sovereign power, providing vitality to senseless, inert matter. In attempting to portray the mechanism of divine sufficiency, Newton returned to the conception of space and the model of mind-body interaction that he had first developed in *De Gravitatione*. He imagined God immediately present in the world, constituting space itself, and the Divine Will acting on matter in a way analogous to the movement of the human body by the will. In the early essay he wrote, "Since each man is conscious that he can move his body at will, and believes further that all men enjoy the same power of similarly moving their bodies by thought alone; the free power of moving bodies at will can by no means be denied to God, whose facility of thought is infinitely greater and more swift."[45] And in a draft of Query 23 for the 1705 edition of the *Opticks*, he stated, "Life and will are active principles. . . . If there be a universal life and all space be the sensorium of a thinking being . . . then laws of motion arising from life or will may be of universal extent."[46] Because of God's omnipresence, He is able to act in every part of the world without exception. "God . . . is everywhere present," Newton wrote in the General Scholium; "He is omnipresent not *virtually* only, but *substantially*. . . . In him are all things contained and moved."[47]

Thus between 1687 and 1704, as he wrestled with the explanation of gravity, Newton came to see not only gravity but also the other animating forces of nature as a manifestation of the immediate presence of God in the world. Even though he never committed himself publicly to an explanation of the cause of gravity, for much of his career he held privately to the view that God caused gravitational attraction by his omnipresent activity according to principles that he had established, called by Newton "active principles" or "laws of motion." Working in accord with these principles, God animated nature, providing life to a world of dead matter. Without Him, there would be no vital force in the world. Samuel Clarke (1675–1729), with whom Newton was in close contact, summed up the latter's view in a letter to Leibniz. There are, Clarke said, "no powers of nature independent of God."[48]

CONCLUSION

The world as Newton described it appeared to be the product of God's action on mindless, inchoate matter. Unlike the world conceived by Aristotle, in which inherent mindlike principles imbued matter with purposive development, the Newtonian world possessed no inherent activity and no inherent direction. Were it not for God's gracious bestowal of active forces such as gravity, the world would have languished inert and purposeless. As the key to the meaning and structure of the new mechanical world, gravity became the mark of power and grace. In the decades after Newton's *Principia,* theologians and religious popularizers latched onto the grace of gravity as a valuable weapon in the ongoing fight against atheism. They accentuated the disparity between dead matter and matter enlivened by gravity, bestowed by the Creator and sustained by his presence. To matter alone they attributed no potential for the making of a universe. To matter animated by God, they attributed the origin, structure, and preservation of the world.

Richard Bentley's *A Confutation of Atheism from the Origin and Frame of the World* (1693), George Cheyne's *Philosophical Principles of Religion Natural and Revealed* (1705), William Derham's *Physico-Theology; or, A Demonstration of the Being and Attributes of God from His Works of Creation* (1711–1712), William Whiston's *Astronomical Principles of Religion Natural and Revealed* (1717), and many similar works turned English Protestant thought in the direction of natural religion based on Newton's system of the world.[49] Rational analysis of nature, they held, showed that the world cannot be explained by natural causes alone but must be the work of God. Newtonian science demonstrated the need for a Creator, who graciously sustains a world totally incapable of sustaining itself. Bentley concluded *A Confutation of Atheism* with the affirmation that "a Power of mutual Gravitation, without contact or impulse, can in no-wise be attributed to mere Matter. . . . Universal Gravitation, a thing certainly existent in Nature, is above all Mechanism and material Causes, and proceeds from a higher principle, a Divine energy and impression."[50] For Bentley and other religious expositors of Newton's work, nature was unambiguously a gift of grace, not a product of necessity. The mechanical worldview, in their hands, became an uncompromising witness to the glory of God.

If my analysis has been correct, the natural religion of the eighteenth century built its case on the radical sovereignty of God found in Reformation theology and developed by the mechanical philosophers. The uncompromising sovereignty of the Protestant God appears to have so overwhelmed the powers of nature in the mechanical worldview that nature, now unable to account for itself, points to the necessity of God. Before concluding too hastily, however, that the notion of radical sovereignty provides an unambiguous link between the Reformation and the natural religion of the eighteenth century, let us reiterate the caution stated earlier. Despite similarities between the thought of the Reformers and of the mechanists, there were also enormous differences. Even though the mechanists' concept of radical sovereignty was technically consistent with that of the Reformers, it did not do justice to the Reformers' *intentions*. In the two hundred years from 1520 to 1720, such a shift of interest and emphasis occurred that the real significance of divine sovereignty in Reformation thought was lost.

For the Reformers, the radical sovereignty of God filled not only intellectual needs but spiritual and pastoral ones as well. Medieval theories of salvation had so stressed the active participation of human beings in their salvation that many believers worried whether they had done enough to be saved. Suffering from this anxiety, Luther saw the radical sovereignty of God as offering the only reliable assurance of salvation. Accepting on faith that God alone saves, the Protestant was freed from doing good works and penance as preconditions of salvation and from the psychological and spiritual traumas that went with them. The same spiritual and pastoral intentions permeate the Reformers' view of God and nature. The emphasis on divine sovereignty in Calvin's discussion of providence in the *Institutes* has the overriding intention of assuaging believers' anxieties about natural occurrences. Because God (and not "Nature") controls the world, Christians need not fear what happens. Belief in the absolute sovereignty of God instills confidence that nature is not indifferent, but that every event has a divine purpose. God's sovereignty over nature puts Him in a position to care for each creature. For the Reformers "general providence," by which God sustains the world order, is secondary to "special providence," by which He cares for individuals. In contrast with a philosophical analysis of the world, Calvin says, "Faith ought to penetrate more deeply, namely, having found Him Creator of all, forthwith to conclude . . . not only that He drives the celestial frame as well as its several parts by a universal motion, but also that he sustains, nourishes, and cares for, everything he has made, even to the least sparrow."[51]

Nothing could contrast more sharply with the mechanists' view of God and the world. For them, although God was sovereign over a world that He created and, in principle, could suspend or change natural laws to accomplish a special purpose, in practice He did not tamper with the laws of nature. He was a God of general providence and only rarely, in the case of miracles, a God of special providence. The needs of the individual are thus subordinated to the general laws by which God maintains the common good. The good of the whole, Boyle reiterated tirelessly, comes first. The good of the individual is a distant second. As a consequence, the mechanists' God, whose existence and attributes Newton's religious expositors zealously proved, only faintly resembled the Reformers' God, despite their common understanding of the notion of sovereignty. In the mechanical worldview, God has become a cosmic legislator—a "Universal Ruler," as Newton said in the General Scholium. He is no longer "my God," as Luther was fond of saying.

Why the difference? No simple answer can be given, but one important factor was the different problems addressed by the Reformers and the mechanists. The Reformers faced a crisis of faith brought about by what they believed was a misconception of divine grace. Addressing the needs of the believer, they effected a theological revolution by focusing on the absolute sovereignty of grace and the assurance of salvation that they thought belief in it would bring. The mechanists faced the very different problem of developing a plausible conception of nature in the light of recent discoveries of mathematical laws of nature. They employed the sovereignty of God to impose laws of nature on the corpuscles of ancient atomism, making atomism into a viable worldview and laying the conceptual basis for mathematical physics. In the process, however, God changed character. The sovereign Redeemer of Luther and Calvin became the sovereign Ruler of the world machine. The Reformers' search for assurance of salvation gave way to the assurance of scientific explanation. The radical sovereignty of God between the Reformation and the Enlightenment followed the course of many concepts in the complex history of religion and science. While the technical dimensions remained the same, the context changed, and so did the meaning.

NOTES

1. Andrew Dickson White, *A History of the Warfare of Science with Theology in Christendom* (1896; reprint, New York: George Braziller, 1955), p. 208.

2. Francis Oakley, "Christian Theology and the Newtonian Science: The Rise of the Concept of the Laws of Nature," in *Creation: The Impact of an Idea*, ed. Daniel O'Connor and Francis Oakley (New York: Scribners, 1969), pp. 53–84; and Eugene Klaaren, *Religious Origins of Modern Science* (Grand Rapids, Mich.: Wm. B. Eerdmans, 1977). The impact of the Condemnations on late medieval science is discussed by Edward Grant in chap. 2 of this volume.

3. B. A. Gerrish, "The Reformation and the Rise of Modern Science," in *The Impact of the Church upon Its Culture*, ed. Jerald C. Brauer (Chicago: Univ. of Chicago Press, 1968), pp. 231–265; and John Dillenberger, *Protestant Thought and Natural Science* (Nashville: Abingdon, 1960); see also Robert Westman's article, chap. 3 of this volume.

4. Cited by Gerrish, "Reformation and the Rise of Modern Science," p. 250.

5. John Calvin, *Commentaries on the First Book of Moses Called Genesis*, trans. John King, 2 vols. (Edinburgh: Calvin Translation Society, 1847–1850), 1:86–87.

6. The more important literature discussing Puritanism and science includes: Dorothy Stimson, "Puritanism and the New Philosophy in 17th Century England," *Bulletin of the Institute of the History of Medicine*, 3 (1935): 321–334; Christopher Hill, *Intellectual Origins of the English Revolution* (Oxford: Oxford Univ. Press, 1965); R. F. Jones, *Ancients and Moderns* (Berkeley and Los Angeles: Univ. of California Press, 1965); R. Hooykaas, *Religion and the Rise of Modern Science* (Edinburgh: Scottish Academic Press, 1972); T. K. Rabb, "Puritanism and the Rise of Experimental Science in England," *Cahiers d'histoire mondiale* 7 (1962): 46–67; Richard Greaves, "Puritanism and Science: The Anatomy of a Controversy," *Journal of the History of Ideas* 30 (1969): 345–368; John Morgan, "Puritanism and Science: A Reinterpretation," *The Historical Journal* 22 (1979): 535–560; and the exchange among Hugh Kearney, Christopher Hill, and T. K. Rabb in issues 28 (July 1964), 29 (Dec. 1964), 31 (July 1965), and 32 (Dec. 1965) of *Past and Present*.

7. Charles Webster, *The Great Instauration: Science, Medicine and Reform 1626–1660* (London: Duckworth, 1975). Webster's study is criticized by Lotte Mulligan, "Puritanism and English Science: A Critique of Webster," *Isis* 71 (1980): 456–469. A well-balanced overview of the problems associated with the study of Puritanism and science, as well as a response to Mulligan, can be found in Webster's article, chap. 7 of this volume.

8. This highlights the methodological problem of many studies in the history of religion and science, including most studies of Protestantism and science. The selection of common themes at the outset such as, for example, the theme of astronomy and Scripture introduces a selective distortion that emphasizes common elements at the expense of the differences. I have tried

to avoid this problem by selecting central motifs of the Reformation and the Scientific Revolution (the doctrine of justification and the mathematization of nature) and asking about the nature of the relation between these motifs.

9. Martin Luther, *D. Martin Luther's Werke: Kritische Gesamtausgabe*, 88 vols. (Weimar: H. Bohlau, 1888–), 39:205, lines 2 ff.

10. *Luther's Works* [hereafter cited as *LW*], ed. Jaroslav Pelikan and Helmut T. Lehman, 56 vols. (Philadelphia: Muhlenberg Press; St. Louis: Concordia Publishing House, 1955), 26:4–5.

11. It should be emphasized that human beings did not *earn* salvation on the medieval view. Only God's grace made salvation possible. Without the initial infusion of grace the pilgrim would not have been able to perform good deeds, and without God's final willingness to honor these deeds salvation would not be a reward. In both steps God was entirely free to act differently. For this reason medieval theologians claimed that God remained sovereign over the process of salvation. He accommodated his control to enable the active involvement of human beings, but He remained in control because their involvement depended on his good will. A clear discussion of medieval teachings on justification and Luther's departure from them is found in Steven Ozment, *The Age of Reform: An Intellectual and Religious History of Late Medieval and Reformation Europe* (New Haven: Yale Univ. Press, 1980), pp. 231–239.

12. *LW* 26:127.

13. Ibid., 31:12.

14. Ibid., 25:152.

15. Ibid., 1:25.

16. Ibid., p. 52.

17. Ibid., p. 127.

18. Jean Calvin, *Commentary on the Book of Psalms*, trans. James Anderson, 5 vols. (Edinburgh: Calvin Translation Society, 1845–1849), 4:154.

19. Calvin, *Commentaries on Genesis* 1:82.

20. Jean Calvin, *Institutes of the Christian Religion* [hereafter cited as *Institutes*], ed. John T. McNeil, 2 vols. (Philadelphia: Westminster, 1960), book 1, chap. 16, sec. 2. Similarly, Luther remarked, "He [God] could give children without using men and women . . . so that it appears to be the work of man and woman and yet He does it under the cover of such masks" (*LW* 14:114).

21. *Institutes* 1.16.2. Compare Luther's remark concerning the tree of knowledge: "This tree was not deadly by nature; it was deadly because it was stated to be so by the Word of God. This Word assigns to all creatures their function . . ." (*LW* 1:95–96).

22. Calvin, *Commentary on Psalms*, p. 152. Discussing the same passage, Calvin said, "The world did not originate from itself, consequently, the whole order of nature depends on nothing else than his [God's] appointment, by which each element has its own peculiar property" (ibid., p. 149).

23. Jean Calvin, *Calvin's New Testament Commentaries*, ed. David W. and Thomas F. Torrance, 12 vols. (Grand Rapids, Mich.: Wm. B. Eerdmans, 1960–), 12:362–363.

24. Aristotle, *The Works of Aristotle Translated into English*, ed. W. D. Ross, 12 vols. (Oxford: Oxford Univ. Press, 1909–1952), vol. 2, 200b10–11.

25. Ibid., 201a10.

26. Thomas Aquinas, *Summa theologiae*, 61 vols. (Cambridge: Blackfriars; New York: McGraw-Hill, 1964–1981), 5:99.

27. Dillenberger, *Protestant Thought and Natural Science*, pp. 50–64; Peter Petersen, *Geschichte der aristotelischen Philosophie im protestantischen Deutschland* (Leipzig: F. Meiner, 1921); E. Weber, *Die philosophische Scholastik des deutschen Protestantismus im Zeitalter der Orthodoxie* (Leipzig: Quelle & Meyer, 1907); Heinrich Heppe, *Reformed Dogmatics: Set Out and Illustrated from the Sources*, rev. and ed. Ernst Bizer (London, 1950; reprint, Grand Rapids, Mich.: Baker, 1978).

28. Marie Boas, "The Establishment of the Mechanical Philosophy," *Osiris* 10 (1952): 425.

29. Bernard Rochot, *Les travaux de Gassendi sur Epicure et sur l'atomisme* (Paris: J. Vrin, 1944); Olivier Bloch, *La philosophie de Gassendi: Nominalisme, matérialisme et métaphysique* (The Hague: Nijhoff, 1971); Richard Popkin, *The History of Scepticism from Erasmus to Descartes* (New York: Harper & Row, 1964), chaps. 5, 7.

30. Walter Charleton, *Physiologia Epicuro-Gassendo-Charltoniana*, ed. Robert Hugh Kargon (London, 1654; reprint, New York: Johnson Reprint Corp., 1966), pp. 12–13. See Kargon's introduction for further information about Charleton and also his article, "Walter Charleton, Robert Boyle, and the Acceptance of Epicurean Atomism in England," *Isis* 55 (1964): 184–192.

31. Robert Boyle, *The Works of the Honorable Robert Boyle*, ed. Thomas Birch, 5 vols. (London: A. Millar, 1744), 4:361.

32. Ibid., p. 366.

33. Ibid., p. 368.

34. Ibid., p. 372.

35. Ibid., p. 362. It is interesting that the active role of angels in the world followed the same fate as "Nature" in the period after the Reformation. Whereas Aquinas gave angels special powers and purposes to act on God's behalf, Calvin said, "Whenever He pleases, He passes them by and performs His own work by a single nod; so far are they from relieving Him of any difficulty" (cited by Stephen Mason, *A History of the Sciences* [New York: Macmillan, 1962], p. 180). Similarly, Protestant scientists uniformly removed angels from tasks in the world that could be done more easily, and with greater glory, by God. "It were a needless thing for Providence to have appointed Angels unto this business," John Wilkins said, "which might have been done as well by the only will of God" (cited by Mason, pp. 187–188).

36. Richard S. Westfall, "The Foundations of Newton's Philosophy of Nature," *British Journal for the History of Science* 1 (1962): 172–182.

37. Isaac Newton, *Unpublished Scientific Papers of Isaac Newton*, ed. A. Rupert Hall and Marie Boas Hall (Cambridge: Cambridge Univ. Press, 1962), p. 142.

38. Ibid.

39. Ibid., p. 144.

40. Isaac Newton, *Sir Isaac Newton's Mathematical Principles of Natural Philosophy and His System of the World*, trans. Andrew Motte, ed. Florian Cajori (Berkeley: Univ. of California Press, 1934), p. 547.

41. Ibid., p. 546.

42. "Isaac Newton to Richard Bentley, February 25, 1692/3," in *Isaac Newton's Papers and Letters on Natural Philosophy*, 2d ed., ed. I. Bernard Cohen (Cambridge, Mass.: Harvard Univ. Press, 1978), pp. 302–303.

43. These two reasons underlying Newton's conception of matter are discussed in Ernan McMullin, *Newton on Matter and Activity* (Notre Dame, Ind.: Univ. of Notre Dame Press, 1978).

44. Isaac Newton, *Opticks; or A Treatise on the Reflections, Refractions, Inflections, and Colours of Light* (New York: Dover, 1952), pp. 399–400.

45. Newton, *Unpublished Scientific Papers*, pp. 138–139.

46. Cambridge University Library, MS. Add. 3970, fol. 619r, cited by J. E. McGuire, "Force, Active Principles, and Newton's Invisible Realm," *Ambix* 15 (1968): 196. Along with McMullin's *Newton on Matter and Activity*, McGuire's article has been a major source for my analysis of Newton's doctrine of active principles and their association with God.

47. Newton, *Mathematical Principles of Natural Philosophy* p. 545.

48. Samuel Clarke, *Leibniz-Clarke Correspondence*, ed. H. G. Alexander (New York: Philosophical Library, 1956), p. 22. On Newton's role in the correspondence see A. Koyré and I. B. Cohen, "Newton and the Leibniz-Clarke Correspondence," *Archives internationales d'histoire des sciences* 15 (1962): 63–126.

49. Hélène Metzger discusses these works in "Attraction universelle et religion naturelle chez quelques commentateurs anglais de Newton," *Philosophie et histoire de la pensée scientifique* 4–6 (1968): 1–223; see also Margaret Jacob's article, chap. 9 of this volume.

50. *Newton's Papers and Letters*, ed. Cohen, pp. 341, 344.

51. *Institutes* 1.16.1.

7

Puritanism, Separatism, and Science

Charles Webster

The period between 1560 and 1660 is one of outstanding interest in English history. This century marked the nation's emergence as a major European political and economic force and the extension of its horizons into the imperial sphere. The population expanded, urbanization increased, and London became the largest and most rapidly growing city in Europe. Finally the tensions generated in this process culminated in revolution. The revolutionary decades, 1640–1660, witnessed the overthrow of the established church, the execution of the king, and the creation of a republic. These events initiated a remarkable phase of unbridled debate and experimentation over alternative forms of social and religious organization. But aspirations were not matched by achievement. No viable or stable form of government emerged under the republic, and the monarchy was restored in 1660.

Among the most noteworthy features of this dramatic landscape were the movements concerned with the reform of religion and the advancement of science, commonly associated with Puritanism and Baconianism. The two movements evolved in parallel, and each left a permanent cultural legacy. Each separately presents challenging problems of interpretation. But we must face the even more difficult question of the precise relationship between them.[1]

Since about 1965 the question of the relationship between Puritanism and science at the time of the English Revolution has been the subject of an undiminishing tide of commentary. This subject has assumed the status of crucial test case in the wider debate concerning the cultural ramifications of the rise of capitalism. The work of Karl Marx forms the background of debate; in the early decades of the twentieth century Ernst Troeltsch, Richard Tawney, and Max Weber contributed an understanding of the social ethic of the rival religious groups; and in 1938 and 1965, respectively, Robert K. Merton and Christopher Hill brought science to the center of the stage, as an indicator of the ideological differences between the different religious groups.[2] Because of the prominence of science in English culture and the sharpness of the religious divisions, most of the discussion has centered on England.

DEFINITIONS

Questions of definition could easily absorb the whole of this brief review. There is no doubt concerning the existence and importance of either Puritanism or science, but difficulties of definition arise because neither existed in unitary form. It must be recognized that both terms refer to a continuous spectrum of practices and beliefs, and it is therefore no simple matter to place limits on their application.

Although lip service is paid to the limitations and inadequacies of older definitions, assessments of pre-Newtonian science nevertheless continue to defer to the mathematical sciences, while chemistry, natural history, and the applied sciences are accorded a lower status; and alchemy, speculative biology, and medicine are largely disregarded, except by specialists concerned entirely with these subjects. This is an important point, because the branches of science least valued by modern commentators were precisely those that were cultivated by the more unorthodox Puritans. Accordingly, the greater the implicit restriction in the definition of science, the more the contribution of Separatists or "left-wing Puritans" will be overlooked. Indefensible restrictions on the definition of science undermine any attempt at a balanced appraisal of the scientific perspective of the various religious groups.

Puritans were known as the "impatient" or "hotter sort" of Protestants, dissatisfied above all else with the compromise form of church government established by Elizabeth at the beginning of her reign. They were, however, never a completely unified group. They represented a whole spectrum of attitudes, ranging from the most moderate reformism, which sought minor adjustments in the management of the church, to extreme separatism, which sought dismemberment of the church, leaving authority firmly in the hands of separate or gathered congregations.

The term *Puritanism* tends to be limited by church historians to reformers who maintained the ideas of a comprehensive church (embracing the whole community), *Separatist* being reserved for those who went beyond this point to limit the church to individual congregations.[3] The treatment of Puritanism and Separatism in isolation from one another, as if they were definable alternatives, owes more to the importance attached to the distinction between "church" and "sect" ideals within Protestantism than it does to historical realities. Especially after 1625 the church authorities lumped together all Protestant reformers, thus driving Separatists and Puritans into close alliance. Congregations influenced by reforming zeal tended to fluctuate in outlook and usually occupied no rigidly distinct position; Puritan and Separatist congregations often differed on relatively inessential points. When, during the English Revolution, the Puritan movement became politically ascendant, the so-called Independents, who dominated the Puritan regime, in practice advocated religious policies that ranged from reformist to separatist. Independents thus sprawled over a considerable part of the territory of Puritanism and Separatism.

Puritanism was in a constant state of flux. Before 1642 the major part of the reformist movement favored some form of presbyterian church organization; Separatists were noisy but insignificant numerically. After 1642 the pendulum increasingly swung against the moderate reformers. As politically radical Independents gained ground, their more extreme allies, the separatist congregations, multiplied and gained influence. When the republic collapsed in 1660, only a small rump of moderate Puritans within the ministry were absorbed into the restored church, while a heterogeneous group of some two thousand clergymen drawn from across the Puritan-Separatist spectrum were deprived of their livings. They and their equally diverse congregations laid the foundations of modern nonconformity.

As would be expected from the state of affairs summarized above, it is unlikely that the Puritan intellectuals involved in science would occupy an immediately definable and fixed point on the Puritan-Separatist spectrum. Responding to a chaotic religious situation, scientists were conspicuous in attempts to redefine religious boundaries with a view to restoring greater unity; this can be seen from the 1620s onward in the irenicism of Samuel Hartlib (d. 1662), John Dury, and Jan Amos Komenský (Comenius), and later in the latitudinarianism of the founders of the Royal Society. Such initiatives by scientists merely add to the difficulty of fitting them into any of the standard denominational compartments. This dilemma produces some tortured characterizations of figures like Robert Boyle, who is described by Hooykaas as "a 'puritan at heart,' if ever there was one, but at the same time a moderate royalist and episcopalian"; others have described him as anything from a "devout Anglican" to a follower of the Cambridge Platonists.[4]

THE PURITAN AND SCIENTIFIC REVOLUTIONS

With the accession of Elizabeth I to the English throne the Protestant settlement was confirmed. But the independent Church of England superintended by the monarch seemed to many an unsatisfactory hybrid, a temporary compromise, making too many concessions to the discredited Roman Catholic church order. There commenced a long and painful struggle to "purify" the church. Since the church occupied such a central place in the nation's cultural life, and because religious questions impinged on almost all aspects of secular life, Puritanism became central to the whole process of religious and secular change. Very little in the tangled web of economic and social debate was free from vocabulary and concepts rooted in religious sources. Accordingly, in view of its importance as an organizing principle and rallying point, it is not surprising that Puritanism has been regarded as central to the ideology of what is commonly called the Puritan or English Revolution. The significance of the religious dimension can be inferred from the fact that the opposition party was firmly identified as "Puritan" by its monarchist and Laudian opponents,[5] while the political groupings of the revolutionary decades took as their labels the names of the segments of the Puritan movement.

There is no consensus on the origins and nature of the revolution. This subject retains its unending fascination and controversy. Among historians of Parliament and most students of "county communities," there exists for the moment some tendency to underplay the role of ideological factors, including religion. But recent county studies of religious nonconformity point in the opposite direction. In any case, no explanation of the English Revolution couched in political terms will retain credibility unless it recognizes the degree to which religious issues acted as the rallying point of opposition. Without the deep penetration of Puritan ideas the opposition movement would have been deprived of the degree of committed support needed to sustain a revolutionary struggle. Puritanism furnished the opposition with a comprehensive and coherent framework of belief, finding support at all levels within the community, and it raised the status of the struggle to that of a holy war providentially ordained to bring about the final overthrow of Antichrist. The internal coherence of Puritanism was sufficient to sustain a revolution, but it was insufficient to guarantee the stability of the republican regime, as the restoration of the monarchy in 1660 revealed. The cultural impact of Puritanism continued after 1660, but in the context of dissenting congregations rather than as the claimant for a position of centrality in the church.

By whatever criterion science is defined, England emerged from a culturally negligible position to one of remarkable prominence in the century ending with the restoration of Charles II in 1660 and the formation of the Royal Society in the same year. Before the accession of Elizabeth the humanistic revival had made a minor impact; English humanists occupied a minor niche on the European scene; and groups of humanists secured a foothold at Oxford and Cambridge. But their literary impact was insignificant, and the model humanistic foundation, the College of Physicians of London, scarcely more than hovered on the edge of extinction. Perhaps with an element of exaggeration, the French reformer Petrus Ramus in 1563 could not recall the name of a single English scholar.

By the end of the sixteenth century the situation had changed radically. The attainment of maturity of English science was marked by the appearance of William Gilbert's *De Magnete* (1600). A new spirit of cultural assertiveness is suggested by Francis Bacon's *Advancement of Learning* (1605). Gilbert had no equals in the College of Physicians; no other English philosopher before Thomas Hobbes matched Bacon's accomplishment. But at the second rank, and among specialists, a strong spirit of innovation and technical expertise was already firmly established; witness, for instance, the defense of Nicolaus Copernicus by Thomas Digges (1576); John Banister's acceptance of Realdo Colombo's theory of the pulmonary circulation of the blood (1578); the highly professional botanical work compiled by William Turner; and especially contributions to mathematics, astronomy, and navigation by John Dee, Thomas Harriot, Henry Briggs, and their associates. Both Bacon and Gilbert drew upon this tradition. Thereafter the English were not relegated to the league of translators and imitators. They entered into an equal partnership with Continental natural philosophers. Some of their most important works were composed in Latin and disseminated widely abroad. Their classic contributions were backed by a vernacular literature of outstanding quality.

Notwithstanding a more turbulent institutional and social setting, the prelude to the Civil War marks no significant setback in levels of commitment to the new science. By 1640 the College of Physicians contained a number of young physiologists keen to exploit the lessons learned from *De Motu Cordis* (1628) of their colleague William Harvey (1578–1657). Apothecaries, led by Thomas Johnson, were engaging in organized botanical exploration; astronomy continued to flourish in Oxford and London; on the eve of the Civil War Jeremiah Horrocks and William Gascoigne seemed set for a major contribution to physical astronomy. And Hobbes was beginning to make his brooding presence felt as a rival to Descartes.

The Civil War and Revolution yet further increased the turbulence; science was affected by all the normal inconveniences occasioned by civil war and changes of regime. Nevertheless, as I shall indicate below, the pace of scientific development quickened. Many embryo scientific organizations were formed, and a strong start was given to the Royal Society when it was founded at the Restoration in 1660. By this date England had possibly already become the major center for organized scientific activity in Europe. The golden age of science witnessed immediately after the Restoration is scarcely credible without recognition of the impetus provided during the revolutionary decades.[6]

SCIENCE AND SOCIAL CHANGE

It might be argued that the parallel evolution of Puritanism and science, and even the close proximity of the dates at which they reached their zenith, is little more than a curious statistical coincidence. This possibility must be kept in mind. It is equally important to recognize that religion is merely one of a number of determinants requiring consideration in an examination of the dynamics of the scientific movement in England. The direction of scientific effort was influenced by a whole range of social and economic factors. For instance, much of the interest in mathematics, the physical sciences, and botany can be related to the search for innovation in the fields of navigation, trade, industry, agriculture, and horticulture. Few of the personnel of science escaped involvement in the applied sciences. Baconianism, the dominant philosophy of English science, owed its appeal to its empiricist and inductive methods, combined with an explicit directive toward economic participation. The provocative essay by Boris Hessen, followed by more rigorous studies by Edgar Zilsel and Robert K. Merton, suggested the close connection between science and capitalist development in Britain.[7] Subsequent investigations by Christopher Hill and myself have confirmed these findings in a wide range of instances.[8] Preliminary studies for the Restoration period are pointing in the same direction.[9] For instance, technical subjects, or "trade," virtually unstudied or occupying a low priority elsewhere, formed in Britain the centerpiece of scientific effort and scientific organization.[10]

Symbolic of the central role of capitalism is Gresham College, founded by the Elizabethan magnate Sir Thomas Gresham, who also built the Royal Exchange. Gresham College was intended as a meeting place for intellectuals and tradesmen. At the turn of the century it excelled as a forum for pure and applied mathematics, and at the Restoration it became the home of the Royal Society, which was more commonly called "Gresham" than by its proper name.[11]

Nonetheless, introduction of the question of economic determination reinforces rather than diminishes the relevance of religion, by virtue of the interpenetration of economic and religious affairs. It may not be possible to defend in absolute terms the theories of Tawney and Weber concerning the dependence of capitalism upon the "Protestant ethic," but they have revealed the degree to which economic action was justified in religious terms.[12] Not only was the church a direct economic force; the social ethic of every religious group defined attitudes to such major problems as usury, enclosure, and monopoly. All men of practical affairs, including scientists, needed to demonstrate that their actions were in accord with the principles of godliness.

SECTARIAN DIVISIONS WITHIN ENGLISH SCIENCE

Acute religious awareness and frequent references to theology are points that stand out in any examination of the sociology of the English scientific movement. A long line of leading figures in science were ordained clergymen, and many occupied important ecclesiastical positions. These clergymen–natural philosophers included such eminent practitioners as William Turner, William Oughtred, Henry More, Ralph Cudworth, Isaac Barrow, John Ray, John Wilkins, John Wallis, and Seth Ward. Boyle and Isaac Newton, although laymen, pursued science with the zeal of a religious mission.

Scientists contributed freely to the literature of religion. From the beginning to the end of the seventeenth century, natural philosophers, beginning with John Napier and ending with Newton and William Whiston, became the acknowledged expert commentators on the prophetic books of the Bible. They created the genre of physicotheology. Sir Thomas Browne's *Religio Medici* (1642–1643) was deeply influential and widely imitated. Scientific writings were habitually interspersed with religious observations or preceded by extensive theological prolegomena. As an extreme example the practical *Treatise of Fruit Trees* by the humble Ralph Austen was accompanied by his ponderous *Spiritual Use of an Orchard*.[13]

The question immediately arises whether this ample body of data relating to the religious activities of the scientists might be exploited to determine which particular religious group was contributing most actively to science. Headcounting would seem the most elegant means of reducing this complex matter to simple order. Such exercises were pioneered by Augustus de Candolle and made current by Jean Pelseneer in an effort to prove that their fellow Protestants created modern science.[14]

In my opinion, however, this approach, whether conducted on a national or a European scale, is confronted by such profound methodological and conceptual difficulties that it is likely to generate conclusions that are either trivial or irresolvably contentious. The complexities of English Puritanism and Separatism constitute an insuperable barrier to the application of such simplistic numerical analysis. It is very difficult to envisage how even the more meaningful quantitative methods will carry as much weight as our present impressionistic assessment. A great deal of wasted labor might be saved if we were to accept that any impartial inspection of the English scientific community in the seventeenth century, with respect to any of the branches of the specialized sciences, is likely to reveal discoveries emanating from every part of the religious spectrum, possibly with minorities such as Roman Catholics contributing more, and Separatists less, than the proportionate share expected on the basis of their numbers. At the same time the presence of Catholics such as the mathematician Thomas Allen, the astronomer William Gascoigne, the polymath Sir Kenelm Digby, the neo-Scholastic Thomas White, and the physicist Richard Towneley, each highly significant but in completely different aspects of science, indicates the hazards involved in quantifying the notion of scientific contribution.

The Catholic list could be expanded, and similar listings might be undertaken for each point along the religious spectrum, as when, for instance, a strong case was made recently for scientific commitment within the Laudian party.[15] William Harvey might have welcomed being included in this category. The greater the number of subdivisions, the harder it becomes to apply the taxonomic criteria. Then we are embarrassed by certain exotic cases, such as that of John Graunt, who seems to have begun as a Separatist and ended as a Catholic. Even violent enthusiasts like John Webster (1610–1682) are known to have drifted into conformity in later life. Attempts to escape the drawbacks of "splitting," by dividing the religious spectrum into two major segments, also run into difficulties. If we assume that the distribution of religious opinion followed a normal curve, as may well be the case, the greatest numbers must congregate around the mean, with the result that the largest number of people will exist in an ambiguous position with respect to our arbitrarily adopted and imaginary line of division. Moreover, by what criteria of religious belief is the division to be made? The results would vary greatly depending on whether attitudes to the episcopacy, or acceptance of Calvinist theology of election, or some other indicator was taken as the criterion.

The headcounting technique, undertaken explicitly or implicitly, whether by "splitting" or by "lumping," has proved counter-productive as a means of establishing the denominational origins of modern science. Seemingly conclusive enumerations of Puritan and Protestant scientists have provoked an assiduous search for exceptions and quarrels over categorization. The end result is confusion, expressed in a recent strong tendency to disclaim any meaningful connection between science and religion. For instance, Adamson prefers to call Henry Briggs rather a "Puritan and scientist than Puritan scientist." Nicholas Tyacke concludes that his researches on the period of Laudian ascendancy point to a "negative correlation between religion and science." And Lotte Mulligan's study of the Royal Society concludes entirely negatively: "science correlated less with puritanism or latitudinarianism than with the waning role of religion"—a return to the old-fashioned view of W. E. H. Lecky that the rise of science was an expression of increasing secularization experienced during the seventeenth century.[16]

PURITANISM AS ANTISCIENTIFIC?

Failed experiments with quantitative methods should not detract from the fact, apparent from the most elementary data, that there existed the deepest interpenetration between science and religion within the English scientific movement, from the date of its origin to its full maturity. Similarly, the existence of major sectarian tensions within the English church should not disguise the fact that English Protestants of whatever conviction shared a large common denominator of belief. Calvinist theology formed the framework of thinking of all parties, notwithstanding many shades of interpretation and divergence from Calvin on specific points. It would therefore be unrealistic to expect the worldview of the Puritans to be totally different from that of other English Protestants. On fundamental issues affecting cosmology and cosmogony, English Protestants drew on common sources and shared similar preconceptions. English Protestants agreed concerning divine providence, the laws of nature, and the relative status of the book of nature and the book of revelation. Anglicans and Puritans argued for witchcraft or against materialism in essentially the same terms, and, significantly, neither group was completely united. Divisions of opinion on such issues did not occur down the Anglican-Puritan divide.

Within English Protestantism there existed a general sanction for the investigation of nature on the grounds that it would glorify God and contribute to the comprehension of his attributes. The experimental sciences in general attained an enhanced status owing to their development in tandem with works devoted to natural religion and physicotheology. Pioneer contributors to this popular genre, including Robert Boyle, Nehemiah Grew, Henry More, John Ray, and John Wilkins, belonged to the middle band of the religious spectrum. Most of them had close relations with the Puritan movement, but the appeal of natural religion also extended to churchmen and nonconformists of all kinds.

Granted a substantial common denominator of belief on points of theology relating to science, it is not unreasonable to expect "Anglican" and "Puritan" versions of natural philosophy to have a certain resemblance. The Puritan botanist William Turner's spiritual successor was the Anglican Thomas Johnson. The Puritan mathematicians and astronomers Henry Briggs and John Bainbridge found Anglican counterparts in William Oughtred and John Greaves. The Puritan astrologer William Lilly struck up a firm friendship with his Anglican counterpart Elias Ashmole. Such examples could be multiplied. Each new significant phase of innovation found its Anglican and Puritan advocates. The two groups spoke broadly a common language, and both needed to defend their position against a body of opinion among their fellows deeply suspicious of the new science.

In the seventeenth century, as in later periods, every sectarian group contained an influential party convinced that the values of religion and science were essentially incompatible. There existed very real antagonism to scientific and philosophical innovation among Anglicans, Puritans, and Separatists, induced by fear of distraction from the central religious goals of life, through the dangers of vain curiosity. Calvinism, like its rivals, could be associated with a rejection of the new science in favor of obsolete knowledge drawn from a body of Scholastically oriented dogmatic theology. The fear of innovation is well expressed in the desperate call by Robert Baillie, the leading Scottish presbyterian academic, for the Protestant universities to compile a body of sound philosophy to combat Cartesianism. Francis Bacon's *Advancement of Learning* was matched by a work of similar title, expressing extreme skepticism about the sciences, emanating from Bacon's Puritan friend Fulke Greville, the first Lord Brooke. The latter's son, the leading parliamentarian Robert Greville, admitted to similar reservations regarding secular knowledge in his celebrated attack on the episcopacy. Similarly, the Separatists constantly argued that the spiritual understanding of the Scriptures came "not by humane learning, by arts and tongues, but by the spirit of God." Such quotations, this from the coachman John Spencer, could be matched among the utterances of the cobbler Samuel How or, archetypically, of the Quaker George Fox.[17] It is thus easy to embellish the time-honored caricature of Puritan bigotry, to project a view of the typical Puritan mentality as being inward-looking and closed to the values of the new science.[18] Nowadays we are faced with a revival of the idea of Puritanism as representing "intellectual narrowness, lack of receptivity to new ideas, . . . dogmatism, the closed mind and a firm attachment to repression." Failure to attach due weight to this evidence is castigated as a "primary methodological error."[19]

Such conclusions are liable to objection at two levels. First, theologically based skepticism of the value of learning, assertions of the supremacy of spiritual goals, denigration of the flesh, and so on must be seen in context. They are rarely intended as a general disincentive to secular learning. More usually they signify commonplace emphasis on the primacy of the spiritual and warning against contamination of revelation by secular learning. Once this point is established, any form of productive secular knowledge may be cultivated without religious constraint. Thus, with respect to the examples previously given, the first Lord Brooke was completely committed to the reform of knowledge in line with the ideas of Ramus and Bacon, while Robert Greville, the second Lord Brooke, was a supporter of the pansophic scheme of Comenius. Expressions precisely like those of the enthusiasts Spencer and How are used by John Webster to preface his critique of the universities for their *neglect* of experimental science and medicine.[20]

Second, the above arguments strike at straw men: the fallacies they denounce are not subscribed to, and they risk denial of self-evident truths by implying that "typical" Puritans could not become involved in scientific activity. No amount of antiscientific feeling emanating from Puritan sources logically entails that all members of that group should come to the same conclusions; neither does it entail that scientific propensities exhibited among Puritans must be divorced from Puritan religious motives. If this weapon is used against Puritanism, it can be used equally well against other religious groups. By accepting the above "methodology," we would be forced to conclude that every religious group was fundamentally antiscientific and that no scientific activity could stem from genuine religious motivation. Any evidence to the contrary would be dismissed as an unrepresentative exception, suitably ignored.

Such negative conclusions are decisively at variance with the declarations of the scientists themselves, whose personal testimonies must be regarded as more than token gestures toward the reconciliation of science and religion. Such testimony unambiguously suggests that Puritans believed their motivation toward science derived from religious sources. This religious spur to scientific activity was not the prerogative of any one sectarian group; each developed the religious rationale for science in a characteristic way and with resultant differences of emphasis in the pattern of science that emerged.

THE PROTESTANT ETHIC AND SCIENCE

We must now attempt to identify features of the value system of Puritanism that help us to understand the Puritan attitude toward science. The main line of approach to this issue, stemming from Weber and adopted by Merton and Hill, credits Puritans with the quintessence of the proscientific virtues of Protestantism.[21] According to Reijer Hooykaas, a recent proponent of this position, the common qualities of Puritanism and the new philosophy are "anti-authoritarianism, optimism about human possibilities, rational empiricism, [and] the emphasis on experience."[22] There is less certainty among these scholars concerning the theological roots of this positive mental attitude toward science. Weber placed his faith in intramundane asceticism (*innerweltliche Askese*). He saw science as a by-product of the performance of good works, deriving from a restless search for a sign of election, made necessary in its turn by the Calvinist doctrines of grace and predestination.

Various critics, even those within the same camp, have urged that the role of predestination within English Puritanism has been exaggerated, and they point out that the Weber thesis faces a variety of inconsistencies in the evidence.[23] In contrast, these critics accept Weber's contention that Calvinists valued good works, asserting that these works were viewed primarily as a means of securing positive signs of God's favor for the elect. Armed with the additional sanction provided by Romans 1:20, English scientists represented experimental science as a form of good works compatible with the ideal of glorification of God advocated in reformed theology. Romans 1:20, and even more the gloss on this verse in the Geneva translation, insisted that "all men have a most cleere and evident glasse wherein to behold

the everlasting and Almightie nature of God, even in his creatures."
A Discourse Concerning the Beauty of Providence (1649) by John Wilkins
(1614–1672), coming close on the heels of his classic Puritan *Ecclesiastes;
or, A Discourse Concerning the Gift of Preaching* (1646), proved to be the
first of a long line of works driving home the essential piety of experimental philosophy.[24]

There is much less good reason to support the view, advanced
occasionally, that the modern idea of immutable laws of nature rests
on the doctrine of predestination.[25] This concept is readily traceable
back beyond the Reformation. Protestants were merely taking over
an idea of providence that was current among medieval nominalists.[26]
Nevertheless, it seems that voluntarism, which stresses the direct
imposition of divine will on a world created by the unconditional
enactment of providential fiat, was given new momentum by Reformation and Calvinist thought. The latter favored the idea of a created world sustained directly by God's will, in which the moral and
natural realms respond to edicts and laws imposed by divine sovereignty. This framework left no room for intermediaries belonging to
the realms neither of matter nor of soul, such as ethers or the "plastic"
or "hylarchic" spirit, which Platonists assigned to the category of
immaterial body. It has been suggested that the Calvinist notion of
laws of nature made familiar by such Puritan theologians as Joseph
Mede, William Perkins, William Ames, and John Preston formed the
basis for the voluntarism of Boyle and Newton.[27]

It is arguable that the above inducements to science represent a
quantitative, rather than qualitative, difference between Puritans and
other churchmen. Similar quantitative differences apply to such
points of doctrine as God's sovereignty, man's impotence, and the
all-sufficiency of the Scriptures. None of these points was unique to
Puritanism, but each achieved a particular intensity of expression at
the hands of the Puritans.

PRIMITIVE PURITY OF THE SCRIPTURES

Insistence on the authority of the Scriptures was fundamental to the
Puritans. This position had widespread intellectual and social implications. At the earliest point in their evolution, Puritans became involved in conflict with orthodox churchmen over the relative authority
of the Scriptures and natural reason. The Anglican position, as enunciated by Richard Hooker, would seem to allow greater scope for
natural reason, with the Scriptures receiving full acknowledgment
but in reality playing a background role. The Scriptures were more

to the forefront in Puritan thinking. It might appear that this would result in a blind derivation of scientific principles from biblical sources. But in practice this danger was avoided by the operation of the equally strong principle that there exists complete harmony between natural and revealed truth. This latter idea was ultimately developed systematically by Comenius (1592–1670), whose *pansophia*, which had widespread appeal in Puritan circles, was based on the idea of the acceptance of those scientific principles that might be firmly based on reason, experiment, and the Scriptures.

A more immediate point of friction between the Anglican church authorities and the Puritans was the lack of biblical sanction for many of the practices and forms of church organization incorporated in the Elizabethan settlement. To varying degrees Puritans took exception to rules governing ceremony and dress, they opposed much of the content of the prayer book, and they found objectionable the structure of authority within the church. In place of this fabric they wanted a simple order in conformity with their ideas about the primitive church, with ministers more truly accountable to their congregations and services more explicitly based on the recital of psalms and exegesis of the Scriptures.[28]

This program struck at the root of the authority of the Church of England. The Puritans repudiated the Anglican view that the church reserved to itself the discretion to legislate on "inessentials." As far as Puritans were concerned, these inessentials, having no scriptural basis, fundamentally corrupted the church with heathen magic. In their writings the rambling and degenerate magical edifice of the Egyptians was contrasted with the purity and simplicity of the early church. Tirades by the Puritans and Separatists against relics of pagan magic provoked the grandiloquent assertion of Weber that Puritanism represented the logical conclusion of the "great historic process in the development of religion, the elimination of magic from the world."[29]

Weber may have exaggerated this antimagical tendency, but the antimagical polemic of Puritans did carry over into the sphere of science. For instance, the whole of the Puritan apparatus was employed by Richard Bostocke (fl. 1580) in his classic defense of Paracelsianism (a new system of medicine self-consciously designed by its author, Paracelsus [1493–1541], to undermine classical medicine on the basis of premises derived from the Bible). Galenism was censured as a corrupt and baseless system of "heathenish Philosophie" contrasting with Paracelsianism, which he represented as a return to the purity of Adamic knowledge. Bostocke thus inaugurated a line of attack against ancient systems of knowledge that became a commonplace in Puritan circles and was adopted as a standard part of the armory of the Baconians.[30]

Church authorities regarded Puritan scripturalism as particularly dangerous because it contested the standing of the ancient structure of the church and encouraged a process of reappraisal that was seen as the pathway to infinite regress. Every individual would be offered the temptation to challenge all traditional forms of authority. At an early stage the archbishop of York identified the Puritans as those "who tread all authority under foot."[31] Puritanism seemed to its critics to involve a reorientation of mental attitudes that would lead inevitably to infinite regress, not only undermining the basic ideal of the historic unity and continuity of the church but also sanctioning all forms of individual assertiveness and antiauthoritarianism. These predictions were to a great degree fulfilled: the church shattered into a multitude of sects, and the spirit of iconoclasm carried over into political and economic life.[32]

One ultimate effect of the Puritan appeal to biblical authority was to increase the intellectual assertiveness of the lower social orders. Increasing numbers of people from humble backgrounds made their voices heard in religious or secular affairs. One of these was William Petty (1623–1687), who offered the opinion that "many now hold the Plough, which might have been made fit to steere the State." True to his severely practical turn of mind, Petty elaborated for the benefit of Hartlib a complex form of technical education that might be made available to all children above the age of seven, "none to be excluded by reason of the poverty and inability of their parents."[33] The writings of Hartlib, Dury, and Comenius convinced younger associates such as Petty that universal education was the first priority in the social program of the Puritan state, and their elaboration of a comprehensive and detailed educational plan constituted their major corporate endeavor. This venture represents one of the most highly developed practical testimonies to the Puritan faith in the worth of individual experience;[34] it was relevant to science by virtue of the strong "realistic" or scientific bias of the form of education proposed for all social classes. A further point of emphasis in the educational schemes was increasing the accessibility of the Scriptures, by means of a variety of endeavors for translation and propagation, embracing the Turkish New Testament, the Lithuanian Bible, the Indian Bible, and the Company for the Propagation of the Gospel in New England. Robert Boyle was involved in all of these projects.[35]

William Petty's career presents an extreme example of audacious self-confidence and success. It also betokens the way in which the new climate of opinion offered inducements to the breaking of traditional barriers and to enterprise in both the secular and religious spheres. Petty selected medicine and practical mathematics as his first vocational choices. It is interesting that both areas had experienced rapid expansion by recruitment from below during the first part of the century. And both were, of course, important for expanding the horizons of the English scientific movement. The medical practitioners opposed Galenism, took up Paracelsus, van Helmont, and other innovators, and expanded involvement in practical chemistry. The mathematical practitioners rapidly made England the center of the making of scientific instruments in Europe. Mathematical practitioners were pioneering a new field of artisan activity untrammeled by monopoly, in which the initiative could be taken without impediment. Medicine, in contrast, involved trespassing into an area traditionally controlled by the College of Physicians, where the intruders faced the authority of the entrenched hierarchy. It is notable that here, as in the sphere of monopolies in general, the same arguments were mobilized on the part of the intruders as were used against the authority of the church. It is important to establish whether the known examples of Puritan and Separatist involvement among the new breed of mathematical and medical practitioners are indicative of a pattern. It is at least likely that radical Puritanism contributed to a favorable climate for developments of this kind in the same way as it encouraged the expansion of interloping trade in the face of the trading monopolies.[36]

EDIFICATION

With the Puritan mission to purify the church went the parallel mission to purify the personal and social life of the community of believers. This ideal resulted in the idea of the covenanted church, under which the basic unit was a group of members bound together by voluntary contract. Such a congregation was portrayed as a living temple, in contrast with the "dead" pagan temples of the traditional church. Members of this temple were pledged to cooperate with one another, so as to utilize their gifts to the maximum effect in the cause of perfecting the organic body in which they were participating.[37] Typically, John Dury (1596–1680) described the aims of the collaborative effort of the English followers of Comenius as the introduction of "all rules, doctrines and inducements which tend unto the apprehension of fundamentall truthes and performances of duties, whereby the consciences of all conscionable men inwardly and their course of life outwardly may be ordered in the feare of God."[38] This application of the idea of "edification," deriving from the Pauline epistles, has been designated by one author as the distinctive Puritan contribution to the understanding of Paul's theology.[39]

The ideal of edification, when pursued to an extreme, resulted in an audacious confidence in the attainability of a millennial utopia founded on the Word of God. Edification in the hands of groups inspired by a sense of operating in a covenant relationship with God provides a context for the understanding of motives underlying the institutionalization of science in mid-seventeenth-century England. Pioneers of organized science, such as John Wilkins, John Wallis, Theodore Haak, and Samuel Hartlib, were nurtured in the context of the "spiritual brotherhood" of Puritan churchmen and their lay patrons.[40] Their scientific outlook was colored by the inspiration of this brotherhood.

Some of the early scientific clubs were analogous to Continental developments, primarily a convenient mechanism for undertaking research requiring collaborative effort, but most betray deeper motivations. Some took on a distinctly utopian flavor, as in the case of Boyle's "Invisible College" or Samuel Hartlib's "Office of Address." These schemes called for the abandonment of self-interest in favor of pooling information, the aim being to make advanced knowledge available to the republic in a form applicable to the solution of pressing economic and social problems. The Office of Address schemes, which attained a degree of official recognition and patronage while attracting a substantial number of committed adherents, presented an ambitious exemplification of the Puritan idea of edification. In this context it is interesting that Robert Boyle, one of the better-known participants in the Office of Address, published as his first work a brief essay calling for the free communication of useful scientific information.[41]

As a final carryover of the utopianism of the Puritan republic, Henry Oldenburg attempted to infuse something of the universalist reformism of the Office of Address into the Royal Society. Realizing the advantages of a transcendental framework for the Royal Society when it came under attack from the High Church, the Society's latitudinarian apologists made good use of millenarian imagery and tried to represent their elitist scientific club as the realization of Solomon's House. Ironically, this propaganda was disseminated partly to protect the reputations of rehabilitated Puritans such as John Wilkins, founder of the Society and brother-in-law of Oliver Cromwell.[42]

PURITANS IN POWER

It is now necessary briefly to consider the impact on science of the transmutation of Puritanism from a position of opposition to one of power (1649–1660). In general, the Puritan ascendancy has been regarded as a dismal setback for developments in the cultural sphere, partly by virtue of the inevitable effects of the breakdown of civil order, partly because of the supposed anti-intellectualism of the Puritans. Granted, not all of the changes occurring under the new Puritan regime operated in favor of science. It is easy to enumerate losses to science occasioned by the revolution. William Gascoigne and Thomas Johnson were killed during the hostilities. William Harvey's scientific papers are supposed to have been destroyed by London mobs. The universities were dislocated. Harvey and a host of minor and aspiring natural philosophers were driven out of Oxford and Cambridge. The College of Physicians was not abolished, but its authority was largely destroyed. Numerous scientists went into retirement or exile. It is even arguable that in the two decades before the restoration of the monarchy in 1660, no major scientific work was published. Such adverse trends might be regarded as a characteristic legacy of Puritanism as it is popularly conceived.

More realistically, the above list of casualties is characteristic of any civil war or revolution. And, as for other revolutions, a case can be made on the other side. The loss of life occasioned by the wars was insignificant. Very few intellectuals on either side were killed. Institutions such as Oxford and Cambridge were disrupted much less by the new parliamentarian authorities than by the royalist occupation. The Fellows of the College of Physicians were left to their own devices. Academic traditions were protected, and the enemies of Parliament were treated lightly. Many returned to academic life or suffered no major inconvenience. Because they were excluded from politics and because the door to ecclesiastical preferment was closed to them, many ambitious young men of royalist conviction were diverted into science as a pastime or, alternatively, entered upon medical careers. For the first time the medical faculties at Oxford and Cambridge became viable and modern in outlook, if anything outstripping every other comparable institution in Europe. Royalists remained active in scientific clubs, within or outside the universities.[43]

The civil service under the parliamentarians drew extensively on the abilities of intellectuals, and such policies of the new regime as the suppression of monopolies, the imposition of the Navigation Act, the settlement of Ireland, and the relaxation of censorship provided fresh career opportunities and other positive inducements to effort in science and technology.[44] The Puritan ascendancy marked the beginning of unhindered pursuit of *philosophia libera,* the "free philosophy," in which adherents of every brand of philosophy, ancient or modern, were allowed totally free expression. This situation contrasts strongly with England before 1640 and with the Continent, where tight restrictions were placed on education, publication, and religious expression by both ecclesiastical and secular authorities.[45]

Perhaps one of the major cultural contributions of Puritanism before 1660 was the constant challenge it offered to authoritarianism within the church and generally in secular life. Before 1640 the Church of England suffered the inconvenience of a crisis of identity; it possessed little internal coherence; and even when assisted by outside authority it failed to control dissent. This open competition was even more pronounced after 1640, and it acted as a spur to initiative for all parties. The support of the people needed to be won by persuasion rather than coercion. The examples cited above suggest that science was one of the beneficiaries of this free trade of ideas brought about by the power of nonconformity and the weakening of the establishment. Detailed examination of the biographies of the leaders of science after the restoration illustrates the strong formative influence of events associated with the revolution.

Notwithstanding the relevance to science of Puritanism and the Puritan revolution, it is important not to exaggerate the unity of outlook of scientists falling within the orbit of Puritan influence. As in other spheres of religious and secular life, the Puritans and Separatists failed to establish a common platform capable of sustaining the coherence of their movement throughout the revolutionary decades. The greatest unifying factor was provided by a generalized adherence to certain ideas of Bacon, whose anti-Scholasticism, inductive methodology, experimental philosophy, natural histories, and utilitarianism attracted widespread enthusiasm. Otherwise the Puritan advocates of the new science, like their nonscientific brethren, represented an unstable coalition of interests, having very different views on religious, social, and scientific questions.

Thus old associations, formed during the broadly based opposition to the regime of Archbishop Laud, dissolved and ended in indifference or active antagonism. The intellectual alignments of 1660 were thus very different from those evident in 1642. Even at the earliest stage, the embryonic scientific organizations suggest a parting of the ways among the Puritan intellectuals. The "1645 Group," the ultimate ancestor of the Royal Society, possessed, in spite of its instigator, Theodore Haak, a firm "modern" bias; its membership overlapped very little with the more utilitarian Office of Address of Samuel Hartlib and the "Invisible College" of Robert Boyle and Benjamin Worsley. The latter two groups coalesced and remained centered in London, while their colleagues from the 1645 Group were conspicuous in securing university preferment. This in turn provided a further point of divergence. Hartlib, Dury, and their colleagues were dissatisfied with the universities, and on matters of policy there was little to separate them from John Webster, the universities' most extreme critic, regarded at the time as a dangerous fanatic. John Wilkins, Seth Ward, Henry More, and their academic colleagues recognized the attack on the universities both as an assault on the idea of a learned ministry and the organized national church and as a threat to social stability. Webster's attack on the Puritan establishment, *Academiarum Examen* (1654), and the reply from Wilkins and Ward, *Vindiciae Academiarum* (1654), are indicators of deep division within the ranks of Puritan natural philosophers.

These differences are reflected in scientific interests and even in philosophical alignments. More and his fellow Platonists moved sharply away from the utilitarianism of Hartlib and Petty; Worsley and the Hartlib group were offended by the "Oxford professors'" lack of sympathy for astrology. Paracelsianism, Helmontian chemistry, and the pansophism of Comenius were central to the outlook of Hartlib's circle, peripheral to that of their colleagues at Oxford. The ideas of Harvey, Galileo, Descartes, and Gassendi were taken up within the universities but largely bypassed by Hartlib's group. Even approaches to the utilitarian application of knowledge show sharp differences, the effort of Hartlib and his associates being organized with respect to their wider political and social program.

In summary, the more radical Puritans, exemplified by Hartlib and Webster, adopted a more Biblicist metaphysical standpoint, and at the practical level their priorities were dictated by their mission of a godly utopia. Puritans with ties to the universities showed more receptivity to the varieties of mechanical philosophy being developed on the Continent, and their practical work increasingly related to problems in the field of the modern physical sciences. Both sides believed that they represented the central position of Puritanism. In this situation it is not surprising to find that Hartlib and his associates drifted into partnership with Separatists and hence into a minority status, as the semiofficial servants of a collapsing republic. In contrast, their colleagues within the universities rapidly made common cause with other occupants of the middle ground within the church, many of whom had remained loyal to the monarchy. Their protection of the fabric of essential institutions earned them rewards at the Restoration. This realignment was symbolized by the association of Wilkins and Ward in replying to critics of the universities. In this process, figures like Petty, Boyle, and Oldenburg were left with divided loyalties, retaining residual links with the more radical Puritans engaged in science for the sake of social engineering, while becoming more deeply involved in problem-solving activities connected with the mechanical philosophy. It is tempting to characterize the divisions that emerged within Puritan science as a dichotomy between occultists and radicals on the one hand and the mechanists and conservatives on the other, the former representing an ideology generated by revolutionary fervor, the latter looking forward to the form of modern science associated with the latitudinarians of the Restoration settlement. The one was eager to generate social change, the other to buttress social stability.[46]

Such an analysis usefully underlines the diversity of Puritan science and emphasizes the degree to which Restoration science was rooted in the experiences of the revolutionary period. It is safe to identify the development of the mechanical philosophy in the "Anglican" middle ground, as long as it is not claimed that the mechanical philosophy was the prerogative solely of this Anglican center. It would also be wrong to overlook the tendency on the part of more conservative natural philosophers to turn decisively against the mechanical philosophy, as did the Cambridge Platonists; and Anglicans might even occupy a frankly occultist standpoint from the outset, as did Elias Ashmole, John Aubrey, Robert Turner, and Robert Plot.

Regardless of the difficulties pointed out above, the temptation to regard occultism as the property of the more radical Puritans and Separatists, and the mechanical philosophy as the creation of the latitudinarian Anglican middle ground, has proved too difficult for current researchers to resist. Such a thesis transforms the mechanical philosophy into a political weapon, self-consciously forged with a view to sweeping away the republic and restoring a stable monarchy. In this interpretation there is an emphasis on the absorption of latitudinarian proponents of the mechanical philosophy into the Restoration establishment and the consigning of occultists to the radical underground.

As has been indicated, a strong case can be made for the fragmentation of the Puritan movement during the republic. Scientists well illustrate this tendency. But the attempt to view such disparate figures as Robert Boyle and Walter Charleton as joint architects during the 1650s of a new "Anglican" scientific synthesis is based on supposition rather than direct evidence.[47] It is also doubtful whether before 1660 English natural philosophers had any real sense that the Restoration was about to occur. Even as late as 2 March 1660, Boyle's close friend Oldenburg was confidently predicting that events were moving toward a republican settlement.[48] At this time Oldenburg's more radical Puritan friends were actively planning for a paradise on earth, for the renewal of the church, and for organization of science for an imminent age of "Universall love, & Universall Commerce, in mutuall peace & noble Communications."[49] There was no expectation of the restoration of any monarchy other than the monarchy of Christ's personal reign on earth, and for these reformers the restoration of the Church of England and formation of a Royal Society must have seemed contrary to the course of history. History, of course, very soon proved the republicans wrong. The events of 1660 firmly closed the door on further social and political experimentation. Out of the ashes of the scientific movement that evolved under Puritanism may have emerged many of the constituent elements in the science of the new age, but the process of absorption was selective. Many of the dominant personalities and themes of the science of the republicans fell into the background; the creative energies of science were redirected, largely, it seems, to the benefit of the modern worldview.

CONCLUSION

It would be totally unrealistic to write the history of the emergence of English science in the period 1560–1660 in terms of monocausal derivation with respect to Protestantism, Anglicanism, or Puritanism, however they are defined. But to equate this history with the story of the great discoveries, or to construe science as an entirely autonomous development, unrelated to the Reformation and the Puritan Revolution or to the socioeconomic framework of which Puritanism was a constituent element, is to eliminate vital factors in the explanatory mosaic. Any truly historical account of the Scientific Revolution must pay due attention to the deep interpenetration of scientific and religious ideas. It would seem perverse to deny religious motivation in the numerous cases where this was made explicit by the scientists themselves, often with painful emphasis. No direction of energy toward science was undertaken without the assurance of Christian conscience, and no conceptual move was risked without confidence in its consistency with the Protestant idea of providence. Protestantism constituted a vigorous directive force, and within English Protestantism, Puritanism and Separatism generated the challenging new ideas of the day. It is therefore hardly surprising that Puritanism and Separatism should provide a dominant cultural context, reference to which is essential for any balanced characterization of the English scientific movement. Puritanism and Separatism, along with the whole set of conditions associated with the revolutionary decades, assume particular importance in explaining the distinctiveness, diversity, and creativity of English science on the eve of the foundation of the Royal Society.

NOTES

1. For general surveys from different angles see Christopher Hill, *The Century of Revolution 1603–1714* (Edinburgh: Nelson, 1961); Conrad Russell, *The Crisis of Parliaments: English History 1509–1660* (London: Oxford Univ. Press, 1971); and Charles Wilson, *England's Apprenticeship 1603–1773* (London: Longmans, 1965).

2. Ernst Troeltsch, *Die Bedeutung des Protestantismus für die Entstehung der modernen Welt* (Munich: R. Oldenbourg, 1911); Richard H. Tawney, *Religion and the Rise of Capitalism* (London: J. Murray, 1926); Max Weber, *The Protestant Ethic and the Spirit of Capitalism*, trans. Talcott Parsons (New York: Charles Scribner's Sons, 1930); Robert K. Merton, "Science, Technology and Society in Seventeenth Century England," *Osiris* 4 (1938): 360–632; reprinted as a book (New York: Harper & Row, 1970); and Christopher Hill, *The Intellectual Origins of the English Revolution* (Oxford: Clarendon Press, 1965).

3. Christopher Hill, *Society and Puritanism in Pre-Revolutionary England* (London: Secker & Warburg, 1964), pp. 13–29; Basil Hall, "Puritanism: The Problem of Definition," in *Studies in Church History*, ed. Geoffrey J. Cuming, 2 vols. (London: Ecclesiastical History Society, 1965), 2:183–196. For the most recent exchange concerning terminology see Paul Christianson, "Reformers of the Church of England under Elizabeth I and the Early Stuarts," *Journal of Ecclesiastical History* 31 (1980): 463–482; Patrick Collinson, "A Comment Concerning the Name Puritan," ibid., pp. 483–488.

4. Reijer Hooykaas, *Religion and the Rise of Modern Science* (Edinburgh: Scottish Academic Press, 1973), p. 143; Charles Webster, ed., *The Intellectual Revolution of the Seventeenth Century* (London: Routledge & Kegan Paul, 1974), pp. 234, 296 (Hugh F. Kearney's article on Boyle's sympathy for the Cambridge Platonists, Barbara Shapiro's on his Anglicanism).

5. The group within the Church of England supporting the policies of William Laud, Archbishop of Canterbury from 1633 until his execution in 1644.

6. Robert G. Frank, *Harvey and the Oxford Physiologists* (Berkeley, Los Angeles, London: Univ. of California Press, 1980); Francis R. Johnson, *Astronomical Thought in Renaissance England* (Baltimore: Johns Hopkins Univ. Press, 1937); and Charles E. Raven, *Natural Religion and Christian Theology*, 2 vols. (Cambridge: Cambridge Univ. Press, 1953).

7. Boris Hessen, "The Social and Economic Roots of Newton's *Principia*," in *Science at the Crossroads*, ed. Nikolai I. Bukharin (London: Kniga, 1931), pp. 149–192; Edgar Zilsel, "The Sociological Roots of Science," *American Journal of Sociology* 47 (1942): 544–562; Zilsel, "The Origins of William Gilbert's Scientific Method," *Journal of the History of Ideas* 2 (1941): 1–32; Merton, "Science, Technology and Society" [citations are to the 1938 ed.], pp. 414–565. For an opposing view see George N. Clark, *Science and Social Welfare in the Age of Newton* (Oxford: Clarendon Press, 1937; new ed., 1970).

8. Hill, *Intellectual Origins*, chap. 2; Charles Webster, *The Great Instauration: Science, Medicine and Reform 1626–1660* (London: Duckworth, 1975), sec. 5.

9. John U. Nef, *The Rise of the British Coal Industry,* 2 vols. (London: Routledge & Kegan Paul, 1932); Michael Hunter, *Science and Society in Restoration England* (Cambridge: Cambridge Univ. Press, 1981), chap. 4.

10. Walter E. Houghton, "The History of Trades: Its Relation to Seventeenth Century Thought," *Journal of the History of Ideas* 2 (1941): 33–60; Margaret Denny, "The Early Program of the Royal Society and John Evelyn," *Modern Language Quarterly* 1 (1940): 481–497.

11. Francis R. Johnson, "Gresham College: Precursor of the Royal Society," *Journal of the History of Ideas* 1 (1940): 413–438; Ian Adamson, "The Royal Society and Gresham College, 1660–1711," *Notes and Records of the Royal Society* 33 (1978): 1–21.

12. Weber, *Protestant Ethic;* Tawney, *Religion and the Rise of Capitalism.*

13. Ralph Austen, *A Treatise of Fruit Trees . . . The Spirituall Use of an Orchard* (Oxford: T. Robinson, 1653).

14. Augustus P. de Candolle, *Histoire des sciences et des savants* (Geneva: H. Georg, 1873); Jean Pelseneer, "La reforme et le progrès des sciences en Belgique au XVI siècle," in *Science, Medicine and History,* ed. Edgar A. Underwood, 2 vols. (London: Oxford Univ. Press, 1953), 1:280–284; Pelseneer, "L'origine protestante de la science moderne," *Lychnos,* 1946–1947:246–248; Pelseneer, "Les influences dans l'histoire des sciences," *Archives internationales d'histoire des sciences* 1 (1948): 348–353.

15. Nicholas Tyacke, "Science and Religion at Oxford before the Civil War," in *Puritans and Revolutionaries: Essays in Seventeenth-Century History Presented to Christopher Hill,* ed. Donald H. Pennington and Keith Thomas (Oxford: Clarendon Press, 1978), pp. 73–93.

16. Tyacke, "Science and Religion at Oxford," pp. 77 (quoting I. Adamson), 93; Lotte Mulligan, "Civil War Politics, Religion and the Royal Society," in *Intellectual Revolution,* ed. Webster, pp. 317–339; W. E. H. Lecky, *History of the Rise and Influence of the Spirit of Rationalism in Europe,* rev. ed., 2 vols. (New York: Appleton, 1889).

17. Robert Baillie, *Letters and Journals,* 3 vols. (Edinburgh: Bannatyne, 1841–1842), 3:268, 274; Fulke Greville, "Treatise of Humane Learning," in *Poems and Dramas of F. Greville,* ed. Geoffrey Bullough, 2 vols. (Edinburgh: Oliver & Boyd, 1939), 1:52–61; Robert Greville, *The Nature of Episcopacy* (1642), quoted from *Tracts on Liberty,* ed. William Haller, 3 vols. (New York: Columbia Univ. Press, 1934), 2:53; John Spencer, *A Short Treatise concerning . . . mans exercising his gift* (London: J. Bales, 1641); Samuel How, *The Sufficiency of the Spirits Teaching* ([London], 1640).

18. Douglas S. Kemsley, "Religious Influence in the Rise of Modern Science," *Annals of Science* 24 (1968): 199–226; John Morgan, "Puritanism and Science: A Reinterpretation," *The Historical Journal* 22 (1979): 535–560; Richard B. Schlatter, "The Higher Learning in Puritan England," *Historical Magazine of the Protestant Episcopal Church* 23 (1954): 167–187; Lotte Mulligan, "Puritanism and English Science: A Critique of Webster," *Isis* 71 (1980): 456–469.

19. Mulligan, "Puritanism and English Science," p. 469; Morgan, "Puritanism and Science," p. 540.

20. Hill, *Intellectual Origins*, pp. 133–137; Ronald A. Rebholz, *The Life of Fulke Greville* (Oxford: Clarendon Press, 1971); Webster, *Great Instauration*, p. 29; John Webster, *Academiarum Examen* (London: G. Calvert, 1654).

21. Above, nn. 2, 7, and 8.

22. Hooykaas, *Religion and the Rise of Modern Science*, p. 143.

23. See Paul Seaver, "The Puritan Work Ethic Revisited," *Journal of British Studies* 19 (1980): 35–53, for a balanced review of this issue from a historical perspective. For the theological issues see Hooykaas, *Religion and the Rise of Modern Science*, pp. 102–105, 107–109; John S. Coolidge, *The Pauline Renaissance in England: Puritanism and the Bible* (Oxford: Clarendon Press, 1970), p. 72 and passim.

24. Hooykaas, *Religion and the Rise of Modern Science*, pp. 101–106; Richard S. Westfall, *Science and Religion in Seventeenth Century England* (New Haven: Yale Univ. Press, 1958), pp. 106–145.

25. Merton, *Science, Technology and Society*, p. 468; Stephen F. Mason, *Main Currents of Scientific Thought* (London: Routledge & Kegan Paul, 1953), pp. 137, 140.

26. Francis Oakley, "Christian Theology and the Newtonian Science: The Rise of the Concept of the Laws of Nature," *Church History* 30 (1961): 433–357; Heiko A. Oberman, *Masters of the Reformation* (Cambridge: Cambridge Univ. Press, 1981), pp. 165–168.

27. J. E. McGuire, "Neoplatonism and Active Principles: Newton and the *Corpus Hermeticum*," in Robert S. Westman and J. E. McGuire, *Hermeticism and the Scientific Revolution* (Los Angeles: William Andrews Clark Memorial Library, 1977), p. 108; Perry Miller, *The New England Mind: The Seventeenth Century* (Cambridge, Mass.: Harvard Univ. Press, 1954), pp. 207–235.

28. For major surveys of Elizabethan Puritanism see P. Collinson, *The Elizabethan Puritan Movement* (London: Cape, 1967); Marshall M. Knappen, *Tudor Puritanism* (Chicago: Univ. of Chicago Press, 1939); Leonard J. Trinterud, ed., *Elizabethan Puritanism* (New York: Oxford Univ. Press, 1971).

29. Weber, *Protestant Ethic*, p. 105.

30. Richard Bostocke, *The Difference betwene the auncient Phisicke, and the latter Phisicke* (London: R. Walley, 1585); Richard F. Jones, *Ancients and Moderns* (Berkeley and Los Angeles: Univ. of California Press, 1965).

31. Edwin Sandys, in *The Zürich Letters*, ed. Hastings Robinson, 3 vols. (Cambridge: Parker Society, 1842), 1:332.

32. Margaret James, *Social Problems and Policy during the Puritan Revolution* (London: Routledge & Kegan Paul, 1930).

33. William Petty, *The Advice of W. P. to Mr. Samuel Hartlib for the Advancement for Some Particular Parts of Learning* (London, 1648).

34. Richard L. Greaves, *The Puritan Revolution and Educational Thought* (New Brunswick, N.J.: Rutgers Univ. Press, 1969); Charles Webster, *Samuel Hartlib and the Advancement of Learning* (Cambridge: Cambridge Univ. Press, 1972); Webster, *Great Instauration*, sec. 3.

35. R. E. W. Maddison, *The Life of the Honourable Robert Boyle* (London: Taylor & Francis, 1969), pp. 111–112.

36. Hill, *Intellectual Origins*, chap. 2; Margaret Pelling and Charles Webster, "Medical Practitioners," in *Health, Medicine and Mortality in the Sixteenth Century*, ed. Charles Webster (Cambridge: Cambridge Univ. Press, 1979), pp. 165–236; Webster, *Great Instauration*, sec. 4; Robert Brenner, "The Civil War Politics of London's Merchant Community," *Past and Present* 58 (1973): 53–107.

37. Coolidge, *Pauline Renaissance*; J. S. McGee, *The Godly Man in Stuart England and the Two Tables 1620–1670* (New Haven: Yale Univ. Press, 1976).

38. Dury to Edward Montagu, Viscount Mandeville, 1638, Trinity College Dublin MS C2.10, fol. 7.

39. Coolidge, *Pauline Renaissance*, p. 147.

40. William Haller, *The Rise of Puritanism* (New York: Columbia Univ. Press, 1938), chap. 2; Webster, *Great Instauration*, sec. 2.

41. Webster, *Great Instauration*, sec. 2; Boyle, "An Epistolical Discourse . . . inviting a free and generous Communication of Secrets and Receipts in Physick," in *Chymical Addresses*, ed. Samuel Hartlib (London: G. Calvert, 1655), pp. 113–150.

42. Michael McKeon, *Poetry and Politics in Restoration England* (Cambridge, Mass.: Harvard Univ. Press, 1975).

43. Webster, *Great Instauration*, pp. 144–178, 300–308; Frank, *Harvey and the Oxford Physiologists*, pp. 45–93.

44. Webster, *Great Instauration*, pp. 77–85 and passim.

45. Ibid., pp. 195 and passim; Christopher Wren, *Parentalia* (London: Osborn & Dodsley, 1750), pp. 205–206: *Philosophia libera* at Gresham College in 1657 "in such a measure hardly to be found in the academes themselves."

46. Christopher Hill, *The World Turned Upside Down* (London: Temple Smith, 1972); James R. Jacob and Margaret C. Jacob, "The Anglican Origins of Modern Science," *Isis* 71 (1980): 251–267.

47. Lindsay Sharp, "Walter Charleton's Early Life 1620–1659, and Relationship to Natural Philosophy in Mid-Seventeenth Century England," *Annals of Science* 30 (1973): 311–340.

48. Oldenburg to Becher, 2 Mar. 1660, in *The Correspondence of Henry Oldenburg*, ed. A. R. Hall and Marie Boas Hall, 9 vols. (Madison: Univ. of Wisconsin Press, 1965–1973), 1:359.

49. John Beale to Hartlib, 28 Nov. 1659, Sheffield University Library, Hartlib Papers, LX.1.

8

The Rise of Science and the Decline of Orthodox Christianity: A Study of Kepler, Descartes, and Newton

Richard S. Westfall

In the relations of science and Christianity, no period seems to me more crucial than the seventeenth century. Western European civilization had taken shape in the Middle Ages as a Christian civilization, its characteristic institutions either directly nurtured by Christianity or profoundly influenced by it during their period of formation. The central events of the sixteenth century, the Reformation and all that flowed from it, lead irresistibly to the conclusion that "Christian" continued to be the single most suitable adjective to describe European civilization when the seventeenth century opened. Not many, I think, would choose the same adjective to describe it at the close of the century. Some might be inclined to call it "scientific." Certainly during the Enlightenment, already under way as the seventeenth century closed and gaining momentum, philosophers turned to science for inspiration, direction, and criteria of truth, and they used science as a weapon to mount the first serious attack that Christianity itself had sustained since European civilization appeared. From that time on, Christianity has become ever more tangential to the living concerns of European civilization, and science ever more central as it has assumed the mantle Christianity once wore. In my perception of Western history, the seventeenth century was the watershed, and the relations of science and Christianity during that time appear to me as a problem the significance of which spreads out over the history of the entire civilization.

If this analysis is correct, it follows immediately that the issue far exceeds the possibility of definitive treatment in the space of one brief paper. I propose merely to illustrate aspects of it by examining the religious beliefs of three of the most prominent scientists, Kepler, Descartes, and Newton. Although I shall confine myself entirely to the realm of ideas, I do not thereby mean to deny the impact of other factors, political, economic, and social, that were operating at the time to undercut the centrality of Christianity. I do contend, however, that there was also a purely intellectual dimension in the seventeenth-century challenge to Christianity, an intellectual dimension which itself contained many facets, though in my opinion the rise of modern science was easily the most important one. Kepler, Descartes, and Newton, three men of deep religious commitment, located chronologically near the beginning, middle, and end of the century, who participated centrally in formulating the distinctive outlook of modern science, illustrate the impact of the tradition they helped to create on their own and on all received religion. Three geniuses, they are more apt to indicate the line of march into the future than to reflect the consensus accepted in their own time. I propose them, not as a representative sample of seventeenth-century scientists, but as an indication of the problems for received Christianity inherent in the rise of modern science.

JOHANNES KEPLER: CHRISTIAN COSMOLOGIST

After his skill in astronomy, religious devotion is probably the best-known characteristic of Johannes Kepler (1571–1630). One is tempted to use him as the example of traditional orthodoxy on the eve of Europe's plunge into the cold bath of skeptical inquiry. Such a use would do scant justice to the intensity of Kepler's religious pilgrimage. Differences on essential doctrines separated him from each of the major denominations and greatly complicated his life in an age of confessional conflict. "Yet it is not my way to become a hypocrite in matters of conscience," he insisted to his former teacher, Michael Maestlin, as he explained his unwillingness to compromise.[1] Whatever we say about Kepler, we shall not dare to present him as an unquestioning supporter of inherited tradition.

Nevertheless, in Kepler's religious thought Christianity remained intact, harmoniously interwoven with his science and scarcely altered by it. His personal piety furnished the background to his work, forcing itself as it were onto the printed page, as though he were unable to contain it. He called book 5 of the *Harmonies of the World* "a sacred sermon, a veritable hymn to God the Creator" in which he would worship, not by offering sacrifices to God, not by burning incense, "but first in learning and then in teaching others how great are His wisdom, power, and goodness."[2] When he came to chapter 9, the climax both of book 5 and of the entire work, where he revealed the ultimate harmonies of the world, he introduced it with a prayer that wove Christian and cosmological themes together in one continuous fabric:

> Holy Father, preserve us in the harmony of mutual love so that we may be one even as you with your Son, our Lord, and the Holy Spirit are one, and as you have through the gentle bonds of harmony made all your works one; and from the renewed concord of your people let the body of your church on earth be built from harmonies as you have constructed the heavens themselves.[3]

He concluded the chapter with a second prayer that his work contain nothing unworthy of God, and he closed the *Harmonies* as a whole with a hymn to the glory of the Creator.

It is true that we can distinguish tendencies in Kepler that point toward a different relation of science with Christianity. Jürgen Hübner has examined these tendencies in considerable detail in his recent study of Kepler's religious thought.[4] The basic change, in Hübner's analysis, was a shift of attention away from the central concerns of medieval Christian theology. These concerns had focused on the redemptive relationship of God to man. God had revealed Himself by coming into the world to restore fallen humanity and had codified that revelation in a written record, the Bible, the source to which mankind must turn for knowledge unto life eternal. In contrast, Kepler fastened his gaze on God the creator. His God also had revealed Himself. He had revealed his wisdom in the act of creation, and Kepler's primary theological interest centered on the wisdom of God. Without denying the concept of redemption, he paid it scant attention, while with rapt devotion he explored the details of the creation. Thus Kepler not only redirected the focus of Christian thought but also elevated nature as a revelation of God to a status equal to that of the Bible. "For you, God entered the world," he wrote to David Fabricius; "for me, nature strives toward God."[5]

Even if we grant Hübner's argument, it does not seriously compromise the original assertion that in Kepler traditional Christianity remained virtually unaltered by the impact of science. To be sure, his

Pythagorean God, who eternally manifested arcane geometrical and harmonic relations in the physical creation, differed clearly enough from the traditional God of Christian theology, but this has to do with another level of thought. Kepler's reverence for the written revelation was so intense that we might well overlook his subtle shift of attention if we were not aware of the future direction of Western thought. Whatever his concern with God the creator, the concept of redemption also played a central role in Kepler's life. Exclusion from the sacrament—that is, in his terms, exclusion from the presence of the spirit of Christ—was a personal tragedy, which he refused to accept but struggled against for the rest of his life. We shall not be wise in pressing his departure from received tradition too far.

When we turn to Kepler's natural philosophy, we find a conception of nature that directly supported his religious position. Of foremost importance is the fact that the universe remained for him a cosmos. It is well known that much of Kepler's significance in the history of science stems from the impulse he gave to causal analyses of phenomena and to the concept of mathematical laws. Kepler's laws were never impersonal laws, however, and the universe in which they worked was not for him the chance product of their blind operation. It was an ordered cosmos consciously contrived. Giordano Bruno's speculative system, "that dreadful philosophy," represented to him the blind operation of impersonal causes.[6] He feared the very idea and fled from it. Where means are adapted to definite purposes, Kepler insisted, "there order exists, not chance; there is pure mind and pure Reason."[7] "The Creator," he informed Maestlin, "does nothing by chance."[8]

It was, of course, Kepler's further conviction that the Creator had used the principles of geometry in constructing his universe. The five regular solids, which define the ratios between six spheres that can be inscribed within and circumscribed around them, and hence (because there are only five regular solids) establish the necessity of the six planets in the Copernican system, were the supreme manifestation of Kepler's geometrically ordered cosmos. They were by no means the sole example. Essentially the same mode of thought presented itself with nearly every question in natural philosophy. Consider the number of days in the year, $365\frac{1}{4}$. It is close to one of the archetypal numbers, 360, and Kepler readily convinced himself that God created the earth's motive force to turn it 360 times a year, not $365\frac{1}{4}$, a "disjointed and ignoble fraction." The presence of the sun, which stimulates the earth's faculty, upsets the pristine purity of the ratio, which the discerning cosmologist can nevertheless perceive.[9] Similarly, on a completely different topic, Galileo's discovery of four satellites around Jupiter immediately led Kepler to inquire into the pattern that would establish the number of satellites around each planet.[10] For God does nothing by chance, and He orders his works according to the mathematical principles that are coeternal with Him.

I need not insist on the ready, and indeed necessary, harmony between such principles and a theistic conception of reality. Theism is not identical with Christianity, of course. Kepler drew heavily on the Platonic concept of a mathematically ordered reality in elaborating his philosophy, not on the Bible. When he used the Christian concept that man is the image of God to explicate human knowledge of the geometric cosmos, he went beyond mere theism, and so also when he insisted on the uniqueness of the solar system in the universe.

The ultimate union of Christianity and science in Kepler's mind, however, lay in a further feature of his conception of nature, a feature possible only because his universe remained an ordered cosmos. Wherever he looked, and he looked everywhere, Kepler saw a universe organized in triads, and not just ordinary triads, but triads that are at the same time unities. It was not by accident that Kepler's universe remained finite, finite and spherical, because to him the sphere represented an embodiment of the Trinity.

> For in the sphere, which is the image of God the Creator and the Archetype of the world . . . there are three regions, symbols of the three persons of the Holy Trinity—the center, a symbol of the Father; the surface, of the Son; and the intermediate space, of the Holy Ghost. So, too, just as many principal parts of the world have been made—the different parts in the different regions of the sphere: the sun in the center, the sphere of the fixed stars on the surface, and lastly the planetary system in the region intermediate between the sun and the fixed stars.[11]

He was prepared to inject the Trinity into purely scientific questions. Thus he was able to calculate the densities of the sun, the sphere of the fixed stars, and the intermediate aether by reasoning that the equality of the three persons of the Trinity demanded an equal division of the matter in the universe among its three principal parts.[12] Likewise, the image contributed to his criticism of Ptolemy (second century A.D.), a pagan, who had considered the stars as visible gods. Such reasoning, he declared, "cannot be tolerated in a Christian discipline."[13]

Kepler did not stop with the mere image of the Trinity. He pursued its implications to the farthest detail, carving from it an extraordinary jewel of many facets, each of which reflected the splendor of Christian doctrine. In the creation, he explained, God expressed the difference between the straight and the curved, the images of the created and the divine. All rectilinear figures are inherently imperfect. Participating in three dimensions, they participate equally in materiality. Described by the motions of points, lines, and planes, they are by nature posterior to points and the space in which points move.[14] The curved is otherwise. A sphere is not generated by the rotation of a circle, because the sphere is prior to the circle. In respect to other figures, the sphere can be called ungenerated in that it is not produced from them but stands before them, the result of a wholly different process, whereby the central point communicates itself equally in all directions. Thus the sphere, the outpouring of a point, constitutes the space that other figures, generated by the finite motions of points, assume. A sphere has, as well, the form of immateriality because it is free of internal solidity. A sphere differs from a globe, which is a sphere filled with solid body.[15]

The sphere was thus to Kepler more than the shape of the universe. As the image of the divine, it was the form that every being that aspires to perfection assumes, as far as it is able to do so. Bodies, which are confined by the limits of their surfaces, nevertheless expand spherically in a vicarious manner through the powers with which they are endowed. The soul, and to Kepler everything was ensouled, pours itself forth from its punctiform abode, both in perceiving external things that surround it in a spherical fashion, and in governing its body, which also lies around it.[16] Inevitably he applied the same analogy to light as one of the foremost powers inherent in bodies.

Is it any wonder, then, if that principle of all beauty in the world, which the divine Moses introduces into scarcely created matter, even on the first day of creation, as (so to speak) the Creator's instrument, by which to give visible shape and life to all things—is it any wonder, I say, if this primary principle and this most beautiful being in the whole corporeal world, the matrix of all animal faculties and the bond between the physical and the intellectual world, submitted to those very laws by which the world was to be formed? Hence the sun is a certain body in which resides that faculty, which we call light, of communicating itself to all things. For this reason alone its rightful place is the middle point and centre of the whole world, so that it may diffuse itself perpetually and uniformly throughout the universe. All other beings that share in light imitate the sun.[17]

He could heighten the trinitarian image still further. A point, the center of a sphere, is invisible; it reveals itself by flowing outward in all directions. The surface is its image, the way to the center. Who sees the surface also sees the center, and in no other way.[18] No doubt the image explains why Kepler insisted that light is not the rays that spread out from luminous and illuminated points. The rays are only the lines of motion. Light itself is the spherical surface that their equal motions constitute, the surface that represents the Son in the trinitarian sphere. Hence in optics as in most of his science, Kepler's contemplation of nature brought him back, not just to theism, but to the very heart of the Gospels. Jesus said, "I am the light of the world."

RENÉ DESCARTES: RELUCTANT SKEPTIC

In René Descartes (1596–1650), who flourished one generation later than Kepler, we meet a different man, different above all in his level of spiritual exaltation. Nevertheless, Descartes was no less committed to Christianity. He was ostentatious in always deferring to the church on questions of faith. He explicitly excluded his religion from the process of systematic doubt. He chose to present *Le monde* as a fantasy that would aid one in comprehending the laws at work in nature "without doing outrage to the miracle of creation,"[19] and he suppressed the work after Galileo's condemnation, though he lived well beyond the reach of the Holy Office. When he did finally publish his natural philosophy in the *Principles,* he not only altered it in order to assert that the earth is at rest, but he insisted once more on his obedience to the church. The work closed with a general assessment of the degree of certainty he had attained, claiming at least moral certainty and going beyond that to assert that some of his demonstrations reached absolute certainty and that his exposition of the general phenomena of nature was the only possible one. "At the same time," he concluded, "recalling my insignificance, I affirm nothing, but submit all these opinions to the authority of the Catholic Church, and to the judgment of the more sage."[20] It is not my business here to examine Descartes's motives. No doubt they were complex and stemmed from more than simple piety. Nevertheless, it is a fact that he was greatly concerned to remain in the good graces of the church, and he took care that his philosophy not appear as an attack on Christianity, either in whole or in part.

Moreover, Descartes did not confine himself to the passive role of not giving offense. He dedicated his *Meditations* to the faculty of theology at the Sorbonne as a demonstration of the two basic points on which Christianity depends: the existence of God and the immaterial nature of the soul.[21] This was no mere gesture, for the two points were as central to his philosophy as they were to Christianity. Without the existence of God, Descartes's epistemology could not stand, and his epistemology, the provision of absolute certainty that would rescue philosophy from the swamp of skepticism in which it had lost its way, was the cornerstone on which he proposed to rebuild the philosophical enterprise. We can translate the final stage of Descartes's systematic doubt, the evil spirit bent on deluding him, into more prosaic terms as the irremovable finitude of human capacities.

> And if we think that an omnipotent God is not the author of our being, and that we subsist of ourselves or through some other [he argued in the *Principles*], yet the less perfect we suppose the author to be, the more reason have we to believe that we are not so perfect that we cannot be continually deceived.[22]

Only by reaching beyond the limits of the human to authority that was by definition not finite could Descartes find the absolute certainty he sought. Both the guarantor of human faculties when they are used aright and the author of the eternal truths that the faculties so used perceive, God was the bedrock on which his epistemology stood. He was equally essential to sustain in being a creation, which in Descartes's view lacked any capacity to maintain itself in existence from one instant to the next.[23] The immateriality of the soul, which entailed its immortality, was a consequence of his dualism, and as such was no less central to his philosophy as a whole than the existence of God.

I may seem to be heading for the conclusion that Descartes's relation to Christianity was nearly identical with Kepler's—if anything, less fraught with change in that he never questioned the Christian denomination in which he was reared. Such is by no means the case. As it appears to me, Descartes bore witness to a movement of thought to a new and different plane. If he rigidly controlled the consequences that he himself would draw, further conclusions remained implicit for later generations to extract.

Consider first of all the process of systematic doubt and with it the objections of the Jesuit Fr. Bourdin to the *Meditations* (Objections VII).[24] On the surface, Bourdin's objections are perverse; they treat systematic doubt as permanent skepticism, whereas Descartes manifestly intended it as a temporary process by which permanently to overthrow skepticism. Nevertheless, let us ask ourselves whether Bourdin might have had some cause for his evident alarm. Systematic doubt was not a self-limiting process. It came to an end when and only when Descartes found a proposition he could not doubt and, using it as a foundation, rebuilt a structure of knowledge. Descartes himself excluded the realm of faith from the process of questioning. If ever there was a position of unstable equilibrium, surely it was this one, where all the matters of secondary importance were reexamined while the one acknowledged as supremely important and thus most in need of a solid foundation remained untouched. Descartes could justify his procedure by treating revelation as a separate realm of knowledge, immediately dependent on the God of truth. As Bourdin understood, the truths of faith could not be permanently insulated from the quest for compelling demonstrations once the quest was initiated. Only natural reason could establish that a pretended revelation did indeed come from God. Natural reason would have to interpret it as well. What an earlier age had readily accepted as truths above reason—that three divine persons are yet one God, that God and man were united in Jesus Christ—might well appear contrary to reason in an age of systematic doubt. I suggest that Bourdin was right in fearing that no body of accepted truths could long remain immune to such a spirit.

We can go further. The new beginning in natural philosophy that Descartes embodied had cast aside that very stone on which Kepler's union of Christianity with science stood. Descartes rejected the concept of a cosmos in order to start, as he explicitly said, with "a chaos as confused as the poets ever feigned" and to show how physical necessity governed by the laws of motion must result in a world like ours.[25] Perhaps nothing displays the difference between the two men better than their discussions of snowflakes. Kepler refused to believe that the hexagonal shape of snowflakes, "this ordered pattern," exists at random.[26] Descartes explained how it necessarily results from neighboring droplets freezing together.[27] Descartes's world, stretching out indefinitely in all directions, devoid of internal structure except for the endlessly repeated pattern of vortices that were a necessary consequence of motion in a plenum, constantly in flux as suns crusted over and died and vortices disappeared, required God to sustain it in being and to prescribe its laws. It revealed, however, no sign of intelligent planning. Descartes argued that knowledge of final causes is beyond human capacity; mankind cannot know the purposes of God.[28] In fact, the impossibility of knowing final causes had a deeper root. There were no final causes in Descartes's universe.

There were also no vestiges of a triune God. Descartes's philosophy was theistic; it required the existence of God. It is difficult to find in it anything specifically Christian. His God was the God of the philosophers, necessary to call the world into being and necessary to sustain it. He was not the God who redeemed mankind with his blood. The whole thrust of Descartes's thought exemplified the characteristic that Hübner found in Kepler; that is, he emphasized God the Creator and Sustainer at the expense of God the Redeemer. This thrust carried over into his ethical philosophy, and theologians had just cause to complain of his Pelagianism (the theological view that man can save himself without the aid of divine grace).[29]

If God did not reveal Himself to Descartes in the ordered structure of the cosmos, He did reveal Himself in the ordered regularity of phenomena. From such came a recognition of law but not a sense of worship and wonder. The sense of wonder repelled Descartes. One of the goals of his natural philosophy was the abolition of wonder by displaying the physical necessity of supposed marvels.

> It is our nature [he explained in the introduction to *Les météores*] to have more admiration for the things above us than for those that are on our level, or below. And although the clouds are hardly any higher than the summits of some mountains, and often we even see some that are lower than the pinnacles of our steeples, nevertheless, because we must turn our eyes toward the sky to look at them, we fancy them to be so high that poets and painters even fashion them into God's throne, and picture Him there, using His own hands to open and close the doors of the winds, to sprinkle the dew upon the flowers, and to hurl the lightning against the rocks. This leads me to hope that if I here explain the nature of clouds, in such a way that we will no longer have occasion to wonder at anything that can be seen of them, or anything that descends from them, we will easily believe that it is similarly possible to find the causes of everything that is most admirable above the earth.[30]

Les météores then proceeded to explanations of all these things (clouds, winds, dew, lightning, and other things as well), explanations that invoked only physical necessity—all intended, as he said in conclusion, to remove "any reason to marvel" about phenomena in the skies.[31]

Descartes did not object so much to wonder as to the concept of God that stood behind it. His God, the God of the philosophers, did not demean Himself to circus entertainment in producing a constant succession of surprises. Eternally unchanging, He revealed Himself rather in the unchangeable laws He ordained.

> For we understand it to be a perfection in God not only that He is in Himself immutable but also that He acts in a manner as constant and immutable as possible, so that, with the sole exception of those instances which the evidence of experience or divine revelation makes certain, and which we perceive or believe to have been brought about without any change in the creator, we must not admit any other alterations in his acts lest any inconsistency be thence inferred in God Himself.[32]

In *Le monde* Descartes briefly spelled out what such a concept of God meant. It was, he specified, an assumption of the world he there described "that God will never perform any miracles, and that neither rational souls, which we will later suppose are present there, nor angels interfere in any way with the ordinary course of nature."[33]

Indeed, the issue of miracles indicates that all his obeisance to the church could not restrain Descartes from quietly modifying Christianity to bring it into line with the dictates of natural philosophy. Apparently the very notion of miracles, the suggestion that God had not been able to make up his mind in the creation, offended Descartes, and frequently he allowed himself to offer naturalistic explanations of presumed miracles, which had, of course, the effect of rendering them nonmiraculous. The wonders that *Les météores* explained away included such. He described, for example, how exhalations could be pressed and formed into matter with the consistency of blood, milk, iron, stone, or corrupted matter that engenders insects; "thus we often read, among the miracles, that it rained iron, or blood, or locusts, or similar things."[34] If the reference to Moses in Egypt were not explicit enough, Descartes had already explained that manna was a form of dew.[35] His explanation of the rainbow led him further. He described how a fountain with oils of differing refractive powers could produce rainbows of differing sizes so that, by combining them all into one complex fountain, we could fill a great part of the sky with color. Then by closing certain jets, we could make parts of the rainbows disappear until the remaining patches of color would "have the shape of a cross, or a column, or some other such thing which gives cause for wonder. But I admit," he continued, "that skill and much work would be necessary in order to proportion these fountains, and to cause the liquids there to leap so high that these figures could be seen from afar by a whole nation, without the trick being discovered."[36] This was to treat a central miracle of the Old Testament and a central miracle in the establishment of Christianity as displays deliberately staged to sway the multitude. Philosophers, who could understand metaphysical arguments, did not require similar trickery. Were any "miracles" immune to such treatment? Was the greatest miracle of all, the Incarnation, immune? Descartes never questioned it. How far could religious thought proceed in his direction before someone did?

ISAAC NEWTON: FOE OF IRRATIONALITY

In fact, not very far. Before the end of the century a number of men had begun to question the divinity of Jesus Christ. Among them was Isaac Newton (1642–1727). One would not conclude as much from

Newton's published works. Here one meets well-known expressions of religious conviction, less frequent than Kepler's but not less impassioned. "This most beautiful system of the sun, planets, and comets," he asserted in the General Scholium, which concludes the *Principia*,

> could only proceed from the counsel and dominion of an intelligent and powerful Being. . . . He is eternal and infinite, omnipotent and omniscient; that is, his duration reaches from eternity to eternity; his presence from infinity to infinity; he governs all things, and knows all things that are or can be done. . . . We know him only by his most wise and excellent contrivances of things, and final causes; we admire him for his perfections; but we reverence and adore him on account of his dominion: for we adore him as his servants; and a god without dominion, providence, and final causes, is nothing else but Fate and Nature. Blind metaphysical necessity, which is certainly the same always and everywhere, could produce no variety of things. All that diversity of natural things which we find suited to different times and places could arise from nothing but the ideas and will of a Being necessarily existing.[37]

Such passages summon up the image of a traditional Christian piety apparently untouched by the rise of modern science. However, when we turn from the published word to the private manuscripts on theology and religion, which he left behind in great abundance, we discover more hidden turmoil than the surface serenity of his words indicates. The manuscripts reveal a Newton who spent his entire adult life probing, questioning, rejecting the received tradition of Christianity. The published words concealed the reality of Newton's heterodoxy, were indeed carefully designed to conceal it by emphasizing his theism, which was, to be sure, both sincere and profoundly felt.

In the early 1670s Newton began serious theological study, which came to focus almost at once on the doctrine of the Trinity. As he read on, with his eye riveted on the allied problems of the nature of Christ and the nature of God, the conviction took hold of him that a monstrous fraud had perverted the nature of Christianity in the fourth and fifth centuries. The fraud had altered the Bible. Newton began to collect evidence that the passages on which Trinitarians relied had been inserted into the Bible in the fourth and fifth centuries. The material thus collected later became the foundation of his letters on "Notable Corruptions of Scripture."[38] The corruption of Scripture stemmed from a corruption of doctrine, primarily the work of Athanasius (a theologian of the fourth century and the principal architect of the doctrine of the Trinity), who denied the original and true form of Christianity represented by Arius (also a theologian of the fourth century, who rejected the Trinity). In the end, every aspect of Christianity was involved in the lapse from truth, from the ecclesiastical structure on the one hand to the moral tone of society on the other. Although he did not say so directly, Newton clearly believed that the Protestant Reformation had only scratched the surface. It had left the source of infection, Trinitarianism, untouched.

By 1675 at least, Newton had become an Arian in the original sense of the word. When I say that he questioned the miracle of the Incarnation, I have his Arianism in mind. As an Arian, he did not consider that Jesus was merely a man like other men, but he did hold that Jesus was not fully God. From this position Newton never retreated. He was still writing Arian definitions of the nature of Christ at the end of his life.

If he moved in any direction from his early Arianism, it was toward a position more radical yet. During the early eighties, in the years immediately before the *Principia*, Newton began to compose a treatise that he called *Theologiae Gentilis Origines Philosophicae (The Philosophical Origins of Gentile Theology)*. The *Origines* advanced the concept of an original religion practiced by the man the Jews called Noah, though the annals of other peoples gave him other names, from whose offspring mankind descended. The religion of Noah, he stated, was "the true religion till ye nations corrupted it."[39] To Newton, Jewish religion was the religion of the sons of Noah purged of the superstitions of gentile theology. When the Jews fell into idolatry as the Egyptians before them had, prophets came to recall them. Jesus was such a prophet, cast in the same mold, one who came not to institute a new religion but to restore an old one. Two precepts constituted its message, the duty to love God and the duty to love one's neighbor. These precepts descended from Noah to Abraham, Isaac, and Jacob. Moses taught them to Israel again. Pythagoras learned them in Egypt and carried them to the West. "This religion," Newton concluded, "may therefore be called the Moral Law of all nations."[40] These two basic commandments, he repeated, "always have and always will be the duty of all nations and the coming of Jesus Christ has made no alteration in them." As often as mankind turned from them, God sent prophets to restore them—Moses, the Jewish prophets, Jesus. "And in all the reformations of religion hitherto made the religion in respect of God and our neighbor is one and the same religion (barring ceremonies and forms of government which are of a changeable nature) so that this is the oldest religion in the world."[41]

The implications of the *Origines* seem to me to go beyond Arianism and to look toward the deist tracts, which rejected the concept of any divine revelation apart from nature, and which would burst upon

England in the following decade. In the *Origines* Newton demoted Christ even from the semidivine status Arianism accorded Him. He was merely one more prophet, who came to restore the true religion after mankind's innate propensity for idolatry had corrupted it. Trinitarianism, the worship of a man as God, had in its turn repeated the pattern of idolatry. The "Christian religion was not more true" than the religion of the children of Noah, he stated, "and did not become less corrupted."[42]

When I consider the role that Arianism played in the early history of Christianity and the role of its offspring, Unitarianism, in the modern world, and when I consider the various forms of expression that Newton employed, his religious quest presents itself to me as an effort to purge Christianity of irrationality. With the later deists, he shared a hatred, which stood at the very heart of his Arianism, of mystery and superstition. Trinitarianism was built on superstition in his view. Athanasius had deliberately contrived it for the easy conversion of the heathens "by bringing into it as much of ye heathen superstition as the name of Christianity would then bear." He referred to "Monstrous Legends, false miracles, veneration of reliques, charmes, ye doctrine of Ghosts or Daemons, and their intercession invocation and worship and such other heathen superstitions as were then brought in."[43]

An allied spirit displaced itself in his tract on "Corruptions of Scripture." The verse in John's Epistle that he took to be corrupted made sense, he argued, without the phrase in question, but not with it.

> If it be said that we are not to determine what's scripture & what not by our private judgments, I confess it in places not controverted: but in disputable places I love to take up with what I can best understand. Tis the temper of the hot and superstitious part of mankind in matters of religion ever to be fond of mysteries, & for that reason to like best what they understand least. Such men may use the Apostle John as they please: but I have that honour for him as to believe that he wrote good sense, & therefore take that sense to be his wch is the best. . . .[44]

The goal of his interpretation of the prophecies, a topic to which he devoted extended attention from the time when he was about thirty years of age until his death more than fifty years later, was to introduce an objective method that would eliminate individual fancy. If the very attempt to interpret the prophecies seems incompatible with this position, understand that the message of Newton's interpretation was Arianism. The Book of Revelation was God's prophecy of the rise of Trinitarianism—"this strange religion of ye west," "the cult of three equal Gods"—and of God's punishments on mankind for whoring after false gods.[45]

Newton did not repeat Descartes's systematic doubt. I am, however, prepared to interpret Descartes's process as a special version of the whole century's experience, what Basil Willey has called the "touch of cold philosophy."[46] A tradition of natural philosophy that had stood for two thousand years had been rejected, and a new beginning made. Like every scientist of the age, Newton was conscious of the change. He had repeated it in his own intellectual life by casting aside the Aristotelianism the university taught, to embrace the new mechanical philosophy. In him, though not solely in him, the step Descartes refused was realized. At his hand, Christian theology felt the touch of cold philosophy. There was much that failed to meet the test.

It is not surprising then that Newton's view of Scripture was considerably different from that of the Christian tradition. Although he accepted the idea of a revealed word of God, what he meant by it differed greatly from what prior Christians had meant. In the *Origines* he treated the historical books of the Old Testament as the record of the Jewish nation, which held no more inherent truth than the records of the Egyptians, Phoenicians, and Chaldeans. Nowhere did he approach the Bible as the revelation of truths above human reason unto life eternal. He was not likely, as an Arian, to hold such views. The heart of the Bible to Newton was prophecy, and the Book of Revelation its key. "There [is] no book in all the scripture so much recommended and guarded by providence as this."[47] What did the prophecies tell about God? Not his act of redeeming love but his dominion over history.

For Newton, who carried further the tendency present in Kepler and Descartes, Nature was the revelation of God as much as the Bible was, perhaps more so. This was part of the message of the *Origines*. The Vesta-like temples in which Noah and his sons worshiped, prytanea with fires in their centers, were symbols of the universe: "The whole heavens they recconed to be ye true & real temple of God & therefore that a Prytanaeum might deserve ye name of his Temple they framed it so as in the fittest manner to represent the whole systeme of the heavens. A point of religion then wch nothing can be more rational."[48] Let me note in passing that the universe depicted by the temple was heliocentric; true philosophy accompanied true religion before corrupting idolatry set in. One purpose of the true religion was to encourage mankind, through the structure of the temple, to study nature "as the true Temple of ye great God they worshipped." "So then the first religion was the most rational of all others till the nations corrupted it. For there is no way (wthout revelation) to come to ye knowledge of a Deity but by ye frame of nature."[49] Newton added the parenthetical phrase, "wthout revelation," above the line, as an afterthought.

When we compare Newton's conception of nature with Descartes's, he appears to have retreated somewhat from Descartes's forthright assertion that everything in the physical universe has been shaped by the necessary operation of impersonal laws. Indeed, one of the decisive turning points in his career had been his conclusion that Cartesian natural philosophy with its autonomous material realm was a recipe for atheism. He had rejected it to pursue a philosophy that embodied the dominance of spirit.[50] To Newton's gaze, nature displayed undoubted marks of design. Hence he accepted final causes and considered that they offered the best argument for the existence of God. Furthermore, he believed that God continues to be active in his creation.

For all of that, Newton's conception of nature still appears to me very similar to Descartes's in the dominance of law within it. Gottfried Wilhelm Leibniz (1646–1716) seized on his bizarre concept of periodic readjustments by God and held it up to ridicule; following Leibniz, historians have emphasized it far beyond its just proportion. It was not prominent in his thought. The immanence of God in Nature had to do overwhelmingly with the maintenance of law. Newton did not believe that the universal gravitational attraction of all bodies, the force by which his *Principia* explained the functioning of the heavenly system, is a power inherent in matter. The meaning of his concept of the world as God's sensorium was that the Creator was the "agent acting constantly according to certain laws" (as he put it to Richard Bentley) that makes bodies move as though they attract each other.[51] Book 1 of the *Principia* contained an implicit argument for the existence of God in its demonstration that only the inverse-square law of attraction, the law book 3 would demonstrate empirically to exist, is compatible with a rationally ordered universe—again an argument that identified God with law. Newton's God was the Pantocrator of the General Scholium who holds dominion over all that is, who reveals Himself in history as well, not by his watchful providence but by a similar dominion over the course of events. David Hume would soon point out that no qualities can properly be ascribed to a God deduced from nature except those from which He is inferred. Newton's God was not solely inferred from nature. It does appear to me, however, that his God was primarily a metaphysical projection of the creation. There can be no doubt that Newton recognized and revered Him with deep emotion. Nevertheless, He had lost many of the characteristics of the redeemer God of Christian tradition. "There is nothing I want to find out and long to know with greater urgency than this," Kepler had written in a letter of 1613: "Can I find God, whom I can almost grasp with my own hands in looking at the universe, also in myself?"[52] Newton also found God in the universe in a similar way; he did not look for Him elsewhere.

CONCLUSION

As I survey the developments in religious thought from Kepler through Descartes to Newton, they appear to me to have been in one sense inevitable. I do not mean that the views of the three were the only responses to the rise of science that were possible. I have in mind rather questions, questions that seem necessarily connected with general tendencies inseparable from modern science. Everyone was not compelled to answer them in the same way or even to admit they had been raised, but the culture as a whole could not avoid them. Kepler, Descartes, and Newton were geniuses of immense stature, who were apt as such to stand in the vanguard, probing questions that became apparent to the general public only later. When following generations and indeed the entire future course of Western civilization bore witness to the same questions at work, we have some cause to consider the developments inevitable.

The new natural philosophy found evidence of God in nature. Even Kepler, though he found the Trinity, could not find the Atonement there. Inevitably, natural philosophers concentrated on what alone natural philosophy could reveal, God the Creator, and they did so increasingly as the scientific revolution progressed. Just as inevitably, given the thrust of the new conception of nature, they found a God who revealed Himself in immutable laws and not in the watchful care of personal providence or in miraculous acts. Rationalism, a probing of the grounds of assent, was a necessary aspect of a philosophical movement founded on the rejection of a tradition as old as Western man; such rationalism was bound in the end to question affirmations of Christianity once held to be above reason. Natural philosophy does not, of course, have to concern itself with God at all. With us it does not. Because the Scientific Revolution occurred in a society dominated by religious concerns, it could not avoid such matters. Its net effect was to question those aspects of Christianity that distinguished it from theism. It remained for a future age, drawing on the same intellectual source, to question theism as well. I do not mean to assert that the Scientific Revolution logically entailed the decline first of

Christianity and then of religion as such. While some would assert that proposition, I find it far from evident. It does appear to me that the Scientific Revolution raised challenges to central aspects of received Christianity, and that such challenges arose inevitably from its very nature.

As I suggested at the beginning, the Scientific Revolution was not an isolated event. Many other changes in Western civilization, including other changes in its patterns of thought, worked at the same time to undermine the dominant position of Christianity. Nevertheless, it was the rise of modern science that confronted Christianity on the most critical ground, its claim to give an account of reality. During the seventeenth century, in the eyes of the leaders of thought, the enchanted world of the medieval church dissolved right away. Responsible thinkers could not ignore the fact. Newton tried to salvage Christianity by purging it of irrationalities. Not many in his age went so far. Nevertheless, when Robert Boyle (1627–1691), after a lifetime spent in the refutation of atheism, left part of his fortune to endow a lecture series to refute it some more, he testified that his assessment of the situation was not far different from Newton's. Two and a half centuries later, one is inclined to think that neither one had fully appreciated the change taking place. With the rise of modern science, as one of its most central results, the age of unquestioned faith was lost to Western man.

NOTES

1. Kepler to Maestlin, 22 Dec. 1616, *Gesammelte Werke*, ed. Walther von Dyck and Max Caspar, 22 vols. (Munich: Beck, 1937–), 17:203. I quote the translation from Carola Baumgardt, *Johannes Kepler: Life and Letters* (New York: Philosophical Library, 1951), p. 107.

2. *Werke* 6:287.

3. Ibid., pp. 330–331.

4. Jürgen Hübner, *Die Theologie Johannes Keplers zwischen Orthodoxie und Naturwissenschaft* (Tübingen: Mohr, 1975); Hübner, "Johannes Kepler als theologischer Denker," in *Kepler Festschrift 1971*, ed. Ekkehard Preuss (Regensburg: Naturwissenschaftlicher Verein Regensburg, 1971), pp. 21–44.

5. Kepler to Fabricius, 4 July 1603, *Werke* 14:421.

6. *Kepler's Conversation with Galileo's Sidereal Messenger*, trans. Edward Rosen (New York: Johnson Reprint, 1965), p. 37.

7. *The Six-Cornered Snowflake*, trans. Colin Hardie (Oxford: Clarendon Press, 1966), p. 33.

8. Kepler to Maestlin, 2 Aug. 1595, *Werke* 13:27.

9. *Epitome of Copernican Astronomy,* in *Great Books of the Western World,* ed. Robert M. Hutchins, vol. 16 (Chicago: Encyclopaedia Britannica, 1952), pp. 916–917.

10. *Conversation,* p. 14.

11. *Epitome, Great Books* 16:853–854.

12. Ibid., p. 885.

13. Ibid., p. 889.

14. *Epitome, Werke* 7:50.

15. Ibid., pp. 50–51.

16. *Harmonice mundi, Werke* 6:275.

17. *Paralipomena, Werke* 2:19. I quote the translation in W. Pauli, "The Influence of Archetypal Ideas on the Scientific Theories of Kepler," in C. G. Jung and W. Pauli, *The Interpretation of Nature and the Psyche* (New York: Pantheon, 1955), pp. 169–170.

18. *Epitome, Werke* 7:51.

19. *Oeuvres,* ed. Charles Adam and Paul Tannery, 12 vols. (Paris: Cerf, 1897–1910), 11:31–32.

20. *The Philosophical Works of Descartes,* trans. Elizabeth S. Haldane and G. R. T. Ross, 2 vols. (Cambridge: Cambridge Univ. Press, 1931), 1:302.

21. Ibid., pp. 134–137. Cf. Preface to the Reader, pp. 137–139.

22. Ibid., p. 220.

23. Ibid., p. 168.

24. Ibid., 2:259–344 (with Descartes's annotations on them).

25. Ibid., 1:107.

26. Kepler, *Snowflake,* p. 33.

27. *Discourse on Method, Optics, Geometry, and Meteorology,* trans. Paul J. Olscamp (Indianapolis: Bobbs-Merrill, 1965), pp. 311–319.

28. *Philosophical Works* 1:173.

29. See Objections II to the *Meditations* and Descartes's reply to the charge: *Philosophical Works* 2:24–51.

30. *Discourse,* p. 263.

31. Ibid., p. 361.

32. *Oeuvres* 8:61.

33. Ibid., 11:48.

34. *Discourse,* p. 329.

35. Ibid., p. 320. For both manna and the Egyptian miracles Descartes could call on passages in the Conimbricensis commentary on Aristotle, though the tone of their comments differed from his. See Étienne Gilson, *Index scolastico-cartésien,* 2d ed. (Paris: Vrin 1979), pp. 166, 234.

36. *Discourse,* p. 345.

37. *Principia,* trans. Andrew Motte, ed. Florian Cajori (Berkeley: Univ. of California Press, 1934), pp. 544–546.

38. In the form of two letters to Locke in 1690, *The Correspondence of Isaac Newton,* ed. W. H. Turnbull et al., 7 vols. (Cambridge: Cambridge Univ. Press, 1959–1977), 3:83–122. He also composed a third letter, which apparently he never sent: ibid., 3:129–142.

39. Yahuda MSS 17.3, fols. 8–10, and 41, fols. 3–4, Jewish National and University Library, Jerusalem. The primary source of the *Origines* is Yahuda MS 16.

40. I quote this passage from *Irenicum*, an offspring of the *Origines* composed much later; Keynes MS 3, p. 27 (King's College, Cambridge).

41. Keynes MS 3, p. 35.

42. Yahuda MS 16.2, fol. 45v.

43. Clarke Library MS (Los Angeles).

44. *Correspondence* 3:108.

45. Yahuda MSS 1.4, fol. 50, and 11, fol. 7. I am referring to his early interpretation, found primarily in Yahuda MS 1, not to the meandering product of his old age, which was published after his death.

46. "The Touch of Cold Philosophy," in R. F. Jones et al., *The Seventeenth Century* (Stanford: Stanford Univ. Press, 1951), pp. 369–376.

47. Yahuda MS 7.2i, fol. 4.

48. Yahuda MS 41, fol. 6.

49. Ibid., fol. 7.

50. See *De Gravitatione et Equipondio Fluidorum*, composed in the late 1660s, in A. R. and M. B. Hall, *Unpublished Scientific Papers of Isaac Newton* (Cambridge: Cambridge Univ. Press, 1962), pp. 90–121; English translation, pp. 121–156.

51. Newton to Bentley, 25 Feb. 1693, *Correspondence*, 3:253–254.

52. Kepler to an unknown Noble, 23 Oct. 1613, *Werke* 17:80. Translation quoted from Baumgardt, *Kepler*, pp. 114–115.

9
Christianity and the Newtonian Worldview

Margaret C. Jacob

All his [Christ's] laws are in themselves, abstracted from any consideration of recompense, conducing to the temporal interest of them that observe them.

—Richard Bentley, 1692

Thus the wise Governour of the World, hath taken Care for the Dispatch of Business. But then as too long Engagement about worldly Matters would take off Mens Minds from God and Divine Matters, so by this Reservation of every Seventh Day, that great Inconvenience is prevented also.

—William Derham, 1714

The interplay between science and religion in seventeenth-century England served to transform both. Far from being in conflict, as historians used to suppose, science and religion (as systems of ideas) modified each other in the course of the century. Mainstream English Protestants gradually embraced a version of the new science that supported traditional Christian metaphysics, while scientists responded to the necessity of protecting an established church and religiosity by significantly modifying the mechanical philosophy of nature and purging it of its materialistic tendencies. But this process, this transformation of ideas, did not occur in minds divorced from everyday reality. Intellectual change does not generally occur in that way. Scientists and churchmen alike were coming to terms with economic and political forces that were new and profoundly unsettling. Today we use words like *capitalism* and *revolution* to describe these forces; in the seventeenth century men (and some women) spoke of nature and God, of laws spiritual and natural, of self-interest or greed, of business, and of the necessity for order and harmony. Both science and religion were seen as being capable of imposing that order, but agreement among the educated as to which version of either would best serve was difficult, if not impossible, to achieve. This failure to agree convinced some thinkers that science and nature, properly understood, were sufficient principles by which human beings might order reality. The resulting "deism," or even "atheism," became a vital part of an intellectual transformation found throughout western Europe in the eighteenth century, commonly described by historians as the "Enlightenment." Almost unwittingly, in the early decades of the eighteenth century, science helped to foster the first generation of intellectuals among whom could be found a significant number of quite articulate opponents of all forms of traditional Christianity.

THE SEVENTEENTH-CENTURY BACKGROUND

The Protestant Christianity embraced by Isaac Newton (1642–1727) and his Newtonian followers had been molded by a new social and economic order that emerged in seventeenth-century England. A powerful market society operating according to the necessities of supply and demand existed in seventeenth-century London and the southern market towns, and any clergyman worthy of a pulpit there had to address that fundamental social and moral reality. Of course, this commercial society, which grew increasingly more conspicuous by the late seventeenth century, had emerged within the context of political revolution. The English Revolution, understood as a matrix of social and political upheaval that began in the 1640s and that culminated in the Revolution of 1688–89, gave increased political power to the landed and commercial classes. By the late 1690s the great London financiers had their Bank, while the landed gentry, with their side interests in commerce and trade, ruled over their parliamentary seats with little interference from the crown.[1] In London and the market towns men of "business and dispatch," as one clergyman in the 1660s described them, represented a new class and a new political force for whom both learning and divinity had to be practical and applicable if they were to be meaningful.

The Christianity that spoke most directly to this postrevolutionary elite was not the rigorous Calvinism of the 1630s and 1640s, which had inspired a generation of revolutionary saints. Rather it was a liberal (at the time one said "latitudinarian") Anglicanism that repudiated predestination, yet continued to define religion as an individual matter wherein the conscience of the laity must be respected, and that firmly subordinated church to state, insisting that bishops serve, not manipulate, the political system. If that liberal Christianity had a birthplace and theological center, it was Cambridge. There as early as the 1650s the Cambridge Platonists, Henry More (1614–1687) and Ralph Cudworth (1617–1688), repudiated the doctrine of predestination, while the young mathematician and clergyman Isaac Barrow (1630–1677), an associate of Newton, recorded privately his belief that religion must address itself not to "cloisters (whence much of it came)" but to "congregations of tradesmen and merchants."[2] In the select circle of liberal Anglicans that Newton frequented, Cambridge was intellectually alive and not the arid wasteland chronicled by commentators[3] who want to downplay the stimulation provided Newton by More and Cudworth or the importance of Isaac Barrow and the Cambridge divines in shaping the irenical, anti-Calvinist, millenarian, and violently antimaterialistic Christianity that became central to Newton's own religiosity.

Not only was this liberal Anglicanism basic to Newton; it was also embraced by a new generation of Cambridge-trained clergymen who used both pulpit and press to articulate for the educated elite what was nothing less than a new version of the Christian message. They addressed themselves to the competitive and self-interested world of the market and found its ethics, when restrained by Christian virtue, compatible with salvation. And for our purposes even more important, they used the new science of the seventeenth century as a foundation upon which this liberal Christianity might rest its case for God's benevolent overseeing of society and commerce. Chance and disorder are only apparent, not real, they argued, and God instills order in a world made complex by competition, market fluctuations, and (not least) political upheaval. Science, liberal Anglicans argued, proves the reality of that inherent, providentially directed, natural harmony. By the late seventeenth century the new science and the new Anglicanism reinforced one another. We should hardly be surprised to find the young Isaac Newton incorporating into his natural philosophy, and hence into his science, definitions of matter, space, and time that were deeply indebted to the liberal Anglicanism of Restoration Cambridge. The Newtonian synthesis entered the eighteenth century as an intellectual construction born in response to the English Revolution. More than any other philosophy of the early modern period, Newtonianism in turn shaped the beliefs and intellectual aspirations of an age we have come to describe as enlightened.

But if liberal Anglicanism was sympathetic to men of business, to the necessities and ethics of the marketplace, to what most people today would call material interests, how could it also have been so violently opposed to materialism in philosophy? In seventeenth-century England philosophical materialism, although derived from a variety of sources and found among very disparate social groups, was uniformly condemned by Christian apologists as "atheism" and as disruptive of the very fabric of social obligation. They condemned it for endorsing the worst aspects of market competition and worldly self-interest, or they associated it with the religious heresies promulgated by lower-class social reformers intent upon undermining the church's privileges, who were oftentimes drawn from the ranks of the people victimized by the new wage market.

Because there were so many varieties of materialism in mid-seventeenth-century England, no one definition identifies all its proponents and their various social beliefs and interests. All did, however, share one common philosophical assumption: while traditional Christian metaphysics argued for a separate spiritual realm, distinct from matter and body—in effect the world of God, angels, and souls—materialists obliterated that distinction. They might argue that souls are in bodies in such a way as to be indistinguishable one from the other, or they might simply assert that there is only matter in the universe. The sources of seventeenth-century materialism were numerous: ancient philosophers like Aristotle or Epicurus, new scientists like Hobbes, or popular heresies and beliefs that saw nature as alive and fertile without the need of divine intervention. Such philosophical heresies were particularly rife during the English Revolution. In the reaction that followed that Revolution, symbolized by the Restoration of Charles II in 1660, progressive churchmen sought to advance the cause of science under royal patronage and still to purge it of any materialistic tendencies. At stake in their enterprise, as they perceived it, was not simply the reconciliation of science and religion. Heresies that eliminated the spiritual realm, and hence its priestly overseers, threatened the very order of society—church, aristocracy, property, and privilege.

In the 1640s and 1650s Levellers, Quakers, Diggers, and Muggletonians—to name the better known sectaries of the period—argued that if God dwelt in Nature (some went so far as to say that God is Nature), then all human beings partake of the divine in this world as well as in the next. And from that metaphysic the radicals drew certain social conclusions. Should not all people share in the riches of the earth? If God dwells in us all, what need have we of clergymen and churches, and are there such things as sin and hell?[4] That sort of pantheistic materialism could justify social leveling, and the Cambridge Platonists waged a violent campaign in pulpit and press against that heretical and dangerous response to social and economic inequality. In the 1660s Newton wrote a manuscript treatise wherein he too condemned the materialism of the "atheists," "the vulgar," who on this occasion were probably followers of a very paganized version of Aristotle's philosophy of nature.[5] Whatever its source, materialism represented the gravest intellectual heresy confronted by the English church.

The philosophical heresies associated with lower-class radicalism had their analogue in another species of materialism believed to be prevalent among the educated classes themselves. The major political philosopher of the English Revolution, Thomas Hobbes (1588–1679), had used the new science and mechanical philosophy to argue that only matter and motion govern the operations of nature, and in that formulation churchmen saw a profound threat to social harmony as well as to Christianity itself. According to Hobbes, desire and passion rule in the heart—we are nothing but matter impelled by force—and as a result, churchmen argued, Hobbes's materialism, which saw the actions of matter as governed only by laws inherent to it, sanctioned the unrestrained use of passion in pursuit of self-interest—to paraphrase Hobbes, the marketplace of the all against the all.[6]

While churchmen read Hobbes as a blatant materialist and atheist, they were also suspicious for different reasons of his French contemporary, René Descartes (1596–1650). Although Descartes was a committed theist, his natural philosophy rested on a radical separation of matter and spirit. This was a separation so radical that the Cambridge Platonists, among others, came to fear that Descartes had freed matter to operate on its own, without the assistance of spiritual agencies. In effect, Descartes defined matter in such a way that it could be seen as part of Hobbes's self-contained material order. Newton himself called Descartes a materialist and argued that his science would undermine all religious belief. At almost precisely the same time the vice-chancellor of Cambridge University, Edmund Boldero of Jesus College, ordered that Descartes's work not be read.[7] Both Hobbes and Descartes addressed the highly educated, and what later seventeenth-century Anglican Christians, including Newton, wanted was an equally sophisticated natural and religious philosophy that would effectively counter materialism of whatever origin while maintaing a liberal stance in matters of doctrine. Churchmen wanted social harmony without the threat of social disorder coming from below, but also without the rapacious self-interest (which ultimately fed the flames of lower-class radicalism) so characteristic of the "crafty ill-principled men," as John Evelyn, one of the founders of the Royal Society, called the ungodly and prosperous.

Under the linkage forged by the Cambridge Platonists, Barrow, Newton, and the Newtonians during the late seventeenth and early eighteenth centuries, Christianity and science entered into an alliance addressed to the moral reality of a market society, the first of its kind (outside of the Netherlands) to exist in one of the highly centralized nation-states of the early modern period. Science and natural philosophy, as interpreted by Newton and his followers, offered a model of the stable, ordered, providentially guided universe within which could occur that competition so basic to the operations of the restrained, yet relatively free, market society.

THE BOYLE LECTURES

Through the efforts of the first generation of Newtonians—Richard Bentley, Samuel Clarke, William Derham, and William Whiston— Newton's natural philosophy was preached from the 1690s onward at the podium provided by a prestigious London lectureship. It was presented as the cornerstone of a liberal, tolerant, and highly philosophical version of Christianity, a natural religion based upon reason and science that came dangerously close to deism but that managed, in Newton's own lifetime, never to slip over that particular ledge. Perhaps the major reason why the early Newtonians remained aggressively Christian, or more precisely Anglican, derived from the active role that Newton took in the promulgation of his natural philosophy. When the great natural philosopher and supporter of the church, Robert Boyle, was in his last illness and the terms of his will establishing what became his famous lectureship became known to his intimates, a close friend of Newton, the Scottish mathematician David Gregory, recorded in a memorandum dated 28 December 1691 a revealing glimpse of Newton's sense of what his philosophy might achieve. From the date and contents of Gregory's memorandum it appears likely that Newton was referring to the projected Boyle lectures. His description of the "public speech" and the contents of "ane Act," that is, a college speech, thesis, or disputation, closely resembles the contents of lectures first given in 1692 by Bentley. Newton, in effect, suggested that his discoveries in celestial physics would show the cosmic qualities in the laws of nature and hence would serve the argument from providential design better than the reliance on the "general contrivance" in animals and plants used by John Ray in his *The Wisdom of God Manifested in the Works of the Creation* (1691). Gregory's memorandum reads:

In Mr Newton's opinion a good design of a publick speech (and which may serve well as ane Act) may be to shew that the most simple laws of nature are observed in the structure of a great part of the Universe, that the philosophy ought ther to begin; and that Cosmical Qualities are as much easier as they are more Universall than particular ones, and the general contrivance simpler than that of Animals Plants etc.[8]

In January 1692 Newton may also have suggested Richard Bentley as the first Boyle lecturer, and earlier, in July 1691, Bentley had already received instructions through another liberal churchman, William Wotton, on how to understand the *Principia*. Wotton took a keen interest in the Boyle lectures, as did his patron and leader of the church party, Heneage Finch. In the autumn of 1692 Bentley developed his version of Newton's philosophy and used it as the underpinning for his social vision. Before publishing those sermons Bentley consulted with Newton, and the first of Newton's four replies began with the now famous words: "When I wrote my treatise upon our Systeme I had an eye upon such Principles as might work with considering men for the beliefe of a Deity and nothing can rejoyce me more than to find it usefull for that purpose."[9] By way of assistance to Bentley, Newton may have written an account of his system of the world; a manuscript version of that draft survives among Newton's unpublished papers.[10]

In the early eighteenth century the numerous editions and translations of the Boyle lectures became the major vehicle for disseminating Newtonian natural philosophy to the educated laity both in England and on the Continent. On the basis of Newton's behind-the-scenes interest in those lectures, his consistent antimaterialism, and his devout, but highly liberal and irenical, Christianity, this foremost English scientist should also be described as a Newtonian in the social and ideological sense. He condoned the Boyle lectures that articulated the social vision of Bentley, Clarke, Derham, and the other liberal divines; and he lent the prestige of his achievement to what became in their hands an enlightened philosophy that supported the pursuit of sober self-interest, that endorsed human domination over nature, and that encouraged the application of scientific learning to the problems posed by navigation, agriculture, and industry. In short, Newtonianism became an ideology that justified commercial capitalism, empire, scientific progress, and a new religiosity geared more to the vicissitudes of this world than the rewards of the next. This is not to say that social factors and political interest can account for Newton's scientific achievements, his mathematical genius, or his philosophical insights into the structure of physical reality. But it is to say that, with his consent, his science served a precise ideological function in the early decades of the eighteenth century. After 1688–1689 it was used to shore up the newly reconstituted monarchy and established church as the bulwarks of order, stability, and prosperity; only strong government, centralized and coordinated by court, placemen, and bishops, would make the pursuit of economic interests possible. The cosmic order and design explicated in the *Principia* became, in the hands of Newton's early followers, a natural model for a Christian society, providentially sanctioned and reasonably tolerant of diverse religious beliefs, provided they did not threaten the stability of the polity (hence the exclusion of Catholics and anti-Trinitarian heretics with their propensity, or so it was imagined, for purely rationalist explanations of supernatural phenomena). Yet the Newtonians argued, against the demands made by contemporary reformers, that no further political reform was necessary beyond that embodied in the so-called Revolution settlement of 1689.

In polemical response to the materialism of Hobbes and the pantheism of the political radicals, Newton's closest friends, Bentley, Clarke, and Whiston, took to their pulpits and in their lectures and writings preached primarily to a London-based and prosperous—often mercantile—audience. They extolled the virtues of self-restraint and public-mindedness, while at the same time assuring their congregations that prosperity came to the virtuous and that divine providence permitted, even fostered, material rewards. The same providence that generates the mechanical laws at work in the universe oversees the workings of society and government, and men must see to it that their political and economic actions conform to the stability and harmony decreed by supernatural authority. While tolerating doctrinal differences among Christians themselves, reasonable people must acknowledge a vast cosmic order, imposed by God, and attempt to imitate it in society and government. In Boyle lectures that were read and admired by eighteenth-century thinkers as diverse as Samuel Johnson and Jean-Jacques Rosseau, Samuel Clarke argued that religion reinforced by science should play a vital role in state policy.[11] Liberal Anglicanism preaches social order and political stability—in other words, that men should not be "extremely and unreasonably solicitous" to change their stations in life and that they should not become, in the words of Bentley, "men of ambitious and turbulent spirits, that [are] dissatisfied . . . with privacy and retirement."[12] The natural rulers should be allowed their positions and stations; they, of course, must practice a moral virtue that is conducive to harmony because God's providence sees to it that it is. There can be no doubting the absolute necessity for social stability and no doubting that the moral laws ordained by God for its attainment are universal and guaranteed to work. The physical order explicated by Newton proclaims order and stability, but this order comes not from matter or nature but directly from God, whose will operates in the universe either directly or through active principles. The "world natural" stands as a model for the "world politick," and Newton's explanation of the first provides a foundation upon which the government of the second should rest. Without that model, what refutation could work against the radicals or the Hobbists, whose prescriptions rested upon observed behavior and upon the experience of political revolution?

In the most influential and consistently republished lectures ever delivered during the eighteenth century, the Newtonians soothed and assured their congregations, but they also simultaneously exhorted them. Wealth, leisure, and power in the hands of the natural rulers of society fulfilled the providential design, yet all had to be used with moderation and in the service of a liberal and tolerant Christianity. Social harmony and political stability complement an ordered universe explicated by Newton, where matter is dead or lifeless, its motion controlled by the will of God; in short, as Clarke explained, "there is no such thing as what men commonly call the course of nature, or the power of nature. [It] is nothing else but the will of God producing certain effects in a continued, regular, constant, and uniform manner."[13] The Newtonians succeeded, as had the Cambridge Platonists before them, in proclaiming the providential and interventionist God who allowed the ordered universe to operate according to discernible laws of nature.

NEWTONIANISM AND DEISM

The charge most commonly leveled against this Newtonian Christianity of the eighteenth century was, and is, that it quickly degenerated into deism. Yet all the evidence we possess about Newton's own religiosity confirms his theistic and providential understanding of God and his biblical sense of history. In his millennial paradise, "the new Jerusalem that [mystical] spiritual building in Sion where of the Chief corner stone is [Christ]," the returned Savior will "rule with a rod of iron."[14] Indeed, Newton discussed events in his own time—for example, the war against France during the reign of Anne—as possible signs leading to the institution of that expected godly paradise.[15] There was nothing remote about Newton's God, and surely if the term *deism* had any meaning in the eighteenth century, it lay in a definition of God that allowed Him to exist but not to participate, and that relegated Christianity to a series of ethical maxims taken less, rather than more, seriously.

Yet after we have pointed to Newton's intensely Christian temper or to the vagaries in defining deism during the eighteenth century, the charge that something less than Christian emerged in church-sponsored, science-based English Protestantism still will not go away. The charge bears relevance not to the religiosity of the first generation of Newtonians—not even to Samuel Clarke, whose anti-Trinitarianism was drawn from his reading of Newton's science[16] but did not, in my reading of his writings, lessen his commitment to a liberal Christianity as he understood it—but rather to the second generation of Newtonians. These were scientists and ideologues who came into their own in the 1720s, in that complacent world of Whig oligarchs that so impressed foreign visitors like Voltaire. In their hands Newtonian science fostered a variety of cultural institutions and philosophical systems that seem to bear little resemblance to the Christianity in which Newton, or Whiston and Clarke for that matter, personally believed.

Not least of these new institutions was Freemasonry, that secret male fraternity officially established in 1717 in London. It grew out of the old artisan guilds but became, under the leadership of Whigs and Newtonians, a totally "speculative" (to use the Masonic term) brotherhood of bourgeois gentlemen and aristocrats dedicated, as their official *Constitutions* proclaim, to religious toleration, Baconian experimentalism, and court-centered government. The leading spirit in British Freemasonry was the Anglican clergyman Jean Theophile Desaguliers (1683–1744), the official experimenter of the Royal Society, who had known Newton well; indeed, Newton stood as a godparent to one of Desaguliers's children.[17] Desaguliers combined a clerical career, which he rather neglected, with an avid dedication to Newtonian science and Freemasonry. He lectured widely in England and the Netherlands on the practical application of Newtonian mechanics to industry and agriculture. He also encouraged the formation of Masonic lodges in the provinces and abroad, while his own London lodge at the Horn Tavern was among the most prestigious in the country and the one to which the French philosopher, Charles Louis de Secondat Montesquieu, proudly belonged.

In the hands of Desaguliers and his Newtonian associates in the new fraternity, in particular Brook Taylor (1685–1731) and Martin Folkes (1690–1754), the London Masonic lodges became places where literate and cosmopolitan men could seek a grounding in the new science and mathematics made simple and participate vicariously in the "Royal Art" of architecture, with its supposedly ancient wisdom still intact, while worshiping the new science-inspired God, the "Grand Architect," as he was called. The official Masonic *Constitutions* of 1723 prescribed that "in ancient Times Masons were charg'd in every Country to be of the Religion of that Country or Nation, whatever it was, yet 'tis now thought more expedient only to oblige them to that Religion in which all men agree, leaving their particular opinions to themselves."[18] Into that fraternal and secretive religiosity a variety of creeds could comfortably fit; indeed, eighteenth-century Freemasonry, in both England and the Continent, housed Newtonians, pantheists, materialists, and deists, with the specific identity of the object of worship revered at lodge meetings under the name of "Grand Architect" known only to the individual worshiper. In effect, the eighteenth-century Freemason could worship Newton's God or Nature, and the difference depended not upon communal experience, which consisted largely of banquets and processions, nor upon rituals and ceremonies, which were largely secular in origin, nor upon doctrine, but solely upon the private meaning attached to language.

As a cultural institution Freemasonry betrays the linkage between Newtonianism, when embraced by the educated laity, and deism. But there were also purely intellectual constructions of Newton's system made by that second generation of Newtonian scientists which further suggest that connection. In particular, the writings of Henry Pemberton (1694–1771) are representative of this "de-Christianized" Newtonianism. Pemberton was educated in Leiden under the great physician and chemist Herman Boerhaave, from whom he probably learned his Newtonianism. Pemberton's willingness to defend that system against the Continental followers of Leibniz brought him to Newton's attention, and by 1725 he was supervising the production of the third edition of the *Principia* (1726). Although various London Freemasons who were publishers and printers were involved in its actual production, and indeed in the general dissemination of Newtonian science, Pemberton, unlike Desaguliers, Folkes, and Taylor, does not appear to have been a Mason.[19]

The writings of Pemberton and his Newtonian colleagues repeated themes made famous by the great Boyle lecturers. Yet this next generation of Newtonians toned down the polemics aimed at freethinkers and materialists, which had been so characteristic of the earlier period. The accomplishment of the Hanoverian Succession in 1714 had engendered a modicum of political complacency. Dedicating his exposition of Newton's philosophy to Robert Walpole, the first prime minister, whose government embodied reason as it did his "masculine perspicuity and strength of argument," Pemberton claimed that Newton had read and approved the greater part of this treatise.[20]

Pemberton's *A View of Sir Isaac Newton's Philosophy* (1728) is a much more straightforward and succinct account of Newton's philosophy of nature, his definitions of matter, space, time, the vacuum, and the law of universal gravitation, than that found in the Boyle lectures. Christian apologetics has been deemphasized in favor of a general, but constant, emphasis on the power of the deity, on a straightforward explanation of Newtonian physics. Whenever Pemberton enters into polemics, it is against the materialists: those who assert that gravity is essential to matter; those who would assert the eternity of the world; those who deny the supremacy of God in every aspect of creation.[21]

In the second quarter of the eighteenth century, during Walpole's era, a fashionable Newtonian and providentialist "deism" can be found among the educated elite, who grew less interested in the doctrinal rigidity of the early Newtonians. Their natural religion was transformed into an ethical system (seldom dwelt upon at any length) buttressed by Newtonian explanations of the universe. And most important, there is no evidence to indicate that Bentley, Clarke, or in the 1720s Newton himself disapproved of this fashionable extrapolation. Nor should they have. This natural religion, so broad as to accommodate Protestants and even "deists" of whatever doctrinal persuasion, at every turn asserted God's benevolent, if somewhat impersonal, relationship to his creation. It was a tested bulwark against materialism in philosophy as well as against the political radicalism associated with the English Revolution. By 1730 most observers declared that church and monarchy rested more securely than they had in previous decades and that the seeds of destruction lay in internal corruption rather than in the schemes of the radicals.

Given the increasingly obvious deemphasizing of religious doctrines in favor of a science-based natural religion championed by the Newtonians, it is understandable that European intellectuals hostile to organized religion, particularly as found in Catholic countries, rushed to embrace the Newtonian synthesis. That was precisely the response of the young Voltaire, who after arriving in England in 1726 became an ardent Newtonian. Indeed, he knew Clarke's Boyle lectures intimately, and with his Newtonian faith in place Voltaire launched violent polemics against clerics, religious persecution, and most forms of organized worship. His contemporary and the leading Dutch Newtonian of the eighteenth century, Willem Jacob s'Gravesande, taught Newtonian physics at Leiden for decades, believed deeply in divine providence, and seems to have had no scruples about associating with pantheists, materialists, and Freemasons—perhaps even joining the last-named organization. The assimilation of Newtonian science into Western thought produced the first generation of European thinkers for whom faith in the order of the universe proved more satisfying than faith in doctrines, creeds, and clerical authority.

CHRISTIAN OPPOSITION TO NEWTONIANISM IN ENGLAND

By the middle of the eighteenth century many English Protestants had become convinced that the growth of deism and materialism, the degeneration of public and private morality, and political corruption should be laid at the door of liberal Anglicanism and its science-supported natural theology. In this age of Whig ascendancy the opponents of Newtonian Christianity predictably came from the political opposition, the Tory or "country" wing of the Anglican church. By the 1740s this Tory disaffection led to the questioning of the most basic tenets of liberal Anglicanism. Tory thinkers became increasingly convinced that the Newtonians, possibly even Newton himself—although few, if any, of his contemporaries outside his circle knew what we now know about his ideological involvements and his religious beliefs—had, by their avowal of the new mechanical philosophy as the foundation of natural religion, effectively undermined all religion. Ironically, in the light of what we know about the ideological uses of seventeenth-century science, they believed that the Newtonians had opened the door to the radicals, to the atheists, deists, and Spinozists. This anti-Newtonian thrust within Tory Anglican thought received its most elaborate explication in the voluminous writings of John Hutchinson (1674–1737) and his many followers.[22] Although primarily given to natural-philosophical explanations of the universe, this anti-Newtonian movement also displayed strongly mystical and spiritualizing tendencies. It sought to keep aspects of Newtonian science, while finding in nature proof for doctrines as diverse as the Fall of Man and the Trinity.

Throughout the eighteenth century the anti-Newtonianism of the devout may have been much more widespread than has as yet been imagined. Methodist preachers could be found who "bitterly inveighed against Newton as an ignorant pretender who had presumed to set up his own ridiculous chimeras in opposition to the sacred philosophy of the Pentateuch."[23] If any thread united such disparate religious positions as those of the Hutchinsonians and the "enthusiastic" Methodists, it was in fact their opposition to establishment culture and its liberal and Newtonian spokesmen. Tory or "country" opposition, in particular its Christian and God-fearing element of whatever sectarian persuasion, saw the materialists as the quintessential symbol of a corrupt age and as the wayward, but inevitable, offspring of their science-deceived elders. Even within Cambridge itself a reaction set in against the alliance of science and religion, and throughout the eighteenth century the college common rooms and lecture halls witnessed isolated attacks on a form of religion now totally dependent upon principles of attraction and inertia and definitions of matter and motion.

A few examples should suffice to illustrate the religious sensibilities of these anti-Newtonian critics and the depth of their dissatisfaction.

George Cheyne (1671–1743), one such critic and one of the finest doctors of his age, became an early convert to the Newtonian natural philosophy and wrote a long treatise (*The Philosophical Principles of Religion*, 1705, 1715) in support of natural religion based upon Newtonian principles. Indeed, Cheyne was so convinced of the argument from design that he believed divine providence to have designed the waters at Bath as the means by which the English might cope with their weather and diet.[24] Apparently Cheyne knew whereof he spoke; he had been a "Free-liver" and suffered from extreme obesity for many years. He then became a pioneer for clean living and careful diet and an expert on gout.

By the 1730s Cheyne had become convinced that the body politic was severely ailing, and he traced its disease to "spurious Freethinkers, active Latitudinarians, and Apostolic Infidels."[25] As Cheyne grew increasingly disaffected from the ruling Whig oligarchy, he spoke more and more bitterly about liberal divines and freethinkers and turned toward Methodism.[26] At precisely the period of his political disaffection Cheyne also grew skeptical of the new science with its emphasis upon induction and calculation. In his search for physical well-being in man and government, Cheyne abandoned the Newtonian synthesis and opted for an increasingly spiritualized understanding of nature and for a contemplative, almost mystical and millenarian, version of Christianity.[27] In the face of the corruption he universally perceived, Cheyne, the young Newtonian, became the disaffected and antiestablishment Methodist. For the first time in Protestant Europe the eighteenth century witnessed a widespread disaffection from the new science, characterized by a growing sense that science had betrayed the very religious sensibility that had done so much during the previous century to foster it.

The rule of the liberal divines in the government of the church further inflamed the clerical (as well as lay) opposition to Whig hegemony in church and state and low-church Anglicanism. Given the power of the latitudinarians, few if any of the opposition clergy ever emerged out of the political and ecclesiastical wilderness to become effective spokesmen against the prevailing order. By the 1720s and 1730s Walpole was said to have found his pope in the Whiggish Edmund Gibson, bishop of London, while the liberal Newtonian Benjamin Hoadly, who had learned his science from Samuel Clarke, incited the Tory opposition by arguing for the subordination of church to state. Hoadly was rewarded with a bishopric for his efforts in support of the Whig interpretation of ecclesiastical government. In contrast, alienated Tory and anti-Newtonian churchmen, such as the Hutchinsonian George Horne (1730–1792), generally kept their opin-

ions to themselves. Only in 1790 did Horne finally obtain high ecclesiastical office as bishop of Norwich; in the interim he confined his
opinions on current events and the state of the church to his private
diary.

Horne's diary is therefore a valuable guide to the Tory and anti-
Newtonian conscience, and it reveals that he believed that "Arianism
and Deism . . . have darkened the sun." In a moment of self-pity he
bitterly recorded: "These [are] poor gentlemen the Hutchinsonians
because they'll never get any preferment. The bishops . . . all entered
into a league never to promote them . . . [yet] we are not of the
numbers of them who preach Christianity for gain or take orders
because we are likely to get more by that than by anything else."[28]
Horne was convinced that the Whigs and liberal churchmen had
invented pernicious political and religious principles—"religion of
nature [is] a chimera"—while Whig principles almost invariably lead
to republicanism.[29] Horne was convinced that mathematics could
never provide ultimate certainty about the nature of reality—"nothing
but revelation can ever set us right, or give us certainty." And to make
the danger to religion even more extreme, Horne believed that the
radicals were everywhere; he observed "a presbyterian who said that
man was not born for serving kings—so chopping his neck with his
hands."[30] Horne knew "ranters" in his own time (a radical sect of the
1650s) who, true to their naturalistic doctrines, make everything god,
which "is the dregs of the old corrupt heathen philosophy."[31] If
Horne's observations were true to a larger reality, perhaps we can
better understand why the guardians of the Whig constitution en-
forced some of the most repressive legislation against disruptive elements ever to be devised in the history of English criminal law.

Despite this catalogue of woes induced by the specter of popular
radicalism and irreligion, Horne reserved enough animosity to list
tersely the many failings of John Tillotson, archbishop of Canterbury
(1691–1695) after the Revolution, who more than any other archbishop
in his century had shifted the church's thinking toward religious toleration, constitutional monarchy, and the new science. Well after 1750
Horne condemns Tillotson as if he were alive and well and charges
that he "denies the divinity of Christ . . . denies the eternity of hell
torments . . . speaks of the Old Testament as not good nor relating
to Christ . . . makes Christianity good for nothing but to keep societies
in order the better that there should be no Christ than that it should
disturb societies."[32] Horne had discerned, as had many of his alienated
lay and clerical contemporaries, the social (but not necessarily the
spiritual) message that lay at the heart of Newtonian natural religion.
That its spokesmen were perceived as putting their blessings on a

corrupt and godless society merely confirmed opposition attempts to find alternative forms of science and Christian worship.

Generally these attempts to find an alternative to Newtonian science and natural religion led to the exercises in baroque metaphysics that we associate with Hutchinson and his writings on science and the Trinity, or to the philosophical idealism of Bishop Berkeley, which was to play an important role in the German Enlightenment. These critics never succeeded, however, in breaking the linkage between Newtonian science and the liberal Christianity of the church's leadership. As a result, late in the eighteenth century William Blake, who was sensitive to that linkage, came to see Newton as a symbol of oppression, as a party to commercial and industrial society and to the endorsement of economic exploitation inherent in the social ideology of liberal Anglicanism.[33]

Only in the nineteenth century did Darwinianism deliver a severe blow, not to Christianity as such, but to science-supported and liberal Anglicanism. Not only did Darwin expose the scientific failings in the argument from design; some of his important followers also called in question that model of social order and benign harmony, born in reaction to revolution, which had for so long denied the realities of commercial society. Yet for nearly a century, beginning in the 1690s, Newton's science had provided the intellectual foundation for a unique version of European Protestantism, one particularly suited to the maintenance of political stability and an unprecedented degree of religious toleration, all within the context of a rapidly expanding commercial society.

NOTES

1. For a discussion of this political process see J. H. Plumb, *The Origins of Political Stability, England, 1675–1725* (Boston: Houghton Mifflin, 1967), pp. 159–189.

2. Margaret C. Jacob, *The Newtonians and the English Revolution 1689–1720* (Ithaca, N.Y.: Cornell Univ. Press, 1976), p. 45. For preachings against predestination in Cambridge during the 1650s see Trinity College, Cambridge, MS R.10.29, notes made by Isaac Barrow on sermons by Benjamin Whichcote, Ralph Cudworth, John Arrowsmith, and others.

3. Richard S. Westfall, "Isaac Newton in Cambridge: The Restoration University and Scientific Creativity," in *Culture and Politics: From Puritanism to the Enlightenment*, ed. Perez Zagorin (Berkeley, Los Angeles, London: Univ. of California Press, 1980), pp. 135–164. For a different perspective see James Jacob and Margaret Jacob, "The Anglican Origins of Modern Science: The Metaphysical Foundations of the Whig Constitution," *Isis* 71 (1980): 251–267.

4. Christopher Hill, *The World Turned Upside Down* (New York: Viking Press, 1972), pp. 112, 114, 176, 318–319.

5. *Unpublished Scientific Papers of Isaac Newton*, ed. A. Rupert Hall and Marie Boas Hall (Cambridge: Cambridge Univ. Press, 1962), pp. 141–142.

6. Jacob, *Newtonians*, pp. 169–171.

7. John Craig to John Conduitt, 7 Apr. 1727, Cambridge University Library, MS Add. 4007, fol. 686. Cf. John Gascoigne, "'The Holy Alliance': The Rise and Diffusion of Newtonian Natural Philosophy and Latitudinarian Theology within Cambridge from the Restoration to the Accession of George II" (D. Phil. diss., University of Cambridge, 1981), p. 115 (citing Bodleian Library, MS Rawlinson C.146, fol. 37). This is a very useful thesis, which documents Newton's relations with other fellows in his university and modifies the account found in Richard S. Westfall, *Never at Rest: A Biography of Isaac Newton* (Cambridge: Cambridge Univ. Press, 1980), chap. 3.

8. *The Correspondence of Sir Isaac Newton*, ed. H. W. Turnbull, 7 vols. (Cambridge: Cambridge Univ. Press, 1959–1977), 3:191. Cf. James E. Force, *William Whiston: Honest Newtonian* (Cambridge: Cambridge Univ. Press, 1985).

9. Jacob, *Newtonians*, p. 156.

10. I. B. Cohen, "Isaac Newton's *Principia*, the Scriptures and Divine Providence," in *Philosophy, Science and Method: Essays in Honor of Ernest Nagel*, ed. S. Morgenbesser, P. Suppes, and M. White (New York: St. Martin's Press, 1969), pp. 523–548.

11. *A Discourse Concerning the Unchangeable Obligations of Natural Religions and the Truth and Certainty of the Christian Religion* (London, 1706), pp. 152–153.

12. *The Works of Richard Bentley*, ed. A. Dyce, 3 vols. (London, 1838), 3:24. For Whiston see Force, *William Whiston*.

13. *A Discourse . . .* , in *A Collection of Theological Tracts*, ed. Richard Watson, 4 vols. (London, 1785), 4:246; a more accessible edition.

14. Frank E. Manuel, *The Religion of Isaac Newton: The Fremantle Lectures, 1973* (Oxford: Clarendon Press, 1974), pp. 132–133. Appendix taken from Newton's manuscripts.

15. Margaret Jacob, "Newton and the French Prophets: New Evidence," *History of Science* 16 (1978): 134–142.

16. Larry Stewart, "Samuel Clarke, Newtonianism, and the Factions of Post-Revolutionary England," *Journal of the History of Ideas* 42 (1980): 53–72.

17. For Desaguliers and Freemasonry in general see Margaret Jacob, *The Radical Enlightenment: Pantheists, Freemasons, and Republicans* (London and Boston: George Allen & Unwin, 1981), pp. 122–126.

18. Ibid., p. 280, in appendix; a reprinting of a portion of the 1723 edition of James Anderson, *The Constitutions of the Freemasons* (London).

19. J. R. Clarke, "The Royal Society and Early Grand Lodge Freemasonry," *Ars Quatuor Coronatorum* 80 (1967): 110–119. Of the two hundred known Masons based in London in the 1720s, one out of four was a Fellow of the Royal Society.

20. Henry Pemberton, *A View of Sir Isaac Newton's Philosophy* (London, 1728), dedication. The subscription list is heavily Whiggish.

21. Ibid., pp. 22, 180–181, 406–407.

22. A. J. Kuhn, "Hutchinson vs. Newton," *Journal of the History of Ideas* 22 (1961): 303–322.

23. Barnard Semmel, *The Methodist Revolution* (New York: Basic Books, 1973), p. 20.

24. See George Cheyne, *An Essay on the Gout, with an Account of the Nature and Qualities of the Bath Waters* (London, 1720).

25. George Cheyne, *Dr. Cheyne's Account of Himself and His Writings: Faithfully Extracted from His Various Works* (London, 1743), p. 21.

26. *An Essay on Regimen . . . Serving to Illustrate the Principles and Theory of Philosophical Medicin, and Point Out Some of Its Moral Consequences* (London, 1740), pp. xiv–xv; *The Letters of Dr. George Cheyne to the Countess of Huntingdon,* ed. Charles F. Mullett (San Marino, Calif.: Huntington Library, 1940), passim.

27. *Essay on Regimen,* pp. viii, 206–208, 227–236.

28. "Commonplace Book I of George Horne, Bishop of Norwich." Owned by Sir Robert Arundel, but now in the possession of the University Library, Cambridge, MS Add. 8134/B/1, fol. 2 (made available by the kindness of Christopher Wilde). Probably written in the 1760s. For further evidence of tension between Hutchinsonians and Newtonians see Walter Wilson, *History and Antiquities of Dissenting Churches and Meeting Houses in London . . . ,* 2 vols. (London, 1808), 2:90. Cf. C. Wilde, "Hutchinsonianism, Natural Philosophy and Religious Controversy in Eighteenth Century Britain," *History of Science* 18 (1980): 1–24.

29. "Commonplace Book," fols. 29, 42–43.

30. Ibid., fol. 70.

31. Ibid., fol. 100.

32. Ibid., fol. 111.

33. David V. Erdman, *Blake: Prophet against Empire* (New York: Doubleday, 1969), pp. 224, 367, 484.

10
Laplace and the Mechanistic Universe

Roger Hahn

It is no easy task to place Pierre Simon Laplace (1749–1827) in the history of the relations of science and Christianity because there exists no historiographical context. To my knowledge no major scholarly treatise stands in need of correction or revision; nor is there even a series of articles linked by a chain of argumentation to provide a framework for our examination.[1] We have no historiographic tradition crying out for analysis, no classic debate requiring judicious settlement. There is merely a tacit agreement that Laplace closed whatever issue might once have existed by asserting that he had no use for God in his system of the world. "I have no need of that hypothesis," he is reported to have announced to Napoleon Bonaparte. So startling an assertion was this that even his quarrelsome interlocutor—who as a young man mastered his scientific manuals—was unable to rebut his friend or even blurt out a clever rejoinder. It was as if Laplace had given the nineteenth century a peremptory command that religious considerations were superfluous for an understanding of nature. An issue that had occupied hundreds of theologians and natural philosophers for centuries was apparently so threadbare that its dismissal failed at first to elicit any serious dissent.

To make matters even more difficult, this Laplacean assertion comes down to us in the form of a colorful anecdote, unsupported by substantive textual evidence but deserving to be taken seriously because it is entirely consistent with his overall intellectual stance.[2] How, then, can one deal with it properly in the absence of documentary confirmation? Perhaps by locating places in his writings where the issue might be joined in a more serious vein. Unfortunately,

Laplace offers no assistance in his major writings. Neither in the famous *Traité de mécanique céleste* (1799–1825) nor in the *Théorie analytique des probabilités* (1812) does he confront the topic head-on. Why should we be surprised? If he truly considered God to be a superfluous hypothesis, Laplace would not have felt the need to deal with the issue at all.

Indeed, why should we discuss it at all ourselves? Appearances notwithstanding, it was a matter of serious concern for Laplace, and one that caused him considerable mental anguish, which he nevertheless managed to hide from the public. Moreover, quite apart from any biographical considerations, the quiet proclamation of the superfluity of God by a scientist marks a significant turn in the course of intellectual history, for it reopened debates on new grounds about the relationship between faith and reason, and hence between those seeking answers to spiritual problems and those aiming to fathom the world of nature. The issue is also significant to remind us that the evolution of scientific knowledge about the cosmos—then as now—remains linked to cultural values despite attempts of positivists like Laplace to establish sharp boundaries between various human activities. The paradox of our modern era is surely that increasingly detailed and accurate knowledge of the material world, including ourselves, has done little to alleviate our persistent quandary about meaning. It has merely shifted the background against which we may vent our puzzlement.

PROGRESS IN ASTRONOMY

A mere century separates the deaths of Isaac Newton (1642–1727) and Laplace. During that time major changes in science and in cultural attitudes occurred, which can provide an initial framework for appreciating the position taken by Laplace and beginning to put it in historical perspective.

At the time of Laplace's birth in 1749, most of Newton's assertions about the system of the world were gaining a secure place in the scientific community. His three laws of motion had been given succinct mathematical expression in the handy language of the calculus by Leonhard Euler. The concept of universal gravitation, though still occasionally challenged by die-hard Cartesians for metaphysical reasons, was proving to be a fruitful working hypothesis. Disagreements existed over the correct mathematical formulation of the law of attraction and the proper coefficients to be employed for calculating various terrestrial and celestial phenomena, but rarely about the possibility of determining them or the power of Newton's synthetic models. All mathematically inclined astronomers, theoreticians and observers alike, were working toward a common goal of developing the fine structure of the Newtonian paradigm for the solar system.

The task was by no means simple or devoid of challenges. There were significant obstacles posed by the language of calculus, particularly the proper manipulation of differential equations, the integration of particular functions, and the difficulties of summing divergent series. Theoreticians were stimulated by the possibility of finding determinate solutions that would square predictions with observational data.[3]

While Laplace was obtaining a standard education in Normandy in the 1760s, two problems that Newton's *Principia* and subsequent treatises had not satisfactorily resolved came under special scrutiny. One was an accurate accounting of the various motions of the earth's axis (precession and nutation), which necessarily affected all the calculations of movements in the heavens, since they are observed from the earth itself as a moving platform. The other was the establishment of a correct theory of the moon's motion, which depends upon ascertaining the shape of the earth and calculating the perturbation of the lunar orbit due to the action of the sun and possibly other planets.[4] Tackling these issues was a small, intense, and competitive group of scientists from various urban centers in Europe who displayed considerable mathematical ingenuity and took pride in meeting various challenges within the Newtonian framework. As they conquered each difficulty, their conviction of the validity of Newton's laws and the gravitational hypothesis was strengthened, redoubling their expectation of future promise. Laplace grew up at a time when astronomers had vivid examples of the progress of their own discipline and confidence in the force of the human mind to settle the remaining riddles of celestial mechanics.

As each advance was registered in the annals of various learned societies, it was also extolled by popularizers as evidence of the power modern science gained from its unique method: the gradual but relentless elucidation of nature pursued by developing and refining mathematical laws derived from the observation of phenomena. The fruitfulness of the approach was reiterated in schools and universities, at countless public occasions, in prefaces to scientific treatises, and even in technical articles. Young minds of Laplace's generation grew up in an atmosphere that expected results from the transference of proper scientific methods to any endeavor that required the use of the human intellect. A rational or "scientific" approach could theoretically be adapted to any subject by anyone who learned from the example of celestial mechanics.

Soon after leaving the University of Caen for Paris, where he was quickly accepted into academic circles in the early 1770s, Laplace turned to problems in celestial mechanics that others had not solved successfully.[5] He sought guidance from the brilliant Euler in St. Petersburg and from his mentor in Paris, Jean Le Rond d'Alembert (1717–1783); and he studied in detail the writings of his colleagues in the Academy of Sciences who followed in their footsteps, especially Joseph Louis Lagrange (1736–1813). Lagrange towered above his generation in the elegance and power of his mathematical solutions to issues in astronomy and physics and, more than anyone else, inspired Laplace to apply his imagination to the knottiest problems of celestial mechanics. They worked on similar puzzles, aware of the competition between them. Often they independently reached partial solutions within months of each other, using different mathematical techniques. Laplace and Lagrange developed a reciprocal sense of respect and admiration, probably tinged with jealousy.

No problem was more refractory for them than demonstrating the stability of the remote parts of the solar system, Jupiter and Saturn. Observational data had indicated that Jupiter was slowly accelerating its course around the sun without any end in sight, while Saturn was decelerating. According to the best calculations then available, the laws of mechanics and the action of universal gravitation were by themselves unable to bring these unruly planets into a self-correcting pattern. Laplace had tried to introduce *ad hoc* hypotheses to bring them into line, but to no avail. No astronomer seriously considered, as Newton had once suggested in the *Opticks*, calling upon the power of the Deity to help bring regularity back whenever it seemed necessary. Astronomers of the eighteenth century assumed that the heavens operated like an accurate clock, requiring no divine intervention once set in motion. If there was a problem, it lay in their techniques of calculation, not in the design of the universe.

Laplace's greatest astronomical feat, offered to the Academy of Sciences in May and July 1786, was his mathematical demonstration that the acceleration of Jupiter was balanced by the deceleration of Saturn and that the two would be reversed in about nine hundred years. The recognition that Jupiter and Saturn, when considered as a system, followed a long, "secular" period of oscillation was a major triumph of contemporary astronomy. Now the last stumbling block to an understanding of the mechanism of the solar system had been removed, and Laplace could begin in earnest to produce his *Traité de mécanique céleste* with knowledge that the principles of Newton were sufficient for an understanding of the functioning of the solar system.

The announcement of the stability of the solar system, which Laplace reiterated before his academic colleagues in April 1788 in a discussion of lunar theory, was greeted with admiration but not surprise. The accomplishment was technically awesome, but its implication far from revolutionary. One might have expected this demonstration to destroy the basis for introducing a divinity into the system of the world. In fact, astronomers and cosmologists had abandoned the concept of an interventionist God long before the evidence and calculations warranted it. To show mathematically the stability of the solar system was merely to confirm the expectations of generations of Newtonian astronomers. Hence it provoked few comments and no controversy.

The issue had been aired, if not settled, in an important debate between Gottfried Wilhelm Leibniz (1646–1716) and Samuel Clarke (1675–1729), which dated from 1715 and had become well known after its publication in 1717.[6] Leibniz had accused Newtonian philosophy of furthering the cause of irreligion, particularly because it diminished God's craftsmanship and foresight by making him adjust the system of the world in the same way that a clockmaker at times must clean and repair his timepiece. Just as the small amount of mending was a measure of the degree of his competence as a workman, so God's intervention attested to his inability to create a perfect world. That, Leibniz asserted, was a dangerous Newtonian misconception of the Deity. Clarke produced a rejoinder that was no less offensive to his accuser. Should the system of the world function like a perpetual-motion machine "without the Continual direction of God the Supreme Governour," then it would inevitably "exclude God out of the World."[7] The mutual accusations of irreligion were in fact not warranted, since both Leibniz and Newton held strong religious convictions and both expected a correct understanding of nature to further the cause of Christianity. But the arguments that each used against the other developed new force when considered in a different intellectual atmosphere several generations later. To understand this we must also take into account the changes brought about by the Enlightenment and the French Revolution. They were of at least equal significance to the transformation in astronomy described above.

CULTURAL CHANGES TO 1750

Considered as a whole, the Enlightenment was a movement that sapped the vitality of traditional Christianity—Catholic and Protestant—as Western thinkers turned increasingly toward secular issues.[8]

Whether one takes the view that it derived its dynamics from classical sources, from the example of natural science, or from the needs of the new state-centered economy, and whether or not the process of altering the significance of religious belief was unconscious, covert, or openly combative, focus on Christianity—to say nothing about strict belief—had weakened measurably by the eve of the French Revolution. The attacks against credulity, fideism, the authority of the Bible, the wisdom of the clergy, and even against natural religion undeniably made their mark on the *mentalité* of the age. In France, where Laplace grew up, the movement was more conspicuous and widespread than elsewhere. In roughly the first half of the century a pronounced attack against superstition and a renewed appreciation of pagan philosophies and values, coupled with a merciless historical criticism of biblical texts, pervaded the intellectual atmosphere. The growth of religious toleration, advocated by John Locke and François Marie Arouet de Voltaire, and the impact of reports from ethical, non-Christian civilizations forced many to doubt the absolute validity of their sectarian convictions, even when stripped of delusions and idolatry. Increasingly, various degrees of latitudinarianism, unitarianism, and deism replaced the better-defined doctrines of Christianity.

A variety of radical positions against established religion was discussed, often in the intimacy of private groups of freethinkers or freemasons, who circulated their views in clandestine manuscripts that occasionally surfaced to scandalize authorities. Most of these discussions involved a substantial scientific component often drawn from recent discoveries used to buttress various arguments. One group of the late 1730s included the artisan Jean Pigeon (1654–1739), his talented daughter, Marie Anne Victoire, and the mathematics lecturer who married her, André Pierre Le Guay de Prémontval (1716–1764). The ideas they exchanged were not in any way original, but typified the current issues that nourished the public philosophical debates of a later period. It was in this circle, for example, that Denis Diderot first came into contact with unorthodox notions about the relationship between knowledge of nature and the Deity.[9]

Pigeon, a self-educated military man with mechanical aptitudes, invented an exceptional orrery, a "spherical globe representing the Copernican system," powered by a pendulum clock, which he presented to Louis XIV at court in 1706. Though the artisan was himself nominally pious, the character of his invention coupled with his native curiosity led him to wonder out loud about the role of God in the universe. He made an analogy between René Descartes's concept of a man-machine and the mechanism of the automaton he had constructed. To be activated, both required the introduction of a motive force: in man, the soul provided by the Creator; in the orrery, a clock invented by a humble artisan. The implication was that the possibility of creating an imitation of the system of the world that ran mechanically diminished the religious mysteries of the cosmos. Perhaps God was to be conceived, in the image of man, merely as a master craftsman! Because of his philosophical bent, Pigeon went on to speculate freely about the relationship between matter and activity, reviewing and criticizing disingenuously the views of Descartes, Nicolas Malebranche, and Leibniz as understood through the simplifying lens of Bernard Le Bovier de Fontenelle's accounts. Pigeon's association with the Cardinal Melchior de Polignac, author of the influential *Anti-Lucretius; sive, De Deo et Natura* (1747), and with the Freemason Comte de Clermont, who presided over an association of scientists and artisans, placed him in a strategic position between the world of notables and the modest community of instrument makers.

Following this tradition, his son-in-law also mediated between the abstruse metaphysical concepts of philosophers and the more mundane concerns of the public. Le Guay de Prémontval, who offered free scientific lectures on Sundays and holidays to Parisian audiences of several hundreds—including, notably, women and artisans—inherited Pigeon's apparatus and philosophical concerns, captivating audiences with physical demonstrations and simplified explanations about the system of the world. No doubt it was the impious allusions with which he laced his lectures that won him the enmity of officials in Paris and forced him into exile. He converted to Protestantism in Basel and moved to Holland, ending his days as a philosopher at the Academy of Sciences and Belles-Lettres in Berlin, where he maintained a keen interest in both the new science and various unorthodox positions. During this later period his main concern was with the consequences of Leibniz's idea of preestablished harmony. But even when he offered metaphysical discourses as an academician, he was still preoccupied, as he had been as a young lecturer, with the limits that various philosophical systems placed on God's power.

Academic discourse of this sort inevitably drifted into the public arena, often by way of published lectures on natural philosophy used as manuals for schools and universities. It became the custom for all the popularizers of Newton, in England as well as on the Continent, to incorporate comments about the implications of the new philosophy for religion in their lectures and writings.

Some of the discussions were variations on positions held earlier. Colin Maclaurin (1698–1746) offered a remarkably clear and succinct defense of Newtonian principles in lectures that he prepared during the last days of his life. He railed against Descartes and his followers, Baruch Spinoza and Leibniz, whom he collectively characterized as holding "rash and crude notions concerning [God's] nature and essence, his liberty and other attributes."[10] They were at fault for assuming that men could "measure the divine omnipotence itself, and the possibility of things, by their own clear ideas concerning them; affirming that God himself cannot make contradictions to be true at the same time. . . ." In contrast, he noted, Newton insisted that He is not merely the creator and contriver of the universe, but at the same time its governor, whose "influence penetrates the inmost recesses of things" and whose repeated "acting and interposing" shows Him to be a free agent, unbounded by any human concept of necessity. According to Maclaurin, the manner by which God continues to operate in nature is not entirely known, but it is clear that He uses "subordinate instruments and agents" such as "gravity, attraction, repulsion, etc. constantly combined and compounded with the principles of mechanism: and we see no reasons why it should not likewise take place in the more subtle and abstruse phaenomena and motions of the system."

To strengthen his case, Maclaurin also added contemporary justifications for the existence of God drawn from the admirable structure of the world. Following the lead of François de Salignac de La Mothe Fénelon, John Ray, and William Derham, an influential group of Dutch popularizers headed by Bernard Nieuwentyt, Willem Jacob van 'sGravesande, and Pieter van Musschenbroek had modernized the argument from design.[11] The old metaphysical position was now infused with a myriad of examples drawn from the observational sciences of nature, punctuated with the sense of awe derived from new discoveries revealed by the microscope. The marvelous contrivances of nature reinforced orthodox beliefs in the wisdom of the Creator, further replacing the traditional view, which had drawn more heavily on metaphysics, by one based on empiricism. Examples from the Newtonian mechanical universe fit perfectly and were used as additional fodder for the argument. Belief in God was thus increasingly grounded in evidence supplied by scientific advances, an approach particularly pleasing to Newtonians still fighting to discredit Descartes by emphasizing the superiority of induction to metaphysics.

The Dutch physicist 'sGravesande (1688–1742) pushed this line of reasoning further, introducing an example of induction expressed mathematically, which buttressed his admiration of the Supreme Being's governance of the universe. He refurbished the arguments that John Arbuthnot presented in 1710 to the Royal Society concerning the improbability that, given the differential birthrate by sex, equal numbers of boys and girls could survive without the intervention of an omniscient God.[12] Crude as it was, this attempt to infer causes from *a posteriori* evidence provided later theorists of probability with still another approach from which to consider the nature of the Deity. The argument was simple enough to grasp: the probability that such a state would exist from chance alone was miniscule; hence it was necessary to posit a purposeful cause, the Supreme Being.

The existence of God was thus once again assured. But 'sGravesande was careful not to claim much more for science. He assured his students that the discovery of various regularities in nature did not offer a means for fathoming the character of God's being.[13] Nothing about the essence of God could be determined inductively, even though it was axiomatic that God had created these very laws of nature. They were a product of his free will. Hence the task of scientists was merely to discover what laws He had chosen, not to divine why He had established them.

CULTURAL CHANGES AFTER 1750

Enlightenment historians have chronicled a notable shift of intellectual concerns near the mid-mark of the century, which coincided with Laplace's birth. The era of the criticism and reassertion of earlier notions gave way to more constructive attempts to establish a new philosophy. Within a short time-span Etienne Bonnot de Condillac and David Hume proposed their original epistemological views, the Comte de Buffon began to publish his *Histoire naturelle*, d'Alembert and Diderot launched the *Encyclopédie*, and Jean-Jacques Rousseau formulated his counterattack against the *philosophes*. The ways in which contemporaries considered the association between belief and the mechanical universe also began to be affected, to a large extent loosening the bond that insured that the mark of the Divine would remain on the universe. As the triumph of Newtonian views elevated the value of induction, debates with Cartesians faded, and science took on a new aspect. Though he was reasonably well informed about earlier arguments, Laplace was raised in a new atmosphere that in France was more optimistic, positive, and secular.

Several features are worthy of our notice. The vigorous debates over metaphysical principles governing the measurement of forces conserved in the universe—the *vis viva* controversy—had been cleverly defused by d'Alembert, who asserted that it was merely a battle of words, which mattered little to a useful understanding of the way the physical world functioned.[14] A century before August Comte he adopted a positivist and operational stance in his scientific works, one that mirrored his disparagement of systematic philosophy in his literary essays. D'Alembert demonstrated both as a scientist and as a *philosophe* that knowledge could progress well without a prior settlement of metaphysical issues, and he recommended deemphasizing ontological issues in favor of epistemological questions. He was less concerned with finding underlying principles in science or religion than with determining how closely one could come to knowing them on rational grounds.

In a separate though parallel context David Hume (1711–1776) argued that man could not expect to reach certainty about the true causes of events but should content himself with the probability of relations between them.[15] Echoing d'Alembert's position, he suggested that humans could profitably operate in a state of suspended skepticism, just as scientists could learn to function without the certainty provided by a knowledge of essences.

Pierre Louis Moreau de Maupertuis (1698–1759), a Breton scientist who settled in Berlin, was among the first to display this new spirit. In his 1756 *Essai de cosmologie* he found fault with current attempts to establish God's existence from scientific evidence. He was worried about contemporary abuse of the design argument and indicated how dangerous it was to draw direct inferences from the perfection of creatures in natural history. After all, he insisted with obvious sarcasm, these life forms could as easily be the product of chance as of design, and for the sake of argument he even sketched a mechanism of natural selection to explain how they might falsely appear to be a product of a purposeful cause.[16] He also warned against the use Newton made of his inability to assign a physical cause for special features of the solar system—such as the fact that all planets move around the sun in a narrow band close to the ecliptic. There was danger in relying on such grounds; for example, someone might find a physical explanation or might claim that the feature in question was the product of chance. He expressed his unhappiness in this way:

> All the philosophers of our time belong to two sects. One group wishes to subjugate nature to a purely material order and to exclude all intelligent principles from it; or at least to banish final causes from the explanation of phenomena. The others, on the contrary, make constant use of these causes to discover through all of nature the views of the Creator, penetrating his intent in the smallest of phenomena. According to the first group, the universe could do without God; or at the very least the marvels of nature do not prove Him to be a necessary agent. According to the latter, the tiniest parts of the universe constitute repeated demonstrations [of his being]: his power, wisdom and goodness are painted on the wings of butterflies and in every spider's web.[17]

But Maupertuis had also published on a related issue, which drew the focus of discussion away from the repetitive and unconvincing arguments of the orthodox Newtonians and Leibnizians. In the article on the laws of nature derived from metaphysical principles, published in 1748, he raised suspicions about his possible atheistic tendencies and provoked a minor debate among German philosophers, particularly Hermann Samuel Reimarus and Jean Henri Samuel Formey.[18] One outcome was the Berlin Academy's decision in 1756 to solicit essays on the topic "Whether the truth of the principles of statics and mechanics are necessary or contingent." The strategic importance of this prize essay question was that while ultimately useful in elucidating God's role in the universe, the question was devoid of overt theological concerns. It could be taken as a simple issue in the metaphysics of science, distinct from its implications for theology.

Unlike others who used the occasion to draw somewhat traditional conclusions for the existence of God, d'Alembert seized on it to further his program of examining the epistemological bases of natural science. In the preface to the second edition of the *Traité de dynamique* (1758), d'Alembert shifted the grounds of the argument by diminishing its importance for settling religious issues.[19] He wrote: "It is not a matter of deciding whether the Author of nature could have provided it with laws other than the ones we observe; as soon as one admits an intelligent being capable of acting on matter, it is evident that this being can at any moment move or stop it at will." In other words, if God exists, He is able but not obliged to intervene in the natural order; hence it is futile to try to induce his definitive existence or his absence by examining nature directly. Neither regularity in nature nor irregularity provides conclusive evidence. What d'Alembert implied was that scientists could add little to the problem conceived in this traditional manner. He transposed the Berlin Academy's question into a much more useful one: "The question raised thus comes down to knowing whether the laws of equilibrium and motion that we observe in nature are different from those which matter, left to itself, would have followed." By comparing laws of nature derived from metaphysical principles, as suggested by Maupertuis, with those induced from empirical evidence, as proposed by Newton, one could promote the proper business of science while accommodating the results to two conceptions of God's nature: as a rational Creator bound by his creation, exercising his omniscience; and as a willful or volitional God exercising his omnipotence. D'Alembert cut the ground out from under earlier reliance on natural philosophy to learn about God, while seemingly remaining a believer. Tongue in cheek, he asserted that comparing laws derived from essences with those induced from observation would yield information useful for the religiously inclined:

If they are different from one another, he [the natural philosopher] will conclude that the laws of statics and mechanics derived from experience are contingent truths, since they follow the particular and express will of the supreme being. If, on the contrary, the laws derived from experience correspond to those determined by reason alone, he will conclude that the observed laws are necessary truths—[of course,] not in the sense that the Creator is prevented from establishing altogether different laws from those resulting from the existence of matter itself.

When he made these assertions in 1758, d'Alembert was coeditor with Diderot of the *Encyclopédie* and commonly associated with an anticlerical position that bordered on atheism. He was accused, along with other *philosophes*, of undermining religious authority and spreading the pagan views of nature of Epicurus, Thomas Hobbes, Spinoza, and contemporary materialists. Whatever he really believed—and we do not know with certainty—his statements on contingency and necessity were taken as another clever and well-placed assault on religious orthodoxy.

LAPLACE'S CONTRIBUTIONS, I: DETERMINISM

Among the many voices raised against this impious philosophy was that of a now-forgotten professor of philosophy at the University of Caen, the abbé Jean Adam (1726–1795). In 1766, he published a pamphlet refuting d'Alembert, entitled *Réflexions d'un logicien adressé à son professeur sur un ouvrage anonyme intitulé Mélanges de littérature, d'histoire et de philosophie.*[20] The work was so little valued in its time that it has been properly forgotten, and no copies have survived. For us, though, it provides the historical link to the young Laplace, who was a student in Adam's classes, preparing for a degree in theology. Laplace later confided to a colleague that Adam's views were so inadequate that they deserved to be forgotten.[21] But it is likely that d'Alembert's framing of the philosophic issues of the day, understood through Adam's witless refutation of them, profoundly shaped his conceptions. Laplace was seventeen or eighteen years old when he studied with Adam, and it was shortly thereafter that he turned for training in the sciences to a rival professor at Caen, one Christophe Gadbled (1731–1782). Gadbled was personally acquainted with d'Alembert and, like the notorious Parisian academician, was reprimanded for allowing dangerous views about the nature of God to creep into his lectures on mathematics and physics.[22] Before Laplace left Caen for Paris, he had already been drawn into an important intellectual dispute. And when he arrived in the capital, he was immediately taken under d'Alembert's wing.

Echoes of d'Alembert's analysis of the question posed by the Berlin Academy were evident in an epistle published in 1768 by a contemporary of Laplace who had also become a devotee of d'Alembert's scientific approach. In his *Letter on the System of the World and on Integral Calculus* the Marquis de Condorcet (1743–1794) rephrased his mentor's statement on natural law:[23]

> Bodies in motion seem to be subject to two essentially different types of laws. One is the necessary consequence of the concept we have of matter, the other seems to be the product of the free will of an intelligent Being who has willed the world to be as it is rather than any other way. The complete assemblage and outcome of necessary laws constitutes mechanics. We call the assemblage and outcome of the other laws, which we could ascertain only if we knew [laws] of all phenomena, the "System of the World."

But Condorcet went one step beyond, insisting that the standard activity of professional astronomers—matching evidence to theory to make them fit one another—ultimately turned on an epistemological rather than an ontological issue. He asserted:

> Perhaps these laws differ among themselves only because, given the present relationship between things and us, we require more or less shrewdness to know them; so that . . . one could conceive [of the universe] at any instant to be the consequence of the initial arrangement of matter in a particular order and left to its own devices. In such a case, an Intelligence knowing the state of all phenomena at a given instant, the laws to which matter is subjected, and their consequences at the end of any given time would have a perfect knowledge of the "System of the World." This understanding is beyond our capabilities, but it is the goal toward which all the efforts of philosophical mathematicians must be directed, and which they will constantly approach without ever expecting to attain.

It was left to Laplace, a few years later, to pursue this formulation and assert in print his famous statement on determinism. The conceptions he used and the very words employed to express them are worth close attention:

> The present state of the system of nature is evidently a result of what it was in the preceding instant, and if we conceive of an Intelligence who, for a given moment, embraces all the relations of being in this Universe, It will also be able to determine for any instant of the past or future their respective positions, motions, and generally their affections.
>
> Physical astronomy, that subject of all our understanding most worthy of the human mind, offers us an idea, albeit imperfect, of what such an

Intelligence would be. The simplicity of the laws by which celestial bodies move, the relationship of their masses and their distances allow us to follow their motions through analysis, up to a certain point; and in order to determine the state of the system of these large bodies in past or future centuries, it is enough for the mathematician that observation provide him with their position and speeds at any given instant. Man owes this advantage to the power of the instrument he uses and to the small number of relations he employs in his calculations; but ignorance of the diverse causes that produce the events and their complexity, taken together with the imperfection of analysis, prevents him from making assertions with the same certitude on most phenomena. For him, therefore, there are many things that are uncertain, and some that are more or less probable. In view of the impossibility of really knowing them, he has tried to compensate by determining their different degrees of likelihood; so that we owe to the feebleness of the human mind one of the most delicate and ingenious of mathematical theories, the science of probabilities.[24]

There is little doubt that the lineage of ideas expressed here, phrased in the words of Condorcet, stemmed from the prize essay question raised by the Berlin Academy. What is equally important is that in a span of fifteen years Laplace carried out the implications of that question far beyond the religious problems that had initially been the focus of attention. In 1773 there was no longer any discussion of the nature of God or any debate about the predominance of his omniscience over his omnipotence, as with Leibniz and Newton. God was not cited! In Laplace's world He does not seem to exist except as a human construct. The Intelligence to which he referred was merely a superhuman calculator. If God exists, it is as a perfect philosophical mathematician. The transposition from man created in the image of God to a supreme intelligence conceived in the image of man is startlingly powerful. It reveals the immense intellectual distance traveled in less than a century.

Laplace chose not to pursue this philosophical line of argument for another four decades, when he again proclaimed the deterministic credo in his *Essai philosophique sur les probabilités* (1814). In the meantime he focused his attention on the very mathematical instrument he had extolled as offering a rigorous technique for inferring causes from the knowledge of events.[25] The idea of using a method of calculation to such ends had been sketched, but without rigor, by Arbuthnot, who had been criticized and corrected successively by Jakob Bernoulli, Abraham De Moivre, and 'sGravesande, with all of whose writings Laplace was familiar. He had also read Daniel Bernoulli's treatise answering a prize essay question of the Paris Academy for the years 1732 and 1734, to determine the "physical cause" of the small mutual inclinations of the planetary orbits, which employed a somewhat more elaborate calculus of probabilities. John Michell made use of similar techniques in 1767, trying to understand why stars are clustered in such an unlikely configuration in the heavens. But it was Thomas Bayes's posthumously published method in 1764 that provided a new mathematical tool for calculating *a posteriori* probabilities. In France it seems to have been forgotten until Condorcet called Laplace's attention to it less than a decade later.

Laplace, perhaps independently of Bayes, developed this new mathematical tool in a landmark paper published by the Paris Academy of Sciences in 1774 on the probability of causes by events. He established there a method of statistical inference that was to serve him well for the next few decades in the solution of key problems in celestial mechanics, including those leading to the demonstration of the stability of the solar system. Thus on the eve of the French Revolution, Laplace, who had already formulated a philosophical position that turned the Supreme Being into an omniscient philosophical mathematician, had also fashioned a mathematical tool to measure how close to perfection the lay mathematician had come in his knowledge of the system of the world. In less than a century, both celestial mechanics and probability theory had been turned on their heads; they no longer served as an essential support for believing in the Deity, but were now put to work to confirm the brilliance of human effort to penetrate nature's secrets.

LAPLACE'S CONTRIBUTIONS, II: THE NEBULAR HYPOTHESIS

In the gradual process that amounted to the amicable divorce of God from the physical universe, Laplace took one other major step, thoroughly in line with his scientific research. He advanced a hypothesis in 1796 to explain the physical origins of the solar system.[26] By doing so, he turned one of Maupertuis's warnings into reality. Newton had used the small likelihood that random chance was responsible for the peculiar arrangement of the planets and their satellites as an argument for belief in Divine Providence. Now Laplace was proposing a reasonable mechanism for these features of the solar system, shortcircuiting the need for God as the direct cause of its peculiar configuration. It was especially for this invention that Laplace was repeatedly taken to task later for being a materialist and an atheist.

At first glance this invention seems to derive logically from his earliest concerns of 1773, following both the implications of the 1756

Berlin Academy prize essay question and the century-long progress of probability theory. In fact, the genesis of the so-called "nebular hypothesis" is both more complex and more revealing. It shows how much Laplace was a product of his environment and how easily his diverse interests fell naturally into place. Most likely Laplace encountered the problem of cosmogony through his astronomy teacher, Gadbled. We know that Gadbled's other noted student, the chevalier Jean Jacques de Marguerie, was led to consider the origins of the solar system in a generally forgotten memoir published at Brest in 1773.[27] Buffon's and Laplace's close friend Bailly had also postulated another physical mechanism for the beginnings of the system of the world, notably the possibility of a comet colliding with the sun.[28]

But Laplace was also heir to the philosophical movement that distinguished secondary causes (*"causes actuelles"* in Buffon's language) from first causes.[29] It was an age-old issue broached by Plato and Aristotle, discussed by humanists who favored atomic theory, and a favorite subject of Descartes, Ralph Cudworth, Spinoza, and John Toland. Newton himself had taken note of the identity between the Supreme Being and the ultimate cause of the universe. More recently, Malebranche, Hume, and d'Alembert had written about the difficulty of determining causes at all and underscored the futility of searching for first causes. Precisely at the time when Laplace arrived in Paris to take up his first teaching post at the Ecole royale militaire in 1769, one of the authors whose books were used as texts there, the abbé Charles Batteux, published his *Histoire des causes premières*, reviewing both the ancient and modern history of the issue.

What distinguished Laplace's treatment was his single-minded determination to use the tools of probability to highlight the significance of his solution to the problem. His hypothesis for the beginnings of the solar system was preceded by a strict calculation of the miniscule likelihood that random chance was responsible for the unidirectional movement and rotation of all planets and their satellites, the small eccentricity of planetary orbits, and the very large eccentricity of cometary orbits. He followed this conclusion with the assertion that the assignment of a single physical cause producing all these phenomena was the task of an astronomer, and advanced with some "misgivings" his own famous but speculative nebular hypothesis.[30] For our purposes it matters little that the theory itself grew in detail as Laplace learned of William Herschel's theory of the evolution of nebulae and revised it accordingly in successive editions of the *Exposition du système du monde*. Much more significant was his deliberate substitution of a physical explanation for what had long been a first cause, God the Creator.

No less than contemporary commentators, Laplace was quick to avow the import of proposing on scientific grounds a first cause for the origins of the solar system. The idea itself and its implications for theology had already stirred up controversy decades earlier when Buffon published his *Epoques de la nature*.[31] Now, in the desacralized atmosphere of the French Revolution, many proclaimed the idea that rational thinking freed from religious censure and ancient superstition would topple God from his pedestal. Diderot's disciple Jacques André Naigeon, for example, argued in the *Encyclopédie méthodique* article "Order of the Universe" that soon God would be exposed as an "excess wheel in the mechanism of the world," relegated, as it were, to the unemployment rolls for his redundancy.[32] Laplace himself, in the introduction to his mathematical lectures at the Ecole normale in 1795, ridiculed attempts by Leibniz to prove the existence of God.[33] In 1800 Laplace was listed as one of the many notables in the *Dictionnaire des athées*.[34] He took his argument a step further in 1802 when he is reported to have maintained before Bonaparte "that a chain of natural causes would account for the construction and preservation of the wonderful system [of the world]."[35] Finally, in the 1813 edition of the *Exposition du système du monde*, he openly distanced himself from traditional Christian opinion by singling out Newton for reprimand. After outlining the nebular hypothesis, Laplace pointedly remarked that "I cannot forgo noting here how Newton strayed on this point from the method that he otherwise used so effectively."[36]

CONCLUSIONS

By the turn of the century, Laplace was taken by many as the archetype of the atheistic scientist. As we have seen, he deserved his reputation as an authority in science who not only excluded religion from his professional work but cast doubt on drawing conclusions about the Deity from natural knowledge. Some contemporaries went on to associate him with the group of French freethinkers in the Revolution who set out to undermine personal belief in the Deity and were thereby responsible for the excesses of the Terror. In the minds of many, especially those in Great Britain brought up on the tradition of natural theology, he was a dangerous "Jacobin" who gave science an ugly name.[37] Rumors also circulated about his personal impiety.[38] These judgments were excessive, obtuse, and biased; but whether or not they were well founded, it must be recognized that his philosophical position was distinct from that of many contemporaries.

Laplace's views about God did not derive either from the d'Holbach materialist group in France or from Hume across the Channel. Though he occasionally shared the materialist or skeptical sentiments of Enlightenment philosophers, Laplace rested his conclusions on different grounds.[39] They were nourished by direct participation in the progress of Newtonian science and the application of Bayesian induction (or statistical inference), which opened up new epistemological horizons. If he is to be associated with any philosophical type, Laplace is in the mold of d'Alembert's natural philosopher or Condorcet's *géomètre philosophe*. He based his understanding on palpable evidence and calculation rather than metaphysical systems of thought of either a Christian or a pagan variety. It was by disentangling his notions from traditional philosophy, all the while refusing to link them to personal, fideist convictions about Christianity, that he was able to forge a new position full of meaning for both philosophy and theology.

Laplace's views about the mechanism of the heavens, the origins of the solar system, and probability were widely known in the nineteenth century, and their implications for the relationship of religion to science were debated with ardor by theologians and philosophers as well as by working scientists.[40] Though his assertions did not close a chapter in the history of thought, they markedly changed the character of the discussion by raising it to a new level.

NOTES

I owe the original inspiration for this article to my teacher, the late Alexandre Koyré. Its composition has benefited much from discussions with colleagues, especially Thomas L. Hankins, Dorinda Outram, and Charles Paul.

1. Important exceptions are Herbert H. Odom, "The Estrangement of Celestial Mechanics and Religion," *Journal of the History of Ideas* 27 (1966): 533–548; and François Russo, "Théologie naturelle et sécularisation de la science au XVIII⁰ siècle," *Recherches de science religieuse* 66 (1978): 27–62.

2. The origins of the anecdote may be traced in print to Augustus de Morgan, *The Athenaeum*, no. 1921 (20 Aug. 1864), p. 247. Its meaning is discussed in Roger Hahn, "Laplace and the Vanishing Role of God in the Physical Universe," in *The Analytic Spirit*, ed. Harry Woolf (Ithaca, N.Y.: Cornell Univ. Press, 1981), pp. 85–95.

3. Alfred Gautier, *Essai historique sur le problème des trois corps* (Paris: Veuve Courcier, 1817).

4. Eric G. Forbes, "Tobias Mayer's Contribution to the Development of Lunar Theory," *Journal for the History of Astronomy* 1 (1970): 144–154; Curtis

A. Wilson, "Perturbations and Solar Tables from Lacaille to Delambre," *Archive for History of Exact Sciences* 22 (1980): 54–304.

5. For details see Charles Gillispie et al., "Laplace, Pierre-Simon, Marquis de," *Dictionary of Scientific Biography*, 15 vols. (New York, 1970–1980), 15:273–403, esp. sec. 17.

6. F. E. L. Priestley, "The Clarke-Leibniz Controversy," in *Methodological Heritage of Newton*, ed. Robert E. Butts and John W. Davis (Toronto: Univ. of Toronto Press, 1970), pp. 34–56; and *Correspondance Leibniz-Clarke*, ed. André Robinet (Paris: Presses Universitaires de France, 1957).

7. *Correspondance Leibniz-Clarke*, p. 31.

8. Georges Gusdorf, *Les sciences humaines et la pensée occidentale*, 8 vols. (Paris: Payot, 1968–1978), vols. 4, 5, and 6; and Simone Goyard-Fabre, *La philosophie des Lumières en France* (Paris: Klincksieck, 1972).

9. Marie A. V. Le Guay de Prémontval, *Le mécaniste philosophe* (The Hague: Pierre van Cleef, 1750); Maurice Pélisson, "Les mémoires d'un professeur au XVIIIe siècle," *Revue pédagogique* 44 (1904): 232–252; and Franco Venturi, *Jeunesse de Diderot (1713–1753)* (Paris: Albert Skira, 1939).

10. Colin Maclaurin, *An Account of Sir Isaac Newton's Philosophical Discoveries* (London: A. Millar & J. Nourse, 1748), p. 380. Quotations below are taken respectively from pp. 379, 381–382, and 389–390.

11. J. Bots, *Tussen Descartes en Darwin: Geloof en natuurwetenschap in de achttiende eeuw in Nederland* (Assen: Van Gorcum, 1972), pp. 49–95.

12. Willem J. van s'Gravesande, *Oeuvres philosophiques et mathématiques*, 2 vols. (Amsterdam: Marc Michel Rey, 1774), 2:221–248.

13. Edward G. Ruestow, *Physics at 17th and 18th Century Leiden* (The Hague: Martinus Nijhoff, 1973), pp. 128–129; Giambattista Gori, *La fondazione dell'esperienza in 'sGravesande* (Florence: La Nuova Italia, 1972), pp. 160–283.

14. Jean Le Rond d'Alembert, *Traité de dynamique*, new. ed. (Paris: David, 1758), p. xxii; and Thomas L. Hankins, *Jean d'Alembert: Science and the Enlightenment* (Oxford: Clarendon Press, 1970), p. 207.

15. Keith A. Baker, *Condorcet: From Natural Philosophy to Social Mathematics* (Chicago: Univ. of Chicago Press, 1975), pp. 129–194.

16. Pierre Louis Moreau de Maupertuis, *Oeuvres*, new ed., 4 vols. (Lyon: Jean-Marie Bruyset, 1756), 1:3–25.

17. Ibid., 1:iv–v.

18. Giorgio Tonelli, "La nécessité des lois de la nature au XVIIIe siècle et chez Kant en 1762," *Revue d'histoire des sciences* 12 (1959): 237.

19. D'Alembert, *Traité*, pp. xxiv–xxv and xxvi–xxvii for the next quotations. These ideas are also discussed in Roger Hahn, *Laplace as a Newtonian Scientist* (Los Angeles: William Andrews Clark Memorial Library, 1967), pp. 13 ff.

20. Edouard Frère, *Manuel du bibliographe normand*, 2 vols. (Rouen: A. Le Brument, 1858–1860), 1:5.

21. [Christophe Gadbled], *Exposé de quelques-unes des vérités rigoureusement démontrées par les géometres, et rejettées par l'auteur du Compendium de physique, imprimé à Caen en 1775* (Amsterdam: Libraires Associés, 1779), pp. 6–7.

22. Caen, Archives départementales du Calvados, MS D1016, fol. 13v.

23. *Le Marquis de Condorcet à d'Alembert sur le système du monde et sur le calcul*

intégral (Paris: Didot, 1768), pp. 4–5; and Roger Hahn "Laplace's First Formulation of Scientific Determinism in 1773," in *Actes du XIe Congrès international d'histoire des sciences*, 6 vols. (Warsaw: Ossolineum, 1968), 2:167–171.

24. *Mémoires de mathématique et de physique presentés à l'Académie royale des sciences par divers savans, année 1773*, 11 vols. (Paris: Imprimerie Royale, 1776), 7:113.

25. Charles C. Gillispie, "Probability and Politics: Laplace, Condorcet, and Turgot," *Proceedings of the American Philosophical Society* 116 (1972): 4–5; Roger Hahn, "Determinism and Probability in Laplace's Philosophy," in *Actes du XIIIe Congrès international d'histoire des sciences*, 11 vols. (Moscow: Nauka, 1974), 1:170–175.

26. *Exposition du système du monde*, 2 vols. (Paris: Cercle Social, an IV [1796]), 2:301–304. The successive changes in the new editions of this work are discussed best in Remigius Stölzle, "Die Entwicklungsgeschichte der Nebularhypothèse von Laplace," in *Abhandlungen aus dem Gebiete der Philosophie und ihrer Geschichte: Eine Festgabe zum 70. Gerburtstage Georg Freiherrn von Hertling* (Freiburg im Breisgau: Herder, 1913), pp. 349–369; and Stanley L. Jaki, "The Five Forms of Laplace's Cosmogony," *American Journal of Physics* 44 (1976): 4–11.

27. "Sur le système du monde," in *Mémoires de l'Académie royale de marine* (Brest: R. Malassis, 1773), pp. 45–46.

28. Stanley L. Jaki, *Planets and Planetarians: A History of Theories of the Origin of Planetary Systems* (New York: John Wiley, 1978), pp. 96–106.

29. Buffon, *Les époques de la nature*, édition critique, ed. Jacques Roger (Paris: Editions du Muséum, 1962), pp. lxxxv–lxxxvii; Victor Monod, *Dieu dans l'univers* (Paris: Fischbacher, 1933), chaps. 3 and 4.

30. Jacques Merleau-Ponty, "Situation et rôle de l'hypothèse cosmogonique dans la pensée cosmologique de Laplace," *Revue d'histoire des sciences* 29 (1976): 46–49.

31. Jean Stengers, "Buffon et la Sorbonne," *Etudes sur le XVIIIe siècle* (Brussels), 1 (1974): 97–127.

32. *Philosophie ancienne et moderne*, vol. 3 (Paris: H. Agasse, an II [1794]), p. 377 n. 1. Because the translation from the original is subject to various readings, I note the original wording: "il viendra . . . un temps . . . où cet être [God] . . . sera regardé comme une roue de luxe dans la machine du monde, et par conséquent comme un hors d'oeuvre et un double emploi."

33. *L'abréviateur universel*, no. 151 (19 Feb. 1795), p. 603, col. 1.

34. Pierre [Sylvain] M[aréchal], *Dictionnaire des athées anciens et modernes* (Paris: Grabit, an VIII [1800]), pp. 231–232.

35. John L. E. Dreyer, ed., *The Scientific Papers of Sir William Herschel*, 2 vols. (London: The Royal Society, 1912), 1:lxii.

36. *Exposition du système du monde*, 4th ed. (Paris: Veuve Courcier, 1813), p. 443.

37. Jack B. Morrell, "Professors Robison and Playfair, and the *Theophobia Gallica*: Natural Philosophy, Religion and Politics in Edinburgh, 1789–1815," *Notes and Records of the Royal Society* 26 (1971): 50–51.

38. See, for example, "Journal d'un genevois à Paris sous le Consulat,"

Mémoires et documents publiés par la Societé d'histoire et d'archéologie de Genève, ser. 2, 5 (1893): 98–133; and Louis Aimé Martin, "Curieuses anecdotes sur Laplace," *L'intermédiaire des chercheurs et curieux* 29 (20 Jan. 1894): 87–88.

39. For his private views see Roger Hahn, "Laplace's Religious Views," *Archives internationales d'histoire des sciences* 8 (1955): 38–40.

40. See the discussions in Ronald L. Numbers, *Creation by Natural Law: Laplace's Nebular Hypothesis in American Thought* (Seattle: Univ. of Washington Press, 1977); Enrico Bellone, *I modelli e la concezione del mondo nella fisica moderna da Laplace a Bohr* (Milan: Feltrinelli, 1973), chap. 1; Dominique Dubarle, "De Laplace à Cournot: Philosophie des probabilités et philosophie du hasard," in *A. Cournot: Etudes pour le centenaire de sa mort (1877–1977)* (Paris: Economica, 1978), pp. 106–118; Maurizio Ferriani, "Dopo Laplace: Determinismo, probabilità, induzione," in *Eredità dell'Illuminismo*, ed. A. Santucci (Bologna: Il Mulino, 1979), pp. 261–304.

11

The Mechanistic Conception of Life

Jacques Roger

The problem of life is very old, and it is likely that when humans began thinking about nature, the most conspicuous and puzzling objects in their environment were living beings, especially animals. They had to fight them and to feed upon them, but they shared so many things in common, the most obvious being life and death, that they could not help thinking that even the feelings and thoughts of animals were similar to their own. For humans, death transformed an active, sentient, and perhaps thinking animal into an inert body, deprived of any reaction, motion, or feeling. If the inner principle of human activity was something called a soul, then it seemed reasonable that animals should also have souls.[1]

Among the many ideas and concepts that Christianity inherited from Greek philosophy, the concept of soul was one of the most important. Plato (427–348/347 B.C.) had declared the human soul to be immortal. But more important perhaps for our present topic, his disciple Aristotle (384–322 B.C.) had elaborated a full theory of the soul as a principle of life, present in all living beings. For Aristotle there were different kinds of souls. Vegetable soul controlled the most fundamental functions of life: nutrition, growth, and reproduction. Animal soul possessed the same powers but was also responsible for motion and feeling. The human soul had, in addition, the special privilege of reason. Although vegetable and animal souls were transmitted from parents to offspring through the process of generation, the human soul, said Aristotle, "came from outside," a formula Christian theologians easily transformed into the statement that it "was especially created by God."[2]

277

From the early Middle Ages, but more particularly after the twelfth century, the Aristotelian conception of life was widely accepted by Western Christians. According to their philosophy, the soul was the guardian of Nature's order, so to speak. Being responsible, on the one hand, for the embryonic development of every living being, the soul ensured the perfect similarity between parents and offspring, that is, the permanence and fixity of species. On the other hand, its power accounted for the perfect adaptation of every organ to the functioning of the whole. According to the nature and way of life of each animal, it gave them the necessary tools to survive: bills and wings to birds, claws and teeth to tigers, and a flexible spine to snakes. In the Christianized version of Aristotelianism, that perfect adaptation of the anatomy of animals to their way of life was but a part of the general harmony of a universe designed and created by God. The search for final causes—that is, for the use of every organ in an animal or plant—therefore became a legitimate and even necessary part of scientific inquiry. Without the knowledge of final causes, one could not hope really to understand a living organism.

There was, however, an ancient Greek tradition of atomism, which considered final causes to be mere illusions and refused to think of the universe as the purposeful creation of a wise God. That tradition, initiated in the fifth century B.C. by Leucippus and Democritus, had been popularized by the Greek philosopher Epicurus (341–270 B.C.) and the Roman poet Lucretius (ca. 95–ca. 55 B.C.), whose didactic poem *De rerum natura* ("On the Nature of Things") enjoyed a lasting fame, even if considered scandalously imbued with atheism. According to the generally accepted version of the atomistic philosophy, everything in the universe, including living beings, was made of very minute particles called *atoms*, the Greek word for *indivisible*. These atoms, swiftly moving through void, collided at random and formed physical aggregates. Living beings were no exception to the rule: they had been formed at random in every possible way, but only those capable of living and reproducing had survived and formed permanent species. Therefore, it was useless to search for design and purpose in the structure of living beings. Eyes had not been created in order to see, but had been formed by chance; and once an animal had eyes, it was impossible for it not to see. Chance and necessity— that is, Nature's law—rather than finality and harmony were thus the ultimate causes of nature's apparent order.[3]

Though neither Epicurus nor Lucretius denied the existence of the gods, those beings never interfered with natural phenomena or human affairs. For all practical purposes the atomists left no room for what is generally called religion, and they based ethics upon merely human considerations, thus making their philosophy unpalatable to Christian theologians. Atomism was known during the Middle Ages almost solely through Aristotle's refutation of it (though in the twelfth century there was some interest in Plato's geometrical atomism), and it was almost never taken seriously as a philosophy of nature. When atomism was revived at the beginning of the seventeenth century, it was through the recovery of ancient primary sources containing a favorable account of the atomic doctrine.

THE MECHANISTIC PHILOSOPHY OF LIFE
IN THE SEVENTEENTH CENTURY

The so-called Scientific Revolution of the sixteenth and seventeenth centuries involved much more than a change in scientific ideas; it also entailed the emergence of a new way of reasoning, modeled on geometry. It would be misleading to regard that movement as directed against Christian thought; on the contrary, it was deeply rooted in a new religious attitude, the main result of which was the Protestant Reformation of the sixteenth century. The most important philosophical problem at that time was probably the relationship between God and his creation, and the general trend was toward emphasizing God's absolute power over the created world and the radical powerlessness of every creature. In the religious sphere this led to the doctrine of salvation preached by Martin Luther and John Calvin, according to which God was the only active power in human justification. For the physical world this meant that Nature had no power of her own, that matter was passive, inert, and incapable of moving or forming anything by itself. God, being the only source of grace and salvation in the spiritual world, was the sole origin of motion and activity in nature (see chapter 6).[4] At this same time more and more scientists were accepting the idea, first borrowed from Platonic philosophy, that mathematics was the key to a real understanding of natural phenomena. As Galileo (1564–1642), one of the founders of the new science, said, "The book of nature is written in mathematical language."[5] In such an atmosphere the branch of physics known as mechanics necessarily became the queen of sciences. Most early-modern scientists and philosophers viewed the universe as being similar to a giant clock, put in motion by God and functioning according to the laws of mechanics. The problem confronting the scientist was to discover how the gears of the clock were arranged and worked with each other, and how the initial motion was transmitted from one to the other.

But there was no question about the clock being the work of a Supreme Clockmaker.

Thus, the fundamental claim of mechanism was that everything in nature could and should be explained in terms of matter and motion. As far as the life sciences were concerned, this assumption at first amounted to suppressing all those traditional entities that, under the name of souls, were formerly considered to be responsible for the order and activity of life and were supposed to direct the embryonic development and the general functioning of every living thing. According to the new mechanical philosophy, the only possible soul was the rational one, which could exist in humans only.[6]

Seventeenth-century philosophers and scientists generally accepted the idea that matter was composed of minute parts endowed with different shapes.[7] For some philosophers those minute parts were the atoms of Epicurean philosophy; but for the majority of scientists they were simply corpuscles, theoretically but not actually divisible. Virtually everybody agreed that all phenomena should be ultimately explained by the various shapes of those corpuscles and the properties of their motions. No experimental evidence could be given for the existence of corpuscles, but they were the only possible way to form a clear, mechanical image of phenomena. Thus, the phenomena of life could be mechanically explained on two different levels: on the macroscopic level it was easy to interpret the newly discovered circulation of the blood, the movements of limbs, or the contractions of the stomach as mechanical phenomena; on the microscopic level, so to speak, it was easy to imagine corpuscles endowed with various shapes and motions in order to explain less visible processes such as the functioning of glands and nerves or embryonic development. Glands, for example, were seen as sieves whose holes had precisely the right shape and size to allow the proper corpuscles to pass. Nerves were hollow tubes through which round corpuscles called "animal spirits" rushed from sensory organs to the brain or from the brain to muscles.[8]

But two basic problems remained to be solved: the activity and order of life. The first question was intimately related to the origin of motion. According to the Epicurean philosophy, atoms were naturally endowed with activity; consequently, there was no need for any other source of motion. Such a philosophy, which could easily lead to atheism, was not absent from seventeenth-century thought, but it seems to have attracted few followers. The majority of scientists and philosophers regarded matter as entirely passive; motion was not one of its essential properties. In their opinion, God, after creating matter, gave it a certain quantity of motion, which was then kept and transmitted from corpuscle to corpuscle. From a scientific point of view both solutions are equally valid, exactly as, from the same point of view, there is no difference between an atom and a corpuscle. The dissimilarity between the two systems is important, but only metaphysical.

The order of life is a much more complicated and difficult problem. Living beings obviously display a very complex structure, without which life could not subsist. In all individuals of a species, this structure is practically identical, having been built the same way, through a process of embryonic development. In addition, there is the classical problem of teleology; the elements of the structure are obviously constructed in such a way that they are able to perform particular functions, without which the life of the whole organism would be difficult or even impossible: the eye is made in order to see, teeth in order to cut and grind aliment, and so forth. Such harmony between structure and function was easily accounted for by the old Aristotelian souls, which were at the same time final and efficient causes of the development of the living being. But how was one to explain it in a mechanistic philosophy if one refused, as most scientists did at that time, to follow the Epicurean doctrine, which denied the existence of any finality in nature?

To such questions there were two different sets of answers in the seventeenth century, each corresponding to different ways of understanding the relationship between God and his creation. The first set of answers was given by the French philosopher René Descartes (1596–1650).[9] Concerning living beings as well as the universe in general, Descartes was an epigeneticist; that is, he was convinced that every natural structure, be it "the wonderful structure of the world" or the structure of a living being, had been brought about by natural processes, namely the movements of corpuscles endowed with different shapes. These movements had been able to build the most complicated living structures because they were regulated very precisely by the laws of motion instituted by God. Thus, according to Descartes, Nature's order is first of all the order of Nature's laws, which are precise enough to account for all the structures that we discover in nature. The marvelous properties of living beings are but the necessary result of the play of the laws of motion. God of course foresaw that result and, to that extent, there is a purpose. For Descartes, however, there are no final causes in nature: teleology resides in God's Wisdom; it does not act in natural processes. Furthermore, since humans are unable to understand God's wisdom in all its depth, it is better for them not to speculate about final causes.

Because of its determinism, its apparent reduction of God's direct creation to matter and motion and its rejection of final causes, Descartes's philosophy has often been interpreted as covert atheism. This is a mistake. On the contrary, God is the keystone of Descartes's thought. Without his warrant, human reason would not be able to reach any certainty; without his will, the world would simply not exist. According to Descartes, it is not enough to say that God created the world once and for all. Only God is a really autonomous being, because He exists by his own power. The created world is not autonomous, because it cannot subsist by itself. At every moment of time its very existence depends on God's will; that is, God's will has to create it anew at every moment. For Descartes, time is a succession of separate instants, and no created being is capable by itself of passing from one instant to the next. By the same token, the constancy of Nature's laws has no foundation other than the constancy of God's will. If, for the sake of human knowledge, the world may be considered to be physically autonomous, one must not forget that, metaphysically, it depends entirely on God's will.

Descartes's way of thinking was very similar to that of many theologians of the first half of the seventeenth century, who thought that humans, as created beings, were incapable of retaining God's grace; therefore, God had to give them his grace anew at every moment. Even in profane literary works, the theme of human fragility as opposed to God's constancy was widely developed, especially by religiously inclined poets, be they Catholics or Protestants. It was indeed one of the most popular themes in the Baroque age.

During much of his adult life Descartes lived in the Netherlands, where he engaged in some bitter controversies with Dutch Calvinist theologians; and after his death French universities were forbidden to teach his philosophy. It seems, however, that his ideas on life and mechanism had little to do with those difficulties, in part because, as far as his biological thought was concerned, Descartes had very few, if any, followers. Contemporary scientists interested in the life sciences, mostly medical doctors, considered his interpretation of life as a gross oversimplification. They were ready to view a living being as a machine, but they could not imagine how such a complicated machine could be built by the mere play of the laws of motion.

The very novelty of the concept of Nature's laws made it difficult for seventeenth-century philosophers and scientists to grasp it. Even for Descartes, Nature's laws had been dictated by God. Clearly they were intended to be obeyed by intelligent beings, but how could nonreasonable beings, such as animals, or inanimate things, such as stones, obey any law? More important perhaps, Nature's laws could not be conceived as precise and powerful enough to exclude chance from natural events, and chance was incompatible with both Christian faith and human reason. Epicurean philosophy had given chance an eminent role in the building of the world, but Epicurus was clearly an atheist. No sensible mind could believe that blind chance was responsible for the marvelous structure of the world in general and living beings in particular.

Such a reaction to Descartes's absolute mechanism is best exemplified by the famous British chemist Robert Boyle (1627–1691), who was very influential in shaping scientific and religious opinions in England at the end of the seventeenth century.[10] In 1667 Boyle wrote:

> I do not at all believe, that either these *Cartesian laws of Motion*, or the *Epicurean casual concourse* of Atoms could bring meer Matter into so orderly and well contriv'd a Fabrick as this World. . . . So that according to my apprehension it was *at the beginning* necessary, that an intelligent and wise Agent should contrive the Universal Matter into the World, (and especially some portions of it into Seminal organs and principles,) and settle the laws, according to which the motions and actions of its parts upon one another should be regulated: without which interposition of the world's Architect, however *moving Matter* may with some *probability* (for I see not in the Notion any certainty) be conceiv'd to be able after numberless occursions of its insensible parts to cast itself into such grand conventions and convolutions as the Cartesians call *Vortices* and as (I remember) Epicurus speaks of under the name of *proskriseis kai dineseis* [or accretions and vortices]; yet I think it utterly improbable that *brute and unguided*, though *moving*, Matter should ever convene into such admirable structures, as the bodies of perfect Animals. But the world being once fram'd and the course of Nature establish'd, the Naturalist (except in some few cases, where God or incorporeal Agents interpose,) has recourse to the first Cause but for its general and ordinary support and influence, whereby it preserves Matter and Motion from annihilation or desition; and in explicating particular Phenomena considers only the Size, Shape, Motion, (or want of it,) Texture, and the resulting qualities and attributes of the small particles of Matter.[11]

This text clearly expresses the kind of mechanism that prevailed at the end of the seventeenth century, in which both the world and living beings were viewed as machines. If we want to understand the working of these machines, we must take into account only the mechanical properties of elementary principles—their size, shape, motion, and the like. To that extent, life is nothing but mechanism. But mechanism cannot build the world, not even a single living being. The order of laws cannot be trusted because it does not exclude chance. Boyle for this reason feigns to see no difference between Descartes and Epicurus. For him the fundamental order of the world is not the order of laws but the order of structures, which must have been directly created by God. Isaac Newton's cosmology perfectly met the requisites of Boyle's brand of mechanism. According to Newton (1642–1727), God had directly created the solar system, putting each new planet at the right distance from the sun, and then set the whole system to work according to the laws of mechanics. Therefore, concluded Newton, it was "unphilosophical" to search for a scientific explanation of the building of the system: God was the only explanation.[12]

It is also clear that a great difference exists between Descartes's and Boyle's ideas of God. As the French mathematician, physicist, and religious writer Blaise Pascal (1623–1662) wrote in his *Pensées*, "The God of Christians is not a God who is merely the author of mathematical truths and the order of the elements"—an obvious reference to Descartes.[13] Like Pascal's, Boyle's God was first of all that of the Bible, the God who had directly spoken to men and had even gone so far as to become a man Himself. Such a God could not have so completely hidden his intentions in creating the world that humans could not discover any final causes in his creation, as Descartes maintained. Boyle himself did not hesitate to search for final causes in nature, especially in the anatomy of living beings. For example, he suggested that the difference of shape between the eyes

> of cats and those of horses could be explained in the following way: the reason may be, that horses and oxen being usually to find their food growing on the ground, they can more conveniently receive the images of the laterally neighbouring grass, etc., by having their pupils transversely placed; whereas cats, being to live chiefly upon rats and mice, which are animals, that usually climb up or run down walls and other steep places, the commodiousest situation of their pupil, for readily discovering and following these objects, was to be perpendicular.[14]

Boyle seemed ready to endorse this explanation, given by "an ingenious cultivator of optics," because God's wisdom must be visible everywhere in nature.

Boyle's kind of restricted mechanism, however, had to overcome two major difficulties, at least as far as living beings were concerned: spontaneous generation and regular generation. Until the middle of the seventeenth century, virtually everybody believed that living beings, at least very simple ones, could spontaneously arise from nonliving matter. Through that process of spontaneous generation Nature seemed able to create a new living being by her own power—an impossibility if one believed that God alone could build such complicated structures. Fortunately, spontaneous generation was easily disposed of: in 1668 the Italian scientist Francesco Redi (1626–1697) published the results of ingenious experiments that demonstrated that worms do not spontaneously appear on corrupted meat, but come from eggs previously laid by flies. The scientific community accepted Redi's results with a surprising rapidity, unanimously interpreting them as evidence that there could be no spontaneous generation of living beings in nature. Redi's work thus sealed the fate of spontaneous generation, which had already been condemned by the prevailing creationist mechanism.[15]

Disposing of regular generation proved more difficult. This idea embarrassed the philosophy of creationist mechanism because, through the natural process of embryonic development, seemingly homogeneous matter was transformed into the exquisite structure of a living being. Because such a transformation appeared to be beyond the powers of Nature, a new theory was formulated in the late 1660s, according to which every living being had been directly created by God at the beginning of the world as a minute germ, which then waited for the proper moment for its development. This so-called theory of preexisting germs also won rapid acceptance, though its only factual basis was a dubious embryological observation made by the Italian anatomist Marcello Malpighi (1628–1694), who himself had been cautious enough not to draw such a bold and general conclusion from what he had seen.[16] But the theory perfectly suited the spirit of the time: it provided scientists with a solution for an apparently insoluble problem and made God the only active cause of generation.

Needless to say, seventeenth-century theologians were delighted with such beautiful agreement between science and Christian faith. It seemed scientifically legitimate to repeat, with Holy Writ and Saint Augustine: "God created everything at the same time." Among British writers such as John Keill (1671–1721) and Richard Bentley (1662–1742), who belonged to Newtonian circles on the eve of the eighteenth century, Boyle's natural philosophy served as a model, while Descartes and all the "world makers" were strongly condemned for impiety.[17] From the Boyle lectures in the beginning of the eighteenth century to the *Bridgewater Treatises* in the 1830s, from John Derham (1657–1735) to William Paley (1743–1805), many Englishmen who were at the same time clerics and scientists published books that developed the theme of "the wisdom of God demonstrated by the marvels of Nature." Continental theologians, especially in Protestant countries, often followed their example.

But agreement between science and Christianity was being gained at the expense of Nature, so to speak. The Christian mechanists assumed that matter was entirely passive and that no natural process was able to bring forth any new being. It is extremely likely that their philosophy had political significance since it developed at a time when few people in Europe were prepared to accept the idea that the source of political power belonged to the people rather than to kings.[18] In any case, new theories appeared by the middle of the eighteenth century that questioned the view of nature and the agreement between mechanism and Christianity characteristic of the late seventeenth century.

NATURE AND LIFE IN THE EIGHTEENTH CENTURY

As far as science was concerned, the limited mechanism I have described left ample room for research. Naturalists were eager to study living beings that they considered to be the work of God. They carefully described many new species, especially among insects, portraying all the delicacy of their anatomical structure and the stupendous precision of their behavior. For example, many regarded bees as being greater geometers than men because they had solved the difficult problem of building cells of the greatest capacity with the minimum quantity of wax. To such writers it seemed that no explanation but a direct intervention of God could account for such marvels. When classifying living beings, naturalists believed that they were discovering the very order of God's creation; since each animal and plant had been individually created, it followed that all relationships had been planned from the beginning by the divine Architect.

Some new discoveries, however, made it less easy to believe in the absolute passivity of Nature. In the early 1740s a young Swiss amateur, Abraham Trembley (1701–1784), discovered a strange little animal, the polyp or freshwater hydra, which, when cut into several pieces, was able to regenerate as an equal number of complete animals. How was such a phenomenon to be reconciled with the theory of preexisting germs? Was it possible to believe that God had foreseen the encounter of the hydra and the naturalist, and put precisely as many preexisting germs in the body of the little animal as were to be necessary to regenerate the missing parts of its body? The theory of preexisting germs also led to endless discussions about monsters and other abnormal beings, since it obliged one to believe either that God was personally responsible for the birth of such unfortunate creatures or that accidents in the natural process of embryonic development were able to prevent the realization of God's will. Some years after Trembley's discovery the Swiss physiologist Albrecht von Haller (1708–1777) discovered a new property of muscular tissue, which he called irritability; when pricked, muscle contracted spontaneously, even if all the connected nerves had been cut off. This property Haller compared to Newtonian gravitation, because no mechanical explanation was available.[19]

Perhaps more than new scientific discoveries, the general trend of Enlightenment philosophy made it difficult for the idea of a passive Nature to survive.[20] Eighteenth-century philosophers generally agreed that nature should be studied directly without reference to a divine Being whose existence could not be ascertained and whose intervention into natural phenomena put a limit, so to speak, on the power of human understanding. The eighteenth century thus witnessed a general tendency to transfer to Nature all the powers traditionally attributed to God. Newton's natural philosophy was the first victim of that tendency. Newton had demonstrated that the force of gravitation pervaded nature. But soon after his discovery, and against his will, others began interpreting that force as an essential property of matter, which transformed matter into an active being. The German philosopher and scientist Gottfried Wilhelm von Leibniz (1646–1716), Newton's famous rival in discovering the calculus, proposed for very metaphysical reasons that the ultimate element of every being was a "monad" endowed with activity and sensitivity. The concept of monad was so difficult to grasp that many philosophers transformed it into the more understandable notion of an active and sensitive atom, similar to that of Epicurean philosophy. As early as 1704 the British philosopher John Toland (1670–1722) in his *Letters to Serena* proposed a philosophy in which the most distinctive feature was the idea of an active and powerful Nature that clearly substituted for God. Other philosophers, such as the British naturalist Nehemiah Grew (1641–1712) and the French Huguenot Jean Le Clerc (1657–1736), found it impossible to explain life without recourse to spiritual principles acting upon nature as God's agents. The German chemist and professor of medicine Georg-Ernst Stahl (1660–1734) argued that life was not understandable without the action of the soul. Thus, under the pressure of both scientific discoveries and novel philosophical ideas, new biological theories began appearing by the middle of the eighteenth century. These new theories significantly altered the mechanistic conception of life.

Among the first developments was a revival of the old Epicurean philosophy, mixed with some tenets of Cartesianism and adapted to the new scientific situation. This type of mechanism was exemplified by the French physician and philosopher Julien Offray de La Mettrie (1709–1751), who had studied medicine in Leiden under the famous and piously orthodox Professor Hermann Boerhaave (1668–1738) and who remained faithful to the mechanistic philosophy of his master,

if not to the latter's religious beliefs.[21] In his *Man-Machine*, first published in 1747, La Mettrie took advantage of the not-yet-published
discovery of irritability by Haller to demonstrate autonomous activity
in living matter. If Nature is spontaneously active, he concluded, there
is no need of God. As for the order that obviously reigns over the
living world, he thought that it, too, could be explained without
recourse to God. In a very Cartesian way La Mettrie stated his belief
in the power of Nature's laws to eliminate chance from natural phenomena: "Suppressing Chance is not demonstrating the evidence of
a supreme Being, since there can be something else that would be
neither Chance nor God, namely Nature."[22]

In another book, the *System of Epicurus* (1750), La Mettrie continued
to develop his ideas by borrowing even more from Epicurean philosophy. Perfect animals, he wrote, are the final outcome of innumerable unsuccessful combinations of matter as well as the necessary
result of natural laws: "Elements of matter, by moving themselves
and mixing with each other, managed to make eyes, and then it was
as impossible not to see as not to see oneself in a mirror." Blind
necessity thus explained everything: "Nature, without seeing, has
made seeing eyes and without thinking has made a thinking
machine."[23]

This apparently was the main point of La Mettrie's philosophy.
Not only did he maintain that living beings are mere machines—a
point on which many naturalists would have agreed with him—but
also that humans are *nothing but machines*, that is, that mechanical
processes are the key to understanding human activity, including
reason. This could be called a reductionist attitude, because it reduces
all the phenomena of life to mere mechanical processes. Scientifically
speaking, La Mettrie's traditional mechanism had no future, but his
reductionism proved to be easily adapted to more sophisticated mechanical theories of life, such as those that prevailed in the nineteenth
century. From that time on, biological mechanism allied with reductionism was available as a weapon against religion.

Less radical and more sophisticated forms of biological mechanism
appeared in the 1740s; however, they shared with La Mettrie's version
a common recognition of spontaneous activity in nature and rejection
of the now classical theory of preexisting germs. According to the
French astronomer and biologist Pierre Louis Moreau de Maupertuis
(1698–1759), for instance, elementary particles of matter must be endowed with something like will, memory, and perception, without
which it would be impossible to explain the phenomena of life naturally. Maupertuis's conception of the relationship between God and
nature was also typical; for him, Nature's laws are the work of God,
so there can be no contradiction between God's will and natural pro-

cesses. On the contrary, one acquires a greater idea of God's power by saying that everything in nature happens through natural processes obeying the laws He has dictated than by imagining Him as a craftsman, fabricating each natural being one after another. The latter belief, he said, could even lead incredulous minds to ask embarrassing questions, such as why did God create snakes, mosquitoes, or poisonous plants. He thought that God's wisdom could be better demonstrated by blind natural processes being able, if guided by his laws, to build such beautifully contrived machines as living beings. John Turberville Needham (1713–1781), a British Roman Catholic priest, was of the same opinion. Many microscopical observations, in which he claimed to have seen clear cases of spontaneous generation, had convinced him of the active power of Nature. A devout Christian, he saw no contradiction between his faith and his philosophy; but in the eyes of many contemporary scientists and philosophers his views appeared to pave the way to atheism.[24]

A more ambiguous case is that of the famous French naturalist Georges Louis Leclerc, Comte de Buffon (1707–1788), whose great *Natural History* appeared from 1749 to 1788.[25] Though a faithful Newtonian, Buffon disagreed with his master about the origin of the solar system, preferring a physical hypothesis—a collision of a comet with the sun—to belief in a direct creation by God. In biology, Buffon denied the theory of preexisting germs, because, like his friend Maupertuis, he believed that it provided a miraculous rather than a scientific explanation. He did not, however, think that simple mechanism could explain the phenomena of life. Thus he supposed the existence of "living matter" made of "organic molecules." He also argued that biological mechanism had to include special "penetrating forces," obviously modeled on Newtonian gravitation, that acted within living organisms. Buffon's biological mechanism is thus much more complicated than the old Cartesian scheme: it is the biological counterpart of the new dynamics created by Newton. But by insisting that Nature is perpetually active, by emphasizing natural processes rather than natural structures, Buffon's thought tended to eliminate God, replacing Him with Nature and history. By combining the active power of Nature with natural mechanism acting through the course of history, Buffon was able to allow for significant alterations of natural structures. Limited as it is, Buffon's theory of evolution introduced a new historical dimension into biological thought, a dimension that increased the explanatory power of biological mechanism at the expense of the traditional idea of creation.

It should be clear that Maupertuis's, Needham's, and Buffon's theories of life, which supposed the existence in matter of psychic qualities or unknown forces, all deviated far from the original biological mechanism of the seventeenth century. This was not far enough, however, for those who wanted to give Nature and life still greater autonomy and thus advocated a vitalist conception of life, which spread rapidly through the European scientific community in the 1760s. Vitalists, such as the German anatomist Caspar Friedrich Wolff (1733–1794), did not deny that living beings were chiefly machines, but they maintained that mechanical and chemical processes could not account for the embryonic development or even the normal functioning of an organism if not guided by a natural "vital force" or "vital principle," the nature of which was unknown. For many partisans of this view, the vital principle explained the most conspicuous property of life, sensitivity, and thus vitalism acquired a definitely materialistic flavor. Despite the brilliant discoveries of the Scottish neurophysiologist Robert Whytt (1714–1766), who identified the "sentient principle" with the soul, the concept of soul continued to disappear slowly from biology. Thus, although the mechanistic conception of life had lost ground by the end of the eighteenth century, it had done so without benefiting a religious conception of nature and science. On the contrary, biologists insisted on the spontaneous activity of life as firmly as their predecessors had during the Renaissance, before the advent of biological mechanism.[26]

LAMARCK AND NINETEENTH-CENTURY REDUCTIONISM

Despite the general acceptance of vitalism by physicians and biologists at the beginning of the nineteenth century, biological mechanism found an outspoken proponent in the person of the French naturalist Jean Baptiste Lamarck (1744–1829).[27] Lamarck is well known as the first naturalist to propose a complete theory of evolution, but his most famous book, *Zoological Philosophy* (1809), was much more than a treatise on evolution. Its real aim was to show how biology—a term Lamarck helped to popularize—could explain everything about animals. The first part of the book dealt chiefly with evolution, but the second part contained a lengthy description of "the physical causes of life"—causes that were entirely mechanical, because Lamarck reduced all biological processes to the various motions of fluids through cellular tissue. The "exciting cause" of those motions he identified with the action of invisible and imponderable fluids. For plants and very simple animals those fluids were mainly heat and electricity, which acted from the outside and pervaded the whole organism. For animals endowed with a nervous system, external fluids were replaced by a nervous fluid of electrical nature. Finally, in the last part of *Philosophical Zoology* Lamarck explained the faculties of the higher animals and humans: sensitivity, perception, memory, and intelligence.

Lamarck was a materialist to the extent that he did not consider it necessary to have recourse to any spiritual principle in order to explain the faculties of the mind, which he thought also exist in higher animals. He was also a deist, because he could not conceive of nature as eternal and preferred to think that it had been created. But his deism remained vague, and his idea of creation did not prevent him from believing that everything in nature, including the highest forms of life, was but the result of natural processes. His materialism was neither aggressive nor antireligious; he simply believed that human feelings and human thought were natural phenomena that could be explained scientifically, that is, by means of biological mechanisms. Thus, his philosophy of life was typically reductionist.

Lamarck's biology is remarkable for the profundity of its theoretical insight and for its total lack of experimental evidence. It is surprising that such a competent naturalist, such a careful observer of minute animals, never made an experiment. His description of the working of fluids on the cellular tissue was sheer fancy; thus, methodologically, his biological mechanism had no future. But his reduction of all biological phenomena to physical processes provided a model that had a far-reaching, though somewhat delayed, influence.

Vitalism continued to dominate European physiology until the 1840s, when a new generation of physiologists, led by the Germans Emil du Bois-Reymond (1818–1896), Karl Ludwig (1816–1895), and Hermann von Helmoltz (1821–1894), rebelled against their teachers and insisted on reducing life to physicochemical processes. Theirs was a new brand of mechanism, which replaced the old Cartesian image of the universe as a clock with a more sophisticated view of the world, in which electricity, thermodynamics, and chemistry played the most important roles. But the new physiologists shared with La Mettrie and Lamarck a common reductionist attitude. They attacked vitalism as a kind of spiritualist philosophy and discarded the soul and the vital principle as unnecessary for a complete explanation of life. To be sure, many members of the new school were not outspoken materialists; as scientists, they merely ignored anything but matter and its properties. But for the most radical members of the school, Karl Vogt (1817–1895), Jacob Moleschott (1822–1893), and Ludwig Büchner (1824–1899), the adoption of a materialist philosophy and the rejection of a spiritualistic worldview were necessary consequences of their interpretation of life. Such philosophers and scientists considered the synthesis of urea, first achieved by the German chemist Friedrich Wohler (1800–1882) in 1827, to be a severe blow against religion, because urea was one of those organic compounds that, according to vitalists, could only be synthesized by living organisms. Since vitalism was considered a spiritualistic philosophy, it followed that if vitalism was wrong, so was Christianity. Such was the logic of biological materialism.[28]

The use of biological mechanism and reductionism as a weapon against religion was a prominent feature of nineteenth-century intellectual life. In reaction, many religious leaders throughout Europe denounced science in general and biology in particular as menaces to religion and public morality. It was in such an atmosphere that Darwinism appeared, and evolution established itself as the ultimate product of a science definitively "liberated from the shackles of superstition." But that is another story.

CONCLUSION

In concluding this brief study of the mechanistic conception of life and its relationships with religious thought from the seventeenth to the nineteenth century, I should point out that the philosophy of biological mechanism created, successively, two major kinds of problems. When it appeared in the seventeenth century, biological mechanism was linked to a conception of nature that deprived matter of any activity. Thus, the first problem involved the extent of God's interference with natural phenomena. If, for example, living beings were able to reproduce naturally, as biologists asserted, it seemed, according to the logic of the time, that God's prerogative was thereby reduced. The temporary alliance between religion and creationist mechanism eventually proved dangerous for religion, because it transformed every scientific advance into a defeat for Christianity. In retrospect, we can see that it would have been safer to allow Nature more power and autonomy under the guidance of the laws dictated by God. This, however, was not generally understood by Christian theologians of any denomination before the end of the nineteenth century, when the evolutionary debate obliged them to think anew about the concept of Creation.

The second problem, which assumed importance in the eighteenth century, concerned the relationship between life and soul. The soul was a very ambiguous notion, indeed, since it could be the name for a vital principle in Aristotelian philosophy, for an autonomous being responsible for the working of human reason according to Plato and Descartes, or for a divine principle given to humans by God. Advocates of biological mechanism first tried to eliminate the Aristotelian soul—only to have it survive under the name of vital principle. Then the mechanists attacked the Cartesian soul, together with the vital principle. It is not at all clear whether theologians were right to identify the Christian concept of soul with the agent of human rational thinking, but they did; and by doing so, they exposed themselves to the attacks of reductionists. Here again, it would have been wiser perhaps not to have linked religion with a changeable philosophy and a transient stage of scientific knowledge. But few can resist the intellectual trends of their age, and, in any case, it is much easier to identify the error of the past than to see the misunderstanding of the present.

NOTES

I wish to thank Professor Phillip Sloan, whose stimulating commentary of the first draft of this paper helped me to complete and clarify my ideas, and Professor Ronald L. Numbers, who took the trouble to carefully correct my English text and gave it a more palatable form without betraying it.

1. For general histories of physiology and the problem of life see Thomas S. Hall, *Ideas of Life and Matter: Studies in the History of General Physiology, 600 B.C.–1900 A.D.*, 2 vols. (Chicago: Univ. of Chicago Press, 1969); and Christopher U. M. Smith, *The Problem of Life: An Essay in the Origins of Biological Thought* (New York: John Wiley & Sons, 1976).

2. On Aristotle's biological thought see Sir William David Ross, *Aristotle*, 5th ed. (London: Methuen, 1964); Marjorie Grene, *A Portrait of Aristotle* (London: Faber & Faber, 1963); G. E. R. Lloyd, *Aristotle: The Growth and Structure of His Thought* (Cambridge: Cambridge Univ. Press, 1968); D. M. Balme, "Development of Biology in Aristotle and Theophrastus: Theory of Spontaneous Generation," *Phronesis* 7 (1962): 91–104; Joseph Owens, "Teleology of Nature in Aristotle," *Monist* 52 (1968): 159–173; Anthony Preus, "Science and Philosophy in Aristotle's Generation of Animals," *Journal of the History of Biology* 3 (1970): 1–52.

3. Cyril Bailey, *The Greek Atomists and Epicurus: A Study* (Oxford: Clarendon Press, 1928).

4. See, for example, E. J. Dijksterhuis, *The Mechanization of the World Picture*, trans. C. Dikshoorn (Oxford: Clarendon Press, 1961).

5. Galileo Galilei, *The Assayer* (1623), in *Discoveries and Opinions of Galileo*, trans. Stillman Drake (Garden City, N.Y.: Doubleday Anchor Books, 1957), p. 238.

6. On the mechanical philosophy see Marie Boas, "The Establishment of the Mechanical Philosophy," *Osiris* 10 (1952): 412–541; and David Kubrin, "Providence and the Mechanical Philosophy: The Creation and Dissolution

of the World in Newtonian Thought" (Ph.D. diss., Cornell University, 1968).

7. See, for example, Robert H. Kargon, *Atomism in England from Hariot to Newton* (Oxford: Clarendon Press, 1966).

8. On physiology and the mechanical philosophy see Theodore M. Brown, "The Mechanical Philosophy and the 'Animal Oeconomy': A Study in the Development of English Physiology in the 17th and Early 18th Century" (Ph.D. diss., Princeton University, 1968).

9. On Descartes see Norman Kemp Smith, *New Studies in the Philosophy of Descartes* (London: Macmillan, 1952); Thomas S. Hall, "Descartes: Physiological Methods," *Journal of the History of Biology* 3 (1970): 53–79; Philip R. Sloan, "Descartes, the Sceptics, and the Rejection of Vitalism in 17th-Century Physiology," *Studies in History and Philosophy of Science* 8 (1977): 1–28.

10. On Boyle see Mitchell Salem Fisher, *Robert Boyle, Devout Naturalist: A Study in Science and Religion in the Seventeenth Century* (Philadelphia: Oshiver Studio Press, 1945); Marie Boas Hall, *Robert Boyle on Natural Philosophy: An Essay with Selections from His Writings* (Bloomington: Indiana Univ. Press, 1966); and J. E. McGuire, "Boyle's Conception of Nature," *Journal of the History of Ideas* 33 (1972): 523–542.

11. Robert Boyle, *The Origine of Formes and Qualities (According to the Corpuscular Philosophy)*, 2d ed. (Oxford: Ric. Davis, 1667), pp. 102–104.

12. On Newton's views see David Kubrin, "Newton and the Cyclical Cosmos," *Journal of the History of Ideas* 28 (1967): 325–346.

13. Pascal's *Pensées*, trans. Martin Turnell (London: Harvill Press, 1962), p. 115.

14. Robert Boyle, *A Disquisition about the Final Causes*, in *The Works of the Honourable Robert Boyle*, 6 vols. (London: J. & F. Rivington, 1772), 5:408.

15. See John Farley, *The Spontaneous Generation Controversy: From Descartes to Oparin* (Baltimore: Johns Hopkins Univ. Press, 1977), chap. 2.

16. François Duchesneau, "Malpighi, Descartes, and the Epistemological Problems of Iatromechanism," in *Reason, Experiment, and Mysticism in the Scientific Revolution*, ed. Maria Luisa Righini Bonelli and William R. Shea (New York: Science History Publication, 1975), pp. 111–130.

17. On Keill see Kubrin, "Providence and the Mechanical Philosophy," chap. 11.

18. On the political significance of the mechanistic philosophy see Margaret C. Jacob, *The Newtonians and the English Revolution, 1689–1720* (Ithaca, N.Y.: Cornell Univ. Press, 1976).

19. Charles Bodemer, "Regeneration and the Decline of Preformationism in 18th-Century Embryology," *Bulletin of the History of Medicine* 38 (1964): 20–31; Aram Vartanian, "Trembley's Polyp, La Mettrie, and 18th-Century French Materialism," *Journal of the History of Ideas* 11 (1950): 259–286; Shirley A. Roe, ed., *The Natural Philosophy of Albrecht von Haller* (New York: Arno Press, 1981).

20. On nature and life in the eighteenth century see Jacques Roger, *Les sciences de la vie dans la pensée française du XVIIIᵉ siècle: La génération des animaux de Descartes à l'Encyclopédie*, 2d ed. (Paris: Armand Colin, 1971). See also Aram Vartanian, *Diderot and Descartes: A Study of Scientific Naturalism in the Enlightenment* (Princeton: Princeton Univ. Press, 1953); Philip C. Ritterbush, *Overtures*

to Biology: The Speculations of Eighteenth-Century Naturalists* (New Haven: Yale Univ. Press, 1964); and Robert E. Schofield, *Mechanism and Materialism: British Natural Philosophy in an Age of Reason* (Princeton: Princeton Univ. Press, 1970).

21. On La Mettrie see Aram Vartanian, ed., *La Mettrie's L'homme machine: A Study in the Origins of an Idea* (Princeton: Princeton Univ. Press, 1960); and Leonora D. C. Rosenfield, *From Beast-Machine to Man-Machine: Animal Soul in French Letters from Descartes to La Mettrie* (New York: Oxford Univ. Press, 1941).

22. Vartanian, *La Mettrie's L'homme machine*, pp. 177–178.

23. Julien Offray de La Mettrie, *Système d'Epicure* (1750), in *Oeuvres philosophiques de La Mettrie*, new ed., 3 vols. (Berlin: C. Tutot, 1796), 2:11, 14.

24. Roger, *Les sciences de la vie*, pp. 457–484; and Jacques Roger, "The Living World," in *The Ferment of Knowledge: Studies in the Historiography of Eighteenth Century Science*, ed. G. S. Rousseau and Roy Porter (Cambridge: Cambridge Univ. Press, 1980), pp. 255–283.

25. On Buffon see Jacques Roger, ed., *Buffon: Les époques de la nature* (Paris: Muséum national d'histoire naturelle, 1962); Otis E. Fellows and Stephen F. Milliken, *Buffon* (New York: Twayne, 1972); John Lyon and Phillip R. Sloan, eds., *From Natural History to the History of Nature: Readings from Buffon and His Critics* (Notre Dame, Ind.: Univ. of Notre Dame Press, 1981); and Peter J. Bowler, "Bonnet and Buffon: Theories of Generation and the Problem of Species," *Journal of the History of Biology* 6 (1973): 259–281.

26. Theodore M. Brown, "From Mechanism to Vitalism in 18th-Century English Physiology," *Journal of the History of Biology* 6 (1973): 259–281; Shirley A. Roe, *Matter, Life, and Generation: Eighteenth-Century Embryology and the Haller-Wolff Debate* (Cambridge: Cambridge Univ. Press, 1981); Roger K. French, *Robert Whytt, the Soul, and Medicine* (London: Wellcome Institute of the History of Medicine, 1969).

27. On Lamarck see Richard W. Burkhardt, Jr., *The Spirit of System: Lamarck and Evolutionary Biology* (Cambridge: Harvard Univ. Press, 1977); and M. J. S. Hodge, "Lamarck's Science of Living Bodies," *British Journal of the History of Science* 5 (1971): 323–352.

28. Frederick Gregory, *Scientific Materialism in Nineteenth Century Germany* (Dordrecht: Reidel, 1977); Owsei Temkin, "Materialism in French and German Physiology of the Early Nineteenth Century," *Bulletin of the History of Medicine* 20 (1946): 322–327; Timothy O. Lipman, "Vitalism and Reductionism in Liebig's Physiological Thought," *Isis* 58 (1967): 167–185; Timothy Lenoir, "Teleology without Regrets: The Transformation of Physiology in Germany, 1790–1847," *Studies in History and Philosophy of Science* 12 (1981): 293–354. On nineteenth-century biology generally, see William Coleman, *Biology in the Nineteenth Century: Problems of Form, Function, and Transformation* (New York: John Wiley & Sons, 1971).

12

The Shape and Meaning
of Earth History

Martin J. S. Rudwick

Archbishop James Ussher, a scholarly Irishman of the seventeenth century, has become unjustly famous as the supposed author of the claim that the creation of the world could be dated to the year 4004 B.C. More than two centuries later, when the classic histories of science and religion were being written in terms of warlike conflicts,[1] similar claims were still being made by some culturally conservative groups in Western societies. Today, routine estimates of the earth's antiquity in terms of several billion years, made by geologists on the basis of radioactivity in rocks, contrast strikingly with the assertions of the small but vocal group of creationists, who retain something like Ussher's calculation in their body of alternative knowledge. It is not surprising, therefore, that this piece of history is still commonly seen as a story of continuous conflict between Christianity and science, in which Christians—with the exception of the so-called fundamentalists—have compromised their traditional beliefs in the face of the triumphant march of scientific knowledge.

This kind of scientific triumphalism is long overdue for critical reappraisal. Its claims to serious attention have been thoroughly demolished in other areas of the history of science, but it survives as an anomaly in the historical treatment of the relation of science to religious belief.[2] This may be because the historians' own attitudes are conditioned by the immature age at which religious beliefs and practices are abandoned by many, though not all, intellectuals in modern Western societies. This common experience may explain why many historians of science seem incapable of giving the religious beliefs of past cultures the same intelligent and empathic respect that

296

they now routinely accord to even the strangest scientific beliefs of the past. Traditional interpretations in terms of conflict and compromise do more, however, than fail to treat religious beliefs seriously. These well-worn categories also encourage the reification of science and religion into contrasting bundles of abstract propositions. The crucial third term, society, is either ignored[3] or else invoked in the most naive form, the contents of religion and science being attributed to two similarly polarized social groups, namely religious believers and scientists.

In contrast with such simplistic treatments I suggest that specific episodes of conflict should be regarded as stories about the interaction of rival *cosmologies*—using that term, as I shall throughout this essay, in its anthropological sense.[4] In other words, they are episodes in which people on both sides appealed to some aspect of nature, such as the origin and history of the earth, in order to support and justify their attempts to propagate their own view of the *meaning* of personal and social life and of the conduct appropriate to that life, whether that meaning was formulated in religious terms or not. In historical studies there should be no place for sweeping generalizations that contrast the progressive outlook of scientists with the reactionary attitudes of Christians. We must expect to find that scientists of varying degrees of originality and competence and Christians of varying degrees of insight and orthodoxy were prominent on *both* sides of many controversies. Furthermore, there is the obvious fact that one and the same individual has frequently been both Christian and scientist (a term I use for convenience, although it is highly anachronistic before the mid-nineteenth century).

In the history of controversies about the age of the earth, few modern scholarly studies of particular episodes take the religious dimension seriously and at the same time give full attention to the social uses to which rival viewpoints were put. What I shall do in this brief essay, therefore, is simply to sketch the main outlines of the changing interpretations of earth history since the Middle Ages and to suggest how rival religious and social meanings have been expressed through those interpretations. In particular, I shall argue that the quantitative figures that have been given at various times for the age of the earth are far less significant than the qualitative patterns that have been discerned in, or attributed to, the whole history of the earth, of life, and of mankind (see fig. 12.1). I shall first summarize the tradition of biblical chronology that formed the temporal component of the geocentric picture of the cosmos. Second, I shall describe the new enterprise that was termed the "theory of the earth" and its relation to the rise of critical methods in biblical interpretation. And

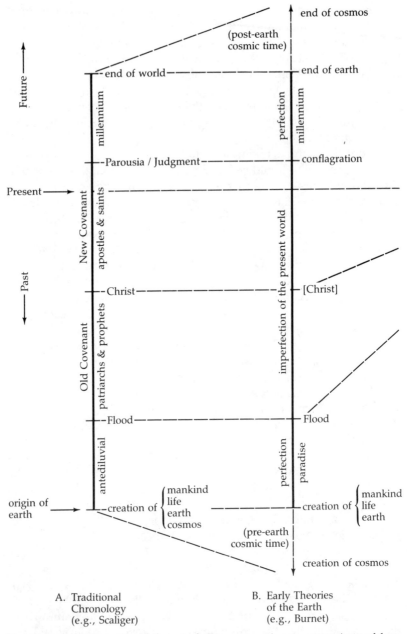

A. Traditional
   Chronology
   (e.g., Scaliger)

B. Early Theories
   of the Earth
   (e.g., Burnet)

Fig. 12.1. Earth histories of the mind. Diagrammatic representations of four successive ways in which the shape of earth history and its most significant events were conceived. Time is shown flowing upward (as in classical geological diagrams). *Quantitative* estimates or calculations of the magnitudes of time involved are deliberately ignored; the span of time from the origin of

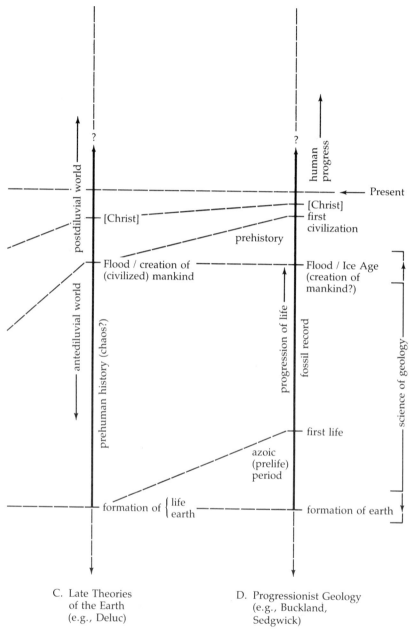

C. Late Theories
of the Earth
(e.g., Deluc)

D. Progressionist Geology
(e.g., Buckland,
Sedgwick)

the earth to the present is represented (arbitrarily) as uniform in all four diagrams, in order to highlight the qualitative changes in the conceptualized pattern of events. Note that eternalistic conceptions of earth history cannot be adequately depicted in this kind of visual representation.

third, I shall outline the way that a new science of geology, with deliberately limited cognitive goals, pushed attributions of cosmological meanings out of the scientific study of the earth and relegated them to the social and cognitive margins of science.

THE GEOCENTRIC COSMOS

The spatial aspect of the picture of the cosmos culturally dominant around the end of the Middle Ages in the West is comparatively familiar. The universe was conceived as a bounded system, with the earth lying immobile at the center of an ascending hierarchy of ceaselessly revolving celestial spheres. The abode of mankind was central in position, but furthest from the divine presence and least in glory. This image embodied and expressed a cosmology that related mankind both to the environment and to the transcendence of God. It also reflected, and justified as natural, an analogous social order of stable hierarchical equilibrium. The temporal pattern that would have matched this spatial structure was one of merely cyclic change, without truly historical development. Up to a point this image of cyclic change was indeed incorporated into the personal and social life of Christendom, as for example in the public celebration of the cycle of the church's year. But a concept of merely cyclic change could all too easily be extrapolated into an image of a cosmos that was eternal, self-maintaining, and—above all—uncreated. This eternalism, which, like the accepted spatial picture, derived principally from Aristotle, was therefore suspect to those who saw themselves as the guardians of the order of nature and society. Conversely, an eternalistic picture of the cosmos was a valuable resource in the hands of any critics of that social order, the more so if the spatial bounds of the conventional cosmos were dissolved into boundless infinity.

Those who sought to maintain the stable order of society, as justified by the order of nature, therefore united a limited acknowledgment of cyclic change with an affirmation of the finite spatial limits of the cosmos and the underlying directional pattern of its history. In this image of world history the cosmos was bounded as much temporally as spatially: it had a clear beginning in Creation, and God's action would bring it to an equally decisive End. It was also structured as much temporally as spatially within these limits (see fig. 1A). It had a unique midpoint in the events surrounding the life of Christ, which divided the old relationship or covenant between mankind and God from the new. On either side of that divide, the particularities of patriarchs and prophets, apostles and saints, were framed by past and future events of global significance, namely the Flood and the Parousia (or Second Coming of Christ). Beyond that frame lay only the swift prelude of the Creation, Paradise, and the Fall in the past, and the expected culmination of the final Judgment and (more controversially) the Millennium in the future. This whole temporal structure imbued the past, present, and future of the cosmos with human meaning: it attributed order to the often chaotic flux of human lives and gave social action a transcendent context and justification.

This picture of earth history was derived, of course, principally from the Bible, the diverse components of which were interpreted in terms of an underlying unity of narrative history. Spiritual methods of interpretation, such as allegory and typology, were built on a substrate of literal historical meaning. The narrative story discerned in the Bible was not simply a religious way of looking at the history of the world. For most members of Western societies it *was* the history of the world, at least in outline. Other secular events, above all the life of society and its constituent persons, received meaning by being seen in their appropriate place within the narrative structure. The brief narratives recorded in the opening passages of Genesis, the first book of the Bible, posed few problems of credibility. It seemed plausible to regard human history as virtually coextensive with earth history, and that with cosmic history; without mankind the earth and the cosmos would have seemed to lack meaning and purpose. The closely integrated Creation of cosmos, earth, and life, the swift sequence of Paradise and the Fall, and the great global action of the Flood together formed an intelligible prelude to the main historical narrative of redemption embodied in the Bible. As Sir Thomas Browne put it, "time we may comprehend; 'tis but five days older than ourselves" (*Religio Medici*, 1635).

CHRONICLES OF THE WORLD

The construction of a single narrative story of cosmic history received new impetus during the period of the Renaissance and Reformation. Improved methods of textual scholarship were used to eliminate apparent discrepancies within the Bible itself. The interest of humanist scholars in the texts and monuments of classical antiquity, later broadened to include those of other ancient civilizations, provided a new wealth of historical information that needed to be integrated into the biblical narrative. A tradition of scholarly chronology grew up, in which that narrative was given quantitative precision by the dating of its events. The scattered calendrical information in the Bible was collated and compared with, for example, astronomical calculations on historically recorded eclipses and conjunctions. The resultant outline of datable history was then enriched by fitting into it whatever was known about the history of the world from nonbiblical sources. The result of this scholarly activity was the production of an outline of world history that had pretensions to being universal and was no longer confined to biblical sources; an example of this genre is J. J. Scaliger's *De Emendatione Temporum* (1583). At first there was little to suggest any marked deviation from traditional estimates of the scale of cosmic history, even back to the Creation. All reliable calculations, despite minor differences of scholarly opinion, could be plotted without strain within a few thousand years.[5] Ussher's famous figure of 4004 B.C., which he did not originate, was only one of many rival scholarly estimates of this kind; it has become the best known—in the English-speaking world—only through its adoption in the marginal notes of some editions of the seventeenth-century King James translation of the Bible.

This scholarly consensus was disturbed, however, by ancient records of Egyptian dynasties that implied a higher antiquity; and these were followed in the seventeenth century by reports of alleged records of Chinese civilization that pushed the history of mankind still further back in time. Moreover, problems of another kind emerged in the wake of European exploration of other continents. It became increasingly difficult to integrate what was becoming known about the distribution of exotic animals and plants—and, above all, of human beings—into the brief narrative framework of the Bible. It was not clear, for example, how the descendants of Noah and of the animal inmates of the ark could have had time to repopulate all the scattered continents after the Flood. Such problems gave rise to an extensive scholarly literature in the sixteenth and seventeenth centuries.[6] Its significance lies in the fact that these problems were used as resources for *either* the defense *or* the criticism of the established view of a temporally finite world. The consensus among scholars held that documented human history could not be carried back in any civilization more than a few thousand years; texts that implied a higher antiquity were regarded as either legendary or fraudulent. Those who claimed on the contrary that such documents were reliable used them to attack the authenticity of the biblical narrative in the interests of alternative, and generally anti-Christian, interpretations of the world. In other words, speculations about a vast antiquity for mankind, about the possible existence of human beings before Adam, and about the inadequacy of the ark as an explanation of organic distribution were never just enlightened and disinterested scholarly inquiries. They were put forward to support specific cosmologies, as were the more literalistic interpretations to which they were opposed.

It would be wholly anachronistic to contrast the opinions of scholarly chronologists with those of contemporary scientists. Natural philosophers, as the latter generally called themselves, also worked within the taken-for-granted assumptions of their societies. For example, even the recognition of fossils as organic remains was highly problematical; the most obviously organic fossils were precisely those that could most readily be attributed to a single large-scale event.[7] The most appropriate recorded event was of course the Flood, the historicity of which seemed to be confirmed by analogous stories in other ancient literatures. For example, the Danish scholar Niels Stensen (1638–1686), better known as Steno, interpreted the rock structure of Tuscany in Italy in terms of a temporal sequence of events; but he inferred that the fossil-bearing strata must have been deposited during the Flood, and he thought they could not be much older than the monuments of the ancient Etruscan civilization that he could see in the same region. Around the same time Robert Hooke (1635–1703) in England argued likewise for the organic origin of many fossils, but he assumed that they represented organisms that would have been almost contemporary with early mankind. When, in a famous phrase, he suggested that it might be possible to "raise a chronology out of them," he meant that fossils might be used to supplement the coins and other artifacts used by antiquarians, thus amplifying the chronology of human history by charting the parallel history of the animate world.[8] Seventeenth-century naturalists such as Steno and Hooke envisaged only dimly, if at all, the possibility of a long *prehuman* history of the earth.

It is easy in retrospect to pour scorn on the tradition of chronology in biblical scholarship and the related work of naturalists such as Steno and Hooke. But its literalism was a simple consequence of the precritical approach to biblical texts, and there was little nonbiblical evidence that threw any serious doubt on the short time scale that it proposed. Chronologists were not responsible for establishing the belief in a short cosmic history; their work merely codified and lent an air of precision to an already-taken-for-granted view of the natural world. What is most significant about that view is not its short timescale by modern standards, but rather its almost unexamined assumption that the history of the cosmos must be virtually coextensive with the history of mankind—indeed, the history of civilized literate mankind. In this way the culturally dominant Christian cosmology, although in principle centered on God, was in practice centered more on mankind. The history of the earth was seen only as the stage for the drama of human history, the drama of the creation, fall, and redemption of a unique set of rational beings.

NEW MODELS OF EARTH HISTORY

Within the traditional temporal image of the cosmos, the origin of the earth could only be regarded as an integral aspect of the creation of the cosmos as a whole. What was religiously important about that primal creation was the assertion, or alternatively the denial, that it had indeed been the work of a transcendent Creator. The origin of the earth could not become an object of inquiry on any other level until the earth could be seen as a part of the cosmos that was not wholly unique. But even the slow acceptance in the seventeenth century of Copernicus's heliostatic system of the cosmos did not have that effect, since it merely altered the position of the earth within a bounded cosmos similar in structure to the earlier geostatic system. A far more radical alternative, however, had continued a submerged existence from earlier centuries. This was the image of a cosmos without center or boundaries, a cosmos that was infinite, eternal, and possibly even uncreated. Giordano Bruno (1548–1600) described such a cosmos in the late sixteenth century, and in the mid-seventeenth century René Descartes (1596–1650) tried to rehabilitate that suspect image. In view of the recent condemnation of Galileo's work, the French philosopher felt obliged to keep a "low profile" in relation to Catholic authority and its localized secular power, and so he framed his speculations in an ambiguously hypothetical style. In *Principiae Philosophiae* (1644) he sketched a possible model of a universe of indefinite limits, within which the earth, and perhaps countless similar bodies, could have had their own origins and histories. He outlined a possible physical history of this hypothetical earth, suggesting natural explanations of its origin and of its main surface features. This account, which left aside the question of the primal creation of the cosmos, was quite compatible with the brief earth history sanctioned both by tradition and by most of the nonbiblical evidence. In this way Descartes effectively detached earth history from cosmic history (see fig. 1B). Following this new model, it became possible to conceive that the history embodied in the biblical narrative, which all agreed had been written primarily for the salvation of mankind, referred to terrestrial events directly relevant to mankind and not to the cosmos as a whole.

The implications of Descartes's model were first articulated by Thomas Burnet (ca. 1635–1715), a Cartesian scholar living in England, which was much freer from intellectual restrictions than absolutist Catholic states. In his *Sacred Theory of the Earth* (1680–1689) Burnet tried explicitly to discover the "true" interpretation of the biblical records of the great physical events of earth history by drawing on the explanatory principles of Cartesian natural philosophy. He was not reconciling Scripture with natural knowledge, for he saw no conflict there; rather, he was using natural knowledge to amplify and illuminate the biblical narrative, which he restated in physical terms (see fig. 1B). The present irregular and "imperfect" state of the earth was framed in the past by the Flood and in the future by the "Conflagration" (or burning of the whole earth) that was widely expected to bring the present order to an end.[9] Beyond those twin catastrophes were the matching "perfections" of Paradise and the Millennium, which in turn were bracketed by the Creation and the final End. The whole symmetrical scheme lay under the sovereignty of Christ as the "alpha and omega" of history, a traditional attribution that now referred only to the earth, not to the cosmos. Burnet conceived the brief and finite history of the earth as being flanked by vast "oceans" of past and future cosmic time. But in asserting the finitude of the earth he explicitly refuted the unnamed eternalists who claimed that the earth and mankind had not been created by the divine will at all.

A PROLIFERATION OF THEORIES

Burnet's work was the prototype of a new kind of writing that became known as the "theory of the earth."[10] This proved to be a highly flexible conceptual resource, in the sense that grand speculative theorizing about the shape of earth history could be, and was, used to support and justify highly diverse cosmologies. In the later seventeenth century, theories of the earth proliferated in great variety, particularly in England, where Burnet's Cartesianism was soon replaced by various aspects of the newer Newtonian natural philosophy. For example, in *A New Theory of the Earth* (1696) the Newtonian William Whiston (1667–1752) used comets to give what he claimed were better explanations of the great physical events of earth history. Above all, the older idea that the earth had decayed from an original perfection gave way to a new emphasis on the way that the harmonious equilibrium of the present earth had been derived from original chaos.[11] Of all such theories, perhaps the most influential was that of John Woodward (1667–1728), who made use of his substantial firsthand knowledge of strata and fossils. In his *Essay towards a Natural History of the Earth* (1695) Woodward claimed that the whole sequence of strata had settled in order of specific gravity out of a chaotic global mixture at the time of the Flood. He thought this would explain the tendency for specific fossils to be embedded in particular strata. This example makes clear the way in which, in this kind of speculation, physical interpretations of events such as the Flood generally diverged far from any literal interpretation of the biblical narratives, even *before* the impact of critical methods of biblical interpretation began to be felt. The basic historicity of the narratives was not necessarily questioned; but it was assumed that behind the conventional or "vulgar" interpretation lay a true or "philosophical" interpretation, which could be discovered by the light of the latest natural philosophy. This attitude was characteristic, for example, of the latitudinarian churchmen in England, who sought to make Christian beliefs acceptable to the enlightened intellects of their age.

It is easy to see how this conception of a privileged interpretation, dependent on scholarly or philosophical knowledge, could lead to a total inversion of the traditional task of biblical interpretation. Traditionally, nonbiblical sources, whether natural or historical, had received their true meaning by being fitted into the unitary narrative of the Bible. This relationship now began to be reversed: the biblical narrative, it was now claimed, received its true meaning by being fitted, on the authority of self-styled experts, into a framework of nonbiblical knowledge. In this way the cognitive plausibility and religious meaning of the biblical narrative could only be maintained in a form that was constrained increasingly by nonbiblical considerations.

The same inverted relationship could equally well be used, however, to promote radically anti-Christian cosmologies. If the biblical narrative were to be interpreted in the light of nonbiblical resources, it could be claimed that it had no validity whatever, except as a record of the superstitions of an unenlightened primitive people. This was the strategy characteristically adopted by the early Enlightenment *philosophes* in France. They generally used the theory of the earth as a means with which to attack Christian orthodoxy and the secular cultural power that it still wielded in many of the Catholic states. For example, Voltaire (1694–1778), in order to remove any evidential foothold for the historicity of the Flood, went so far as to deny the natural emplacement of fossils altogether. He failed to win support for that view, however, since anyone who had observed fossils in strata could see at once that it was untenable. Later theorists in this tradition therefore focused their attention on denying the validity of the supposed evidence for the Flood, claiming, for example, that it had been merely local or that, if universal, it had mysteriously failed to leave any traces and therefore could be ignored for all scientific purposes.

Another line of argument with similar cosmological goals involved reviving the older eternalistic model of the cosmos and applying it to the earth. The earth, it was claimed, had always been and would always be under the dominion of the same purely natural laws. Its history stretched indefinitely or even infinitely into past and future and involved no unique and unexplained events such as the Flood; indeed, earth history was "without vestige of a beginning, without prospect of an end." That famous phrase appeared in James Hutton's *Theory of the Earth* (1795), but the sentiment had often been foreshadowed earlier, particularly in continental Europe, in such works as the Baron d'Holbach's *Système de la nature* (1770). Writers such as Holbach and Hutton generalized the present relative stability of the earth into a permanent feature of the terrestrial system, past and future. This was often given meaning in deistic terms by being attributed to a wise and providential design directed toward the permanent well-being of mankind. Most significantly, the virtual eternalism of such theories was extended, often explicitly, to the history of mankind— for example, in George Toulmin's *The Antiquity and Duration of the World* (1780). Mankind could thus be claimed as uncreated and therefore not subject to any of the traditional moral and social constraints.[12] These theories were far from anticipating modern geology, despite their casual references—for example, in Jean-Baptiste Lamarck's *Hydrogéologie* (1802)—to "millions of centuries" for the history of the earth. Such vast spans of time were invoked primarily as an essential component of eternalistic theories that had clear and generally overt cosmological goals.

PREHUMAN EARTH HISTORY

Meanwhile, however, the bulk of empirical studies of the earth was taking a different direction. Such studies were not necessarily integrated into any high-level theory of the earth. Rather, they were often directed toward more mundane and practical goals, such as the discovery of mineral resources. In such work the implausibility of Woodward's explanation of the strata soon became clear, but his emphasis on the strata as a temporal sequence was retained and enlarged. It became commonplace among eighteenth-century naturalists to distinguish the most ancient, or "Primary," rocks, having no fossils, from the regular sequences of "Secondary" fossil-bearing strata; these were distinguished in turn from irregular and patchy superficial deposits containing the bones of exotic animals such as elephants. The record of the biblical Flood or Deluge was now identified only with these relatively recent deposits. Admittedly they did not suggest the kind of episode recorded in Genesis, and they contained no human remains; but they did seem to be the product of some exceptional catastrophe, and they were difficult to explain away in terms of ordinary observable processes. Since these superficial deposits were identified as "diluvial" (that is, dating from the Flood), the regular sequence of Secondary strata was necessarily described as "antediluvial" or pre-Flood. Since it too contained no human remains, it gradually came to be accepted as a record of *prehuman* earth history (fig. 1C).

This implicit separation of the origin of the earth from the origin of mankind had profound consequences. It created a new kind of history, a history without human documents, which required new conceptual tools. These were borrowed by naturalists from human historiography.[13] Antiquarians had already concluded that "monuments"—a term that covered artifacts such as coins as well as architectural remains—were more trustworthy as historical evidence than textual documents, and in the eighteenth century this term was appropriated by naturalists. They argued that fossils and strata should be more reliable monuments than human artifacts, since Nature could hardly be suspected of historical bias or forgery. In this way, natural monuments were transformed from being merely a source of evidence to supplement the annals of human history, as they had been for Steno, into evidence for a long history that predated mankind altogether. By the late eighteenth century, fossils and strata were routinely described as monuments or as "Nature's archives"; they helped to define "epochs" of local validity, which gave greater precision to the global categories of Primary and Secondary. The naturalists who pioneered this new kind of earth history rarely attempted to quantify its time scale. On occasion this may have been a matter of prudence, to avoid disturbing readers who still took the traditional biblical chronology for granted.[14] But a more general reason was the scarcity of evidence to go on, beyond the impression given by thick piles of strata that seemed to have been deposited slowly on a former seafloor. Nonetheless, such evidence was sufficiently compelling by the late eighteenth century for many naturalists to assume implicitly—and sometimes explicitly, if only in passing—that prehuman earth history must be reckoned at least in tens or hundreds of thousands of years.

This view of a prehuman earth history of inconceivable duration was seized upon for diverse cosmological purposes. For example, the posthumous publication of Gottfried Wilhelm von Leibniz's theory of the earth *Protogaea* (1749), which had originally been intended as a prelude to a conventional human history of his patron's territories, provided a useful model for interpretations of earth history that stressed natural causes but were not eternalistic.[15] Thus the French naturalist Georges Louis Leclerc, Comte de Buffon (1707–1788), abandoned the virtual eternalism of his earlier theorizing and worked out a directional model based on analogical experiments with cooling globes. This led him to date the successive "epochs of nature," past and future, with an impressive air of precision; in his *Epoques de la nature* (1778) he gave a total of about a hundred thousand years.[16]

Although Buffon's work could seem like a secular parody of the Creation narrative, other naturalists sought to harness recent empirical results to the cause of defending the plausibility of the traditional Christian viewpoint. For example, the Swiss naturalist Jean-André Deluc (1727–1817) conceded the vast time-scale of prehuman earth history; and, even though he regarded it as peripheral to the main issues of religious concern, he absorbed it into the biblical narrative at least to his own satisfaction. He criticized eternalistic theorists like Hutton, above all for implicitly denying the biblical account of the origin and early history of mankind. In *Lettres physiques et morales* (1779) he focused his attention on the detailed evidence of "natural chronometers" derived from the observable rates of natural processes, believing these indicated that an exceptional physical disturbance—which he identified with the biblical Flood—had affected many areas of Europe only a few thousand years ago, turning seafloors into land areas. In effect, Deluc believed that in the study of the earth the issues of concern to Christians could be narrowed down to those affecting the creation and history of mankind. Within that narrowed limit, the tradition of biblical chronology remained in his opinion valid; outside it, for the epochs before the Flood and before mankind, a more symbolic interpretation of Genesis was quite acceptable (see fig. 1C). This was no simplistic compromise between Christianity and science; rather, Deluc, in seeking to defend traditional Christian beliefs from the skeptical attacks of openly antireligious *philosophes*, was trying to define just what areas of natural philosophy were of legitimate concern in maintaining those beliefs as valid guides to the meaning and conduct of life.

The inference that earth history as a whole had been inconceivably lengthy, even if human beings were relative newcomers to the scene, was not very widespread outside the small circles of naturalists engaged in this kind of study. Such conclusions certainly remained suspect among some conservative religious groups in Western societies; but this was at least partly because high estimates of the earth's antiquity were tainted by their long association with eternalistic cosmologies. Some social groups, however, found it possible to accept the idea of a high antiquity for the earth without rejecting the religious authority of the biblical writings. This was due above all to the emergence of the new critical school of biblical scholarship centered in the German cultural area. Unlike much earlier work of biblical criticism, this was not necessarily directed toward rationalistic or antireligious goals. Its conclusions could indeed be used to argue reductively that the Bible was now more worthless than ever. But alternatively it could be claimed that the new critical perspective gave even the "legendary" parts of the Bible their truly religious meaning. They could now be regarded as a precious record of early *religious* insights into the relation between mankind, the created world, and God. In any case, since the new methods treated the biblical texts as the products of diverse periods and cultures, the early chapters of Genesis, bearing a close relation to physical and historical events for which there was nonbiblical evidence, became a natural early focus of debate, as for example in J. G. Eichhorn's *Die Urgeschichte* (1779).[17]

But even if the new biblical criticism was not used in the service of antireligious cosmologies, it altered profoundly the traditional concerns of theories of the earth, because the search for physical evidence that would confirm, or undermine, the more or less literal meaning of the opening biblical narratives became irrelevant from this perspective. The Flood could be taken to have been a purely local event, and the narrative of Creation could be regarded as a prescientific story designed primarily to express in religious terms the creaturehood of the natural world and mankind. Above all, the time scale of earth history became religiously irrelevant. For those who abandoned the traditional precritical approach to the biblical texts, and with it the idea of a total earth history of only a few thousand years, it made no difference to religious belief and practice whether naturalists estimated that history in tens of thousands or hundreds of millions of years. The only religious problem was now that of finding some human meaning in those vast spans of prehuman history.

THE NEW SCIENCE OF GEOLOGY

Toward the end of the eighteenth century many naturalists engaged in the study of the earth tried to dissociate themselves from the use of their work by rival cosmological interests. In the three main cultural areas of Europe, the preferred terms for the study of the earth became *Geognosie, géographie physique,* and (somewhat later) *geology.* Such terms marked a firm rejection of large-scale theorizing and a new emphasis on the value of cumulative observation, at a time when the economic value of mineral surveying was becoming apparent. The new empiricist rhetoric was therefore not socially neutral. It expressed an attempt to establish the study of the earth as a practical pursuit that would be free of cultural pressures from *either* side: from the traditional concerns of biblical chronologists *and* from the secularizing concerns of eternalistic theorists. Empiricism was justified at the time on the grounds that earlier theories of the earth had signally failed to lead to any clear progress in knowledge. But after the revolution in France in the late eighteenth century it was strongly reinforced by widespread political suspicion of the naturalistic speculations of the *philosophes* and their antireligious cosmological goals.[18]

The new science of geology therefore emerged in the early nineteenth century as a strongly bounded field of knowledge, conspicuous for what it did *not* contain. Geologists (as they may now at last be called without anachronism) excluded as unscientific almost all that had previously made the earth rich in cosmological meaning: the origin of the earth, its ultimate fate, and, above all, the origin and early history of mankind (see fig. 1D). Within its self-imposed frontiers, however, geology developed its cognitive heartland with great practical success. Local sequences of strata were classified in terms of a programmatically global sequence of Systems (Carboniferous, Silurian, etc.), which were accepted as the records of a sequence of corresponding Periods of literally immeasurable length. Deluc's unique, recent diluvial event was generalized into a notion that such catastrophes had been a repeated feature of the earth's history; and this was used by the French zoologist Georges Cuvier (1769–1832) and others to account for the apparently abrupt changes in fossil animals and plants between adjacent sets of strata. Far from bringing the supernatural into geology, this so-called catastrophism turned even the puzzling Flood or Deluge into one of a series of natural events, as can be seen, for example, in Léonce Elie de Beaumont's *Sur les révolutions du globe* (1829–1830). Geology, with its carefully maintained cosmological neutrality, was prized as a science in which Christians of all denominations, together with freethinkers and those who were later termed agnostics, could cooperate amicably. At least in Europe, if not in America, those geologists who regarded themselves as Christians generally accepted the new biblical criticism and therefore felt the age of the earth to be irrelevant to their religious beliefs. The more sensitive issue of the origin of mankind—and, by implication, the nature of human beings as creatures in God's image— was effectively excluded by the newly drawn boundaries of geology.

It should be added, however, that this did not seem at the time to be avoiding the issue, because human remains were conspicuously absent from even the geologically recent diluvial deposits.

In the early nineteenth century, therefore, geologists opened up with increasing self-assurance an astonishing drama of vanished worlds that had been inhabited by strange, extinct organisms. They set this drama within an assumed time-scale that dwarfed even the whole history of civilization (see fig. 1D). In popularized form this new drama of earth history was eagerly absorbed by many among the wider public. But not all were prepared to accept on trust what ran so strongly counter to both tradition and common sense.

MOSAIC GEOLOGY

In conscious opposition to the self-styled philosophical (i.e., scientific) geologists, a so-called scriptural or Mosaic geology emerged, in which the cognitive validity of the biblical narrative was reasserted in terms inherited from the biblical chronology of the sixteenth and seventeenth centuries. Mosaic geology was so called because its proponents retained the precritical view that Genesis and the rest of the Pentateuch had been written under divine inspiration by Moses himself. It flourished more in the English-speaking world, including the United States, than in continental Europe, probably because critical methods of interpretation were accepted earlier and more widely among intellectual Christians on the Continent. Mosaic geologies ranged from work by erudite, though precritical, biblical scholars down to the most unsophisticated popularizations, from theories supported by at least some empirical fieldwork down to books by those who had never studied a rock or a fossil at first hand. What united all these writers was the conviction that Genesis, if rightly interpreted, embodied an authoritative narrative account of the origin and history of the earth and mankind. But the contrast that they frequently expressed between the "fanciful" theories of the geologists and their own "commonsense" conclusions shows that more was involved than simple religious or social conservatism. The geologists' startling assertions about earth history were indeed derived from increasingly esoteric inferences that the ordinary person could no longer follow easily. Mosaic geology was, therefore, in part a cultural reaction to the social and cognitive exclusion of all but self-styled experts from an area of speculation that, in the heyday of theories of the earth, had been open to all.

The scientific geologists claimed to regard Mosaic geology as marginal to science and worthy only of derision. But in fact they took very seriously its threat to the cognitive and social status of their own enterprise. This is shown particularly by their reaction to any work from within their own social circle that transgressed the tacit boundaries of the science. Early in the century, for example, Cuvier's extension of Deluc's arguments for the historicity of a recent Flood event was widely criticized on just these grounds. Cuvier argued for the low antiquity of civilization—and, by implication, of mankind—by comparing the records of all ancient civilizations. Although he was probably no orthodox Christian, and although he used the biblical records with all the scholarly impartiality of the German biblical critics, his excursion into chronology seemed to others to imperil the cosmological neutrality of geology.[19] This was particularly the case because, when imported into the English-speaking world in Robert Jameson's edition of the *Theory of the Earth* (1813), Cuvier's work was used openly to reassert the literal authority of the Bible. Cuvier's English follower William Buckland (1784–1856) met with a similar critical response, when he argued in *Reliquiae Diluvianae* (1823) for the historicity of a recent, though nonmiraculous, Flood event, basing his case in large part on a detailed study of a supposedly antediluvial hyena den. Such episodes seem, however, to reflect highly specific social circumstances. Buckland's diluvialism, for example, was evoked by a local situation at Oxford, in which he felt he had to defend the new science of geology from the old charge that such speculations encouraged religious skepticism. Once that social threat receded, he quietly dropped his claim that geology gave evidence of a universal Flood event, and later became one of the first geologists to support Louis Agassiz's (1807–1873) theory of a recent Ice Age as a better explanation of the puzzling diluvial phenomena.[20]

The famous remark by the British geologist Charles Lyell (1797–1875) that he was determined to "free the science from Moses" therefore needs to be interpreted in its proper context. Other geologists, whether Christians or freethinkers, agreed with Lyell that the cognitive boundaries of geology needed to be maintained in order to exclude Mosaic geology and its practitioners. They also agreed that scientific geologists such as Buckland, who—for whatever reason—transgressed those boundaries, did the science a disservice. But this exercise in boundary maintenance reflected a conflict not between science and religion but between one social group and another. The geologists were struggling for a cultural place in the sun, for greater social recognition of their cultural authority, in competition with older elites. In the early nineteenth century they did not represent antire-ligious interests but rather those of a pragmatic alliance between lib-eral Christians, whom even Lyell accepted as "enlightened saints," and a varied assortment of freethinkers; both groups valued geology especially for its potential practical utility.

SCIENTIFIC NATURALISM

Within the cognitive boundaries of early-nineteenth-century geology, one cosmological gloss won widespread acceptance because it was not socially divisive. This related not to Genesis but to natural the-ology. Geology, or more particularly the analysis of extinct organisms preserved as fossils, gave a new temporal dimension to the sense of divine design in the world. The traditional static concept of design was dramatically enlarged by the understanding that divine provi-dence had underlain equally all the successive phases of earth history, even before the existence of mankind, a view expressed, for example, in Buckland's Bridgewater treatise on *Geology and Mineralogy Consid-ered with Reference to Natural Theology* (1836). In this way cosmological meaning could be attributed to the vast prehuman history that geology had opened up. Rather than being socially divisive, this perspective, because it was so broad, acted as a social cement between conflicting religious groups.[21] It was acceptable to a deistically inclined geologist like Lyell, with his uniformitarian or virtually eternalistic theory of earth history, as well as to a quite explicitly Christian geologist such as Adam Sedgwick. And any geologist privately inclined to a more materialistic viewpoint, like the young Charles Darwin (1809–1882), could simply omit the rhetoric of design, leaving his geology unim-paired in the eyes of others.

A second cosmological interpretation of geology was, however, more debatable and had more divisive implications. The general belief among geologists that the earth had cooled gradually in the course of its history seemed at first to be an adequate explanation of an observed directional change in the character of its faunas and floras. This could readily be assimilated within the new sense of a dynamic providential design. In the middle decades of the century, however, evidence began to emerge that could be made to support the view that the history of life had been not only directional but progressive, moving from "lower" to "higher" forms independently of environ-mental change.[22] Indeed, it was possible for geologists such as Agassiz and Richard Owen (1804–1892) to attribute this to the progressive unfolding of an overarching divine design, by which the living world had slowly been prepared for its culmination in the creation of mankind. But this kind of progressionist interpretation could be radically transformed into a strictly naturalistic image of earth history. This possibility first became apparent in the *Vestiges of the Natural History of Creation* (1844) by the Scottish writer Robert Chambers (1802–1871), notwithstanding his substantial use of providentialist arguments. Chambers used the nebular hypothesis of Pierre Simon Laplace (1749–1827), in a new context of progressionist geology and evolutionary biology, to provide a naturalistic explanation of the origin of the earth and the progressive evolution of life toward mankind. It is significant that such reinterpretations of geology (and biology) in terms of the cosmology of scientific naturalism first arose among generalists like Chambers, outside the social circle of the geological specialists; for of course any such theory transgressed the cognitive boundaries that had been defined by that circle. Because such theories could not simply be ignored—Chambers's work was extremely popular among the general public—they forced open the tacit boundaries of the science and obliged geologists to respond to them in kind. If those with an ax to grind in the interests of scientific naturalism claimed that the latest geological discoveries supported that cosmology, then those concerned to defend a Christian cosmology were obliged to show how the same evidence could be interpreted differently, and to do so on the same popular level; Hugh Miller's *Footprints of the Creator* (1847) exemplifies such an effort.

In the middle decades of the nineteenth century, therefore, the frontiers of geology were reopened, as it were, at both ends of the time scale (see fig. 1D). The question of the origin of the earth was forced back into scientific discourse, though it is significant that this opening was first exploited not by geologists themselves but by physicists such as William Thomson, later Lord Kelvin (1824–1907). At the other end of their temporal territory, geologists at last accepted the evidence that human beings must have coexisted with extinct mammals in a geologically recent (but humanly remote) period, because stone implements were found with those animals' bones in circumstances that could no longer be doubted. These discoveries opened up a new conceptual space of prehistory, between the relatively well-established history of civilized literate mankind and the strictly geological history of prehuman periods (see fig. 1D). The question of the origin and antiquity of mankind could thus no longer be tacitly cordoned off from scientific geology. Yet that question, like the origin of the earth, was debated in the later nineteenth century not in terms of conflict between science and religion but between rival cosmologies. The naturalistic interpretation of human origins was neither neutral nor disinterested: it was generally used in the service of the often strident cosmology of scientific naturalism. And scientific naturalism was itself the cosmology of specific social groups, including the self-consciously professionalizing scientists, who used it as a means of wresting cultural power from the hands of older social elites, particularly, of course, the clergy.[23]

These conflicts in the later nineteenth century were more directly concerned with the relation of mankind to the rest of the animal world than with the earth as such. At this point, therefore, they pass beyond the strict limits of this essay. The specific question of the age of the earth did arise once more in the mid-nineteenth century, but only in this biological context was it of cosmological significance. Ever since the rise of geology with its self-imposed cognitive limitations, there had been a tacit embargo on quantitative estimates of geological time. As the Prussian naturalist Alexander von Humboldt (1769–1859) had put it in his *Essai géognostique* (1823), such estimates belonged to "géologues hebraizans," that is, to Mosaic geologists. Geologists got on very well without quantitative estimates; and by the middle of the century Lyell's explanatory use of unquantified but virtually limitless time had been assimilated into much routine geological practice. The quantitative magnitude of the time scale reemerged into scientific discourse only after Darwin in *The Origin of Species* (1859) hitched his concept of natural selection to a Lyellian concept of geological time and used natural selection in the service of a far-reaching naturalistic theory of species change and, implicitly, of the origin of mankind. Darwin rashly committed himself in print to a "guesstimate" of geological time that even modern geologists would find extravagant.[24] This gave his contemporaries the opportunity to attack his theory at a weak point on impeccably scientific grounds, though in reality their reasons for doing so were no more disinterested cosmologically than his. On the basis of observed rates of sedimentation, for example, geologists such as John Phillips (1800–1874) estimated the total age of all preserved strata to be on the order of a hundred million years. They found this estimate gratifyingly compatible with those proposed by Kelvin for the total age of the earth, using the quite independent evidence of the thermodynamic history of the sun.[25] In the face of such a consensus on the relatively limited time scale of earth history, natural selection seemed to be eliminated from being a plausible motor for evolutionary change. But the dynamic behind this criticism lay in opposition not to evolutionary theories in general but to the particular form of Darwin's theory, in which "blind chance" seemed to play such a crucial role and providential design was apparently excluded from organic nature. Still less was the scientists' opposition to Darwin's geological time scale rooted in any desire to reinstate the time scale of precritical biblical chronology. Such an attempt did indeed continue throughout the nineteenth century, but only in the tradition of Mosaic geology, not among those whose work was accepted within the circle of scientists. And even Mosaic geology was pushed inexorably into an increasingly marginal position, both cognitively and socially, as the intellectual spokesmen for Christian opinion, even in the English-speaking world, abandoned precritical forms of biblical interpretation and restated their beliefs in terms that took account of the newer critical methods.

CONCLUSION

Soon after 1900 Kelvin's ever more restrictive estimates of geological time were burst open by the discovery of radioactivity in rocks. But by then the question had lost all its earlier associations with rival religious and secularist cosmologies. The great expansion of estimates of the age of the earth during the twentieth century (to their present level of several billions of years) facilitated the revival of Darwinian interpretations of evolutionary theory, but it had no new religious implications. For Christians who accepted critical methods of interpretation in their understanding and practical use of the biblical documents, the religious meaning of texts such as the Creation narrative remained undisturbed by changing estimates of the quantitative magnitude of earth history or the history of mankind. Some individual scientists did assert that those histories bore a deeper cosmological meaning; the Catholic priest and paleontologist Pierre Teilhard de Chardin (1881–1955), for example, argued for a religious interpretation, while the French biologist Jacques Monod (1910–1976) favored an antireligious one. But neither assertion found general support among scientists; to most of them, either conclusion seemed evidently imposed on the scientific evidence rather than derived from it. More clearly than ever, any such cosmological gloss could be seen to represent an individual decision to attribute a certain set of values to a scientific story of earth history that in itself was geared to far more limited cognitive goals.

Yet this modest and perhaps tame conclusion continues to be challenged from two opposed directions. On the one hand there are the successors of the strident nineteenth-century proponents of scientific naturalism, such as Monod, who insist that the scientific story does carry an intrinsic cosmological implication, namely an atheistic one. And on the other hand there are the successors of the equally strident nineteenth-century proponents of biblical literalism, who insist that the scientific story is radically false because it is incompatible with their own "scientific" evidence and with a precritical method of interpreting the Bible. Such Christian fundamentalism, including its component strand of creationism, has become in recent years a powerful cultural force in some Western societies—for example, in the United States and the Netherlands (see chapter 16). But it has been evoked, at least in part, by the way that a few scientists have made well-publicized and often arrogant claims to a privileged monopoly in the attribution of human meaning to the natural world.

Late-twentieth-century Christians who reject the precritical assumptions of the fundamentalists find it necessary to steer a difficult middle course between this Scylla and Charybdis. But so do late-twentieth-century agnostics who reject the arrogant scientistic pretensions of the new scientific naturalists. Being in the same boat, those two groups can probably agree about the present outcome of the earlier debates on the origin and history of the earth and of mankind's place in it, namely that Christian beliefs about the meaning and conduct of human lives have no legitimate point of contact of any significance with the modern scientific story of earth history. This is not because mainstream Christian theology has compromised with atheistic secularism, as the fundamentalists claim. Nor is it because orthodox Christianity has been defeated in a conflict with science, as the new scientific naturalists claim. The true reason, I suggest, is twofold. First, earth scientists as a social group have *collectively* chosen the historical option of abandoning any cosmological ambitions, as the most effective route to the achievement of more limited cognitive and technical goals. And second, mainstream Christian theologians have recognized that the religious meaning of biblical texts is to be found in terms of whatever input from a "God-labeled" source (that is, in traditional language, revelation) may be embodied in the religious insight of the ancient cultures that produced those texts.[26] Of course the Christian and the agnostic are likely to differ profoundly in their estimate of the cognitive and practical value of that insight for the construction of individual and social lives in the modern world. But that is another story.

NOTES

I am under an obligation to state that the work for this paper was begun while I was still Professor of the History and Social Aspects of Science at the Vrije Universiteit, Amsterdam, the Netherlands. Preliminary versions of the paper were given to colloquia at the Science Studies Unit, Edinburgh University, and the Department of History and Philosophy of Science, Cambridge University; I am grateful to those who made helpful comments and suggestions on these earlier occasions, as well as at the conference at Madison. Neal Gillespie and Jim Moore made valuable written comments on the draft discussed at the conference.

1. James R. Moore, *The Post-Darwinian Controversies: A Study of the Protestant Struggle to Come to Terms with Darwin in Great Britain and America, 1870–1900* (Cambridge: Cambridge Univ. Press, 1979), part 1, gives a valuable account of the polemical contemporary context of these works.

2. For further discussion of this point of view see Martin Rudwick, "Senses of the Natural World and Senses of God: Another Look at the Historical Relation of Science and Religion," in *The Sciences and Theology in the Twentieth Century*, ed. A. R. Peacocke (London: Routledge & Kegan Paul, 1981), pp. 241–261.

3. This point is well made by Mary Hesse, "Criteria of Truth in Science and Theology," in her *Revolutions and Reconstructions in the Philosophy of Science* (Hassocks: Harvester Press, 1980), chap. 10.

4. For work that explores the extension of the term *cosmology* beyond its original anthropological setting see, for example, Mary Douglas, *Implicit Meanings* (London: Routledge & Kegan Paul, 1975). The same notion is used in the context of the history of science in Barry Barnes and Steven Shapin, eds., *Natural Order: Historical Studies of Scientific Culture* (Beverly Hills, Calif.: Sage Publications, 1979). I deliberately avoid the contentious term *ideology* in this context.

5. See Anthony T. Grafton, "Joseph Scaliger and Historical Chronology: The Rise and Fall of a Discipline," *History & Theory* 14 (1975): 156–185; and J. D. North, "Chronology and the Age of the World," in *Cosmology, History, and Theology*, ed. Wolfgang Yourgrau and Allen D. Breck (New York: Plenum Press, 1977), pp. 307–333.

6. See Don Cameron Allen, *The Legend of Noah: Renaissance Rationalism in Art, Science and Letters* (Urbana: Univ. of Illinois Press, 1949); Arnold Williams, *The Common Expositor: An Account of the Commentaries on Genesis, 1527–1633* (Chapel Hill: Univ. of North Carolina Press, 1948); and Janet Browne, *The Secular Ark: Studies in the History of Biogeography* (New Haven: Yale Univ. Press, 1983).

7. See Martin Rudwick, *The Meaning of Fossils: Episodes in the History of Palaeontology*, 2d ed. (New York: Science History Publications, 1976), chaps. 1 and 2.

8. On the close relation between naturalists and antiquarians see Cecil J. Schneer, "The Rise of Historical Geology in the Seventeenth Century," *Isis* 45 (1954): 256–268; and Paolo Rossi, *The Dark Abyss of Time: The History of the Earth and the History of Nations from Hooke to Vico* (Chicago: Univ. of Chicago Press, 1984).

9. The political context of Burnet's chiliastic expectation of an imminent millennium is explored in Margaret C. Jacob and Wilfrid A. Lockwood, "Po-

litical Millenarianism and Burnet's *Sacred Theory*," *Science Studies* 2 (1972): 265–279. Burnet's scheme is elegantly summarized in visual form in the frontispiece of his book, which is reproduced in Rudwick, *Meaning of Fossils*, p. 79.

10. See the important interpretative synthesis in Jacques Roger, "La theorie de la terre au XVIIe siècle," *Revue d'histoire des sciences* 26 (1973): 23–48. See also Roy Porter, "Creation and Credence: The Career of Theories of the Earth in Britain, 1660–1820," in *Natural Order*, ed. Barnes and Shapin, pp. 97–123; and "The Terraqueous Globe," in *The Ferment of Knowledge: Studies in the Historiography of Eighteenth-Century Science*, ed. G. S. Rousseau and Roy Porter (Cambridge: Cambridge Univ. Press, 1980), pp. 285–324.

11. See Marjorie H. Nicolson, *Mountain Gloom and Mountain Glory: The Development of the Aesthetics of the Infinite* (Ithaca, N.Y.: Cornell Univ. Press, 1959); and Gordon L. Davies, *The Earth in Decay: The History of British Geomorphology* (London: Macdonald, 1969).

12. Roy Porter, "George Hoggart Toulmin's Theory of Man and the Earth in the Light of the Development of British Geology," *Annals of Science* 35 (1978): 339–352.

13. I am grateful to Dr. Rhoda Rappaport for allowing me to draw on her unpublished research in this section.

14. On the absence of any consensual view see Rhoda Rappaport, "Geology and Orthodoxy: The Case of Noah's Flood in Eighteenth-Century Thought," *British Journal for the History of Science* 11 (1978): 1–18.

15. Bernhard Sticker, "Leibniz' Beitrag zur Theorie der Erde," *Sudhoffs Archiv* 51 (1967): 244–259.

16. Jacques Roger, ed., "Buffon: Les epoques de la nature, edition critique," *Mémoires du Muséum d'histoire naturelle*, n.s., ser. C, 10 (1962). Privately, Buffon suspected that the true time scale was even longer.

17. My interpretation of the precritical concept of biblical narrative, and of the way it was supplanted by critical methods of interpretation, is much indebted to Hans W. Frei, *The Eclipse of Biblical Narrative: A Study in Eighteenth and Nineteenth Century Hermeneutics* (New Haven: Yale Univ. Press, 1974).

18. See Roy Porter, *The Making of Geology: Earth Science in Britain, 1660–1815* (Cambridge: Cambridge Univ. Press, 1977).

19. See Dorinda Outram, *Georges Cuvier: Vocation, Science and Authority in Post-Revolutionary France* (Manchester: Manchester Univ. Press, 1984).

20. See Nicolaas A. Rupke, *The Great Chain of History: William Buckland and the English School of Geology, 1814–1849* (Oxford: Clarendon Press, 1983); Martin Rudwick, "The Glacial Theory," *History of Science* 8 (1970): 136–157.

21. See John H. Brooke, "The Natural Theology of the Geologists: Some Theological Strata," in *Images of the Earth: Essays in the History of the Environmental Sciences*, ed. L. J. Jordanova and Roy S. Porter (Chalfont St. Giles: British Society for the History of Science, 1979), pp. 39–64.

22. For the earlier interpretation of progression see Martin Rudwick, "Uniformity and Progression: Reflections on the Structure of Geological Theory in the Age of Lyell," in *Perspectives in the History of Science and Technology*, ed. Duane H. D. Roller (Norman: Univ. of Oklahoma Press, 1971), pp. 209–227; for the later or true progressionism see Peter J. Bowler, *Fossils and Progress:*

Paleontology and the Idea of Progressive Evolution in the Nineteenth Century (New York: Science History Publications, 1976).

23. See, for example, Frank M. Turner, "The Victorian Conflict between Science and Religion: A Professional Dimension," *Isis* 69 (1978): 356–376.

24. J. D. Burchfield, "Darwin and the Dilemma of Geological Time," *Isis* 65 (1974): 300–321.

25. See Joe D. Burchfield, *Lord Kelvin and the Age of the Earth* (New York: Science History Publications, 1975).

26. For a reinterpretation of revelation framed in these terms see John Bowker, *The Sense of God: Sociological, Anthropological and Psychological Approaches to the Origin of the Sense of God* (Oxford: Clarendon Press, 1973).

13
Geologists and Interpreters of Genesis in the Nineteenth Century

James R. Moore

Let no man upon a weak conceit of sobriety or an ill-applied moderation think or maintain, that a man can search too far, or be too well studied in the book of God's word, or in the book of God's works, divinity or philosophy; but rather let men endeavor an endless progress or proficience in both; only let men beware . . . that they do not unwisely mingle or confound these learnings together.

Our saviour saith, "You err, not knowing the scriptures, nor the power of God"; laying before us two books or volumes to study, if we will be secured from error; first the scriptures, revealing the will of God, and then the creatures expressing his power; whereof the latter is a key unto the former: not only opening our understanding to conceive the true sense of the scriptures, by the general notions of reason and rules of speech; but chiefly opening our belief, in drawing us into a due meditation of the omnipotency of God, which is chiefly signed and engraven upon his works.
—Sir Francis Bacon, 1605

THE BACONIAN COMPROMISE

When Sir Francis Bacon (1561–1626), the new counsel to King James I, set forth his doctrine of the "two books" in 1605, he served writ on the Renaissance universe. Previously philosophers seldom drew the sharp distinction between the visible marks that God had stamped upon the surface of the earth, so that its inner secrets could be known, and the legible words that the Scriptures set down in the books preserved by tradition. In nature and the Bible there were simply "signs to be discovered and then, little by little, made to speak." The signs formed "one vast single text," and their truth, correctly deciphered (*divinatio*) or read (*eruditio*), was "everywhere the same: coeval with the institution of God."[1] But Bacon held no brief for this method of interpretation. It mistook the resemblance of things for reality, it made idols of mere words, and it impeded physical discovery. Things and words, Bacon believed, must be carefully distinguished, for things themselves cannot speak directly to the mind; and words, which are invented, merely represent them more or less accurately. Things must be studied in their own right, empirically and systematically, in order to restore through human words the cognitive harmony between mind and nature that was disrupted by the Fall. The true and certain knowledge thus gained will elicit religious belief by articulating the divine omnipotence "chiefly signed and engraven" on God's works in nature. It will also elicit understanding of God's own words, "understanding to conceive the true sense of the scriptures, by the general notions of reason and rules of speech." For Bacon the book of God's works is "a key" to the book of God's word; students of nature may therefore instruct interpreters of the Bible. To reverse the relationship and attempt to make things in nature conform to words in the Scriptures would be to "unwisely mingle or confound these learnings together."[2]

The doctrine of the two books was a *modus vivendi*, a political compromise offering illustrations of the divine omnipotence, the true sense of the Scriptures, and recovery from the noetic effects of the Fall in exchange for the freedom of students of nature from harassment by interpreters of biblical texts. Commended by the salutary example of Galileo, and by his pleading in the "Letter to the Grand Duchess Christina" (1615)—"having arrived at any certainties in physics, we ought to utilize these as the most appropriate aids in the true exposition of the Bible"—the Baconian compromise became a convention in English-speaking scholarship for more than two hundred years: the basis of congenial relations between naturalists and exegetes, and a chief sanction for the growth in volume and expertise of physical research.

In the seventeenth century, natural philosophers like Robert Boyle and Isaac Newton adhered to the Baconian compromise, while Thomas Sprat employed it apologetically in likening the new-formed Royal Society to the Church of England: "each of them passing by the *corrupt Copies,* and referring themselves to the perfect *Originals* for their instruction; the one to the Scripture, the other to the large Volume of the *Creatures.*" The authors of speculative cosmogonies, or "theories of the earth," which remained in vogue through the seventeenth and eighteenth centuries, seldom agreed among themselves, but they were united in support of the doctrine of the two books. Their attempts at collation differed notoriously because few of the theorists felt compunctions about stretching Genesis every which way to fit natural-historical facts. By the early years of the nineteenth century the Baconian compromise had been consolidated in the nascent science of geology. Empirical and exegetical investigations were more carefully differentiated (a few lingering Christian cosmogonists to the contrary notwithstanding), and a sober preference for facts over fruitless theories was seen as most becoming in those who would guard their increasingly specialist knowledge from association with contentious religious and political issues.[3]

If the evidence of James Hutton (1726–1797) should compel acceptance of the earth's great antiquity, then a theologian like Thomas Chalmers (1780–1847) would obligingly prize apart the first two verses of Genesis—the so-called "gap theory"—to allow for extra time. Or if the strict empiricism of Georges Cuvier (1769–1832) should punctuate prehistory with a series of sudden geographical upheavals, then Christian geologists like Robert Jameson (1774–1854) and William Buckland (1784–1856) would rush to vindicate their emerging profession by baptizing the latest of the "*révolutions*" as the Genesis Flood. Ill considered though these accords proved to be, they promoted the autonomy and respectability of a scientific discipline—the very "advancement of learning"—by observing the Baconian compromise. Geologists would gladly expound God's word and exhibit God's works if left to get on with their job. Buckland may have been overzealous in construing Cuvier's localized evidence to be that of a universal deluge, but he nevertheless sought to justify his endeavor with Bacon's famous text. One did not "unwisely mingle or confound" the two books, he argued, by showing that geological phenomena are "in no way inconsistent with the *true* spirit of the Mosaic cosmogony." Geology, after all, could prove the fact of a universal deluge "had we never heard of such an event from Scripture, or any other authority."[4]

In Victorian Britain and America Bacon achieved beatification for his belief in progress, for his utilitarian and empirical philosophy, and for his inductive method, which was heralded as the bulwark of traditional views in science and the universal means of acquiring truth.[5] Considering the strength of his reputation, one might naturally suppose that the doctrine of the two books was also well received.

But on the contrary: in an age when Bacon was specially honored, perhaps as never before, his historic compromise erupted into controversies over the jurisdiction of interpreters of Genesis in geological inquiry, and, conversely, over the jurisdiction of geologists in delimiting the "true sense" of Genesis. How and why this happened, and how the controversies were resolved, are the main themes of this essay.

TOWARD A CRITICAL HERMENEUTICS

The story of "Genesis and geology" has become part of the mythology of the history of science. Ancient ideas and modern theories did battle for half a century or more as geology was progressively liberated from the shackles of the primitive Hebraic cosmogony. Around 1800 "Vulcanists" and "Neptunists" argued over the primacy of fire and water as agents of geological change, while naturalists and theologians pondered the extinct fossil species being uncovered in the earth's crust. Those who favored a watery extermination saw the Mosaic Deluge as the universal solvent for geological problems, but after 1830 others were convinced that earth history had been a good deal longer and more complex. Had the causes of geological change been "uniform" or "catastrophic," natural or miraculous? Had they produced an eternal steady state or did the emerging geological column reveal a progressive historic process? Whatever the case, Genesis had to be reinterpreted so as not to conflict with the discoveries of modern science. By midcentury nearly everyone who wrote on the subject agreed that the global Flood should be drained of its influence—a "partial" inundation somewhere in the Fertile Crescent would fit the Genesis narrative just as well. They also agreed that earth history had been unimaginably vast—the aeons could be interpolated in a pre-Adamic creation (the "gap theory" again), by extending the Genesis "days" (the "day-age theory"), or through loopholes in the genealogies preceding the Flood narrative. The book of Genesis, after all, had been "accommodated" to the viewpoint of its original audience. One should not seek there what can now be discovered by scientific methods.

This story, hallowed by repetition, is not entirely wrong, but it is scarcely the last word. Increasingly historians, like the critic of Hegelian philosophy, have viewed it as "a ballet of bloodless categories." In recent years there has been a movement not only to blur the distinction between the putatively "religious" and "scientific" aspects of the debates but to humanize and, more important, to socialize the various partisans caricatured in the conventional account. If science may be said to represent a special kind of politics, then the history of science can be nothing less than the history of the power blocs and interest groups who constitute society's knowledge. On this premise, or something like it, historians have begun remaking the story of Genesis and geology, and the present essay is intended to assist with the task.

Having established the prevalence of the Baconian compromise— the doctrine of the two books—at the beginning of the nineteenth century, it is necessary to situate the problem of interpreting the book of Genesis within the history and philosophy of hermeneutics. Hermeneutics is the science of interpretation. In this science, as in others, it had long been customary to regard the object of inquiry as something quite distinct from the inquiring subject. The question of *how* a text should be understood, for example, was settled traditionally by appeal to formal rules of interpretation or to agreed historical and philological techniques. *Who* might interpret a text was of little consequence for understanding it, provided that the person had the requisite skills and could relate imaginatively and sympathetically to the author. The foremost advocate of such objectively and universally valid interpretation of texts was the German theologian Friedrich Schleiermacher (1768–1834), but by the end of the nineteenth century his "scientific hermeneutics" was being seriously questioned. Philosophers had come to realize that *who* interprets a text has everything to do with *how* it is interpreted; and in the twentieth century this insight led some to assert the radical historicity of every textual interpretation either in relation to the interpreter's linguistic "tradition" or, more recently, in relation to the social "interests" that the language of each tradition represents. This latter approach to the interpretation of texts, known as "critical hermeneutics," proposes the difficult but hopeful task of connecting text and interpretation with the patterns of "language, labour, and domination" that shape the interpreter's ideology and social identity.[6]

Now when the book of Genesis is viewed in a "critical" perspective, the text immediately appears both as a prime piece of ideological property and as a strategic territory for turning to further ideological account. Starting at the beginning, as the uninitiated are apt to read the Bible, Genesis is the first document they encounter. And every story, without exception, that they read in the first eleven chapters has been understood to furnish some rationale or etiological explanation for the existing arrangements of nature and society. The uniqueness of human beings (1:26–27; 2:7, 21–23), their warrant to populate and dominate the earth (1:28), their willfulness as the source of natural and moral evil (3:1–22), and their obligation to labor as the penalty for sin (3:17–19)—these are the fundamental doctrines. Then on this basis of Creation and Fall an entire social system takes shape: marriage and the family (2:24; 4:1–25; 5:1–5), sexual modesty (2:25; 3:7, 11, 20; 9:22–27), the subordination of females (2:18, 3:16) and of Negroes as slaves (9:22–27), observance of the Sabbath (2:1–3), retributive justice (3:14–19; 4:11–12; 6:7, 12–13), and capital punishment (9:5–6), all within a promised secure natural order (8:21–22; 9:11–17). The legitimating power of the Genesis stories, moreover, may be thought to depend on their historicity, not simply because so-called mythical people like Adam and Noah can have no place in the genealogies of real ones, like Jesus and oneself, but because in the New Testament the stories provide analogues of critical historical events like the Crucifixion (Romans 5:12–17) and the Last Judgment (Matthew 24:37–39), events that serve in turn as the bases of further ethical injunctions, such as the appeal to lead godly and otherworldly lives (2 Peter 2:5–9; 3:5–13). What is at stake, therefore, in the interpretation of Genesis cannot be merely the historicity of ancient narratives, or the doctrine of biblical inspiration, or even the systems of theology based on an inspired historical record of Creation, Fall, and Deluge. From a critical perspective it can be argued that the ultimate issue is nothing less than the social order, its character and sanctions, as dependent on human nature, created and corrupt.[7]

If the interpretation of Genesis takes on significance primarily because of the text's outstanding potential for ideological development, then it makes sense to ask about the collective identities of those who have shown a proprietary interest in the matter. It is well known, for example, that courtly exegetes in the antebellum southern United States interpreted the so-called Hamitic curse of Genesis 9 as the divine sanction for a social institution otherwise justified by science: the enslavement of Negroes as a race. And lately historians have begun to show how, a century earlier, John Hutchinson (1674–1736) and his High Church followers devised an anti-Newtonian "biblical" natural philosophy, based on the opening verses of Genesis, as an "ideological response" to the alliance of Latitudinarian politics with Newtonianism after the revolution of 1688/89.[8] Further studies of these episodes in the history of interpretation might be undertaken from the standpoint of a critical hermeneutics, but the work to date clearly suggests the possibility of a critical perspective on the Victorian controversies among geologists and interpreters of Genesis. The main themes of this essay will therefore be pursued in answering the question: What social groupings become apparent among these individuals as the controversies unfold?

PROFESSIONAL DISPARITIES

Geologists first forged a collective identity at the turn of the nineteenth century. The Geological Society of London, founded in 1807, provided a genteel atmosphere for hammering out conceptual and methodological problems in a normative discourse that proclaimed its members' interest in the independence and objectivity of their research. Prominent among the coterie of gentlemen and academics who dominated the Society in its early decades was Charles Lyell (1797–1875), a former law student who had studied geology with Buckland at Oxford. Lyell, seeing that there was yet some confusion as to the "principle of reasoning" in the science, undertook to define what it would mean henceforth for geological explanations to be "scientific." His principle of extreme actualism—only those causes have operated in earth history that are now observed to operate, and only with the intensities now observed—was formulated in the late 1820s and applied systematically in his *Principles of Geology* (1830–1833). Far from polarizing the community of geologists, the book integrated the domain of professional knowledge and gave masterly expression to a growing consensus about geological method. If Lyell did not convert everyone to his actualistic principle, or anyone to his steady-state interpretation of geohistory, he nevertheless "cornered the market in three volume textbooks in the Earth sciences." His personal determination "to make science a profession" contributed decisively to making a profession of his science.[9]

In order to define and circumscribe geological expertise Lyell thought it necessary to rewrite the history of geology as though every path of inquiry in the science had been blocked repeatedly with Noah's ark, every thread of induction had routinely been snapped with a divine creative fiat. His polemical account, containing a scarcely veiled and indiscriminate attack on some of his colleagues, appeared in the introductory chapters of the first volume of *Principles*. As a liberal Christian Lyell was both reverent and discreet: he practically ignored the Genesis stories.[10] But those who failed to do so—or worse, tried to make Genesis teach geology—were treated with the same withering disdain that had regaled the Tory intelligentsia who read an article of his in the *Quarterly Review* three years before. Full of wonder that "such transcendent importance should be attached to every point of supposed discrepancy or coincidence between the phenomena of nature and the generally-received interpretations of the Hebrew text," Lyell had written:

> We cannot sufficiently deprecate the interference of a certain class of writers on this question who have lately appeared before the public. . . . While

they denounce as heterodox the current opinions of geologists, with respect to the high antiquity of the earth and of certain classes of organic beings, they do not scruple to promulgate theories concerning the creation and the deluge, derived from their own expositions of the sacred text, in which they endeavour to point out the accordance of the Mosaic history with phenomena which they have never studied, and to judge of which every page of their writings proves their consummate incompetence.

The threat that geological incompetence would achieve popularity led Lyell in conclusion to pass on verbatim Bacon's "admirable piece of advice" about the two books.[11] In context it reads less like Buckland's earlier self-justification, still less as it was originally intended, a prescription for social harmony, than as the challenge of an adolescent professionalism.

Although Lyell's challenge to "scriptural geologists," as his "certain class of writers" came to be called, was not overtly anticlerical, it might as well have been, judging from the controversies that ensued. A few clergymen had indeed shown themselves to be fully competent members of the Geological Society—Buckland, William Conybeare (1787–1857), and Adam Sedgwick (1785–1873), for example. But Lyell realized that in general the disparity between the expertise of clergymen as interpreters of prehistory, even from biblical texts, and that of geologists, who studied the subject in the book of nature, was of such a degree as amounts to a difference in kind. The clerical profession in the early nineteenth century offered pastoral and denominational credentials rather than scholarly ones. Its members, though educated beyond the average, had little or no specialist proficiency even in the subjects of their training.

In the United States congregational polities, evangelical priorities and the needs of an expanding frontier conspired to ensure that up to the early twentieth century half the nation's clergy had never received a professional education, or any general education beyond high school. Great steps had been taken, it is true, to enlarge and improve ministerial education in the nineteenth century through the founding of some 140 denominational colleges and universities, and more than 50 denominational seminaries, before the Civil War. The number of trained ministers rose dramatically; but for lack of qualified instruction, among other things, their standard of knowledge remained low. Biblical studies tended to be practical and dogmatic rather than critical, to be conducted in the English texts rather than the Hebrew and Greek. Where a classical education could be presupposed, often the New Testament alone was studied in the original, sometimes in conjunction with the "lower criticism," or the analysis of textual variants in order to establish authoritative readings. Methodologically, the most sophisticated exegetical theology (apart from that of the solitary Edward Robinson and a small Unitarian elite) was purely inductive and unhistorical: the assembling and classification of authoritative texts and the scrupulous generalization of their teachings. This was an enterprise not unlike that of the collectors, taxonomists, and system-builders who studied the book of nature in the century before Lyell.[12]

Biblical studies in Great Britain, where prominent, were conducted in much the same manner, but generally they suffered in direct proportion to the social status of the clergy. It was Scottish and Nonconformist churchmen, barred from Oxford and Cambridge by religious tests, who appeared after midcentury on the vanguard of professional biblical scholarship. Divinity students in Scotland began studying abroad in the 1840s. They returned from German universities full of advanced opinions, which they taught (though often apologetically) from chairs of biblical criticism established at Edinburgh in 1847, at Aberdeen in 1860, at Glasgow in 1861, and at St. Andrews about 1868. Likewise in the same period several Unitarian clergymen and lay scholars availed themselves of German expertise in writing learned critical works.[13]

In 1856 the Congregationalist minister Samuel Davidson (1807–1898), professor of biblical literature in the Lancashire Independent College at Manchester, espoused the views of German scholars in a treatise that rejected the Mosaic authorship of the entire Pentateuch. Indicted by the college authorities and various clergymen, among whom the Liverpool minister John Kelly became a spokesman, Davidson was obliged to resign his post within the year. Numerous sympathetic friends and colleagues subscribed a testimonial of three thousand pounds, and the Reverend Thomas Nicholas (1820–1879), the young, German-educated professor of biblical literature in the Presbyterian College, Carmarthen, undertook his defense against the Reverend Kelly:

> Dr. Davidson happens to be a biblical critic of long standing; and we must ask what are Mr. Kelly's qualifications? The work he . . . offhandedly pronounces upon, has been spoken of with respect by men of real attainment in this country and on the Continent. . . . Though most probably not free from many defects—what a marvel if it were!—it is yet a very remarkable production, dealing with manifold questions of great difficulty, presenting a body of erudite discussion rather unusual, and forming a *resumé* of countless opinions and theories, which none but a *literateur* [sic] thoroughly versed in modern criticism, and capable of handling it, could so speedily, (for the volume was very quickly written) and so skilfully adjust into shape. And, behold, the Rev. John Kelly is the man to take

this book in hand, form the estimate, and communicate with the author, "suggesting the course!" We must again ask, what, in all decency, must have been this gentleman's qualifications?

Kelly's own meager writing on biblical questions gave evidence of "an imperfect professional education," yet he was considered, as he considered himself, fit to assess the "critical and scholarly qualifications" of an "accomplished Professor." In these matters, Nicholas concluded, the "science" of biblical criticism must be judged in the manner of "geology, chemistry, and all experimental and natural sciences," that is, according to the prevailing "state of opinion" among learned and qualified men. Nicholas went on to become a governor of the new University College of Wales at Aberystwyth, Davidson to serve as Scripture examiner in the nonsectarian University of London. In 1893 he received a civil service pension from the High Church prime minister, W. E. Gladstone, for his lifelong contributions to biblical studies.[14]

But Davidson and Nicholas were atypical. Perhaps their case exemplifies less the enhanced prospects of biblical scholarship among Dissenters than the emerging disparity within the clerical profession between amateur exegetes and hermeneutic specialists. Among the Anglican clergy, at any rate, the disparity was even more pronounced. Educated as gentlemen at Oxford and Cambridge, they studied the classics, perhaps some mathematics, and picked up divinity along the way from several well-worn "standard" works of doctrine and apologetics. Their professors, few in number, were notoriously lax in lecturing. Voluntary examinations, though easily passed by cramming, remained unpopular until after midcentury, often being avoided as potential tests of orthodoxy or as degrading to divinity. German scholarship was ignored, Hebrew was an unfavored option, and the combined inadvertence can be explained by the likes of the Reverend E. B. Pusey, Regius Professor of Hebrew at Oxford from 1828 until his death in 1882, who recoiled from a youthful flirtation with German Old Testament criticism and, beginning in the 1830s, led the movement back to an authoritarian Mother Church.

The intellectual backwardness of Pusey's Anglo-Catholic movement and the older Evangelical party, whose members tended to value piety or zeal above learning, was both cause and consequence of the agitation for social reform during the 1830s. This agitation elicited a spate of arguments on behalf of an improved "professional education" for clergymen. One result of such arguments can be seen in the founding, within forty years, of seventeen new centers of specialized theological and pastoral instruction outside the universities. These institutions, however, were largely dominated by Anglo-Catholics and Evangelicals; they lacked the culture and facilities that in the chief universities conduced increasingly toward hermeneutic specialism. At Oxford and Cambridge officials were dilatory in taking up the liberalizing recommendations of the Royal Commissions that inquired into their academic affairs in the 1850s, but the establishment in 1869 of an honors school of theology at Oxford and the beginning of the Cambridge theological tripos in 1871, coupled with the virtual abolition of religious tests at both universities in the latter year, were perhaps the main preconditions for the emergence in England of professional biblical scholarship. Meanwhile the influential few who promoted this end joined with their Scottish and Nonconformist colleagues in importing scholarly skills.[15]

GERMANIZATION

From Germany came the hermeneutic expertise by which professional Old Testament scholars in Great Britain and America eventually distinguished themselves from clerical exegetes of Genesis. The German clergy were not of the ruling class but functioned as an educational civil service, in most cases employed by the state. Neither the state nor the Protestant churches required them to subscribe a statement of belief, and thus in the theological faculties of the great universities there had been for many years a freedom of scholarship almost unknown in British and American institutions, where professors were bound by denominational creeds through most of the nineteenth century. It was in these German theological faculties, especially at Halle, Göttingen, and Berlin, that the Old Testament first came to be studied critically and professionally, without regard for the practical needs of the ministry. The publication by J. G. Eichhorn of *Die Urgeschichte* (1779), an analysis of the early chapters of Genesis, and of his pioneering "introduction" to the Old Testament (1780–1783), marks the beginning of the modern critical movement and, indeed, of the "higher criticism," or the analysis of the composite character of the Old Testament books and the order in which they and their constitutive documents were assembled. By the early decades of the nineteenth century, when efforts had just begun to improve the education of British and American clergymen, the Old Testament was being studied in Germany with a critical intensity and professionalism matched only by that of the sciences in Britain and America. Genesis in the one land was being studied in the manner of geology in the others.[16]

Intellectually, the transition to professional parity between geologists and interpreters of Genesis in the English-speaking lands can be seen as a process of "Germanization" (a term suggested by Pusey). The Germanizing tendency in American biblical scholarship still awaits its historian, but clearly in the late 1870s the study of the Old Testament in the major eastern divinity schools and universities was being undertaken in the German manner, as "a neutral science closely allied with the fields of oriental research and the history of religions." In 1876, for example, Charles A. Briggs, who had studied at Berlin and Göttingen, became professor of Hebrew in Union Theological Seminary. The Society of Biblical Literature and Exegesis was founded in 1880, and two years later Paul Haupt, a brilliant twenty-five-year-old German scholar, began a lifetime career as director of the Oriental Seminary at Johns Hopkins University, a graduate institution established on the German model in 1876.[17]

In Britain the principal, if not initially the most prominent, Germanizers of Old Testament scholarship belonged to a network of professional scientists and Broad Churchmen who had considerable influence at Oxford and Cambridge. This network of friends, colleagues, and (for the most part) Whiggish political allies has been identified as "the progressive center of English thought" in the mid-nineteenth century. The members "were not the only, or always the best, creative individuals of the period, but it was they who established or maintained—in London scientific circles, . . . in learned societies and on government advisory committees—a common professional standard of debate." Among those connected with Cambridge were the Reverend Adam Sedgwick, Woodwardian Professor of Geology, and the Reverend William Whewell (1794–1866), professor of mineralogy, then Master of Trinity College, both of whom welcomed Lyell's *Principles of Geology*, though not uncritically. Sedgwick served with the mathematician John Herschel (1792–1871) and the Reverend George Peacock (1791–1858), Lowndean Professor of Astronomy, on the Royal Commission that investigated the state of education at Cambridge. The thrust of their alliance may be judged from the fact that Peacock, their leader, had already called for the appointment of a professor of biblical criticism ten years earlier. Whewell, while opposing the Commission, agreed that the theological teaching at Cambridge was most inadequate, and in this, rather than in his defense of religious tests, he sided with his and Sedgwick's old student, Connop Thirwall (1797–1875), the first English translator of Schleiermacher and later bishop of St. David's.[18]

Like Sedgwick, Whewell, and Peacock, Thirwall was a Fellow of Trinity in the heyday of Germanophilia at the College. Together with

Julius Hare, another Fellow, he stimulated an enthusiasm for the critical historian Barthold Niebuhr (1776–1831), and for German scholarship generally, which penetrated into Oxford through the influence of the Reverend Thomas Arnold (1795–1842) and his associates. Arnold, to whom as headmaster of Rugby School the creation of a "professional ideology" in Victorian Britain has been ascribed, became the first explicit Germanizer of biblical hermeneutics in his *Essay on the Right Interpretation and Understanding of the Scriptures,* published in 1831, the year Arnold's brother "Noetic" from Oriel College, Edward Copleston, now bishop of Lllandaff, helped secure Lyell's short-lived appointment as professor of geology in King's College, London. Subsequently the *Essay* had a formative influence on A. P. Stanley (1815–1881), Arnold's favorite pupil and master-biographer, who gave currency to the term *Broad Church* as early as 1850 and became its archetypal representative as Regius Professor of Ecclesiastical History at Oxford from 1856 to 1863, and as dean of Westminster thereafter until his death. Stanley, a family friend of Sedgwick's, was secretary of the Commission of inquiry into academic affairs at Oxford, serving with the Reverend Baden Powell (1796–1860), Savilian Professor of Geometry, another of the Oriel Noetics. The Commission's recommendations were influenced, as in the case of Cambridge, by the ideal of the German university, not least because of Stanley's involvement and the evidence secured from the Reverend Benjamin Jowett (1817–1893), tutor and, much later, Master of Balliol. Jowett's desiderata—admission of Dissenters, competitive examinations, greater dependence on the state, new professorships of Hebrew, ethnology, and comparative philology *inter alia*—owed much to an acquaintance with the German university system obtained at first hand with his bosom friend, Stanley, in the summers of 1844 and 1845.[19]

In 1860 Jowett and Powell appeared among the contributors to *Essays and Reviews,* the notorious manifesto and apotheosis of Germanizing Anglican theologians that deflected criticism for a time from a book published a few months earlier, *On the Origin of Species.* Powell's essay dispensed with miracles on the venerable principle, maintained throughout the Germanizing network, that "records written in the characters of a long past epoch are left to be deciphered by the advancing light of learning and science." Jowett's contribution, "On the Interpretation of Scripture," was the longest and most important essay in the book. "Here the great sea-change of nineteenth-century theology, the passage from a sacred hermeneutic to a secular one, occurred." Taking for granted the results of German critical scholarship, Jowett—now Regius Professor of Greek—followed Schleiermacher in declaring that biblical interpretation must be empirical and actualistic. *"Interpret the Scripture like any other book"* was his principle of reasoning in hermeneutic science, a principle, not unlike Powell's, that would claim the biblical text from amateur exegetes on behalf of those who possessed the critical expertise already developed among German philologists and historians. Strategically, that is to say, Jowett's principle served the professionalization of biblical scholarship in roughly the same way as Lyell's *Principles* had served that of geology. Lyell laid claim to the book of nature, Jowett to the Scriptures, for empirical, actualistic, and specialist interpretation. Henceforth the two books could be studied professionally, in isolation, on a common methodological basis but according to an agreeable division of labor. Geologists and interpreters of Genesis need no longer compromise; now they might freely cooperate or conspire.[20]

THE BACONIAN COMPROMISE IN JEOPARDY

The Baconian compromise, like all political compromises, could be maintained only so long as the parties concerned fulfilled its terms and pursued compatible ends. So long as naturalists proved their biblical orthodoxy by furnishing evidence of God's wisdom, goodness, and power; so long as exegetes accepted from naturalists the "true sense" of the natural historical portions of the Scriptures; and so long as naturalists and exegetes alike remained content with the social relations that sustained and were sanctioned by their endeavors—to that extent the compromise prevailed. And to an overwhelming extent it did, from Bacon's time until the early decades of the nineteenth century. Biblical exegesis was indeed a naturalist's legitimate avocation—the case of Newton is well known—and clergymen typically took the lead in studying natural history. The interpretation of Bacon's two books, singly or together, was a gentlemanly pursuit to which the few were called and chosen from the upper reaches of society.

But in the context of rapid industrialization, as those of a "lofty, dignified brow and commendable horny-handedness" began, like others, to parade the independent authority of their hard-won expertise and the professionalism of their interpretations of earth history, the Baconian compromise fell into jeopardy for several decades.[21] The outcome was the dissolution of the doctrine of the two books into the division of labor that it had adumbrated from the start. For when geologists had at last distinguished themselves from amateurs

Interpreters of Genesis

Naturalists-and-Exegetes
believe
Nature interprets
Genesis*

C. 1630–1830: Baconian compromise

Scriptural Geologists	*Harmonizers*
(exegetes)	(older professional
believe	geologists)
Genesis interprets	believe
Nature	Nature interprets
	Genesis*

C. 1830–1860: Baconian compromise in jeopardy

Amateurs		*Professionals*	
scriptural	harmonizers	(Lyell	(Germanized
geologists	believe	and younger	Old Testament
believe	Nature interprets	geologists)	scholars)
Genesis interprets	Genesis*	all believe	
Nature		Nature interprets Genesis*	

C. 1860–present from compromise to hegemony

* = natural history portions only

and "practical men," their theories and techniques from those of a gentlemanly past, interpreters of Genesis had scarcely any acquaintance with the hermeneutic skills of their professional counterparts in Germany. A generation or more was to pass before Orientalists, Semitic philologists, and higher critics in Britain and America began to distinguish themselves professionally from clerical exegetes of Genesis by their academic credentials and imported skills of interpretation. In so doing they joined with geologists and other scientific professionals, not in a renewed compromise, but in an outright alliance against the common foe of meddlesome, censorious amateurs. In hermeneutics as elsewhere, the dominion of wealth and rank gave way but controversially to the hegemony of merit and expertise.

The interval between the emergence of a conceptually and methodologically integrated geological profession and the onset of the professionalization of Old Testament scholarship can be marked conveniently at 1832 by Lyell's adopted maxim, "The physical part of Geological inquiry ought to be conducted as if the Scriptures were not in existence," and at 1860 by Jowett's leading motto, "Interpret the Scriptures like any other book." This interval witnessed the efflorescence of the so-called scriptural geologists, who studied the Bible more than nature, and their opponents, the harmonizers of Genesis and geology. Scriptural geologists rejected the traditional Baconian compromise with a radical assertion of their own competence to interpret earth history from the book of Genesis alone, sometimes with geological facts (usually obtained at second hand) brought in by way of illustration. They were largely preprofessionals or members of the older professions—classically educated and genteel laymen, versed in polite literature; clergymen, linguists, and antiquaries—those, in general, with vested interests in mediating the meaning of books, rather than rocks, in churches and classrooms. To them a sound classical education, with logic, perhaps mathematics as well, and a proven ability in inductive reasoning were the sole requisite skills not only for interpreting Genesis but for assessing the explanations of geologists and arbitrating among them. Thus their typical ploy of ransacking geological works for contradictory assertions, for passages of which no real understanding is shown but which serve admirably to exercise and display the interpreter's own proficiency in logic and linguistics.[22]

Many scriptural geologists no doubt were also deeply concerned that ordinary people should be able to extract a true history of the earth from the Bible, which was after all the most widely read and circulated book at the time. With an eye on the progress of "infidelity" among the restive workers, and a troubled glance at the rising and increasingly well-educated middle classes, they foresaw only too clearly the social consequences of a general questioning or abandonment of the literal historicity of the early chapters of Genesis. Thus for scriptural geologists to lay claim to geohistory in the name of biblical inspiration or some other doctrine was hardly a matter of disinterestedly pursuing theological truth. Nor perhaps was it merely an attempt to ensure continued recognition for their traditional hermeneutic skills. It was also arguably an urgent bid to maintain socially needful interpretations of the Genesis stories, hitherto dependent on their own mediation and lately, it seemed, threatened by a band of upstarts, self-regarding professionals, who proposed to go about their work as if Genesis did not exist.[23]

The obvious recourse for many older geologists, who as yet lived by the Baconian compromise, was to vindicate their profession by pointing out how little, or how edifyingly, the results of geological inquiry affected traditional interpretations of Genesis. In recent years they had perhaps been negligent in proffering the "true sense" of the Scriptures, too comfortable in the belief that the truth of both "books" would ultimately coincide. Now, for their own good and society's— geologists also feared incompetence and infidelity—they would have to show how the Genesis narrative could be harmonized with the record in the rocks. "The earlier attempts, to square the facts to the narrative," as Baden Powell wryly observed, "have been succeeded by those to square the narrative to the facts."[24]

While in Germany an older division of labor had long since left the reconciling to a few conservative theologians, in mid-Victorian Britain and America the outstanding harmonizers of Genesis and geology were among the most eminent professional geologists. Buckland, Conybeare, and Gideon Mantell (1790–1852), as well as the popular Hugh Miller (1802–1856) and the leading naturalists of the Germanizing network, Sedgwick and Whewell, did not each condone detailed schemes of reconciliation, but all were at pains on more than one occasion to reassure their audiences, by precept or example, that although the Bible had not been intended to teach scientific truths, its statements would always be shown to harmonize with properly demonstrated theories. Indeed, this conviction was expounded by "higher geologists and higher theologians" alike (to use Miller's phrase), and the former made sure to praise the latter—most notably John Pye Smith (1774–1851)—for thus defending their profession. In North America the same conviction was advanced unremittingly through most of the century by a kind of apostolic succession of evangelical geologists: Benjamin Silliman (1779–1864), the Reverend Edward Hitchcock (1793–1864), Arnold Guyot (1807–1884), James Dwight Dana (1813–1895), and the Canadian J. W. Dawson (1820–1899). Each of them labored in one or more popular books—Dawson in a dozen—to uphold established geological theories through an acceptable reinterpretation of Genesis.[25]

But "who shall decide when a new theory is completely demonstrated, and the old interpretation become untenable?" Whewell, for one, thought the answer would "not be very difficult"; then he proceeded to gloss it. Others were less uncertain. The question went to the heart of the Baconian compromise and it would have to be settled controversially. The Reverend Moses Stuart (1780–1852), professor of sacred literature in Andover Theological Seminary, claimed not to find any geology in Genesis, and on that account he upbraided Hitchcock in 1836 for interpreting Genesis in its light. Geology was as yet an immature science. Only an exegete and philologist like Stuart could validly interpret what Moses meant, writing under divine inspiration in the common language of his time. Geologists would simply have to decide whether or not to believe the sacred writer. What Moses (Stuart) meant of course was creation in six solar days *et cetera*.[26]

Or consider the politics and pugnacity of William Cockburn (1773–1858) on the return of the British Association for the Advancement of Science in 1844 to the place of its birth at York, where he was dean of the cathedral. Eight years had passed since Buckland at Oxford quietly conceded his prize evidence for a catastrophic deluge in a footnote to his Bridgewater Treatise. Cockburn had taken him to task in a pamphlet at the time, but now Buckland's appointment to succeed Samuel Wilberforce as dean of Westminster was in the offing, and the perpetrator was none other than Cockburn's brother-in-law, the Tory prime minister Robert Peel. Apart from his crowd of followers Cockburn embarrassed nearly everyone in the Geological Section with a paper scorning Buckland's theory of creation and spinning a theory of his own, which was ostensibly faithful to the literal sense and traditional chronology of Genesis. "Oh Oxford!" he lamented; "so long the seat of learning, religion, and orthodoxy—who could have believed that out of thee should come a cherished voice leading the children committed to thy care directly to infidelity and indirectly to atheism?" Sedgwick, in response, amused the audience at Cockburn's expense. Cockburn countered with *The Bible Defended against the British Association* (1844). The pamphlet ran through four editions within a year, but Buckland got his job.[27]

And so the political struggle over hermeneutic jurisdiction went on. Locked in debate with Silliman in 1854, the Reverend Gardiner Spring (1785–1873), a prominent Presbyterian minister in New York City, felt constrained "to suspend . . . judgement on all questions which put any other construction than that which a sound philology puts upon the Mosaic narrative." The next year Tayler Lewis (1802–1877), professor of Greek and oriental literature in Union College, took up the theme with a scathing attack on the harmonizers in his *Six Days of Creation*. Geologists were expendable, just like most other nineteenth-century innovations. "Faithful and exact exegesis" alone has the right to pronounce on the meaning of Genesis. Lewis, unlike Stuart, reached the geologically acceptable conclusion that the Mosaic "days" were extended periods of time, but his viewpoint rankled none the less. In 1856 Dana, Silliman's son-in-law, struck back at Lewis acrimoniously on behalf of Buckland, Lyell, and Miller, defending geology as an independent guide to biblical interpretation. His professional colleagues applauded.[28]

Miller himself had his innings posthumously in a chapter of his *Testimony of the Rocks* (1857) entitled "The Geology of the Anti-Geologists." "As men descend in the scale of accomplishment or intellect," he began, "a nearer and yet nearer approximation takes place between their conceptions of the causes of the occult processes of nature, and the common and obvious motives which influence large masses of their fellows; until at length the sublime contrivances of the universe sink, in their interpretations of them, into the clumsy expedients of a bungling mechanism." This, however, coming from a self-educated Scottish stonemason, was a clear opening for his social superiors, and from the frontiers of biblical professionalism, at Oxford, Powell retorted loftily that although Miller had been a pioneer amid "popular prejudice," he was a "greatly overrated" man. In his speculations "the very last possible resources of biblical interpretation must be regarded as thoroughly exhausted. They are the very ghost of a defunct Biblical geology." Jowett, for the future, remarked in *Essays and Reviews:* "He who notices the circumstance that the explanations of the first chapter of Genesis have slowly changed, and, as it were, retreated before the advance of geology, will be unwilling to add another to the spurious reconcilements of science and revelation."[29]

FROM COMPROMISE TO HEGEMONY

After 1860 the fatuity and irrelevance of the scriptural geologists was plain for all to see—as witness, for example, the writings of Benjamin Wills Newton (1806–1899), an English Plymouth Brother, and of Charles Coffin Adams (1810–1888), an Episcopal clergyman in the United States. By dint of piety, prestige, and perseverance the harmonizers had secured the independent authority of the geological profession and the prerogative of its members to interpret Genesis. Whether geologists would now renew the Baconian compromise was, however, another matter. With their social role secure they could resume working "as if the Scriptures were not in existence"; and the majority of younger geologists, whom Jowett aptly characterized, found the prospect inviting. Also, as Charles Darwin was relieving naturalists of the obligation, under the compromise, to glorify God from his works, the chief supporters of this obligation, the professional harmonizers, were rapidly becoming extinct. By 1866 Mantell, Jameson, Buckland, Miller, Conybeare, Hitchcock, Silliman, Whewell, and Pye Smith had died. Dana was turning into an evolutionist, and Guyot, his mentor in matters pertaining to biblical interpretation, did not complete a book-length harmony until the eve of his passing in 1884. This left the superannuated Sedgwick, who died in 1873, and that most provincial of Presbyterians, Dawson, a solitary figure holding forth from the heights of Montreal until he and his century expired. The harmonizers would henceforth be amateurs: popular preachers and miscellaneous writers—the likes of Thomas Cooper (1805–1892), a Chartist turned Baptist, and Luther Townsend (1838–1922), an American Methodist minister—some of whom would now seek, ironically, to defend Genesis from higher critics by showing its accord with geology. Professionals had other interests and obligations, such as mutual defense against bands of marauding laymen.

Essays and Reviews precipitated the professional alliance. The book went through thirteen editions in five years, called forth in reply more than four hundred books, pamphlets, and articles, and caused Anglo-Catholics and Evangelicals at Oxford jointly to sponsor a declaration reaffirming the inspiration and authority of the Bible. After the judicial committee of the Privy Council cleared two of the authors (Rowland Williams and H. B. Wilson) of heresy charges in 1864, 11,000 clergymen signed the declaration—nearly half the clergy in England and Ireland—and the dissenting bishops on the Council were memorialized with 137,000 lay signatures. In London about the same time a group of minor scientists circulated a declaration of their own, affirming that "it is impossible for the Word of God, as written in the book of nature, and God's Word written in Holy Scripture, to contradict one another, however much they may appear to differ." The declaration was neutral as between harmonizers and scriptural geologists, skirting the issue of hermeneutic jurisdiction; and eventually 717 men, most of questionable scientific achievement, attached their names.[30]

In 1865 a number of the signatories joined in founding the "Victoria Institute, or Philosophical Society of Great Britain." The organization was intended to combat "scientific coteries" and defend "the great truths revealed in Holy Scripture . . . against the opposition of Science, falsely so-called," by giving "greater force and influence to proofs and arguments which might be regarded as comparatively weak and valueless, or be little known, if put forward merely by individuals." The membership at once became an epitome of evangelical amateurism, despite the presence of a minority with some claim to scientific professionalism. Merchants, doctors, solicitors, manufacturers, clergymen, civil servants, and military personnel graced the list of members at the first annual general meeting in 1867, among them scriptural geologists such as the founder and first principal of an Anglican theological college, Joseph Baylee, and Patrick McFarlane, an eccentric Scot. Indeed, one of the Institute's vice-presidents, Philip Henry Gosse, was the most notorious scriptural geologist at the time. Some of the names could be found as late as 1882 in the list of subscribers in Samuel Kinns's *Moses and Geology; or, The Harmony of the*

Bible with Science, a conceited volume of five hundred pages that reached a seventh edition two years later. Kinns, the principal of a preparatory college, reprinted the entire scientists' declaration of 1864 in an appendix. But at the head of the book he furnished to his personal credit the names of 15 bishops, 10 other peers, 16 members of Parliament, 64 lesser clergymen, 18 military men, perhaps a dozen marginal scientists, one or two of note, and 341 other individuals of no particular distinction.[31]

So the political threat was clear. "The ignorance of the so-called educated classes," as T. H. Huxley (1825–1895) would later call it, might well prevail over the theories of self-defining expertise if professionals did not join in upholding each other's authority. Thus in February 1861 Lyell's father-in-law, Leonard Horner (1785–1864), raised a paean to Powell in his presidential address to the Geological Society of London. Powell, a lately deceased Fellow, could scarcely have bettered Horner's subsequent bold assertion—gratuitous but for the circumstances—of geologists' jurisdiction over clerical exegetes in fixing the age of the earth. The other authors of *Essays and Reviews,* still very much alive, also received support during the month when a number of prominent scientists, including Lyell, Horner, and Darwin, subscribed an address welcoming the essayists' "attempts to establish religious teaching on a firmer and broader foundation."[32]

Then in 1862 appeared *The Pentateuch and Book of Joshua Critically Examined* by J. W. Colenso (1814–1883). It added to the furor over *Essays and Reviews*—a spate of pamphlets and the like—not least because the Germanizing author was the missionary bishop of Natal. Colenso, a small-time Hebrew scholar, had been at Cambridge in the 1830s, but he claimed to have begun a serious study of the higher criticism only after a Zulu native asked him whether he really believed the story of the Flood. The upshot was this "strict scientific treatment," in five parts, and the social ostracism of the author and his family on their return to England. But to the rescue came Sir Charles and Lady Lyell. Lyell introduced Colenso at his club, the Athenaeum, even as the bishop was being ousted from a vice-presidency of the Society for the Propagation of the Gospel; and thereafter the Lyells remained the family's closest friends and most faithful supporters in England. Colenso gave Lyell his professional dues in the last part of the *Pentateuch;* Lyell gave Colenso financial assistance when he sought redress from the Crown after an unsuccessful attempt to deprive him of his see. Other contributions to his legal expenses came from Dean Stanley, whose *Lectures on the History of the Jewish Church* (1863–1865) was then popularizing the German critic Georg Ewald, and from Huxley the episcophagous, who in reality was making episcopal friends.[33]

In 1863, as Lyell's *Antiquity of Man* and the second part of Colenso's *Pentateuch* appeared together on the book stands, the second volume of William Smith's monumental *Dictionary of the Bible* at last carried the substance of a postponed article on the Deluge. The Reverend F. W. Farrar (1831–1903), lately a student and friend of Whewell's and a Fellow of Trinity College, had written an article for the first volume maintaining that the Deluge was not universal. This view the editors found unacceptable; they first delayed, then declined to publish the piece, inserting "Deluge: see Flood," then "Flood: see Noah," at the appropriate places. When "Noah" came to hand, time had run out and the article was, if anything, worse. It not only gave up the universal Deluge; it questioned the unity and Mosaic authorship of Genesis, cited Lyell and German critics as authorities, and thanked Professor Huxley "especially, for much valuable information on the scientific questions touched upon in this article." The author was an accomplished Hebraist, the Reverend J. J. S. Perowne, vice-principal of the theological college in Thirwall's diocese and later the bishop's biographer and himself bishop of Worcester. Farrar, whose piece had been dropped, was elected a Fellow of the Royal Society in 1864 for his studies of the origin of language. His candidacy had been supported by Darwin.[34]

The "conflict between religion and science" of the late 1860s and after was an undoubted social reality, but little evidence of it seems to exist among the professional scientists and professionalizing Old Testament interpreters who were supporting, nay embracing, one another at the time. When Huxley and seven freethinking professional colleagues—together with Herbert Spencer—had constituted themselves the "X Club" in late 1864, they soon cheered up the forlorn Colenso at one of their monthly soirees. Twenty years later the same prestigious group welcomed Britain's first fully professional Old Testament scholar, the brilliant William Robertson Smith (1846–1894), who had recently undergone the sordid litigation that deprived him of his chair of oriental languages and Old Testament exegesis in the Free Church College, Aberdeen. Meanwhile Dean Stanley at Westminster served as virtual chaplain to the scientific establishment, officiating at the marriage of the X Club's John Tyndall in the Abbey and interring Herschel, Sedgwick, and Lyell there with befitting pulpit eloquence. Farrar joined Stanley as a canon in 1876 and remained after the dean's death to bear Darwin's coffin in 1882 and sermonize glowingly on his grave.[35]

Three years later Farrar delivered the Bampton Lectures at Oxford, published as *History of Interpretation* (1886). Here was no censure of science, nor timid acquiescence, but a celebration of its "irrefragable conclusions" in their bearing on biblical exegesis, an account worthy of H. T. Buckle and J. W. Draper that would beguile A. D. White into repeating its mistakes, a history of the "triumph of light over darkness, of truth over error, of faith and freedom over tyranny and persecution." Beginning in utter "incompetency"—witness the "foolish exegesis" of Genesis—biblical interpretation has passed in these latter days, according to a "law" of "eternal progress," into the hands of German theologians and their English representatives, among them Thirwall, Hare, Arnold, and Stanley. These, like the "great discoverers" of science, have been reviled and condemned by the "religious world," but withal "it remains certain that true science and true religion are twin sisters, each studying her own sacred book of God." "Let them study in mutual love and honour side by side," advised the canon and Fellow of the Royal Society, "and pronounce respecting those things which alone she knows."[36]

"Those things which alone she knows." And to think at the very time Huxley was trying to outbid the octogenarian Gladstone in the pages of the *Nineteenth Century* for the assent of "average opinion," to upstage the "copious shuffler," who had made "ignorance" a political force, by invoking the "assured results of modern biblical criticism" as to the interpretation of Genesis. "I need hardly say that I depend upon authoritative Biblical critics, whenever a question of interpretation of the text arises," Huxley confidently noted in another essay, appending a list of German names. The irony ascends when it is realized that this amateur exegete, if ever there was one, substantially devoted the last two years of his life to preparing, first, a series of workingmen's lectures, then a book for young people, on the history of biblical religion in the light of modern "scientific" scholarship. Two books and twin sisters indeed.[37]

But ironies entertained too lightly obscure real contradictions or underlying continuities. The doctrine of the two books was ever a piece of ideology, the Baconian compromise a political settlement from the start. In reality the "sister" who successfully imposes her definition of what may be known, and how, defines what the other one knows. By 1890 Huxley and his professional colleagues could interpret Genesis on their own epistemological terms, with the full complicity of professional Old Testament scholars. A view of human nature and historical progress, and a concern to uphold the freedom and prerogatives of professional experts, united them. Indeed, as keepers of the cosmology of an industrial and imperial social order, professional interpreters of the "two books" shared economic and social interests that, it may be argued, were well served by interpreting Genesis as a "primitive" account of the beginning of the world.[38]

Whether my interpretation in this essay seems promising, or even relevant, will depend in some measure on the value one attaches to a critical hermeneutics. It will also depend importantly on how one interprets latter-day challenges to the hegemony of professionals— among them, geologists and interpreters of Genesis.

NOTES

1. Michel Foucault, *The Order of Things: An Archaeology of the Human Sciences* (London: Tavistock Publications, 1970), pp. 33–34, 43. The epigraph is from Bacon's *The Advancement of Learning* (1605), 1.1.3, 1.6.16.

2. Foucault, *Order of Things*, pp. 51–52; Paolo Rossi, *Francis Bacon: From Magic to Science*, trans. Sacha Rabinovitch (Chicago: Univ. of Chicago Press, 1968), chap. 4; Lisa Jardine, *Francis Bacon: Discovery and the Art of Discourse* (Cambridge: Cambridge Univ. Press, 1974).

3. Charles E. Raven, *Natural Religion and Christian Theology*, 2 vols. (Cambridge: Cambridge Univ. Press, 1953), vol. 1, chap. 6; Frank E. Manuel, *The Religion of Isaac Newton* (Oxford: Clarendon Press, 1974), chap. 2; A. R. Peacocke, *Creation and the World of Science* (Oxford: Clarendon Press, 1979), chap. 1; Roland Mushat Frye, "The Two Books of God," *Theology Today* 39 (1982): 260–266; Rhoda Rappaport, "Geology and Orthodoxy: The Case of Noah's Flood in Eighteenth-Century Thought," *British Journal for the History of Science* 11 (1978): 13–14; Roy Porter, "Creation and Credence: The Career of Theories of the Earth in Britain, 1660–1820," in *Natural Order: Historical Studies of Scientific Culture*, ed. Barry Barnes and Steven Shapin (Beverly Hills, Calif.: Sage Publications, 1979), pp. 98–102, 107–108; Roy Porter, *The Making of Geology: Earth Science in Britain, 1660–1815* (Cambridge: Cambridge Univ. Press, 1977), pp. 196–202.

4. Martin J. S. Rudwick, *The Meaning of Fossils: Episodes in the History of Paleontology* (London: Macdonald, 1972), pp. 131–139; John Hedley Brooke, "The Natural Theology of the Geologists: Some Theological Strata," in *Images of the Earth: Essays in the History of the Environmental Sciences*, ed. L. J. Jordanova and Roy S. Porter (Chalfont St. Giles: British Society for the History of Science, 1979), pp. 39–64; William Buckland, *Vindiciae Geologicae; or, The Connexion of Geology with Religion Explained . . .* (Oxford: At the University Press for the author, 1820), pp. 23, 29, emphasis added.

5. Harold Stolerman, "Francis Bacon and the Victorians, 1830–1885" (Ph.D. diss., New York University, 1969); Theodore Dwight Bozeman, *Protestants in an Age of Science: The Baconian Ideal and Antebellum American Religious Thought* (Chapel Hill: Univ. of North Carolina Press, 1977).

6. Wilhelm Dilthey, "The Rise of Hermeneutics," and Hans-Georg Gadamer, "The Historicity of Understanding," in *Critical Sociology: Selected Readings*, ed. Paul Connerton (Harmondsworth: Penguin Books, 1976), pp. 104–116, 117–133; Jürgen Habermas, *Knowledge and Human Interests*, trans. Jeremy J. Shapiro, 2d ed. (London: Heinemann, 1978), pp. 309–313; Habermas, quoted in David Held, *Introduction to Critical Theory: Horkheimer to Habermas* (London: Hutchinson, 1980), p. 316. See also Michael Ermarth, "The Trans-

formation of Hermeneutics: 19th Century Ancients and 20th Century Moderns," *The Monist* 64 (1981): 175–194.

7. See Adrian Cunningham, "Myth, Ideology, and Lévi-Strauss: The Problem of the Genesis Story in the Nineteenth Century," in *The Theory of Myth: Six Studies,* ed. Adrian Cunningham (London: Sheed & Ward, 1973), pp. 132–136.

8. H. Shelton Smith, *In His Image, but . . . : Racism in Southern Religion, 1780–1910* (Durham, N.C.: Duke Univ. Press, 1972); E. Brooks Holifield, *The Gentlemen Theologians: American Theology in Southern Culture, 1795–1860* (Durham, N.C.: Duke Univ. Press, 1978); William Stanton, *The Leopard's Spots: Scientific Attitudes toward Race in America, 1815–1859* (Chicago: Univ. of Chicago Press, 1960); William McKee Evans, "From the Land of Canaan to the Land of Guinea: The Strange Odyssey of the 'Sons of Ham,'" *American Historical Review* 85 (1980): 15–43; C. B. Wilde, "Hutchinsonianism, Natural Philosophy, and Religious Controversy in Eighteenth Century Britain," *History of Science* 18 (1980): 11; G. N. Cantor, "Revelation and the Cyclical Cosmos of John Hutchinson," in *Images of the Earth,* pp. 3–22. See also Richard Popkin, "Biblical Criticism and Social Science," *Boston Studies in the Philosophy of Science* 14 (1974): 339–360, for the contribution of seventeenth-century critics of Genesis to the assumptions of modern social science, and George P. Landow, "The Rainbow: A Problematic Image," in *Nature and the Victorian Imagination,* ed. U. C. Knoepflmacher and G. B. Tennyson (Berkeley, Los Angeles, London: Univ. of California Press, 1977), pp. 341–369, for Genesis 9:12–17 in Victorian art and interpretation. Landow's *Victorian Types, Victorian Shadows: Biblical Typology in Victorian Literature, Art, and Thought* (Boston: Routledge & Kegan Paul, 1980) appeared too late to prove useful in this essay.

9. Porter, *Making of Geology,* pp. 202–215; J. B. Morrell, "London Institutions and Lyell's Career: 1820–1841," *British Journal for the History of Science* 9 (1976): 137–143; Martin J. S. Rudwick, "The Strategy of Lyell's 'Principles of Geology,'" *Isis* 61 (1970): 11; Michael Bartholomew, "The Singularity of Lyell," *History of Science* 17 (1979): 290. The quoted words "cornered the market . . . " are from Bartholomew.

10. Roy Porter, "Charles Lyell and the Principles of the History of Geology," *British Journal for the History of Science* 9 (1976): 91–103; Rudwick, "Strategy of Lyell's 'Principles,'" pp. 8–11; Rudwick, *Meaning of Fossils,* pp. 168–174.

11. [Charles Lyell], review of *Memoir on the Geology of Central France . . . ,* by G. P. Scrope, *Quarterly Review* 36 (Oct. 1827): 482–483.

12. Willard L. Sperry, *Religion in America* (Cambridge: Cambridge Univ. Press, 1945), p. 176; Donald G. Tewksbury, *The Founding of American Colleges and Universities before the Civil War, with Particular Reference to the Religious Influences Bearing upon the College Movement* (Hamden, Conn.: Archon Books, 1965), pp. 78–91; Robert L. Kelly, *Theological Education in America: A Study of One Hundred Sixty-One Theological Schools in the United States and Canada* (New York: George H. Doran Co., 1924); "Theological Education," in *The New Schaff-Herzog Encyclopedia of Religious Knowledge,* 12 vols. (New York: Funk & Wagnalls Co., 1910–1912), 11:335; Jerry Wayne Brown, *The Rise of Biblical Criticism in America, 1800–1870* (Middletown, Conn.: Wesleyan Univ. Press, 1969),

pp. 116–117, 124, 180–182; Bozeman, *Protestants in an Age of Science,* chap. 7. See also Donald M. Scott, *From Office to Profession: The New England Ministry, 1750–1850* (Philadelphia: Univ. of Pennsylvania Press, 1978).

13. Willis B. Glover, *Evangelical Nonconformists and Higher Criticism in the Nineteenth Century* (London: Independent Press, 1954), chap. 2; Andrew L. Drummond and James Bulloch, *The Church in Victorian Scotland, 1843–1874* (Edinburgh: St. Andrew Press, 1975), chap. 9; Dennis G. Wigmore-Beddoes, *Yesterday's Radicals: A Study of the Affinity between Unitarianism and Broad Church Anglicanism in the Nineteenth Century* (Cambridge: James Clarke & Co., 1971), chap. 2.

14. Thomas Nicholas, *Dr. Davidson's Removal from the Professorship of Biblical Literature in the Lancashire Independent College, Manchester, on account of Alleged Error in Doctrine: A Statement of Facts, with Documents; Together with Remarks and Criticisms* (London: Williams & Norgate, 1860), pp. 109, 112, 113–114, 128; Glover, *Evangelical Nonconformists and Higher Criticism,* p. 47.

15. Robert Towler and A. P. M. Coxon, *The Fate of the Anglican Clergy: A Sociological Study* (London: Macmillan Press, 1979), chap. 1; M. A. Crowther, *Church Embattled: Religious Controversy in Mid-Victorian England* (Newton Abbot: David & Charles, 1970), chap. 9; F. W. B. Bullock, *A History of Training for the Ministry of the Church of England in England and Wales from 1800 to 1874 . . .* (St. Leonards-on-Sea, Sussex: Budd & Gillatt, 1955); Brian Heeney, *A Different Kind of Gentleman: Parish Clergy as Professional Men in Early and Mid-Victorian England* (Hamden, Conn.: Archon Books, 1976).

16. Crowther, *Church Embattled,* chap. 2; Charles Augustus Briggs, *History of the Study of Theology,* 2 vols. (London: Duckworth & Co., 1916), vol. 2, chap. 4; Hans W. Frei, *The Eclipse of Biblical Narrative: A Study in Eighteenth and Nineteenth Century Hermeneutics* (New Haven, Conn.: Yale Univ. Press, 1974), chap. 8; T. K. Cheyne, *Founders of Old Testament Criticism: Biographical, Descriptive, and Critical Studies* (London: Methuen & Co., 1893), chap. 2. See also Lenore O'Boyle, "Learning for Its Own Sake: The German University as Nineteenth Century Model," *Comparative Studies in Society and History* 25 (1983): 3–25, and John Rogerson, *Old Testament Criticism in the Nineteenth Century: England and Germany* (London: SPCK, 1984), which appeared too late to prove useful in this essay.

17. George Ernest Wright, "The Study of the Old Testament," in *Protestant Thought in the Twentieth Century: Whence and Whither?* ed. Arnold S. Nash (New York: Macmillan Co., 1951), pp. 17–18. See also Ernest W. Saunders, *Searching the Scriptures: A History of the Society of Biblical Literature, 1880–1980* (Baltimore, Md.: Scholar's Press, 1980); Jurgen Herbst, *The German Historical School in American Scholarship: A Study in the Transference of Culture* (Ithaca, N.Y.: Cornell Univ. Press, 1965); Walter P. Metzger, *Academic Freedom in the Age of the University* (New York: Columbia Univ. Press, 1960), chap. 3; and Carl Diehl, *Americans and German Scholarship, 1770–1870* (New Haven, Conn.: Yale Univ. Press, 1978), pp. 77–86.

18. W. F. Cannon, "Scientists and Broad Churchmen: An Early Victorian Intellectual Network," *Journal of British Studies* 4 (1964): 65–71, 76–81, 86–88; Susan Faye Cannon, *Science in Culture: The Early Victorian Period* (New York:

Science History Publications, 1978), chap. 2; Bullock, *History of Training for the Ministry,* pp. 52–53, 66.

19. W. F. Cannon, "Scientists and Broad Churchmen"; S. F. Cannon, *Science in Culture,* chap. 2; Daniel Duman, "The Creation and Diffusion of a Professional Ideology in Nineteenth Century England," *Sociological Review,* n.s., 27 (1979): 117–122; Martin J. S. Rudwick, "Charles Lyell, F.R.S. (1797–1875) and His London Lectures on Geology, 1832–1833," *Notes and Records of the Royal Society of London* 29 (1975): 231–263; Evelyn Abbott and Lewis Campbell, *The Life and Letters of Benjamin Jowett, M.A., Master of Balliol College, Oxford,* 2 vols. (London: John Murray, 1897), 1:89 ff., 178 ff., 201. See John Burrow, "The Uses of Philology in Victorian England," in *Ideas and Institutions of Victorian Britain: Essays in Honour of George Kitson Clark,* ed. Robert Robson (London: G. Bell & Sons, 1967), pp. 180–204.

20. Crowther, *Church Embattled,* p. 64; W. F. Cannon, "Scientists and Broad Churchmen," pp. 82–84; Baden Powell, "On the Study of the Evidences of Christianity," in *Essays and Reviews,* 4th ed. (London: Longman, Green, Longman & Roberts, 1861), pp. 143–144; Ieuan Ellis, "'Essays and Reviews' Reconsidered," *Theology* 74 (1971): 401–402; Benjamin Jowett, "On the Interpretation of Scripture," in *Essays and Reviews,* p. 377. See also Duncan Forbes, *The Liberal Anglican Idea of History* (Cambridge: Cambridge Univ. Press, 1952), pp. 108, 147–148, and Burrow, "Uses of Philology in Victorian England." Ieuan Ellis's *Seven against Christ: A Study of "Essays and Reviews"* (Leiden: E. J. Brill, 1980) appeared too late to prove useful in this essay.

21. David Elliston Allen, *The Naturalist in Britain: A Social History* (Harmondsworth: Penguin Books, 1978), p. 59. See also Roy Porter, "The Industrial Revolution and the Science of Geology," in *Changing Perspectives in the History of Science: Essays in Honour of Joseph Needham,* ed. Mikuláš Teich and Robert Young (London: Heinemann, 1973), pp. 340–343.

22. Lyell, quoting "an excellent writer and skillful geologist," perhaps the Reverend John Fleming, in an extract from a lecture delivered at King's College, London, 4 May 1832, reprinted in Martin J. S. Rudwick, "Charles Lyell Speaks in the Lecture Theatre," *British Journal for the History of Science* 9 (1976): 150; Milton Millhauser, "The Scriptural Geologists: An Episode in the History of Opinion," *Osiris* 2 (1954): 65–86; Francis C. Haber, *The Age of the World: Moses to Darwin* (Baltimore: Johns Hopkins Press, 1959), pp. 219–264; Bozeman, *Protestants in an Age of Science,* chap. 5.

23. Edward Royle, *Victorian Infidels: The Origins of the British Secularist Movement, 1791–1866* (Manchester: Manchester Univ. Press, 1974), pp. 75, 119–120; Drummond and Bulloch, *Church in Victorian Scotland,* p. 222.

24. Charles Coulston Gillispie, *Genesis and Geology: A Study in the Relations of Scientific Thought, Natural Theology, and Social Opinion in Great Britain, 1790–1850* (Cambridge, Mass.: Harvard Univ. Press, 1951), pp. 223–224; Leroy E. Page, "Diluvialism and Its Critics in Great Britain in the Early Nineteenth Century," in *Toward a History of Geology,* ed. Cecil J. Schneer (Cambridge, Mass.: MIT Press, 1967), pp. 263 ff.; Baden Powell, *Christianity without Judaism: A Second Series of Essays . . .* (London: Longman, Brown, Green, Longmans & Roberts, 1857), p. 62.

25. Haber, *Age of the World*, p. 239; Martin Guntau, "The Emergence of Geology as a Scientific Discipline," *History of Science* 16 (1978): 284–287; Hugh Miller, *The Testimony of the Rocks; or, Geology in Its Bearings on the Two Theologies, Natural and Revealed* (Edinburgh: Thomas Constable & Co., 1857), p. 265; Herbert Hovenkamp, *Science and Religion in America, 1800–1860* (Philadelphia: Univ. of Pennsylvania Press, 1978), chap. 7; Ronald L. Numbers, "Arnold Guyot and the Harmony of Science and the Bible," *Proceedings of the XIVth International Congress of the History of Science* (Tokyo, 1975), 3:239–242; Michael Laurent Prendergast, "James Dwight Dana: The Life and Thought of an American Scientist" (Ph.D. diss., University of California, Los Angeles, 1978); Charles F. O'Brien, *Sir William Dawson: A Life in Science and Religion* (Philadelphia: American Philosophical Society, 1971), chap. 3.

26. William Whewell, *The Philosophy of the Inductive Sciences, Founded upon Their History*, new ed., 2 vols. (London: John Parker, 1847), 1:691; Conrad Wright, "The Religion of Geology," *New England Quarterly*, 14 (1941): 344–345; Brown, *Rise of Biblical Criticism*, pp. 101–102; Stanley M. Guralnick, "Geology and Religion before Darwin: The Case of Edward Hitchcock, Theologian and Geologist (1793–1864)," *Isis* 63 (1972): 531–532; Hovenkamp, *Science and Religion*, pp. 63–66.

27. O. J. R. Howarth, *The British Association for the Advancement of Science: A Retrospect, 1831–1931*, 2d ed. (London: British Association, 1931), pp. 58–60; Owen Chadwick, *The Victorian Church*, 2 vols. (New York: Oxford Univ. Press, 1966–1970), 1:562; William Cockburn, *The Bible Defended against the British Association . . .*, 5th ed. (London: Whittaker & Co., 1845), p. 42.

28. Gardiner Spring to Benjamin Silliman, 26 July 1854, quoted in Haber, *Age of the World*, pp. 261–262; Wright, "Religion of Geology," pp. 353–356; Morgan B. Sherwood, "Genesis, Evolution, and Geology in America before Darwin: The Dana-Lewis Controversy, 1856–1857," in *Toward a History of Geology*, pp. 305–316; John C. Greene, "Science and Religion," in *The Rise of Adventism: Religion and Society in Mid-Nineteenth-Century America*, ed. Edwin S. Gaustad (New York: Harper & Row, 1974), pp. 61–67; Hovenkamp, *Science and Religion*, pp. 142–143; Joseph L. Blau, "Tayler Lewis: True Conservative," *Journal of the History of Ideas* 13 (1952): 218–233; Franklin David Steen, "Tayler Lewis on Scripture: A Defense of Revelation and Creation in Nineteenth-Century America" (Th.D. diss., Westminster Theological Seminary, 1971).

29. Miller, *Testimony of the Rocks*, p. 384; Powell, *Christianity without Judaism*, pp. 255, 257; Jowett, "Interpretation of Scripture," p. 341.

30. Ellis, "'Essays and Reviews,'" p. 396; Chadwick, *Victorian Church* 2:83–84; W. H. Brock and R. M. MacLeod, "The Scientists' Declaration: Reflexions on Science and Belief in the Wake of 'Essays and Reviews,' 1864–5," *British Journal for the History of Science* 9 (1976): 39–66.

31. Brock and MacLeod, "Scientists' Declaration"; and *Journal of the Transactions of the Victoria Institute* 1 (1867): 1–36. The agitation of laymen in America might be traced in the formation of the American Institute of Christian Philosophy in 1881, in a dreary series of litigations and heresy trials that racked the major denominations in the decades after the Civil War, and in the founding of chairs or lectureships devoted to the harmony of science and religion

in Columbia Theological Seminary (1856), the College of New Jersey (1865), Amherst College (1868), Andover Theological Seminary (1879), and Oberlin College (1892). In Scotland science lectureships were established in the Free Church theological college at Glasgow in 1845 and in New College, Edinburgh, in 1858.

32. [Leonard Horner], "The Anniversary Address of the President," *Quarterly Journal of the Geological Society of London* 17 (1861): lxx; Horace G. Hutchinson, *Life of Sir John Lubbock, Lord Avebury* . . . , 2 vols. (London: Macmillan & Co., 1914), 1:57–58; Brock and MacLeod, "Scientists' Declaration," p. 45.

33. John William Colenso, *The Pentateuch and Book of Joshua Critically Examined*, People's ed. (London: Longman, Green, Longman, Roberts & Green, 1865), pp. 5, 8, 363–364; Peter Hinchliff, *John William Colenso, Bishop of Natal* (London: Thomas Nelson & Sons, 1964), pp. 104–105, 140–141.

34. Reginald Farrar, *The Life of Frederic William Farrar* . . . (New York: Thomas Y. Crowell & Co., 1904), pp. 112–113; [J. J. S. Perowne], "Noah," in *A Dictionary of the Bible: Comprising Its Antiquities, Biography, Geography, and Natural History*, ed. William Smith, 3 vols. (London: John Murray, 1861–1863), 2:563–576; Thomas H. Huxley, *Science and Hebrew Tradition* (London: Macmillan & Co., 1893), p. 317.

35. Roy M. MacLeod, "The X Club: A Social Network of Science in Late-Victorian England," *Notes and Records of the Royal Society of London* 24 (1970): 305–322; J. Vernon Jensen, "The X Club: Fraternity of Victorian Scientists," *British Journal for the History of Science* 5 (1970): 63–72; J. Vernon Jensen, "Interrelationships within the Victorian 'X Club,'" *Dalhousie Review* 51 (1971–1972), 539–552; A. S. Eve and C. H. Creasey, *Life and Work of John Tyndall* (London: Macmillan & Co., 1945), pp. 205–207; Farrar, *Life of Frederic William Farrar*, pp. 109–110.

36. Frederic W. Farrar, *History of Interpretation* . . . (London: Macmillan & Co., 1886), pp. 34, 422–428.

37. Huxley, *Science and Hebrew Tradition*, pp. 170, 294n; Leonard Huxley, *The Life and Letters of Thomas Henry Huxley*, 2 vols. (London: Macmillan & Co., 1900), 2:345.

38. See Frank M. Turner, "Public Science in Britain, 1880–1919," *Isis* 71 (1980): 589–608.

14

Christianity and the Scientific Community in the Age of Darwin

A. Hunter Dupree

Science, religion, and Charles Darwin (1809–1882) interacted strongly from the very earliest period of the naturalist's life. In the early nineteenth century in the English-speaking countries that were the scene for the opening acts of the Darwinian drama, science and religion, specifically Christianity, fitted together in a close and seemingly harmonious relationship. Many naturalists were clergymen, and many of those who were not saw the study of nature as a sure way to a greater appreciation of the acts of the Creator. The texts from which the students of the day learned their natural theology—for example, those written by William Paley (1743–1806)—not only inferred the existence of God from the evidence of exquisite design in nature but provided the most credible explanation of why organisms were so perfectly adapted to their environments. Even when intellectuals of skeptical tendencies—such as Joseph Priestley or Erasmus Darwin in the midlands of England in the 1780s—could not go along with the established church, they were not completely outside a generally theistic position or, in the case of Priestley, outside his own definition of Christianity.

Small wonder, then, that the skeptical Dr. Robert Waring Darwin (1766–1848) would contemplate the clergy as a career for his son Charles when the amiable young man found medicine at the University of Edinburgh distinctly uncongenial. During his years on the *Beagle,* sharing a cabin with the intensely orthodox Captain Robert Fitzroy (1805–1865), Charles remained formally true to both his faith and his calling, and with Fitzroy wrote a defense of British missionaries in Tahiti and New Zealand.[1] Darwin and Darwinism came out of a profoundly Christian culture. The scientific community of the early nineteenth century was also embedded in that culture and even depended on Christianity both for a rationale of its social usefulness and for direct economic support.

The foregoing paragraphs do not agree with the major thrust of the book that has set the tone for the discussion of the relation of Darwinism and Christianity ever since its publication in 1896. Andrew D. White's *History of the Warfare of Science with Theology in Christendom*, born of the effort to create the modern secular university, proposed, in the words of its author, "to present an outline of the great, sacred struggle for the liberty of science—a struggle which has lasted for so many centuries and which yet continues."[2] This book, written by a historian, not a scientist, set the opposition between science and a constricting Christian theology on a centuries-long basis that saw organized religion as the oppressor of science long before Darwin. According to White, the influence of Christianity on the scientific community largely disappeared in the age of Darwin. The few vestiges of Christian influence that survived the publication of Darwin's *Origin of Species* in 1859 were the rationalizations of scientists from an older era who could not throw off their theological upbringing. They failed to recognize that the tide of history was against them, that the institutions of learning were to be reconstituted on a secular basis both in England and the United States. All efforts to reconcile science and religion, to save the obscurantist traditions of Christianity while admitting the obvious conclusion that science provided a complete picture of all that could be known about the universe, were illogical.

The purpose of this paper is to show not only that Darwin's theories came out of a predominantly Christian culture but also that representatives of all shades of response to Darwinian ideas within the scientific communities of the English-speaking world were massively influenced by Christian symbolism regardless of their stand toward organized religion. This nonrevolutionary view of the effect of Darwin's ideas on scientists' philosophical and religious views calls attention to the simple proposition that the influence of Christianity was felt in the debates following 1859 and has persisted to the present.

THE CRISIS OF 1859

Darwin, shortly after his return from the *Beagle* voyage, while he was working on his voluminous collections made in five years in and around South America, came to doubt that species were constant. From 1837 he shaped his scientific work as an argument for the proposition that species of organisms arose from other species. To explain the changes that gave rise to new species, he developed the concept of natural selection, by which he meant that in changed conditions of life some organisms will be better adapted than others because of random variations, and they will leave more offspring in the next generation. Darwin had his theory in essentially complete form as early as 1844, but it took him another fifteen years to mature the theory to the point where he was willing to publish it. The book's full title was *On the Origin of Species by Means of Natural Selection; or, The Preservation of Favoured Races in the Struggle for Life.*[3] Darwin, fully aware that he was proposing a revolution in the way scientists thought about biology, was careful and persistent in shaping his argument and his evidence to meet all objections.

For botanists, zoologists, and geologists, and to a lesser degree for other scientists as well, the years just before and after the publication of the *Origin of Species* in 1859 provided an extraordinary experience. A scholar turning through the collections of correspondence of the scientists of those years finds in case after case a similar pattern. Through most of the 1850s the exchange of letters goes on at a steady pace, often concerning mundane affairs and occasionally reaching a level of high sophistication with just a hint that great things are coming. Nevertheless, the implicit framework of shared assumptions never quite breaks down. Then with the publication of the *Origin* there is a period of intense excitement, and scientists who have never risen above the level of taxonomic detail begin to talk of philosophy, religion, the nature of man, and the shape of the cosmos. Some of this sudden theorizing is brilliant and insightful, some is clumsy and inept, but almost never is discourse informed by the rigor of the professional philosopher. Scientists have already become so specialized and so driven by the standards of their disciplines that they seem to be stepping unprepared and unaware into the limelight on the intellectual stage of the nineteenth century.

Shortly after Darwinism made its appearance, it joined the ongoing streams of social evolution and materialism that were already gathering momentum. When confronted with the great issues of philosophy and theology that the anomalous situation unleashed, scientists fell back upon the concepts that their culture afforded them. Whatever position the scientists of the 1859 generation ultimately achieved, the symbol set that exerted the most powerful influence on them in every case was the tradition with which they entered the crisis.

In the years following 1859, talk of conversion to Darwinism was on everyone's tongue, and to the extent that conversion was from one scientific concept to another, one can speak of revolution. Some scientists resisted to death scientific Darwinism. Others went part way scientifically but stopped short of complete conversion. A third group rallied to Darwin with enthusiasm and set the style for what rapidly became a new model, at least as far as evolution itself was concerned. There was room for more than a century of debate on most subsidiary points, such as the mechanism of natural selection, but the change in attitude associated with 1859 is one of those rare shifts that have occurred only half a dozen times in the whole of intellectual history.

If one looks not at the shift of opinion within science but to the division over the meaning of Darwin for religion, the same actors are on the same stage as in the scientific debate, but the drama has an entirely different plot. Conversion now consists of giving up one's religion and swearing (if that is possible) allegiance to science. Thus the metaphor of war between religion and science dominated the discussion of Darwin's influence until scholars began, recently, to question both the appropriateness of the metaphor and the reality of the opposition between religion and science even in the era of the Darwinian debates.

The Christians of the English-speaking world in the early nineteenth century used a wide variety of patterns of symbols in both Scripture and tradition to send the messages of Creation, Fall from grace, the coming of the Messiah, Crucifixion, Resurrection, and ultimate salvation in the Second Coming and the Last Judgment. However, the arguments of natural theology shaped in the eighteenth century had put the story of creation into sharp relief as the one symbol necessary for all order in nature and all beneficence and moral structure in the universe. Ironically, the creation myth of the Christians, which came to occupy such a crucial place, was a Judaic rather than New Testament conception. And in addition to the meanings that the creation story in Genesis may have had for believers who saw it as emanating from God, it served the same purpose among the Hebrews that other creation myths, nearly universal among the peoples of the world, did in their cultures.[4]

Not the particular story found in Genesis but the idea of a Creator and his natural creation made such works as Paley's *Natural Theology* (1802) a mainstay of moral education. According to Paley, just as the harmonious parts of a watch found in a desert place argued a watchmaker, so the exquisite adaptations of nature indicated the existence of God. To Darwin's generation, however, the long chains of evidence put forward as designs that argued the Creator presented, as soon as one was willing to admit the necessity of the Creator, the most credible explanation for biological adaptation. Hence the literature of natural theology played a dual role. It gave to the Christian believer evidence from nature that stood on the same plane as evidence from Scripture. At the same time it gave to the naturalist, in the absence of evidence to the contrary, a reasonable hypothesis for the observed distinctness in kinds of organisms. It further connected the structure of those organisms to their stations in the economy of nature in a harmonious way. God could thus be cited as the author of harmony in nature.

The adoption of science as a religion, replacing Christianity, involved the shattering of an old belief system and the conversion to a new one. Like the metaphor of war, the metaphor of conversion obsessed the Victorian mind. The experience of conversion to science could approach the deep mystical exaltation of Saul on the road to Damascus or of Mohammed. The nineteenth-century German materialists—Karl Vogt, Ludwig Büchner, Jacob Moleschott—showed this kind of zeal.[5] Darwin's British publicists, such as Thomas Henry Huxley (1825–1895), used violent language in tilting with bishops, but the cordial ties of sophisticated debate that joined Huxley to the establishments of church and state in Victorian society reveal implicitly the common culture that made that warfare a tempest in a teacup.

In spite of all the dramatic anecdotes of conflict, the suspicion will not down that instead of converting from the religion of their ancestors to a pure belief in science, the principals on all sides of the Darwinian debate showed a mark of continuity in their pattern of religious thought before and after 1859. Part of the difficulty to recognizing this continuity stems from the complexity and rapid transformation of the religious traditions themselves. The crisis over Darwin and the crisis over higher criticism of the Bible so nearly coincided that a complete separation of factors is impossible.

Instead of making a survey of the response of scientists, I have chosen to pick a few representative figures from among the many available and look for the continuation or lack of continuation of their religious position before and after 1859. An equal list of others might well be selected, but the inclusion of some from outside the Darwin circle, some from within it, and of Darwin himself, makes the list weighted for relevance to the debate. All were professional scientists. All reached maturity before 1859. All lived long enough thereafter to react fully to the publication of the *Origin of Species* and the attendant debates. All are selected from the English-speaking world, for it was there that the primary Darwinian debate took place.

OPPONENTS OF DARWIN

A clear example of the scientist of an old religious orthodoxy who practiced the old subordination of the study of nature to theology and who carried his beliefs, both scientific and theological, unchanged into opposition to Darwin was William Dawson (1807–1899).[6] Born in Nova Scotia and raised a Presbyterian, he became one of the two geologists worthy of the name in Canada in the nineteenth century. He poured much of his life into the development of McGill University, where he made the sciences rather than the liberal arts the bulwark of his educational philosophy. According to his biographer,

> his historical relevance in carrying on the search for a synthesis of the two theologies—natural and revealed—is much greater than his contributions to either education or natural science. . . . His deep involvement in the two theologies' tradition led Dawson into controversy. The reassuring synthesis of science and religion that was so convincing in his youth seemed to be crumbling on all sides as he grew older. Attempting to reaffirm this synthesis, Dawson became one of the last great spokesmen for the two theologies' tradition. . . . His very life was woven out of controversy over what he regarded as the Word and Work of God.[7]

Dawson, who carried the pre-1859 synthesis of religion and science into the Darwinian era and linked it to an uncompromising anti-Darwinian scientific stand represents the pure type of a scientist who lived through the Darwinian era without succumbing to the winds of change. At the same time he was an investigator of talent and an institution-builder who helped to shape the ideal of science into its characteristic late-nineteenth-century embodiment—the university. Thus, even though he did not change either his religious or his scientific orthodoxy from the pre-1859 to the post-1859 periods, he nevertheless responded at the intellectual and institutional level to the explosion of research in the wake of the *Origin* by contributing to the stream of geological knowledge, even in opposition to evolution, and to the building of the new home of science, the secular university.

Superficially, the example of Louis Agassiz (1806–1873) seems to conform closely to that of Dawson, but on a much more cosmopolitan stage than that occupied by the isolated Canadian. The son of a Protestant minister in the French part of Switzerland, Agassiz had developed a major European reputation in geology and zoology by the time he came to the United States in 1846.[8] From his education in German universities and his having been a disciple of Georges Cuvier, he brought with him a full-blown philosophy of natural history based on successive creations of organisms separated by catastrophes. While these creations showed a strong pattern of development within the boundaries of four basic types of animals, the connections between organisms even within the types and within single species were, according to Agassiz, ideal and not material. The Creator did his task by thinking a plan rather than by materially shaping his handiwork. Such a view put Agassiz in the forefront of creationists in the English-speaking world after his decision to reside permanently in the United States.

When the first copies of the *Origin of Species* crossed the Atlantic in late 1859, Agassiz had been solidifying his intellectual position for more than a decade and indeed was so overloaded with institution-building that he participated in the debates over Darwin with a thinly veiled attitude of irritation at having his own labors interrupted. Once he reluctantly admitted that Darwinism was not a fad, however, he used his great powers as a lecturer and writer of popular science to carry on one of the most broadly publicized and persistent campaigns against Darwin's ideas that was mounted on either side of the Atlantic. Since in the latter period of his life his large popular audiences, drawn widely from the American middle class, contained many churchgoing people, Agassiz's dramatic opposition to Darwin was in their eyes an enthusiastic defense of biblical as well as scientific creationism. His childhood in the home of a pastor became the all-embracing explanation for why this major figure in science set himself off decisively from most of his fellows, including his own students. Even his son Alexander (1835–1910), also a zoologist, discreetly adopted Darwin's scientific ideas.

This easy rationalization of Agassiz's anti-Darwinian position in terms of his early religious training does not stand close examination. For all his emphasis on the Creator, he was interested in developing a consistent scientific system rather than a theological position. Except for the Creation, he used little Christian symbolism, and he was never in America closely associated with organized religion. Indeed, when he came to the United States, he made many orthodox Protestants in the North distinctly uneasy, because he argued on scientific grounds that the human races were separately created species, and because this opinion brought him into close association with the freethinking Southern protagonists of the proslavery argument—for example, Josiah Nott (1804–1873), of Mobile, Alabama—who saw the antislavery views of many churchmen as a distinct threat to the freedom of science.

Just before Agassiz was to lecture in New York in 1847, a rumor spread that he was going to say that the Negro and Malay races had not descended from the sons of Noah but had a separate origin. Agassiz's explanation was that the Caucasian races had descended from the sons of Noah, and that it did not violate the Scriptures to say that Negroes and Malays were separately created. The botanist Asa Gray (1810–1888), who was sponsoring Agassiz's lecture tour, defended the Swiss visitor's right to speak and to have his own biblical interpretation. Gray himself felt free to disagree with the scientific interpretation that the human races were separate species both by his own reading of the biological evidence and his own reading of the Scriptures. As a scientific believer in the unity of the human races and as an ardent antislavery advocate, Gray was in a position to appreciate the religious objections to slavery as overriding Agassiz's implicit use of science to make a proslavery argument.[9] When the general discussion of Darwinism picked up in America after the Civil War, the issues of the slavery debate were so transformed that church people could see Agassiz with more friendly eyes, even though the scientific ideas on which he based his arguments against Darwin were precisely the same as those he had used for the multiple origin of races before 1859.

Agassiz's position as an anti-Darwinian is thus clearly that of one who did not accept Darwin for scientific reasons. He was quite willing to gain popular acclaim from religious people and play to a popular audience, as indeed he had always done in behalf of science. He continued his frantic research career and his institution-building until his death in 1873. As a charismatic teacher he had brought into science a large number of gifted students. Despite his tendency to be autocratic in relation to them, Agassiz had to be aware that by the time of his death many of them had become evolutionists.

A CHRISTIAN DARWINIST

As Darwin in the 1850s undertook to shape his theories on the transmutation of species and natural selection into a book, he worked not alone but with the help of highly talented friends, to whom he turned for both evidence and advice. Of the four friends whom Darwin consulted most freely, two of them, the geologist Charles Lyell (1797–1875) and the botanist Joseph Hooker (1817–1911), played more of a role in giving scientific advice than in discussing the strategy for developing a posture toward religion. Lyell was hesitant fully to accept scientific Darwinism and was preoccupied with the special position of man in the evolutionary scale. Hooker had no taste for theological and philosophical speculation. Thus the major influences on Darwin from within his own circle came from two men who presented clear-cut alternatives. Asa Gray, an American botanist, put forward the proposition, to use Darwin's own phrase, "Natural Selection not Inconsistent with Natural Theology." T. H. Huxley, in contrast, as early as 1860 became the major spokesman for evolution, elevating truth revealed by science to a position superior to truth revealed by religion. By comparing Gray and Huxley we can examine whether in their eyes the Christian tradition could coexist with the comprehensive picture of man's and life's place in nature as conceived by Darwin in the *Origin of Species.*

The elements that went into Asa Gray's structure of religion and science come out clearly from the sources. Raised a Presbyterian in upstate New York, he escaped the fervor of the great revival of 1827. In his days as a physician in the village of Bridgewater, New York, Gray encountered Sir William Lawrence's *Lectures on Physiology, Zoology, and the Natural History of Man* (1819), a work that also influenced the young Darwin. Lawrence ruled miracle (though not design) out of science, the soul out of physiology, and asserted a sweeping credo of the freedom of inquiry.[10] Describing Lawrence as "a materialist— after my own fashion completely,"[11] Gray imbibed a full dose of eighteenth-century rationalism, a distrust of orthodox religion, and a dislike of the suppression that was threatening Lawrence in the British courts. This materialist and anticlerical period of Gray's life, brief as it was, came at a crucial time in his intellectual development and suggests a posture toward rationalism, empiricism, and freedom of thought that would mesh well with Darwin when their intellectual trajectories intersected in 1855.

In the mid-1830s Gray moved to New York City to collaborate on a *Flora of North America* with John Torrey (1796–1873), the leading botanist of the United States at the time. The Torrey family were devout New School Presbyterians, and Gray lived in their household for a time. His experience in the city, therefore, pushed him in the direction of membership in both the scientific community and the religious community at the same time. The lack of any social group that would reinforce the materialist signals of the Bridgewater period made it almost impossible for Gray to maintain his stand with Lawrence for very long. The genuineness of Gray's conversion to Presbyterianism is not open to doubt.

During the late 1830s Gray was pious, evangelical, and Sabbatarian. He maintained his orthodoxy when he moved to the predominantly Unitarian Harvard faculty in 1842, although in 1848 he chose to marry a member of a prominent Unitarian family of Boston rather than one of the orthodox Torrey daughters. Little evidence exists of a strong interaction between Gray and theological circles of any denomination in the 1850s. As he came up to the trials of the late 1850s, Gray described himself as orthodox in both religion and science, but he was, in these middle years of a busy life, so swamped with collections from an expanding America that he spent most of his time and thought on taxonomic botany. One presupposition of classification was creation, at some time and in some form, but a much more important presupposition was the fixity of species. Naturalists of all philosophical persuasions needed fixity as a working principle, and when Gray said he was orthodox scientifically he had fixity in mind. However much he, as an empiricist, might differ with his Harvard colleague Agassiz, the idealist, Gray could communicate with him in the lingua franca of natural history—the system of nomenclature going back to Carl Linnaeus (1707–1778).

Gray emerged from the debates of 1859 having changed his position on the fixity of some species by following a rigorous line of statistical reasoning, which he learned from Darwin, about the distribution of plants in Eastern Asia and Eastern North America. He was now willing to accept natural selection as an agent and the breaking of the barrier between species in individual cases. He wrote to J. D. Hooker, "I am quite ready to believe that any particular cognate species so called originated by variation, wherever you say so."[12] He was not ready to expand this mode of change to the whole of the vegetable kingdom, but it pleased him the more that his results enlarged the realm of organic phenomena that could be attributed to natural causes rather than to Agassiz's idealist prescription of thoughts in the mind of the Creator, a dead end scientifically in the eyes of the botanist. Gray was a champion of Darwin the scientist, and the method of the one was as positivistic as the other in the chains of reasoning that led to natural selection.

Gray indicated promptly, however, that he was not going to go beyond the evidence to a belief that science would necessarily replace his whole philosophical and religious position. It was possible to push back the chain of secondary causes in nature a very long way, and he expected that in the future, research would continue to do so. Still, even if "you carry out this view to its ultimate and legitimate results," he felt himself left with the necessity of connecting his science, itself incorporating evolution and natural selection, with his philosophical and theological positions "into a consistent whole."[13] This determination to hold the domains of science and of religion together shaped Gray's course for the rest of his life. That his position did not hold its place in the intellectual competition of the late nineteenth century is a problem of importance in the history of a period that increasingly considered science the sole route to knowledge and that denied both metaphysics and religion any alternative way to knowledge.

Ironically, Gray, in his published writings and in his correspondence with Darwin, tried to tie the domains of science and religion together by falling back on the argument from design. He needed some way of connecting the action of Providence with the action of natural selection. In the old natural history the assumption of design had fulfilled that role. As a taxonomist Gray also was very much aware of order in nature, portrayed by structure in organisms—a structure that showed relative stability even after Darwin. There was an observed design in the adaptations of organisms, however one explained them.

Casual readers, from T. H. Huxley to the present, have usually dismissed Gray's thought as being based on a fallacy already refuted by the Scottish philosopher David Hume (1711–1776) and in any case doomed, along with teleology, to play no role in the biology of the future. Darwin knew the argument from design much better than Gray, who had in his education no counterpart of Cambridge, and he could turn around such contrivances as the eye and the hand advanced by Paley as arguing Providential design into arguments for natural selection. Gray, in contrast, made the process of evolution itself the object of design by the Creator.

He thought he found his opportunity to unite science and religion in his correct insistence that the causes of variation were completely unknown. Lacking all evidence, Gray felt free to assume that variations had been led along certain beneficial lines. An order, a guidance, must move across the boundary from the sphere of religion to the sphere of science. Darwin, in the last paragraph of *Variation of Plants and Animals under Domestication* (1868), apparently said his definitive word: "However much we may wish it, we can hardly follow Professor Asa Gray in his belief 'that variation has been led along certain beneficial lines,' like a stream 'along definite and useful lines of irrigation.'"[14]

Much as Gray may have later wished to back off from the beneficent stream of variations, he had opted with that metaphor to challenge the trend of thought called positivism, or scientific naturalism, or by T. H. Huxley agnosticism. Gray dismissed those currents of thought and was in turn dismissed by them, even though as a practical scientist his methods were identical with those of the positivists. More important than design was Gray's original proposition that the philosophy of science and the philosophy of religion should be tied together across the boundary between them.

In post-Darwinian thought the boundary between the domain of science and the domain of both metaphysics and theology became effectively sealed. Very little traffic crossed through the checkpoints on the boundary in either direction. So lively was the action within the institutions of science, so persuasive was its methodology, even so emotionally exciting were the structures that composed the results of science—for example, the metaphor of the tree of life—that some in the Darwinian generation developed the vision of a truth entirely based on science. This vision had little attraction for the steady, prosaic Asa Gray, but it placed many of his contemporaries in the terrible dilemma of choosing between a reality based on the truth of science and a reality based on a revelation that had lost all persuasiveness. A respectable continuation of traditional religious culture, including Christianity, had in the late nineteenth century little theoretical justification in science or philosophy. Asa Gray's brave try, as Darwin's niece Julia Wedgwood pointed out to him, was not strong enough to overcome the polarized emotions of those who rejected religious reality *in toto* and those who fell back on tradition with a conscious rejection of science.

AGNOSTICISM AND THE USES OF CHRISTIAN SYMBOLISM

Long before 1868, when Darwin published his polite disagreement with Asa Gray, the course away from Christian Darwinism had been set by T. H. Huxley. As the leading spokesman for scientific Darwinism he had also definitely shaped the choice of the truth of science over the truth of any revealed religion and had engaged the spokesmen for organized religion in an almost continuous debate. His acrimonious encounter with Bishop Samuel Wilberforce (1805–1875) of Oxford in 1860 has set the tone, and Huxley had at one stroke removed religion from the active role within science that it had played in the argument from design. He also denied to organized religion the role of arbiter of truth on the basis of revelation. Many of his most famous debates with spokesmen for religion had to do with the validity of Christian revelation, particularly as interpreted by the Church of England. In 1869 Asa Gray was in England but refused to go to the meeting of the British Association in Exeter to "keep from *Darwinian* discussions—in which I desire not to be at all 'mixed up' with the Huxley set, and the prevailing and peculiarly English Materialistic-positivistic line of thought. . . ."[15]

Huxley recognized the awkwardness of not having a name for his point of view and coined the word *agnostic*. Scientists and others, Darwin among them, could now choose an alternative to Christian or theist on the one side and atheist on the other. Huxley's characterization of the new category is worth quoting extensively:

> Agnosticism, in fact, is not a creed, but a method, the essence of which lies in the rigorous application of a single principle. That principle is of

great antiquity; it is as old as Socrates; as old as the writer who said, "Try all things, hold fast by that which is good"; it is the foundation of the Reformation, which simply illustrated the axiom that every man should be able to give a reason for the faith that is in him; it is the great principle of Descartes; it is the fundamental axiom of modern science. Positively the principle may be expressed: In matters of the intellect, follow your reason as far as it will take you, without regard to any other consideration. And negatively: In matters of the intellect, do not pretend that conclusions are certain which are not demonstrated and demonstrable. That I take to be the agnostic faith, which if a man keep whole and undefiled, he shall not be ashamed to look the universe in the face, whatever the future may have in store for him.[16]

A belief in the truth of science was all that a Darwinian needed. Huxley could be as hard on the French positivist Auguste Comte (1798–1857), whom he called a Catholic without Christianity, and on materialism as he was on bishops. With the option open for a clear choice between science and religion, however, any third alternative, such as Asa Gray's, had little appeal. The late nineteenth century in the English-speaking world was a period in which both the adherents of Protestant Christianity and those of agnosticism could only see warfare.

Huxley's rhetoric, in spite of its belligerency, resembles nothing so much as that of his ecclesiastical adversaries. As an old man, he recalled: "I remember turning my pinafore wrongside forwards in order to represent a surplice, and preaching to my mother's maids in the kitchen" as nearly as possible in the manner of the vicar.[17] As we read the texts of Huxley's agnosticism, we become more and more aware that he is modeling his declaration of independence from Christianity point by point on Christian symbolism. The examples in his rhetoric are pervasive—lay sermons, the church scientific, a new Reformation.

The fall of the design argument had taken out the Creator and with it both Genesis as scriptural evidence and nature as evidence of God. The metaphor of the tree of life that evolution supplied in its place was finally strong enough as a metaphor to provide the Western world with an alternative creation myth. But the symbols of the scientific worldview owe their form, as Huxley's definition of agnostic clearly displayed, to older traditions. Saint Paul and Martin Luther as well as philosophers who recognized a metaphysical reality—Socrates and Descartes—provided a reservoir of images for Huxley to mold with his rhetoric of science. The culture of Western civilization, Christianity included, was embedded in the language of Huxley, the apostle of Darwin.

In 1860, shortly after Huxley's famous exchange with the Bishop of Oxford and with the debate over the *Origin* in full force, the Huxleys' son Noel, just four years old, died of scarlet fever. That liberal and scientifically literate clergyman, Charles Kingsley (1819–1875), evoked from Huxley at a time of supreme testing an eloquent statement of faith:

> If that great and powerful instrument for good or evil, the Church of England, is to be saved from being shivered into fragments by the advancing tide of science—an event I should be sorry to witness, but which will infallibly occur if men like Samuel of Oxford are to have the guidance of her destinies—it must be by the efforts of men who, like yourself, see your way to the combination of the practice of the Church with the spirit of science. Understand that all the younger men of science whom I know intimately are *essentially* of my way of thinking. (I know not a scoffer or an irreligious or an immoral man among them, but they all regard orthodoxy as you do Brahmanism.) Understand that this new school of prophets is the only one that can work miracles, that it is right and you will comprehend that it is of no use to try to barricade us with shovel hats and aprons, or to talk about our doctrines being "shocking."[18]

What was new in Huxley was the belief that science could completely take the place of revelation in an essentially Christian matrix drawn from the best of Victorian culture. With the rapid expansion of the sphere of positive science, it could put itself forward as the only source of truth. Give it time and it would fill the whole universe. There was no transcendent sphere from which a Creator could act. It was despite the cold comfort of Huxley's reasoning that his rhetoric imported much of the structure of the Christian worldview into agnosticism. The shared culture of Huxley and his adversaries made their gladiatorial combats marvels of civilized discourse.

Charles Darwin, who lived until 1882, was the center of a personal network that included not only his scientific friends and correspondents, Gray and Huxley among them, but also his family. His wife and many of his Wedgwood relatives remained devoted to Christianity, and he remained affectionately respectful of their views. He himself reported in his autobiography that "disbelief crept over me at a very slow rate, but was at last complete. The rate was so slow that I felt no distress, and have never doubted even for a single second that my conclusion was correct."[19] Although he may have lost his belief in the New Testament in the late 1830s, his mode of thinking about design associated with creation lasted much longer, into the period around 1859. As the thrust and parry of his correspondence with Asa Gray shows, he gave up his belief in design slowly. Recent scholarship emphasizes that long after he had conceived of natural selection as a mechanism for evolution he continued to think of nature as harmonious. Only when he began to see that superfecundity and random variation plus natural selection would lead to divergent and unpredictable paths did he begin to shake free of design as an operating principle in biology.[20] While Darwin differed with Gray about design, he did not deny him the right to join his science with religion. In a letter of 9 May 1879 Darwin summed up his conclusion concerning Gray's position, Huxley's position, and his own position all at the same time:

> It seems to me absurd to doubt that a man may be an ardent theist & an evolutionist. You are right about Kingsley. Asa Gray, the eminent botanist, is another case in point. What my own views may be is a question of no consequence to anyone except myself. But, as you ask, I may state that my judgment often fluctuates. Moreover, whether a man deserves to be called a theist depends on the definition of the term, which is much too large a subject for a note. In my most extreme fluctuations I have never been an atheist in the sense of denying the existence of a God. I think that generally (& more & more as I grow older) but not always, that an agnostic would be the most correct description of my state of mind.[21]

THE LATE-NINETEENTH-CENTURY ACCOMMODATION

When Huxley told Kingsley that younger men of science were "essentially of my way of thinking," he was speaking prophetically. Dawson was the last uncompromising adherent to the orthodoxy that reigned before 1859. Agassiz's extravagant idealism came close to dying before he did. There is some evidence that Asa Gray's Christian Darwinism had a long life in the colleges and churches of the United States and contributed to the introduction of Darwinian scientific ideas into distinctly Christian intellectual environments.[22] But by 1900 the public stance of scientists in the English-speaking world (including some who followed Gray in botany) had overwhelmingly come to resemble the views of Huxley. Since World War II, however, with the evidence piling up that a rapid accommodation on the part of Protestant Christianity to the ideas of Darwin actually took place, and that scientists both ceased to fear and ceased to ponder theological questions and scriptural accounts, the metaphor of the warfare of science and theology has been under attack.

A superficially attractive way out of the dilemma left by the undoubted power of agnosticism and the undoubted persistence of traditional religion is to consider that science itself is a religion. If all the followers of this religion had the theological acumen and the moral awareness of Huxley, such a religion might have swept the world along with modern technology. However, if science functions as a self-correcting matrix of information structured by instrumental rules, it does not determine absolute answers to any questions and does not determine any answers at all to ultimate questions. It can scarcely be called a religion in the sense of the traditional faiths. Certainly evolution can hardly provide a symbolic picture of the universe beyond the beginning and the end of its course. The concepts of science can achieve both clarity and harmony, but these characteristics lead to further fruitful concepts, not to ultimate truth.

Huxley in his lay sermons and elsewhere was fond of referring to the church scientific, a term that had in it a double meaning. Strictly it applied only to the scientific community itself, and it was just here in the circles of consensus that made up the disciplines that many found in their faith in science a true religion. Not everyone could qualify for the strict scientific community, however, and those who tried to force their way in without initiation were to be repelled as impostors and quacks. To get beyond the small circle of the qualified required a Herbert Spencer or a Karl Marx or the Continental materialists to develop a religion of science that could be shared with the masses. Huxley could lecture to workingmen, but he could not evangelize them directly. He could introduce science into the public schools, but only when he participated in founding the secular University of London did he provide an embodiment of the church scientific, and even then he was forced by the definition of academic freedom to make room for other methods than the one on which he based his faith. Huxley, as usual, himself recognized the problem:

> Religions rise because they satisfy the many and fall because they cease to satisfy the few.
>
> They have become the day dreams of mankind and each in turn has become a nightmare from which a gleam of knowledge has waked the dreamer.
>
> The religion which will endure is such a day dream as may still be dreamed in the noon tide glare of science.[23]

If science itself became the dream, whence would come the glare that would enlighten it as the afternoon wore on toward the postivists' time of dogmatic slumber? The prospect is the nightmare with which the twentieth century is all too familiar. Having learned from Huxley the lesson of authoritarian absolutism in religion, the world after Darwin faces the problem of how not to repeat the tragedy with an authoritarianism based on the worship of science.

NOTES

1. Paul H. Barrett, ed., *The Collected Papers of Charles Darwin* (Chicago: Univ. of Chicago Press, 1977), pp. 19–38.

2. Quoted in James R. Moore, *The Post-Darwinian Controversies: A Study of the Protestant Struggle to Come to Terms with Darwin in Great Britain and America, 1870–1900* (Cambridge: Cambridge Univ. Press, 1979), p. 36.

3. London: John Murray, 1859. A facsimile of the first edition of *The Origin of Species*, with an introduction by Ernst Mayr, was published by Harvard Univ. Press in 1964.

4. Edmund R. Leach, "Genesis as Myth," in *Myth and Cosmos: Readings in Mythology and Symbolism*, ed. John Middleton (Garden City, N.Y.: Natural History Press, 1967), pp. 1–14; Frank E. Manuel and Fritzie P. Manuel, "Sketch for a Natural History of Paradise," in *Myth, Symbol, and Culture*, ed. Clifford Geertz (New York: W. W. Norton, 1971), pp. 83–128.

5. Frederick Gregory, *Scientific Materialism in Nineteenth Century Germany* (Dordrecht: Reidel, 1977).

6. Sir William Dawson, *Modern Ideas of Evolution*, ed. William R. Shea and John F. Cornell (New York: Prodist, 1977); Charles F. O'Brien, *Sir William Dawson: A Life in Science and Religion* (Philadelphia: American Philosophical Society, 1971).

7. Ibid., pp. 3, 5.

8. Edward Lurie, *Louis Agassiz: A Life in Science* (Chicago: Univ. of Chicago Press, 1960).

9. A. Hunter Dupree, *Asa Gray, 1810–1888* (Cambridge, Mass.: Harvard Univ. Press, Belknap Press, 1959), pp. 152–153.

10. Both Howard Gruber and Edward Manier have now pointed to the influence of Lawrence on the young Darwin, impressing him, according to Gruber, with the high price of dangerous ideas. Howard E. Gruber, with Paul H. Barrett, *Darwin on Man: A Psychological Study of Scientific Creativity* (New York: E. P. Dutton, 1974), pp. 204–205; Edward Manier, *The Young Darwin and His Cultural Circle* (Dordrecht: Reidel, 1978), pp. 64–66.

11. Dupree, *Asa Gray*, p. 20.

12. Asa Gray to J. D. Hooker, 18 Oct. 1859, quoted in Dupree, *Asa Gray*, p. 266.

13. Ibid.

14. Charles Darwin, *Variation of Plants and Animals under Domestication*, 2 vols. (New York: Orange, Judd, 1868), 2:516.

15. Dupree, *Asa Gray*, p. 340.

16. T. H. Huxley, "Agnosticism," in his *Science and Christian Tradition* (New York: D. Appleton, 1896), pp. 245–246.

17. T. H. Huxley, *Autobiography and Selected Essays*, ed. A. L. F. Snell (Boston: Houghton Mifflin, 1909), p. 4.

18. Leonard Huxley, *Life and Letters of Thomas Henry Huxley*, 2 vols. (New York: D. Appleton, 1901), 1:238.

19. Charles Darwin, *Autobiography,* ed. Nora Barlow (New York: Harcourt, Brace, 1959), p. 87.

20. Dov Ospovat, *The Development of Darwin's Theory: Natural History, Natural Theology, and Natural Selection, 1838–1859* (Cambridge: Cambridge Univ. Press, 1981).

21. John Fordyce, *Aspects of Skepticism: With Special Reference to the Present Time* (London: E. Stock, 1883), p. 190; referred to in Owen Chadwick, *The Victorian Church,* 2 vols. (London: A. and C. Black, 1970), II, 20.

22. For example, Isabelle Baird Sprague, "Creationism and Evolutionary Theory at Mount Holyoke Seminary," *Mount Holyoke Alumni Quarterly,* Winter, 1981, pp. 14–17; Philip Dorf, *Liberty Hyde Bailey: An Informal Biography* (Ithaca, N.Y.: Cornell University Press, 1956), pp. 100–101.

23. Quoted in Cyril Bibby, *T. H. Huxley: Scientist, Humanist and Educator* (London: Watts, 1959), p. 48.

15

The Impact of
Darwinian Evolution on
Protestant Theology in the
Nineteenth Century

Frederick Gregory

As the eighteenth century drew to a close, the German thinker Immanuel Kant (1724–1804) formulated in the most philosophical of terms a distinction that represented what many biological scientists felt instinctively to be true. According to Kant, living organisms, the concept of which could not be grasped unless it contained an element of purpose, could not be produced by mechanical means alone; nor could the constitution of living things be accounted for by explanations that contained no appeal to the active and spontaneous properties of mind. In making his claim Kant was not challenging the understanding of scientific explanation that had been developed over the preceding years. He was, in effect, arguing that complete scientific explanation was impossible in biology.

The understanding of scientific explanation had undergone substantial development from the seventeenth to the eighteenth century. If René Descartes and other "mechanical philosophers" of the seventeenth century had urged that nature must be thought of as a machine, thereby abandoning Aristotle's metaphor of nature as organism and excluding from scientific explanations all reference to the spontaneous attributes of mind, Isaac Newton had forced a reformulation of how the certainty and unalterability of nature was to be expressed. Newton had rejected the strict mechanical philosophy of his day in favor of a natural philosophy based on active forces. In the wake of the successful treatment of the heavens in the *Principia*, Newton's followers in the eighteenth century incorporated force into their understanding of proper scientific explanation. They did not, as Newton himself had done, view the primacy of force as an indication of the undeniable presence of spirit or mind in nature. To them the important feature of Newton's dynamical system was not his conception of the *nature* of force but his demonstration of the *laws* of force. For many of his disciples in the Age of Enlightenment Newton's laws removed all uncertainty and spontaneity from scientific explanation just as Descartes's exclusion of mind had done a century earlier. In spite of the central role played by force in their "Newtonian" understanding of nature, the world still operated as a mindless machine, and scientific explanation could rightfully be called mechanical explanation. Even Kant believed that explanations based on the interaction of material forces were the only kind available to the natural scientist as a scientist.

By the middle of the eighteenth century, then, Aristotle's older organic perception of nature was no longer viable to many as a scientific conception of the natural world. Scientific explanation had come more and more to mean mechanical explanation, so much so that even reference to "naturalistic" explanation could be intended to connote the exclusion of final cause. The real question now was whether mechanical explanations could be as successful in explaining organic nature as they had been in inorganic nature.

When Kant declared that the world of living organisms could not be captured by scientific explanation, he precipitated a debate among his followers. One of them, Jakob Fries (1773–1843), identified his mentor's claim as an unfortunate error, unfortunate because otherwise Kant's philosophy represented to Fries a definite advance over all previous attempts to examine our knowledge of nature. Organisms *could*, argued Fries, be explained by the same mechanical laws that the scientist appealed to in physics.[1] Others in the German scientific community of the Romantic Period adopted Kant's approach to the explanation of organism. In their teleomechanical program the presence of final cause was acknowledged, but only because it conditioned unavoidably the knowledge of organism from *outside* of what Kant called genuine science (*eigentliche Wissenschaft*).

For the most part this debate was confined to a small segment of the German intellectual community, but before the nineteenth century had ended, not only philosophers, but scientists and theologians everywhere, would address the issue in their own ways. As far as the relationship between biological science and religion was concerned, the possibility of a complete mechanical account of organism, where there was no direct reference to mind or any of its attributes, became the central issue.

Of course, not all scientists and few if any theologians agreed with the Kantians that scientific explanation was confined to mechanical explanation. Scientists in particular were perfectly capable of ignoring philosophical conclusions when they threatened to undermine or challenge working assumptions. Just as scientists in the early nineteenth century remained relatively unaffected by David Hume's devastating critique of the traditional understanding of causality, so too did biological scientists in the first half of the nineteenth century, with the exception of Germans, fail to concern themselves with the implications of the Kant-Fries disagreement for their work.

It was not merely that scholars in France, England, and America had not read these German works, although most in fact had not. The issue had been addressed many times before, if not in the explicit and detailed manner of the German philosophers. On the one side there had been the historical materialistic position, perhaps best represented by Julien Offray de La Mettrie's *Man-Machine* (1747), in which it was argued, at least by implication, that a mechanical account of organism was possible. Opposing this view was the widespread conviction that because organisms involved adaptation to their environment and, among animals, a component of volition, no adequate scientific account of living things could be given that did not allow for final causation, a requirement that a strictly mechanical account did not seem able to provide. As indicated above, both of these positions were represented in the early nineteenth century, but in each case their status remained one of belief. Kant might give the impression that a teleological interpretation of organism was unavoidable for human knowledge, but, as Fries argued, Kant's position could be opposed by a strictly mechanical account. One could prove neither a mechanistic nor a teleological view. This disagreement contributed significantly to the confusion and the lack of consensus among scientists and theologians concerning the demarcation between scientific and religious explanation.

Scholars have shown recently how, in the decades prior to the *Origin of Species* in 1859, English scientists came more and more to accept as "scientific" only those explanations that rested on natural law, even when they seemed to undermine belief in God's capacity to interrupt the operations nature. In an oft-cited letter written to the geologist Charles Lyell some twenty-three years before the *Origin*, the astronomer John Herschel argued that even the origination of new species could in theory be explained scientifically, because, if and when it was accounted for, it "would be found to be a natural in contradistinction to a miraculous process."[2]

But it was the publication of the *Origin* itself that ultimately brought the matter to a head. Eventually it became understood that this work not only ignored teleological factors but purported to explain the order and design evident in organic nature by mechanical means. To an age becoming more and more convinced that scientific explanations should be strictly naturalistic and mechanical, Darwin's theory of evolution by natural selection came to represent a ruthless consistency that tolerated little fence-sitting. If the scientific community found itself challenged by Charles Darwin (1809–1882) to live up to its claim that scientific explanation need not resort to divine intervention, the religious community was even more challenged to respond to the implicit assertion that God was not necessary in the physical history of life on earth.

THE HISTORICAL SETTING

The *Origin* may ultimately have forced scientists and theologians to reassess the limits of their respective territories, but it did not do so overnight. There is a tendency among scholars to overestimate the immediate impact that Darwin's book had on the religious community. In England there was a much greater row about the publication of the *Essays and Reviews* in 1860, in which the *Origin* was mentioned only once, than there had been about the *Origin* itself one year earlier. A book in which nine clerics wrote approvingly about the methods of the German higher critics and their implications for Christian doctrine was much more easily assimilated by most people as a threat to religion than was the hypothesis of some relatively unknown scientist. Even up to the first decades of the present century some Anglicans, nearly all official Catholics, and most simple worshipers among the poor either knew nothing of evolution or continued to feel able to reject it on religious or scientific grounds.[3]

This delay in the theological response to Darwin is understandable once one closely investigates the historical setting. For one thing, the *Origin* was not the first indication of a potential conflict between science and religion. Well before 1859 the feeling had been growing in Europe and America that natural science supported a naturalistic, as opposed to a supernaturalistic, point of view. Ronald L. Numbers has demonstrated that in America Pierre Simon Laplace's nebular hypothesis, which explained the evolution of the solar system, helped prepare the way for the *Origin* by forcing educated Americans to assess their belief in the biblical account of creation and in supernatural explanation in general.[4] In Germany the major works of the so-called scientific materialists all predated the *Origin*, and the materialists themselves saw no discontinuity between their position and

Darwin's after 1859.[5] In England the scandalous *Vestiges of the Natural History of Creation*, published anonymously in 1844, depicted a naturalistic evolution that was denounced by both the scientific and religious communities.

Nor were theologians themselves taken by complete surprise when Darwin's work appeared. A two-century-old tradition of natural theology, in which human reason moved from creation to Creator, had always been intended to function as an apology for the Christian faith precisely because the notion of a godless and autonomous nature lurked ever in the background. Further, English clerics had been discussing the relationship between geology and biblical chronology at least since the 1800 Bampton Lectures.[6] Thus the church was hardly a stranger to the claim that natural science was undermining religious authority. At first glance the *Origin* appeared to be just another in a series of scientific works that gave "the ordinary man the uncomfortable feeling that somehow, he knew not how, science favored a materialistic philosophy of life, though no scientist known to fame was a materialist." Initially, Darwin led more to a renewal of old quarrels than to new debates.[7]

Another reason why it took time for the severity of Darwin's challenge to religion to sink in was that the church, especially in England, was occupied with other matters. At midcentury the ecclesiastical controversy within the Anglican Church that had pitted Catholic sympathizers in the so-called Oxford Movement against their critics was beginning to wane. But largely as a result of this internal controversy, the party structure within the Church of England was changing at the time Darwin wrote the *Origin*. Within the High Church a new faction, led by the original tractarians E. B. Pusey and John Keble, was gaining ground in 1860, prompting the old High Church to continue to denounce the lingering ritualism it saw as the trademark of the Catholic sympathizers.[8] The Low Church, or Evangelicals, put Scripture ahead of church organization and personal devotion ahead of priestly mediation. In 1860 the Evangelicals were at the height of their influence. Not only did a majority of bishops display Evangelical inclinations, but the years following 1860 were a time of great religious revival in England.[9]

Cutting across these lines was the Broad Church. Though not an organized church party, the various members of the Broad Church movement all agreed that the authority of the Bible, so important to Evangelicals, and the authority of the church, vital to both factions of the High Church, could be subjected to historical and systematic criticism. The Broad Church, through such ventures as the *Essays and Reviews* of 1860, questioned the very notion of religious authority.

These Anglican party conflicts attracted enormous attention among nineteenth-century Englishmen, so much so that the *Spectator* reported in 1861 that "of all tastes common among the middle class, the taste for discussing half-understood theology is perhaps the most pronounced."[10] In such a climate the appearance of the *Essays and Reviews*, with its theological focus, was bound to have more of an impact than Darwin's ponderous scientific tome. The church had a sufficient number of challenges facing it from within.

All of these considerations relate, of course, to merely intellectual matters. One might think that the church would have been so preoccupied with the exploding population, increasing urbanization and industrialization, and attendant social problems that it could have little time for theological arguments. In fact, when the bishop of London identified the problems facing the church in 1862, he listed social problems third in priority behind the critical spirit of the age and Catholicism.[11] In addition, the growing demand of dissenting sects to be treated before the law on a par with the established church made the search for a new basis for church authority ever more complicated.

For Darwin's countrymen, however, the primary mission of the church clearly remained theological, not social; and although Darwin himself was not a theologian, nor was his book perceived immediately to be a devastating blow to the church, eventually his ideas would prove to have a major impact on the future of Christian theology.

THE ORTHODOX RESPONSE TO DARWIN

In one sense it is possible to analyze the theological reactions to Darwinian evolution in terms of the degree to which natural selection was confronted head-on. Of course in the nineteenth century not even Darwin claimed that natural selection was the exclusive mechanism of evolutionary development. But natural selection came to represent a rigorous naturalism in which no external agency was required either to direct the course of development or to guarantee that a transcendent purpose was being realized as species changed over time.

For many theologians living during the aftermath of the *Origin*, the issue was not at all so sharply drawn as this. If scientists themselves argued over the relative importance of natural selection as opposed to the inheritance of characteristics acquired by use and disuse, how were theologians to presume that teleological factors were not involved? If scientists argued about the status of natural selection as a hypothesis, and philosophers could not distinguish sharply between fact, law, theory, and hypothesis, how was the theologian to formulate definitive new doctrinal positions?

To rigidly orthodox Christians, however, there was no confusion about the matter. At stake was the existence and nature of God, the role of the Scriptures, and the authority of religious truth. In the eyes of traditional Christian theologians the issue centered on the assertion that natural selection could account for design in the organic world without reference to a deity.

In the 1860s it was not difficult to hear facile denunciations of Darwin's theory as a menace to religion. But these attacks were generally directed toward Darwinism as yet another scientific theory that had encroached on religious territory; they rarely involved a specific and reasoned objection to evolution by natural selection. The issue was always the same: how could the audacious claims of modern science be compatible with a proper understanding of the Bible? As the Episcopalian *American Quarterly Church Review* put it in 1865: if Darwin's hypothesis is true, then the Bible is "an unbearable fiction" and Christians have been duped by "a monstrous lie" for nearly two thousand years.[12]

Not until 1874 did a serious spokesman for the orthodox position emerge, and then it was in America, not in England, that the reply originated. In general the *Origin* made little direct impact on American theology in the years immediately following 1859.[13] At the New York international meeting of the Evangelical Alliance in 1873, however, Darwinism was dealt with on its own, in conscious separation from the higher criticism of the Bible to which it had often been subordinated. Early in the meeting there prevailed a mood of supreme confidence that the dangers of skepticism and rationalism were losing their battle with theology. In contrast with European delegates, who warned of the need to defend the fundamentals of the faith against higher critics through a sound view of Scripture, American conservatives boasted that a worthy liberal opponent was hard to find, so strong was the state of Christian apologetics in America.[14]

Into the midst of this optimism penetrated, unexpectedly, the recently published scientific ideas of the Englishman Darwin. In an unscheduled floor debate, the president of Princeton College, James McCosh (1811–1894), suggested that the notion of biological evolution, which as late as the *Vestiges* in 1844 had not been taken seriously by virtually anyone, was not necessarily incompatible with Christian doctrine, that science and Scripture could be reconciled as parallel revelations.

As Charles Hodge (1797–1878), also from Princeton and the most influential Presbyterian theologian of the day, rose in reply, the orthodox Christian community listened to a summary of what would be fully argued the following year in Hodge's *What Is Darwinism?* The issue, said Hodge, was whether one believed in an intellectual process guided by God or a material process ruled by chance. One had to choose between the two views; they were not compatible.[15] In his book Hodge elaborated this view. After an extended description of Darwin's theory taken from the most recent edition of the *Origin* available to him, Hodge identified what he thought were its three components: evolution, natural selection, and natural selection without design. Most people, wrote Hodge, knew that evolution was not original with Darwin. Citing William Wells (1757–1817) and Patrick Matthew (1790–1874), Hodge asserted that natural selection also predated the *Origin*. Only the third component, natural selection resulting from unintelligent causes, was peculiar to Darwin's theory; it was also its most important element.[16]

Hodge had studied Darwin's book carefully. He provided copious documentation from the *Origin* showing that Darwin's whole drift was to assert that all organs of plants and animals, as well as their instincts and mental capacities, could be accounted for without any intention, purpose, or cooperation of God. He quoted the German scientific materialist Ludwig Büchner (1824–1899) to illustrate that Darwin's theory was "the most thoroughly naturalistic that can be imagined, and far more atheistic than that of his predecessor Lamarck."[17] Why, asked Hodge, had evolution been unacceptable at the time of the *Vestiges* but was now acceptable? The answer was that Darwin's unique emphasis had made evolution palatable to that state of mind which excluded design.[18]

In his book Hodge went beyond his position at the New York meetings. Now the problem was more than merely a matter of incompatible and conflicting beliefs: Darwinism was not even a possible option. To Hodge, it had become the mark of scientists to ignore deliberately that the adaptation of means to achieve an end irresistibly led to the conviction that such adaptation was the work of mind. "No man does doubt it, and no man can doubt it," he wrote.[19] Like Kant and unlike Fries, Hodge simply could not admit that his position, a belief based on an assumption, *could* be replaced by its opposite. "To any ordinarily constituted mind," he wrote, "it is absolutely impossible to believe that the eye is not a work of design."[20]

Hodge thought that Darwin, not he, was being dogmatic. Scientists, of course, had the right to demand to be heard in their areas of expertise, but Darwin's presumption that design could be accounted for mechanistically overstepped scientific limits, even as a hypothesis. Hodge argued that hypotheses, which unavoidably involved a degree of belief, should not be tolerated if the belief they required was impossible; and to Hodge, the idea that chance could generate design was rationally self-contradictory and therefore impossible. We have the right, he wrote, "to reject all speculations, hypotheses, and theories which come into conflict with well-established truths. It is ground [*sic*] of profound gratitude to God that He has given to the human mind intuitions which are infallible, laws of belief which men cannot disregard any more than laws of nature."[21]

Hodge's position was heralded and echoed in journals such as the Episcopalian *American Church Review* and even the Unitarian *Religious Magazine and Monthly Review.* To many, including some Catholics, Hodge's critique of Darwin's new theory was impressively reasoned and moderate, yet devastating. To them, the statement at the end of *What Is Darwinism?* summed up the crux of the issue. "The conclusion of the whole matter," Hodge had written, "is that the denial of design in nature is virtually the denial of God."[22]

If anything, such an unequivocal judgment about Darwin by a well-known and highly respected theologian gave confidence to the orthodox community that their initial hostility toward evolutionary theory had been proper. In another sense, however, following Hodge seemed to imply that one was left with an either/or choice: either Darwin was wrong or God did not exist. Hodge made it very clear that the middle ground some were trying to establish was not defensible.

The essential motivation behind Hodge's hard-line stance was to preserve the authority of the Bible, not only its account of the origin of life but its statements regarding the Fall, the Virgin Birth, the divinity of Christ, and the Christian scheme of redemption and immortality. In addition, he believed that there was everything to lose and nothing to gain if the point of God's intervention were removed to the level of secondary causes, unless, of course, God was understood to be in constant control of secondary causes through his mental forces. To Hodge, secondary causes acting somehow on their own went against the fact that we see everywhere the constant activity of mind. A schema with an absentee God, though technically theistic, was to him atheistic.[23]

In England the Evangelicals, or Low Church, shared with American orthodoxy a high reverence for Scripture. But the English Evangelicals did not produce an informed repudiation of Darwin of the stature of Hodge's *What Is Darwinism?* Their activities had for some time been largely negative—against Catholic sympathizers, against the Broad Church, against the spread of the critical spirit. It is therefore not surprising that Evangelicals failed to develop a positive theology that was widely acceptable after Darwin. Increasingly they were seen to be holding on to mere phrases, more through sheer commitment than through personal conviction.[24] As a result, the focus of the theological response to Darwinian evolution shifted away from these conservative circles, and attention increasingly went to those religious thinkers who treated evolutionary theory in a more tolerant and sympathetic manner.

ATTEMPTS TO RECONCILE
EVOLUTION AND THEOLOGY

Some Protestant writers refused to accept the choice set forth in English and American conservative thought. More liberal minds felt the need to explain why orthodox theologians incorrectly assumed that the traditional doctrines of Christianity could not be retained in any recognizable form if evolution by natural selection was embraced.

The liberal attempt to reconcile evolution and Christian theology began in the wake of the initial hostile reaction to Darwin in the 1860s and early 1870s. The liberal theologians included men who resented the denunciation of the prerogatives of modern learning that arose in response to the *Essays and Reviews* and to the increasing respect for Darwin's accomplishment among scientists. In England some, like Frederick Temple (1821–1902), had themselves helped to introduce higher critical methods into the study of the Christian religion. In America the reassessment of the relationship between science and religion by theologians of this ilk had played a part in prompting Hodge to speak out against the dangers inherent in such an endeavor. And in Germany the third edition of Hermann Ulrici's *Gott und die Natur* (1875) took full cognizance of Darwinism, which, Ulrici wrote, "far from setting theology aside, confirms it, so long as one will examine it clearly and without materialistic presuppositions."[25] Not until the 1880s, however, did the theological spotlight shift away from the conservative rejection of evolution to an acknowledgment of its value or even to an enthusiastic appropriation of evolution as a concept pregnant with theological potential.

All the would-be reconcilers had to face squarely the issue raised by Hodge: natural selection, based as it was on chance variation, appeared to be incompatible with God's purposeful activity in nature. Their manner of handling the contradiction involved agreeing, for the most part, with Hodge that natural selection, so understood, was incompatible with divine intent, but disagreeing with him that the essential aspect of evolutionary theory was natural selection, Darwin to the contrary notwithstanding. Since the *Origin* numerous scientists had criticized natural selection but accepted evolution, often of a Lamarckian variety; in fact, this reaction appeared to many to be the majority opinion. "It would seem at first sight," wrote the American philosopher Chauncy Wright, "that Mr. Darwin has won a victory, not for himself but for Lamarck."[26]

The pressing question for liberals was how to appropriate the concept of evolution for theological use. There seemed to be no *a priori* reason why evolution and religion should be incompatible, especially if evolution was understood as a synonym for development. The myth of evolution fitted perfectly into the general atmosphere of progress that permeated Victorian society, allowing some to gloss over contradictions that Darwinian evolution might present. Lord Arthur Balfour recalled how even his barber had talked of "the doctrine of evolution, Darwin and Huxley and the lot of them—hashed up somehow with the good time coming and the universal brotherhood and I don't know what else."[27]

The theological reconcilers appeared in at least three guises. Some believed that importing evolution into theology, while it would change some things, would not so alter orthodox thought that it would become unrecognizable. Others felt less concern about conserving the traditional expressions of Christianity than about reformulating Christian doctrine in a manner in tune with the times. Still others made evolution the very cornerstone of their theological perspective. All three groups adjusted biblical chronology as needed and preserved some form of an argument from design; but where the first faction gave the appearance of being forced into such reconciliation, the latter two reveled in the newfound opportunity to revitalize doctrines that were beginning to tax the loyalty of modern Christians. Typical of the first approach were the American theologians James McCosh and A. H. Strong (1836–1821); the second group found an articulate spokesman in the Anglican clergyman Frederick Temple; and the third viewpoint was represented by the American preacher Henry Ward Beecher (1818–1887) and the Anglican clerics who published a sequel to the *Essays and Reviews* entitled *Lux Mundi* (1889).

In his *Systematic Theology* A. H. Strong, who was then president of Rochester Theological Seminary, wrote: "We grant the principle of evolution, but we regard it as only the method of divine intelligence."[28] He was unambiguous about how Christians should treat evolution, pointing out that natural selection, if assumed to be the only factor in evolution, would imply an irrational hypothesis that was atheistic and nonteleological. So far he stood in agreement with Hodge. But Strong conceded that humankind had had a brute ancestry, though he made it clear why this fact was not damaging: "The wine in the miracle was not water because water had been used in the making of it, nor is man a brute because the brute has made some contributions to his creation."[29]

Earlier, James McCosh had similarly struggled with the significance of evolution for theology. On the boat bringing him from Scotland to America to take up duties as president of Princeton College, he had pondered whether he should let his convictions be known immediately or keep them in abeyance because of the prevailing tendency in evangelical circles.[30] He decided not to hold back and made public his belief that even natural selection was not incompatible with a religious view. According to McCosh, natural selection was but one of several means by which evolution proceeded, and even natural selection was consistent with supernatural design. Darwin, he wrote, had wrongly contrasted the two concepts as opposites. The mechanism revealed design, so that "supernatural design produces natural selection."[31] It is instructive to note that both Charles Hodge and Charles Darwin vehemently objected to this claim of McCosh.

If McCosh was less cautious than Strong would later be, he was even more bold about the key concern of evangelicals everywhere: how to harmonize evolution and the Bible? McCosh did not shy away from the demand that evolution must be shown to be compatible with Scripture. Like Strong, he portrayed evolution as "the method of God's procedure," but he emphasized that, understood in this light, "it is in no way inconsistent with Scripture."[32] The Bible, he wrote, was not concerned with the question of the absolute immutability of species, and even orthodox scholars were harmonizing Genesis and geology by demonstrating correspondences between the classification of historical periods and the six days of creation.[33]

Exactly what had McCosh and Strong conceded in their flirtation with evolutionary theory? Clearly they no longer demanded that the world was a mere six thousand years old or that new species appeared only as a result of special and repeated creative fiats of God. But they retained a belief in divine purpose that was compatible with their understanding of natural science and the Bible. To them, natural law, as the method of God's regular activity, did not preclude unique exertions of God's power to secure his purpose in creation, that is, "miracles" that could in theory be traced to natural causes. Here was a restatement of the age-old conviction that God's superintendence of his creation was immediate, direct, and continuous. Further, since these men saw no incompatibility between their views and a biblically based Christianity, essential doctrines such as the sovereignty of God, the inspiration of Scripture, the Trinity, the Atonement, and the existence of heaven and hell could remain in place.

Liberal theologians already engaged in a reexamination of the doctrine of Scripture at the time of Darwin's *Origin* appeared neither committed nor disposed to the evangelical motivations of McCosh, Ulrici, or Strong. For example, Frederick Temple, later archbishop of Canterbury, contributed a harmless chapter to the controversial *Essays and Reviews,* and refused to give in to pressure from Bishop Samuel Wilberforce and others to repudiate the remaining contributors, who were charged with maligning Scripture.

When in 1884 Temple gave the Bampton Lectures, he made clear his position on the relation between evolution and religion. Evolution, he said, could be understood and used in ways different from those suggested by more conservative minds. Temple identified the foundation of evolution not as God but as a determinism in which the present condition of the universe as a whole was the necessary outcome of its former condition. In fact, he implied that God did not interfere in nature at all. Most people, he wrote, accepted this scientific determinism; even Catholics, "who say God intervenes in nature," kept the interference to a minimum.[34] God's superintendence of evolution was, for Temple, not to be found in his repeated manipulation of natural law to achieve his purpose; rather, divine governance resided in an original decree in which superintendence was contained from the beginning. Temple asserted that the doctrine of evolution left the argument for an intelligent creator and governor stronger than before. However, the execution of God's purpose was now seen to belong more to the original act of creation than to acts of government since that event.[35]

On a linear spectrum of theological opinion about evolution in the late nineteenth century, Hodge's vehement rejection of Darwin would obviously be located to the far right. Next to it, still considerably to the right of center, would fall the views of McCosh and Strong. Temple's position, a moderate stance, which nevertheless substantially qualified Darwin's views and boldly suggested purely scientific conclusions at variance with those of informed evolutionary naturalists, would come next. Temple emphasized what he saw as epistemological weaknesses in Darwin's scheme. Darwin, for example, openly declined to explain the causes of variation, an approach that, to Temple, left fundamental scientific questions unaddressed. Reasoning from effects to causes was not only perfectly appropriate in natural science, according to Temple, but any schema that deliberately broke the inductive chain was scientifically incomplete.[36]

The strength of causal explanation could not, however, overcome its limitation. Temple did not believe in the possibility of a complete scientific explanation of the history of humankind. In an unwitting appeal to the argument that one cannot derive more from an effect than is contained in the cause, Temple declared that Laplacian and Darwinian evolution could not explain how life or morality originated, adding that while it was understandable that scientists had to treat these questions as unsolved puzzles, they could not insist beforehand that such problems were soluble. The evidence was in fact against the scientist, since empirical observation suggested that life came only from antecedent life.[37]

In spite of his criticism of Darwin, Temple crossed over the line on the spectrum of opinion dividing left from right. His position was qualitatively different from that of McCosh and Strong in at least two important respects. He replaced the immediacy of God's superintendence by a governance more distant; God acted through a history perfectly programmed rather than through a history corrected by natural laws in midcourse. Second, Temple portrayed evolution not merely as a concept that could be harmonized with Christian doctrine but as a notion that afforded positive insight into the nature of God's relation to the world. Temple conceded that evolution may have cut away some of the old arguments for God's existence, but he welcomed the new theological foundations he believed evolution had provided.[38]

Other reconcilers, farther to the left than Temple, expressed even greater enthusiasm for the new life they saw evolution breathing into Christian doctrine. In America the prosperity of the eighties made it easier for such theologians to interpret evolution in a manner thoroughly consistent with the general atmosphere of progress and optimism. The public, too, displayed an enormous interest in evolutionary theology. When Henry Ward Beecher preached a series of sermons on evolution in May of 1885 at Plymouth Church in Brooklyn, hundreds had to be turned away. The sermons themselves were telegraphed to Boston and Chicago, and at least two papers published full reports on the front page every Monday.[39]

There was, however, an inverse relation between belief in the positive theological value to be derived from evolution and an acceptance of Darwin's exposition, based on natural selection and the struggle for existence. Beecher's hero, for example, was the philosopher Herbert Spencer (1820–1903), not Darwin, because Spencer had interpreted evolution on a cosmic scale. And Beecher's successor at Plymouth Church, Lyman Abbott (1835–1922), eventually embraced a view that specifically repudiated the war of all against all. In The Theology of an Evolutionist (1897) he portrayed God as the antithesis of natural selection, a creative and directing force in complete control of all phenomena.

By the turn of the century, liberal theologians had reached a consensus that the gospel had to be reinterpreted in terms of evolutionary thought. This consensus was already evident in the compilation of studies on religion, entitled *Lux Mundi*, written by eleven Anglican clergymen.[40] There was even an attempt shortly after the turn of the century to harmonize Christianity and evolution by showing how Christianity was itself but a phase of a great evolutionary law.[41]

Coincident with this consummation of the liberal reconciliation of evolution and Christianity was a shift back from the deistic tendencies of Temple's absentee God to a reformulation of the doctrine of God's immanence. The writers of the *Lux Mundi*, for example, reinterpreted the doctrine of the Atonement by suggesting that the Incarnation be viewed as the culmination of a long process that itself accomplished the reconciliation of God and man.[42] Divine creation was no longer a single act God performed, after which He rested, but a mysterious and permanent relationship between the infinite and finite. If God never stepped in from the outside, wrote Carl Patton, "then God must be inside the process or disappear entirely. So came the new and fruitful conception of the immanence of God."[43] In this way evolution was credited both with rendering a final blow to the old deism of the eighteenth century and with lending weight to a vital element in the Christian doctrine of the Incarnation.[44]

Unquestionably, the attempt to reconcile evolution and Christianity depended on a rejection of natural selection as the mechanism of evolution. A few writers, for example Asa Gray and George Frederick Wright, claimed that natural selection was not incompatible with a divinely ordered creation, but after Hodge, theologians for the most part abandoned the attempt to reconcile natural selection and design.[45]

THE RADICAL SEPARATION
OF SCIENCE AND RELIGION

Although one must never lose sight of the diverse factors that helped to shape the changing theological traditions of the nineteenth century, particularly the impact of German higher criticism, the emergence of a consensus among many theologians that natural selection must be rejected in order to harmonize science and religion, coupled with a simultaneous appropriation of the concept of evolution, reveals the central role Darwin's work played. Between the publication of the

Vestiges in 1844 and the writings of the reconcilers in the last two decades of the century, evolution had been transformed from a dangerous threat into a new theological opportunity. In this process the *Origin of Species* marked the turning point.

Although the majority of theologians became convinced that no reconciliation of Darwinian evolution, if understood to rest on natural selection alone, with traditional Christianity was possible, few, not even Darwin, argued that evolution depended solely on natural selection. In fact, the increasing scientific objection to natural selection had bolstered the theologians' confidence that they were justified in basing their inferences elsewhere.

But all that was beside the point, for natural selection had become much more than a scientific hypothesis. It had come to stand for an attitude, a ruthless mechanical naturalism that required no intervention or preestablished design. Of course it also represented a belief, though not, as we have seen, a new belief. But Darwin made belief in evolution more credible than at any time previous. By providing an example of how mechanisms might, at least in theory, fully account for the constitution and purposive activity of organisms, Darwin challenged those who, like Kant, held that human reason had no other option than a fundamentally teleological explanation of organism.

Hodge understood intuitively what Darwin's *Origin* represented. He appreciated that a matter of belief was at stake. To him it was a question not of reconciliation but of choice. Hodge was not willing to base his conclusions on the objections of scientists to natural selection, even though he knew that by the standards of the philosophy of science natural selection was far from scientific fact. It was as if he distrusted those reconcilers who did not face up to the choice confronting them because at best they were relying on disagreements within the scientific community, and he knew from history the danger of such a stance. Because Hodge recognized the confrontation for what it was, Neal Gillespie observes that he "was and remains one of the most astute writers on the theological implications of Darwin's work."[46]

Gillespie has shown how Darwin's work completed the establishment of what he has labeled thoroughly positivistic science.[47] In the face of the transition from an older, theologically grounded science to a new, positivistically grounded one, the warfare between science and Christianity in the nineteenth century was undeniably real, so long as religion tried to remain traditional. Both Darwin and Hodge saw the encounter between science and religion in this way. "Do not, I beg," Darwin wrote to Lyell in early September 1859, "be in a hurry in committing yourself (like so many naturalists) to go a certain length and no further; for I am deeply convinced that it is absolutely necessary to go the whole vast length, or stick to the creation of each species."[48] "Religion," wrote Hodge fifteen years later, "has to fight for its life against a large class of scientific men."[49]

The appearance of the concept of natural selection in the debate over the transmutation of species represents, therefore, more than merely another indication of the positivistic understanding of natural science that had been under way for some time. In the aftermath of the *Origin*, theologians were more and more confronted with a choice that, since Laplace's nebular hypothesis, had been merely disconcerting but was not profoundly disturbing and unavoidable: either reject the conclusions or the positivistic methods that had come to dominate science, including biology, or fundamentally redefine the essence of Christianity so that it did not at all intersect with science.

Those here described as reconcilers never acknowledged that Darwin's challenge was so fundamental. The objections to the use of the metaphor of a warfare between science and religion raised of late by historians of nineteenth-century thought are indeed appropriate with regard to these theologians. They were, after all, sympathetic to the increasing scope and power of scientific explanation, and as a result the liberal ones among them were increasingly willing to prevent tension by shifting the emphasis away from natural theology, miracles, and the Genesis account of creation to a knowledge of God that lay in the heart or conscience and to a revaluation of traditional views of sin and redemption.[50] But this redefinition of religion did not permit a complete separation of science and religion by removing religion from the physical and into the moral realm. A proper religious outlook, according to the reconcilers, still allowed, even demanded, that one see design in nature, though it was conceded that the old argument from design à la William Paley must be abandoned. The reconcilers did not view natural science as a completely positivistic endeavor devoid of all final causation. They never relinquished their hold on some form of premeditated design in the universe. And they were absolutely convinced that they were not participating in a fight to the finish with natural science. Thus their efforts are only inappropriately described in the language of warfare.

The nineteenth century was not, however, without religious thinkers who agreed that the scientific enterprise was consistently and totally positivistic, even when it treated organism and design in nature. Their challenge, one especially visible in post-Darwinian German theological thought, was to redefine the domain and prerogatives of religion in such a way that scientific explanations did not clash with religious expression. This task implied that religion could no longer restrict, determine, or even condition scientific explanations; knowledge of the physical world per se no longer involved a religious dimension. According to this view, the relation between science and religion is not adversarial; there simply is no relation between the two. The language of warfare is inappropriate not because science and religion are viewed as compatible but because they have nothing to do with each other.

The roots of this development in nineteenth-century theology lie deep in the German Romantic Era in the thought of Friedrich Schleiermacher (1768–1834) and Jakob Fries, and found expression in the post-Darwinian period in the work of their respective disciples, Albrecht Ritschl (1822–1889) and Rudolf Otto (1869–1937). These liberal German theologians viewed the accommodation of reconcilers like McCosh as superficial because they insisted that theology retain the right to make metaphysical assertions about nature. Religion was naive, wrote Otto, if it represented the supernatural and the natural as planes of being and action that variously intersect one another.[51] In contrast with this position, Ritschl, Otto, and others saw Christianity as an ethical and social teaching born from and acting upon human feeling, not knowledge.[52]

Naturally, this radical reshaping of religion did not much concern itself with science. Ritschl wished to purify religion from philosophical and scientific elements that in his view corrupted it, but he willingly conceded that Darwin's cosmos no longer contained adequate symbols of the classical Christian heritage. In response to Darwin he reshaped that heritage so that, in John Dillenberger's words, "the vertical and depth dimension within man and the cosmos" was broken. Ritschlian religion dealt with humans in their relationship to humans; it relinquished all claim to dictate knowledge of the physical world.[53]

But in separating religion from science neither Ritschl nor Otto wished to imply that one could not be subordinated to the other. Otto credited Fries with solving the problem of the proper relation between the supernatural and the natural, a solution Otto expressed in the conclusion of an essay on Darwinism and religion: "There are certainly no means for discovering God and his purposes through natural science; but if we know of them from other sources, then the strictly causative explanation of the origin of our world, presented by natural science, becomes subsidiary to them."[54] Ritschl, too, acknowledged the positivistic nature of scientific explanation and subordinated science to religion. According to Ritschl, the fact that a materialistic interpretation of the world suggested only chance as a moving force of the ultimate causes of the world revealed its irrelevance and subordination to a moral interpretation of experience.[55]

Nor was this tendency confined to Germany. It can also be found, for example, in Leslie Stephen's *Essays on Freethinking and Plainspeaking* (1873). Stephen (1832–1904), man of letters and first editor of the monumental *Dictionary of National Biography*, was, as he put it, willing to grant Darwin everything, because he regarded Darwin's theory as unimportant. "The one main fact is that somehow or other I am here." Religion, he wrote, still existed, as evidenced by the human need to love one another, to elevate the future over the past, and to rise above purely sensual wants. Like Ritschl, Stephen declared that religions thrive to the extent that they express our deepest feeling, not to the extent they express our abstract reasoning.[56]

CONCLUSION

The theological traditions of the nineteenth century were not equally influential. Those scholars who wished radically to separate science from religion attracted the smallest following. In the late nineteenth and early twentieth centuries a desire to reconcile science and religion in some fashion found widespread expression among educated circles, while the story of Adam and Eve continued to meet the needs of the masses. Since that time each of these traditions has faced fundamental challenges. Those who have wanted to remain orthodox in their religion have found that their demand that the positivistic assumptions of natural science be rejected whenever they clashed with a traditional understanding of Scripture has been less and less heeded as science has enjoyed increasing success. Those who have wished to promote harmony between religion and science by reinterpreting Christian doctrine, while at the same time insisting on religion's right to interpret nature teleologically, have lived in constant danger that the evidence for nature's *telos* will become ever less persuasive and appear ever more arbitrary as natural science, especially biological science, proceeds without even acknowledging any such religious prerogative. Finally, those who have felt forced by Darwin to admit that God has no reference to nature have made theology unrecognizable as theology to the majority of believers for whom a demythologized Christianity is no real Christianity at all. Protestant theology in the twentieth century owes its development to many factors, one of the most important of which is the *Origin of Species*. After Darwin the relation between God, man, and nature could never again be as clear as once it had been.

NOTES

1. Immanuel Kant, *Kritik der Urteilskraft*, vol. 5 of *Gesammelte Schriften* (Berlin: Reimer, 1908), p. 373; Jakob Fries, *Reinhold, Fichte und Schelling*, vol. 24 of *Sämtliche Schriften* (Aalen: Scientia Verlag, 1976), pp. 179–180. The best accounts by far of the implications of Kant's treatment of biology occur in Reinhard Löw, *Die Philosophie des Lebendigen: Der Begriff des Organischen bei Kant* (Frankfurt: Suhrkamp, 1980), pp. 127–270, and Timothy Lenoir, *The Strategy of Life: Teleology and Mechanics in Nineteenth-Century German Biology* (Dordrecht: Reidel, 1982), pp. 17–36.

2. Herschel's statement is discussed by Neal C. Gillespie, *Charles Darwin and the Problem of Creation* (Chicago: Univ. of Chicago Press, 1979), pp. 30–31, and by Michael Ruse, "The Relation between Science and Religion in Britain, 1830–1870," *Church History* 44 (1975): 508–510.

3. Owen Chadwick, *The Victorian Church*, 2 vols. (New York: Oxford Univ. Press, 1970), 2:10–11, 23–24.

4. Ronald L. Numbers, *Creation by Natural Law: Laplace's Nebular Hypothesis in American Thought* (Seattle: Univ. of Washington press, 1977).

5. Frederick Gregory, *Scientific Materialism in Nineteenth-Century Germany* (Dordrecht: Reidel, 1977), chap. 8.

6. Bernard Reardon, *From Coleridge to Gore: A Century of Religious Thought in Britain* (London: Longman, 1971), pp. 286–287. The subject came up again in the lectures for 1805, 1811, and 1833.

7. Chadwick, *Victorian Church* 2:34; Harry Paul, "Religion and Darwinism: Varieties of Catholic Reaction," in *The Comparative Reception of Darwinism*, ed. Thomas F. Glick (Austin: Univ. of Texas Press, 1972), pp. 403–436 at 415.

8. Margaret Anne Crowther, *The Church Embattled: Religious Controversy in Mid-Victorian England* (Hamden, Conn.: Archon Books, 1970), pp. 24, 27.

9. Desmond Bowen, *The Idea of the Victorian Church* (Montreal: McGill Univ. Press, 1968), p. 160; Crowther, *Church Embattled*, p. 22.

10. Quoted in Crowther, *Church Embattled*, p. 22.

11. Ibid., p. 13.

12. Quoted in Paul F. Boller, Jr., *American Thought in Transition: The Impact of Evolutionary Naturalism, 1865–1900* (Chicago: Rand McNally & Co., 1969), p. 24.

13. Winfred Ernest Garrison, *The March of Faith: The Story of Religion in America since 1865* (Westport, Conn.: Greenwood Press, 1961), p. 90.

14. George M. Marsden, *Fundamentalism and American Culture: The Shaping of Twentieth-Century Evangelicalism, 1870–1925* (Oxford: Oxford Univ. Press, 1980), p. 18; see also p. 233, n. 31.

15. Ibid., p. 19.

16. Charles Hodge, *What Is Darwinism?* (New York: Scribner, Armstrong & Co., 1874), pp. 48–51.

17. Ibid., p. 85.

18. Ibid., pp. 146, 149. For pre-Darwinian theological attacks against the *Vestiges* see Edward J. Pfeifer, "United States," in *Comparative Reception of Darwinism*, ed. Glick, pp. 170 ff.

19. Hodge, *What Is Darwinism?* p. 169.

20. Ibid., p. 60.

21. Ibid., p. 139.

22. Ibid., p. 173.

23. Ibid., pp. 43–46.

24. Bowen, *Idea of the Victorian Church*, p. 151.

25. Hermann Ulrici, *Gott und die Natur*, 3d ed. (Leipzig: Weigel, 1875), p. 387; see also p. 410.

26. Quoted in Gillespie, *Darwin and the Problem of Creation*, p. 147. For the growth of neo-Lamarckian thought at the end of the nineteenth century see Peter Bowler, *The Eclipse of Darwinism: Anti-Darwinian Evolution Theories in the Decades around 1900* (Baltimore: Johns Hopkins Univ. Press, 1983).

27. Walter E. Houghton, *The Victorian Frame of Mind* (New Haven: Yale Univ. Press, 1957), p. 38.

28. A. H. Strong, *Systematic Theology*, 3 vols. (Westwood, N.J.: Fleming Revell, 1907), 2:473.

29. Ibid., p. 472.

30. James McCosh, *The Religious Aspect of Evolution*, 2d ed. (New York: Scribner's Sons, 1890), pp. viii–ix. See also J. David Hoeveler, Jr., *James McCosh and the Scottish Intellectual Tradition: From Glasgow to Princeton* (Princeton, N.J.: Princeton Univ. Press, 1981), chap. 6.

31. McCosh, *Religious Aspect*, p. 7; see also pp. 16–17.

32. James McCosh, "Autobiographical Statement," in *The Life of James McCosh*, ed. William Milligan Sloane (New York: Scribner's Sons, 1896), p. 234.

33. McCosh, *Religious Aspect*, p. 27.

34. Frederick Temple, *The Relations between Religion and Science* (London: Macmillan & Co., 1885), p. 101.

35. Ibid., pp. 122–123.

36. Ibid., p. 173.

37. Ibid., pp. 169–170. See also A. O. J. Cockshut, *Religious Controversies of the Nineteenth Century* (Lincoln: Univ. of Nebraska Press, 1966), pp. 257–258.

38. Temple, *Relations between Religion and Science*, pp. 108–109.

39. Boller, *American Thought in Transition*, p. 32.

40. Bowen, *Idea of the Victorian Church*, pp. 174–175.

41. Samuel Louis Phillips, *Agreement of Evolution and Christianity* (Washington, D.C.: The Phillips Co., 1904).

42. Leonard Elliot-Binns, *English Thought, 1860–1900: The Theological Aspect* (Greenwich, Conn.: Seabury Press, 1956), p. 244.

43. Carl S. Patton, "The American Theological Scene: Fifty Years in Retrospect," *Journal of Religion* 16 (1936): 452–453; see also P. N. Waggett, "The Influence of Darwin upon Religious Thought," in *Darwin and Modern Science*, ed. A. C. Seward (Cambridge: Cambridge Univ. Press, 1909), p. 490.

44. Leonard Elliot-Binns, *Religion in the Victorian Era* (London: Lutterworth Press, 1953), p. 157.

45. The historian Stow Persons goes so far as to assert that after Hodge "no one undertook seriously to reconcile natural selection with design" ("Evolution and Theology in America," in *Evolutionary Thought in America*, ed. Stow Persons [New Haven: Yale Univ. Press, 1950], p. 426). For an eloquent and articulate exposition of the position of Gray and Wright see James R. Moore, *The Post-Darwinian Controversies: A Study of the Protestant Struggle to Come to Terms with Darwin in Great Britain and America, 1870–1900* (Cambridge: Cambridge Univ. Press, 1979). For an excellent recent study of the shift away from Hodge's strict rejection of natural selection to a qualified acceptance of Lamarckian evolution in the conservative theological tradition see David H. Livingstone, "The Idea of Design: The Vicissitudes of a Key Concept in the Princeton Response to Darwin," *Scottish Journal of Theology* 37 (1984): 329–357.

46. Gillespie, *Darwin and the Problem of Creation*, p. 112. Obviously the perspective represented here precludes agreement with Cynthia Russett that Asa Gray was "a shrewder mind than Hodge" (Russett, *Darwin in America: The Intellectual Response, 1865–1912* [San Francisco: W. H. Freeman, 1976], p. 270).

47. Gillespie, *Darwin and the Problem of Creation*, pp. 53, 76.

48. Charles Darwin, *The Life and Letters of Charles Darwin*, ed. Francis Darwin, 2 vols. (New York: D. Appleton & Co., 1896), 2:519.

49. Hodge, *What Is Darwinism?* p. 142. On Hodge's heritage in the twentieth century see chap. 16 of this volume.

50. Chadwick, *Victorian Church* 2:30–33.

51. Rudolf Otto, "Darwinism and Religion," in his *Religious Essays*, trans. Brian Lunn (London: Oxford Univ. Press, 1931), pp. 128–129.

52. James Ward Smith, "Religion and Science in American Philosophy," in *The Shaping of American Religion*, ed. J. W. Smith and A. L. Jamison (Princeton: Princeton Univ. Press, 1961), pp. 423–424.

53. John Dillenberger, *Protestant Thought and Natural Science: A Historical Interpretation* (Nashville: Abingdon Press, 1960), p. 253.

54. Otto, "Darwinism and Religion," p. 139.

55. Albrecht Ritschl, *Die christliche Lehre von der Rechtfertigung und Versöhnung*, 3 vols. (Bonn: Marcus, 1874); see especially vol. 3, trans. H. R. Mackintosh and A. B. Macaulay as *The Christian Doctrine of Justification and Reconciliation* (Clifton, N.J.: Reference Book Publishers, 1966), p. 209.

56. Leslie Stephen, *Essays on Freethinking and Plainspeaking* (New York: G. P. Putnam's Sons, 1905), p. 86. First published in 1873. On the heritage of this radical reshaping of theology see chap. 18 of this volume.

16

The Creationists

Ronald L. Numbers

Scarcely twenty years after the publication of Charles Darwin's *Origin of Species* in 1859 special creationists could name only two working naturalists in North America, John William Dawson (1820–1899) of Montreal and Arnold Guyot (1806–1884) of Princeton, who had not succumbed to some theory of organic evolution. The situation in Great Britain looked equally bleak for creationists, and on both sides of the Atlantic liberal churchmen were beginning to follow their scientific colleagues into the evolutionist camp. By the closing years of the nineteenth century evolution was infiltrating even the ranks of the evangelicals, and, in the opinion of many observers, belief in special creation seemed destined to go the way of the dinosaur. But contrary to the hopes of liberals and the fears of conservatives, creationism did not become extinct. The majority of late-nineteenth-century Americans remained true to a traditional reading of Genesis, and as late as 1982 a public-opinion poll revealed that 44 percent of Americans, nearly a fourth of whom were college graduates, continued to believe that "God created man pretty much in his present form at one time within the last 10,000 years."[1]

Such surveys failed, however, to disclose the great diversity of opinion among those professing to be creationists. Risking oversimplification, we can divide creationists into two main camps: "strict creationists," who interpret the days of Genesis literally, and "progressive creationists," who construe the Mosaic days to be immense periods of time. But even within these camps substantial differences exist. Among strict creationists, for example, some believe that God created all terrestrial life—past and present—less than ten thousand years ago, while others postulate one or more creations prior to the seven days of Genesis. Similarly, some progressive creationists believe in numerous creative acts, while others limit God's intervention to the creation of life and perhaps the human soul. Since this last species of creationism is practically indistinguishable from theistic evolutionism, this essay focuses on the strict creationists and the more conservative of the progressive creationists, particularly on the small number who claimed scientific expertise. Drawing on their writings, it traces the ideological development of creationism from the crusade to outlaw the teaching of evolution in the 1920s to the current battle for equal time. During this period the leading apologists for special creation shifted from an openly biblical defense of their views to one based largely on science. At the same time they grew less tolerant of notions of an old earth and symbolic days of creation, common among creationists early in the century, and more doctrinaire in their insistence on a recent creation in six literal days and on a universal flood.

THE LOYAL MAJORITY

The general acceptance of organic evolution by the intellectual elite of the late Victorian era has often obscured the fact that the majority of Americans remained loyal to the doctrine of special creation. In addition to the masses who said nothing, there were many people who vocally rejected kinship with the apes and other, more reflective, persons who concurred with the Princeton theologian Charles Hodge (1797–1878) that Darwinism was atheism. Among the most intransigent foes of organic evolution were the premillennialists, whose predictions of Christ's imminent return depended on a literal reading of the Scriptures. Because of their conviction that one error in the Bible invalidated the entire book, they had little patience with scientists who, as described by the evangelist Dwight L. Moody (1837–1899), "dug up old carcasses . . . to make them testify against God."[2]

Such an attitude did not, however, prevent many biblical literalists from agreeing with geologists that the earth was far older than six thousand years. They did so by identifying two separate creations in the first chapter of Genesis: the first, "in the beginning," perhaps millions of years ago, and the second, in six actual days, approximately four thousand years before the birth of Christ. According to this so-called gap theory, most fossils were relics of the first creation, destroyed by God prior to the Adamic restoration. In 1909 the *Scofield Reference Bible*, the most authoritative biblical guide in fundamentalist circles, sanctioned this view.[3]

Scientists like Guyot and Dawson, the last of the reputable nineteenth-century creationists, went still further to accommodate science by interpreting the days of Genesis as ages and by correlating them with successive epochs in the natural history of the world. Although they believed in special creative acts, especially of the first humans, they tended to minimize the number of supernatural interventions and to maximize the operation of natural law. During the late nineteenth century their theory of progressive creation circulated widely in the colleges and seminaries of America.[4]

The early Darwinian debate focused largely on the implications of evolution for natural theology; and so long as these discussions remained confined to scholarly circles, those who objected to evolution on biblical grounds saw little reason to participate. But when the debate spilled over into the public arena during the 1880s and 1890s, creationists grew alarmed. "When these vague speculations, scattered to the four winds by the million-tongued press, are caught up by ignorant and untrained men," declared one premillennialist in 1889, "it is time for earnest Christian men to call a halt."[5]

The questionable scientific status of Darwinism undoubtedly encouraged such critics to speak up. Although the overwhelming majority of scientists after 1880 accepted a long earth history and some form of organic evolution, many in the late nineteenth century were expressing serious reservations about the ability of Darwin's particular theory of natural selection to account for the origin of species. Their published criticisms of Darwinism led creationists mistakenly to conclude that scientists were in the midst of discarding evolution. The appearance of books with such titles as *The Collapse of Evolution* and *At the Death Bed of Darwinism* bolstered this belief and convinced antievolutionists that liberal Christians had capitulated to evolution too quickly. In view of this turn of events it seemed likely that those who had "abandoned the stronghold of faith out of sheer fright will soon be found scurrying back to the old and impregnable citadel, when they learn that 'the enemy is in full retreat.'"[6]

For the time being, however, those conservative Christians who would soon call themselves fundamentalists perceived a greater threat to orthodox faith than evolution—higher criticism, which treated the Bible more as a historical document than as God's inspired word. Their relative apathy toward evolution is evident in *The Fundamentals*, a mass-produced series of twelve booklets published between 1910 and 1915 to revitalize and reform Christianity around the world. Although one contributor identified evolution as the principal cause of disbelief in the Scriptures and another traced the roots of higher criticism to Darwin, the collection as a whole lacked the strident antievolutionism that would characterize the fundamentalist movement of the 1920s.[7]

This is particularly true of the writings of George Frederick Wright (1838–1921), a Congregational minister and amateur geologist of international repute. At first glance his selection to represent the fundamentalist point of view seems anomalous. As a prominent Christian Darwinist in the 1870s he had argued that the intended purpose of Genesis was to protest polytheism, not teach science. By the 1890s, however, he had come to espouse the progressive creationism of Guyot and Dawson, partly, it seems, in reaction to the claims of higher critics regarding the accuracy of the Pentateuch. Because of his standing as a scientific authority and his conservative view of the Scriptures, the editors of *The Fundamentals* selected him to address the question of the relationship between evolution and the Christian faith.[8]

In an essay misleadingly titled "The Passing of Evolution" Wright attempted to steer a middle course between the theistic evolution of his early days and the traditional views of some special creationists. On the one hand, he argued that the Bible itself taught evolution, "an orderly progress from lower to higher forms of matter and life." On the other hand, he limited evolution to the origin of species, pointing out that even Darwin had postulated the supernatural creation of several forms of plants and animals, endowed by the Creator with a "marvelous capacity for variation." Furthermore, he argued that, despite the physical similarity between human beings and the higher animals, the former "came into existence as the Bible represents, by the special creation of a single pair, from whom all the varieties of the race have sprung."[9]

Although Wright represented the left wing of fundamentalism, his moderate views on evolution contributed to the conciliatory tone that prevailed during the years leading up to World War I. Fundamentalists may not have liked evolution, but few, if any, at this time saw the necessity or desirability of launching a crusade to eradicate it from the schools and churches in America.

THE ANTIEVOLUTION CRUSADE

Early in 1922 William Jennings Bryan (1860–1925), Presbyterian layman and thrice-defeated Democratic candidate for the presidency of the United States, heard of an effort in Kentucky to ban the teaching of evolution in public schools. "The movement will sweep the country," he predicted hopefully, "and we will drive Darwinism from our schools."[10] His prophecy proved overly optimistic, but before the end of the decade more than twenty state legislatures did debate antievolution laws, and four—Oklahoma, Tennessee, Mississippi, and

Arkansas—banned the teaching of evolution in public schools. At times the controversy became so tumultuous that it looked to some as though "America might go mad." Many persons shared responsibility for these events, but none more than Bryan. His entry into the fray had a catalytic effect and gave antievolutionists what they needed most: "a spokesman with a national reputation, immense prestige, and a loyal following."[11]

The development of Bryan's own attitude toward evolution closely paralleled that of the fundamentalist movement. Since early in the century he had occasionally alluded to the silliness of believing in monkey ancestors and to the ethical dangers of thinking that might makes right, but until the outbreak of World War I he saw little reason to quarrel with those who disagreed. The war, however, exposed the darkest side of human nature and shattered his illusions about the future of Christian society. Obviously something had gone awry, and Bryan soon traced the source of the trouble to the paralyzing influence of Darwinism on the human conscience. By substituting the law of the jungle for the teaching of Christ, it threatened the principles he valued most: democracy and Christianity. Two books in particular confirmed his suspicion. The first, Vernon Kellogg's *Headquarters Nights* (1917), recounted firsthand conversations with German officers that revealed the role Darwin's biology had played in persuading the Germans to declare war. The second, Benjamin Kidd's *Science of Power* (1918), purported to demonstrate the historical and philosophical links between Darwinism and German militarism.[12]

About the time that Bryan discovered the Darwinian origins of the war, he also became aware, to his great distress, of unsettling effects the theory of evolution was having on America's own young people. From frequent visits to college campuses and from talks with parents, pastors, and Sunday-school teachers, he heard about an epidemic of unbelief that was sweeping the country. Upon investigating the cause, his wife reported, "he became convinced that the teaching of Evolution as a fact instead of a theory caused the students to lose faith in the Bible, first, in the story of creation, and later in other doctrines, which underlie the Christian religion." Again Bryan found confirming evidence in a recently published book, *Belief in God and Immortality* (1916), by the Bryn Mawr psychologist James H. Leuba, who demonstrated statistically that college attendance endangered traditional religious beliefs.[13]

Armed with this information about the cause of the world's and the nation's moral decay, Bryan launched a nationwide crusade against the offending doctrine. In one of his most popular and influential lectures, "The Menace of Darwinism," he summed up his case against evolution, arguing that it was both un-Christian and unscientific. Darwinism, he declared, was nothing but "guesses strung together," and poor guesses at that. Borrowing from a turn-of-the-century tract, he illustrated how the evolutionist explained the origin of the eye:

> The evolutionist guesses that there was a time when eyes were unknown—that is a necessary part of the hypothesis. . . . a piece of pigment, or, as some say, a freckle appeared upon the skin of an animal that had no eyes. This piece of pigment or freckle converged the rays of the sun upon that spot and when the little animal felt the heat on that spot it turned the spot to the sun to get more heat. The increased heat irritated the skin—so the evolutionists guess, and a nerve came there and out of the nerve came the eye!

"Can you beat it?" he asked incredulously—and that it happened not once but twice? As for himself, he would take one verse in Genesis over all that Darwin wrote.[14]

Throughout his political career Bryan had placed his faith in the common people, and he resented the attempt of a few thousand scientists "to establish an oligarchy over the forty million American Christians," to dictate what should be taught in the schools.[15] To a democrat like Bryan it seemed preposterous that this "scientific soviet" would not only demand to teach its insidious philosophy but impudently insist that society pay its salaries. Confident that nine-tenths of the Christian citizens agreed with him, he decided to appeal directly to them, as he had done so successfully in fighting the liquor interests. "Commit your case to the people," he advised creationists. "Forget, if need be, the high-brows both in the political and college world, and carry this cause to the people. They are the final and efficiently corrective power."[16]

And who were the people who joined Bryan's crusade? As recent studies have shown, they came from all walks of life and from every region of the country. They lived in New York, Chicago, and Los Angeles as well as in small towns and in the country. Few possessed advanced degrees, but many were not without education. Nevertheless, Bryan undeniably found his staunchest supporters and won his greatest victories in the conservative and still largely rural South, described hyperbolically by one fundamentalist journal as "the last stronghold of orthodoxy on the North American continent," a region where the "masses of the people in all denominations 'believe the Bible from lid to lid.'"[17]

The strength of Bryan's following within the churches is perhaps more difficult to determine, because not all fundamentalists were creationists and many creationists refused to participate in the crusade against evolution. However, a 1929 survey of the theological beliefs of seven hundred Protestant ministers provides some valuable clues. The question "Do you believe that the creation of the world occurred in the manner and time recorded in Genesis?" elicited the following positive responses:

Lutheran	89%
Baptist	63%
Evangelical	62%
Presbyterian	35%
Methodist	24%
Congregational	12%
Episcopalian	11%
Other	60%

Unfortunately, these statistics tell us nothing about the various ways respondents may have interpreted the phrase "in the manner and time recorded in Genesis," nor do they reveal anything about the level of political involvement in the campaign against evolution. Lutherans, for example, despite their overwhelming rejection of evolution, generally preferred education to legislation and tended to view legal action against evolution as "a dangerous mingling of church and state." Similarly, premillennialists, who saw the spread of evolution as one more sign of the world's impending end, sometimes lacked incentive to correct the evils around them.[18]

Baptists and Presbyterians, who dominated the fundamentalist movement, participated actively in the campaign against evolution. The Southern Baptist Convention, spiritual home of some of the most outspoken foes of evolution, lent encouragement to the creationist crusaders by voting unanimously in 1926 that "this Convention accepts Genesis as teaching that man was the special creation of God, and rejects every theory, evolution or other, which teaches that man originated in, or came by way of, a lower animal ancestry." The Presbyterian Church contributed Bryan and other leaders to the creationist cause but, as the above survey indicates, also harbored many evolutionists. In 1923 the General Assembly turned back an attempt by Bryan and his fundamentalist cohorts to cut off funds to any church school found teaching human evolution, approving instead a compromise measure that condemned only materialistic evolution. The other major Protestant bodies paid relatively little attention to the debate over evolution; and Catholics, though divided on the question of evolution, seldom favored restrictive legislation.[19]

Leadership of the antievolution movement came not from the organized churches of America but from individuals like Bryan and interdenominational organizations such as the World's Christian Fundamentals Association, a predominantly premillennialist body founded in 1919 by William Bell Riley (1861–1947), pastor of the First Baptist Church in Minneapolis. Riley became active as an antievolutionist after discovering, to his apparent surprise, that evolutionists were teaching their views at the University of Minnesota. The early twentieth century witnessed an unprecedented expansion of public education—enrollment in public high schools nearly doubled between 1920 and 1930—and fundamentalists like Riley and Bryan wanted to make sure that students attending these institutions would not lose their faith. Thus they resolved to drive every evolutionist from the public-school payroll. Those who lost their jobs as a result deserved little sympathy, for, as one rabble-rousing creationist put it, the German soldiers who killed Belgian and French children with poisoned candy were angels compared with the teachers and textbook writers who corrupted the souls of children and thereby sentenced them to eternal death.[20]

The creationists, we should remember, did not always act without provocation. In many instances their opponents displayed equal intolerance and insensitivity. In fact, one contemporary observer blamed the creation-evolution controversy in part on the "intellectual flapperism" of irresponsible and poorly informed teachers who delighted in shocking naive students with unsupportable statements about evolution. It was understandable, wrote an Englishman, that American parents would resent sending their sons and daughters to public institutions that exposed them to "a multiple assault upon traditional faiths."[21]

CREATIONIST SCIENCE AND SCIENTISTS

In 1922 William Bell Riley outlined the reasons why fundamentalists opposed the teaching of evolution. "The first and most important reason for its elimination," he explained, "is the unquestioned fact that evolution is not a science; it is a hypothesis only, a speculation." Bryan often made the same point, defining true science as "classified knowledge . . . the explanation of facts."[22] Although creationists had far more compelling reasons for rejecting evolution than its alleged unscientific status, their insistence on this point was not merely an obscurantist ploy. Rather it stemmed from their commitment to a once-respected tradition, associated with the English philosopher Sir Francis Bacon (1561–1626), that emphasized the factual, nontheoretical nature of science. By identifying with the Baconian tradition, creationists could label evolution as false science, could claim equality with scientific authorities in comprehending facts, and could deny the charge of being antiscience. "It is not 'science' that orthodox Christians oppose," a fundamentalist editor insisted defensively. "No! no! a thousand times, No! They are opposed only to the theory of evolution, which has not yet been proved, and therefore is not to be called by the sacred name of *science*."[23]

Because of their conviction that evolution was unscientific, creationists assured themselves that the world's best scientists agreed with them. They received an important boost at the beginning of their campaign from an address by the distinguished British biologist William Bateson (1861–1926) in 1921, in which he declared that scientists had *not* discovered "the actual mode and process of evolution." Although he warned creationists against misinterpreting his statement as a rejection of evolution, they paid no more attention to that caveat than they did to the numerous proevolution resolutions passed by scientific societies.[24]

Unfortunately for the creationists, they could claim few legitimate scientists of their own: a couple of self-made men of science, one or two physicians, and a handful of teachers who, as one evolutionist described them, were "trying to hold down, not a chair, but a whole settee, of 'Natural Science' in some little institution."[25] Of this group the most influential were Harry Rimmer (1890–1952) and George McCready Price (1870–1963).

Rimmer, Presbyterian minister and self-styled "research scientist," obtained his limited exposure to science during a term or two at San Francisco's Hahnemann Medical College, a small homeopathic institution that required no more than a high-school diploma for admission. As a medical student he picked up a vocabulary of "double-jointed, twelve cylinder, knee-action words" that later served to impress the uninitiated. After his brief stint in medical school he attended Whittier College and the Bible Institute of Los Angeles for a year each before entering full-time evangelistic work. About 1919 he settled in Los Angeles, where he set up a small laboratory at the rear of his house to conduct experiments in embryology and related sciences. Within a year or two he established the Research Science Bureau "to prove through findings in biology, paleontology, and anthropology that science and the literal Bible were not contradictory." The bureau staff—that is, Rimmer—apparently used income from the sale of memberships to finance anthropological field trips in the west-

ern United States, but Rimmer's dream of visiting Africa to prove the
dissimilarity of gorillas and humans failed to materialize. By the late
1920s the bureau lay dormant, and Rimmer signed on with Riley's
World's Christian Fundamentals Association as a field secretary.[26]

Besides engaging in research, Rimmer delivered thousands of lectures, primarily to student groups, on the scientific accuracy of the
Bible. Posing as a scientist, he attacked Darwinism and poked fun at
the credulity of evolutionists. To attract attention, he repeatedly offered one hundred dollars to anyone who could discover a scientific
error in the Scriptures; not surprisingly, the offer never cost him a
dollar. He also, by his own reckoning, never lost a public debate.
Following one encounter with an evolutionist in Philadelphia, he
wrote home gleefully that "the debate was a simple walkover, a mas-
sacre—murder pure and simple. The eminent professor was simply
scared stiff to advance any of the common arguments of the evolutionists, and he fizzled like a wet fire-cracker."[27]

George McCready Price, a Seventh-day Adventist geologist, was
less skilled at debating than Rimmer but more influential scientifically.
As a young man Price attended an Adventist college in Michigan for
two years and later completed a teacher-training course at the provincial normal school in his native New Brunswick. The turn of the
century found him serving as principal of a small high school in an
isolated part of eastern Canada, where one of his few companions
was a local physician. During their many conversations, the doctor
almost converted his fundamentalist friend to evolution, but each time
Price wavered, he was saved by prayer and by reading the works of
the Seventh-day Adventist prophetess Ellen G. White (1827–1915),
who claimed divine inspiration for her view that Noah's flood accounted for the fossil record on which evolutionists based their theory.
As a result of these experiences, Price vowed to devote his life to
promoting creationism of the strictest kind.[28]

By 1906 he was working as a handyman at an Adventist sanitarium
in southern California. That year he published a slim volume entitled
Illogical Geology: The Weakest Point in the Evolution Theory, in which he
brashly offered one thousand dollars "to any one who will, in the
face of the facts here presented, show me how to prove that one kind
of fossil is older than another." (Like Rimmer, he never had to pay.)
According to Price's argument, Darwinism rested "logically and historically on the succession of life idea as taught by geology" and "if
this succession of life is not an actual scientific fact, then Darwinism
. . . is a most gigantic hoax."[29]

Although a few fundamentalists praised Price's polemic, David
Starr Jordan (1851–1931), president of Stanford University and an

authority on fossil fishes, warned him that he should not expect "any geologist to take [his work] seriously." Jordan conceded that the unknown author had written "a very clever book" but described it as

a sort of lawyer's plea, based on scattering mistakes, omissions and exceptions against general truths that anybody familiar with the facts in a general way cannot possibly dispute. It would be just as easy and just as plausible and just as convincing if one should take the facts of European history and attempt to show that all the various events were simultaneous.[30]

As Jordan recognized, Price lacked any formal training or field experience in geology. He was, however, a voracious reader of geological literature, an armchair scientist who self-consciously minimized the importance of field experience.

During the next fifteen years Price occupied scientific settees in several Seventh-day Adventist schools and authored six more books attacking evolution, particularly its geological foundation. Although not unknown outside his own church before the early 1920s, he did not attract national attention until then. Shortly after Bryan declared war on evolution, Price published *The New Geology* (1923), the most systematic and comprehensive of his many books. Uninhibited by false modesty, he presented his "great *law of conformable stratigraphic sequences* . . . by all odds the most important law ever formulated with reference to the order in which the strata occur." This law stated that "*any kind of fossiliferous beds whatever, 'young' or 'old,' may be found occurring conformably on any other fossiliferous beds, 'older' or 'younger.'*"[31] To Price, so-called deceptive conformities (where strata seem to be missing) and thrust faults (where the strata are apparently in the wrong order) proved that there was no natural order to the fossil-bearing rocks, all of which he attributed to the Genesis flood.

A Yale geologist reviewing the book for *Science* accused Price of "harboring a geological nightmare." But despite such criticism from the scientific establishment—and the fact that his theory contradicted both the day-age and gap interpretations of Genesis—Price's reputation among fundamentalists rose dramatically. Rimmer, for example, hailed *The New Geology* as "a masterpiece of REAL science [that] explodes in a convincing manner some of the ancient fallacies of science 'falsely so called.'"[32] By the mid-1920s Price's byline was appearing with increasing frequency in a broad spectrum of conservative religious periodicals, and the editor of *Science* could accurately describe him as "the principal scientific authority of the Fundamentalists."[33]

THE SCOPES TRIAL AND BEYOND

In the spring of 1925 John Thomas Scopes, a high-school teacher in the small town of Dayton, Tennessee, confessed to having violated the state's recently passed law banning the teaching of human evolution in public schools. His subsequent trial focused international attention on the antievolution crusade and brought William Jennings Bryan to Dayton to assist the prosecution. In anticipation of arguing the scientific merits of evolution, Bryan sought out the best scientific minds in the creationist camp to serve as expert witnesses. The response to his inquiries could only have disappointed the aging crusader. Price, then teaching in England, sent his regrets—along with advice for Bryan to stay away from scientific topics. Howard A. Kelly, a prominent Johns Hopkins physician who had contributed to *The Fundamentals*, confessed that, except for Adam and Eve, he believed in evolution. Louis T. More, a physicist who had just written a book on *The Dogma of Evolution* (1925), replied that he accepted evolution as a working hypothesis. Alfred W. McCann, author of *God—or Gorilla* (1922), took the opportunity to chide Bryan for supporting prohibition in the past and for now trying "to bottle-up the tendencies of men to think for themselves."[34]

At the trial itself things scarcely went better. When Bryan could name only Price and the deceased George Frederick Wright as scientists for whom he had respect, the caustic Clarence Darrow (1857–1938), attorney for the defense, scoffed: "You mentioned Price because he is the only human being in the world so far as you know that signs his name as a geologist that believes like you do. . . . every scientist in this country knows [he] is a mountebank and a pretender and not a geologist at all." Eventually Bryan conceded that the world was indeed far more than six thousand years old and that the six days of creation had probably been longer than twenty-four hours each— concessions that may have harmonized with the progressive creationism of Wright but hardly with the strict creationism of Price.[35]

Though one could scarcely have guessed it from some of his public pronouncements, Bryan had long been a progressive creationist. In fact, his beliefs regarding evolution diverged considerably from those of his more conservative supporters. Shortly before his trial he had confided to Dr. Kelly that he, too, had no objection to "evolution before man but for the fact that a concession as to the truth of evolution up to man furnishes our opponents with an argument which they are quick to use, namely, if evolution accounts for all the species up to man, does it not raise a presumption in behalf of evolution to include man?" Until biologists could actually demonstrate the evolution of one species into another, he thought it best to keep them on the defensive.[36]

Bryan's admission at Dayton spotlighted a serious and long-standing problem among antievolutionists: their failure to agree on a theory of creation. Even the most visible leaders could not reach a consensus. Riley, for example, followed Guyot and Dawson (and Bryan) in viewing the days of Genesis as ages, believing that the testimony of geology necessitated this interpretation. Rimmer favored the gap theory, which involved two separate creations, in part because his scientific mind could not fathom how, given Riley's scheme, plants created on the third day could have survived thousands of years without sunshine, until the sun appeared on the fourth. According to the testimony of acquaintances, he also believed that the Bible taught a local rather than a universal flood. Price, who cared not a whit about the opinion of geologists, insisted on nothing less than a recent creation in six literal days and a worldwide deluge. He regarded the day-age theory as "the devil's counterfeit" and the gap theory as only slightly more acceptable. Rimmer and Riley, who preferred to minimize the differences among creationists, attempted the logically impossible, if ecumenically desirable, task of incorporating Price's "new geology" into their own schemes.[37]

Although the court in Dayton found Scopes guilty as charged, creationists had little cause for rejoicing. The press had not treated them kindly, and the taxing ordeal no doubt contributed to Bryan's death a few days after the end of the trial. Nevertheless, the antievolutionists continued their crusade, winning victories in Mississippi in 1926 and in Arkansas two years later. By the end of the decade, however, their legislative campaign had lost its steam. The presidential election of 1928, pitting a Protestant against a Catholic, offered fundamentalists a new cause, and the onset of the depression in 1929 further diverted their attention.[38]

Contrary to appearances, the creationists were simply changing tactics, not giving up. Instead of lobbying state legislatures, they shifted their attack to local communities, where they engaged in what one critic described as "the emasculation of textbooks, the 'purging' of libraries, and above all the continued hounding of teachers." Their new approach attracted less attention but paid off handsomely, as school boards, textbook publishers, and teachers in both urban and rural areas, North and South, bowed to their pressure. Darwinism virtually disappeared from high-school texts, and for years many American teachers feared being identified as evolutionists.[39]

CREATIONISM UNDERGROUND

During the heady days of the 1920s, when their activities made front-page headlines, creationists dreamed of converting the world; a decade later, forgotten and rejected by the establishment, they turned their energies inward and began creating an institutional base of their own. Deprived of the popular press and frustrated by their inability to publish their views in organs controlled by orthodox scientists, they determined to organize their own societies and edit their own journals.[40] Their early efforts, however, encountered two problems: the absence of a critical mass of scientifically trained creationists and lack of internal agreement.

In 1935 Price, along with Dudley Joseph Whitney, a farm journalist, and L. Allen Higley, a Wheaton College science professor, formed a Religion and Science Association to create "a united front against the theory of evolution." Among those invited to participate in the association's first—and only—convention were representatives of the three major creationist parties, including Price himself, Rimmer, and one of Dawson's sons, who, like his father, advocated the day-age theory. But as soon as the Price faction discovered that its associates had no intention of agreeing on a short earth history, it bolted the organization, leaving it a shambles.[41]

Shortly thereafter, in 1938, Price and some Seventh-day Adventist friends in the Los Angeles area, several of them physicians associated with the College of Medical Evangelists (now part of Loma Linda University), organized their own Deluge Geology Society and, between 1941 and 1945, published a *Bulletin of Deluge Geology and Related Science*. As described by Price, the group consisted of "a very eminent set of men. . . . In no other part of this round globe could anything like the number of scientifically educated believers in Creation and opponents of evolution be assembled, as here in Southern California."[42] Perhaps the society's most notable achievement was its sponsorship in the early 1940s of a hush-hush project to study giant fossil footprints, believed to be human, discovered in rocks far older than the theory of evolution would allow. This find, the society announced excitedly, thus demolished that theory "at a single stroke" and promised to *"astound the scientific world!"* But despite such activity and the group's religious homogeneity, it, too, soon foundered—on "the same rock," complained a disappointed member, that wrecked the Religion and Science Association, that is *"pre-Genesis time for the earth."*[43]

By this time creationists were also beginning to face a new problem: the presence within their own ranks of young university-trained scientists who wanted to bring evangelical Christianity more into line with mainstream science. The encounter between the two generations often proved traumatic, as is illustrated by the case of Harold W. Clark (b. 1891). A former student of Price's, he had gone on to earn a master's degree in biology from the University of California and taken a position at a small Adventist college in northern California. By 1940 his training and field experience had convinced him that Price's *New Geology* was "entirely out of date and inadequate" as a text, especially in its rejection of the geological column. When Price learned of this, he angrily accused his former disciple of suffering from "the modern mental disease of university-itis" and of currying the favor of "tobacco-smoking, Sabbath-breaking, God-defying" evolutionists. Despite Clark's protests that he still believed in a literal six-day creation and universal flood, Price kept up his attack for the better part of a decade, at one point addressing a vitriolic pamphlet, *Theories of Satanic Origin*, to his erstwhile friend and fellow creationist.[44]

The inroads of secular scientific training also became apparent in the American Scientific Affiliation (ASA), created by evangelical scientists in 1941.[45] Although the society took no official stand on creation, strict creationists found the atmosphere congenial during the early years of the society. In the late 1940s, however, some of the more progressive members, led by J. Laurence Kulp, a young geochemist on the faculty of Columbia University, began criticizing Price and his followers for their allegedly unscientific effort to squeeze earth history into less than ten thousand years. Kulp, a Wheaton alumnus and member of the Plymouth Brethren, had acquired a doctorate in physical chemistry from Princeton University and gone on to complete all the requirements, except a dissertation, for a Ph.D. in geology. Although initially suspicious of the conclusions of geology regarding the history and antiquity of the earth, he had come to accept them. As one of the first evangelicals professionally trained in geology, he felt a responsibility to warn his colleagues in the ASA about Price's work, which, he believed, had "infiltrated the greater portion of fundamental Christianity in America primarily due to the absence of trained Christian geologists." In what was apparently the first systematic critique of the "new geology" Kulp concluded that the "major propositions of the theory are contraindicated by established physical and chemical laws." Conservatives within the ASA not unreasonably suspected that Kulp's exposure to "the orthodox geological viewpoint" had severely undermined his faith in a literal interpretation of the Bible.[46]

Before long it became evident that a growing number of ASA members, like Kulp, were drifting from strict to progressive creationism and sometimes on to theistic evolutionism. The transition for many involved immense personal stress, as revealed in the autobiographical testimony of another Wheaton alumnus, J. Frank Cassel:

First to be overcome was the onus of dealing with a "verboten" term and in a "non-existent" area. Then, as each made an honest and objective consideration of the data, he was struck with the validity and undeniability of datum after datum. As he strove to incorporate each of these facts into his Biblico-scientific frame of reference, he found that—while the frame became more complete and satisfying—he began to question first the feasibility and then the desirability of an effort to refute the total evolutionary concept, and finally he became impressed by its impossibility on the basis of existing data. This has been a heart-rending, soul-searching experience for the committed Christian as he has seen what he had long considered the *raison d'être* of God's call for his life endeavor fade away, and as he has struggled to release strongly held convictions as to the close limitations of Creationism.

Cassel went on to note that the struggle was "made no easier by the lack of approbation (much less acceptance) of some of his less well-informed colleagues, some of whom seem to question motives or even to imply heresy."[47] Strict creationists, who suffered their own agonies, found it difficult not to conclude that their liberal colleagues were simply taking the easy way out. To both parties a split seemed inevitable.

CREATIONISM ABROAD

During the decades immediately following the crusade of the 1920s American antievolutionists were buoyed by reports of a creationist revival in Europe, especially in England, where creationism was thought to be all but dead. The Victoria Institute in London, a haven for English creationists in the nineteenth century, had by the 1920s become a stronghold of theistic evolution. When Price visited the institute in 1925 to receive its Langhorne-Orchard Prize for an essay on "Revelation and Evolution," several members protested his attempt to export the fundamentalist controversy to England. Even evangelicals refused to get caught up in the turmoil that engulfed the United States. As historian George Marsden has explained, English evangelicals, always a minority, had developed a stronger tradition of theological toleration than revivalist Americans, who until the twentieth century had never experienced minority status. Thus while the displaced Americans fought to recover their lost position, English evangelicals adopted a nonmilitant live-and-let-live philosophy that stressed personal piety.[48]

The sudden appearance of a small but vocal group of British creationists in the early 1930s caught nearly everyone by surprise. The central figure in this movement was Douglas Dewar (1875–1957), a Cambridge graduate and amateur ornithologist, who had served for decades as a lawyer in the Indian Civil Service. Originally an evolutionist, he had gradually become convinced of the necessity of adopting "a provisional hypothesis of special creation . . . supplemented by a theory of evolution." This allowed him to accept unlimited development within biological families. His published views, unlike those of most American creationists, betrayed little biblical influence. His greatest intellectual debt was not to Moses but to a French zoologist, Louis Vialleton (1859–1929), who had attracted considerable attention in the 1920s for suggesting a theory of discontinuous evolution, which antievolutionists eagerly—but erroneously—equated with special creation.[49]

Soon after announcing his conversion to creationism in 1931, Dewar submitted a short paper on mammalian fossils to the Zoological Society of London, of which he was a member. The secretary of the society subsequently rejected the piece, noting that a competent referee thought Dewar's evidence "led to no valuable conclusion." Such treatment infuriated Dewar and convinced him that evolution had become "a scientific creed." Those who questioned scientific orthodoxy, he complained, "are deemed unfit to hold scientific offices; their articles are rejected by newspapers or journals; their contributions are refused by scientific societies, and publishers decline to publish their books except at the author's expense. Thus the independents are today pretty effectually muzzled." Because of such experiences Dewar and other British dissidents in 1932 organized the Evolution Protest Movement, which after two decades claimed a membership of two hundred.[50]

HENRY M. MORRIS AND THE REVIVAL OF CREATIONISM

In 1964 one historian predicted that "a renaissance of the [creationist] movement is most unlikely." And so it seemed. But even as these words were penned, a major revival was under way, led by a Texas engineer, Henry M. Morris (b. 1918). Raised a nominal Southern Baptist, and as such a believer in creation, Morris as a youth had drifted unthinkingly into evolutionism and religious indifference. A thorough study of the Bible following graduation from college convinced him of its absolute truth and prompted him to reevaluate his belief in evolution. After an intense period of soul-searching he concluded that creation had taken place in six literal days, because the Bible clearly said so and "God doesn't lie." Corroborating evidence came from the book of nature. While sitting in his office at Rice Institute, where he was teaching civil engineering, he would study the butterflies and wasps that flew in through the window; being familiar with structural design, he calculated the improbability of such complex creatures developing by chance. Nature as well as the Bible seemed to argue for creation.[51]

For assistance in answering the claims of evolutionists, he found little creationist literature of value apart from the writings of Rimmer and Price. Although he rejected Price's peculiar theology, he took an immediate liking to the Adventist's flood geology and incorporated it into a little book, *That You Might Believe* (1946), the first book, so far as he knew, "published since the Scopes trial in which a scientist from a secular university advocated recent special creation and a worldwide flood." In the late 1940s he joined the American Scientific Affiliation—just in time to protest Kulp's attack on Price's geology. But his words fell largely on deaf ears. In 1953 when he presented some of his own views on the flood to the ASA, one of the few compliments came from a young theologian, John C. Whitcomb, Jr., who belonged to the Grace Brethren. The two subsequently became friends and decided to collaborate on a major defense of the Noachian flood. By the time they finished their project, Morris had earned a Ph.D. in hydraulic engineering from the University of Minnesota and was chairing the civil engineering department at Virginia Polytechnic Institute; Whitcomb was teaching Old Testament studies at Grace Theological Seminary in Indiana.[52]

In 1961 they brought out *The Genesis Flood*, the most impressive contribution to strict creationism since the publication of Price's *New Geology* in 1923. In many respects their book appeared to be simply "a reissue of G. M. Price's views, brought up to date," as one reader described it. Beginning with a testimony to their belief in "the verbal inerrancy of Scripture," Whitcomb and Morris went on to argue for a recent creation of the entire universe, a Fall that triggered the second law of thermodynamics, and a worldwide flood that in one year laid down most of the geological strata. Given this history, they argued, "the last refuge of the case for evolution immediately vanishes away, and the record of the rocks becomes a tremendous witness . . . to the holiness and justice and power of the living God of Creation!"[53]

Despite the book's lack of conceptual novelty, it provoked an intense debate among evangelicals. Progressive creationists denounced it as a travesty on geology that threatened to set back the cause of Christian science a generation, while strict creationists praised it for making biblical catastrophism intellectually respectable. Its appeal, suggested one critic, lay primarily in the fact that, unlike previous creationist works, it "looked *legitimate* as a scientific contribution," accompanied as it was by footnotes and other scholarly appurtenances. In responding to their detractors, Whitcomb and Morris repeatedly refused to be drawn into a scientific debate, arguing that "the real issue is not the correctness of the interpretation of various details of the geological data, but simply what God has revealed in His Word concerning these matters."[54]

Whatever its merits, *The Genesis Flood* unquestionably "brought about a stunning renaissance of flood geology," symbolized by the establishment in 1963 of the Creation Research Society. Shortly before the publication of his book Morris had sent the manuscript to Walter E. Lammerts (b. 1904), a Missouri-Synod Lutheran with a doctorate in genetics from the University of California. As an undergraduate at Berkeley Lammerts had discovered Price's *New Geology,* and during the early 1940s, while teaching at UCLA, he had worked with Price in the Creation-Deluge Society. After the mid-1940s, however, his interest in creationism had flagged—until awakened by reading the Whitcomb and Morris manuscript. Disgusted by the ASA's flirtation with evolution, he organized in the early 1960s a correspondence network with Morris and eight other strict creationists, dubbed the "team of ten." In 1963 seven of the ten met with a few other like-minded scientists at the home of a team member in Midland, Michigan, to form the Creation Research Society (CRS).[55]

The society began with a carefully selected eighteen-man "inner-core steering committee," which included the original team of ten. The composition of this committee reflected, albeit imperfectly, the denominational, regional, and professional bases of the creationist revival. There were six Missouri-Synod Lutherans, five Baptists, two Seventh-day Adventists, and one each from the Reformed Presbyterian Church, the Reformed Christian Church, the Church of the Brethren, and an independent Bible church. (Information about one member is not available.) Eleven lived in the Midwest, three in the South, and two in the Far West. The committee included six biologists, but only one geologist, an independent consultant with a master's degree. Seven members taught in church-related colleges, five in state institutions; the others worked for industry or were self-employed.[56]

To avoid the creeping evolutionism that had infected the ASA and to ensure that the society remained loyal to the Price-Morris tradition, the CRS required members to sign a statement of belief accepting the inerrancy of the Bible, the special creation of "all basic types of living things," and a worldwide deluge. It restricted membership to Christians only. (Although creationists liked to stress the scientific evidence for their position, one estimated that "only about five percent of evolutionists-turned-creationists did so on the basis of the over-whelming evidence for creation in the world of nature"; the remaining 95 percent became creationists because they believed in the Bible.) To legitimate its claim to being a scientific society, the CRS published a quarterly journal and limited full membership to persons possessing a graduate degree in a scientific discipline.[57]

At the end of its first decade the society claimed 450 regular members, plus 1,600 sustaining members, who failed to meet the scientific qualifications. Eschewing politics, the CRS devoted itself almost exclusively to education and research, funded "at very little expense, and . . . with no expenditure of public money." CRS-related projects included expeditions to search for Noah's ark, studies of fossil human footprints and pollen grains found out of the predicted evolutionary order, experiments on radiation-produced mutations in plants, and theoretical studies in physics demonstrating a recent origin of the earth. A number of members collaborated in preparing a biology textbook based on creationist principles. In view of the previous history of creation science, it was an auspicious beginning.[58]

While the CRS catered to the needs of scientists, a second, predominantly lay organization carried creationism to the masses. Created in 1964 in the wake of interest generated by *The Genesis Flood*, the Bible-Science Association came to be identified by many with one man: Walter Lang, an ambitious Missouri-Synod pastor who self-consciously prized spiritual insight above scientific expertise. As editor of the widely circulated *Bible-Science Newsletter* he vigorously promoted the Price-Morris line—and occasionally provided a platform for individuals on the fringes of the creationist movement, such as those who questioned the heliocentric theory and who believed that Einstein's theory of relativity "was invented in order to circumvent the evidence that the earth is at rest." Needless to say, the pastor's broad-mindedness greatly embarrassed creationists seeking scientific respectability, who feared that such bizarre behavior would tarnish the entire movement.[59]

SCIENTIFIC CREATIONISM

The creationists revival of the 1960s attracted little public attention until late in the decade, when fundamentalists became aroused about the federally funded Biological Sciences Curriculum Study texts, which featured evolution, and the California State Board of Education voted to require public-school textbooks to include creation along with evolution. This decision resulted in large part from the efforts of two southern California housewives, Nell Segraves and Jean Sumrall, associates of both the Bible-Science Association and the CRS. In 1961 Segraves learned of the U.S. Supreme Court's ruling in the Madalyn Murray case protecting atheist students from required prayers in public schools. Murray's ability to shield her child from religious exposure suggested to Segraves that creationist parents like herself "were entitled to protect our children from the influence of beliefs that would be offensive to our religious beliefs." It was this line of argument that finally persuaded the Board of Education to grant creationists equal rights.[60]

Flushed with victory, Segraves and her son Kelly in 1970 joined an effort to organize a Creation-Science Research Center (CSRC), affiliated with Christian Heritage College in San Diego, to prepare creationist literature suitable for adoption in public schools. Associated with them in this enterprise was Henry Morris, who resigned his position at Virginia Polytechnic Institute to help establish a center for creation research. Because of differences in personalities and objectives, the Segraveses in 1972 left the college, taking the CSRC with them; Morris thereupon set up a new research division at the college, the Institute for Creation Research (ICR), which, he announced with obvious relief, would be "controlled and operated by scientists" and would engage in research and education, not political action. During the 1970s Morris added five scientists to his staff and, funded largely by small gifts and royalties from institute publications, turned the ICR into the world's leading center for the propagation of strict creationism.[61] Meanwhile, the CSRC continued campaigning for the legal recognition of special creation, often citing a direct relationship between the acceptance of evolution and the breakdown of law and order. Its own research, the CSRC announced, proved that evolution fostered "the moral decay of spiritual values which contribute to the destruction of mental health and . . . [the prevalence of] divorce, abortion, and rampant venereal disease."[62]

The 1970s witnessed a major shift in creationist tactics. Instead of trying to outlaw evolution, as they had done in the 1920s, antievolutionists now fought to give creation equal time. And instead of appealing to the authority of the Bible, as Morris and Whitcomb had done as recently as 1961, they consciously downplayed the Genesis story in favor of what they called "scientific creationism." Several factors no doubt contributed to this shift. One sociologist has suggested that creationists began stressing the scientific legitimacy of their enterprise because "their theological legitimation of reality was no longer sufficient for maintaining their world and passing on their world view to their children." But there were also practical considerations. In 1968 the U.S. Supreme Court declared the Arkansas antievolution law unconstitutional, giving creationists reason to suspect that legislation requiring the teaching of biblical creationism would meet a similar fate. They also feared that requiring the biblical account "would open the door to a wide variety of interpretations of Genesis" and produce demands for the inclusion of non-Christian versions of creation.[63]

In view of such potential hazards, Morris recommended that creationists ask public schools to teach "only the scientific aspects of creationism," which in practice meant leaving out all references to the six days of Genesis and Noah's ark and focusing instead on evidence for a recent worldwide catastrophe and on arguments against evolution. Thus the product remained virtually the same; only the packaging changed. The ICR textbook *Scientific Creationism* (1974), for example, came in two editions: one for public schools, containing no references to the Bible, and another for use in Christian schools that included a chapter on "Creation According to Scripture."[64]

In defending creation as a scientific alternative to evolution, creationists relied less on Francis Bacon and his conception of science and more on two new philosopher-heroes: Karl Popper and Thomas Kuhn. Popper required all scientific theories to be falsifiable; since evolution could not be falsified, reasoned the creationists, it was by definition not science. Kuhn described scientific progress in terms of competing models or paradigms rather than the accumulation of objective knowledge. Thus creationists saw no reason why their flood-geology model should not be allowed to compete on an equal scientific basis with the evolution model. In selling this two-model approach to school boards, creationists were advised:

> Sell more SCIENCE. . . . Who can object to teaching more science? What is controversial about that? . . . do not use the word "creationism." Speak only of science. Explain that withholding scientific information contradicting evolution amounts to "censorship" and smacks of getting into the province of religious dogma. . . . Use the "censorship" label as one who is against censoring science. YOU are for science; anyone else who wants to censor scientific data is an old fogey and too doctrinaire to consider.

This tactic proved extremely effective, at least initially. Two state legislatures, in Arkansas and Louisiana, and various school boards adopted the two-model approach, and an informal poll of school-board members in 1980 showed that only 25 percent favored teaching nothing but evolution. In 1982, however, a federal judge declared the Arkansas law, requiring a "balanced treatment" of creation and evolution, to be unconstitutional.[65] Three years later a similar decision was reached regarding the Louisiana law.

Except for the battle to get scientific creationism into public schools, nothing brought more attention to the creationists than their public debates with prominent evolutionists, usually held on college campuses. During the 1970s the ICR staff alone participated in more than a hundred of these contests and, according to their own reckoning, never lost one. Although Morris preferred delivering straight lectures—and likened debates to the bloody confrontations between Christians and lions in ancient Rome—he recognized their value in carrying the creationist message to "more non-Christians and noncreationists than almost any other method." Fortunately for him, an associate, Duane T. Gish, holder of a doctorate in biochemistry from the University of California, relished such confrontations. If the mild-mannered, professorial Morris was the Darwin of the creationist movement, then the bumptious Gish was its Huxley. He "hits the floor running" just like a bulldog, observed an admiring colleague; and "I go for the jugular vein," added Gish himself. Such enthusiasm helped draw crowds of up to five thousand.[66]

Early in 1981 the ICR announced the fulfillment of a recurring dream among creationists: a program offering graduate degrees in various creation-oriented sciences. Besides hoping to fill an anticipated demand for teachers trained in scientific creationism, the ICR wished to provide an academic setting where creationist students would be free from discrimination. Over the years a number of creationists had reportedly been kicked out of secular universities because of their heterodox views, prompting leaders to warn graduate students to keep silent, "because if you don't, in almost 99 percent of the cases you will be asked to leave." To avoid anticipated harassment, several graduate students took to using pseudonyms when writing for creationist publications.[67]

Creationists also feared—with good reason—the possibility of defections while their students studied under evolutionists. Since the late 1950s the Seventh-day Adventist Church had invested hundreds of thousands of dollars to staff its Geoscience Research Institute with well-trained young scientists, only to discover that in several instances exposure to orthodox science had destroyed belief in strict creationism. To reduce the incidence of apostasy, the church established its own graduate programs at Loma Linda University, where George McCready Price had once taught.[68]

TO ALL THE WORLD

It is still too early to assess the full impact of the creationist revival
sparked by Whitcomb and Morris, but its influence, especially among
evangelical Christians, seems to have been immense. Not least, it has
elevated the strict creationism of Price and Morris to a position of
apparent orthodoxy. It has also endowed creationism with a measure
of scientific respectability unknown since the deaths of Guyot and
Dawson. Yet it is impossible to determine how much of the creationists' success stemmed from converting evolutionists as opposed to
mobilizing the already converted, and how much it owed to widespread disillusionment with established science. A sociological survey
of church members in northern California in 1963 revealed that over
a fourth of those polled—30 percent of Protestants and 28 percent of
Catholics—were already opposed to evolution when the creationist
revival began.[69] Broken down by denomination, it showed:

Liberal Protestants (Congregationalists, Methodists, Episcopalians, Disciples)	11%
Moderate Protestants (Presbyterians, American Lutherans, American Baptists)	29%
Church of God	57%
Missouri-Synod Lutherans	64%
Southern Baptists	72%
Church of Christ	78%
Nazarenes	80%
Assemblies of God	91%
Seventh-day Adventists	94%

Thus the creationists launched their crusade having a large reservoir
of potential support.

But has belief in creationism increased since the early 1960s? The
scanty evidence available suggests that it has. A nationwide Gallup
poll in 1982, cited at the beginning of this paper, showed that nearly
as many Americans (44 percent) believed in a recent special creation
as accepted theistic (38 percent) or nontheistic (9 percent) evolution.
These figures, when compared with the roughly 30 percent of northern California church members who opposed evolution in 1963, suggest, in a grossly imprecise way, a substantial gain in the actual
number of American creationists. Bits and pieces of additional evidence lend credence to this conclusion. For example, in 1935 only 36
percent of the students at Brigham Young University, a Mormon
school, rejected human evolution; in 1973 the percentage had climbed

to 81. Also, during the 1970s both the Missouri-Synod Lutheran and Seventh-day Adventist churches, traditional bastions of strict creationism, took strong measures to reverse a trend toward greater toleration of progressive creationism. In at least these instances, strict creationism did seem to be gaining ground.[70]

Unlike the antievolution crusade of the 1920s, which remained confined mainly to North America, the revival of the 1960s rapidly spread overseas as American creationists and their books circled the globe. Partly as a result of stimulation from America, including the publication of a British edition of *The Genesis Flood* in 1969, the lethargic Evolution Protest Movement in Great Britain was revitalized; and two new creationist organizations, the Newton Scientific Association and the Biblical Creation Society, sprang into existence.[71] On the Continent the Dutch assumed the lead in promoting creationism, encouraged by the translation of books on flood geology and by visits from ICR scientists. Similar developments occurred elsewhere in Europe, as well as in Australia, Asia, and South America. By 1980 Morris's books alone had been translated into Chinese, Czech, Dutch, French, German, Japanese, Korean, Portuguese, Russian, and Spanish. Strict creationism had become an international phenomenon.[72]

NOTES

I would like to thank David C. Lindberg for his encouragement and criticism, Rennie B. Schoepflin for his research assistance, and the Graduate School Research Committee of the University of Wisconsin-Madison for financial support during the preparation of this paper. An abridged version appeared as "Creationism in 20th-Century America" in *Science* 218 (1982): 538–544.

1. "Poll Finds Americans Split on Creation Idea," *New York Times*, 29 Aug. 1982, p. 22. Nine percent of the respondents favored an evolutionary process in which God played no part, 38 percent believed God directed the evolutionary process, and 9 percent had no opinion. Regarding Dawson and Guyot, see Edward J. Pfeifer, "United States," in *The Comparative Reception of Darwinism*, ed. Thomas F. Glick (Austin: Univ. of Texas Press, 1974), p. 203; and Asa Gray, *Darwiniana: Essays and Reviews Pertaining to Darwinism*, ed. A. Hunter Dupree (Cambridge: Harvard Univ. Press, 1963), pp. 202–203. In *The Darwinian Revolution: Science Red in Tooth and Claw* (Chicago: Univ. of Chicago Press, 1979), Michael Ruse argues that most British biologists were evolutionists by the mid-1860s, while David L. Hull, Peter D. Tessner, and Arthur M. Diamond point out in "Planck's Principle," *Science* 202 (1978): 721, that more than a quarter of British scientists continued to reject the evolution of species as late as 1869. On the acceptance of evolution among religious

leaders see, e.g., Frank Hugh Foster, *The Modern Movement in American The-*
ology: Sketches in the History of American Protestant Thought from the Civil War
to the World War (New York: Fleming H. Revell Co., 1939), pp. 38–58; and
Owen Chadwick, *The Victorian Church*, Part 2, 2d ed. (London: Adam &
Charles Black, 1972), pp. 23–24.

2. William G. McLoughlin, Jr., *Modern Revivalism: Charles Grandison Finney*
to Billy Graham (New York: Ronald Press, 1959), p. 213. In *Protestant Christianity*
Interpreted through Its Development (New York: Charles Scribner's Sons, 1954),
p. 227, John Dillenberger and Claude Welch discuss the conservatism of the
common people. On the attitudes of premillennialists see Robert D. Whalen,
"Millenarianism and Millennialism in America, 1790–1880" (Ph.D. diss., State
University of New York at Stony Brook, 1972), pp. 219–229; and Ronald L.
Numbers, "Science Falsely So-Called: Evolution and Adventists in the Nineteenth Century," *Journal of the American Scientific Affiliation* 27 (March 1975):
18–23.

3. Ronald L. Numbers, *Creation by Natural Law: Laplace's Nebular Hypothesis*
in American Thought (Seattle: Univ. of Washington Press, 1977), pp. 89–90;
Bernard Ramm, *The Christian View of Science and Scripture* (Grand Rapids,
Mich.: Wm. B. Eerdmans, 1954), pp. 195–198. On the influence of the *Scofield*
Reference Bible see Ernest R. Sandeen, *The Roots of Fundamentalism: British and*
American Millenarianism, 1800–1930 (Chicago: Univ. of Chicago Press, 1971),
p. 222.

4. Charles F. O'Brien, *Sir William Dawson: A Life in Science and Religion*
(Philadelphia: American Philosophical Society, 1971). On Guyot and his in-
fluence see Numbers, *Creation by Natural Law*, pp. 91–100. On the popularity
of the Guyot-Dawson view, also associated with the geologist James Dwight
Dana, see William North Rice, *Christian Faith in an Age of Science*, 2d ed. (New
York: A. C. Armstrong & Son, 1904), p. 101; and Dudley Joseph Whitney,
"What Theory of Earth History Shall We Adopt?" *Bible Champion* 34 (1928):
616.

5. H. L. Hastings, preface to the 1889 edition of *The Errors of Evolution: An*
Examination of the Nebular Theory, Geological Evolution, the Origin of Life, and
Darwinism, by Robert Patterson, 3d ed. (Boston: Scriptural Tract Repository,
1893), p. iv. On the Darwinian debate see James R. Moore, *The Post-Darwinian*
Controversies: A Study of the Protestant Struggle to Come to Terms with Darwin in
Great Britain and America, 1870–1900 (Cambridge: Cambridge Univ. Press,
1979).

6. G. L. Young, "Relation of Evolution and Darwinism to the Question of
Origins," *Bible Student and Teacher* 11 (July 1909): 41. On anti-Darwinian books
see "Evolutionism in the Pulpit," in *The Fundamentals*, 12 vols. (Chicago:
Testimony Publishing Co., 1910–1915), 8:28–30. See also Peter J. Bowler, *The*
Eclipse of Darwinism: Anti-Darwinian Evolution Theories in the Decades around
1900 (Baltimore: Johns Hopkins Univ. Press, 1983).

7. Philip Mauro, "Modern Philosophy," in *The Fundamentals* 2:85–105;
and J. J. Reeve, "My Personal Experience with the Higher Criticism," ibid.,
3:98–118.

8. G. Frederick Wright, *Story of My Life and Work* (Oberlin, Ohio: Bibliotheca
Sacra Co., 1916); idem, "The First Chapter of Genesis and Modern Science,"

Homiletic Review 35 (1898): 392–399; idem, introduction to *The Other Side of Evolution: An Examination of Its Evidences*, by Alexander Patterson (Chicago: Winona Pub. Co., 1902), pp. xvii–xix.

9. George Frederick Wright, "The Passing of Evolution," in *The Fundamentals* 7:5–20. The Scottish theologian James Orr contributed an equally tolerant essay, "Science and Christian Faith," ibid., 4:91–104.

10. Lawrence W. Levine, *Defender of the Faith—William Jennings Bryan: The Last Decade, 1915–1925* (New York: Oxford Univ. Press, 1965), p. 277.

11. Ibid., p. 272. The quotation about America going mad appears in Roland T. Nelson, "Fundamentalism and the Northern Baptist Convention" (Ph.D. diss., University of Chicago, 1964), p. 319. On antievolution legislation see Maynard Shipley, *The War on Modern Science: A Short History of the Fundamentalist Attacks on Evolution and Modernism* (New York: Alfred A. Knopf, 1927); and idem, "Growth of the Anti-Evolution Movement," *Current History* 32 (1930): 330–332. On Bryan's catalytic role see Ferenc Morton Szasz, *The Divided Mind of Protestant America, 1889–1930* (University: Univ. of Alabama Press, 1982), pp. 107–116.

12. Levine, *Defender of the Faith*, pp. 261–265.

13. Ibid., pp. 266–267. Mrs. Bryan's statement appears in Wayne C. Williams, *William Jennings Bryan* (New York: G. P. Putnam, 1936), p. 448.

14. William Jennings Bryan, *In His Image* (New York: Fleming H. Revell Co., 1922), pp. 94, 97–98. "The Menace of Darwinism" appears in this work as chap. 4, "The Origin of Man." Bryan apparently borrowed his account of the evolution of the eye from Patterson, *The Other Side of Evolution*, pp. 32–33.

15. Paolo E. Coletta, *William Jennings Bryan*, vol. 3, *Political Puritan, 1915–1925* (Lincoln: Univ. of Nebraska Press, 1969), p. 230.

16. "Progress of Anti-Evolution," *Christian Fundamentalist* 2 (1929): 13. Bryan's reference to a "scientific soviet" appears in Levine, *Defender of the Faith*, p. 289. Bryan gives the estimate of nine-tenths in a letter to W. A. McRae, 5 Apr. 1924, box 29, Bryan Papers, Library of Congress.

17. "Fighting Evolution at the Fundamentals Convention," *Christian Fundamentals in School and Church* 7 (July–Sept. 1925): 5. The best state histories of the antievolution crusade are Kenneth K. Bailey, "The Enactment of Tennessee's Antievolution Law," *Journal of Southern History* 16 (1950): 472–510; Willard B. Gatewood, Jr., *Preachers, Pedagogues and Politicians: The Evolution Controversy in North Carolina, 1920–1927* (Chapel Hill: Univ. of North Carolina Press, 1966); and Virginia Gray, "Anti-Evolution Sentiment and Behavior: The Case of Arkansas," *Journal of American History* 57 (1970): 352–366. Ferenc Morton Szasz stresses the urban dimension of the crusade in "Three Fundamentalist Leaders: The Roles of William Bell Riley, John Roach Straton, and William Jennings Bryan in the Fundamentalist-Modernist Controversy" (Ph.D. diss., University of Rochester, 1969), p. 351.

18. George Herbert Betts, *The Beliefs of 700 Ministers and Their Meaning for Religious Education* (New York: Abingdon Press, 1929), pp. 26, 44; Milton L. Rudnick, *Fundamentalism and the Missouri Synod: A Historical Study of Their Interaction and Mutual Influence* (St. Louis: Concordia Publishing House, 1966), pp. 88–90; Sandeen, *Roots of Fundamentalism*, pp. 266–268, which discusses

the premillennialists. Lutheran reluctance to join the crusade is also evident in Szasz, "Three Fundamentalist Leaders," p. 279. For examples of prominent fundamentalists who stayed aloof from the antievolution controversy see Ned B. Stonehouse, _J. Gresham Machen: A Biographical Memoir_ (Grand Rapids, Mich.: Wm. B. Eerdmans, 1954), pp. 401–402, and William Bryant Lewis, "The Role of Harold Paul Sloan and his Methodist League for Faith and Life in the Fundamentalist-Modernist Controversy of the Methodist Episcopal Church" (Ph.D. diss., Vanderbilt University, 1963), pp. 86–88.

19. Edward Lassiter Clark, "The Southern Baptist Reaction to the Darwinian Theory of Evolution" (Ph.D. diss., Southwestern Baptist Theological Seminary, 1952), p. 154; James J. Thompson, Jr., "Southern Baptists and the Antievolution Controversy of the 1920's," _Mississippi Quarterly_ 29 (1975–1976): 65–81; Lefferts A. Loetscher, _The Broadening Church: A Study of Theological Issues in the Presbyterian Church since 1869_ (Philadelphia: Univ. of Pennsylvania Press, 1954), p. 111; John L. Morrison, "American Catholics and the Crusade against Evolution," _Records of the American Catholic Historical Society of Philadelphia_ 64 (1953): 59–71. Norman F. Furniss, _The Fundamentalist Controversy, 1918–1931_ (New Haven: Yale Univ. Press, 1954), includes chapter-by-chapter surveys of seven denominations.

20. T. T. Martin, _Hell and the High School: Christ or Evolution, Which?_ (Kansas City: Western Baptist Pub. Co., 1923), pp. 164–165. On Riley see Marie Acomb Riley, _The Dynamic of a Dream: The Life Story of Dr. William B. Riley_ (Grand Rapids, Mich.: Wm. B. Eerdmans, 1938), pp. 101–102; and Szasz, _The Divided Mind of Protestant America_, pp. 89–91. George M. Marsden, _Fundamentalism and American Culture: The Shaping of Twentieth-Century Evangelicalism, 1870–1925_ (New York: Oxford Univ. Press, 1980), pp. 169–170, stresses the interdenominational character of the antievolution crusade. On the expansion of public education see Kenneth K. Bailey, _Southern White Protestantism in the Twentieth Century_ (New York: Harper & Row, 1964), pp. 72–73.

21. Both quotations come from Howard K. Beale, _Are American Teachers Free? An Analysis of Restraints upon the Freedom of Teaching in American Schools_ (New York: Charles Scribner's Sons, 1936), pp. 249–251.

22. [William B. Riley], "The Evolution Controversy," _Christian Fundamentals in School and Church_ 4 (Apr.–June 1922): 5; Bryan, _In His Image_, p. 94.

23. L. S. K[eyser], "No War against Science—Never!" _Bible Champion_ 31 (1925): 413. On the fundamentalist affinity for Baconianism see Marsden, _Fundamentalism and American Culture_, pp. 214–215.

24. William Bateson, "Evolutionary Faith and Modern Doubts," _Science_ 55 (1922): 55–61. The creationists' use of Bateson provoked the evolutionist Henry Fairfield Osborn into repudiating the British scientist; see Osborn, _Evolution and Religion in Education: Polemics of the Fundamentalist Controversy of 1922 to 1926_ (New York: Charles Scribner's Sons, 1926), p. 29. On proevolution resolutions see Shipley, _War on Modern Science_, p. 384.

25. Heber D. Curtis to W. J. Bryan, 22 May 1923, box 37, Bryan Papers, Library of Congress. Two physicians, Arthur I. Brown of Vancouver and Howard A. Kelly of Johns Hopkins, achieved prominence in the fundamentalist movement, but Kelly leaned toward theistic evolution.

26. William D. Edmondson, "Fundamentalist Sects of Los Angeles, 1900–1930" (Ph.D. diss., Claremont Graduate School, 1969), pp. 276–336; Steward G. Cole, *The History of Fundamentalism* (New York: Richard R. Smith, 1931), pp. 264–265; F. J. B[oyer], "Harry Rimmer, D.D.," *Christian Faith and Life* 45 (1939): 6–7; "Two Great Field Secretaries—Harry Rimmer and Dr. Arthur I. Brown," *Christian Fundamentals in School and Church* 8 (July–Sept. 1926): 17. Harry Rimmer refers to his medical vocabulary in *The Harmony of Science and Scripture*, 11th ed. (Grand Rapids, Mich.: Wm. B. Eerdmans, 1945), p. 14.

27. Edmondson, "Fundamentalist Sects of Los Angeles," pp. 329–330, 333–334. Regarding the $100 reward, see "World Religious Digest," *Christian Faith and Life* 45 (1939): 215.

28. This and the following paragraphs on Price closely follow my account in "'Sciences of Satanic Origin': Adventist Attitudes toward Evolutionary Biology and Geology," *Spectrum* 9 (Jan. 1979): 22–24.

29. George McCready Price, *Illogical Geology: The Weakest Point in the Evolution Theory* (Los Angeles: Modern Heretic Co., 1906), p. 9. Four years earlier Price had published his first antievolution book, *Outlines of Modern Science and Modern Christianity* (Oakland, Calif.: Pacific Press, 1902).

30. David Starr Jordan to G. M. Price, 5 May 1911, Price Papers, Andrews University Library.

31. George McCready Price, *The New Geology* (Mountain View, Calif.: Pacific Press, 1923), pp. 637–638. Price first announced the discovery of his law in *The Fundamentals of Geology and Their Bearings on the Doctrine of a Literal Creation* (Mountain View, Calif.: Pacific Press, 1913), p. 119.

32. Charles Schuchert, review of *The New Geology*, by George McCready Price, *Science* 59 (1924): 486–487; Harry Rimmer, *Modern Science, Noah's Ark and the Deluge* (Los Angeles: Research Science Bureau, 1925), p. 28.

33. *Science* 63 (1926): 259.

34. Howard A. Kelly to W. J. Bryan, 15 June 1925; Louis T. More to W. J. Bryan, 7 July 1925; and Alfred W. McCann to W. J. Bryan, 30 June 1925, box 47, Bryan Papers, Library of Congress. Regarding Price, see Numbers, "'Sciences of Satanic Origin,'" p. 24.

35. Numbers, "'Sciences of Satanic Origin,'" p. 24; Levine, *Defender of the Faith*, p. 349.

36. W. J. Bryan to Howard A. Kelly, 22 June 1925, box 47, Bryan Papers, Library of Congress. In a letter to the editor of *The Forum* 70 (1923): 1852–1853, Bryan asserted that he had never taught that the world was made in six literal days. I am indebted to Paul M. Waggoner for bringing this document to my attention.

37. W. B. Riley and Harry Rimmer, *A Debate: Resolved, That the Creative Days in Genesis Were Aeons, Not Solar Days* (undated pamphlet); [W. B. Riley], "The Creative Week," *Christian Fundamentalist* 4 (1930): 45; Price, *Outlines*, pp. 125–127; idem, *The Story of the Fossils* (Mountain View, Calif.: Pacific Press, 1954), p. 39. On Rimmer's acceptance of a local flood see Robert D. Culver, "An Evaluation of *The Christian View of Science and Scripture* by Bernard Ramm from the Standpoint of Christian Theology," *Journal of the American Scientific Affiliation* 7 (Dec. 1955): 7.

38. Shipley, "Growth of the Anti-Evolution Movement," pp. 330–332; Szasz, *The Divided Mind of Protestant America*, pp. 117–125.

39. Beale, *Are American Teachers Free?* pp. 228–237; Willard B. Gatewood, Jr., ed., *Controversy in the Twenties: Fundamentalism, Modernism, and Evolution* (Nashville: Vanderbilt Univ. Press, 1969), p. 39. The quotation comes from Shipley, "Growth of the Anti-Evolution Movement," p. 330. See also Judith V. Grabiner and Peter D. Miller, "Effects of the Scopes Trial," *Science* 185 (1974): 832–837; and Estelle R. Laba and Eugene W. Gross, "Evolution Slighted in High-School Biology," *Clearing House* 24 (1950): 396–399.

40. Joel A. Carpenter, "Fundamentalist Institutions and the Rise of Evangelical Protestantism, 1929–1942," *Church History* 49 (1980): 62–75, provides an excellent analysis of this trend. For a typical statement of creationist frustration see George McCready Price, "Guarding the Sacred Cow," *Christian Faith and Life* 41 (1935): 124–127. The title for this section comes from Henry M. Morris, *The Troubled Waters of Evolution* (San Diego: Creation-Life Publishers, 1974), p. 13.

41. "Announcement of the Religion and Science Association," Price Papers, Andrews University; "The Religion and Science Association," *Christian Faith and Life* 42 (1936): 159–160; "Meeting of the Religion and Science Association," ibid., p. 209; Harold W. Clark, *The Battle over Genesis* (Washington: Review & Herald Publishing Association, 1977), p. 168. On the attitude of the Price faction see Harold W. Clark to G. M. Price, 12 Sept. 1937, Price Papers, Andrews University.

42. Numbers, "'Sciences of Satanic Origin,'" p. 26.

43. Ben F. Allen to the Board of Directors of the Creation-Deluge Society, 12 Aug. 1945 (courtesy of Molleurus Couperus). Regarding the fossil footprints, see the *Newsletters* of the Creation-Deluge Society for 19 Aug. 1944 and 17 Feb. 1945.

44. Numbers, "'Sciences of Satanic Origin,'" p. 25.

45. On the early years of the ASA see Alton Everest, "The American Scientific Affiliation—The First Decade," *Journal of the American Scientific Affiliation* 3 (Sept. 1951): 33–38.

46. J. Laurence Kulp, "Deluge Geology," ibid., 2, no. 1 (1950): 1–15; "Comment on the 'Deluge Geology' Paper of J. L. Kulp," ibid., 2 (June 1950): 2. Kulp mentions his initial skepticism of geology in a discussion of "Some Presuppositions in Evolutionary Thinking," ibid., 1 (June 1949): 20.

47. J. Frank Cassel, "The Evolution of Evangelical Thinking on Evolution," ibid., 11 (Dec. 1959): 26–27. For a fuller discussion see Ronald L. Numbers, "The Dilemma of Evangelical Scientists," in *Evangelicalism and Modern America*, ed. George M. Marsden (Grand Rapids, Mich.: Wm. B. Eerdmans, 1984), pp. 150–160.

48. Numbers, "'Sciences of Satanic Origin,'" p. 25; George Marsden, "Fundamentalism as an American Phenomenon: A Comparison with English Evangelicalism," *Church History* 46 (1977): 215–232; idem, *Fundamentalism and American Culture*, pp. 222–226.

49. Douglas Dewar, *The Difficulties of the Evolution Theory* (London: Edward Arnold & Co., 1931), p. 158; Arnold Lunn, ed., *Is Evolution Proved? A Debate*

between Douglas Dewar and H. S. Shelton (London: Hollis & Carter, 1947), pp. 1, 154; *Evolution Protest Movement Pamphlet No. 125* (Apr. 1965). On Vialleton see Harry W. Paul, *The Edge of Contingency: French Catholic Reaction to Scientific Change from Darwin to Duhem* (Gainesville: University Presses of Florida, 1979), pp. 99–100.

50. Douglas Dewar, "The Limitations of Organic Evolution," *Journal of the Victoria Institute* 64 (1932): 142; "EPM—40 Years On; Evolution—114 Years Off," supplement to *Creation* 1 (May 1972): no pagination.

51. R. Halliburton, Jr., "The Adoption of Arkansas' Anti-Evolution Law," *Arkansas Historical Quarterly* 23 (1964): 283; interviews with Henry M. Morris, 26 Oct. 1980 and 6 Jan. 1981. See also the autobiographical material in Henry M. Morris, *History of Modern Creationism* (San Diego: Master Book Publishers, 1984).

52. Interviews with Morris; Henry M. Morris, introduction to the revised edition, *That You Might Believe* (San Diego: Creation-Life Publishers, 1978), p. 10.

53. John C. Whitcomb, Jr. and Henry M. Morris, *The Genesis Flood: The Biblical Record and Its Scientific Implications* (Philadelphia: Presbyterian & Reformed Pub. Co., 1961), pp. xx, 451.

54. Henry M. Morris and John C. Whitcomb, Jr., "Reply to Reviews in the March 1964 Issue," *Journal of the American Scientific Affiliation* 16 (June 1964): 60. The statement regarding the appearance of the book comes from Walter Hearn, quoted in Vernon Lee Bates, "Christian Fundamentalism and the Theory of Evolution in Public School Education: A Study of the Creation Science Movement" (Ph.D. diss., University of California, Davis, 1976), p. 52. See also Frank H. Roberts, review of *The Genesis Flood*, by Henry M. Morris and John C. Whitcomb, Jr., *Journal of the American Scientific Affiliation* 16 (Mar. 1964): 28–29; J. R. Van de Fliert, "Fundamentalism and the Fundamentals of Geology," ibid., 21 (Sept. 1969): 69–81; and Walter E. Lammerts, "Introduction," Creation Research Society, *Annual*, 1964, no pagination. Among Missouri-Synod Lutherans, John W. Klotz, *Genes, Genesis, and Evolution* (St. Louis: Concordia Publishing House, 1955), may have had an even greater influence than Morris and Whitcomb.

55. Walter E. Lammerts, "The Creationist Movement in the United States: A Personal Account," *Journal of Christian Reconstruction* 1 (Summer 1974): 49–63. The first quotation comes from Davis A. Young, *Creation and the Flood: An Alternative to Flood Geology and Theistic Evolution* (Grand Rapids, Mich.: Baker Book House, 1977), p. 7.

56. Names, academic fields, and institutional affiliations are given in *Creation Research Society Quarterly* 1 (July 1964): [13]; for additional information I am indebted to Duane T. Gish, John N. Moore, Henry M. Morris, Harold Slusher, and William J. Tinkle.

57. *Creation Research Society Quarterly* 1 (July 1964): [13]; [Walter Lang], "Editorial Comments," *Bible-Science Newsletter* 16 (June 1978): 2. Other creationists have disputed the 5-percent estimate.

58. Lammerts, "The Creationist Movement in the United States," p. 63; Duane T. Gish, "A Decade of Creationist Research," *Creation Research Society*

Quarterly 12 (June 1975): 34–46; John N. Moore and Harold Schultz Slusher, eds., *Biology: A Search for Order in Complexity* (Grand Rapids, Mich.: Zondervan Publishing House, 1970).

59. Walter Lang, "Fifteen Years of Creationism," *Bible Science Newsletter* 16 (Oct. 1978): 1–3; "Editorial Comments," ibid., 15 (Mar. 1977): 2–3; "A Naturalistic Cosmology vs. a Biblical Cosmology," ibid., 15 (Jan.–Feb. 1977): 4–5; Gerald Wheeler, "The Third National Creation Science Conference," *Origins* 3 (1976): 101–102.

60. Bates, "Christian Fundamentalism," p. 58; "15 Years of Creationism," *Five Minutes with the Bible and Science*, supplement to *Bible-Science Newsletter* 17 (May 1979): 2; Nicholas Wade, "Creationists and Evolutionists: Confrontation in California," *Science* 178 (1972): 724–729. Regarding the BSCS texts see Gerald Skoog, "Topic of Evolution in Secondary School Biology Textbooks: 1900–1977," *Science Education* 63 (1979): 621–640; and "A Critique of BSCS Biology Texts," *Bible-Science Newsletter* 4 (15 Mar. 1966): 1. See also John A. Moore, "Creationism in California," *Daedalus* 103 (1974): 173–189; and Dorothy Nelkin, *The Creation Controversy: Science or Scripture in the Schools* (New York: W. W. Norton, 1982).

61. Henry M. Morris, "Director's Column," *Acts & Facts* 1 (June–July 1972): no pagination; Morris interview, 6 Jan. 1981.

62. Nell J. Segraves, *The Creation Report* (San Diego: Creation-Science Research Center, 1977), p. 17; "15 Years of Creationism," pp. 2–3.

63. Bates, "Christian Fundamentalism," p. 98; Henry M. Morris, "Director's Column," *Acts & Facts* 3 (Sept. 1974): 2. See also Edward J. Larson, "Public Science vs. Popular Opinion: The Creation-Evolution Legal Controversy" (Ph.D. diss., University of Wisconsin-Madison, 1984).

64. Morris, "Director's Column," p. 2; Henry M. Morris, ed., *Scientific Creationism*, General Edition (San Diego: Creation-Life Publishers, 1974).

65. The quotation comes from Russel H. Leitch, "Mistakes Creationists Make," *Bible-Science Newsletter* 18 (Mar. 1980): 2. Regarding school boards, see "Finding: Let Kids Decide How We Got Here," *American School Board Journal* 167 (Mar. 1980): 52; and Segraves, *Creation Report*, p. 24. On Popper's influence see, e.g., Ariel A. Roth, "Does Evolution Qualify as a Scientific Principle?" *Origins* 4 (1977): 4–10. In a letter to the editor of *New Scientist* 87 (21 Aug. 1980): 611, Popper affirmed that the evolution of life on earth was testable and, therefore, scientific. On Kuhn's influence see, e.g., Ariel A. Roth, "The Pervasiveness of the Paradigm," *Origins* 2 (1975): 55–57; Leonard R. Brand, "A Philosophic Rationale for a Creation-Flood Model," ibid., 1 (1974): 73–83; and Gerald W. Wheeler, *The Two-Taled Dinosaur: Why Science and Religion Conflict over the Origin of Life* (Nashville: Southern Publishing Association, 1975), pp. 192–210. For the judge's decision see "Creationism in Schools: The Decision in McLean versus the Arkansas Board of Education," *Science* 215 (1982): 934–943.

66. Henry M. Morris, "Two Decades of Creation: Past and Future," *Impact*, supplement to *Acts & Facts* 10 (Jan. 1981): iii; idem, "Director's Column," ibid., 3 (Mar. 1974): 2. The reference to Gish comes from an interview with Harold Slusher and Duane T. Gish, 6 Jan. 1981.

67. "ICR Schedules M.S. Programs," *Acts & Facts* 10 (Feb. 1981): 1–2. Evidence for alleged discrimination and the use of pseudonyms comes from: "Grand Canyon Presents Problems for Long Ages," *Five Minutes with the Bible and Science,* supplement to *Bible-Science Newsletter* 18 (June 1980): 1–2; interview with Ervil D. Clark, 9 Jan. 1981; interview with Steven A. Austin, 6 Jan. 1981; and interview with Duane T. Gish, 26 Oct. 1980, the source of the quotation.

68. Numbers, "'Sciences of Satanic Origin,'" pp. 27–28; Molleurus Couperus, "Tensions between Religion and Science," *Spectrum* 10 (Mar. 1980): 74–88.

69. William Sims Bainbridge and Rodney Stark, "Superstitions: Old and New," *Skeptical Inquirer* 4 (Summer, 1980): 20.

70. "Poll Finds Americans Split on Evolution Idea," p. 22; Harold T. Christensen and Kenneth L. Cannon, "The Fundamentalist Emphasis at Brigham Young University: 1935–1973," *Journal for the Scientific Study of Religion* 17 (1978): 53–57; "Return to Conservatism," *Bible-Science Newsletter* 11 (Aug. 1973): 1; Numbers, "'Sciences of Satanic Origin,'" pp. 27–28.

71. Eileen Barker, "In the Beginning: The Battle of Creationist Science against Evolutionism," in *On the Margins of Science: The Social Construction of Rejected Knowledge,* ed. Roy Wallis, Sociological Review Monograph 27 (Keele: University of Keele, 1979), pp. 179–200, who greatly underestimates the size of the E.P.M. in 1966; [Robert E. D. Clark], "Evolution: Polarization of Views," *Faith and Thought* 100 (1972–1973): 227–229; [idem], "American and English Creationists," ibid., 104 (1977): 6–8; "British Scientists Form Creationist Organization," *Acts & Facts* 2 (Nov.-Dec. 1973): 3; "EPM—40 Years On; Evolution—114 Years Off," supplement to *Creation* 1 (May 1972): no pagination.

72. W. J. Ouweneel, "Creationism in the Netherlands," *Impact,* supplement to *Acts & Facts* 7 (Feb. 1978): i–iv. Notices regarding the spread of creationism overseas appeared frequently in *Bible-Science Newsletter* and *Acts & Facts.* On translations see "ICR Books Available in Many Languages," *Acts & Facts* 9 (Feb. 1980): 2, 7.

17

Modern Physics and Christian Faith

Erwin N. Hiebert

From the sixteenth through the eighteenth centuries the physical sciences occupied center stage in discussions of the relationship between Christianity and science. During the nineteenth century, however, the spotlight shifted to the life sciences, particularly to the implications of organic evolution for Christian theology. Even such theologically pregnant questions as the origin of the solar system provoked relatively little religious discussion in an age more concerned about the origin of species.[1] In the physical sciences, nevertheless, issues of religious significance continued to be raised.

From the mid-nineteenth century on, the newly postulated laws of thermodynamics—namely, the principles of conservation of energy and of the increase of entropy—gave rise to considerable discussion in which religious questions played a leading role. The Irish physicist and science popularizer John Tyndall (1820–1893), for example, championed the principle of conservation of energy with evangelical enthusiasm. In an address of 1874 he ranked "the doctrine of the Conservation of Energy," which "asserts itself everywhere in nature," above the "theory of the origin of species," arguing that the former possessed a "wider grasp and more radical significance" and that it held implications for "ultimate philosophical issues which are as yet but dimly seen."[2]

Toward the latter part of the century the idea of the "heat death" of the universe—a necessary consequence of prediction from the second law of thermodynamics regarding the increase of entropy—sparked vigorous debates about the beginning and end of time, creation, the sphere of God's action in history, and the final destiny of the individual soul. Unfortunately for those concerned about such issues, the theological message of thermodynamics remained ambiguous. For some writers the notion of a decaying universe undermined belief in a beneficent God; for others it provided evidence of a Creator and served as a bulwark against evolution.

THE USES AND ABUSES
OF THERMODYNAMICS

In the 1840s several European scientists independently enunciated the general principle of conservation of energy. According to this principle, later referred to as the first law of thermodynamics, all forms of energy—for example, mechanical, thermal, chemical, electrical— are qualitatively transformable and quantitatively indestructible. As Hermann von Helmholtz (1821–1894), who gave the law its most elegant expression, said, "the quantity of all forces which can be put into action in the whole of nature is unchangeable and can be neither increased nor decreased." The second law of thermodynamics, formulated shortly after midcentury, stipulated that the total entropy within a closed system (that is, the quantity of energy available for work) decreases for all spontaneous processes. Thus, systems in nature move spontaneously from order to disorder, from lesser to greater randomness. Rudolph Clausius (1822–1888), one of the architects of the second law, expressed the first and second laws of thermodynamics in the simple verbal form: "The energy of the universe is constant. The entropy of the universe tends toward a maximum."[3]

Although the scientific community at first greeted these laws with considerable skepticism, by the end of the nineteenth century thermodynamics had taken its place alongside mechanics and the electromagnetic theory of light as one of the main theoretical pillars of classical physics. It had transformed and unified the study of chemistry, heat theory, heat engines, radiation, electricity, and magnetism—and prompted countless discussions regarding the significance of thermodynamic concepts for such issues as the source of the sun's energy, the origin of the solar system, and biological evolution.

Some scientists, such as the German physical chemist and Nobel Prize-winner Wilhelm Ostwald (1853–1932), drew on the first law to construct a nontheistic cosmology in which there were no more barriers "between inner and outer life, between the life of the present and that of the future, between the existence of the body and that of the soul, and which comprehends all these things in a single unity that extends everywhere and leaves nothing outside its scope." But more commonly the law of conservation of energy was invoked to bolster the argument for the existence of a Deity who had ordered the world with perfect foresight, wisdom, and economy of action. The correlation of forces, declared one American scientist, allowed humans to "see more clearly the beautiful harmonies of bounteous nature; that on her many-stringed instrument force answers to force, like the notes of a great symphony; disappearing now in potential energy, and anon reappearing as actual energy, in a multitude of forms."

As long as the laws of science were not seen to be so thoroughly successful in their account of the nature of things as to make God a mere benevolent, absentee landlord, the argument for a world of law, order, and timeless permanence served theology well. However, when it appeared that there was no potential limit to the accomplishments of nineteenth-century thermodynamics in explaining the mysteries of inanimate and animate processes in nature, the energy concept, like the philosophy of mechanism in an earlier age, emerged as a threat for those who were unwilling to relegate to the scientist the description and resolution of the workings of nature down to the smallest details. Such persons considered thermodynamics, with its analytical jurisdiction over conversions and redistributions of energy without losses and without divine interference, to be no less tyrannical than mechanism had been—a suspicion amply confirmed by writers like Ostwald. Thus around the turn of the century there was an immensely spirited debate over the implications of thermodynamics for religious belief. Just how far, some wondered, did the energy concept reach into vital life processes, the motor or sensory nerve cells of the brain, problems of volition, consciousness, the nature of the human soul, the relation of the soul to the body, questions of moral freedom, and divine interference in the form of miracles?

The second law of thermodynamics raised theological issues of a different character. If the principle of the increase of entropy of any operating system was extended to include the entire world or the universe, then the universe was moving toward a configuration of maximum randomness, a condition of minimum availability of energy. This irreversible process would lead inevitably to a degradation of the accessible energy sources and ultimately to that pessimistic state of affairs called the "heat death" of the universe in which freezing temperatures would extinguish all life. Thermodynamics accordingly predicted an end to everything as a function of time—a prospect that could hardly be ignored by theologians or scientists.

Although the second law appeared to be fatal to any meaningful view of the ultimate relation between the world and intelligent beings, some conservative thinkers welcomed it as a confirmation of their apocalyptic theology. After all, argued William Ralph Inge (1860–1954), the so-called "gloomy Dean" of St. Paul's in London, this world "was never meant to be a pleasure garden." Besides, in Inge's opinion, thermodynamics seemed to argue for the traditional Christian doctrine that God created the world out of nothing. If the universe was running down like a clock, he reasoned, the clock must have been wound up at some specific time; and if the second law predicted an end in time for the world, then the world must have had a beginning in time. Conservatives like the Dean also derived satisfaction from the notion that the modern philosophy of progress, based on evolution, was "wrecked on the Second Law of Thermodynamics." Since the universe was moving inexorably toward its "heat death," both biological evolution and the idea of progress seemed to be illusions.

Less pessimistic persons attempted to avoid the implications of the second law in a variety of ways. Ostwald, for example, completely ignored the gloomier aspects of the second law. William Thomson, later Lord Kelvin (1824–1907), who helped to formulate the second law, excluded living organisms from its domain. The Swedish Nobel Prize-winning chemist Svante Arrhenius (1859–1927) admitted the universality of the law but thought that rare exceptions might occur leading to the rebuilding of worlds—perhaps by some conscious "Maxwellian demon," which could sort out individual molecules and thereby create a temperature difference without expending energy. The American philosopher-psychologist William James (1842–1910) simply forced an optimistic interpretation on the second law. He wrote: "Though the ultimate state of the universe may be its vital and physical extinction, there is nothing in physics to interfere with the hypothesis that the *penultimate* state might be the millennium. . . . The last expiring pulsation of the universe might be—I am so happy and perfect that I can stand it no longer."

Such responses demonstrate that no matter how good, how secure, or how elegant a scientific theory is, it is never immune to being used in ways that transgress the limits of credulity to the point of sheer ridiculousness—at least in the eyes of subsequent generations. In the garden of thermodynamics, as in other areas of science, all kinds of private metaphysics and theology have grown like weeds.

THE NEW PHYSICS

Toward the end of the nineteenth century physical scientists in general believed that much still remained to be learned about the detailed inner workings of the physical world. They were fully aware of the fact that not all of the far-flung domains of physics and chemistry hung together in one unified physical worldview. Nevertheless, the enormous analytical power and predictive potential embodied in the classical mathematically expressed mechanical (or, as some would have wanted it, electromagnetic) worldview created an aura of self-centered acquiescence in the status quo that has been characterized as the physics of refinement of known laws and data. As Albert A. Michelson (1852–1931), the first American Nobel laureate, said in his Lowell lectures of 1899, "The more important fundamental laws and facts of physical science have all been discovered, and these are now so firmly established that the possibility of their ever being supplanted in consequence of new discoveries is exceedingly remote. . . . Our future discoveries must be looked for in the sixth place of decimals."[4]

Such complacency about the immutability of the mechanical world of classical Newtonian physics, characterized by absolute space, time, and motion, an all-pervading ether, and strict causality, clearly was accompanied by theological implications. Since there was increasingly little room for divine activity, some writers argued that the only respectable position for a scientist to maintain was a severe form of deism. Unfortunately, at least from a traditional Christian perspective, this left little maneuverability for the messages of the Old and New Testament, or for a God who is active in history and in the lives of individuals. It also undercut belief in any relationship between man and God that went beyond the unidirectional praise and adoration of God for having ordered the world in so lawlike a manner.

There were, however, some major attempts to evade the adverse implications of the mechanistic philosophy for Christianity. In some scientific circles, especially among British physicists, the turf on which Christianity was defended shifted from a mechanistic to an electromagnetic perspective. This took the form of expositions and arguments linked with the electromagnetic, the gravitational, and the luminiferous ethers: signals sent through matterless space, possessing only nonmaterial force fields. It was assumed that on these premises man might be able to free himself from the prison of the mechanical philosophy of "matter in motion under the influence of forces." Thus one might discover a more amicable and compatible scientific environment within the philosophy of the spirit, the mental, and the psychic.

The most outspoken interpreter of this "spiritualized-ether" philosophy was the physicist Sir Oliver Lodge (1851–1940), whose pioneering investigations into electromagnetic wave theory had earned him a substantial reputation. In the 1880s he became preoccupied with telepathy, telekinesis, communication with the dead, and the belief in personal immortality. Over a period of about three decades he turned out a prolific literature of some twenty books related in one way or another to his spiritualistic hypothesis and its bearing on religion.[5]

Both this worldview and the more widespread mechanical picture suffered substantial demolition at the hands of the new physics between 1895 and the 1930s. The new physics rested on radically modified conceptions of space, time, motion, simultaneity, causality, the dynamics of energy changes, and the wave-particle nature of both matter and radiation. It entirely eliminated the ethers. During this same period the spontaneous and induced transmutation of atoms gave rise to "the new alchemy." The discovery of argon forced chemists to admit into the periodic table new chemical elements that had no chemical properties. Physical scientists also demonstrated that electrons were discrete particles of negative charge and small mass. The discovery of other elementary particles suggested their use as projectiles to study the nucleus and the structural features of molecules, atoms, and nucleons. Refinements in cryogenic techniques allowed scientists to study the strange properties of matter in the vicinity of the absolute zero of temperature. And with the enunciation of a third law of thermodynamics, by Walther Nernst (1864–1941) in 1906, it became possible to calculate theoretically the feasibility of physical and chemical processes.[6]

By the 1920s Albert Einstein (1879–1955) had eliminated the notions of absolute space, time, and motion, postulated a four-dimensional universe, and laid out the general theory of relativity. He also, along the way, had introduced the equation that gives the magnitude of energy involved in the annihilation of matter. However, his relativity theory attracted little attention until 1919, when a solar eclipse allowed astronomers to confirm his prediction about deflected starlight. The Irish dramatist and critic George Bernard Shaw (1856–1950), in his play *Too True to Be Good*, greeted the theory of relativity with disillusionment:

> The Universe of Isaac Newton, which has been an impregnable citadel of modern civilization for three hundred years, has crumbled like the walls of Jericho before the criticism of Einstein. Newton's universe was the stronghold of rational Determinism: . . . Everything was calculable: everything happened because it must: the commandments were erased from the tables of the law; and in their place came the cosmic algebra: the equations of the mathematicians. Here was my faith: here I found my dogma of infallibility. . . . And now—now—what is left of it? All is caprice: the calculable world has become incalculable.[7]

The period beginning in 1895 has been referred to as "the golden age of physics" because of the revolutionary nature of the experimental and theoretical advances associated with the discovery of X rays and radioactivity; the enunciation of relativity, the quantum theory, and the photon theory of light; and the study of the nature and properties of the internally structured atom. The statement by Niels Bohr (1885–1962) in 1927 of the principle of complementarity, which elucidated the enigma introduced by wave-particle duality, initiated vigorous discussions among both scientists and theologians. As Hans Bethe has indicated, although the thirties were politically anything but happy, for physics they were in fact "the happy thirties."[8]

As might be expected, the turn-of-the-century revolution in the physical sciences prompted considerable theological debate, especially in scientific circles. Although some persons were thoroughly confused and deeply disturbed by the apparent need for so radical a conceptual switch to accommodate the new findings and ideas, others gloried in the outcome. Some writers argued that the hitherto satisfactory conceptual world of nature had been cut loose from age-old and tested moorings, and that henceforth scientists would be set adrift in an uncharted intellectual sea destined for worlds unknown, in which the average Christian would be hard pressed to survive. Others turned the argument on its head by asserting that the hand of God should be in evidence everywhere in nature, including the very large, in cosmology, and the very small, in the subatomic constituents of matter. Many scientists, in the process of designing the new physics, came to realize that arrogance about scientific knowledge, assertions about absolute and rock-bottom truths, and talk about having discovered all the great laws of physics had become passé.

The new physics, like the classical physics, was invoked both to defend and to attack traditional Christian doctrine. By and large, however, it came to be seen by Christians as an ally of faith, offering freedom from the implied determinism and materialism of the Newtonian worldview. The British physicist James Jeans (1877–1946) expressed the joy with which many greeted the new physics:

> The Classical physics seemed to bolt and bar the door leading to all freedom of will; the new physics hardly does this; it almost seems to suggest that the door may be unlocked if we could only find the handle. The old physics showed us a universe which looked more like a prison than a dwelling place. The new physics shows us a universe which looks as though it might conceivably form a suitable dwelling place for free man, and not a mere shelter for him—a home in which it may at least be possible for us to mould events to our desires and live lives of endeavour and achievement.[9]

Radioactive transformation could be used to argue either that God was still at work as a Creator or that calculations for the age of the earth did not square with estimates from organic evolution. Some writers saw in radioactivity a means of escaping the dire fate predicted by the second law of thermodynamics. The American physicist Robert A Millikan (1868–1953), for example, found comfort in the fact that X rays and radioactivity had finally compelled people "to begin to think in terms of a universe which is changing, living, growing, even in its elements—a dynamic instead of a static universe." When Millikan confirmed the existence of cosmic rays in the 1920s, he identified them as the "birth-cries" of atoms, evidence that the Creator was "continually on the job." He felt that just as God intervenes in the process of biological evolution, so also he has a hand in the evolution of the chemical elements: "This whole work constitutes, then, very powerful evidence that creative or atom-building process is continually going on all about us, possibly even on earth, and that such an event is broadcast through the heavens in the form of the appropriate cosmic ray." Millikan assumed that "in the interior of heavy atoms, occasionally a negative electron gets tired of life at the pace it has to live in the electron world, and decides to end it all and commit suicide; but, being paired by Nature in electron-fate with a positive, he has to arrange a suicide pact with his mate, and so the two jump into each other's arms in the nucleus, and the two complementary electron lives are snuffed out at once; but not without letting loose of a terrific death-yell." Thus cosmic rays are generated.[10]

Relativity, too, was invoked—without much regard for Einstein's specific use of the word—to undermine mechanistic materialism or to show that the idea of relativity of knowledge was harmful to the Christian ideals of fixed morality. When Einstein visited England in 1921, the archbishop of Canterbury quizzed the now-famous guest about the implications of relativity for theology. "None," replied Einstein. "Relativity is a purely scientific matter and has nothing to do with religion."[11] But where Einstein refused to tread, others rushed in. The British astronomer Arthur Stanley Eddington (1882–1944), who saw in relativity evidence for the existence of mind in nature, likened Einstein's response to Charles Darwin's saying that because the theory of natural selection was purely scientific, it had no theological implications. "The compartments into which human thought is divided are not so water-tight that fundamental progress in one is a matter of indifference to the rest," declared the Cambridge scientist. "It seems to me unreasonable to maintain that the working out of these wider implications of the new conception of the physical universe should be left entirely to those who do not understand it."[12]

Christian theologians, often confusing the language of relativity with its scientific content, used Einstein's theories to support doctrines ranging from immortality to the existence of the Holy Spirit. "If the idea of time as a fourth dimension is valid, then the difference between this mortal life and the 'other life' is not a difference in the time nor in the quality of the life," observed one theologian. "It is only a difference in our view of it—our ability to see it whole. While we are limited to three-dimensional understandings, it is mortal life. Where we perceive it in four dimensions, it is eternal life."[13]

A British physicist-theologian, whose aim was to demonstrate that the connection between science and Christianity is so close that there should be trust, understanding, and cooperation instead of hostility, wrote: "If the Christian view is true, surely we should expect to find the evidence of the Holy Spirit in the physical sphere in just such signs of dynamic energy and activity as are indicated by modern physics. If energy is the essential basis of the whole material world, this to the Christian is a clear manifestation of the active, creative Spirit of God in the physical realm."[14]

The thrust toward a new synthesis of matter and spirit, a reconciliation of science and Christianity, and a true reciprocity between materialistic and religious philosophies was endorsed explicitly in the critical reflections of the Yale plant morphologist Edmund Ware Sinnott (1888–1968). He suggested that the "revolution introduced by relativity, quantum mechanics, and nuclear physics" had forced science to modify its earlier conclusions and thus had transformed physics from the enemy to the ally of religion. The world being "more complex than it seemed to be in Newton's or Darwin's time," scientists had adopted a more open-minded attitude toward idealistic philosophies. "For three centuries a confidently advancing science seemed to undermine the very foundations of faith, and religion was forced to modify its position in many ways or lose the support of its more thoughtful partisans. The tide, however, has begun to turn, and an aggressive idealism is going over from the defense to the attack."[15]

Eddington, a Quaker, stated the case more dramatically. He felt that the conclusion to be drawn from examining the developments of modern science was "that religion first became possible for a reasonable scientific man about the year 1927," the year of "the final overthrow of [the yoke of] strict causality by Heisenberg, Bohr, Born and others."[16]

No aspect of the new physics captured the imagination of Christian apologists more than the principle of uncertainty, put forth by Werner Heisenberg (1901–1976) in 1927. Because natural laws could not precisely predict the behavior of subatomic particles, some writers concluded that the universe was not deterministic, that there was still room for human freedom and divine activity. The year after Heisenberg's announcement, Eddington wrote: "In so far as supernaturalism is associated with the denial of strict causality I can only answer that that is what the modern scientific development of the quantum theory brings us to." (A decade later he described his earlier reasoning on this point as "nonsense.") In contrast with Eddington's early view, the physicist Philipp Frank (1884–1966) declared outright that "between Newtonian mechanics and twentieth-century subatomic mechanics . . . the difference is completely irrelevant for the problem of free will."[17]

More recently the nuclear physicist and Episcopal priest William G. Pollard (b. 1911) has clung resolutely to the principle of uncertainty as a bulwark against determinism, but without claiming that the indeterminacy principle provides a basis for freedom of the will. In fact, he admits to having "grave doubts that there is any relationship at all between them." Rather, the thrust of his argument is that not only all scientific knowledge has a statistical character but that "indeterminacy, alternative, and chance are real aspects of the fundamental nature of things, and not merely the consequence of our inadequate and provisional understanding." Thus the key to the puzzle of "the Biblical idea of providence . . . is to be found in the appearance of chance and accident in history." Pollard writes: "In the capacity of history to steer a purposeful and meaningful course through the shoals of chance and accident, those who have participated in history as members of this tradition have seen the hand of God in events." According to these views God exercises his providential control of the world at the subatomic level, where secular minds see only chance at work.[18]

Twentieth-century developments in astronomy, like those in physics, have been used both to support and to undermine orthodox religion. On balance, however, the published reflections of astronomers seem to reveal the same sympathetic shift toward religion as is evidenced by physicists. As an extreme case we might cite the grandiose and undaunted bravado of the American astronomer Robert Jastrow, who, in discussing the big bang theory in a book entitled *God and the Astronomers* (1978), wrote: "Now we see how the astronomical evidence leads to a biblical view of the origin of the world. The details differ, but the essential elements in the astronomical and biblical accounts of Genesis are the same: the chain of events leading to man commenced suddenly and sharply at a definite moment in time, in a flash of light and energy." In a much-quoted statement, he concluded: "For the scientist who has lived by his faith in the power of reason, the story ends like a bad dream. He has scaled the mountains of ignorance; he is about to conquer the highest peak; as he pulls himself over the final rock, he is greeted by a band of theologians who have been sitting there for centuries."[19]

The intricate and variegated interactions between modern physics and Christian faith cut across so many social factors and specific denominational beliefs and practices that generalizations are difficult to make. We do know, however, that for reasons not entirely clear, physical scientists in the twentieth century have remained more orthodox theologically than their colleagues in the biological, behavioral, and social sciences.[20] A number of physical scientists, including some of the most prominent members of the scientific community, have written extensively on the relationship between science and Christianity. Three of the most common views—what I call monism, dualism, and pluralism—will be illustrated by means of case studies of individual physical scientists. My intent is to focus on the self-image of the scientist as interpreter and practitioner of religion, not to portray the scientist as theologian. To this end I will explore how specific scientists have sought to correlate their work with religion and how some of them have managed, on their own terms, to be both scientific and religious at the same time.

THE MONISM OF
SIR WILLIAM HENRY BRAGG

On issues relating to science and religion physical scientists of the past century have taken a variety of positions, the most common being monism, dualism, and pluralism. Monists stress the unity, oneness, and harmony of reality and knowledge. Although conflict between science and religion may appear at times, it is only apparent; in the end harmony will be revealed, even if it comes at the expense of religion or science. Dualists, undoubtedly the most numerous group among nineteenth- and twentieth-century scientists, insist on a radical separation of the physical and the mental, of body and soul, of science and religion. Because there is no interaction between science and religion, there can be no conflict. In contrast with monists, who force all knowledge into one domain, and dualists, who divide science and religion into mutually exclusive domains, pluralists allow for a multiplicity of interpretations—complementary methods of observing, classifying, and arranging the available information about nature. Science and religion may not always be in agreement, but, because they represent equally valid perspectives, neither are they incompatible.

Representative of the monist outlook was the English physicist William Henry Bragg (1862–1942), who, with his son William Lawrence, won the Nobel Prize in physics in 1915 for "their services in the analysis of crystal structure by means of X-rays."[21] Born into a family of yeoman farmers and merchant seamen in northwestern England, the elder Bragg enrolled as a teenager in Trinity College, Cambridge, where for three years he studied nothing but mathematics. At first his studies suffered because of the distraction of a "wave of religious experience" that swept through the college. The meetings and discussions, the horrible talk about eternal damnation, and inane efforts to interpret biblical passages literally absorbed his time and left him permanently disillusioned with dogmatic religion. For many years, he later recalled, "the Bible was a repelling book which I shrank from reading." Nevertheless, he never abandoned the Christian faith, and during later life he repeatedly spoke and wrote about the relationship between science and religion.[22]

Upon completing his studies at Cambridge, Bragg accepted a post in mathematics and physics at the University of Adelaide in Australia, where he remained for over two decades. At first he devoted himself exclusively to teaching, but at age 41, inspired by the new advances in X rays and radioactivity, he began a series of original scientific investigations that won international acclaim—and a professorship back in England, first at the University of Leeds, later at University College, London. In 1923 Bragg succeeded Sir James Dewar (1842–1923) in the Fullerian Professorship at the Royal Institution, London.

As a physicist, Bragg stressed the importance of experiments over theories, which latter he regarded as nothing more than makeshift hypotheses designed and built around experimental results, which dictated whether theories should be retained, modified, or abandoned. This principle guided him in practice as well as in theory. For example, after experimenting for years to prove the corpuscular nature of X rays, he rejected the corpuscular theory when experiments demonstrated conclusively the wave nature of X rays. He adopted a similar approach toward religion, repeatedly emphasizing that both scientific and religious knowledge were to be won with the help of theories, hypotheses, and constructs that experiment would subsequently render obsolete.

From the beginning of his career as an experimental physicist, science served as the driving force in Bragg's life. It may, as he maintained, have represented only one half of his life, but it was the half that established the essential criteria for judging the other half, including religion. "From religion comes a man's purpose; from science, his power to achieve it," he told a juvenile audience at the Royal Institution, London, in 1919. "Sometimes people ask if religion and science are not opposed to one another. They are: in the sense that the thumb and fingers of my hand are opposed to one another. It is an opposition by means of which anything can be grasped."[23]

In later years Bragg spelled out more explicitly his views on the relation of science and religion. In 1940, for example, he identified "two sad mistakes" current in science-religion debates: "The one is to suppose that science, that is to say, the study of Nature, leads to . . . materialism. . . . The other that the worship of God . . . can be carried on without the equipment which science provides." It was dangerous, he warned, to assume that life arose from dead matter just because no other explanation seemed plausible. "Other and better explanations [might] appear which we had not thought of previously, possibly for the reason that our knowledge was imperfect, possibly through lack of mental capacity."[24]

Despite such cautions, Bragg staunchly defended a restricted materialism and mechanistic view of the universe not only in physics and chemistry but also in biology. To illustrate his position, he asked readers to imagine "that a motor car were a novel object, and its driver hidden." By means of various probes, tests, and arguments, an engineer might try to explain the phenomena associated with the operation and motion of the car. "He could go on enquiring for ever [but] in the end he will come across the driver, and will now say that he has an explanation of why the car moves and acts with seeming intelligence. He will probably lose interest in the theories he may have formed provisionally." Although Bragg stopped short of predicting that the Driver of the universe would be discovered, he did not rule out the possibility. But such a discovery would be scientific in nature and could conceivably square with a mechanistic interpretation of life. Mechanical sequence, in his opinion, did not rule out free will any more than a corpuscular theory of light ruled out a wave theory. He was, however, reluctant to invoke Heisenberg's uncertainty principle as an escape route for free will via physics.[25]

Although Bragg's language sometimes hinted at a pluralist position, such was not the case. He remained convinced that knowledge is of one kind acquired only by experience. He conceded that many theories could be useful in achieving "a higher level of thought" or "an explanatory truth now hidden from us," but he consistently rejected the pluralist view that complementary, but mutually exclusive, theoretical constructs could be used with near finality to describe the same domain of phenomena.

The year before his death Bragg delivered a lecture on "Science and Faith" in which he once again emphasized the experimental basis of scientific and religious knowledge:

Science is experimental, moving forward step-by-step, making trial and learning through success and failure. Is not this also the way of religion, and especially of the Christian religion? The writings of those who preach the religion have from the very beginning insisted that it is to be proved by experience. If a man is drawn towards honour and courage and endurance, justice, mercy, and charity, let him follow the way of Christ and find out for himself that it leads him where he could go. No findings in science hinder him in that way, nor do they give any direct proof that it is the right way to follow. Indirectly science is of primary importance because a man who tries to help his neighbor must know how to do it, and science in these days constitutes a large part of the knowledge that is required.

Because of the provisional nature of both scientific theories and theological dogma, no one could afford to be doctrinaire in either area; yet one could act on the basis of present knowledge. "I should think that the theologian's dogma is now becoming more like the scientist's hypothesis," he wrote, "so probable of course that he accepts it and acts upon it always."[26]

In his own life Bragg seems to have adopted a liberal interpretation of religion that stressed the social gospel—that is, helping one's neighbors. By this means he was able to test his religious beliefs as experimentally as he tested his scientific theories in the laboratory. As far as Bragg was concerned, there was—or at least he felt that there should be—no possible conflict between science and religion properly conceived. The cumulative experiences derived from religion and science constituted for him the composite source of knowledge available for designing incomplete, tentative, but extremely significant hypotheses for attaining desirable and potentially achievable aims. To this end the Scriptures, which he knew so well, were to be taken not literally but as one possible source of information about religious experiences. Thus he avoided discussions of doctrine, the existence of God, spiritual matters, miracles, supernaturalism, the plenary inspiration of the Bible, immortality, salvation, and organized religion.[27]

For Bragg there was one complicated, interconnected world of phenomena awaiting to be discovered, uncovered, related, and interpreted. The role of hypotheses—religious and scientific—was to pave the way for additional discoveries at a deeper level. In his search for knowledge, science occupied the determinative position. Religion, of course, was neither in conflict with science nor irrelevant to human endeavors and goals. But this harmonious compatibility resulted in part from Bragg's choosing to highlight only those components of religion that were considered to be compatible, in principle, with the sciences. He thus championed a monism of knowledge (in its substantive content), a monism of method (which ruled out private techniques for getting at what is), and a monism of goals (the fascination of the search).

The monism of Bragg is revealed pointedly in his comments about Michael Faraday (1791–1867), who had spent his entire scientific career at the Royal Institution and for whom Bragg had an enormous admiration as scientist and Christian. But Faraday clearly was a dualist who espoused the strictest separation of his religion from his science. Queried about his religion, Faraday replied that he belonged to "a very small and despised sect of Christians, known—if known at all— as Sandemanians; and our hope is founded on the faith as it is in Christ." In a Broadcast National Lecture in 1931, Bragg said:

> If this complete separation of . . . [Faraday's] religion from his science seems strange, we must remember that it would not seem so strange to any of us if we could put ourselves back into his days: and I think it may be added that to some of us it would not seem strange even now, if we consider what Faraday may have meant by it. Remember that he himself was filled with a vision; he had actually been himself the first to see the workings of some of the great laws of the universe, and the unity of it all possessed him. Here were facts in natural accordance with the universal presence and power of the One God he had been taught to believe in. But his experiments could tell him nothing more of the qualities of that God. They fitted perfectly into their place, but they were trifles in comparison with the wider vision which he believed that his own spirit could ponder on and hope to see. This he sought in the quiet of his fellowship. We do not know, of course, to what extent he was satisfied.[28]

THE DUALISM OF PIERRE DUHEM

Pierre Duhem (1861–1916) was a versatile and influential French physical chemist, historian of science, and philosopher of science who, partly because of a penchant for controversy, spent his professional career at the provincial universities of Lille, Rennes, and Bordeaux rather than in Paris. A rigid ultra-Catholic, he liked to identify himself as a Christian positivist, one who believed that sensory perception provided the only basis of scientific knowledge.[29] Although he wrote prolifically on subjects ranging from thermodynamics and hydrodynamics to the history of medieval science, he published little on the relations of science and religion. A notable exception was a 1905 essay on the "Physics of a Believer," written in response to an accusation by the Sorbonne professor of the history and philosophy of science Abel Rey (1873–1940) that Duhem's scientific writings betrayed his religious beliefs.[30]

The implication that his theology influenced his physics aroused Duhem's indignation. He happily acknowledged his Christian faith: "Of course, I believe with all my soul in the truths that God has revealed to us and that He has taught us through his Church. . . . In this sense it is permissible to say that the physics I profess is the physics of a believer." But he resented the suggestion "that one must be a believer, not to mention being a perspicacious one, in order to adopt altogether the principles as well as the consequences of the doctrine that I have tried to formulate concerning physical theories." Duhem felt particularly injured because he had "constantly aimed to prove that physics proceeds by an autonomous method absolutely independent of any metaphysical opinion." The theories that summarize and classify the discoveries achieved by this autonomous method, he asserted in positivistic fashion, have no "ability to penetrate beyond the teachings of experiment or any capacity to surmise realities hidden under data observable by the senses." Physics, he argued, could be pursued equally well by "positivists and metaphysicians, materialists and spiritualists, non-believers and Christians."[31]

Duhem left no doubt that metaphysics and religion had nothing at all to offer physics. But—except at the level of "objective reality"— he was unwilling to say that physics had nothing to contribute to metaphysics and religion. The expectations of many that the basic doctrines of the Catholic faith would soon crumble "under the ramming blows of scientific systems" he attributed to a failure to understand the fundamental difference between physical theory and religious dogma. Propositions such as "Man is free," "The soul is immortal," and "The Pope is infallible in matters of faith," he argued, all relate to objective reality, "affirming or denying that a certain real being does or does not possess a certain attribute." Since physical theories have no objective reality but merely summarize and classify laws established by experiment, they can neither agree nor disagree with such propositions. In short, because physical theories can be neither true nor false, they have *"no part to play in metaphysical or theological discussions."* And because science and theology have nothing in common at this level, there can be no conflict.[32]

In spite of the subjective and contingent nature of physical theory, Duhem urged metaphysicians and theologians not to distrust science. It was important, he wrote, that "the metaphysician should know physical theory in order not to make an illegitimate use of it in his speculations." Above all, the metaphysician should be able to distinguish between the *theories* of physics, which have no objective reality, and the *facts and laws* of physics, which are "rich in objective truth." Doing this, of course, was tricky business, impossible for anyone having only a superficial acquaintance with physics. Only the "subtle mind," "sharpened by long practice . . . by profound and detailed study of theory," could hope to make the necessary distinctions. Duhem thus ends up maintaining on the one hand that metaphysics and religion are irrelevant for doing physics—the physics of the believer is just physics, nothing more—while on the other hand arguing that "it is necessary for the metaphysician to have a very exact knowledge of physical theory in order to recognize it unmistakably when it crosses the boundaries of its domain and tries to penetrate into the territory of cosmology." In this respect Duhem credited the Catholic church with having "on many occasions helped powerfully . . . to maintain human reason on the right road, even when this reason strives for the discovery of truths of a natural order."[33]

It was not uncommon among Duhem's positivist compatriots in France and elsewhere to treat scientific theories as repositories for propositions that are elegant, comprehensive, economical, simple, and convenient, but "essentially subjective, contingent, and variable with time, with schools, and persons" and therefore "stripped of all objective existence."[34] But it certainly was rare to find so prestigious a scholar as Duhem reserve for metaphysics and theology the status of truth and objective reality independent of science. His ultra-Catholic positivism, combined with his bellicose temperament, brought him considerable intellectual isolation and opposition, among both scientists and clerics. Nevertheless, he held firmly to his rigid, disputatious, and unique brand of science-faith dualism until his death.

THE PLURALISM OF
CHARLES A. COULSON

Charles A. Coulson (1910–1974), a tall, imposing British scientist, enjoyed a brilliant career that straddled mathematics, physics, and chemistry.[35] Trained in mathematics and physics at Trinity College, Cambridge, he later applied his mathematical skills with uncanny wizardry to solving problems in wave mechanics and molecular-structure theory. At various times in his life he held professorships in physics, mathematics, and chemistry, ending his career as professor of theoretical chemistry at Oxford University.

As one might guess from his *curriculum vitae*, Coulson had little use for disciplinary boundaries. Similarly, he resisted efforts to separate science and religion, so popular among British intellectuals in the 1920s and 1930s. Although raised in the Methodist church, he remained only a nominal Christian until age nineteen, when he experienced a conversion. At this time, he later recalled, "God became real to me—utterly real—I knew Him and I could talk with Him as I had never imagined it possible before." Prayers with his Christian friends became the highlight of his day, and life took on new meaning and purpose.[36] Shortly after his conversion he became an accredited lay preacher in the Methodist church, and he subsequently devoted much of his life to religious and humanitarian causes, especially ones connected with the social and ethical responsibility of scientists. His practical outlook, reflected in both his scientific and religious activities, is captured in the lines of William Butler Yeats's poem "A Prayer for Old Age," which Coulson often quoted:

> God guard me from the thoughts men think
> In the mind alone;
> He that sings a lasting song,
> Thinks in a marrow bone.

During his last decades he spent almost as much time on religion as on science, writing so much on the relation of science and religion— about fifty pamphlets and articles and three major books—that London newspapers began referring to him as the holder of the Chair of Theological Physics.[37]

In 1954 Coulson summed up his conclusions about science and religion in the John Calvin McNair Lectures at the University of North Carolina, published the following year under the title *Science and Christian Belief*. In this book he addressed the question of how Christianity could survive "in an age so profoundly influenced by scientific discovery and scientific thought." In opposition to the monist view that science and religion are the same thing and the dualist opinion that they represent different domains of truth, he argued that science is one component of the revelation of God, "consonant in its insistence on value and person with the traditional Christian conception, but adding certain elements which we could not otherwise ever know." In other words, science and religion provided complementary perspectives.[38]

Coulson explicitly rejected all religious responses to the challenge of modern science that involved "clinging to the past." He particularly disliked attempts to "take refuge in metaphysics—a situation which seems not infrequently to follow the discovery that physics is not sufficiently accommodating to our personal whim." As an example of this unfortunate tendency he cited the work of Karl Heim (1874–1959), a prominent Protestant professor of systematic theology in Tübingen, who tried to protect theology from scientific encroachment by removing it from the physical world. Einstein might eliminate the concepts of absolute space, time, and motion, argued Heim, but he could not touch the concept of an absolute God. This type of religious defense, said Coulson bluntly, "cuts no ice with the professional scientist who feels hamstrung right away when told to accommodate his science to some reality beyond his reach." Scientists, he explained, must "follow uncompromisingly wherever we are led, into whatever abyss or on to whatever height, and accept whatever we may meet upon the way." If science were recognized as a revelation from God rather than as a threat to religion, Christianity would be imbued with fresh air "sweeping away the cobwebs of metaphysical dogmatism."[39]

Coulson expressed equal contempt for attempts to harmonize science and religion by marking out autonomous regions for each. "It has always been one of our major temptations to try to divide our experience into two (or more) parts and grant science control of the one part, while allowing religion to maintain its authority in the other," he wrote. But such "intellectual partitioning" was "a fatal step" that invited science "to discover new things and thence gradually to take possession of that which religion once held." Scientists, he argued, have little need of a "God of the Gaps" whose role in the world shrank with each new scientific discovery; "either God is in the whole of Nature, with no gaps, or He's not there at all."[40]

To illustrate the way in which science had been abused by Christian apologists, Coulson cited various authors who appealed to Heisenberg's uncertainty principle to justify belief in free will and divine involvement, who (in the words of E. N. da C. Andrade) believed that "the electron leads us to the doorway of religion." In Coulson's opinion this way was not only bad physics but bad religion, resulting from an ambiguous use of language that gave the false impression that an electron was a tiny "particle." Rather than leading to the gateway of religion, he wrote, the electron "leads us to think a little more deeply about science, and to modify our fundamental concepts to bring them into line with the increasing variety of our experiments. Once we admit that the electron need not be pictured as a tiny particle, the uncertainty relation has nothing more to say about free will."[41]

To avoid the pitfalls he described, Coulson urged Christians to view science and religion as complementary activities, to recognize that "science is one aspect of God's presence, and scientists therefore part of the company of His heralds." The model upon which he drew to illustrate the relationship between science and religion was Bohr's concept of complementarity, designed to explain the wave-particle duality of the nature of light and electrons. According to Bohr, light and electrons are not *both* waves *and* particles; rather the dualism derives from "our integration [and from] the language and concepts that we use to give meanings and pattern to our experiments in optics and spectroscopy." Similarly, science is not religion and religion is not science; they are merely two ways, among many, of explaining the world we see around us.[42]

Coulson's position on the complementary relation between science and religion is perhaps best understood by looking at the rules and functions that he assigned to each. Although science does not recognize God *in* its work, it is nevertheless religious to the extent that it recognizes God in the act of reflection *upon* its scientific work. Religion, too, recognizes God, but from a very different perspective. The accounts of science and of religion are not identical; it is in "the putting together of two or more partial views" that a genuine complementarity emerges.[43] Coulson's interpretation of nature thus boils down to a pluralism of perspectives, a unity born of integrating complementary viewpoints, with religion occupying the most significant vantage point for constructing as nearly as possible a total picture of the environment.

CONCLUSION

In this essay I have attempted to clarify a number of issues that have arisen at the intersection of religion and science. Within the limited framework of recent developments in the physical sciences I have tried to identify the self-image of the scientist as an interpreter-practitioner of religion and to discover, where possible, the means by which a rapprochement was achieved that might illuminate the scientific dimensions of religion or the religious dimensions of science.

As we have seen, one attractive option for scientists was to adopt the premise that the principles of science are nonessential to Christian belief and vice versa. To those who embraced this position, however, neither science nor religion necessarily appeared to be irrelevant to the life and thought of the scientist as believer. By contrast, among scientists who assumed science and religion to be interdependent in some meaningful way, it was common to invoke arguments to demonstrate the connection, by restructuring either their views on religion to fit their science or their views on science to fit their religion. The latter strategy, in its exaggerated form, was characteristic of religious fundamentalists. The former emphasis was dominant among scientists who identified strongly with the beliefs, customs, and biases of the established scientific community. The views expressed by the scientists discussed in this paper were conceived largely from within a mental framework intrinsically tilted toward science. Indeed, our scientists invariably championed science as the model for religious discourse.

For centuries, both monist and dualist positions have been advocated in works devoted to analyzing the reciprocity between science (or natural philosophy) and the Christian religion. By the twentieth century the complexion and interchanges that earlier had converged so myopically on the warfare of science and religion, with science characteristically on the defensive and religion on the offensive, had shifted to accommodate, in one way or another, radically new scientific conceptions both in regard to nature as observed in its pristine state and in regard to the world of nature created by humans. The three scientists singled out for analysis—Bragg, Duhem, and Coulson—confronted an expansive mosaic of fundamentally novel questions and dilemmas concerning the concepts of space, time, motion, simultaneity, continuity, determinism, and a number of apparently independent hierarchies of existence and lawlike behavior within matter.

Both monism and dualism, of course, survived. In fact, in some quarters, as we have seen, both took on new life by virtue of being able to draw upon an ostensibly limitless reserve of new ways of thinking made available by relativity theory, quantum theory, and the new frontiers associated with the internal structure of the atom. Simultaneously, scientific pluralism, which had never occupied a prominent position in the annals of science, came into fashion for a number of circumstantial reasons. For example, arguments in favor of overarching unitary conceptions meant to encompass all of existence increasingly seemed forced and feeble. And a two-tier compartmentalization of natural-spiritual phenomena was seen to be flawed in the face of richly successful, nonoverlapping, but mutually complementary conceptions within science proper. Thus religion, too, it was argued, could provide a complementary way of interpreting nature—especially when emphasis was placed on humans as a part of nature. Although markedly divergent in their emphases, the scientists mentioned in this paper moved with considerable flexibility back and forth between the two mirror-image models of how science promotes religion and how religion promotes science.

NOTES

I acknowledge with sincere thanks the criticisms and suggestions Ronald Numbers has made during the process of revising this paper.

1. See, e.g., Ronald L. Numbers, *Creation by Natural Law: Laplace's Nebular Hypothesis in American Thought* (Seattle: Univ. of Washington Press, 1977).

2. John Tyndall, Inaugural Address, British Association in Belfast, *Nature* 10 (20 Aug. 1874): 316.

3. This section is abstracted from Erwin N. Hiebert, "The Uses and Abuses of Thermodynamics in Religion," *Daedalus* 95 (1966): 1046–1080. Although the words *force* (*Kraft*) and *energy* (*Energie*) often were used interchangeably in the nineteenth century, it is not difficult to recognize from the context of Helmholtz's statement that he meant *energy* (as the action of force through distance), not simply *force*.

4. A. A. Michelson, *Light Waves and Their Uses* (Chicago: Univ. of Chicago Press, 1903), pp. 23–24.

5. The writings of Oliver Lodge include *Life and Matter: A Criticism of Professor Haeckel's "Riddle of the Universe"* (London: Williams & Norgate, 1905); *Science and Human Progress* (London: George Allen & Unwin, 1927); *Beyond Physics; or, The Idealization of Mechanism* (New York: Greenberg, 1931); *My Philosophy: Representing My Views on the Many Functions of the Ether of Space* (London: Ernest Benn, 1933).

6. See, e.g., Erwin N. Hiebert, "The State of Physics at the Turn of the Century," in *Rutherford and Physics at the Turn of the Century*, ed. Mario Bunge and William R. Shea (New York: Dawson & Science History Publications, 1979), pp. 3–22; Hiebert, "Developments in Physical Chemistry at the Turn of the Century," in *Science, Technology and Society in the Time of Alfred Nobel*, ed. C. G. Bernard, E. Crawford, and P. Sörbom (Oxford: Pergamon, 1982), pp. 97–115; and Hiebert, "Historical Remarks on the Discovery of Argon: The First Noble Gas," in *Noble Gas Compounds*, ed. Herbert H. Hyman (Chicago: Univ. of Chicago Press, 1963), pp. 3–20.

7. George Bernard Shaw, *Too True to Be Good: A Political Extravaganza* (New York: Dodd, Mead & Co., 1934), p. 105.

8. Quoted in Roger H. Stuewer, ed., *Nuclear Physics in Retrospect: Proceedings of a Symposium on the 30's* (Minneapolis: Univ. of Minnesota Press, 1979), p. 11.

9. James Jeans, *Physics and Philosophy* (Cambridge: Cambridge Univ. Press, 1943), p. 216.

10. Robert Andrews Millikan, *Evolution in Science and Religion* (New Haven: Yale Univ. Press, 1928), pp. 13–14; Millikan and G. Harvey Cameron, "Evidence for the Continuous Creation of the Common Elements out of Positive and Negative Electrons," *Proceedings of the National Academy of Sciences* 14 (1928): 449; Millikan, "Present Status of Theory and Experiment as to Atomic Disintegration and Atomic Synthesis," *Annual Report of the Smithsonian Institution*, 1931:280.

11. Philipp Frank, *Einstein: His Life and Times* (New York: Alfred A. Knopf, 1947), pp. 189–190.

12. Sir Arthur Eddington, *The Philosophy of Physical Science* (New York: Macmillan, 1939), pp. 7–8.

13. Quoted in Frank, *Einstein*, p. 264.

14. Canon Arthur F. Smethurst, *Modern Science and Christian Beliefs* (New York: Abingdon Press, 1955), p. 81.

15. Edmund Ware Sinnott, *Two Roads to Truth: A Basis for Unity under the Great Tradition* (New York: Viking Press, 1953), p. 105.

16. Arthur Eddington, *The Nature of the Physical World* (Cambridge: Cambridge Univ. Press, 1928), p. 350.

17. Ibid., p. 347; Eddington, *Philosophy of Physical Science*, p. 182; Philipp Frank, *Philosophy of Science: The Link between Science and Philosophy* (Englewood Cliffs, N.J.: Prentice-Hall, 1957), p. 254.

18. William G. Pollard, *Chance and Providence: God's Action in a World Governed by Scientific Law* (London: Faber & Faber, 1959), pp. 53–54, 66, 72.

19. Robert Jastrow, *God and the Astronomers* (New York: W. W. Norton, 1978), pp. 14, 116.

20. James H. Leuba, *The Belief in God and Immortality: A Psychological, Anthropological and Statistical Study* (Boston: Sherman, French & Co., 1916), pp. 275–280; Leuba, "Religious Beliefs of American Scientists," *Harper's Monthly Magazine* 169 (1934): 291–300.

21. On Bragg's life and work see E. N. da C. Andrade, "William Henry Bragg, 1862–1942," *Obituary Notices of Fellows at the Royal Society* 4 (1943): 277–292; Sir Lawrence Bragg and Mrs. G. M. Caroe [Gwendolen Bragg], "Sir William Bragg, F.R.S. (1862–1942)," *Notes and Records of the Royal Society of London* 17 (1962): 169–182; Mrs. Alban Caroe [Gwendolen Bragg], "The Royal Institution in Sir William Bragg's Time," *Proceedings of the Royal Institution of Great Britain* 40 (1965): 398–416; Paul Forman, "William Henry Bragg," *Dictionary of Scientific Biography*, ed. Charles C. Gillispie, 16 vols. (New York: Charles Scribner's Sons, 1970–1980), 2:397–400; Gwendolen M. Caroe, *William Henry Bragg, 1862–1942: Man and Scientist* (Cambridge: Cambridge Univ. Press, 1978).

22. Bragg and Caroe, "Sir William Bragg," pp. 171–172; Andrade, "William Henry Bragg," p. 278.

23. W. H. Bragg, *The World of Sound* (London: G. Bell & Sons, 1920), pp. 195–196.

24. W. H. Bragg, "Science and the Worshipper: In Response to Sir Richard Tute," *The Hibbert Journal* 38 (1940): 289–295.

25. Ibid.

26. W. H. Bragg, *Science and Faith* (London: Oxford Univ. Press, 1941), pp. 16–18.

27. In light of Bragg's position on these matters it is not surprising to discover that there seems to be no reference to his having attached himself formally, as an adult, to any denomination or church group.

28. William Jerome Harrison, "Faraday, Michael (1791–1867)," *Dictionary of National Biography* 6 (1917): 1065; William H. Bragg, *Michael Faraday* (London: British Broadcasting Corporation, 1931), p. 35.

29. On Duhem's life and work see Donald G. Miller, "Pierre-Maurice-Marie Duhem," *Dictionary of Scientific Biography* 4:225–233; and R. Niall D. Martin, "The Philosophy of Pierre Duhem: A Historical and Critical Essay on the

Philosophy and Historiography of a Catholic Physicist" (Ph.D. diss., London School of Economics, 1981).

30. Pierre Duhem, "Physique de Croyant," *Annales de philosophie chrétienne,* 4th ser., 4 (1905): 44–67, 133–159, an English translation of which appears in Pierre Duhem, *Aim and Structure of Physical Theory* (Princeton: Princeton Univ. Press, 1954), pp. 273–311; Abel Rey, "La philosophie scientifique de M. Duhem," *Revue de métaphysique et de morale* 12 (1904): 699–744. Some of the discussion that follows draws on Hiebert, "The Uses and Abuses of Thermodynamics in Religion."

31. Duhem, *Aim and Structure,* pp. 273–279.

32. Ibid., pp. 283–286.

33. Ibid., pp. 291–293, 311. On the relationship between Duhem's ideas and those of the seventeenth-century French philosopher-scientist Blaise Pascal, see Martin, "The Philosophy of Pierre Duhem."

34. Duhem, *Aim and Structure,* pp. 285, 288.

35. The best sources regarding Coulson's life and work are S. L. Altmann and E. J. Bowen, "Charles A. Coulson: 1910–1974," *Obituary Notices of Fellows of the Royal Society* 20 (1974): 75–134; and P. E. Hodgson, "C. A. Coulson: Scientist and Man of Faith," *Epworth Review* 2 (1975): 19–25.

36. Hodgson, "C. A. Coulson," p. 20.

37. Coulson's books on science and religion include *Christianity in an Age of Science* (Oxford: Oxford Univ. Press, 1954); *Science and Christian Belief* (Chapel Hill: Univ. of North Carolina Press, 1955); and *Science, Technology and the Christian* (Nashville: Abingdon Press, 1960).

38. Coulson, *Science and Christian Belief,* pp. 2–3.

39. Ibid., pp. 16–18. See also Karl Heim, *Christian Faith and Natural Science* (London: SCM Press, 1953; first published in German in 1949).

40. Coulson, *Science and Christian Belief,* pp. 19–22, 28.

41. Ibid., pp. 22–25.

42. Ibid., pp. 29–30, 70–71.

43. Ibid., pp. 84–85.

18

Protestant Theology
and Natural Science
in the Twentieth Century

Keith E. Yandell

At the turn of the twentieth century, liberalism dominated the theological scene. Liberals saw the Bible as one of many religious writings, Jesus as one of many religious teachers; they viewed progress as inevitable, human nature as essentially good, and morality as the heart of religion. By the late teens and early twenties, World War I had challenged the notions of inevitable progress and essential goodness, and many theologians were finding a morality-centered theology too thin to provide a basis for preaching or living during troubled times. Thus various theologians, most clearly united by their opposition to liberalism, attempted to find middle ground between liberalism and traditional orthodoxy, a viewpoint soon called neoorthodoxy. First influential in Europe, and in the United States by the early thirties, these neoorthodox theologians, in fact if not by intent, built a wall between science and theology. At the same time more conservative thinkers developed an articulate orthodox theology, which they saw as having bridges to science. Neoorthodoxy dominated the Protestant theological scene until the sixties, and because of its central position its leading spokesmen are featured in the account that follows. Some attention, however, is also devoted to orthodox, or evangelical, theology, which enjoyed a renaissance in America in the seventies, and to process theology, which has had some impact on the American scene.

FROM LIBERALISM
TO NEOORTHODOXY

The liberalism against which neoorthodoxy rebelled originated with such figures as Immanuel Kant (1724–1804), Georg Wilhelm Friedrich Hegel (1770–1831), David Strauss (1808–1874), and Friedrich Schleiermacher (1768–1834).[1] Kant's *Religion within the Limits of Reason Alone* (1793) claimed that the basic significance of Christianity lay not in theology or dogmatics but in morality; the Bible was seen as more popularly presenting the same rationally discernible morality that one finds in Kant's ethical works. Hegel developed a "philosophy of Absolute Spirit" that denied (or was seen as denying) ultimate religious significance to any particular historical person or event; his *Lectures on the Philosophy of Religion* (1832) appeared to replace the orthodox doctrine of the Incarnation (that God became also human in the person of Jesus Christ, at a particular time and place) by a metaphysical, nonhistorical doctrine of divine immanence. Strauss wrote *The Life of Jesus* (1835), a work representative of biblical criticism that called in question the historical accuracy of the biblical records.[2] Schleiermacher's two-volume *Christian Faith* (1821, 1822) based religious claims not on revelation but on religious experience. Through the influence of such writers a liberalism came to dominate Protestant theology for which religious experience (not revelation) was central, which taught salvation by works and good moral character (not divine grace), for which Jesus was an outstanding moral teacher (not the Son of God), and which based nothing of particular religious importance on the overall historical accuracy of the Scriptures. H. Richard Niebuhr's famous remark that according to liberalism a God without wrath brought men without sin into a kingdom without judgment through the ministrations of a Christ without a cross captured both the thrust of liberalism and the core of conservative and neoorthodox opposition to it.[3]

Within a liberal perspective, then, if genuine conflict between science and theology occurred, theology must give way, because the Bible had no special status or religious authority. Further, given the favor the notions of inevitable progress and inherent human goodness found within liberalism, science and technology appeared as resources by which human effort could usher in the kingdom of God. In the prewar period of the twentieth century it appeared that liberalism had captured the strongholds of Protestantism in both Europe and the United States. Then the war came, followed by the depression, and liberalism was soon overshadowed by neoorthodoxy.

The towering figure of neoorthodoxy was Karl Barth. Emil Brunner tended to agree with Barth but also held that reason has something positive to teach about God. Rudolph Bultmann collapsed theology into existentialist philosophy. Paul Tillich collapsed theology into impersonalist metaphysics. Richard and Reinhold Niebuhr endeavored to state theology in terms compatible with their understanding of change, culture, and history. Because these were the most influential neoorthodox figures, a section is devoted to each of them.[4]

KARL BARTH (1886–1968)

Trained by liberal theologians, Barth, a Swiss pastor who later taught at various universities in Germany and Switzerland, found the optimism of liberalism to be neither consonant with the tragedy of World War I nor adequate to the message he found in the New Testament, particularly in Saint Paul's Epistle to the Romans. Influenced by Søren Kierkegaard (1813–1855), whose thought, in reaction to Hegel, emphasized the transcendence of God, Barth in *The Epistle to the Romans* (1919) challenged liberal theology and reinstated revelation, sin, and judgment as basic theological categories. Kierkegaard's insistence on a qualitative distinction between finite and infinite, time and eternity (the contrastive categories through which Kierkegaard characteristically expressed his view of divine transcendence), stressed an impassable ontological gulf between creature and creator. Barth's view of revelation emphasized an impassable epistemological gulf between revelation and the results of human inquiry of any sort, including science.[5]

Orthodox Christianity had long insisted that many, if not all, of the basic Christian doctrines are known only through revelation— only by God's having taken the initiative and imparted them to persons who would never have discovered them by research. Barth's neoorthodoxy gave this thesis a new (and, the orthodox claimed, inconsistent) embodiment. Influenced by Kierkegaard's existentialism, Barth insisted that revelation is not given unless it is received; a person whose life is not challenged to its depths by revelation has not encountered revelation, even if he or she has read the Bible through. Influenced also by higher criticism of the Bible, Barth denied that the Bible is itself revelation; rather, he held, it points to revelation that occurred in actions by God in history, which it fallibly reports. Such divine action was not accessible to historical methodology, which could only confirm such events as David's having been crowned or

Jesus' having been crucified. *Heilsgeschichte* (holy, or sacred, history), which revealed that God had chosen David and that Jesus had died for our sins, could be discerned only by those to whom God made it known. For Barth, revelation is not conceived as propositional or expressible in statements, since God cannot be an "object"; rather, it is "truth as encounter." Even the capacity to receive revelation is newly created by God, and such content as revelation possesses is not viewed as continuous with what persons know from nonrevelational sources.

Not surprisingly, given this perspective, Barth asserted that an adequate Christian theology must satisfy two criteria: it must be church theology, directed to and satisfactory for internal dialogue among Christian believers, and it must be Christocentric theology, understanding assertions about God and his actions in terms of the life, death, and resurrection of Christ. Even without discussing how those criteria might apply in particular cases, it is clear that the application of these criteria may decide whether a theology is genuinely Christian, but it will not decide whether it is true.

Since he held that knowledge of God is possible only through special revelation, he denied that one could reflect on human nature or natural order and obtain knowledge of God. The Gifford Lectures— a series established by Lord Gifford specifically to deal with natural theology or a "science of God" independent of supernatural revelation—included Barth's *The Knowledge of God and the Service of God* (1938) only because he was allowed to explain why he rejected natural theology. Barth expressed astonishment that a "science of God" should exist. "I am convinced," he told his Gifford audience, "that so far as it has existed and still exists, it owes its existence to a radical error."[6]

The net result of Barth's theology was to build a wall between science and theology. Science, in contrast with theology, makes statements concerning observable or inferred objects, deals with finite items, and arises from a methodology developed by humans. Science and theology, he infers, thus deal with different realms and so are incommensurate.

EMIL BRUNNER (1899–1966)

Emil Brunner, a Swiss Reformed minister and longtime professor of theology at the University of Zurich, shared much of Barth's perspective. He agreed with Barth that Christianity rests on a revelation from God that carries its own authority rather than requiring justification by appeal to the arguments of natural theology or the reports of personal religious experience. Further, this revelation is soteriological; its purpose is the salvation of the persons to whom it is addressed.[7]

But there also are differences between Barth's theology and Brunner's. Barth held the radical view that so devastating is the effect of sin that in order to communicate with a person God has first to create in that person the capacity to receive revelation, whereas Brunner held that, having been created in God's image, persons are able to receive a communication from God without his having to create within them again the capacity to do so. In theological terms the image of God, for Barth, was effaced by the Fall; for Brunner it was only marred. Brunner was also prepared to grant that some knowledge of God is available without special revelation, though this knowledge is not sufficient to redeem persons from their sins. Moreover, persons, by virtue of being persons, share an ethical common ground that makes possible recognition by believers and nonbelievers alike of some basic rights and duties.[8]

Brunner saw the cause of sin to be desire for freedom from God— to be one's own master apart from any norms established by creation or revelation and in denial of one's dependence on God for one's existence and powers. He viewed attempts at such self-sufficiency as denials of our nature as *human* persons and as rebellion against the divine Person. The effects of such attempts blight all aspects of life and culture, but they affect mathematics and natural science least, since these, Brunner suggests, least affect our notion of what a human being is; and they affect the social sciences, the humanities, and religion most, since there our views of what persons are become most explicit.

At least two themes developed here seem relevant to Brunner's view of natural science. One is that, within limits, Brunner finds point in the view that the soteriological completes or perfects the natural. Not only does the process of receiving special, soteriological revelation involve the use of preexisting capacities, but the content of that revelation illumines what was previously known; further, the development of a systematic theological perspective requires that one consider what is known independent of revelation as one tries to unfold the meaning of revelation itself. Another theme is that natural science, whether viewed as method or as product, is not unaffected by sin but is less devastatingly affected than most other areas of human inquiry and less likely to be perverted into a basis for a false autonomy. "The less a truth has to do with the center of personality, the more autonomous is reason within it; that is, the difference, or the contrast between the point of view of the believer or of the unbeliever, comes out in it less and less," Brunner wrote in *Man in Revolt*.[9]

In principle, then, science can correct or purify theology, though not revelation. In fact, Brunner suggests, this sometimes occurs. Referring to views that posit a literal, historical Adam who was not descended from previous forms of life, he writes:

> The whole picture of "the first man" has been finally and absolutely destroyed for us today. The conflict between the teaching of history, natural science, and palaeontology, on the origins of the human race, and that of the ecclesiastical doctrine, waged on both sides with the passion of a fanatical concern for truth, has led, all along the line, to the victory of the scientific view, and to the gradual but inevitable decline in the ecclesiastical view. Upon the plane of empirical research, whether that of history or of natural science, which in the wide field of pre-history often merge into one another, no facts have been left which could support the Augustinian ecclesiastical view of the historical "first man," or which could prove that the empirical origin of the human race was to be sought on a specially elevated plane of spiritual existence.[10]

In this case (and, presumably, the same would hold in other cases where ecclesiastical conflicts with scientific claims) theology is the better for having abandoned claims that conflict with well-established scientific conclusions. Indeed, in such cases science serves to do for theology what theology should have done for itself, namely restrict itself to purely theological claims. "The abandonment of the historical form of the doctrine is not a loss, nor is it a trifle, but it is a necessary purification of the Christian doctrine for its own sake, not for the sake of science," Brunner wrote. "Science stimulates us to find a positive and adequate form for the Biblical message of the origin of Creation and the Fall of man."[11]

The core of the doctrine of Creation, for Brunner, is that persons depend for their existence on God, in whose image they are made, and the core of the doctrine of the Fall is that persons seek, or suppose they have, an autonomy that ignores the Creator/creature distinction. These claims do not conflict, or compete, with the claims of natural science.

Another aspect of the connection between science and theology, as Brunner conceived it, should be noted here. Brunner writes:

> By clinging to the historical framework the actual fundamental content of the Christian doctrine of the origin of man has been either concealed or buried. So long as the historico-theological interest was maintained on the plane of empirical history, the central Biblical truth remained concealed

behind a story which was perceived to be impossible. To one who thought in scientific terms there remained only the two other alternatives which do not conflict with historical research: a theory of evolution conceived in either naturalistic or idealistic terms; that is, a modified Darwinian or Hegelian view—and from the very outset the Hegelian view was only possible for a small circle of philosophical thinkers.[12]

Brunner's suggestion, apparently, is this: by treating the doctrine of Creation as a scientific hypothesis, one both discredited it (since no data supported it) and furthered the doctrine's genuine competitors (the Hegelian view that nature flows from the Absolute, or the dogmatic naturalism that denies any place to theology by claiming that what can be said about persons, science alone says). Instead, Brunner argued that the doctrine of Creation should provide a context within which the scientific data can be placed interpretatively, though its basic thrust remains soteriological. A corollary is that if natural science is supplemented by what is really a religious or philosophical doctrine (Hegelian, naturalistic, or other), a conflict with Christian theology will result; the conflict, however, will not be with natural science but with the philosophical or religious context within which science has been placed.

In North America Brunner's influence was greater even than Barth's, in part because his views were less radical but also because of closer personal ties, some of which were formed while he was serving as a visiting professor at Princeton Seminary in the late 1930s.

RUDOLPH BULTMANN (1884–1976)

One of the most influential twentieth-century theologians was Rudolph Bultmann, a professor of New Testament at the University of Marburg in Germany, who sought to demythologize the message of the New Testament. In contrast with the mechanistic view of the world constructed by scientists (a view, incidentally, more characteristic of nineteenth- than of twentieth-century science), Bultmann contended that the New Testament authors described the world as a scene of conflict between God and demons and as a place where miracles occur. These views, he suggested, could be accommodated in the following way:

> In faith I realize that the scientific world-view does not comprehend the whole reality of the world and of human life, but faith does not offer another general world-view which corrects science in its statements on its

own level. Rather, faith acknowledges that the world-view given by science is a necessary means for doing our work within the world. Indeed, I need to see the worldly events as linked by cause and effect not only as a scientific observer, but also in my daily living. In doing so there remains no room for God's working. This is the paradox of faith, that faith "nevertheless" understands as God's action here and now an event which is completely intelligible in the natural or historical connection of events.[13]

Since, in Bultmann's opinion, the mechanistic view was inescapable for persons living in the twentieth century, it followed that if there were to be Christians in the twentieth century, a version of Christianity must be found that did not conflict with science. This, he held, could be best produced by demythologizing the Christian message, making it a call to "authentic" existence.

Demythologizing in Bultmann's hands became a wide-ranging enterprise. For example, he interpreted the doctrine of divine judgment, with a heaven to be gained and a hell to be shunned, as saying (and *only* as saying) that we all face death and that, in our everyday decisions, either we realize our authentic potential or else we live inauthentically. The doctrine of Christ's atoning death and resurrection, he argued, should be interpreted along the lines (and *only* along the lines) of one's experiencing a sense of forgiveness and new life when one forgoes security and risks authenticity. However, Bultmann did, with dubious consistency, stop short of demythologizing the New Testament portrayal of God, although in general his existential version of Christian theology became consistent with whatever science happened to say.

PAUL TILLICH (1886–1965)

Like the other neoorthodox theologians we have been discussing, Paul Tillich, a German professor who in the early 1930s left his homeland to join the faculty of Union Theological Seminary in New York, saw no reason why science and theology should come into conflict. In response to the question "What is the relationship of theology to the special sciences?" he answered:

If nothing is an object of theology which does not concern us ultimately, theology is unconcerned about scientific procedures and results, and vice versa. Theology has no right and no obligation to prejudice a physical or historical, sociological or psychological, inquiry. And no result of such an inquiry can be directly productive or disastrous for theology. The point of contact between scientific research and theology lies in the philosophical element of both, the sciences and theology. Therefore, the question of the relation of theology to the special sciences merges into the question of the relation between theology and philosophy.[14]

For Tillich this latter relationship (that is, between theology and philosophy) was characterized by clear boundaries that distinguished sources, methods, and content.

Tillich viewed theology as both less concrete and less objective—as both more abstract and more existential—than philosophy or science. In "Science and Theology: A Discussion with Einstein," he wrote:

> Theology, above all, must leave to science the description of the whole of objects and their interdependence in nature and history, in man and his world. And beyond this, theology must leave to philosophy the description of the structures and categories of being itself and the *logos* in which being becomes manifest. Any interference of theology with these tasks of philosophy and science is destructive for theology itself.[15]

Theology, by contrast, was to concern itself with the ground of being or being itself, an activity that seemed unlikely to generate conflicts with scientific claims.

On might expect a professor of Christian theology to hold that theology has something to do with God and with God's actions—with the Lord of nature and history. Instead, Tillich maintained that

> the concept of a "Personal God," interfering with natural events, or being "an independent cause of natural events," makes God a natural object besides others, an object among others, a being among beings, maybe the highest, but nevertheless *a* being. This, indeed, is the destruction, not only of the physical system, but even more the destruction of any meaningful idea of God. It is the impure mixture of mythological elements (which are justified in their place, namely, in the concrete religious life) and of rational elements (which are justified in their place, namely, in the theological interpretation of religious experience). No criticism of this distorted idea of God can be sharp enough.[16]

This looks curiously like a rejection of the existence of the deity of the Bible and the Christian creeds. In any case, there is for Tillich no problem of relating claims about what God has done, is doing, or will do, to any statements about natural laws or events, for the simple reason that he thinks there is no divine agent, and so no divine activity.

For Tillich, the object of theology is what concerns us ultimately. The notion of an object of ultimate concern is ambiguous. It may refer to what does in fact concern someone ultimately; then it will vary from person to person depending on what someone feels is "really important" (and might be something that conflicts with science). Or it may refer to that which Tillich thinks ought to concern everyone ultimately, namely the "Ground of being" which is otherwise beyond all description. Then there will be no claims about the object of ultimate concern that might conflict with science.

REINHOLD NIEBUHR (1892–1971) AND H. RICHARD NIEBUHR (1894–1962)

Among the foremost American neoorthodox theologians were Reinhold Niebuhr (who disliked the label) and his brother, H. Richard. Reinhold viewed the doctrine of creation—in which God is viewed as the underived rational power or Logos on whom the derived physical universe depends—as "a necessary presupposition for the whole Christian view of life and history." This doctrine enables Christianity to escape identifying finitude with evil and to avoid deifying the human mind. Further, Niebuhr suggested, "while the Biblical idea of creation did not anticipate the modern discovery of the emergence of novelty in time, it is actually much more compatible with the view of an evolutionary process than the Greek concept of temporal occurrence."[17]

Perhaps three features of Reinhold Niebuhr's discussion most deserve emphasis here. First, he focuses on theological motifs, the general implications of basic theological concepts, and does not develop particular, detailed connections between theological doctrines and scientific data. Second, those motifs that dominate our contemporary scientific age he subjects to a theological critique. Third, his discussion of science is implicitly a critique of scientism but also endeavors to interpret theological themes compatibly with scientific results.

Niebuhr thought that the notion of religious myth was helpful in relating theology to science. "It is the genius of true myth," he wrote, "to suggest the dimension of depth in reality and to point to a realm of essence which transcends the surface of history, on which the cause-effect sequences, discovered and analyzed by science, occur. Science can only deal with this surface of nature and history, analysing, dividing, and segregating its detailed phenomena and relating them to each other in terms of their observable sequences. . . ."[18] His treatment of myth was not patently consistent, since he claimed both that the creation of the world by God calls "attention to the fact that the temporal process is not self-explanatory, though there are always particular explanations for particular events," and also describes the doctrine of creation (which he regards as myth) as marking the limits of rationality and being the dividing line between intelligibility and mystery.[19] It would seem that if the doctrine of creation calls attention to the fact that the temporal process is not self-explanatory, it does so by offering an explanation of the fact that there is a world. But if it offers an explanation, it can hardly be unintelligible, though Niebuhr's remarks question its full intelligibility. Nonetheless, it is his view that creation and natural causation "are not contradictory but complementary." He approvingly quotes from Erich Frank to the effect that theology "does not infringe upon the precincts of natural science . . . a confusion of the two spheres would endanger not only scientific understanding but religious truth as well."[20]

Perhaps it is H. Richard Niebuhr who took most seriously an issue that concerned all of the neoorthodox theologians. He wrote that "we are aware today that all philosophical ideas, religious dogmas and moral imperatives are historically conditioned." "This awareness," he continued "tempts us to a new agnosticism. I have found myself unable to avoid the acceptance of historical relativism yet I do not believe that the agnostic consequence is necessary."[21]

The problem of how to develop a reliable theology that was nonetheless historically conditioned was shared by all of the neoorthodox. Niebuhr is sensitive to the self-defeating character of the view that all views are historically conditioned and so discredited. He attempts to develop a reliable theology by distinguishing between internal and external history. Basic to this distinction is the fact that historical events can be viewed and described "from the outside" by observers whose communities are unaffected by their consequences, and they can also be viewed and described "from within" by those who participate in them and whose communities are vitally affected by their outcome. Both internal and external descriptions can be true, so they can be complementary rather than contradictory. Revelation consists of events crucial to the believing community that are described from within. The theology that recounts these events is confessional or church theology, and it is possible to describe these events from a secular viewpoint that brings out none of their religious significance.

This internal/external distinction is relevant to the relation between science and theology in two ways. It conceives theological and scientific descriptions, in principle and sometimes in practice, as complementary and noncompeting descriptions of the same things,

though from different points of view. This option has seemed attractive to orthodox thinkers as well (as is clear from the discussion below
of D. M. MacKay's views). It also implies that in some manner scientific and theological claims have different epistemological sources
and sanctions, though not in such a way as to require them to be
incommensurate. Because there is not space here to discuss the details of Niebuhr's program for developing a valid theology that is
historically conditioned, it must suffice to note that he thinks that his
dual-aspect analysis of history (and, by implication, of phenomena
generally) allows one to offer secular historical (or scientific) descriptions of events without threatening the possibility of providing theological descriptions of the same events.

NEOORTHODOXY AND SCIENCE

As we have seen, the neoorthodox theologians attempted to build a
wall between theology and science. Perhaps their desire to do so
reflected, in part, such factors as compartmentalization in academia.
During the twentieth century both science and theology have experienced rapid changes, and times of ferment within a discipline are
not conducive to interdisciplinary integration. But I suspect that more
significant were reasons intrinsic to the ways in which theology itself
was perceived and pursued by theologians. For example, if history
is perceived as being of only tangential relevance to Christianity, it is
not likely that science will be perceived as more relevant; science will
probably be thought to have no theological relevance at all, which is
what many of neoorthodox concluded.

If we ask, then, what factors intrinsic to neoorthodox theology itself
served to build a wall between theology and science, it seems clear
that the following should be included. First, there was a strong desire
that religious belief be certain—that a believer's convictions not be at
the mercy of the higher critic, the historian, or the scientist. This
supported the requirement, or at least hope, that theological doctrines
not depend on—not only not be *falsified* but also not *falsifiable* by—
the results of scientific inquiry. Second, the neoorthodox followed a
theme favored by ancient Greek philosophers and insisted that nothing spatial or temporal, and so nothing historical, can possess ultimate
religious significance; if, then, one both agrees with this judgment
and supposes that anything *does* have such significance, one must
hold that there is something nonspatial and nontemporal beyond the
range of scientific inquiry or concern, which is the subject of religious

and theological interest. Given the close connections between Christian doctrine and history, this emphasis was perhaps surprising, but its influence was pervasive. Third, the view that (a) revelation is one source of knowledge, reason or sensory experience another—supplemented by the contentions that (b) nothing known through one source is also known through another, and that (c) if X is known through revelation and Y through reason (and/or sensory experience), then X and Y are different *kinds* of things—does not logically entail the mutual irrelevance of science and theology. Psychologically, however, it seems to be very easy to move from these theses to the claim that science and theology are mutually irrelevant. Fourth, there was a tendency in neoorthodoxy to suppose that revelation somehow is nonpropositional so that its object—that which is revealed—cannot be described and thereby escapes all possible rational scrutiny. Fifth, at least early neoorthodoxy strongly emphasized the transcendence of God, involving the radical difference between God and everything else. Because this belief was not sufficiently balanced by emphasis on the immanence of God or an admission that God is similar to any of his creatures, it contributed still further to an intellectual mapping that placed science and theology in different hemispheres. Putting all this together, one views theology as yielding certainty about the nontemporal, which is known through revelation, is transcendent, and has ultimate religious significance, though perhaps it cannot be described at all, and science as dealing with the temporal, which is known through reason and sensory experience, is describable, nontranscendent, tentative, and of no ultimate religious significance. In sum: from the discontinuity between God and creation is derived a discontinuity between theology and science.

It is not clear that there must be a wall between theology and science, nor that there has always been one—even in the twentieth century. It is exceedingly difficult to have any Christian theology at all that is not somehow related to, and does not require the existence of, Jesus of Nazareth; but the evidence regarding the claim that Jesus actually lived, was crucified, and died is, of course, historical. The difference between a theological claim's depending for its truth on a miniscule core of historical claims and its depending for its truth on a larger core is a difference in degree, not in kind. Further, there seems to be no way of telling what implications for science a developed theology might have, or what implications for theology a developed science might have; informed opinions on that type of issue seem plainly *a posteriori*, formed only after looking at the relevant data.

THE ORTHODOX THEOLOGY
OF ERIC MASCALL

Orthodox theologians in the twentieth century, with some exceptions, have seen the science-theology relationship in terms rather of bridges than of walls—though of course bridges can be the locus of either communication or conflict. A good example of an attempt to relate orthodox theology to the natural sciences is the work of the British Anglican thinker Eric Mascall (b. 1905).

In *Christian Theology and Natural Science* (1957) Mascall develops a very different perspective on theology and science from that of the neoorthodox. The most obvious difference is that Mascall deals with details as well as motifs. For example, he explains prehuman disorder by angelic sin, asserts that the unity of the human race (implied or presupposed by the doctrines of Creation and Redemption) does not require the descent of all humans from a single pair of parents, and chooses creationism (the idea that God creates each new soul) over traducianism (the notion that one's soul is inherited from one's parents), though he thinks that the latter fits nicely with data concerning nonhuman species. In connection with the doctrine of the Virgin Birth of Christ, he raises the question of natural parthenogenesis, which he regards as possible but theologically irrelevant, and he discusses determinism in the context of classical and quantum physics. In these and other ways Mascall relates theological claims and scientific details.

There is, as these examples suggest, considerable distance between Mascall's and the basic neoorthodox perspective. For one thing, Mascall believes that natural theology retains solid prospects; his books *He Who Is* (1943) and *Existence and Analogy* (1949) endeavor to prove God's existence without making any appeal to special revelation. For another, being a neo-Thomist, that is, a follower of the medieval theologian Thomas Aquinas, he is convinced of the basic correctness of Saint Thomas's philosophy, though he is willing to revise that view when revision seems required. Thus Christian theology and Thomistic philosophy combine to create a rather detailed position that interacts with the details of various relevant natural sciences to create positions like the ones just described. Mascall is fully alert to the fact that science changes, that theories come and go, and that theology and philosophy themselves are not static, but views this as no reason not to ask how Thomistic theology connects with science at any given time.

In discussing the epistemological status of scientific theories, Mascall rejects the view that scientific models are "straightforward literal descriptions of the real constitution of the world." Rather, he argues,

The maps or models which science uses, whether constructed out of physical images or purely mathematical concepts, are no more than deductive
systems whose function is to co-ordinate and to predict empirical observations. There is a large margin of arbitrariness as to which theory we
adopt in any particular case, and there is no reason to suppose that logical
necessity in the structure of a model implies any kind of necessity in the
structure of the facts which it depicts.[22]

Nonetheless, Mascall's epistemology is critically realistic; scientific
theories are intended to be true and to interact interpretatively with
perceptual experience.

For Mascall, physics (and science generally) supplements metaphysics. Referring to Oxford philosopher Michael B. Foster's explanation of the *contingency* of the natural world by reference to divine
freedom, and Cambridge and Harvard philosopher Alfred North
Whitehead's explanation of the intelligible *regularity* of the natural
world by reference to divine *rationality*, he remarks:

> Foster explains why modern science did not arise in ancient Greece, White-
> head why it did not arise in India; but this difference only serves to bring
> out more clearly the point at issue, which is that it is precisely the *com-
> bination* of the two notions, and not either of them in isolation, which is
> presupposed by the application of the modern scientific method. For em-
> pirical science to arise at all, there must be the belief—or at least the
> presumption—that the world is both contingent and regular. There must
> be regularities in the world, otherwise there will be nothing for science to
> discover; but they must be contingent, otherwise they . . . could be
> thought out *a priori*.[23]

In this way Mascall seeks to integrate theology (both natural and
revealed) with science, both by way of setting the scientific enterprise
(and its object, a contingently existing, orderly world) in a theistic
explanatory context and by way of placing particular, determinate
interpretations of Christian doctrines into interpretative interaction
with specific scientific theories.

OTHER ORTHODOX PROPOSALS

In America orthodox, or evangelical, theologians have tended to react
more against hyperorthodoxy, or fundamentalism, than against
neoorthodoxy, and they have done so in a variety of ways. In *The
Christian View of Science and Scripture* (1954) Bernard Ramm (b. 1916),
an influential Baptist theologian and philosopher of science who for

a time studied in Europe with Barth, argues that a harmonization of Christian theology and science is an "imperative necessity." A sampling of the problems with which Ramm deals provides considerable insight into his conception of the relationship between science and theology. His chapter on anthropology, for example, considers the unity of the human race, its antiquity and its origin, the location of paradise, the nature of the Fall, the origin of races and languages, and the longevity of Methuselah and other antediluvians (over nine hundred years). Under "geology" he considers creation and the Noachian flood. Creation also appears under "astronomy," as do the long day of Joshua, the dial of Ahaz, and the star of Bethlehem. The Virgin Birth of Christ is considered under "biology." All of this reveals a very different attitude toward higher criticism, the biblical text, the miraculous, and the relationship between science and theology from that which we found in neoorthodoxy. Ramm, who is neither closed-minded nor antiscientific, willingly considers interpretations of biblical texts that produce no apparent conflicts with science; for example, he suggests that perhaps antediluvian ages were recorded on a scale other than ours, so that "nine hundred years" on the Genesis scale is not nine hundred of our years. But what matters for present purposes is the general perspective he represents, as reflected in the fact that he looks for resolutions of such issues.

Ramm emphasizes that orthodoxy is not committed to a 4004 B.C. creation of earth or humanity, to an earth-centered astronomy, to opposing evolutionary theory, or to finding scientific claims in the Bible. Biblical statements about nature, he maintains, are phenomenal or from the "ordinary person's" point of view: "The Bible does not teach final scientific theory, but teaches final theological truth from the culture-perspective of the time and place in which the writers of the Bible wrote. . . . *The theological and eternal truths of the Bible are in and through the human and the cultural.*"[24] Those taking this perspective often distinguish between what the Bible teaches, or what the biblical authors *intended* to teach, and the culture-bound way in which it is said; for example, a literal doctrine of Final Judgment is expressed in language that involves reference to a three-tiered universe.

A different way of relating science and theology is commended by Gordon H. Clark (b. 1902), a Presbyterian philosopher and one of the leading defenders of theological orthodoxy in America. He utilizes a view of science called instrumentalism or operationalism, which denies that scientific theories, properly understood, give (or even purport to give) an account of the physical universe. The laws that appear in such theories serve only to correlate our observations, to retrodict, and to predict, and the models that occur in scientific theories serve only to provide a better grasp of the laws with which they are associated; they do not correspond to any physical realities. On this view, then, such theoretical terms as *atoms, particles, quarks,* and the like do not refer to theoretical entities; they do not refer at all. As one physicist and operationalist put it, "Physics is the science of meter readings." Its laws map relationships that hold between, not unobserved and inferred items, but our observations themselves.

According to this view, science is not a potential competitor to theology. In an essay entitled "The Limits and Uses of Science," Clark's particular development of this point is expressed by his slogan that "science is always false, but often useful":

> Experimentation never discovers how nature works. Every law of physics is an equation, and, if viewed as a description of natural processes, false. The law is indubitably unprovable; it may also be called false because, even aside from a strictly mechanical view, the chance of selecting the true description from among all the laws observation allows is one in infinity, or zero.[25]

Citing Albert Einstein's opinion that "the real nature of things— that we shall never know, never," Clark concludes that science "can never prove or disprove any metaphysical or theological assertion."[26] Thus operationalism, originally developed by philosophers without the slightest concern for any impact it might have on the relationship between science and theology, serves as a basis for denying that any such relationship obtains because there are no scientific propositions to be related to theological claims.

One "old-fashioned" strategy for relating theology and science involved invoking divine activity to account for whatever the science of the moment could not explain. Once science explained a particular phenomenon, divine activity was no longer invoked; but since other phenomena were always waiting to be explained, one could continue to invoke divine activity on their behalf. This "god-of-the-gaps" strategy is theologically inelegant; it thrives on our ignorance and fears our knowledge, and thus has been rejected by most, perhaps all, of twentieth-century theology. To avoid this god-of-the-gaps approach, D. M. MacKay (b. 1922), a professor of communications at the University of Keele, England, has proposed complementarity as a way of seeing the connections between science and theology.[27]

Any overt human action has an essential bodily component that can be given a purely physical description. The difference between a deliberate action and a sheer physical event—gnashing one's teeth versus one's teeth gnashing, to use a standard example—is not the presence of gaps in the physical description of the former and the absence of gaps in the physical description of the latter. It is rather that there are nonphysical descriptions involving intentions that are true of the one and no such descriptions that are true of the other. Similarly, the historical claims *Jesus died from crucifixion* and *Jesus died on the cross for our sins* are not incompatible, and normally the latter would be taken to entail the former.

Such examples, presumably, illustrate *complementary* descriptions. MacKay writes,

> I call two or more statements complementary when (a) they purport to have a common reference, (b) they make different allegations, yet (c) all are justifiable in the sense that each expresses something about the common reference [referent?] which could not (for one reason or another) be expressed in the terms of the others—the commonest reason being, as I have indicated, that the terms belong to different logical categories.[28]

MacKay uses complementarity, a principle borrowed from physics, to insist that the possibility, in principle, of giving an exhaustive physical description of the universe (or a complete physical description, and explanation, of an event) does not tell us, one way or another, whether the universe is also dependent for its existence on an omnicompetent Creator. Neither human freedom nor divine providence requires gaps in physical descriptions or explanations, so the lack (in fact or in principle) of such gaps is no problem for theology.

It should be noted, however, that the truth of some physical descriptions does rule out the truth of certain nonphysical descriptions, and *perhaps* some physical descriptions of events rule out certain theological descriptions of them—both in the sense that *God moved Mount Sinai* is false if Mount Sinai has not moved, and in other, more subtle, ways. The interest and significance of the notion of complementarity, of course, does not preclude this, but neither does appeal to complementarity, by itself, answer the questions about how science and theology are related.

As we have seen, there are a number of ways in which orthodox theologians can view science. One possibility, illustrated by Mascall and Ramm, involves relating particular theological doctrines and particular scientific claims, endeavoring to discover a coherent perspective that includes both. This may be done within a specific, detailed philosophical framework (Mascall) or without appeal to such a framework (Ramm). Operationalism is consistent with orthodox theology, though whether it is a defensible account of science is strongly disputed; since one who accepts it finds no substantial claims in science, there is nothing to relate. A bridge from theology to science would be a bridge to nowhere; a wall between theology and science would wall theology off from nothing.

MacKay's appeal to complementarity attempts to provide a general way of looking at the connections between theology and science, but it, too, is not without problems. Nevertheless, the general picture seems clear: save for those who embrace operationalism, orthodox theologians want bridges, not walls, between theology and science. They seek a view of the world that integrates the theological and the scientific.

PROCESS THOUGHT

Not every perspective on science and theology in the twentieth century has been neoorthodox or orthodox; process theology is neither. The classic text of philosophical process thought is Alfred North Whitehead's (1861–1947) *Process and Reality* (1929). Process philosophy is given something more of a religious, or at least philosophy-of-religion, direction by Charles Hartshorne (b. 1897), who claims that the orthodox concept of God is inadequate and proposes to replace it with panentheism (a term he uses to indicate that he is neither a traditional pantheist nor a traditional monotheist), which holds that "God [is] both an all-independent all-causative factor *and* the totality of effects for theism."[29] Although it is questionable whether his perspective is in any significant way continuous with Christian theology, some have tried to construct a Christian theology on process foundations.

In any case, Hartshorne's thought does illustrate another way of relating science and (something like) theology. In part, he develops a view of God and the World that takes a model derived from science and extrapolates a worldview that follows the pattern of the model. The motivation is apparently to provide a sort of scientific sanction or justification for the resultant account of God in relation to the world, though in fact it is not clear that any actual justification is involved.

Like MacKay, Hartshorne employs the notion of complementarity:

> As the long argument between those who said that light was corpuscular and those who said it was a set of waves seems, in our time, to have ended with the admission that it is both, in each case with qualifications; so the longer argument between those who said, there is nothing higher than relative being (and thus either there is no God or he is relative), and

those who said, there is a highest being who is absolute, is perhaps to be ended by showing a way in which both statements may consistently be made.[30]

For Hartshorne, God and the world are interdependent; indeed, the world is so much an "aspect" of God that "God inherits reality and value from our lives and actions. In ultimate perspective all life other than divine is purely contributive [to the life of God]."[31]

Hartshorne, in various works, defends his version of the ontological argument for God's existence as an essential part of his perspective; thus he holds that *God exists* is a necessary truth. Further, Hartshorne's version of the argument, like many others, contends that *God exists* is *either* a necessary truth *or* a necessary falsehood or contradiction. As a consequence, empirical evidence, and so scientific evidence, is irrelevant to the existence of God. Thus Hartshorne writes: "If I am correct in denying that the divine existence is an empirical matter, subject to conceivable empirical disproof, it must not be possible for any result of science, if it is really that, to conflict with theism."[32]

The "a priori knowledge of God," he goes on to argue,

is at most only an understanding of His purely abstract aspect; while all that is concrete in His reality is to be known, so far as it can be known, through observation, scientific or personal . . . through scripture, religious tradition or ritual, partly through science, certainly not through any proof. Proofs can only show that there is a divine actuality for these more concrete or experiential means to reveal, thus giving us an infinitely bare yet balanced, seemingly consistent, and intelligible *outline* which all our life can joyously fill with contingent, more particular values, meanings and surmises."[33]

For process theology, then, God has two aspects. One is abstract and not accessible to empirical inquiry, and the statements that express it are necessary truths if they are true at all. The other is concrete and accessible (in principle) to scientific observation. This suggests that process theology wants both a wall and a bridge between theology and science. But little is done by way of placing particular theological claims and particular scientific statements in juxtaposition, whether by way of contrast or complement. The connection between theology and science seems to come mainly through the use of the notions of process and complementarity in filling in the general outline provided by Whiteheadian philosophical theology.

CONCLUSION

We have been concerned with how representative twentieth-century theologians and philosophers have conceived relations between Protestant theology and natural science. (How things look in this regard to scientists and laypersons is another story.) Not surprisingly, views of the theology-science relationship depend on perspectives on the nature of science itself. Most contemporary theologians have assumed that the natural sciences include claims about the existence and properties of physical objects and systems. If (as instrumentalism asserts) science includes no such claims, there is no point in building walls or bridges between theology and science. Since most contemporary theologians have done one or the other, they have assumed a realistic view of science.

The nature of theology is also relevant to how theology and science are related. Broadly speaking, neoorthodoxy, orthodoxy, and process theology disagree on this issue, and there is considerable diversity even within neoorthodox thought. While each perspective has its own positive content, each consciously arose against its own particular adversary: neoorthodoxy against liberalism, American (in contrast with British) orthodoxy against hyperorthodoxy (or evangelicism against fundamentalism), process theology against orthodoxy.

Process theology, in effect, rejects the notion of revelation; it rests its abstract segment on metaphysical reflection and its concrete portion on the varieties of experience. Neoorthodoxy, on the whole, retains the notion of revelation, though against certain internal pressures to the contrary. If revelation is somehow nonpropositional, then there will be no revealed propositions to which the results of science might be related; but the notion of nonpropositional revelation was powerfully criticized. The desire of the neoorthodox that religious belief be in principle unfalsifiable, and their tendency to view revelation as somehow nonpropositional, in fact called in question the possibility of a revelation, so conceived, having any content. Those among the neoorthodox who were attracted to the view that nothing historical can possess ultimate religious significance were hard pressed to retain what traditionally was viewed as the basic Christian message. The transcendence of God was so emphasized that the very knowledge of God on which the claim that He was transcendent rested was called in question. In these ways neoorthodoxy flirted with a sort of theological instrumentalism. Perhaps most pervasively among the neoorthodox, the premise that revelation was one source of knowledge and that reason and experience were another led to the conclusion that theological propositions and scientific propositions somehow occupy different epistemological realms. Hence the neoor-thodox wall between theology and science.

Orthodoxy, in general, granted the premise and denied the con-clusion. Mostly, it assumed a realistic view of science, and hence it has been willing to explore possible relationships between theological doctrines and scientific theories. Agreeing with such neoorthodox thinkers as Reinhold Niebuhr on the importance of general themes or motifs in both theology and science, most of the orthodox thinkers we considered also were willing to reflect on the possible connections between particular theological claims and particular scientific state-ments. Hence the orthodox bridge between theology and science.

NOTES

1. On this period see three books by James Collins: *The Emergence of Phi-losophy of Religion* (New Haven: Yale Univ. Press, 1967); *God and Modern Phi-losophy* (Chicago: Henry Regnery Co., 1959); and, on the existentialists, *The Existentialists* (Chicago: Henry Regnery Co., 1952).

2. See Stephen Neill, *The Interpretation of the New Testament, 1861–1961* (Oxford: Oxford Univ. Press, 1964).

3. On the historical background of liberal views see John Herman Randall, Jr., *The Making of the Modern Mind* (Boston: Houghton Mifflin Co., 1940); and Carl F. H. Henry, *Remaking the Modern Mind* (Grand Rapids, Mich.: Wm. B. Eerdmans, 1946). See also William R. Hutchison, *The Modernist Impulse in American Protestantism* (Cambridge, Mass.: Harvard Univ. Press, 1976).

4. A good *first* book to read on neoorthodoxy is William Hordern, *A Lay-man's Guide to Protestant Theology* (New York: Macmillan, 1968); G. C. Ber-kouwer, *A Half Century of Theology* (Grand Rapids, Mich.: Wm. B. Eerdmans, 1978) is a good *second* book. Hordern (p. 95) suggests that "America at first could not understand the strange theology of Barth and Brunner that was born across the Atlantic, but after the depression of 1929 it commenced to search its own soul."

5. On Barth see Geoffrey W. Bromiley, *Introduction to the Theology of Karl Barth* (Grand Rapids, Mich.: Wm. B. Eerdmans, 1979); G. C. Berkouwer, *The Triumph of Grace in the Theology of Karl Barth* (Grand Rapids, Mich.: Wm. B. Eerdmans, 1956).

6. Karl Barth, *The Knowledge of God and the Service of God* (London: Hodder & Stoughton, 1938), pp. 3–4. See also George Casalis, *Portrait of Karl Barth* (Garden City, N.Y.: Doubleday & Co., 1963).

7. On Brunner see Paul K. Jewett, *Emil Brunner's Concept of Revelation* (London: James Clarke & Co., 1954); Emil Brunner, *Truth as Encounter* (Phil-adelphia: Westminster Press, 1964).

8. Emil Brunner, *Christianity and Civilisation*, 2 vols. (London: Nisbet & Co., 1948–1949). See also the clash between Barth and Brunner, who were

friends, in their exchange entitled *Natural Theology* (London: Geoffrey Bles, 1946).

9. Emil Brunner, *Man in Revolt* (Philadelphia: Westminster Press, [1947]), p. 85. The first English edition of this work appeared in 1939.

10. Ibid.

11. Ibid., p. 88.

12. Ibid., p. 86.

13. Rudolph Bultmann, *Jesus Christ and Mythology* (New York: Charles Scribner's Sons, 1958), p. 65. Bultmann also produced significant, if challengeable, work as a New Testament critic, but only his theological work is of interest here. On Bultmann's theology see John MacQuarrie, *The Scope of Demythologizing* (London: SCM Press, 1960); Karl Jaspers and Rudolph Bultmann, *Myth and Christianity* (New York: Noonday Press, 1958).

14. Paul Tillich, *Systematic Theology*, 3 vols. (Digswell Place, Welwyn, Hertfordshire: James Nisbet & Co., 1951–1963), 1:21. On Tillich see also Kenneth Hamilton, *The System and the Gospel* (London: SCM Press, 1963); William Rowe, *Religious Symbols and God* (Chicago: Univ. of Chicago Press, 1968).

15. Paul Tillich, *Theology of Culture*, ed. Robert C. Kimball (New York: Oxford Univ. Press, 1964), p. 129.

16. Ibid., p. 132.

17. Reinhold Niebuhr, *Faith and History* (New York: Charles Scribner's Sons, 1949), pp. 46–47.

18. Reinhold Niebuhr, *An Interpretation of Christian Ethics* (New York: Harper & Brothers, 1935), p. 21. Note that Niebuhr's remarks here reject the possibility of theological claims precluding particular scientific results.

19. George Hammar, *Christian Realism in Contemporary American Theology* (Uppsala: Lundequistska Bokhandeln, [1940]), pp. 241 ff.; Edward John Carnell, *The Theology of Reinhold Niebuhr* (Grand Rapids, Mich.: Wm. B. Eerdmans, 1950), pp. 144 ff.

20. Erich Frank, *Philosophical Understanding and Religious Truth* (New York: Oxford Univ. Press, 1945), pp. 56–58, as quoted in Niebuhr, *Faith and History*, p. 48.

21. H. Richard Niebuhr, *The Meaning of Revelation* (New York: Macmillan, 1941), p. vii.

22. Eric Mascall, *Christian Theology and Natural Science* (London: Longmans, Green & Co., 1957), p. 89.

23. Ibid., p. 98. See also M. B. Foster, "The Christian Doctrine of Creation and the Rise of Modern Natural Science," *Mind*, n.s., 43 (1934): 446–468; M. B. Foster, "Christian Theology and Modern Science of Nature," *Mind*, n.s., 44 (1935): 439–466, and 45 (1936): 1–27; and A. N. Whitehead, *Science and the Modern World* (New York: Macmillan, 1925), chap. 1.

24. Bernard Ramm, *The Christian View of Science and Scripture* (Grand Rapids, Mich.: Wm. B. Eerdmans, 1954), pp. 348–349.

25. Gordon H. Clark, "The Limits and Uses of Science," in *Horizons of Science*, ed. Carl F. H. Henry (New York: Harper & Row, 1978), p. 271. For a bibliography of Clark's writings and a discussion of his views see R. H.

Nash, ed., *The Philosophy of Gordon H. Clark* (Philadelphia: Presbyterian & Reformed Publishing Co., 1968).

26. Henry, *Horizons of Science*, p. 265. See also Gordon H. Clark, *The Philosophy of Science in God* (Nutley, N.J.: The Craig Press, 1964). Instrumentalism, or operationalism, is presented in Percy Bridgman, *The Nature of Physical Theory* (Princeton: Princeton Univ. Press, 1936); and is criticized by Ernst Nagel, *The Structure of Science* (New York: Harcourt, Brace & World, 1961).

27. See D. M. MacKay, *The Clockwork Image* (Downer's Grove, Ill.: Inter-Varsity Press, 1974); and D. M. MacKay, ed., *Christianity in a Mechanistic Universe* (London: Billing & Sons, Ltd., 1965).

28. D. M. MacKay, "Complementary Descriptions," *Mind*, n.s., 66 (1957): 390–394. See also D. M. MacKay, "Complementarity," *Aristotelian Society Supplementary Volume 32* (1958); and Peter Alexander, "Complementary Descriptions," *Mind*, n.s., 65 (1956): 145–165.

29. Charles Hartshorne and William L. Reese, eds., *Philosophers Speak of God* (Chicago: Univ. of Chicago Press, 1935).

30. Charles Hartshorne, *The Divine Relativity* (New Haven: Yale Univ. Press, 1948), p. x.

31. Perry Le Feure, ed., *Philosophical Resources for Christian Thought* (Nashville: Abingdon Press, 1968), p. 52.

32. Charles Hartshorne, *A Natural Theology for Our Time* (LaSalle, Ill.: Open Court Publishing Co., 1967), p. 92. For his defense of the ontological argument see his *The Logic of Perfection* (LaSalle, Ill.: Open Court Publishing Co., 1962) and *Anselm's Discovery* (LaSalle, Ill.: Open Court Publishing Co., 1965).

33. Hartshorne, *Anselm's Discovery*, p. 300.

A Guide to Further Reading

The following list, though far from exhaustive, offers a sample of the most influential, valuable, and representative historical literature on science and Christianity in the English language. Titles are arranged by category.

GENERAL

Barbour, Ian G. *Issues in Science and Religion.* Englewood Cliffs, N.J.: Prentice-Hall, 1966. The first third of this book, by a physicist-theologian, surveys relations between science and religion since the seventeenth century.

Dillenberger, John. *Protestant Thought and Natural Science: A Historical Interpretation.* Garden City, N.Y.: Doubleday, 1960. Sees the relative authority and interpretation of nature and Scripture in theological matters as "the fundamental problem."

Draper, John William. *History of the Conflict between Religion and Science.* New York: D. Appleton, 1874. An influential polemic against the Roman Catholic church.

Feuer, Lewis. *The Scientific Intellectual: The Psychological and Sociological Origins of Modern Science.* New York: Basic Books, 1963. A bold but flawed attempt to portray modern science as a product of the hedonist-libertarian ethic.

Jaki, Stanley L. *The Road of Science and the Ways to God.* Chicago: University of Chicago Press, 1978. A scientist-priest argues unconvincingly that "belief in creation and the Creator . . . formed the bedrock on which science rose."

Koestler, Arthur. *The Sleepwalkers: A History of Man's Changing Vision of the Universe.* New York: Macmillan, 1959. A readable, though idiosyncratic and unreliable, study of the interaction between theology and physics from antiquity to the late seventeenth century, when they "parted ways not in anger, but in sorrow."

Moore, James R. "Historians and Historiography." In *The Post-Darwinian Controversies: A Study of the Protestant Struggle to Come to Terms with Darwin in Great Britain and America, 1870–1900*, part 1. Cambridge: Cambridge University Press, 1979. A splendid 100-page historiographical essay that traces the life of the warfare metaphor and identifies its fallacies.

Numbers, Ronald L. "Science and Religion." *Osiris*, 2d Ser., 1(1985): 59–80. A historiographical survey of science and religion in America.

Raven, Charles E. *Natural Religion and Christian Theology*. 2 vols. Cambridge: Cambridge University Press, 1952–1953. Sees a generally harmonious relationship prevailing until the nineteenth century, when conflict broke out in geology and biology.

Rudwick, Martin J. S. "Senses of the Natural World and Senses of God: Another Look at the Historical Relation of Science and Religion." In *The Sciences and Theology in the Twentieth Century*, edited by A. R. Peacocke, pp. 241–261. Notre Dame, Ind.: University of Notre Dame Press, 1981. Evaluates the applicability of the "strong programme" in the sociology of science for understanding the historical relations of science and religion.

Russell, C. A., ed. *Science and Religious Belief: A Selection of Recent Historical Studies*. London: University of London Press, 1973. A useful collection of essays, covering the period from Copernicus to Darwin.

White, Andrew Dickson. *A History of the Warfare of Science with Theology in Christendom*. 2 vols. New York: D. Appleton, 1896. The classic statement of the warfare thesis.

ANCIENT AND MEDIEVAL

Armstrong, A. H., ed. *The Cambridge History of Later Greek and Early Medieval Philosophy*. Cambridge: Cambridge University Press, 1970. Contains excellent studies of the church fathers and philosophy in the patristic period.

Armstrong, A. H., and R. A. Markus, *Christian Faith and Greek Philosophy*. London: Darton, Longman & Todd, 1960. A little-known but extremely valuable study of early Christian attitudes toward nature.

Chenu, M.-D., O.P. *Nature, Man, and Society in the Twelfth Century: Essays on New Theological Perspectives in the Latin West*. Edited and translated by Jerome Taylor and Lester K. Little. Chicago: University of Chicago Press, 1968. A provocative account of the relationship between theology and other aspects of culture, including natural philosophy, in the twelfth century.

Cochrane, Charles N. *Christianity and Classical Culture: A Study of Thought and Action from Augustus to Augustine*. Oxford: Clarendon Press, 1940. Brilliantly analyzes the impact of Christianity on the Greco-Roman world.

Gilson, Etienne. *Reason and Revelation in the Middle Ages*. New York: Charles Scribner's Sons, 1938. A dated and somewhat oversimplified, but useful and lucid, introductory account.

Grant, Edward. "The Condemnation of 1277, God's Absolute Power, and Physical Thought in the Late Middle Ages." *Viator* 10 (1979): 211–244. Analyzes a critical encounter between theology and natural philosophy.

————. *Much Ado about Nothing: Theories of Space and Vacuum from the Middle Ages to the Scientific Revolution.* Cambridge: Cambridge University Press, 1981. Places conceptions of space and vacuum within a theological context.

Grant, Robert. *Miracle and Natural Law in Graeco-Roman and Early Christian Thought.* Amsterdam: North-Holland, 1952. Still the only book-length study of science and the early church.

Hooykaas, Reijer. "Science and Theology in the Middle Ages." *Free University [of Amsterdam] Quarterly* 3 (1954): 77–163. Concludes that medieval theology was not an obstacle to the development of science.

Laistner, M. L. W. *Christianity and Pagan Culture in the Later Roman Empire.* Ithaca, N.Y.: Cornell University Press, 1951. Treats the decline of pagan culture and the development of a Christian educational system.

Lindberg, David C., ed. *Science in the Middle Ages.* Chicago: University of Chicago Press, 1978. Offers a comprehensive survey of science in Western Christendom.

McEvoy, James. *The Philosophy of Robert Grosseteste.* Oxford: Clarendon Press, 1982. A masterly examination of the interaction of science and theology in a key medieval philosopher.

Murdoch, John E., and Edith D. Sylla, eds. *The Cultural Context of Medieval Learning: Proceedings of the First International Colloquium on Philosophy, Science, and Theology in the Middle Ages—September 1973.* Boston Studies in the Philosophy of Science, vol. 26. Dordrecht: Reidel, 1975. Contains several excellent essays on theology and natural philosophy.

Olson, Richard. *Science Deified and Science Defied: The Historical Significance of Science in Western Culture from the Bronze Age to the Beginnings of the Modern Era ca. 3500 B.C. to ca. A.D. 1640.* Berkeley, Los Angeles, London: University of California Press, 1982. A perceptive account of the relationship between science and religion.

Pieper, Josef. *Scholasticism: Personalities and Problems of Medieval Philosophy.* Translated by Richard and Clara Winston. New York: Pantheon, 1960. An introductory treatment of medieval Scholasticism.

Steneck, Nicholas H. *Science and Creation in the Middle Ages: Henry of Langenstein (d. 1397) on Genesis.* Notre Dame, Ind.: University of Notre Dame Press, 1976. An examination of a representative medieval Christian natural philosopher.

Walsh, James J. *The Popes and Science: The History of the Papal Relations to Science during the Middle Ages and Down to Our Own Time.* New York: Fordham University Press, 1908. A reply to A. D. White's account of alleged Catholic opposition to science, especially medieval and biomedical.

White, Lynn, Jr. *Machina ex Deo: Essays in the Dynamism of Western Culture.* Cambridge: MIT Press, 1968. Contains White's contentious but influential essay, "The Historical Roots of our Ecological Crisis," which places the blame on Christianity.

SCIENTIFIC REVOLUTION

Allen, Don Cameron. *The Legend of Noah: Renaissance Rationalism in Art, Science, and Letters.* Illinois Studies in Language and Literature, vol. 33, nos. 3–4. Urbana: University of Illinois Press, 1949. Centers on attempts in the six-teenth and seventeenth centuries to prove the actuality of a universal flood.

Burtt, Edwin A. *The Metaphysical Foundations of Modern Physical Science.* Rev. ed. New York: Harcourt, Brace & Co., 1932. A classic exploration of the metaphysical (including theological) roots of modern science.

Dick, Steven J. *Plurality of Worlds: The Origins of the Extraterrestrial Life Debate from Democritus to Kant.* Cambridge: Cambridge University Press, 1982. Shows how the concept of other worlds was transformed from heresy to orthodoxy in Western thought.

Hall, A. Rupert. "Merton Revisited or Science and Society in the Seventeenth Century." *History of Science* 2 (1963): 1–16. A rebuttal of the Merton thesis, attacking social explanations of scientific progress.

Hannaway, Owen. *The Chemists and the Word: The Didactic Origins of Chemistry.* Baltimore: Johns Hopkins University Press, 1975. Examines the role of religion in the emergence of chemistry as a distinct discipline.

Hobart, Michael E. *Science and Religion in the Thought of Nicolas Malebranche.* Chapel Hill: University of North Carolina Press, 1982. An analysis of Male-branche's attempt to synthesize Cartesian science and Catholic theology.

Hodgen, Margaret T. *Early Anthropology in the Sixteenth and Seventeenth Cen-turies.* Philadelphia: University of Pennsylvania Press, 1964. Stresses the biblical context in which discussions of human history took place.

Hooykaas, Reijer. *Religion and the Rise of Modern Science.* Grand Rapids, Mich.: Wm. B. Eerdmans, 1972. Apologetic in tone, this brief work maintains that modern science is a product of a biblical worldview, especially Calvinist Puritanism.

Jacob, James R. *Robert Boyle and the English Revolution.* New York: Burt Frank-lin, 1977. Situates Boyle's integration of science and religion within the context of the English revolution.

Klaaren, Eugene M. *Religious Origins of Modern Science.* Grand Rapids, Mich.: Wm. B. Eerdmans, 1977. Using Boyle as a key illustration, the author tries to show that the theology of creation was crucial to the rise of modern science.

Kocher, Paul H. *Science and Religion in Elizabethan England.* San Marino, Calif.: Huntington Library, 1953. Searches for areas of harmony and tension, focusing on the relationship between spirit and matter.

Koyré, Alexandre. *From the Closed World to the Infinite Universe.* Baltimore: Johns Hopkins Press, 1957. Theology is omnipresent in this excellent study.

Kubrin, David. "Newton and the Cyclical Cosmos: Providence and the Me-chanical Philosophy." *Journal of the History of Ideas* 28 (1967): 325–346. Shows that Newton's worldview, in private if not in public, was not a static one.

Langford, Jerome J. *Galileo, Science and the Church.* Rev. ed. Ann Arbor: University of Michigan Press, 1971. An introductory account of Galileo's condemnation, which attempts to soften the stereotype of Galileo as a victim of injustice and narrow-mindedness.

Manuel, Frank E. *The Religion of Isaac Newton.* Oxford: Clarendon Press, 1974. Contends that Newton's religion was primarily historical and scriptural, not metaphysical.

Merton, Robert K. "Science, Technology and Society in Seventeenth Century England." *Osiris* 4 (1938): 360–632. Several reprintings. The classic statement of a close relationship between Puritanism and the rise of modern science.

Morgan, John. "Puritanism and Science: A Reinterpretation." *The Historical Journal* 22 (1979): 535–560. A subtle analysis of Puritan attitudes toward reason in the prerevolutionary period.

Pedersen, Olaf. "Galileo and the Council of Trent: The Galileo Affair Revisited." *Journal for the History of Astronomy* 14 (1983): 1–29. A synthetic account, stressing the theological issues.

Popkin, Richard H. *The History of Scepticism from Erasmus to Descartes.* Rev. ed. New York: Humanities Press, 1964. Treats the relationship of "fideism" and "skepticism" and their impact on science.

Redwood, John. *Reason, Ridicule and Religion: The Age of Enlightenment in England 1660–1750.* Cambridge, Mass.: Harvard University Press, 1976. Discusses the influence of science on changing religious beliefs.

Santillana, Giorgio de. *The Crime of Galileo.* Chicago: University of Chicago Press, 1955. Sees Galileo's condemnation as resulting from confusion and conspiracy within a small segment of the Catholic church.

Shapiro, Barbara J. *Probability and Certainty in Seventeenth-Century England: A Study of the Relationships between Natural Science, Religion, History, Law and Literature.* Princeton: Princeton University Press, 1983. In both science and religion the quest for certainty gave way to an acceptance of probable knowledge.

Thomas, Keith. *Religion and the Decline of Magic.* New York: Charles Scribner's Sons, 1971. A much-cited social history of magic and witchcraft in sixteenth- and seventeenth-century England, which explores the influence of Reformation thought on supernatural belief and practice.

Webster, Charles. *From Paracelsus to Newton: Magic and the Making of Modern Science.* Cambridge: Cambridge University Press, 1982. Suggests that questions of science and religion continued to be inseparable during the Scientific Revolution.

―――― . *The Great Instauration: Science, Medicine and Reform 1626–1660.* London: Duckworth, 1975. A meticulous examination of the impact of Puritan millennialism on English science, with emphasis on practical achievements.

―――― , ed. *The Intellectual Revolution of the Seventeenth Century.* London: Routledge & Kegan Paul, 1974. An important collection of papers on science and Christianity in seventeenth-century England.

Westfall, Richard S. *Science and Religion in Seventeenth-Century England.* New Haven: Yale University Press, 1958. A lucid review of the opinions of the scientific "virtuosi" regarding the relationship between science and Christianity.

Westman, Robert S. "The Melanchthon Circle, Rheticus, and the Wittenberg Interpretation of the Copernican Theory." *Isis* 66 (1975): 164–193. A seminal article on the Protestant response to Copernicanism.

———, ed. *The Copernican Achievement.* Berkeley, Los Angeles, London: University of Caifornia Press, 1975. Includes several essays on the religious response to Copernican astronomy and cosmology.

Willey, Basil. *The Seventeenth Century Background: Studies in the Thought of the Age in Relation to Poetry and Religion.* London: Chatto & Windus, 1934. Science created a rationalistic Christianity in its own image.

Williams, Arnold. *The Common Expositor: An Account of the Commentaries on Genesis, 1527–1633.* Chapel Hill: University of North Carolina Press, 1948. Shows that Genesis commentaries were a widely used forum for the discussion of science and the natural order in the Renaissance.

NEWTON TO DARWIN

Bozeman, Theodore Dwight. *Protestants in an Age of Science: The Baconian Ideal and Antebellum American Religious Thought.* Chapel Hill: University of North Carolina Press, 1977. Shows how Old School Presbyterians used the Baconian philosophy to monitor science without opposing it.

Brooke, John Hedley. "Natural Theology and the Plurality of Worlds: Observations on the Brewster-Whewell Debate." *Annals of Science* 34 (1977): 221–286. Illustrates that even before Darwin natural theology was not a "static, autonomous and monolithic set of presuppositions about the existence of design in nature."

Browne, Janet. *The Secular Ark: Studies in the History of Biogeography.* New Haven: Yale University Press, 1983. From seventeenth-century attempts to verify the biblical account of Noah's ark to nineteenth-century uses of biogeography in the development of evolutionary theory.

Cannon, Susan Faye. *Science in Culture: The Early Victorian Period.* New York: Science History Publications, 1978. A collection of individualistic essays, including an influential one on an intellectual network of scientists and Broad Churchmen.

Coleman, William. *Georges Cuvier, Zoologist: A Study in the History of Evolution Theory.* Cambridge, Mass.: Harvard University Press, 1964. Cuvier's insistence on the fixity of species stemmed from scientific rather than religious considerations.

Fleming, Donald. *John William Draper and the Religion of Science.* Philadelphia: University of Pennsylvania Press, 1950. A biography of the scientist-historian who wrote a *History of the Conflict between Religion and Science* (1874).

Gillespie, Neal C. "Preparing for Darwin: Conchology and Natural Theology in Anglo-American Natural History." *Studies in History of Biology* 7 (1983):

93–145. A model exposition of the problems that the working naturalist faced, viewed from the double perspective of natural theology and emerging evolutionary ideas.

Gillispie, Charles Coulston. *Genesis and Geology: A Study of the Relations of Scientific Thought, Natural Theology, and Social Opinion in Great Britain, 1790–1850.* Cambridge, Mass.: Harvard University Press, 1951. A seminal study that emphasizes "religion in science" rather than "religion *versus* science."

Frängsmyr, Tore, ed. *Linnaeus: The Man and His Work.* Berkeley, Los Angeles, London: University of California Press, 1983. Includes discussions of how this eighteenth-century natural philosopher reconciled his scientific and religious beliefs.

Greene, John C. *The Death of Adam: Evolution and Its Impact on Western Thought.* Ames: Iowa State University Press, 1959. Traces the growth of evolutionary ideas from the seventeenth through the nineteenth century.

Haber, Francis C. *The Age of the World: Moses to Darwin.* Baltimore: Johns Hopkins Press, 1959. A history of ideas that focuses on the period from the seventeenth through the nineteenth century.

Hovenkamp, Herbert. *Science and Religion in America, 1800–1860.* Philadelphia: University of Pennsylvania Press, 1978. Surveys how the Protestant "honeymoon with science" turned into "a pitched battle."

Jacob, Margaret C. *The Newtonians and the English Revolution 1689–1720.* Ithaca, N.Y.: Cornell University Press, 1976. Argues that Newtonian science triumphed because of its utility as a bulwark of the political and social order installed in power by the "Glorious Revolution."

_____ . *The Radical Enlightenment: Pantheists, Freemasons, and Republicans.* London: George Allen & Unwin, 1981. Explores the relationship between the Scientific Revolution and the rise of pantheistic materialism.

LeMahieu, D.L. *The Mind of William Paley: A Philosopher and His Age.* Lincoln: University of Nebraska Press, 1976. Discusses each of Paley's major works and his influence on nineteenth-century thought.

Millhauser, Milton. *Just before Darwin: Robert Chambers and Vestiges.* Middletown, Conn.: Wesleyan University Press, 1959. Shows how the *Vestiges* broke down scientific and religious resistance to evolution.

_____ . "The Scriptural Geologists: An Episode in the History of Opinion." *Osiris* 11 (1954): 65–86. Looks at writers in the first half of the nineteenth century who argued that Scripture is geology.

Numbers, Ronald L. *Creation by Natural Law: Laplace's Nebular Hypothesis in American Thought.* Seattle: University of Washington Press, 1977. By showing development over long periods of time and by promoting modifications of natural and revealed theology, the nebular hypothesis helped to prepare the way for organic evolution.

Odom, Herbert H. "The Estrangement of Celestial Mechanics and Religion." *Journal of the History of Ideas* 27 (1966): 533–548. Traces the decline of natural theology between Newton and Laplace.

Ospovat, Dov. *The Development of Darwin's Theory: Natural History, Natural Theology, and Natural Selection, 1838–1859.* Cambridge: Cambridge University Press, 1981. Demonstrates the influence of natural theology in the development of Darwin's thought.

Page, Leroy E. "Diluvialism and Its Critics." In *Towards a History of Geology*, edited by Cecil J. Schneer, pp. 259–271. Cambridge, Mass.: MIT Press, 1969. Most geologists in the early nineteenth century agreed that religion should not be entangled with geology.

Popkin, Richard H. "Pre-Adamism in 19th Century American Thought: 'Speculative Biology' and Racism," *Philosophia* 8 (1978–1979): 205–239. Argues that "from the mid-17th century onward, pre-Adamism was . . . the most fundamental challenge to the Judeo-Christian tradition to arise from the 'new science.'"

Porter, Roy. *The Making of Geology: Earth Science in Britain, 1660–1815*. Cambridge: Cambridge University Press, 1977. A revisionistic account of the rise of geology as an independent discipline and its changing relationship with religion.

Rappaport, Rhoda. "Geology and Orthodoxy: The Case of Noah's Flood in Eighteenth-Century Thought." *British Journal for the History of Science* 11 (1978): 1–18. Maintains that religious orthodoxy did not inhibit geologists, who reduced the flood to one of a series of natural upheavals.

Rudwick, Martin J. S. *The Meaning of Fossils: Episodes in the History of Paleontology*. 2d ed. New York: Science History Publications, 1976. The best source for information about changing interpretations of fossils from the Renaissance to the late nineteenth century.

Rupke, Nicolaas A. *The Great Chain of History: William Buckland and the English School of Geology (1814–1849)*. Oxford: Clarendon Press, 1983. A first-rate study showing that Buckland tried to harmonize science and religion because of institutional constraints, not religious orthodoxy.

Stanton, William. *The Leopard's Spots: Scientific Attitudes toward Race in America, 1815–59*. Chicago: University of Chicago Press, 1960. Focuses on American ethnologists who discarded the story of Adam and Eve and lengthened human history.

Vartanian, Aram. *Diderot and Descartes: A Study of Scientific Naturalism in the Enlightenment*. Princeton: Princeton University Press, 1953. Describes efforts between 1650 and 1750 to free science from metaphysics and theology.

Willey, Basil. *The Eighteenth Century Background*. London: Chatto & Windus, 1940. On the idea of nature in relation to religion and other aspects of thought.

SINCE 1859

Betts, John Rickards. "Darwinism, Evolution, and American Catholic Thought, 1860–1900." *Catholic Historical Review* 45 (1959–1960): 161–185. Nineteenth-century American Catholics embraced biological evolution slowly and reluctantly.

Bowler, Peter J. *The Eclipse of Darwinism: Anti-Darwinian Evolution Theories in the Decades around 1900.* Baltimore: Johns Hopkins University Press, 1983. Includes a discussion of the decline of theistic evolutionism.

Chadwick, Owen. *The Secularization of the European Mind in the Nineteenth Century.* Cambridge: Cambridge University Press, 1975. An important assessment of Darwin's contribution to secularization.

Cosslett, Tess, ed. *Science and Religion in the Nineteenth Century.* Cambridge: Cambridge University Press, 1984. A convenient collection of nineteenth-century documents dealing primarily with the Darwinian controversy.

Dupree, A. Hunter. *Asa Gray, 1810–1888.* Cambridge, Mass.: Harvard University Press, 1959. A superb biography of the American botanist who sought to reconcile Darwinism and Christianity.

Ellegård, Alvar. *Darwin and the General Reader: The Reception of Darwin's Theory of Evolution in the British Periodical Press, 1859–1872.* Gothenburg, Sweden: Elanders Boktryckeri Aktiebolag, 1958. Argues that religious and ideological beliefs influenced the response of the general public.

Gatewood, Willard B., Jr., ed. *Controversy in the Twenties: Fundamentalism, Modernism, and Evolution.* Nashville: Vanderbilt University Press, 1969. A useful collection of sources accompanied by an introductory essay.

Gillespie, Neal C. *Charles Darwin and the Problem of Creation.* Chicago: University of Chicago Press, 1979. Examines the shift from a creationist "episteme," which unified science and theology, to a positivist "episteme," which interpreted nature exclusively in terms of secondary laws.

Greene, John C. *Darwin and the Modern World View.* Baton Rouge: Louisiana State University Press, 1961. Three lectures surveying Darwin's impact on biblical studies, natural theology, and social science.

Gregory, Frederick. *Scientific Materialism in Nineteenth Century Germany.* Dordrecht: Reidel, 1977. Focuses on three German scientists who used science to defend materialism in the wake of Feuerbach's *The Essence of Christianity.*

Gruber, Howard E., and Paul H. Barrett. *Darwin on Man.* New York: E. P. Dutton & Co., 1974. Includes a discussion of Darwin's views on religion.

Gruber, Jacob W. *A Conscience in Conflict: The Life of St. George Jackson Mivart.* New York: Columbia University Press, 1960. Biography of a British biologist who tried, unsuccessfully, to harmonize Darwinism and Catholicism.

Irvine, William. *Apes, Angels, and Victorians: The Story of Darwin, Huxley, and Evolution.* New York: McGraw-Hill Book Co., 1955. A graceful, comprehensive interpretation by a student of Victorian literature.

Kelly, Alfred. *The Descent of Darwin: The Popularization of Darwinism in Germany, 1860–1914.* Chapel Hill: University of North Carolina Press, 1981. Shows how popular Darwinism was used as a weapon against Christianity.

Larson, Edward J. *Trial and Error: The American Controversy over Creation and Evolution.* New York: Oxford University Press, 1985. A dispassionate survey of the legal history of creationism.

Lucas, J. R. "Wilberforce and Huxley: A Legendary Encounter." *The Historical Journal* 22 (1979): 313–330. Challenges the common interpretation of this notorious event.

Marsden, George M. *Fundamentalism and American Culture: The Shaping of Twentieth Century Evangelicalism.* New York: Oxford University Press, 1980. An outstanding treatment of fundamentalists and their attitudes toward evolution.

Moore, James. R. "1859 and All That: Remaking the Story of Evolution-and-Religion." In *Charles Darwin, 1809–1882: A Centennial Commemorative,* edited by Roger G. Chapman and Cleveland T. Duval, pp. 167–194, 361–363. Wellington, N.Z.: Nova Pacifica, 1982.

_____ . *The Post-Darwinian Controversies: A Study of the Protestant Struggle to Come to Terms with Darwin in Great Britain and America, 1870–1900.* Cambridge: Cambridge University Press, 1979. The starting place for any discussion of the religious response to Darwin.

Morrison, John L. "American Catholics and the Crusade against Evolution." *Records of the American Catholic Historical Society of Philadelphia* 64 (1953): 59–71. During the 1920s Catholics were more concerned about the kind of evolution taught than about evolution as such.

Nelkin, Dorothy. *The Creation Controversy: Science or Scripture in the Schools.* New York: W. W. Norton, 1982. A convenient, though historically flawed, account of recent creationist activities.

O'Brien, Charles F. *Sir William Dawson: A Life in Science and Religion.* Philadelphia: American Philosophical Society, 1971. An influential harmonizer and one of the last prominent scientists to reject evolution.

Paul, Harry W. *The Edge of Contingency: French Catholic Reaction to Scientific Change from Darwin to Duhem.* Gainesville: University Presses of Florida, 1979. Describes a broad spectrum of Catholic responses to science.

_____ . "Religion and Darwinism: Varieties of Catholic Reaction." In *The Comparative Reception of Darwinism,* edited by Thomas F. Glick, pp. 403–436. Austin: University of Texas Press, 1974. Surveys the responses of European Catholics to Darwinism.

Ruse, Michael. *The Darwinian Revolution: Science Red in Tooth and Claw.* Chicago: University of Chicago Press, 1979. The best recent introduction to the subject, although largely restricted to the British scene.

Stephens, Lester D. *Joseph LeConte: Gentle Prophet of Evolution.* Baton Rouge: Louisiana State University Press, 1982. A biography of one of America's most influential popularizers of theistic evolution.

Szasz, Ferenc Morton. *The Divided Mind of Protestant America, 1880–1930.* University: University of Alabama Press, 1982. Looks at the response of conservative Protestants to higher criticism and evolution.

Turner, Frank Miller. *Between Science and Religion: The Reaction to Scientific Naturalism in Later Victorian England.* New Haven: Yale University Press, 1974. Studies six Englishmen who rejected the dogmas of both religion and science.

_____ . "The Victorian Conflict between Science and Religion: A Professional Dimension." *Isis* 69 (1978): 356–376. A ground-breaking essay that places the conflict not between science and religion as such, but between professionalizing scientists and the clerical establishment and its allies.

Turner, James. *Without God, without Creed: The Origins of Unbelief in America.* Baltimore: Johns Hopkins University Press, 1985. Argues that religion, not science, caused unbelief.

Waggoner, Paul M. "The Historiography of the Scopes Trial." *Trinity Journal,* n.s., 5(1984): 155–174. Argues that the trial did *not* represent a turning point in the fundamentalist controversy.

White, Edward A. *Science and Religion in American Thought: The Impact of Naturalism.* Stanford, Calif.: Stanford University Press, 1952. A somewhat dated study that focuses on the ways in which six American thinkers— Draper, White, Fiske, James, Jordan, and Dewey—viewed the relationship between science and religion.

Young, Robert M. "The Historiographic and Ideological Contexts of the Nineteenth-Century Debate on Man's Place in Nature." In *Changing Perspectives in the History of Science: Essays in Honour of Joseph Needham,* edited by Mikuláš Teich and Robert M. Young, pp. 344–438. London: William Heinemann, 1973. A programmatic and influential call for religious and ideological "factors" to be seen as constitutive, rather than merely contextual, in the nineteenth-century debate.

MEDICINE AND CHRISTIANITY

Amundsen, Darrel W. "Medicine and Faith in Early Christianity." *Bulletin of the History of Medicine* 56 (1982): 326–350. Christians displayed the same range of attitudes toward medicine and healing as did pagans.

———. "Medieval Canon Law on Medical and Surgical Practice by the Clergy." *Bulletin of the History of Medicine* 52 (1978): 22–44. Contrary to common belief, the church did not formally forbid the practice of medicine by clerics.

Buck, Peter. *American Science and Modern China, 1876–1936.* Cambridge: Cambridge University Press, 1980. A novel interpretation of "missionary science" and medical missionaries.

Burnham, John C. "The Encounter of Christian Theology with Deterministic Psychology and Psychoanalysis." *Bulletin of the Menninger Clinic* 49 (1985): 321–352. The best introduction to this underexplored subject.

Cipolla, Carlo M. *Faith, Reason, and the Plague in Seventeenth-Century Tuscany.* Ithaca, N.Y.: Cornell University Press, 1979. A case study of conflict between religious leaders and public-health authorities.

MacDonald, Michael. *Mystical Bedlam: Madness, Anxiety, and Healing in Seventeenth-Century England.* Cambridge: Cambridge University Press, 1981. Illustrates the fusion of natural and supernatural theories of insanity.

Marty, Martin E., and Kenneth L. Vaux. *Health/Medicine and the Faith Traditions: An Inquiry into Religion and Medicine.* Philadelphia: Fortress Press, 1982. Contains 110 pages of historical survey by Darrel W. Amundsen, Gary B. Ferngren, Ronald L. Numbers, and Ronald C. Sawyer.

Numbers, Ronald L. *Prophetess of Health: A Study of Ellen G. White.* New York: Harper & Row, 1976. Popular science in the service of religion, illustrated by the founder of Seventh-day Adventism.

Numbers, Ronald L., and Janet S. Numbers. "Millerism and Madness: A Study of 'Religious Insanity' in Nineteenth-Century America." *Bulletin of the Menninger Clinic* 49 (1985): 289–320. A case study.

Rosenberg, Charles E. *The Cholera Years: The United States in 1832, 1849, and 1866.* Chicago: University of Chicago Press, 1962. The best case study of the changing relationship between medical theory and religious belief.

Sheils, W. J., ed. *The Church and Healing.* Studies in Church History, vol. 19. Oxford: Basil Blackwell, for the Ecclesiastical History Society, 1982. A collection of historical essays on topics ranging from the early church to the twentieth century.

Whorton, James C. *Crusaders for Fitness: The History of American Health Reformers.* Princeton: Princeton University Press, 1982. Identifies the religious roots of the health-reform movement, which fashioned a "Christian physiology."

Contributors

WILLIAM B. ASHWORTH, JR. (b. 1943) earned the Ph.D. in history of science at the University of Wisconsin in 1975 and is currently Associate Professor of History at the University of Missouri—Kansas City. He has published articles on seventeenth-century astronomy, natural history, and scientific illustration, and is completing book manuscripts entitled *Leibniz and Seventeenth-Century Geological Thought* and *Allegorical Images of the Scientific Revolution*.

GARY B. DEASON (b. 1945) received the Ph.D. from Princeton Theological Seminary, in conjunction with the Program in History and Philosophy of Science, Princeton University. He is Associate Professor of Religion and Philosophy at St. Olaf College, where he teaches courses on science and religion. He has recently completed a book tentatively entitled *Religion, Politics, and Science in the Work of Francis Bacon*.

A. HUNTER DUPREE (b. 1921), George L. Littlefield Professor of History (emeritus) at Brown University, received the Ph.D. in history from Harvard University in 1952. His publications include *Science in the Federal Government: A History of Politics and Activities to 1940* (1957) and *Asa Gray, 1810–1888* (1959). He is a member of the American Academy of Arts and Sciences, a corresponding member of the Académie internationale d'histoire des sciences, recipient of the Presidential Award of the New York Academy of Sciences, and holder of several distinguished fellowships.

EDWARD GRANT (b. 1926) was awarded the Ph.D. in history of science by the University of Wisconsin in 1957. He is Distinguished Professor of History and Philosophy of Science at Indiana University. A former fellow of the Guggenheim Foundation and the American Council of Learned Societies and a past member of the Institute for Advanced Study (Princeton), he is currently a fellow of the Medieval Academy of America and president of the History of Science Society. His books include *Physical Science in the Middle Ages* (1971), *Nicole Oresme and the Kinematics of Circular Motion* (1971), *A Source Book in Medieval Science* (1974), and *Much Ado about Nothing: Theories of Space and Vacuum from the Middle Ages to the Scientific Revolution* (1981).

FREDERICK GREGORY (b. 1942) earned a B.D. degree from Gordon-Conwell Theological Seminary in 1968 and a Ph.D. in history of science from Harvard University in 1973. He is Associate Professor of History of Science at the University of Florida. He has been a fellow of the Alexander von Humboldt Stiftung and is author of *Scientific Materialism in Nineteenth Century Germany* (1977). At present he is writing an intellectual biography of the German philosopher-scientist Jakob Fries.

ROGER HAHN (b. 1932) received the certificate of the Ecole pratique des hautes études, Paris, in 1955 and the Ph.D. in history from Cornell University in 1962. He is Professor of History, University of California, Berkeley. He is also a fellow of the AAAS, member of the Académie internationale d'histoire des sciences, and past president of the American Society for Eighteenth-Century Studies. He has published *Laplace as a Newtonian Scientist* (1967), *Calendar of the Correspondence of Pierre Simon Laplace* (1982), and *The Anatomy of a Scientific Institution: The Paris Academy of Sciences, 1666–1803* (1971), which won the book prize of the Pacific Coast Branch of the American Historical Association.

ERWIN N. HIEBERT (b. 1919), who received the Ph.D. in physical chemistry and the history of science from the University of Wisconsin in 1954, is Professor of the History of Science at Harvard University. He is president of the International Union of the History and Philosophy of Science, past president of the History of Science Society, and former member of the Institute for Advanced Study (Princeton). He is also a fellow of the American Academy of Arts and Sciences and a corresponding member of the Académie internationale d'histoire des sciences. His publications include *The Impact of Atomic Energy* (1961), *Historical Roots of the Principle of Conservation of Energy* (1962), and *The Conception of Thermodynamics in the Scientific Thought of Mach and Planck* (1968).

MARGARET C. JACOB (b. 1943) earned the Ph.D. in history from Cornell University in 1968. Dean of Lang College and University Professor of History, Graduate Faculty, New School for Social Research, she has also been a visiting scholar at Harvard University and the University of Amsterdam and a member of the Institute for Advanced Study (Princeton). She has held fellowships from the National Science Foundation, the National Endowment for the Humanities, the American Council of Learned Societies, and the Fulbright Commission for the Netherlands. Her books are *The Newtonians and the English Revolution, 1689–1720* (1976), which won the Gottschalk Prize of the American Society for Eighteenth-Century Studies, *The Radical Enlightenment: Pantheists, Freemasons and Republicans* (1981), and a forthcoming work entitled *The Integration of Science into Western Culture, 1600–1800*.

DAVID C. LINDBERG (b. 1935), who received the Ph.D. in history and philosophy of science from Indiana University in 1965, is Evjue-Bascom Professor of the History of Science at the University of Wisconsin. He has been a

Guggenheim Fellow and a member of the Institute for Advanced Study (Princeton) and the Institute for Research in the Humanities at the University of Wisconsin; he is also a fellow of the Medieval Academy of America. His books include *John Pecham and the Science of Optics* (1970), *Theories of Vision from al-Kindi to Kepler* (1976), *Science in the Middle Ages* (1978), and *Roger Bacon's Philosophy of Nature* (1983).

JAMES R. MOORE (b. 1947) received the M.Div. from Trinity Evangelical Divinity School in 1972 and the Ph.D. in ecclesiastical history in 1975 from the University of Manchester, where he was a Marshall Scholar. He is Lecturer in History of Science and Technology in The Open University, where he has been responsible for courses on "Science and Belief." His publications include *The Post-Darwinian Controversies: A Study of the Protestant Struggle to Come to Terms with Darwin in Great Britain and America, 1870–1900* (1979), *Beliefs in Science: An Introduction* (1981), and *The Future of Science and Belief: Theological Views in the Twentieth Century* (1981). He is preparing a book on Charles Darwin.

RONALD L. NUMBERS (b. 1942) earned the Ph.D. in history at the University of California, Berkeley, in 1969. He is Professor of the History of Medicine and the History of Science, University of Wisconsin, and, during 1983–85, Fellow in Interdisciplinary Studies, The Menninger Foundation. He has been a fellow of the Guggenheim Foundation and the Josiah Macy, Jr. Foundation. His books include *Prophetess of Health: A Study of Ellen G. White* (1976), *Creation by Natural Law: Laplace's Nebular Hypothesis in American Thought* (1977), *Almost Persuaded: American Physicians and Compulsory Health Insurance, 1912–1920* (1978), and a forthcoming history of twentieth-century creationism.

JACQUES ROGER (b. 1920) was educated at the Sorbonne, receiving the Doctorat ès lettres in 1963. He is Professor of the History of Science at the University of Paris I, Director of the Centre international de synthèse and the Centre Alexandre Koyré, and sometime Andrew Dickson White Visiting Professor in the Humanities at Cornell University. He is the recipient of the Grand Prix Gobert of the Académie française in 1964 and past president of the Société française d'histoire des sciences et des techniques. His publications include *Les sciences de la vie dans la pensée française du 18ᵉ siècle* (1963) and a critical edition of Buffon's *Les époques de la nature* (1962).

MARTIN J. S. RUDWICK (b. 1932) received the Ph.D. in geology from the University of Cambridge in 1958. Formerly Professor of the History and Social Aspects of Science at the Vrije Universiteit, Amsterdam, he is currently Professor of History of Science at Princeton University. He is a fellow of the Geological Society of London and a corresponding member of the Académie internationale d'histoire des sciences. His publications include *Living and Fossil Brachiopods* (1970), *The Meaning of Fossils: Episodes in the History of Paleontology* (1972), and *The Great Devonian Controversy: The Making of Scientific Knowledge among Gentlemanly Specialists* (1985).

WILLIAM R. SHEA (b. 1937) studied philosophy and theology at the Gregorian University in Rome and received the Ph.D. in philosophy from the University of Cambridge in 1968. He is Professor of History and Philosophy of Science at McGill University and secretary general of the International Union of the History and Philosophy of Science. Among his publications are *Galileo's Intellectual Revolution: Middle Period, 1610–1632* (1972) and *Basic Issues in the Philosophy of Science* (1976).

CHARLES WEBSTER (b. 1936), who received the D.Sc. from the University of London in 1973, is Reader in the History of Medicine, University of Oxford, and Director of the Wellcome Unit for the History of Medicine, Oxford. Among his publications are *Samuel Hartlib and the Advancement of Learning* (1970), *From Paracelsus to Newton* (1982), and a prizewinning book on Puritan science, *The Great Instauration: Science, Medicine and Reform, 1626–1660* (1975).

RICHARD S. WESTFALL (b. 1924) earned the Ph.D. in history from Yale University in 1955. He is Distinguished Professor of History and Philosophy of Science at Indiana University. In addition to winning the Leo Gershoy Award of the American Historical Association and the Pfizer Award of the History of Science Society (twice), he has received many fellowships and served as president of the History of Science Society. Among his publications are *Science and Religion in Seventeenth-Century England* (1958), *Force in Newton's Physics: The Science of Dynamics in the Seventeenth Century* (1971), *The Construction of Modern Science: Mechanisms and Mechanics* (1971), and *Never at Rest: A Biography of Isaac Newton* (1980).

ROBERT S. WESTMAN (b. 1941), who received the Ph.D. in history from the University of Michigan in 1971, is Professor of History at the University of California, Los Angeles. A former fellow of the American Council of Learned Societies and the Guggenheim Foundation, he is editor of *The Copernican Achievement* (1975) and coauthor (with J. E. McGuire) of *Hermeticism and the Scientific Revolution* (1977). He is coeditor (with D. C. Lindberg) of a forthcoming collection, *Reappraisals of the Scientific Revolution*, and is currently completing a book entitled *The Copernicans: Universities, Courts and the Disciplines, 1543–1700*.

KEITH E. YANDELL (b. 1938) received the Ph.D. in philosophy from Ohio State University in 1966. He is Professor of Philosophy and of South Asian Studies at the University of Wisconsin, where he specializes in the philosophy of religion. He has been the recipient of fellowships from the National Endowment for the Humanities and the Institute for Research in the Humanities at the University of Wisconsin. In addition to many articles on a variety of philosophical topics, he has published *Basic Issues in the Philosophy of Religion* (1971), *Problems in Philosophical Inquiry* (1971, with J. R. Weinberg), *God, Man and Religion* (1973), and *Christianity and Philosophy* (1984).

Index

489